THE NIV
APPLICATION
COMMENTARY

From biblical text . . . to contemporary life

THE NIV APPLICATION COMMENTARY SERIES

EDITORIAL BOARD

THE NIV APPLICATION COMMENTARY

From biblical text . . . to contemporary life

J. ANDREW DEARMAN

ZONDERVAN™

GRAND RAPIDS, MICHIGAN 49530

ZONDERVAN™

The NIV Application Commentary: Jeremiah and Lamentations
Copyright © 2002 by J. Andrew Dearman

Requests for information should be addressed to:
Zondervan, *Grand Rapids, Michigan 49530*

Library of Congress Cataloging-in-Publication Data

Dearman, J. Andrew.
      Jeremiah and Lamentations / J. Andrew Dearman.
         p. cm. — (The NIV application commentary)
      Includes bibliographical references and indexes.
      ISBN: 0–310–20616–2
      1. Bible. O.T. Jeremiah — Commentaries. 2. Bible. O.T. Lamentations — Commentaries.
      I. Title. II. Series.
      II. Series.
      BS1525.53.D43 2002
      224'.2077 — dc21
                                              2001005613
                                                    CIP

This edition printed on acid-free paper.

Printed in the United States of America

03 04 05 06 07 08 /❖ DC/ 10 9 8 7 6 5 4 3

This volume is dedicated to my sister Jan Dearman:

A missionary among the nations,

she is one who can boast in the Lord (see Jer. 9:23–24).

Table of Contents

The NIV Application Commentary Series

When complete, the NIV Application Commentary
will include the following volumes:

Old Testament Volumes

Genesis, John H. Walton
Exodus, Peter Enns
Leviticus/Numbers, Roy Gane
Deuteronomy, Daniel I. Block
Joshua, Robert Hubbard
Judges/Ruth, K. Lawson Younger
1-2 Samuel, Bill T. Arnold
1-2 Kings, Gus Konkel
1-2 Chronicles, Andrew E. Hill
Ezra/Nehemiah, Douglas J. Green
Esther, Karen H. Jobes
Job, Dennis R. Magary
Psalms Volume 1, Gerald H. Wilson
Psalms Volume 2, Gerald H. Wilson
Proverbs, Paul Koptak
Ecclesiastes/Song of Songs, Iain Provan
Isaiah, John N. Oswalt
Jeremiah/Lamentations, J. Andrew Dearman
Ezekiel, Iain M. Duguid
Daniel, Tremper Longman III
Hosea/Amos/Micah, Gary V. Smith
Jonah/Nahum/Habakkuk/Zephaniah,
    James Bruckner
Joel/Obadiah/Malachi, David W. Baker
Haggai/Zechariah, Mark J. Boda

New Testament Volumes

Matthew, Michael J. Wilkins
Mark, David E. Garland
Luke, Darrell L. Bock
John, Gary M. Burge
Acts, Ajith Fernando
Romans, Douglas J. Moo
1 Corinthians, Craig Blomberg
2 Corinthians, Scott Hafemann
Galatians, Scot McKnight
Ephesians, Klyne Snodgrass
Philippians, Frank Thielman
Colossians/Philemon, David E. Garland
1-2 Thessalonians, Michael W. Holmes
1-2 Timothy/Titus, Walter L. Liefeld
Hebrews, George H. Guthrie
James, David P. Nystrom
1 Peter, Scot McKnight
2 Peter/Jude, Douglas J. Moo
Letters of John, Gary M. Burge
Revelation, Craig S. Keener

To see which titles are available,
visit our web site at www.zondervan.com

NIV Application Commentary
Series Introduction

THE NIV APPLICATION COMMENTARY SERIES is unique. Most commentaries help us make the journey from our world back to the world of the Bible. They enable us to cross the barriers of time, culture, language, and geography that separate us from the biblical world. Yet they only offer a one-way ticket to the past and assume that we can somehow make the return journey on our own. Once they have explained the *original meaning* of a book or passage, these commentaries give us little or no help in exploring its *contemporary significance*. The information they offer is valuable, but the job is only half done.

Recently, a few commentaries have included some contemporary application as *one* of their goals. Yet that application is often sketchy or moralistic, and some volumes sound more like printed sermons than commentaries.

The primary goal of the NIV Application Commentary Series is to help you with the difficult but vital task of bringing an ancient message into a modern context. The series not only focuses on application as a finished product but also helps you think through the *process* of moving from the original meaning of a passage to its contemporary significance. These are commentaries, not popular expositions. They are works of reference, not devotional literature.

The format of the series is designed to achieve the goals of the series. Each passage is treated in three sections: *Original Meaning, Bridging Contexts,* and *Contemporary Significance.*

THIS SECTION HELPS you understand the meaning of the biblical text in its original context. All of the elements of traditional exegesis—in concise form—are discussed here. These include the historical, literary, and cultural context of the passage. The authors discuss matters related to grammar and syntax and the meaning of biblical words.[1] They also seek to explore the main ideas of the passage and how the biblical author develops those ideas.

---

1. Please note that in general, when the authors discuss words in the original biblical languages, the series uses a general rather than a scholarly method of transliteration.

After reading this section, you will understand the problems, questions, and concerns of the *original audience* and how the biblical author addressed those issues. This understanding is foundational to any legitimate application of the text today.

THIS SECTION BUILDS a bridge between the world of the Bible and the world of today, between the original context and the contemporary context, by focusing on both the timely and timeless aspects of the text.

God's Word is *timely*. The authors of Scripture spoke to specific situations, problems, and questions. The author of Joshua encouraged the faith of his original readers by narrating the destruction of Jericho, a seemingly impregnable city, at the hands of an angry warrior God (Josh. 6). Paul warned the Galatians about the consequences of circumcision and the dangers of trying to be justified by law (Gal. 5:2–5). The author of Hebrews tried to convince his readers that Christ is superior to Moses, the Aaronic priests, and the Old Testament sacrifices. John urged his readers to "test the spirits" of those who taught a form of incipient Gnosticism (1 John 4:1–6). In each of these cases, the timely nature of Scripture enables us to hear God's Word in situations that were *concrete* rather than abstract.

Yet the timely nature of Scripture also creates problems. Our situations, difficulties, and questions are not always directly related to those faced by the people in the Bible. Therefore, God's word to them does not always seem relevant to us. For example, when was the last time someone urged you to be circumcised, claiming that it was a necessary part of justification? How many people today care whether Christ is superior to the Aaronic priests? And how can a "test" designed to expose incipient Gnosticism be of any value in a modern culture?

Fortunately, Scripture is not only timely but *timeless*. Just as God spoke to the original audience, so he still speaks to us through the pages of Scripture. Because we share a common humanity with the people of the Bible, we discover a *universal dimension* in the problems they faced and the solutions God gave them. The timeless nature of Scripture enables it to speak with power in every time and in every culture.

Those who fail to recognize that Scripture is both timely and timeless run into a host of problems. For example, those who are intimidated by timely books such as Hebrews, Galatians, or Deuteronomy might avoid reading them because they seem meaningless today. At the other extreme, those who are convinced of the timeless nature of Scripture, but who fail to discern its timely element, may "wax eloquent" about the Melchizedekian priest-hood to a sleeping congregation, or worse still, try to apply the holy wars of the Old Testament in a physical way to God's enemies today.

The purpose of this section, therefore, is to help you discern what is time-less in the timely pages of the Bible—and what is not. For example, how do the holy wars of the Old Testament relate to the spiritual warfare of the New? If Paul's primary concern is not circumcision (as he tells us in Gal. 5:6), what *is* he concerned about? If discussions about the Aaronic priesthood or Melchizedek seem irrelevant today, what is of abiding value in these passages? If people try to "test the spirits" today with a test designed for a specific first-century heresy, what other biblical test might be more appropriate?

Yet this section does not merely uncover that which is timeless in a pas-sage but also helps you to see *how* it is uncovered. The authors of the com-mentaries seek to take what is implicit in the text and make it explicit, to take a process that normally is intuitive and explain it in a logical, orderly fash-ion. How do we know that circumcision is not Paul's primary concern? What clues in the text or its context help us realize that Paul's real concern is at a deeper level?

Of course, those passages in which the historical distance between us and the original readers is greatest require a longer treatment. Conversely, those passages in which the historical distance is smaller or seemingly nonex-istent require less attention.

One final clarification. Because this section prepares the way for dis-cussing the contemporary significance of the passage, there is not always a sharp distinction or a clear break between this section and the one that fol-lows. Yet when both sections are read together, you should have a strong sense of moving from the world of the Bible to the world of today.

THIS SECTION ALLOWS the biblical message to speak with as much power today as it did when it was first written. How can you apply what you learned about Jerusalem, Ephesus, or Corinth to our present-day needs in Chicago, Los Angeles, or London? How can you take a message originally spoken in Greek, Hebrew, and Aramaic and com-municate it clearly in our own language? How can you take the eternal truths originally spoken in a different time and culture and apply them to the sim-ilar-yet-different needs of our culture?

In order to achieve these goals, this section gives you help in several key areas.

(1) It helps you identify contemporary situations, problems, or questions that are truly comparable to those faced by the original audience. Because

contemporary situations are seldom identical to those faced by the original audience, you must seek situations that are analogous if your applications are to be relevant.

(2) This section explores a variety of contexts in which the passage might be applied today. You will look at personal applications, but you will also be encouraged to think beyond private concerns to the society and culture at large.

(3) This section will alert you to any problems or difficulties you might encounter in seeking to apply the passage. And if there are several legitimate ways to apply a passage (areas in which Christians disagree), the author will bring these to your attention and help you think through the issues involved.

In seeking to achieve these goals, the contributors to this series attempt to avoid two extremes. They avoid making such specific applications that the commentary might quickly become dated. They also avoid discussing the significance of the passage in such a general way that it fails to engage contemporary life and culture.

Above all, contributors to this series have made a diligent effort not to sound moralistic or preachy. The NIV Application Commentary Series does not seek to provide ready-made sermon materials but rather tools, ideas, and insights that will help you communicate God's Word with power. If we help you to achieve that goal, then we have fulfilled the purpose for this series.

The Editors

General Editor's Preface

THE THEME OF RIGHTEOUS KINGS, aided by powerful religious figures and reforming wayward people groups, is not an uncommon one in Middle Eastern and Asian history. One thinks, for example, of Asoka in Buddhist India, Constantine in Christian Rome, and Saladin in Islamic Palestine.

Typically, these righteous kings did not attempt to become religious leaders themselves by usurping power from bhikkhus, priests, and imams. Instead, they attempted reform of declining and/or wayward religious institutions. They rebuilt dilapidated religious buildings—or built brand new ones. They replaced immoral religious leaders with moral ones. They convened councils of religious leaders to articulate doctrine more fully in the face of new challenges. Often, they reemphasized religion's privileged place in the life of their cultures. In general they acted as the consciences of drifting religious people.

As J. Andrew Dearman shows us in this commentary, the initial period of the book of Jeremiah is set in the context of such a king, Josiah. With the help of the prophet Jeremiah, Josiah attempted to restore not only the political but also the spiritual life of his nation, Judah. Unlike Asoka, Constantine, and Saladin, however, Josiah's reforms failed. To be sure, he did achieve some short-term successes. These successes, however, were temporary, as evidenced by the growing failures of Josiah's successors to maintain Israel's fidelity to their agreement with God. That failure had disastrous effects. Eventually Babylon conquered Judah and took thousands of Judeans into exile.

How are we to understand this unusual series of events? What lessons do they teach us? Should we pray for a modern "king-prophet" tandem to rise up and cleanse us? What would make them successful?

The common wisdom is that biblical stories of king-prophet alliances in attempting to keep their societies on the straight and narrow have as their common theme that spiritual faithfulness is more important than political good fortune. Although prophets frequently label political meltdowns as God's judgment and political successes as evidence of God's blessings, they also manage to elevate the importance of the spiritual over the political. Thus, even though Josiah's political strategies ultimately fail at the hands of his Egyptian killers, his attempts at moral reform earn him the label of ruler without equal (2 Kings 23:25).

At least that is the common wisdom. But to read the prophets—and Jeremiah is no exception—is to read over and over again that spiritual faithfulness and political good fortune go hand in hand in a cause-effect relationship (and vice versa, spiritual unfaithfulness leads to political calamities). The spiritual task of faithfully upholding one's end of the covenant leads to God's protection from political enemies and economic ruin. The common wisdom that spirituality is more important than political expertise doesn't measure up to the frequency with which these judgments are made, and one is left feeling that a broader understanding is needed.

That broader understanding must acknowledge two things before it becomes useful for us today. (1) The identification between spiritual faithfulness and political success was much greater in Jeremiah's day than in ours. The Israelites were not too far from theocracy, rulership by God himself, as managed by priests. Even after they began to have kings, it was made clear that the kings ruled by God's choice and at God's sufferance. No political ruler today even comes close to having such a mandate.

(2) Today, even after we realize this first difference, we must clearly prioritize the two factors: spirituality first, politics second. Or better, we should see politics as a fruit of spirituality, not its root or its synonym. The Bible is clear that "politics" by any name is temporal while all the roads that lead to God usher us into the presence of eternity. Blessings along the way are nice—and to some extent needed for the journey. But they are just rest stops. Great "kings" are like hoteliers, themselves making life more comfortable and faithful, but always ready to move us on—and eventually move on themselves.

—Terry C. Muck

Abbreviations

AB	Anchor Bible
ABD	*Anchor Bible Dictionary*
Ant.	Josephus, *Jewish Antiquities*
AUSS	*Andrews University Seminary Studies*
BA	*Biblical Archaeologist*
BAR	*Biblical Archaeology Review*
Bib	*Biblica*
BZAW	Beihefte zur Zeitschrift für die alttestamentliche Wissenschaft
IEJ	*Israel Exploration Journal*
ITC	International Theological Commentary
JBL	*Journal of Biblical Literature*
JNSL	*Journal of Northwest Semitic Languages*
JSOT	*Journal for the Study of the Old Testament*
JSOTSup	Journal for the Study of the Old Testament Supplement Series
LXX	Septuagint (Greek translation of the Old Testament)
MT	Masoretic Text
NCB	New Century Bible
NICOT	New International Commentary on the Old Testament
NIDOTTE	*New International Dictionary of Old Testament Theology and Exegesis*
NIV	New International Version
NIVAC	NIV Application Commentary
OTL	Old Testament Library
RB	*Revue biblique*
RevQ	*Revue de Qumran*
RHR	*Revue de l'histoire des religions*
SBLDS	Society of Biblical Literature Dissertation Series
Taʿan.	*Taʿanit*
TynBul	*Tyndale Bulletin*
VT	*Vetus Testamentum*
WBC	Word Biblical Commentary
WMANT	Wissenschaftliche Monographien zum Alten und Neuen Testament
ZAW	*Zeitschrift für die alttestamentliche Wissenschaft*

Introduction to Jeremiah

The Transmission and Collection of Jeremiah's Message

THE BOOK OF JEREMIAH in Hebrew is the second-longest book in the Old Testament, exceeded only by the Psalter. The Greek version of Jeremiah, however, is about one-sixth shorter than the Hebrew and its contents are arranged differently,[1] two of several reasons why the textual analysis of Jeremiah is complicated. No consensus exists as to the reasons for the disparity in versions. Probably it goes back to the exilic communities who received and transmitted collections of Jeremiah's oracles that the prophet had delivered repeatedly in previous years.

Already in the fifth year of Jehoiakim Jeremiah had instructed Baruch, his scribal companion, to produce a written scroll of his oracles (604 B.C.; Jer. 36:2, 9). When that scroll was destroyed by Jehoiakim, another was produced with additional oracles (36:32; cf. 45:1). During the reign of Zedekiah Jeremiah corresponded with Judeans in Babylon (ch. 29). After Gedaliah's murder he and Baruch were still engaged in prophetic activity in Egypt, where there was a substantial Judean community (chs. 43–44). Thus, there were likely written copies of some of Jeremiah's oracles in Palestine, Egypt, and Babylonia even before the prophet's death, along with people in each of these regions who had known Jeremiah and were interested in preserving his words after his death. We should also reckon with the possibility that oral tradition, derived from both Jeremiah and Baruch, accompanied the earlier collections and continued to be passed among disciples after Jeremiah's death until its inclusion in the scroll.

The circle(s) responsible for the final form of Jeremiah are not well known, even though some who helped Jeremiah preserve and disseminate his oracles are named in the book. Baruch certainly had a major role in preserving the Jeremiah traditions (i.e., oracles, sermons, and narratives about Jeremiah); perhaps it was even a family affair, since Baruch's brother

---

1. For additional details see the discussions of E. Tov, "The Literary History of the Book of Jeremiah in the Light of Its Textual History," in *Empirical Models for Biblical Criticism*, ed. J. Tigay (Philadelphia: Univ. of Pennsylvania Press, 1985), 211–37; idem, "Some Sequence Differences Between the MT and LXX and Their Ramifications for the Literary Criticism of the Bible," *JNSL* 13 (1987): 151–60; and W. Holladay, *Jeremiah* (2 vols.; Hermeneia; Minneapolis: Fortress, 1989), 2:1–8.

Seraiah (a Judean official) also assisted Jeremiah with the deliverance of a prophetic message to Babylon (51:59–64).[2] In addition to these scribal companions, there must have been disciples who learned the gist of his message and who passed along his words in the aftermath of Jerusalem's fall.

It remains difficult, however, to reconstruct the stages through which the book of Jeremiah passed to reach its final Hebrew and Greek forms or to determine the dates of the final forms. Clearly in the case of the Hebrew text the date was not before the reference to Jehoiachin's release (52:31–34), which can be dated to 561 B.C. By this time both Jeremiah and Baruch were likely dead. Since the book itself does not claim an author (i.e., the final author is anonymous), interpreters are simply left with few clues as to the production of the book in its final form(s).[3] Most English versions (including the NIV) follow the Hebrew text and its arrangement of chapters.

The vantage point of the final compilers of the book was similar to that of the historical Jeremiah and Baruch in one very important respect: They too lived after the tragic fall of Judah. Virtually every line in the book is preserved to help explain the recent past to readers. How could God's people fall to the Babylonians? Was God impotent to deal with the power of Babylon, was he simply uncaring, or did he judge Judah by allowing the state to bring this tragedy upon itself? In seeking to explain the past, the book also instructs readers in exercising their faith for their own day. The book presents plenty of things to be avoided (e.g., idolatry, injustice) as well as things to be emulated (e.g., repentance, hope). Finally, the book points to a future that lies open to the action of God in history, even though some of the hopes for that future are as yet unrealized.

These three things, then—explanation of the past, instruction for the present, and hope for future transformation—are the primary functions of the book of Jeremiah.

The Arrangement of the Book's Contents

WHOEVER WAS RESPONSIBLE for the book of Jeremiah did not arrange its contents chronologically. This causes consternation on the part of some read-

---

2. N. Avigad, "Baruch the Scribe and Jerahmeel the King's Son," *IEJ* 28 (1978): 52–56; idem, "The Seal of Seraiah (Son of) Neriah," *Eretz Israel* 14 (1978): 86–87 [in Hebrew]; J. R. Lundbom, "Baruch, Seraiah, and Expanded Colophons in the Book of Jeremiah," *JSOT* 36 (1986): 89–114; J. Andrew Dearman, "My Servants the Scribes: Composition and Context in Jeremiah 36," *JBL* 109 (1990): 403–21.

3. The discovery of fragments of Jeremiah at Qumran have made the textual history of Jeremiah even more intriguing and difficult to reconstruct. Included in the Hebrew fragments are texts in Hebrew that are closer to the Greek versions than the Masoretic Text. See the discussion of E. Tov, "The Jeremiah Scrolls from Cave 4," *RevQ* 2 1989): 189–206.

ers. Indeed, no theory about the process of the book's composition has reached consensus among interpreters. One can point, however, to subunits within the book that are collections of traditions united thematically (e.g., chs. 2–20; 27–29; 30–32; 37–44). Readers will often recognize links (both verbal and thematic) between proximate chapters, even if reasons for the structure and arrangement of the book as a whole eludes them.

At one level of reading, the book's arrangement is not unlike that of a snowball: It is a collection of materials brought together by a movement of repeating the prophet's words and re-presenting his life.[4] Those who compiled the book seem more interested in collecting a full measure of Jeremiah traditions than in arranging the materials according to some comprehensive scheme.[5] It is finally a statement of faith to conclude that God, who raised up Jeremiah, also raised up anonymous editors who have left us with authoritative portraits of the prophet and reliable summaries of his oracles.

Although there is no scholarly consensus about the composition and arrangement of the book, the final form of the Hebrew version does suggest some major structural divisions and an overall theme to the collection of oracles. The book begins with God's promise to make Jeremiah a prophet to the nations (ch. 1), and it ends with oracles about other nations (chs. 46–51) and another report[6] about the fall of Judah (ch. 52). Thus the theme of "prophet to the nations" does describe the stance of the book as a whole and its portrait of Jeremiah. The fate of Judah—which is on center stage throughout most of the book—is set in the context of God's lordship over the nations as a whole. The God who has called Israel as a people is none other than the Creator of the world and moral Judge of all nations.[7]

One can see a major structural element in Jeremiah by a division of the book in two sections (chs. 1–25; 26–52). Within the first section there is a

---

4. In his commentary W. McKane describes the compilation of the book of Jeremiah as a "rolling corpus" (*A Critical and Exegetical Commentary on Jeremiah* (2 vols.; ICC; Edinburgh: T. & T. Clark, 1986), l–lxxxiii.

5. One of the striking things about the book of Jeremiah is the number of doublets and repeated phrases and allusions. This phenomenon seems to reflect a goal of presenting, and even re-presenting, a full measure of Jeremiah's public prophecies. See the analysis of G. H. Parke-Taylor, *The Formation of the Book of Jeremiah: Doublets and Recurring Phrases* (Atlanta: Society of Biblical Literature, 2000).

6. For sequential readers, a description of Jerusalem's fall (and thus the end of the kingdom of Judah) is given in Jer. 39. Chapter 52 is anticlimactic in several ways. Apparently the account of Judah's fall was attached to the prophet's oracles against other nations as another indication of his prophetic work.

7. Associated with the theme of God's lordship over the nations is the announcement initially revealed in Jeremiah's call that God watches over his word to pluck up and to tear down, to build and to plant (1:10). These words and their elaboration run like a thread through various parts of the book.

mixture of literary genres (see below), but the material is united in theme (largely judgmental on Israel and Judah) and by a persistent lack of regnal dates to situate the oracles in a more precise historical context. Chapter 25 is a summary of judgmental prophecy and may at some point have ended an early collection of Jeremiah's prophecies. Further structural divisions within chapters 1–25 may be identified, but they offer few clues to the overall shape of the book.

The second section has three major subsections (chs. 26–36; 37–44; 46–51). Chapters 26 and 36 are "bookends" that have the rejection of God's word as their theme. Within this subsection, however, is the "book of consolation" (chs. 30–31) and other hopeful material that looks beyond immediate historical disaster toward renewal. The narratives in chapters 37–44 cluster around the fall of Jerusalem and its aftermath, as even the surviving remnants are caught up in self-destructive activities. Chapters 46–51 are oracles against and about other nations.

Literary Characteristics of the Book's Contents

THE BOOK CONTAINS different types of literature in its collection of materials. Poetry and prose are the two most common types of literature, and these two broad categories can be subdivided. In the poetry are such things as judgment speeches, individual laments, and prophecies of future salvation. In the prose are sermons and biographical accounts. In his groundbreaking work, S. Mowinckel describes Jeremiah as comprised of three different sources: poetic oracles (A), biographical narratives (B), and prose sermons (C).[8] The poetry of source A is largely that of Jeremiah, the biographical narratives go back to Baruch and others, and source C is influenced by Deuteronomy and derives from Jeremiah's exilic editors.

A number of scholars have followed Mowinckel's lead either in whole or in part.[9] Others, in reaction, have seen the prose vocabulary of the sermons and biographic narratives as part of the scribal prose of the era—related to Deuteronomy and the books of Kings—but not something that should be divorced necessarily from the prophet himself and his early circle of

---

8. S. Mowinckel, *Zur Komposition des Buches Jeremia* (Oslo: Dybwad, 1914). Chapter 2 is an example of a collection of poetic oracles; ch. 36 is an example of biographical prose; and ch. 7 is an example of a prose sermon.

9. E. Nicholson, *Preaching to the Exiles: A Study of the Prose Tradition in the Book of Jeremiah* (Oxford: Basil Blackwell, 1970); W. Thiel, *Die deuteronomistische Redaktion von Jeremia 1–25* (WMANT 41; Neukirchen-Vluyn: Neukirchener Verlag, 1973); idem, *Die deuteronomistische Redaktion von Jeremia 26–52* (WMANT 52; Neukirchen-Vluyn: Neukirchener Verlag, 1981).

disciples.[10] The issue is not that of faith or skepticism: God, who raised up Jeremiah, can also use the creativity of editors! In the opinion of the present author there is no compelling reason to doubt that Jeremiah (and Baruch) could employ prose forms of expression or that they could be influenced by a work like Deuteronomy.

The attention to literary types and forms of expression in Jeremiah helps us to see what is unique to Jeremiah, especially when compared with other prophetic books. On the one hand, Jeremiah has judgment speeches and prophecies of salvation in common with other prophetic books. On the other hand, three things stand out by comparison: the individual prayers Jeremiah offers, his prose sermons, and the number and range of biographical accounts. No other prophet offers lamentation and confession to God about his circumstances in the manner of Jeremiah, although the language and tone are similar to the laments in the Psalter.[11] No other prophetic book has prose sermons like those of Jeremiah (so similar in tone to Deuteronomy and the hortatory material in 1–2 Kings). More biographical accounts exist for Jeremiah than for any other prophetic figure in the Latter Prophets. For all the difficulty in accounting for the shape of the book of Jeremiah, we know more about this prophet's prayers and events than about any other prophet.

The Interpretation of the Book of Jeremiah and Its Influence[12]

IT IS WORTH noting that the influence of both Jeremiah and Baruch continued well past the compiling of this book.[13] In postbiblical Jewish traditions, Baruch, 2 *Baruch*, 3 *Baruch*, and 4 *Baruch* (also called the *Paraleipomena Ieremiou*) as well as the so-called Epistle of Jeremiah[14] each indicates how the figures

---

10. H. Weippert, *Die Prosareden des Jeremiabuches* (BZAW; Berlin: de Gruyter, 1973). The two-volume Hermeneia commentary by Holladay represents this viewpoint.

11. The bibliography on Jeremiah's "confessions" is large; see M. S. Smith, *The Laments of Jeremiah and Their Contexts: A Literary and Redactional Study of Jer 11–20* (Atlanta: Scholars Press, 1990), and the comments in the commentary on Jer. 11:18–12:17.

12. See further A. H. W. Curtis and T. Römer, *The Book of Jeremiah and Its Reception* (Leuven: Leuven Univ. Press, 1997); and A. Siedlecki, "Jeremiah, Book of (Interpretation Through the 19th-Century)," in *Dictionary of Biblical Interpretation*, ed. J. H. Hayes (2 vols.; Nashville: Abingdon, 1999), 1:564–70.

13. Jeremiah is mentioned in 2 Chron. 35:25 and 36:21, and his oracles influenced a variety of postexilic biblical texts, noncanonical literature, and the New Testament. See Holladay, *Jeremiah* 2:85–93. For more details, see C. Wolff, *Jeremia im Frühjudentum und Urchristentum* (Berlin: Akademie Verlag, 1976).

14. One may find introductions to and descriptions of these works in volumes of the *Anchor Bible Dictionary*, ed. D. N. Freedman (New York: Doubleday, 1992). See the various entries under "Baruch," "Jeremiah (Additions to)," and "Jeremiah, Epistle of."

of Jeremiah and Baruch continued to be of interest to Jews and Christians and how centuries after the compiling of Jeremiah's book the two figures were employed to interpret the faith for believing communities.

(1) The New Testament joins in this interpretive enterprise. When Jesus instructed his disciples about the prophet's reward (Matt. 5:11–12), he could have used Jeremiah as a prime example. It is also the case that the canonical portraits of Jesus as the suffering Messiah are shaped, in part, by the biographical accounts of the persecution and rejection of Jeremiah. Some of the closest parallels in the canon to the narratives of Jesus' ministry are the prose biographical accounts of the prophets—particularly of their witness to and rejection by contemporaries.[15] Through the Gospels the accounts of Jeremiah's prophetic suffering are retroactively illuminated as pointers to the fulfillment of the ministry of Christ.

For Christian instruction, Jeremiah is to be read as part of the canonical record of God's self-revelation. Interpretation is aided by historical or literary methods by which any reader may understand better this prophet and book. The goal of a theological interpretation of Jeremiah, however, is not only to grasp the book's particular witness to God's self-revelation but also to see that particular witness as an integral part of Scripture as a whole. Thus my comments in the Bridging Contexts and Contemporary Significance sections will make references to other scriptural texts as indications of Jeremiah's place in the larger biblical-theological enterprise.

(2) Reading Jeremiah as instruction for Christian faith means reading the book as the revelation of the God and Father of Jesus Christ, as an anticipation of the gospel revealed in and through Christ the Redeemer, and in dependence on the Holy Spirit, who convicts one of sinfulness and assures one of forgiveness in Christ. Stated differently, a Christian hermeneutic for interpreting Scripture should be consistent with God's triunity, a formulation of the early church that ultimately makes a doctrine of God specifically Christian. An adequate mode of interpreting Scripture for Christian faith, therefore, places Christ at the center of confession while affirming that the Old Testament revelation is an authoritative disclosure of God in pre-Christian form. One of the most surprising (and encouraging) developments in the second half of the twentieth century has been the revival of Trinitarian theology among both mainline Protestant and evangelical churches.[16]

---

15. See M. Knowles, *Jeremiah in Matthew's Gospel: The Rejected Prophet Motif in Matthean Redaction* (Sheffield: JSOT Press, 1993).

16. Perusing the catalog of a theological library will amply confirm that reflection on the Trinity has made a remarkable resurgence. Good sources for further thought are: M. Erickson, *God in Three Persons: A Contemporary Interpretation of the Trinity* (Grand Rapids: Baker, 1995); T. F. Torrance, *The Christian Doctrine of God: One Being in Three Persons* (Edinburgh: T. & T. Clark, 1996); and P. Toon, *Our Triune God: A Biblical Portrayal of the Trinity* (Wheaton: Victor, 1996).

A related way to grasp the link between the Old and New Testaments and to affirm Christ as the true scope[17] of Scripture is to see him in his threefold office as the true prophet, priest, and king of God's people. This is an interpretation that goes back to the patristic and Reformation periods, particularly among the churches who are heir to the legacy of John Calvin, but it has been adopted by other schools of thought as well. It need not be thought of in rigid dogmatic terms but as one way among others to see Christ as the culmination of what God began through the prophetic movement, the priestly ministry, and the royal house in Israel.[18]

(3) Christians should read Jeremiah ecclesiologically, since much of the book is in the form of corporate addresses to Israel, Judah, or remnants thereof. To be sure, individuals can profit spiritually from the book, but the primary audience for the compilers is a significant indicator of the categories in which Jeremiah thought (and thus through which God intended to communicate). A "bridging" mechanism employed in this commentary is the conviction that an address to Israel or Judah should be directed to the church through Christ and in light of the gospel. The church inherits the promises made to and essential responsibilities expected of Israel in the Old Testament.

The New Testament witness proclaims that in Christ there is a fulfillment "already" of Israel's covenants and promises, yet it is restrained in projecting a "not-yet fulfillment" of future hope in a people called Israel.[19] Thus Israel's future restoration, so gloriously depicted in the Old Testament, is organically related to the church in the unfolding plan of salvation. Thus, it is in the church (= people of God) that such prophecies have found and will find fulfillment.[20]

---

17. Christ as the *scope* of Scripture is a favorite theme of the church fathers. Although some of their exegetical methods appear arbitrary, the substance of their claim is still valid. See the essays on patristic biblical interpretation in P. Blowers, ed., *The Bible in Greek Christian Antiquity* (Notre Dame, Ind.: Univ. of Notre Dame Press, 1997). Three modern biblical scholars whose work presupposes Trinitarian doctrine with a Christological center are: B. Childs, *Biblical Theology of the Old and New Testaments* (Minneapolis: Fortress, 1993); F. Watson, *Text and Truth: Redefining Biblical Theology* (Grand Rapids: Eerdmans, 1997); and C. Seitz, *Word Without End: The Old Testament As Abiding Theological Witness* (Grand Rapids: Eerdmans, 1998).

18. For a treatment of the threefold office in both historical and contemporary theology, see G. Wainwright, *For Our Salvation: Two Approaches to the Work of Christ* (Grand Rapids: Eerdmans, 1997), 99–186. One may interpret Christ as the culmination of prophecy, priesthood, and royalty whether beginning with a historical-critical analysis or typological, intertextual, and even sociological readings.

19. There is future hope for Israel in the New Testament (cf. Rom. 11:25–36). I do not think it wise to give priority to a literal reading of Old Testament prophecies concerning the future of Israel when the New Testament does not do so.

20. Some examples would be J. Bright, *The Kingdom of God* (Nashville: Abingdon, 1953); P. E. Hughes, *Interpreting Prophecy* (Grand Rapids: Eerdmans, 1976); H. LaRondelle, *The Israel*

Likewise, Israel's covenant responsibilities revealed in Torah and the Prophets and set forth in institutional life have their typological counterparts in the church, where Christ, the mediator of the new covenant through his blood, has created a fellowship of disciples through the power of the Spirit.[21]

Since there are clear differences between ancient Israel and the modern church, interpreters should not expect a one-to-one correspondence between the message to ancient Israel and that to the church. An Old Testament text should be heard through Christ and in light of the gospel. The reason is simple enough, even if the process of interpretation is complicated: For Christians there can be no other foundation than that laid in Christ. What the Law or the Prophets (indeed, the Old Testament as a whole!) could not do—although they bear authoritative witness to it—Christ has done. Nevertheless, both ancient Israel and modern church are graciously called "the people of God," so that God's word through Jeremiah to his people of old can be interpreted as a word to the current generation of his people as they seek to be obedient to the gospel.

Christians have developed other methods for interpreting Old Testament prophecy for and about the church. Some of these may put more emphasis on the distinction between Israel and the modern church and on the fulfillment of Old Testament prophetic hope in a spiritually renewed Israel within the bounds of the ancient promised land (complete with a millennial reign of Christ in Jerusalem). Readers are invited to investigate for themselves the advantages of other approaches.[22]

The Last Years of the Judean State: Jeremiah's Historical Context

Reconstructing Chronology[23]

ACCORDING TO 1:2, God called Jeremiah to his task in the thirteenth year of King Josiah. This simple reference masks more than one chronological diffi-

---

of God in Prophecy (Berrien Springs, Mich.: Andrews Univ. Press, 1983); W. VanGemeren, *The Story of Salvation: The Story of Salvation from Creation to the New Jerusalem* (Grand Rapids: Zondervan, 1988); idem, *Interpreting the Prophetic Word* (Grand Rapids: Zondervan, 1990).

21. See further, D. L. Baker, *Two Testaments, One Bible*, 2d ed. (Downer's Grove: InterVarsity, 1992). His discussions of typology and promise and fulfillment are especially helpful.

22. Two excellent discussions of hermeneutics, dispensational and otherwise, are J. S. Feinberg, ed., *Continuity and Discontinuity: Perspectives on the Relationship Between the Old and New Testaments: Essays in Honor of S. Lewis Johnson, Jr.* (Westchester, Ill.: Crossway, 1988); C. A. Blaising and D. L. Bock, ed., *Dispensationalism, Israel, and the Church: The Search for Definition* (Grand Rapids: Zondervan, 1992).

23. For discussion of a difficult subject, see E. R. Thiele, *The Mysterious Numbers of the Hebrew Kings* (3d ed.; Grand Rapids: Zondervan, 1983); more briefly, M. Cogan, "Chronology

culty in the modern calculation of dates in antiquity. Quite apart from the task of establishing the thirteenth year of King Josiah according to modern reckoning (essentially the calendar year 627 B.C.; see below), some scholars have concluded that the "call" of Jeremiah narrated in 1:2 is actually the date of Jeremiah's birth, not the beginning of his prophetic career.[24] If Jeremiah was born in the thirteenth year of Josiah, then his delivery of public oracles probably did not begin until the end of Josiah's thirty-one-year reign. This would account for the fact that little in the book is explicitly dated to Josiah's reign.

For other scholars, the thirteenth year of Josiah is indeed the commencement of Jeremiah's prophetic ministry, while he was a young man (probably a teenager).[25] The few references to Josiah in Jeremiah (3:6; 25:3; 36:2) do assume that he actually prophesied during Josiah's reign, even if no other specific dates or settings from Josiah's reign are provided. Perhaps his public speaking during Josiah's reign was sporadic, with interludes of silence, and largely supportive of the king's reforming efforts. Since a primary aim of this book is to account for Judah's fall to the Babylonians, much of the prophet's preaching before 605 may have been left out. In any case, some of the undated oracles in chapters 2–20 may come from the period of Josiah's reign and before the rise of Babylon to power in 605.[26] What is clear from the book is that the dated oracles fall almost exclusively in the reigns of Jehoiakim, Jehoiachin, and Zedekiah, and during the brief governorship of Gedaliah (i.e., from ca. 609 to 585 B.C.).

(Hebrew Bible)," in *ABD*, 1:1005–11; and G. Galil, *The Chronology of the Kings of Israel and Judah* (Leiden: Brill, 1996). Each work takes the scriptural texts seriously in an attempt to present an absolute chronology where possible. The fact that each presents a different chronology in places (and the fact that there are still other competing schemes) urges caution upon the interpreter. For Babylonian and Egyptian dates see D. J. Wiseman, *Chronicles of Chaldean Kings (626–556 B.C.) in the British Museum* (London: British Museum, 1956); A. Spalinger, "Egypt and Babylon: A Survey (620–550 BC)," *Studien zur altägyptische Kultur* 5 (1977): 228–44.

24. The two-volume commentary on Jeremiah by William Holladay is based on a reconstruction of Jeremiah's career that assumes the thirteenth year of Josiah (ca. 627 B.C.) as the prophet's birth. Holladay provides a full bibliography of others, pro and con, who discuss the date of the prophet's birth and the commencement of his public ministry.

25. For a defense of the thirteenth year as the beginning of Jeremiah's prophetic career, assuming a date for his birth ca. 640 B.C. or earlier, see J. R. Lundbom, *The Early Career of the Prophet Jeremiah* (Lewiston, N.Y.: Edwin Mellen, 1993). Lundbom proposes that Jeremiah was called, as a teenager, in Josiah's thirteenth year, but that he did not commence his public prophecy until a few years later, prompted by the discovery of the book of the Torah in Josiah's eighteenth year (622 B.C.).

26. It is also possible that some of the oracles in chs. 30–31, concerned with the reconstitution of Israel (i.e., the northern kingdom), come from the early period of Jeremiah's ministry. According to 2 Kings 23, Josiah's reforming measures included parts of the former northern kingdom (= Israel), and Jeremiah may have supported these efforts

Jeremiah 1:2 (thirteenth year of Josiah) also represents the most common type of chronological difficulty for interpretation, that is, the reconstruction of an absolute date. Changes in political hegemony or in dynastic rule, coupled with differing customs as to the beginning of a calendar year (spring or autumn) or the dating of an initial year of rule (accession year or new-year dating), mean that many events are dated by approximation and/or are given in overlapping years.[27] Thus interpreters will see among scholarly reconstructions such dates as 628, 627, or 626 B.C. for Josiah's thirteenth year, or sometimes the double reference 628/627 or 627/626 B.C.

Perhaps the biggest discussion of a date in Jeremiah's lifetime concerns the time of Jerusalem's destruction by the Babylonians. Some scholars conclude that it took place in 587 B.C.; others have claimed 586.[28] The date depends on the reckoning of the date of Jehoiachin's exile to Babylon, the related dating(s) of Zedekiah's reign, the references to exiles taken to Babylon in both Nebuchadnezzar's eighteenth year (52:29) and nineteenth year (52:12; cf. 2 Kings 25:8), and the evidence of the Babylonian Chronicles. In a commentary of this nature, it is less important to argue which year is preferable and more important to ask about the significance assigned by the prophet to the city's destruction.

Judean Kings and Political History[29]

JOSIAH IS CELEBRATED as a king without a peer in Judah (2 Kings 23:25). In summary, he ascended the throne (ca. 640 B.C.) at the age of eight, and during his reign of thirty-one years he instituted a nation-wide religious reform as well as extricated Judah from its status as vassal to the Assyrians. He died in battle with the Egyptians (609 B.C., 2 Kings 23:29–30). Josiah was not the only casualty in the struggle between Egypt and Babylon that developed in the last years of the seventh century. Ultimately the whole region of Syria-Palestine was affected by the struggle.

To grasp the significance of Josiah's reign, its tragic aftermath, and its influence on the period of Jeremiah's public ministry, we must consider briefly Judah's dealings with Assyria. For at least fifty years previously, Assyria had

---

with prophecies about the restoration of Israel. If so, the oracles in chs. 30–31 have been updated and are placed in a context where they point to a new future for all of God's people.

27. See Cogan, "Chronology," 1:1006, for brief explanations of these terms.

28. See briefly ibid., 1:1008; Galil, *Chronology of the Kings*, 108–18.

29. See the two articles by A. Malamat, "The Last Kings of Judah and the Fall of Jerusalem: An Historical-Chronological Study," *IEJ* 18 (1968): 137–56; "The Twilight of Judah: In the Egyptian-Babylonian Maelstrom," *VT* 25 (1975): 123–45; also Galil, *Chronology of the Kings*, 108–18.

held Judah as its vassal (just as it held virtually all of the eastern Mediterranean states). Even earlier the prophets Amos and Hosea had announced divine judgment on Israel and Samaria, and in the last quarter of the eighth century the Assyrians laid siege to Samaria. The city and what remained of the nation fell in 722/721 B.C.

Judah managed to escape destruction when Ahaz submitted to the Assyrian ruler Tiglath-pileser III and became his vassal (2 Kings 16:1–17:6). His wickedness was partially overcome by his son Hezekiah, who instituted a religious reform and rebelled against the Assyrians (2 Kings 18:1–7). The Assyrians attacked Hezekiah and Jerusalem in 701, and although the Lord miraculously spared the city and dynasty from destruction (2 Kings 18:13–19:37), Judah would soon enter Assyrian vassal status and remain there until Josiah's reign.

Although there were earlier signs of weakness in Assyria, its dissolution accelerated rapidly by 627 B.C. The death of its last strong king, Assurbanipal, came in that year or perhaps a little earlier. Soon after, the young Josiah began movements toward political independence. By 612 B.C. the Assyrian capital city of Nineveh had fallen to rebels, and efforts to reconstitute the Assyrian army were futile. Josiah was killed in battle in 609 B.C. in an attempt to keep an Egyptian army from moving north to Syria to support the remnants of the Assyrian army.[30] The year of Assurbanipal's death and the commencement of Jeremiah's prophetic career essentially coincide. Also, Josiah had recently begun an effort at religious reform, a theme dear to the heart of the biblical authors.[31] The stage was thereby set for a tumultuous period in the ancient world, marked on the one hand by political chaos and destruction and on the other hand by the rise of prophetic figures like Jeremiah, Habakkuk, and Ezekiel.

In Josiah's eighteenth year (622 B.C.), repairs at the Jerusalem temple complex brought to light a scroll of the "Law in the temple of the LORD" (2 Kings 22:8), a "covenant" document that proved to be a catalyst for a more thoroughgoing reform (2 Kings 23). Scholars have debated the identity of the scroll for years; since the description of Josiah's reforming efforts reflects the criticisms of the book of Deuteronomy regarding idolatry and polytheism, the best conclusion appears to be Deuteronomy or an earlier form of it. In

---

30. Apparently the Egyptians stood to inherit Assyrian title to the region of Syria-Palestine if they supported the Assyrians in their struggle with the Babylonian rebels (see Malamat, "The Twilight of Judah," 124–29).

31. According to 2 Chron. 34:3–4, Josiah's physical maturation also resulted in a spiritual maturation. In the eighth year of his reign (632 B.C.) he began to seek the Lord in earnest fashion, and in his twelfth year (628 B.C.) he began a religious reform in Judah and Jerusalem.

spite of the prominence given Josiah by the biblical writers, it is not clear how successful (i.e., how thorough) his religious reforms actually were. Jeremiah's criticisms of the people during the reigns of Jehoiakim and Zedekiah indicate that those practices opposed by Josiah (and Deuteronomy) had not been eradicated. Perhaps in a perverse way, Josiah's untimely death contributed to their rebirth.

Jeremiah is not mentioned in 2 Kings or 2 Chronicles as a prophetic figure during Josiah's reform measures. The prophet's criticisms of Judean idolatry and polytheism (e.g., Jer. 2–3), however, leave no doubt that he agreed with the essential aims of the reform as presented in 2 Kings 23. Also, Jeremiah's commendation of Josiah (Jer. 22:15) indicates an appreciation of the king's moral stance.[32]

When Josiah died, the "people of the land" (probably Judean landowners) made his son Jehoahaz king in his stead (2 Kings 23:30–33; 2 Chron. 36:1–4).[33] Jehoahaz was not the oldest son, and after a three-month reign he was removed by the Egyptians in favor of his older brother Eliakim (2 Kings 23:34–37; 2 Chron. 36:4–8). They even changed his name to Jehoiakim at his accession. Apparently Jehoiakim represented a policy more in line with Egyptian wishes, whereas Jehoahaz may have preferred a more independent course like that of his father.

Jehoiakim reigned for eleven years (ca. 609–598 B.C.). Jeremiah opposed his policies completely. During Jehoiakim's reign his Egyptian handlers were defeated by the Babylonians in a decisive battle at Carchemish in northern Syria (summer, 605 B.C.). In the same year the Babylonian crown prince Nebuchadnezzar, who was the architect of the Egyptian defeat, succeeded his father on the Babylonian throne.[34]

Babylon's rise to political power was a major shift in political relations for all the states in the region. During the years 604–601 B.C., Nebuchadnezzar

---

32. According to 2 Chron. 35:25, Jeremiah offered a lament for Josiah upon his death.

33. Jehoahaz is also called Shallum in Jer. 22:11–12.

34. According to Dan. 1:1 Nebuchadnezzar also moved against Jehoiakim in the latter's third year and took some Judeans into exile (e.g., Daniel and his friends). Nothing about this action is recorded elsewhere in the Bible or in the Babylonian Chronicles. It may be, however, that the notice in Daniel follows an accession-year form of reckoning. See M. K. Mercer, "Daniel 1:1 and Jehoiakim's Three Years of Servitude," *AUSS* 27 (1989): 179–92; T. Longman, *Daniel* (NIVAC; Grand Rapids: Zondervan, 1999), 43–45. If so, then the third year of Jehoiakim in Dan. 1:1 in an accession-year dating scheme would be 605 B.C. According to Jer. 46:2, the battle against the Egyptians (605) was in Jehoiakim's fourth year. The fourth year would be reckoned on a nonaccession-year scheme. Nebuchadnezzar was made king soon after the battle, and the campaign of the Babylonians in the region continued through the year. Thus the reference in Dan. 1:1 likely refers to Babylonian activity that took place sometime not long after the summer of 605.

campaigned in the west, taking cities on or near the Palestinian coast. In the winter of 604 Ashkelon was attacked and burned (cf. Jer. 36:9).[35] About this time or soon after, Jehoiakim paid tribute to Nebuchadnezzar and served three years as a Babylonian vassal. In the winter of 601/600 Egypt and Babylon fought a bloody and indecisive battle. Perhaps Jehoiakim rebelled against Nebuchadnezzar after the latter's battle with Egypt; in any case, the Babylonian king organized a campaign against Jehoiakim and Judah. With the Babylonians at the gate in Jerusalem, Jehoiakim died in December 598.[36]

According to 2 Kings 24:8, Jehoiachin,[37] son of Jehoiakim, became king and ruled three months in Jerusalem. On March 16, 597 B.C.,[38] Jehoiachin surrendered to Nebuchadnezzar and was taken to Babylon along with thousands of other Judeans. He would stay there until his death. The last reference to him comes thirty-seven years later in the accession year of the Babylonian king Evil-Merodach (561 B.C.; 2 Kings 25:29–30; Jer. 52:31–34).[39]

Nebuchadnezzar appointed Mattaniah, another son of Josiah, as the next "king" in Jerusalem (2 Kings 24:17; 2 Chron. 36:10–13). His reign lasted eleven years (ca. 597–586 B.C.). He was an uncle of the exiled Jehoiachin. Nebuchadnezzar changed Mattaniah's name to Zedekiah. Eventually Zedekiah conspired against Nebuchadnezzar (cf. Jer. 27) and then formally rebelled against him. In Zedekiah's ninth year, the Babylonian army again came against Judah and Jerusalem and laid siege to the city. A feeble attempt by the Egyptians to intimidate the Babylonians failed (Jer. 37:7–38:28), and in the eleventh year of Zedekiah's reign the city fell to the besiegers. Depending on one's reckoning, it was either August of 587 B.C. or, more likely, the same month in 586. Zedekiah was captured, blinded, and taken to Babylon. The temple was looted, the city was burned, and thousands more were taken into exile.

For those who remained in the land, Nebuchadnezzar appointed Gedaliah as governor.[40] Gedaliah was from the family of Shaphan, who had been a high

---

35. Wiseman, *Chronicles of Chaldean Kings*, 69.

36. According to 2 Chron. 36:6 Jehoiakim was in the custody of Nebuchadnezzar. The various biblical references do not provide details of his mysterious death. See A. R. Green, "The Fate of Jehoiakim," *AUSS* 20 (1982): 103–9.

37. Jeremiah calls him Coniah (22:24) and Jeconiah (24:1).

38. The date is calculated from Babylonian records. See Wiseman, *Chronicles of Chaldean Kings*, 72–73. Among the Judeans taken into exile at this time was Ezekiel.

39. In an astounding coincidence, archaeologists discovered ration tablets from the Babylonian administration that mention Jehoiachin and his five sons; see W. F. Albright, "King Jehoiachin in Exile," *BA* 5 (1942): 49–55.

40. There are two clay bullae from the time period that likely refer to this Gedaliah. The first is from Lachish and reads, "Belonging to Gedaliah [w]ho is over the house." The provenance of the second is not known; it reads, "Belonging to Gedaliah, servant of the king." For bibliography see N. Avigad, *Hebrew Bullae from the Time of Jeremiah: Remnants of a Burnt Archive* (Jerusalem: Israel Exploration Society, 1986), 25.

government official under Josiah. Shaphan's son Ahikam, Gedaliah's father, had supported Jeremiah after a disastrous sermon during the reign of Jehoiakim (Jer. 26:24). Jeremiah does not criticize Gedaliah the way that he did Jehoiakim, Jehoiachin, and Zedekiah. Gedaliah was assassinated by disaffected Judeans, and the curtain comes down on affairs in Palestine (Jer. 40–44).

Jeremiah's Place in the Last Years of the Judean State and Its Destruction

JEREMIAH WAS FROM a priestly family who lived just north of Jerusalem in the village of Anathoth. Centuries earlier the priest Abiathar was ousted by Solomon from his post in the royal administration and removed to Anathoth (1 Kings 2:26–27). It is likely, therefore, that Jeremiah and his family were exposed to many traditions of Israelite and Judean history. Nothing else is known about his family except that they were skeptical of his prophetic activity and some members conspired against him (Jer. 12:6; cf. 11:21).

As a young man during Josiah's reign, Jeremiah had a religious experience in which he was called to the prophetic office (Jer. 1). Associated with his call was an announcement of a threat to Judah from the north (1:14). The identity of the foe from the north is not revealed, although the image of the foe appears periodically in Jeremiah's oracles (e.g., 4:6; 5:15–17; 6:1–5). Scholars have debated its identity. Proposals include the Scythians, the Assyrians, or the Babylonians, depending on an early or late date assigned to Jeremiah's "call" and the nature of his early prophetic career.[41] In any case, the threatening foe from the north is eventually seen to be Babylon, which arose to dominance in the region in 605 B.C.

Little in this book relates explicitly to the earlier years of Jeremiah's prophetic activity, although his preaching against idolatry and polytheism is complementary to the reforming efforts undertaken by King Josiah (see above). Jeremiah seems particularly influenced by the eighth-century prophet

---

41. Because of the constraints of geography, an attacking army would often approach Israel or Judah from the north. Thus it is possible that Jeremiah intentionally did not name the northern threat, but simply emphasized its menacing profile and left its identity to the startled imagination of his hearers. Since Babylonian resurgence had not begun in 627 B.C.—the traditional or early date for the prophet's call—those who look for a likely foe at this time have suggested either the Scythians or the Assyrians. For the discussion see H. Cazelles, "Zephaniah, Jeremiah, and the Scythians in Palestine," in *A Prophet to the Nations: Essays in Jeremiah Studies*, ed. L. Perdue and B. Novacs (Winona Lake, Ind.: Eisenbrauns, 1984), 129–49. Some scholars have even concluded that Jeremiah wrongly threatened Judah with invading hordes of Scythians or Assyrians in 627 and that later his editors used the prophecies as indications of the coming Babylonian threat.

named Hosea, who also opposed idolatry and polytheism and who understood the covenant between God and Israel to be like that of a marriage.[42]

The majority of Jeremiah's dated prophetic oracles come in the reigns of Jehoiakim and Zedekiah, uttered from 609 to 586 B.C. In these prophecies the corporate life of Judah is described and criticized. The political history sketched above is necessary for the interpretation of the prophet and his book, but it is primarily background material. It is the same for the narratives about Jeremiah. The political history is presupposed but often not cited directly. Readers are told, for example, that Jeremiah preached a difficult "sermon" at the beginning of Jehoiakim's reign (Jer. 26; cf. Jer. 7), but we are told nothing about the Egyptian appointment of Jehoiakim or of the tragic death of Josiah at the hands of the Egyptians. We are also told that Jeremiah was forbidden to preach at the temple complex (Jer. 36), but there is no direct reference to why the fifth year of Jehoiakim was significant for the message he preached.[43]

More often the narrative accounts are concerned to tell about the suffering and rejection of Jeremiah rather than relating his persecution directly to the larger political horizon.[44] It is clear, however, that Jeremiah announced God's decisive judgment on Judah and Jerusalem through the historical agency of Babylon and its ruler, Nebuchadnezzar. History was not only the medium of revelation; it also produced the agent of God's judgment.

Jeremiah's circumstances in the first siege of Jerusalem in the winter of 598/597 B.C. are not known, although his opinion that the siege was divine judgment on Judah is made clear. Also clear is his opposition to the political policies, moral commitments, and spiritual sensibilities of Jehoiakim, Jehoiachin, and Zedekiah. He was convinced that Judah had not heeded the lessons of 598/597, so his message of judgment continued throughout his career. Particularly memorable were his wearing of a yoke to symbolize servitude to Babylon and his confrontations with Hananiah, a prophet who opposed him (Jer. 27–28).

Jeremiah was already under arrest by the order of King Zedekiah when the walls were breached by the Babylonians. This had not been his first

---

42. In addition to the brief sketch of Jeremiah's theology provided in the introductory sections of this commentary, one may consult the detailed study of M. Schulz-Rauch, *Hosea und Jeremia: Zur Wirkungsgeschichte des Hoseabuches* (Stuttgart: Calwer Verlag, 1996).

43. Jer. 36:9. As noted above, Nebuchadnezzar's army campaigned in the region during this year, destroying Ashkelon in the winter of 604. As an Egyptian appointee, Jehoiakim's future and perhaps that of Judah hung in the balance.

44. There are a number of accounts in the book concerned with Jeremiah's persecution at the hands of Judeans. They range from laments about his circumstances (e.g., 15:10–21) to accounts of beatings and imprisonments (e.g., 37:14–15).

encounter with Judean authorities, nor would it be the last time that his prophetic counsel was sought and then rejected. The Babylonian victors released him from imprisonment, and he briefly joined the circle of Judeans around Gedaliah at Mizpah. When Gedaliah was assassinated, Jeremiah and his scribal companion, Baruch, were taken to Egypt by a band of Judeans (Jer. 40–44).[45] They professed interest in his prophetic counsel but refused to follow it. There he continued to offer prophetic oracles, and (apparently) he, Baruch, and others collected his previous oracles. The reference to his presence in Egypt is the latest notice preserved about him in the book. Scripture offers no information about his last days and his death. Jeremiah, like most prophets, would be more influential in death than in life.

Chronological Chart

Historical event	Date	Scripture
13th year of Josiah	627	Jer. 1:2
18th year of Josiah/discovery of book of the law	622	2 Kings 22
Fall of Nineveh	612	
31st year of Josiah/his death	609	2 Kings 22:1
3-month reign of Shallum/Jehoahaz	609	2 Kings 23:31
1st year of Jehoiakim (Egyptian appointee)	609	2 Kings 23:34–36
Battle of Carchemish/ Nebuchadnezzar made king	605	
Babylonian threat against Judah and Jehoiakim, Daniel and others taken into exile	605	Dan. 1:1
Babylonian campaigns in Syria-Palestine	604–601	
Destruction of Ashkelon by Babylonians	604	
Jehoiakim becomes a vassal of Babylon	604–603	2 Kings 24:1
Babylonian defeat on Egyptian border	601	
Jehoiakim revolts against Nebuchadnezzar	ca. 601	2 Kings 24:1
11th year of Jehoiakim/his death	598	
3-month reign of Jehoiachin in Jerusalem	597	2 Kings 24:8
Jerusalem besieged by Babylonians	598/597	2 Kings 24:10
Jerusalem surrenders/ Jehoiachin and people taken in exile	597	2 Kings 24:12–16

---

45. In his oracles against Moab and Ammon (48:1–49:6), Jeremiah may reflect knowledge of Babylonian campaigns in Transjordan after the fall of Jerusalem and his forced relocation to Egypt. Josephus records that Babylon campaigned in Ammon as a reprisal for the murder of Gedaliah (*Ant.* 10.9.7). This campaign may be the setting for a 3d group of Judean exiles taken to Babylon in Nebuchadnezzar's 23d year (Jer 52:30).

Zedekiah/Mattaniah made king by Nebuchadnezzar	597	2 Kings 24:17–18
Regional conference in Jerusalem	ca. 594	Jer. 27
Zedekiah rebels against Nebuchadnezzar	ca. 594	2 Kings 24:20
Babylonians besiege Jerusalem	588	2 Kings 25:1; Jer. 39:1
Jerusalem falls in 11th year of Zedekiah	586	2 Kings 25:3–11
Gedaliah appointed governor by Babylonians	586	2 Kings 25:22
Gedaliah assassinated	586?	2 Kings 25:25/Jer. 41
Jeremiah and Baruch taken to Egypt	586?	Jer. 43
Another group taken in exile	582/581	Jer. 52:30
Jehoiachin released from house arrest	561	2 Kings 25:27
Babylon falls to Cyrus	539	cf. Ezra 1:1; Dan. 5:31

Aspects of Jeremiah's Theology

A THEOLOGICAL ANALYSIS of the book of Jeremiah should concern itself primarily with what the book claims about God. To paraphrase a wise Bible teacher from the past: If someone thinks rightly about God, that person will be pointed in the right direction about any other matter. Thus, if we grasp the basic claims about God in the book of Jeremiah, we should gain some clarity about the other matters addressed in the book. We should not mistake the following sketches as substitutes for an extended examination of the biblical texts themselves or think that Jeremiah's theology can be reduced to a collection of ideas. Form and content go together.

As an indispensable part of Scripture, Jeremiah bears authoritative witness to the one God of creation, revealed consummately in Jesus Christ and known through the work of the Holy Spirit. The sketches that follow can only indicate in briefest fashion how Jeremiah contributes to the unfolding drama of God's self-revelation.[46]

God As Creator

THAT GOD IS THE CREATOR of the world is assumed and confessed rather than argued (4:23–28; cf. the "echo" of Gen. 1:2 in 4:23; 10:12–16; 32:17; 51:15, 19). Three main lines of thought follow from this confession about God. (1) By virtue of being Creator, God is also the Lord of all nations. Jeremiah himself is called as a prophet to the "nations" (1:10), and his words are

---

46. A perceptive sketch of elements of Jeremiah's theology is in Appendix A of D. Kidner's *The Message of Jeremiah* (Downers Grove, Ill.: InterVarsity, 1987), 163–72. This appendix is entitled "Sin, Judgment, Repentance, Grace and Salvation in the Preaching of Jeremiah." See also L. Perdue, "The Book of Jeremiah in Old Testament Theology," *Troubling Jeremiah*, ed. A. R. Pete Diamond et al. (Sheffield: Sheffield Academic Press, 1999), 320–38.

used by God not only to interpret history but in a mysterious way also to form events and historical processes. There are extended oracles directed to and against other nations (chs. 46–51), where they are weighed in the moral balance and judged. There are universal standards to which God holds all nations accountable. Even Nebuchadnezzar is called God's "servant" (25:9) because God employs him to chastise his people; yet Babylon too will fall under God's righteous judgment. What moderns might call the "historical process" is a part of God's revelatory interplay with creation.

(2) God is Lord of the processes that sustain or affect creation. God can send drought (14:1–6) as a sign of Judah's faithlessness. Clouds and wind serve him (4:11–13). Wild beasts serve as his rod of judgment (5:6). The constancy of night and day testify to his goodness (31:35–36; 33:25). Fertility is one of his gifts (31:27).

(3) God can renew creation or bring something new to it. The enigmatic saying of 31:22 proclaims that God will create (*br³*) something new. God is like a potter who may rethrow the clay if not satisfied (18:1–11). The book of consolation (chs. 30–31) is predicated on the affirmation that God can restore the physical and spiritual conditions of his people. Within that corpus, the announcement of a new or everlasting covenant (31:31–34; 32:40) underscores the commitment of God to renew completely his relationship to his people and their relationships with one another. A provisional fulfillment of these hopes comes with the restoration of a remnant from Babylonian exile. It is a foretaste of grander reconciliation yet to come.

In all these things the book of Jeremiah plays a role in the biblical depiction of God as Creator.[47] For the most part, creation is simply assumed as the arena of God's self-revelation, so that Jeremiah advances little that is new or distinctive. The main thrust of the book is to apply the belief in God as Creator and Lord to the issues facing the people of Judah and Jerusalem. In the third point noted above, Jeremiah prepares for the broader eschatological horizon revealed in the New Testament. God has promised to make all things new!

God Calls Israel to His Service

GOD CHOSE ISRAEL (through its ancestors) as a recipient of his covenant (*bᵉrit*) and his gracious loyalty (*ḥesed*).[48] Israel was called out of Egypt (7:22; 11:4; 23:7–8). God's choice of and resulting bond with Israel comprise the essence of *his* covenant (*bᵉrit*; 11:1–7; 31:31–32). Jeremiah will never describe the covenant as Israel's; it belongs to God and is extended as a gift to Israel. Mar-

---

47. See further R. Simkins, *Creator and Creation: Nature in the Worldview of Ancient Israel* (Peabody, Mass.: Hendrickson, 1994).

48. Jeremiah's convictions on this matter are similar to those of Hosea and Deuteronomy.

riage is a metaphor for the covenant (2:2–3; 31:32), as is the family image of the people as the Lord's "house" (12:7–9). As God's "chosen," Israel owes God exclusive worship and wholehearted obedience. Through the prophet, God often designates Israel/Judah as "my people."[49]

All of Jeremiah's criticism of the people for their failures is predicated on the two convictions that God had chosen Israel as his people and expected loyalty and obedience on their part (cf. 22:9). The corporate failure of Israel/Judah, complete with all its institutions and leadership, is the dominant theme of this book. That failure, however, can only be understood in light of the presupposition of a gracious covenant given to them and subsequently broken by them.

God calls leaders to serve his people. The prophet calls them shepherds (2:8; 3:15; 23:1) and watchmen (6:17), since God has entrusted the education and care of the people to them. More specifically the leaders are kings and princes, priests, prophets, and wise men. Monarchs in Judah are descended from David and occupy David's seat (22:2). As such the kings and princes are recipients of God's promises to David's "house,"[50] and they are called to uphold justice and righteousness (21:11–12; 22:1–30). Priests are responsible to instruct the people in matters of faith and to act as mediators between God and the people in sacrificial service (2:8; 5:31; 18:18). The priesthood is the recipient of a covenant from God (33:21). Prophets provide the people with God's word (2:8; 18:18; 23:9–40) and communicate his will. When rightly engaged in ministry, they are God's "servants" (7:25; 25:4). Insight is a gift from God, and the wise who perceive the truth should offer counsel (18:18).

A fundamental assumption of Jeremiah's judgmental prophecies is that the leadership of the people had been in the forefront of corporate failure. Monarchy, priesthood, and prophecy all stood against him and diverted the people away from God's word through the prophet to them. Nevertheless, after judgment God's resolve to bless included a new David (23:5–6; 33:19–22), a renewed priesthood (33:19–22), and faithful prophets like Jeremiah (and Uriah, 26:20–23). In the broader unfolding of God's revelation, Christ becomes the culmination of the promises to David's house, the ministries of the priesthood, and the prophetic work among God's people.[51]

As an Old Testament book, Jeremiah's emphases are corporate, institutional, and political. Theological analysis comes in and through these

---

49. Jer. 2:11, 32; 4:22; 5:26, 31; 7:12; 8:7; 12:14, 16; 15:7; 23:13, 22, 27, 32; 29:32; 30:3, 22; 33:24; 50:6; 51:45.

50. Cf. 2 Sam. 7.

51. Christ embodies the hopes of Israel in his "threefold office" as prophet, priest, and king. See the introductory comments on interpreting the book of Jeremiah.

emphases. They are the primary ways in which Jeremiah addresses the matter of ecclesiology, that is, the doctrine of God's people and their life before him. From the covenant graciously given to Israel, later readers can extrapolate a way of understanding the Christian church as yet another and later corporate form of God's people. Judah and Israel represent an earlier type of the corporate identity of God's people.

Jeremiah also points to the broader biblical theme of the remnant. Even where there is chaos and massive failure (as in the prophet's day), there was also a remnant saved by grace. This paradigm shows itself time and again in the unfolding historical drama of redemption, from the family of Noah saved from the Flood down through the pages of church history.

God Gives Gifts to Sustain His People

A COROLLARY TO the confession that God chose Israel as his people and delivered them from Egyptian bondage is the confession that God guided the people through the desert and granted them land (2:7). Israel's settlement in the land of Canaan was actually a settlement in God's earthly inheritance (*nahala*; so 2:7). As God's inheritance it was not Israel's to do with as they pleased; instead, Israel honored the gift of the land by serving God while in it (12:7–9). The great polemic in Jeremiah against the defiling nature of Israel's (and Judah's) sin should be seen against the background of God's call to Israel to live a life of holiness in God's heritage. Exile was, in a sense, the cleansing of the land as well as judgment on its inhabitants for their failure.

Within his heritage God provided two centers of holiness, both of which mediated divine presence and guidance to the people. The first was the city of Jerusalem. In line with the affirmation of the Psalter that God had chosen Jerusalem/Zion (Ps. 78; 132; Jer. 2:2), Jeremiah assumes a special role for the city. Jerusalem was metaphorically God's daughter,[52] the object of God's tender affection and mercy. Jerusalem/Zion was also the location of the temple (the second center of holiness, located in Jerusalem). Characteristically it is referred to as "the LORD's house" or "the house, which bears my Name."[53] The perversion of Jerusalem and the temple was a result of the people's sinfulness, aided and abetted by their leaders. It is in the context of Judah's perversion of these good gifts that the language of divine anguish and anger reaches it peak.

---

52. Jer. 3:14; 6:2, 23; 8:19; 9:19; 14:19; 26:18; 30:17; 31:6, 12; 50:5, 28; 51:10, 35. Cities are personified as feminine in the Old Testament. Jeremiah also uses the phrase "my daughter people" in 6:26; 8:11, 19–22; 9:1, 7; and the phrase "virgin daughter people" in 14:17. It is not clear whether the people as a whole are personified as God's daughter or just the people of Jerusalem are thus personified.

53. Cf. Jer. 7:2; 19:14; 20:1–2; 26:2; 28:1; 35:4; the phrase "which bears my Name" occurs in 7:11.

If it is true that a common and corporate perversion leads to judgment, it is also true that God's resolve to restore is such that people, Jerusalem, and the temple all had a place in the future beyond exile. The claim of God's everlasting covenant with the priests (33:19–22) presupposed the restoration of the temple. Sacrifices and gifts of thanksgiving would be offered again (33:11). Jerusalem (31:38–40) too would be rebuilt as part of the remnant's return from exile.

Beyond the postexilic period and the unfolding drama of the Old Testament witness, the restored temple becomes the occasion for a new word about Christ as the fleshly temple-presence of God (John 2:13–22). Jerusalem serves as a symbol of the true home of Christians (Gal. 4:21–5:1; Rev. 21–22), and the land-as-God's-inheritance is transformed into Christian adoption as sons (and daughters) and heirs of God's eternal glory (Rom. 8:14–17). Jeremiah's words, therefore, about Jerusalem, land, and inheritance serve as signposts along the way toward the unveiling of the gospel. His words should not be used as evidence for any modern claims with respect to the state of Israel, the current predicament regarding Jerusalem, or the fate of Arab Palestinians.

God As Unique Among the Gods

JEREMIAH CONTAINS POLEMICAL language against polytheism, idolatry, and syncretism on the part of God's people (e.g., 2:20–28). The book assumes that God's covenant with the people forbids the worship of other deities, as the first two commandments of the Decalogue assert (Ex. 20:2–6; Deut. 5:6–10).[54]

In common with other Old Testament books, Jeremiah contains polemic against Canaanite deities known as Baal.[55] This title was used for popular weather and fertility deities in Canaan. In the middle of the ninth century the worship of Baal in Israel provoked a crisis in Israel and occasioned the prophetic ministry of Elijah (1 Kings 18–21). Hosea likewise polemicized against Baal deities in the middle of the eighth century. Jeremiah's own critique is similar to and probably influenced by Hosea. Both the singular and

---

54. Jeremiah's assessments of polytheism and syncretism are similar to those of Zephaniah and Ezekiel.

55. The Hebrew word *ba'al* means master, owner, and even husband. It is a not a proper name but a title or appellative for a deity who may also have a personal name. In addition to Bible dictionary and encyclopedia entries on Baal, cf. also J. A. Dearman, "Baal in Israel: The Contribution of Some Place Names and Personal Names to an Understanding of Early Israelite Religion," in *History and Interpretation: Essays in Honour of John H. Hayes*, ed. M. P. Graham et al. (Sheffield: JSOT Press, 1993), 173–91.

plural form of the title Baal occur in Jeremiah, along with slur-like comparisons for the deity, such as shame and worthless.[56]

There seem to have been several related problems with Baal deities. Some people in Israel wanted to use the title for the God of Israel (cf. Hos. 2:18 [Eng. 2:16]) or, similarly, assumed that the Lord was just like a Baal deity. Others wanted to worship both the Lord and Baal as part of their polytheistic worldview. There was a grain of truth in the identity of the Lord as Baal, for the God of Israel was indeed concerned about fertility and rain. What gets rejected in the witness of the Old Testament are the overt sexual terms associated with divine procreation, gender identity for the deity, and the a/immoral acts associated with fertility cults.

Jeremiah notes also that some Judeans worshiped the Queen of Heaven (7:17–19; 44:15–19). She too was likely known by a personal name (perhaps Astarte or Asherah) as well as by her title. The emphasis of her devotees in chapter 44 is that she provided better care than the Lord (see comments on ch. 44). Most likely she was also venerated for her supposed powers of fertility. According to 17:2, some Judeans worshiped Asherim, a plural term the NIV translates as "Asherah poles." The singular form of the term is Asherah (cf. 2 Kings 23:4–6).

Rituals associated with child sacrifice are referred to in a place known as the Topheth (Jer. 7:30–32; 19:5; 32:35). Two different deities are named as recipients; Baal and Molech. Since Molech, like Baal, is a title[57] and not a personal name, it is not at all clear whether one deity or more was involved in the cult. The Topheth was located in a valley just south of the temple area in Jerusalem, so it is possible that some participants associated the Lord with these sacrifices in spite of the Lord's vehement protests otherwise (e.g., 7:31).

Jeremiah mentions a number of deities worshiped by other peoples with whom Judah had contact. Among them are Egyptian, Ammonite, Moabite, and Babylonian deities.[58] These are often mentioned in prophecies of judgment to come upon "their" people, a judgment brought about by the Lord, the God of Israel. There is even mention on occasion of those people or territories being restored—again as an indication that God is the Lord of all creation and the processes of history. Jeremiah contains no real discussion over

---

56. Baal in the singular is in Jer. 2:8; 7:9; 11:13, 17; 12:16; 19:5; 23:13, 27; 32:29, 35; in the plural, 2:23; 9:14 (cf. Hos. 2:15 [13], 19 [17]; 11:2); for Baal as "shame" and "worthless," see Hos. 9:10; Jer 2:8.

57. The verb "to rule, be king" in Hebrew is *malak*. A noun derived from the verb, meaning "king," is *melek*. Molech is from the same word and indicates a (divine) monarch or ruler. See the commentary discussion on chs. 7, 19, and 32 for additional details on this cult.

58. Egyptian deities: 43:12; 46:25; Moabite deity: 48:13, 46; Ammonite deity: 49:3; Babylonian deities: 50:2.

the question of the existence of these deities. It is simply assumed that they have no influence over the fate of Judah or on the Lord's activity within the orders of creation.

According to Jeremiah, therefore, the Lord God of Israel has no rival in the divine world, and his people have no need to worship any other deity. To put it in a colorless phrase, Jeremiah represents God as both unique and comprehensive in person and scope. God's *uniqueness* does not translate necessarily into the affirmation that God is utterly different from human conceptions of other deities. The true concerns of religion, any religion, will find an appropriate counterpart in the *comprehensiveness* of the Lord. If, for example, the sacrifice of children in Canaan was for the personal crises of families or to express devotion to Molech/Baal, then a proper counterpart in nonhuman sacrifice was available to those who wanted to worship the Lord. For those families enacting fertility rites or praying to Baal for rain, there was an appropriate counterpart in the merciful care of the Lord. As Jeremiah put it in an unforgettable phrase: The Lord is a "spring of living water" (2:13; 17:13) for those who trust in him.

The other deities of Jeremiah's time play a role analogous to the "principalities and powers" unmasked by the apostle Paul. They provide historical illustration from the period of the "old covenant" of the broad biblical teaching: "You shall have no other gods before me" (Ex. 20:3). Jeremiah's strictures against other deities are also timely warnings applicable in any age, given the human tendency to "hedge one's bets" or to divide one's allegiance among several powers as a safety precaution. The book claims (and rightly so!) that the Lord is sufficient for all the needs of his people and that there is self-incurred danger in worshiping other powers.

Outline of Jeremiah

I. Judgment and Hope (Jer. 1–25)
 A. Call of Prophet (ch. 1)
 B. Corporate Failures Identified (chs. 2–6)
 C. Sermon at Temple (7:1–8:3)
 D. Corporate Failures Identified (8:4–10:25; 13:12–14:22)
 E. Sermon on Covenant Breaking (11:1–17)
 F. Threats to Prophet and His Laments (11:18–12:17; 15:11–21;
  16:14–17:27; 18:13–23; 20:7–18)
 G. Signs of Judgment
  1. Loincloth (13:1–11)
  2. No Prayer (15:1–10)
  3. No Marriage (16:1–13)
  4. Potter (18:1–12)
  5. Broken Pots (19:1–15)
  6. Prophet in Stocks (20:1–6)
  7. Basket of Figs (ch. 24)
 H. Judgment on Leaders (chs. 21–23)
 I. Nebuchadnezzar and Exile (ch. 25)
II. Judgment and Hope (Jer. 26–52)
 A. Narratives about Judean Failures (26–28)
 B. Letter to First Wave of Exiles (ch. 29)
 C. Hope and Consolation (chs. 30–33)
 D. Oppression of Slaves (ch. 34)
 E. Sign of the Rechabites (ch. 35)
 F. Writing and Burning of First Scroll (chs. 36; 45)
 G. Narratives During and After the Final Siege of Jerusalem
  (chs. 37–44)
 H. Oracles About and Against Other Nations, Including
  Babylon (chs. 46–51)
 I. Rehearsal of Jerusalem's Fall and Note of Jehoiachin's Release
  (ch. 52)

Bibliography

Bogaert, P. M., ed. *Le livre de jérémie: le prophète et son milieu, les oracles et leur transmission*. Leuven: Leuven Univ. Press, 1981; 2d ed. with supplements, 1997.

Brueggemann, W. *To Build and To Plant: A Commentary on Jeremiah 26–52*. Grand Rapids: Eerdmans, 1991.

_____. *To Pluck and To Tear Down: A Commentary on Jeremiah 1–25*. Grand Rapids: Eerdmans, 1988.

Carroll, R. *Jeremiah: A Commentary*. OTL. Philadelphia: Westminster, 1986.

Clements, R. *Jeremiah*. Interpretation. Atlanta: John Knox, 1988.

Craigie, P., P. Kelley, and J. Drinkard. *Jeremiah 1–25*. WBC. Waco, Tex.: Word, 1991.

Curtis, A. H. W., and T. Römer. *The Book of Jeremiah and Its Reception*. Leuven: Leuven Univ. Press, 1997.

Diamond, A. R. P., K. M. O'Connor, and L. Stulman. *Troubling Jeremiah*. Sheffield: Sheffield Academic Press, 1999.

Gross, W., ed. *Jeremia und die "deuternomistische Bewegung."* Weinheim: Atheneum, 1995.

Hill, J. *Friend or Foe? The Figure of Babylon in the Book of Jeremiah MT*. Leiden: Brill, 1999.

Holladay, W. *Jeremiah*. 2 vols. Hermeneia. Philadelphia: Fortress, 1986, 1989.

Keown, G., P. Scalise, and T. Smothers. *Jeremiah 26–52*. WBC. Waco, Tex.: Word, 1994.

Kidner, D. *The Message of Jeremiah: Against Wind and Tide*. Downers Grove, Ill.: InterVarsity, 1987.

McKane, W. *A Critical and Exegetical Commentary on Jeremiah*. 2 vols. ICC. Edinburgh: T. & T. Clark, 1986.

Parke-Taylor, G. *The Formation of the Book of Jeremiah: Doublets and Recurring Phrases*. Atlanta: Scholars Press, 2000.

Perdue, L., and B. Kovacs, eds. *A Prophet to the Nations: Essays in Jeremiah Studies*. Winona Lake, Ind.: Eisenbrauns, 1984.

Thompson, H. O. *The Book of Jeremiah: An Annotated Bibliography*. Lanham, Md.: Scarecrow, 1996.

Thompson, J. A. *The Book of Jeremiah*. NICOT. Grand Rapids: Eerdmans, 1980.

Bibliography

Jeremiah 1:1–3

THE WORDS OF Jeremiah son of Hilkiah, one of the priests at Anathoth in the territory of Benjamin. [2]The word of the LORD came to him in the thirteenth year of the reign of Josiah son of Amon king of Judah, [3]and through the reign of Jehoiakim son of Josiah king of Judah, down to the fifth month of the eleventh year of Zedekiah son of Josiah king of Judah, when the people of Jerusalem went into exile.

LIKE MOST PROPHETIC books, Jeremiah begins with a superscription (i.e., a heading) indicating the time of the prophet's ministry. Dates in Judah were reckoned in accordance with the reign of a monarch, a common procedure in the ancient world.[1] As noted in the introduction, the forty plus years given for Jeremiah's ministry (ca. 627–584 B.C.) cover some of the most tumultuous and tragic events of the nation's history. Included among them were rebellions against foreign control, the death of Judean kings at the hands of foreign powers, the demise and virtual destruction of the nation itself, and the forced descent of the prophet into Egypt in the aftermath of the destruction.

Jeremiah was from a priestly family of Anathoth, a village about three miles north of Jerusalem, the capital city of Judah. Anathoth was part of the Benjamite inheritance and assigned as a Levitical city (Josh. 21:18).[2] It was also the home of the priest Abiathar, who centuries earlier had served David faithfully but who had backed Adonijah, Solomon's brother and rival for the throne, at David's death. Anathoth became the home in exile of Abiathar (1 Kings 2:26), and thus Jeremiah's hometown likely had deep roots in the priestly and Levitical traditions of the nation, providing the future prophet with an education suited to his task.

King Josiah attempted to free Judah from the control of Assyria and to set Judah on the road to spiritual reform. His thirteenth year coincides with the demise of Assyria's last strong king Assurbanipal and probably also includes his initial steps to alter Judah's politically subservient and religiously

---

1. See the comments on chronology and difficulties in reckoning chronology in the introduction on the life and times of Jeremiah.

2. For discussion of the location of biblical Anathoth near the modern Arabic village of Anata, see J. L. Peterson, "Anathoth," ABD, 1:227–28.

degenerate path. The eleventh year of Zedekiah is among the most somber in all of biblical history. Jerusalem was captured and destroyed by the Babylonians, Zedekiah himself was seized and blinded, and many Judeans were taken into exile by their captors (Jer. 52; cf. 2 Kings 25).

JEREMIAH'S MINISTRY IS embedded in the convulsive events leading to Judah's tragic demise. This is typical of the timely nature of biblical prophets and the books that record their work. The heading to the book also bears a significant cultural marker: Time itself is reckoned according to the regnal years of a Davidic monarch. Eventually much of the world will adopt a chronological scheme that is dated to the birth of a descendant from David's line, that is, Jesus of Nazareth. These Davidic kings in Jeremiah 1:1–3, therefore, are in a chosen line of great significance; nevertheless, each of them failed in varying degrees to lead God's people from the paths of syncretism and idolatry.

The search for the original meaning of biblical prophecy is based on the conviction that the words and deeds of a prophet first address the pressing issues of a prophet's own day. Indeed, Jeremiah's life story is a reflection of the pain of Judah's failure, and his own suffering mirrors that of the people. But the very fact that a book of Jeremiah is still being read after 2,500 years is evidence that it was intended to instruct later readers through its portrayal of past events and its predictions of God's transforming moments to come. By God's grace and in light of subsequent biblical revelation, readers are also invited to find new light coming forth from the same words of the prophetic book, reflecting the transcendent quality of God's Word and his intention to instruct all generations of his people in the twin contexts of their common humanity and their inheritance among the saints.

Scripture provides additional contexts in which to place the words of Jeremiah. In the Old Testament the prophetic books of Zephaniah, Habakkuk, Nahum, and Ezekiel address audiences whose life spans overlap with those first addressed by Jeremiah. Previous prophetic models in Scripture include the accounts of Elijah and the prophecies of Amos, Isaiah, Micah (cf. Jer. 26), and Hosea. The covenant and Torah about which the prophet will speak are subjects well known to his audience. Whether they grasped the significance of either is debatable. Jeremiah certainly regards their adherence to them as inadequate!

The prophecy of Jeremiah not only interprets the significance of historical events; it offers specific judgments on corporate failure and includes promises that God would see the people through their self-generated demise in order to heal the consequences of their failures. This pattern of historical judgment and redemption in Jeremiah is intended as more than a historical report about the past; it is also typological and analogical instruction for later generations, who are to see themselves corporately addressed as God's people of their day.

ACCORDING TO APOSTOLIC preaching, God "has not left himself without testimony" (Acts 14:17). The manner of God's self-revelation varies according to divine discretion. Jeremiah's historical rootedness is testimony to one facet of God's revelation, a timely witness intended not only for the generation to which it was first delivered but for subsequent generations as well. Jeremiah the prophet and the book called by his name are chosen vessels, brought forth in specific contexts, to communicate God's timely truth.

The prophetic superscription reflects a form of incarnational theology. Just as God's supreme revelation was his Word become flesh in Jesus Christ, so God's Word took historical form in the life of Jeremiah and acquired written form in a book. It is by consideration of God's revelation through the prophet Jeremiah and in his book that subsequent generations of God's people continue to find divine instruction.

For the people of God, the timely nature of Jeremiah's ministry takes on the primary character of corporate address, inviting the church to consider God's judging and redeeming activity within the historical process. For individual reflection, Jeremiah's words provide testimony that God uses both people and events to further his purposes and to instruct the faithful.

Jeremiah 1:4–19

The word of the Lord came to me, saying,

⁵"Before I formed you in the womb I knew you,
   before you were born I set you apart;
   I appointed you as a prophet to the nations."

⁶"Ah, Sovereign Lord," I said, "I do not know how to speak; I am only a child."

⁷But the Lord said to me, "Do not say, 'I am only a child.' You must go to everyone I send you to and say whatever I command you. ⁸Do not be afraid of them, for I am with you and will rescue you," declares the Lord.

⁹Then the Lord reached out his hand and touched my mouth and said to me, "Now, I have put my words in your mouth. ¹⁰See, today I appoint you over nations and kingdoms to uproot and tear down, to destroy and overthrow, to build and to plant."

¹¹The word of the Lord came to me: "What do you see, Jeremiah?"

"I see the branch of an almond tree," I replied.

¹²The Lord said to me, "You have seen correctly, for I am watching to see that my word is fulfilled."

¹³The word of the Lord came to me again: "What do you see?"

"I see a boiling pot, tilting away from the north," I answered.

¹⁴The Lord said to me, "From the north disaster will be poured out on all who live in the land. ¹⁵I am about to summon all the peoples of the northern kingdoms," declares the Lord.

"Their kings will come and set up their thrones
   in the entrance of the gates of Jerusalem;
they will come against all her surrounding walls
   and against all the towns of Judah.
¹⁶I will pronounce my judgments on my people
   because of their wickedness in forsaking me,
in burning incense to other gods
   and in worshiping what their hands have made.

¹⁷"Get yourself ready! Stand up and say to them whatever I command you. Do not be terrified by them, or I will terrify you before them. ¹⁸Today I have made you a fortified city, an iron pillar and a bronze wall to stand against the whole land— against the kings of Judah, its officials, its priests and the people of the land. ¹⁹They will fight against you but will not overcome you, for I am with you and will rescue you," declares the LORD.

THE REST OF chapter 1 contains an account of Jeremiah's call and appointment to prophesy (1:4–10), followed by two divine oracles (1:11–12 and 1:13–19) assuring the prophet that God is with him as he delivers a judgmental word to Judah.

Jeremiah's call is cast in poetic form. Verse 5 has paired phrases indicating that God's decision to use Jeremiah came prior to his birth. The phrase translated in the NIV as "set apart" is a rendering of the Hebrew verb *qdš*, whose basic meaning is to be holy. Holiness can be a property, like clean or unclean, and it can be related to ethical activity and spiritual dedication; but the term assumes that what God designates as holy is reserved for (i.e., set apart for) a particular task. Otherwise said, God's choice of Jeremiah, his designation of him as prophet, is the reason he is sanctified. It is not the other way around, as if Jeremiah's moral and spiritual attributes are the impetus for God's selection of him as prophet.

Verse 5 concludes with the affirmation that God has appointed Jeremiah a "prophet to the nations." Jeremiah's protest that he is too young and inexperienced is countered by God's assurances to be with Jeremiah, to deliver him, and to place his words in Jeremiah's mouth. Each of these assurances is a way to define a prophet. He or she is designated by God for a task and is granted his presence and guidance, and what is spoken by the prophet is God's word for the occasion in which it is given.

In the call's conclusion, verse 10 offers an elaboration on the phrase "prophet to the nations," with the comment that Jeremiah's appointed activities are to tear down and to overthrow as well as to build and to plant. How might this young man become a prophet to the nations, since Jeremiah holds no political office and his words to kings are widely ignored? It seems that, in reality, Jeremiah's "appointment" describes the function of the words God gives him to deliver. A prophet's defining is functional: When the words from God do what they are called to do, they define what it is to be a prophet.

Through oracles the prophet will announce in the Lord's name that nations will be judged and found wanting, that these nations will be overthrown by the Lord, and that beyond the judgment to fall on Judah as part of this process, the Lord will rebuild his people and replant them in the Promised Land. Jeremiah becomes a prophet to the nations by virtue of what he says, not through a job given him in Jerusalem or by popular vote. The book of Jeremiah does not offer a generic definition of what it means to be a prophet; instead, it describes who Jeremiah will be as the prophet to his generation.

The verbs of 1:10 describe succinctly what Jeremiah's words will do. They will tear down much that his audience believes, and only after the terrible toll of Judah's failures has been reckoned will his positive words begin to build up and plant. These verbs appear later in the book (12:14–17; 18:7–10; 24:4–7; 42:10; 45:4), although not all six of them together. Tearing down and building up is a leading motif in this book as it presents the prophet to readers and hearers.

The first oracle of assurance (1:11–12) is a pun in Hebrew. The Hebrew word for almond tree sounds like the Hebrew verb to watch (cf. NIV note). The almond tree becomes a sign to Jeremiah that God is watching over his word to bring it to fulfillment. This is another way to define the work of a prophet. The prophet is called to obedience, and God is responsible for using the word for his own purposes.

The second oracle (1:13–19) concerns the effects of an overturned pot of boiling liquid. The pot is a metaphor for the threat to come on Jerusalem and Judah because of the people's disobedience. There is also an initial reference to those who will oppose Jeremiah (v. 19); there will be much more in the book about them. Finally, the repetition of the assurance from verse 8 reminds the reader that God will be with Jeremiah to deliver him from his opponents. As the book will eloquently display, Jeremiah is not immune from human suffering or doubt; his security does not reside in his cleverness or physical stamina, but in the fact that God is with him.

THE CALL OF Jeremiah to a prophetic ministry has similarities to other accounts of persons called into God's service. These similarities are no doubt intentional and communicate a pattern to both ancient and modern readers. God prevails on Moses in spite of the latter's objections (Ex. 3:1–15), assuring Moses that he will be with him.[1] Ezekiel swallows a scroll given him through divine revelation (Ezek. 2:1–3:11), clearly a sign that the prophetic words to come forth from his mouth have

---

1. W. Holladay points out (*Jeremiah*, 1:26–31) that the call of Jeremiah is close in form to that of Moses in Ex. 3:1–15; furthermore, Jeremiah may be a "prophet like [Moses]" (Deut. 18:18) for Judah and Jerusalem.

divine origin. Jeremiah 1:9 makes a similar point where the Lord touches Jeremiah's mouth and declares: "I have put my words in your mouth" (cf. Isa. 6:1–8). Human frailty (e.g., youth or difficulty in speech) is no excuse before God's expressed will to grant a person the words to say and the opportunities to deliver them.

Elements of this commissioning pattern can be seen in the New Testament as well. The risen Christ declares to his first followers that they are to teach his word to other disciples and that he will be with them until the end of the age (Matt. 28:18–20). The apostle Paul perceives his own life in light of God's call and even more particularly describes God as One who has set him apart from his mother's womb in order to preach Christ among the Gentiles (i.e., non-Jewish nations; see Gal. 1:13–17). There are clear parallels between Paul's autobiographical description and the prophetic model of Jeremiah, set apart from his mother's womb to be a prophet to the nations. John the seer is told by the risen Christ to write a prophecy in a book and not to fear the persecution to come (Rev. 1:9–19). The human fears and frailties common to those who are called are not ultimately barriers to their service because God has declared he will be with them.

Undergirding the commissioning pattern is the electing work of God, who sets people apart in order to use them as messengers of his Word. They are chosen on behalf of others. This is a primary implication of what is meant by "election" in the Bible: A person or persons are chosen by God in order to affect the lives of others. Such an emphasis should keep later readers from speculating unduly about Jeremiah's personal characteristics or his psychological make-up (how he "felt" about his experience). The account of his call is given primarily to persuade people about the significance of the material that follows his call.

GOD'S CALL. THE account of God's call to Jeremiah is not meant as a model of God's call to believers in the sense that we should all seek an experience with God like that of Jeremiah. Instead, Jeremiah's call is narrated first of all to tell prospective readers why they should have any interest in the words that follow. Believers are asked to trust Jeremiah's experience of God as instructive for them. Jeremiah is a chosen vessel, set apart before his birth, to deliver God's words concerning the nations of his day. Jeremiah's book likewise is a chosen vessel intended for the instruction of later generations. His call and commissioning come at the beginning of the book to indicate what kind of message and what kind of authority the book contains.

God does not call all believers to be prophets; some, however, are called to engage in prophetic activity, and all are called to trust the efficacy of the prophetic word in Scripture. Two related elements in Jeremiah 1 have continuing significance for understanding prophetic activity: dependence on God for vindication rather than popularity among one's contemporaries, and the likelihood that such activity will result in opposition. Old and New Testament alike indicate that prophets face strong opposition from their contemporaries, that they owe the preservation of their words (and even their very lives) to God, and that future generations will often look on them differently from their own generation.

The value of human life. The account of God's call of Jeremiah is also relevant to the contemporary debates over abortion, euthanasia, assisted suicide, and the "value of human life." Let's admit, of course, that the account of Jeremiah's call is not intended initially as a polemic against abortion or euthanasia, nor does the text answer all the complicated questions facing modern societies over these and related issues. Nevertheless, Jeremiah is known to God even before his conception, and his preparation for prophetic work begins before his birth. Thus even in the womb Jeremiah is valued. Furthermore, the account assumes that God is the author of Jeremiah's life and the One who shapes his historical destiny in spite of his reluctance.

These claims do function as powerful confessions that human life is God's gift and subject to God's discretion—more particularly, that the womb is the home of a person known to God. In Jeremiah's case, his bitterness over treatment by his contemporaries and even his frustration with his treatment by God eventually lead him Job-like to curse the day of his birth (20:14–18; cf. 15:10) and to think that his life is worthless. God, of course, would not agree that Jeremiah's life is worthless. Nevertheless, God's call of Jeremiah and the assurance of protection does not mean that Jeremiah is spared the humiliation that often goes with the prophetic office or self-doubt; on the contrary, God's power is made manifest through his human weakness.

Jeremiah is not being called to judge the effectiveness of his work or the significance of his life. He is called to deliver God's word; God will see to its effectiveness as well as to the vindication of Jeremiah's life in ways he himself will never see. In God's good but inscrutable providence, this can be the experience of the saints in any generation. God not only works his will through their words and deeds, but he also uses their lives to touch future generations in ways the saints themselves would not know.

The following account of a convicted criminal was passed along to me by a friend engaged in prison ministry. This criminal, a relatively young man in his late twenties, had been the product of a broken home. Actually, he was born out of wedlock and learned early on that he was not particularly wanted by either his mother or his father (the latter he hardly even knew). After landing in prison for violent criminal activity, he was led by the grace of God, along with the sincere efforts of some lay Christians, to realize that he had been called by God, first to a saving relationship with Jesus Christ and then to a form of ministry to other inmates in prison. Part of his emotional and spiritual healing came in the tearful realization that God had called him and set him apart for the task of ministry. For him this meant that God wanted him, even if his biological parents did not, that God had set him apart for a task, and therefore that God would be with him as he carried out his new-found call.

In the case of this inmate, his incarceration did not end with his newly formed faith. He hoped his time in jail would end so that he could do some form of ministry, but then saw instead his incarceration as the place where God had put him and as the place where God would be with him in the difficulties (and joys!) ahead. One of his first tasks was to learn study habits, so that he might retain more effectively the things he read in the Bible and present them more effectively.

Jeremiah 2:1–37

THE WORD OF the LORD came to me: ²"Go and proclaim in the hearing of Jerusalem:

"'I remember the devotion of your youth,
   how as a bride you loved me
and followed me through the desert,
   through a land not sown.
³ Israel was holy to the LORD,
   the firstfruits of his harvest;
all who devoured her were held guilty,
   and disaster overtook them,'"

                                        declares the LORD.

⁴ Hear the word of the LORD, O house of Jacob,
   all you clans of the house of Israel.

⁵ This is what the LORD says:

"What fault did your fathers find in me,
   that they strayed so far from me?
They followed worthless idols
   and became worthless themselves.
⁶ They did not ask, 'Where is the LORD,
   who brought us up out of Egypt
and led us through the barren wilderness,
   through a land of deserts and rifts,
a land of drought and darkness,
   a land where no one travels and no one lives?'
⁷ I brought you into a fertile land
   to eat its fruit and rich produce.
But you came and defiled my land
   and made my inheritance detestable.
⁸ The priests did not ask,
   'Where is the LORD?'
Those who deal with the law did not know me;
   the leaders rebelled against me.
The prophets prophesied by Baal,
   following worthless idols.

⁹"Therefore I bring charges against you again,"

declares the LORD.

"And I will bring charges against your children's children.

¹⁰Cross over to the coasts of Kittim and look,
　　send to Kedar and observe closely;
　　see if there has ever been anything like this:

¹¹Has a nation ever changed its gods?
　　(Yet they are not gods at all.)
　But my people have exchanged their Glory
　　for worthless idols.

¹²Be appalled at this, O heavens,
　　and shudder with great horror,"

declares the LORD.

¹³"My people have committed two sins:
　They have forsaken me,
　　the spring of living water,
　and have dug their own cisterns,
　　broken cisterns that cannot hold water.

¹⁴Is Israel a servant, a slave by birth?
　　Why then has he become plunder?

¹⁵Lions have roared;
　　they have growled at him.
　They have laid waste his land;
　　his towns are burned and deserted.

¹⁶Also, the men of Memphis and Tahpanhes
　　have shaved the crown of your head.

¹⁷Have you not brought this on yourselves
　　by forsaking the LORD your God
　　when he led you in the way?

¹⁸Now why go to Egypt
　　to drink water from the Shihor?
　And why go to Assyria
　　to drink water from the River?

¹⁹Your wickedness will punish you;
　　your backsliding will rebuke you.
　Consider then and realize
　　how evil and bitter it is for you
　when you forsake the LORD your God
　　and have no awe of me,"

declares the Lord, the LORD Almighty.

²⁰"Long ago you broke off your yoke
   and tore off your bonds;
   you said, 'I will not serve you!'
Indeed, on every high hill
   and under every spreading tree
   you lay down as a prostitute.
²¹I had planted you like a choice vine
   of sound and reliable stock.
How then did you turn against me
   into a corrupt, wild vine?
²²Although you wash yourself with soda
   and use an abundance of soap,
   the stain of your guilt is still before me,"
                     declares the Sovereign LORD.
²³"How can you say, 'I am not defiled;
   I have not run after the Baals'?
See how you behaved in the valley;
   consider what you have done.
You are a swift she-camel
   running here and there,
²⁴a wild donkey accustomed to the desert,
   sniffing the wind in her craving—
   in her heat who can restrain her?
Any males that pursue her need not tire themselves;
   at mating time they will find her.
²⁵Do not run until your feet are bare
   and your throat is dry.
But you said, 'It's no use!
   I love foreign gods,
   and I must go after them.'

²⁶"As a thief is disgraced when he is caught,
   so the house of Israel is disgraced—
they, their kings and their officials,
   their priests and their prophets.
²⁷They say to wood, 'You are my father,'
   and to stone, 'You gave me birth.'
They have turned their backs to me
   and not their faces;
yet when they are in trouble, they say,
   'Come and save us!'

²⁸ Where then are the gods you made for yourselves?
    Let them come if they can save you
    when you are in trouble!
For you have as many gods
    as you have towns, O Judah.

²⁹ "Why do you bring charges against me?
    You have all rebelled against me,"

                        declares the LORD.

³⁰ "In vain I punished your people;
    they did not respond to correction.
Your sword has devoured your prophets
    like a ravening lion.

³¹ You of this generation, consider the word of the LORD:

"Have I been a desert to Israel
    or a land of great darkness?
Why do my people say, 'We are free to roam;
    we will come to you no more'?
³² Does a maiden forget her jewelry,
    a bride her wedding ornaments?
Yet my people have forgotten me,
    days without number.
³³ How skilled you are at pursuing love!
    Even the worst of women can learn from your ways.
³⁴ On your clothes men find
    the lifeblood of the innocent poor,
    though you did not catch them breaking in.
Yet in spite of all this
³⁵   you say, 'I am innocent;
    he is not angry with me.'
But I will pass judgment on you
    because you say, 'I have not sinned.'
³⁶ Why do you go about so much,
    changing your ways?
You will be disappointed by Egypt
    as you were by Assyria.
³⁷ You will also leave that place
    with your hands on your head,
for the LORD has rejected those you trust;
you will not be helped by them.

CHAPTER 2 IS a collection of Jeremiah's undated poetic utterances, and as the first collection of oracles presented in the book, it also serves as an introduction to his public speaking. (Jeremiah 1:4–19, though intended ultimately for readers as well, is addressed directly to Jeremiah.) Perhaps it is helpful to think of these oracles in chapter 2 as a "sampler," since the topics taken up reappear time and again in his book. The primary themes are about Judah's defection from following the Lord and the importance of maintaining obedience to his revealed will. The same basic themes continue into chapter 3.

It is clear from the Hebrew text that chapter 2 alternates the manner in which the audience is addressed. Unfortunately English words do not offer a similar kind of specificity in translation because the English pronoun "you" can refer to masculine singular, feminine singular, and corporate entities, whereas these are all differentiated in Hebrew. As a result, at some points readers cannot tell from the translation of the NIV when the identity of the addressee has shifted. In fact, the NIV does not always render the different Hebrew pronouns literally, as the following outline will show. It is important to recall, however, that the change in addressee used by the prophet is for poetic effect. The people of Judah and Jerusalem are the real audience, regardless of the poetry or metaphor being used by the prophet.

A. 2:1–2 address Jerusalem (cities are personified as female in Hebrew) as the bride of the Lord.

B. 2:3 refers to Israel. To keep the continuity with the address to Jerusalem as bride, the NIV refers to Israel as "her" in verse 3, even though the Hebrew text follows the grammatical shift to masculine Israel and uses "him."

C. 2:4–13 is for the people who are addressed with a plural "you."

D. 2:14–16 continues the address to Israel (cf. B).

E. 2:17–25 shifts the address back to Jerusalem (cf. A). The NIV translates "yourselves" in verse 17, even though the Hebrew text has the feminine singular "you."

F. 2:26–32 addresses Israel and Judah, both of which are corporate designations of the people.

G. 2:33–37 addresses Jerusalem again (cf. A). The Hebrew text has the feminine singular "you."

Readers can see from the outline above that the collected oracles in chapter 2 vary the way the people are addressed. Since gender roles in the ancient world influence the way that poetry and metaphor characterize an entity, it is necessary to keep in mind the alternation listed above.

2:2–3. Jerusalem is reminded of her beginnings as the young bride of the Lord. Here the gender role of the poetry is significant. Cities are personified as female in Northwest Semitic cultures (of which Israel was a part). Jerusalem represents the people, just as Washington, D.C., or Beijing represent respectively the Unites States of America and the People's Republic of China. It is her gender that provides the metaphor of Jerusalem as the bride of the Lord.

Verse 3 switches abruptly to address the people by their covenant name "Israel," even though Israel is grammatically masculine singular. The combined imagery of 2:2–3 is that of Israel's devotion to and dependence on the Lord for both identity and sustenance. It recalls by inference the exodus from Egypt into the desert, the covenant ceremony at Mount Sinai, and God's sustaining of his people in the arid desert. This period of intimacy is contrasted with the estrangement from God depicted for Jeremiah's contemporaries in the rest of the chapter.

2:4–13. Israel is defined here inclusively (i.e., in covenantal terms, not political terms) as "my people" (2:13; i.e., the people of God). Note the double address as "house of Jacob" and "clans of the house of Israel." Corporately Israel is accused of having defected from its first love in order to pursue "worthless idols," that is, other deities. Baal, a popular Canaanite deity, is named specifically in verse 8.[1]

Also in verse 8 Jeremiah singles out Judah's leadership for particular criticism (cf. 2:26). It is leadership of a particular kind. "Priests" had the sacred task of interpreting God's presence and will among the people and having facility with Torah (NIV "law"). The word translated as "leaders" is more literally rendered as "shepherds." God, who is the great Shepherd of his people, demands that the leadership of the people share in this shepherding role. Finally, the "prophets" are singled out for their perfidy in seeking inspiration from Baal rather than the Lord.

The Lord's historic faithfulness in the events of Exodus, desert wandering, and entry to the Promised Land (2:6–7) is contrasted with the emptiness of Baal and other idolatries. Succinctly stated: "My people have exchanged their Glory for worthless idols" (v. 11) and have committed two evils: They have rejected the Lord and attempted vainly to support themselves (v. 13). The image of broken cisterns in verse 13 is telling, since the care of cisterns was a laborious job in the hill country of Palestine, where earthquake tremors occurred periodically. Jeremiah compares the labor-intensive work of repairing cisterns with the idolatry of following other gods, whereas the Lord is a fountain of living water.

---

1. Jer. 2:23 refers to the Baals in the plural. Cf. also the references to multiple deities in 2:25, 28.

2:14–19. These verses are addressed to two entities, each of whom represents the people. Verses 14–16 speak directly of "Israel," and the "you" of verses 17–19 is addressed to Jerusalem. The tragic example of Israel (here, the northern kingdom) serves to highlight the precarious position of Jeremiah's contemporaries in Judah. The defection from Yahweh shows itself institutionally in the political realm as Judah has become entangled with Egypt and Assyria (for historical details, see the introduction). This indictment presupposes a close relationship between an idolatrous and false worship on the one hand, and a disastrous political agenda on the other. Just as Judah seems willing to trust any deity in the Canaanite pantheon, so the state seems willing to grasp at straws in an attempt to save itself by making deals with Egypt and Assyria. Verse 19 predicts that Judah's wicked acts will also be the measure of its judgment.

2:20–25. Because of their defection from the Lord, the people are depicted through a personification of Jerusalem as a prostitute. By analogy she/they are also like animals in heat who are unrestrained in seeking a mate. The valley mentioned in verse 23—where the people seek the Baals—is likely the Valley of Hinnom, which runs on the southern and western sides of the city of Jerusalem. It is also the probable site of child sacrifice to Molech or Baal (see also 7:30–34).

2:26–32. In matters of religious devotion, Jeremiah describes the people as calling on other gods through the symbols of trees and stones, with Judah having as many gods as towns (vv. 26–28). Perhaps the prophet employs sarcasm in his description of the wood as father and the stone as mother, for he reverses a widespread symbolic understanding in polytheism. In fertility cults, a tree is often the symbol of female fertility and a stone (in the form of a pillar; Heb. *maṣṣēbot*) the symbol of male fertility. The consequences are severe: The Lord has rejected those forces in which Judah has put its trust.

In verses 29–32 the prophet carries on a dialogue or dispute with the people. Apparently some among them have accused God of negligence, while God, through the agency of prophets, has accused the people of defection— which earlier in the chapter was described as prostitution. The people are also accused of forgetting God. Modern readers should not take this charge as implying that memory or recognition of God has faded in Judah. Forgetting is associated with not honoring God or with being disobedient, just as remembering is associated with doing what is expected. If one "remembers," one will act appropriately; thus, forgetting is tantamount to an inappropriate or nonresponsive act.

2:33–37. Jerusalem is again addressed, now personified as a prostitute or an adulteress. Verse 34 understands the prostitution as more than a defection from the worship of the Lord. The image is that of blood spattered on a garment, blood from innocent people whose lives have been consumed by the adulterous activities of Jerusalem. This adds the element of what can be called social criticism. Injustice and unrighteousness also flow from a defective understanding of who the Lord is and what he desires from his covenant partner.

The final image is that of personified Jerusalem walking away with her hands on her head. This is the posture of mourning and resignation, and it probably refers to the posture used by captives who are being led away. The activities of Jerusalem are leading to unpleasant consequences. Those entities (e.g., Assyria, Egypt) in whom she has trusted will be unable to help her in time of need.

A "SAMPLER" ROLE. The thrust and tenor of these prophetic oracles are common to the book of Jeremiah. They possess two characteristics that define their particular role in the book: their placement at the beginning of Jeremiah's words to his audience, and their profile as corporate address to the people as a whole. Both characteristics are important for interpretation. Like an introductory paragraph for an essay, Jeremiah's initial words set the tone and substance of what follows. The fact that dates for the oracles are lacking suggests that the chapter is intended to "paint with a broad brush" and to function as a "sampler," a term used in the previous section to describe the role of this collection. The overall thrust of the oracles is to paint God's people in their totality as rebellious against the Lord, who brought them into existence.

The mortal folly of the people is a constant theme of Jeremiah's public ministry. In keeping with the corporate nature of the address, the critique has to do with social institutions, political choices, and national character—that is, those things that make the audience a particular people. It is also a thoroughly theological analysis, reflecting Jeremiah's judgmental words to God's covenant partner. This is not just any state or group of people but those defined by election and covenant. Their fundamental identity is not that of a state but of a community of the Lord's people, who also have a political shape to their corporate existence.

God's people yesterday and today. The specifics of Judah's situation do not need exact replication among God's people in another time and place for them to be relevant to the faithful. Certainly God's people today should read the criticisms (and the expectations) of ancient Israel and ask if they apply to them, but the essential point is covenantal and ecclesiological. These oracles question the fitness of Judah to serve as God's covenant partner; they question the validity of the people's identity as the beloved bride of the Lord. A congregation, a church body, can hear this text question their own role as God's people.

In all parts these utterances assume the identity of Jeremiah's audience to be the people of God. This identity is the common element with Jerusalem (v. 2), the house of Jacob and all the clans of Israel (v. 4), and Judah (v. 28). It takes precedence over the various political forms Israel or Judah might take. God declares the audience to be "my people" (v. 13); through their ancestors they became God's bride (v. 2), rescued from Egypt (v. 6) and given a place in God's land (v. 7). They began as holy to the Lord (v. 3), set apart for his service.[2] They originated as a choice vine (v. 21), selected for the fruit they would bear (cf. Isa. 5:1–7).

Spurning the Lord from the heart. The text also assumes the faithlessness of God's people at that time to their *formative identity*. By their actions they have defiled God's land (v. 7), ignored his teaching (v. 8), and sought the protection of other deities (vv. 26–28). Instead of acting like a faithful spouse, they have prostituted themselves (vv. 20–25), frantically seeking protection from other gods or a political advantage through diplomatic intrigue (v. 36). This rejection of God is couched in *personal terms*. The failure to be obedient is also the rejection of an intimate relationship. One sees this in the anguished query of verse 29: "Why do you bring charges against me?" It is the basis of the charge in verse 13, "My people . . . have forsaken me," and the incredulity of verse 32, "My people have forgotten me."

Readers who conclude that Judah is accused only of not following God's instructions or making unwise political decisions have missed the most important claim here. It is not the failure to maintain an external norm that is at the heart of the criticism—though disobedience to God's revealed will is primary to the criticism; rather, it is the astounding claim that the Lord himself has been spurned, that the "spring of living water" himself has been rejected by the people in a foolhardy attempt to redefine themselves. One discerns the pain of rejection and anger over infidelity in the divine voice infusing the text. Such is the intensity of emotion where God has lost an intimate partner to the seductions of alien suitors, who will be unable to support her.

THE SHAPE OF LIFE. Such a critique of the life of God's people invites every generation of his people to reexamine its own commitments. As is common with the prophetic critique, the criticisms in Jeremiah 2 do more than explain what was wrong in Jeremiah's day; they also intend to ask subsequent generations to examine the corporate nature of their life and witness.

---

2. A form of the same Hebrew word (*qodeš*) is used to describe God's setting Jeremiah apart for service in 1:5.

This can be done in various ways. A church or Christian fellowship ought to ask if the shape of its life portrays some of the failings of Judah, perhaps in more subtle forms than a blatant idolatry or overt polytheism. Since the church is not identical with a state, the problem may not be alliances with a modern Egypt or Assyria, but the seeking of security and advantage among social and political forces may be detrimental to the church's life.

In the United States, for example, churches are often invited (tempted?) to make alliances for gain or influence. Conservative churches may unite with a Republican or a politically conservative figure (e.g., Jerry Falwell) and more liberal churches with a Democrat or a more politically liberal figure (e.g., Jesse Jackson). Thus in political campaigns collections are taken up in congregations. The question here is: Who is using whom? Are not both parties using the other? Is it possible that there will be long-term pain for short-term gain in these alliances? The answer may not be simple or obvious, but it is important to ask the questions of primary identity and covenant loyalty.

Contemporary idolatry. What makes idols worthless? The short answer is that they are not divine and they cannot save! Idols are a substitute for the real thing; they may be attractive and appealing to people with heightened religious longings. Idols offer theological rewards, but they cannot save. One of the fascinating (and scary) things about Jeremiah's day was the fervor with which his contemporaries sought to be religious, as if more religious activities and devotion to more deities would usher in a more secure future.

Among some non-Western churches, idolatry and animism may be real issues with which to struggle. I have observed this matter firsthand in Africa, where there is much debate about reincorporating indigenous religious customs among churches. Western missionaries who brought the gospel to the continent also taught that many of the indigenous customs (e.g., dancing, polygamy, ancestor veneration, witchcraft) were wrong. In some respects these missionaries were more "Western" than "Christian," but in other respects they were correct to oppose pagan practices. Among most Western Christians, idolatry is just as pernicious as in Jeremiah's day, but the objects of attachment are more symbolic and subtle in nature.

It is frequently observed that people in Western society who do not worship the triune God are often not without religious activities and other fundamental commitments. Instead of believing in nothing, they are tempted to believe a little in everything in their search for "solutions." Technology and individual "do-it-yourself" spirituality are two seductions facing Western Christians.

The stock markets of developed countries are good examples of a kind of secular polytheism in the modern world. Money, fervor, and alliances follow the trail of power and economic productivity. It is a remarkably amoral endeavor. One switches allegiances (i.e., investments) quickly in the search for profit. There are no lasting commitments other than immediate benefit. This can be a similar logic to that of combined polytheism and political machinations castigated by Jeremiah.

The name of modern counterparts to ancient polytheism is legion, for they are many (Mark 5:9). As public acceptance of traditional Judeo-Christian standards continues to erode, the growth of "new" religions and an emphasis on generic spirituality in contemporary society are nothing short of phenomenal. Without a firm foundation from which to proceed in important matters, people are tempted to commit themselves to a variety of ventures. It appears risky to trust all things to one Lord and more prudent to diversify. Monotheism has always appeared risky to some and narrow to others, whether in Jeremiah's day or ours. Contemporary Christianity faces a genuine threat from cultural forces like generic spirituality, which seeks to water down or dilute orthodox piety. It is now common in certain Christian circles to incorporate prayers to the great spirit or the mother goddess and to downplay the uniqueness of the gospel in favor of a more generic religiosity.

Polytheism in contemporary Western life may manifest itself in subtle ways, as when people compartmentalize fundamental issues, look to experts (theological and otherwise) who advise on their specialties, and refuse to see their lives as interconnected wholes before a sovereign God. Christians are not immune either from the temptations of self-help, which may lead them astray from devotion to their true Lord.

Living water. The New Testament builds on the theme of God as a fountain of living water (2:13). Jesus informs the Samaritan woman that he can give her "living water ... welling up to eternal life" (John 4:10, 14). To any who believe in him, Jesus declares that "streams of living water" will proceed from them (7:38). To reject his claim is to reject the offer of life that only God can grant. This is the same dynamic of Jeremiah's own day but put in a Christological context.

Jeremiah 3:1–4:2

1 "If a man divorces his wife
    and she leaves him and marries another man,
  should he return to her again?
    Would not the land be completely defiled?
  But you have lived as a prostitute with many lovers—
    would you now return to me?"

                                    declares the LORD.

2 "Look up to the barren heights and see.
    Is there any place where you have not been ravished?
  By the roadside you sat waiting for lovers,
    sat like a nomad in the desert.
  You have defiled the land
    with your prostitution and wickedness.
3 Therefore the showers have been withheld,
    and no spring rains have fallen.
  Yet you have the brazen look of a prostitute;
    you refuse to blush with shame.
4 Have you not just called to me:
    'My Father, my friend from my youth,
5 will you always be angry?
    Will your wrath continue forever?'
  This is how you talk,
    but you do all the evil you can."

6 During the reign of King Josiah, the LORD said to me, "Have you seen what faithless Israel has done? She has gone up on every high hill and under every spreading tree and has committed adultery there. 7 I thought that after she had done all this she would return to me but she did not, and her unfaithful sister Judah saw it. 8 I gave faithless Israel her certificate of divorce and sent her away because of all her adulteries. Yet I saw that her unfaithful sister Judah had no fear; she also went out and committed adultery. 9 Because Israel's immorality mattered so little to her, she defiled the land and committed adultery with stone and wood. 10 In spite of all this, her unfaithful sister Judah did not return to me with all her heart, but only in pretense," declares the LORD.

¹¹The LORD said to me, "Faithless Israel is more righteous than unfaithful Judah. ¹² Go, proclaim this message toward the north:

"'Return, faithless Israel,' declares the LORD,
   'I will frown on you no longer,
for I am merciful,' declares the LORD,
   'I will not be angry forever.
¹³ Only acknowledge your guilt—
   you have rebelled against the LORD your God,
you have scattered your favors to foreign gods
   under every spreading tree,
   and have not obeyed me,'"

declares the LORD.

¹⁴"Return, faithless people," declares the LORD, "for I am your husband. I will choose you—one from a town and two from a clan—and bring you to Zion. ¹⁵Then I will give you shepherds after my own heart, who will lead you with knowledge and understanding. ¹⁶In those days, when your numbers have increased greatly in the land," declares the LORD, "men will no longer say, 'The ark of the covenant of the LORD.' It will never enter their minds or be remembered; it will not be missed, nor will another one be made. ¹⁷At that time they will call Jerusalem The Throne of the LORD, and all nations will gather in Jerusalem to honor the name of the LORD. No longer will they follow the stubbornness of their evil hearts. ¹⁸In those days the house of Judah will join the house of Israel, and together they will come from a northern land to the land I gave your forefathers as an inheritance.
¹⁹"I myself said,

"'How gladly would I treat you like sons
   and give you a desirable land,
   the most beautiful inheritance of any nation.'
I thought you would call me 'Father'
   and not turn away from following me.
²⁰But like a woman unfaithful to her husband,
   so you have been unfaithful to me, O house of Israel,"
      declares the LORD.

²¹A cry is heard on the barren heights,
   the weeping and pleading of the people of Israel,
because they have perverted their ways
   and have forgotten the LORD their God.

²²"Return, faithless people;
    I will cure you of backsliding."

"Yes, we will come to you,
    for you are the LORD our God.
²³ Surely the idolatrous commotion on the hills
    and mountains is a deception;
surely in the LORD our God
    is the salvation of Israel.
²⁴ From our youth shameful gods have consumed
    the fruits of our fathers' labor—
their flocks and herds,
    their sons and daughters.
²⁵ Let us lie down in our shame,
    and let our disgrace cover us.
We have sinned against the LORD our God,
    both we and our fathers;
from our youth till this day
    we have not obeyed the LORD our God."

⁴:¹ "If you will return, O Israel,
    return to me,"

                    declares the LORD.

"If you put your detestable idols out of my sight
    and no longer go astray,
² and if in a truthful, just and righteous way
    you swear, 'As surely as the LORD lives,'
then the nations will be blessed by him
    and in him they will glory."

THIS SECTION IS comprised of various oracles, both poetic and prose, concerned with the faithless acts of Israel and Judah, their folly in rejecting the Lord, and calls for the people to repent. They are not given any precise setting in Jeremiah's own life,[1] and as a continuation of the theme of prostitution from chapter 2, they likely represent samples of public proclamation from more than one period in Jeremiah's prophetic work. There are several rhetorical plays on the Hebrew word *šub* (turn, return, repent) in the section that provide a thematic link to the prophecies.

---

1. There is a reference in 3:6 to prophecy during the days of Josiah. Some material in this section, therefore, may reflect Jeremiah's earliest public preaching.

The manner in which the audience is addressed varies in this collection, as it did in chapter 2. The following outline presents the "figures" of speech that comprise those addressed. An underlying metaphor is the identity of the people as members of the Lord's household or family. Thus they can be depicted as "Jerusalem," as the "spouse" or covenant partner of the Lord, as unfaithful sisters who are "married" to the Lord, and as children who have rebelled against the dictates of the Lord, the head of the household.

> A. 3:1–5. Following the last section of chapter 2, the opening figure in chapter 3 is Jerusalem.
> B. 3:6–10. This prose section represents "faithless Israel" and "unfaithful . . . Judah" as adulterous sisters.
> C. 3:11–13. Israel (i.e., the adulterous northern kingdom) is addressed in a poetic oracle in verses 12b–13.
> D. 3:14–18. The people, scattered because of their sinfulness, are addressed as God's children and called to resettle the area of Judah and Jerusalem.
> E. 3:19–20. Jerusalem is addressed (the "you" in Hebrew is feminine singular).
> F. 3:21–22a. The people are addressed as wayward children from the house/family of the Lord.
> G. 3:22b–25. The people, personified as prodigal children, offer a liturgy of repentance.
> H. 4:1–2. The voice of the Lord concludes this section with a statement about repentance.

3:1–5. Jeremiah uses the relationship of a husband and his divorced wife as an analogy of the relationship between the Lord and his disobedient covenant people. Jerusalem is the female personification of the people; that is, she is the feminine "you" castigated in 3:1. The analogy builds on the claims of 2:2, where the relationship between the Lord and his people is compared to the marriage relationship.

This passage also presupposes the instruction of Deuteronomy 24:1–4 concerning divorce and remarriage. That text from the Torah raises the question whether a woman once married but then divorced and married to another man, can then remarry her "first husband." The answer is *no*. Although the text offers no other reason than that the wife has become "defiled" to the first husband, the scenario likely presupposes some other factors not stated explicitly in forbidding the remarriage. It is not necessary to go into these other factors, since the important thing is the answer given in Torah, an answer presupposed in the rhetorical question of Jeremiah 3:1.

The question in 3:1, "Should [a former husband] *return* to [his wife] again after she had married another?" contains the first use of the verb *šub* in this section. As noted above, the answer is no. Jerusalem, representing the people of Judah, is the spouse who has married many lovers in her defection from the Lord. As a result she is in a defiled state, estranged from her first husband and incapable of mending the relationship. The language of verse 2 contains a Hebrew term so uncompromising and harsh in its depiction of adultery that the scribes who compiled the Masoretic Text provided a substitute word to be used in public reading. The NIV choice of "ravish" catches something of the physical and offensive nature of the term, but it is acceptable for public reading.

Jeremiah uses both rhetorical questions and accusations to engage his audience. Obviously the charge of flagrant prostitution and adultery is offensive to the people, as is the conclusion that once "divorced," the people are unable on their own to effect a reconciliation.

3:6–10. In this prose section, perhaps compiled as an interpretive comment for readers of the poetic oracle in 3:1–5, the fate and infidelity of Israel are compared to the (worse) circumstances of Judah. Israel and Judah are described as sisters who have both committed adultery against their spouse (cf. Ezek. 16:44–58; 23:1–49).[2] The adjective "faithless" used for Israel is *mᵉšuba*, a form of the verb *šub* and a part of the wordplay on the concept of turning/repenting. Literally, one could translate the phrase as "turning Israel," as if she is constantly turning this way and that in seeking lovers.

Surprisingly, Judah has learned nothing from the fall of Israel to the Assyrians (cf. 2 Kings 17). Josiah was a reforming king (2 Kings 22–23), whose covenant renewal measures were good but short-lived and ultimately inadequate. Elsewhere Jeremiah expresses admiration for Josiah (Jer. 22:15–16). Judah did not return (*šub*) "with all her heart" to the Lord. Such language reflects Deuteronomy 6:5 and the renewal ceremony of 2 Kings 23:3.[3]

3:11–13. The Lord calls faithless Israel to return (*šub*) to the Lord. This oracle is preserved as part of an autobiographical section, beginning with: "The LORD said to *me*" (3:11). The oracle is directed explicitly to the north; that is, it is intended for remnants of the former northern kingdom. God promises to be gracious and receptive, foregoing the anger proper to a spurned spouse. Although no date is given for this oracle, it probably fits early in Jeremiah's prophetic ministry, during the time when King Josiah made overtures to remnants of the covenant people in the territory of the former

---

2. Ezekiel 23:1–49 is an extended treatment of the two-sisters metaphor. It is so long and developed that it presupposes a narrative form and so functions like a parable.

3. Jeremiah Unterman has proposed that 3:6–13 and 3:19–4:2 fit best in the days of Josiah's reforming efforts, when the prophet Jeremiah thought that wholehearted repentance might effect real change in Judah's national life. See his *From Repentance to Redemption: Jeremiah's Thought in Transition* (JSOTSup 54; Sheffield: JSOT Press, 1987), esp. 23–38, 176–79.

northern kingdom (cf. 2 Kings 23:15–23; 2 Chron. 35:1–19). The prophet will also evidence a concern for these Israelite remnants in the hopeful prophecies in Jeremiah 30–31.

3:14–18. The analogy of Judah as an adulterous wife is here changed to that of wayward rebellious children; both analogies are part of a root metaphor that identifies the people as comprising part of the household of the Lord. The NIV attempts to keep the metaphor of marriage by translating the Hebrew term for master/owner as "husband." The passage begins with an address to children, however, and not to a personified entity who plays the role of spouse (as in 3:1–5 and somewhat differently in 3:6–10). It assumes a form of exile and resulting loss of land. Restoration, therefore, is concrete. The Lord will bring back the prodigal children and establish them in their homeland.

These verses contain a vision in prose of restoration in the land of promise. One way to grasp the significance of the ark of the covenant is its portrayal as the throne (or royal footstool) of the cosmic Lord. Yet in the future, in a renewed Jerusalem, no one will long for the lost ark because the whole city will be "The Throne of the LORD." Remnants from both Israel and Judah will inhabit the city and surrounding land. Even other nations will come to the city (cf. Isa. 2:1–5). This restoration will come about even though the initial passage of the section (3:1) assumed that according to the Torah, "remarriage" was impossible.

3:19–20. Both the marriage ("unfaithful wife") and familial metaphors (children able to inherit) are again used to indicate Judah's sin. The covenantal term "house of Israel" is also used to describe the people.

3:21–25. The language of "returning" (*šub*) and of healing the people's "faithlessness" and "backsliding" are used in the promises of these verses. The metaphor of the people as wayward children is employed in verse 22. They offer confession of sin and repentance in 3:22b–25. Apparently the passage depicts a state of affairs to come after the judgment of the Exile.

4:1–2. When that time comes, God calls for a sincere return (*šub*) to him. The future restoration of God's people will lead other nations into finding a blessing in the Lord. This last element plays on the foundational promise of Genesis 12:3, that all the nations of the earth will find a blessing in Abraham's descendants.

PUNISHMENT AND REPENTANCE. As noted above, only a general reference to Josiah (3:6) provides a context in Jeremiah's own life, and it is likely that in this section we have prophecies from different stages in the prophet's ministry, all linked by the common themes of Israel and Judah's failure to return to their Lord. The artful collection of these prophecies is already an example of "bridging contexts," designed for recipients of Jeremiah's book. In their original contexts, these oracles indicated the nature of Israel and Judah's failures and the consequences to come. For readers/hearers they indicate why Israel and Judah fell to foreign nations: God was judging his people for their failure to turn to him in true worship and heartfelt obedience.

Punishment for infidelity was inevitable. But beyond that, restoration and healing required a wholehearted return to the Lord. Perhaps this section reflects a development in Jeremiah's message over the decades of his ministry; as a result of calls for corporate repentance, Jeremiah learns that Judah is inherently unable to change her ways. Although this makes judgment on the people unavoidable, it is not the last word. God himself will bring about change among his people and thus offer a new beginning for future generations.

In this section we have no facile preaching of repentance, as if one simply calls the people to change, and by their own efforts they do so. Judah appears heedless of the danger to its existence, taking no instruction from the failure (and exile) of her sister Israel (3:6–7). The first passage (3:1–5) indicates the impossibility of Judah's return to the Lord because she has "married" many lovers in her apostasy, and the Torah (Deut. 24:1–4) makes remarriage an impossibility. In other words, the essential point of judgment is that Judah will not only not "return" but will finally be unable to return to the Lord.

This arrangement of oracles is designed to bridge contexts from the initial audience of Jeremiah to that of subsequent generations, who will read and reflect on the justified demise of Judah. Each generation of God's people is asked to account for Judah's fall as the inevitable consequence of apostasy, resulting in the Lord's righteous judgment. Moreover, each generation is asked to search its own life to see where changes need to be made. Gracious words about the future are a reminder that God is committed to the transformation of his people.

Jesus' public ministry too was marked by explicit calls for repentance (e.g., Matt. 4:17) and reminders of the cost of discipleship. In these actions Jesus brought a major element of prophecy under the old covenant to its culmination. Like Jeremiah, Jesus' call for repentance was not about change for change's sake but for the sake of knowing God and the joy of obedience to his revealed will. Like Jeremiah, Jesus spoke to a generation of God's people who had heard the word of the Lord but who had not responded. Moreover, Jesus' proclamation too was ignored by some and heard by others, with a result that the audiences of both would become examples for generations to come. Finally, like the proclamation of Jeremiah to his audience (3:22), Jesus taught that what God demands by way of repentance and reorientation is something he graciously enables, "because the Lord disciplines those he loves" (Heb. 12:6).

Healing and restoration. In addition to righteous judgment on Israel and Judah for their faithlessness, this section is also about healing and future restoration that only God can provide. Note the emphasis on divine activity: "I will choose ... [I will] bring ... I will give ... I will cure" (Jer. 3:14–15, 22). As everywhere in the Bible, so here too God is the author of salvation. His depiction of restoration is a corporate one because the judgment indicated in these prophecies is a corporate one. Jerusalem is to be repopulated and become the center of divine revelation for all (cf. Isa. 2:2–4; Mic. 4:1–3). Ezekiel, Jeremiah's younger contemporary, likewise has an expansive concluding section to his book where in visionary style he portrays Jerusalem as the holy city and medium of divine revelation (Ezek. 40–48). And John, the seer and prophet of the risen Christ, beholds the heavenly Jerusalem as the eternal home of the redeemed from every generation of God's people (Rev. 21–22), where the Lamb dwells, and death is no more.

One encounters in these prophecies, therefore, two elements in particular that remain instructive to subsequent generations. The first is the call to turn to the living God and recognize the consequences of failure to do so. The second is the prophetic depiction that God will heal the consequences of his people's failures and restore them again in the land promised to their ancestors. When portions of the exilic community returned to Judah and Jerusalem during the Persian period, it was understood as a fulfillment of Jeremiah's prediction that God would restore his people (cf. Dan. 9:2). Yet that return did not exhaust the significance of the prophecy, as later Old Testament prophets and New Testament writers demonstrate.

These oracles, taken as a whole, give a radical witness to the freedom and grace of God. Legal custom forbade the remarriage of a husband and wife, once the wife had been divorced and gone to marry another man. That law is used here to demonstrate the impossibility of Israel and Judah's removing the effects of their sinfulness by simply deciding to do better and return to their first Lord. That same law, however, will not keep *God* from healing the people from his side. It is important to note that his "overrule" of the Torah does not make the law bad or its principles invalid. The better analogy is the Pauline claim that what the law could not do, God has seen fit to do—all for the sake of those he loves (cf. Rom. 8:1–4).

THE VIEW OF THE HUMAN CONDITION. Jeremiah's words should evoke reflection in our hearts. We begin with God's view of the human condition. God formed his people in order that they might have an intimate and exclusive relationship with him (note the analogy of Jeremiah, along with Hosea, of marriage/family). Behind this assumption of an exclusive bond lie the claims of divine choice, the "first" commandment of the Decalogue ("you shall have no other gods before me," Deut. 5:7), and the "great" commandment ("love the LORD your God with all your heart and with all your soul and with all your strength," Deut. 6:5; cf. Mark 12:29–30).

Christians are the bride of Jesus Christ, God's Son. Christ's disciples are bound to him through his resurrection, and the working of the Holy Spirit is present within them and the church, the corporate body of Christ. Disobedience ("sin") is not just failure to observe a norm of behavior, but the breaking of a bond and an affront to one's Lord. Adultery in theological terms is a crime against grace; it is infidelity against God who in Christ has called us into an intimate fellowship and who has formed a church as the holy bride of Christ.

Judgment is the inevitable consequence of failure to turn to the Lord in faith and obedience. Human beings cannot have it both ways: Either one is on intimate exclusive terms with God through Jesus Christ, or one has other gods—other things that capture one's commitments and ultimate allegiance. In Israel's case, God judged them by giving them over to the other lords they seemed to desire (i.e., other "deities," the freedom of immorality, and historical deliverance through political alliances). Communal destruction and exile were the result. Christian reflection should begin with a search for those things that seduce believers from allegiance to Christ, things of a personal nature and a corporate nature. What is it, for example, about modern Western society that pulls Christians from their relationship with Christ and robs them of the joy of obedience to their Lord? What things in our lives, both personal and corporate, should be seen as warning bells announcing that not all is right in Zion? Are there not signs that warn that failure has consequences?

Repentance. Jeremiah's repeated use of the term *šub* urges exploration of the nature and function of repentance in the Christian life. There are rich resources in the history of Christian piety on this subject. Fasting, self-denial, acts of charity, and spiritual disciplines such as *lectio divina* and frequent prayer have all been classical means for turning and returning to the Lord. But repentance first of all means turning from an activity toward God and engaging in obedience to his revealed will. In Christian terms it is not just the rejection of sinful activity but the embracing of the good revealed in Jesus Christ.

Repentance may go on to mean self-renunciation, the setting aside of idols, rejection of evil deeds, and a turning from worldly values (all classical characteristics). It also includes the positive steps of discipleship. Peter urged his hearers to "repent, then, and turn to God, so that your sins may be wiped out, that times of refreshing may come from the Lord. . . . When God raised up his servant, he sent him first to you to bless you by turning each of you from your wicked ways" (Acts 3:19, 26). Repentance is not just a listing of vices to be avoided but the positive movement toward a new life in Christ. Repentance is not simply an act that occurs at the beginning of Christian discipleship, something in Christian experience to be relegated to the past, but a way of life, a mark of discipleship.

Repentance not only has the embrace of God as its goal; it has God as its author. Thus, repentance is not only an event and an act of the will; it is also a process, a positive lifestyle, through which God matures and strengthens his children. If Jeremiah can call on Judah to return to the Lord, he can also proclaim that God will cure Judah's sickness and overcome its chronic infidelity. The judgment of the Exile will lead to the new beginning of restoration. Similarly, the judgment of the cross ushers in the transformation of resurrection. An acknowledgment of a sinful estate is the first step in the turning toward the living God, who makes all things new.

The unveiling of God's character. Within the repeated call to Judah to turn resides the promise that God will do what the divine law (Deut. 24:1–4) says is legally impermissible: to restore a sinful spouse who has apostatized and legally married another. It is a profound theological claim that God's ability to restore is not limited by human inability to heal broken relationships. Even the Deuteronomic law regulating divorce—when read prophetically—points to the God of grace beyond human culpability and its consequences. In New Testament terms, even the curse of the law on disobedience is born by God's Son in order that the blessing promised to Abraham can be received through faith (Gal. 3:13–14). What the law weakened by human fallibility cannot do, God has done in Jesus Christ.

Jeremiah 4:3–6:30

THIS IS WHAT the LORD says to the men of Judah and
to Jerusalem:

"Break up your unplowed ground
   and do not sow among thorns.
⁴Circumcise yourselves to the LORD,
   circumcise your hearts,
   you men of Judah and people of Jerusalem,
or my wrath will break out and burn like fire
   because of the evil you have done—
   burn with no one to quench it.

⁵"Announce in Judah and proclaim in Jerusalem and say:
   'Sound the trumpet throughout the land!'
Cry aloud and say:
   'Gather together!
   Let us flee to the fortified cities!'
⁶Raise the signal to go to Zion!
   Flee for safety without delay!
For I am bringing disaster from the north,
   even terrible destruction."

⁷A lion has come out of his lair;
   a destroyer of nations has set out.
He has left his place
   to lay waste your land.
Your towns will lie in ruins
   without inhabitant.
⁸So put on sackcloth,
   lament and wail,
for the fierce anger of the LORD
   has not turned away from us.

⁹"In that day," declares the LORD,
   "the king and the officials will lose heart,
the priests will be horrified,
   and the prophets will be appalled."

¹⁰Then I said, "Ah, Sovereign LORD, how completely you
have deceived this people and Jerusalem by saying, 'You will
have peace,' when the sword is at our throats."

¹¹At that time this people and Jerusalem will be told, "A scorching wind from the barren heights in the desert blows toward my people, but not to winnow or cleanse; ¹²a wind too strong for that comes from me. Now I pronounce my judgments against them."

> ¹³ Look! He advances like the clouds,
>> his chariots come like a whirlwind,
> his horses are swifter than eagles.
>> Woe to us! We are ruined!
> ¹⁴ O Jerusalem, wash the evil from your heart and be saved.
>> How long will you harbor wicked thoughts?
> ¹⁵ A voice is announcing from Dan,
>> proclaiming disaster from the hills of Ephraim.
> ¹⁶ "Tell this to the nations,
>> proclaim it to Jerusalem:
> 'A besieging army is coming from a distant land,
>> raising a war cry against the cities of Judah.
> ¹⁷ They surround her like men guarding a field,
>> because she has rebelled against me,'"
>
>> declares the LORD.
>
> ¹⁸ "Your own conduct and actions
>> have brought this upon you.
> This is your punishment.
>> How bitter it is!
>> How it pierces to the heart!"
>
> ¹⁹ Oh, my anguish, my anguish!
>> I writhe in pain.
> Oh, the agony of my heart!
>> My heart pounds within me,
>> I cannot keep silent.
> For I have heard the sound of the trumpet;
>> I have heard the battle cry.
> ²⁰ Disaster follows disaster;
>> the whole land lies in ruins.
> In an instant my tents are destroyed,
>> my shelter in a moment.
> ²¹ How long must I see the battle standard
>> and hear the sound of the trumpet?
>
> ²² "My people are fools;
>> they do not know me.

They are senseless children;
    they have no understanding.
They are skilled in doing evil;
    they know not how to do good."

²³ I looked at the earth,
    and it was formless and empty;
and at the heavens,
    and their light was gone.
²⁴ I looked at the mountains,
    and they were quaking;
all the hills were swaying.
²⁵ I looked, and there were no people;
    every bird in the sky had flown away.
²⁶ I looked, and the fruitful land was a desert;
    all its towns lay in ruins
before the LORD, before his fierce anger.

²⁷This is what the LORD says:

    "The whole land will be ruined,
        though I will not destroy it completely.
²⁸ Therefore the earth will mourn
    and the heavens above grow dark,
because I have spoken and will not relent,
    I have decided and will not turn back."

²⁹ At the sound of horsemen and archers
    every town takes to flight.
Some go into the thickets;
    some climb up among the rocks.
All the towns are deserted;
    no one lives in them.
³⁰ What are you doing, O devastated one?
    Why dress yourself in scarlet
    and put on jewels of gold?
Why shade your eyes with paint?
    You adorn yourself in vain.
Your lovers despise you;
    they seek your life.

³¹ I hear a cry as of a woman in labor,
    a groan as of one bearing her first child—
the cry of the Daughter of Zion gasping for breath,
    stretching out her hands and saying,

"Alas! I am fainting;
　　my life is given over to murderers."

⁵:¹"Go up and down the streets of Jerusalem,
　　look around and consider,
　　search through her squares.
If you can find but one person
　　who deals honestly and seeks the truth,
　　I will forgive this city.
²Although they say, 'As surely as the LORD lives,'
　　still they are swearing falsely."

³O LORD, do not your eyes look for truth?
　　You struck them, but they felt no pain;
　　you crushed them, but they refused correction.
They made their faces harder than stone
　　and refused to repent.
⁴I thought, "These are only the poor;
　　they are foolish,
for they do not know the way of the LORD,
　　the requirements of their God.
⁵So I will go to the leaders
　　and speak to them;
surely they know the way of the LORD,
　　the requirements of their God."
But with one accord they too had broken off the yoke
　　and torn off the bonds.
⁶Therefore a lion from the forest will attack them,
　　a wolf from the desert will ravage them,
a leopard will lie in wait near their towns
　　to tear to pieces any who venture out,
for their rebellion is great
　　and their backslidings many.

⁷"Why should I forgive you?
　　Your children have forsaken me
　　and sworn by gods that are not gods.
I supplied all their needs,
　　yet they committed adultery
　　and thronged to the houses of prostitutes.
⁸They are well-fed, lusty stallions,
　　each neighing for another man's wife.

⁹ Should I not punish them for this?"
declares the LORD.
"Should I not avenge myself
on such a nation as this?

¹⁰ "Go through her vineyards and ravage them,
but do not destroy them completely.
Strip off her branches,
for these people do not belong to the LORD.
¹¹ The house of Israel and the house of Judah
have been utterly unfaithful to me,"
declares the LORD.

¹² They have lied about the LORD;
they said, "He will do nothing!
No harm will come to us;
we will never see sword or famine.
¹³ The prophets are but wind
and the word is not in them;
so let what they say be done to them."

¹⁴ Therefore this is what the LORD God Almighty says:

"Because the people have spoken these words,
I will make my words in your mouth a fire
and these people the wood it consumes.
¹⁵ O house of Israel," declares the LORD,
"I am bringing a distant nation against you—
an ancient and enduring nation,
a people whose language you do not know,
whose speech you do not understand.
¹⁶ Their quivers are like an open grave;
all of them are mighty warriors.
¹⁷ They will devour your harvests and food,
devour your sons and daughters;
they will devour your flocks and herds,
devour your vines and fig trees.
With the sword they will destroy
the fortified cities in which you trust.

¹⁸ "Yet even in those days," declares the LORD, "I will not destroy you completely. ¹⁹ And when the people ask, 'Why has the LORD our God done all this to us?' you will tell them, 'As you have forsaken me and served foreign gods in your own land, so now you will serve foreigners in a land not your own.'

²⁰"Announce this to the house of Jacob
      and proclaim it in Judah:
²¹ Hear this, you foolish and senseless people,
      who have eyes but do not see,
      who have ears but do not hear:
²² Should you not fear me?" declares the LORD.
      "Should you not tremble in my presence?
   I made the sand a boundary for the sea,
      an everlasting barrier it cannot cross.
   The waves may roll, but they cannot prevail;
      they may roar, but they cannot cross it.
²³ But these people have stubborn and rebellious hearts;
      they have turned aside and gone away.
²⁴ They do not say to themselves,
      'Let us fear the LORD our God,
   who gives autumn and spring rains in season,
      who assures us of the regular weeks of harvest.'
²⁵ Your wrongdoings have kept these away;
      your sins have deprived you of good.
²⁶"Among my people are wicked men
      who lie in wait like men who snare birds
      and like those who set traps to catch men.
²⁷ Like cages full of birds,
      their houses are full of deceit;
   they have become rich and powerful
²⁸   and have grown fat and sleek.
   Their evil deeds have no limit;
      they do not plead the case of the fatherless to win it,
      they do not defend the rights of the poor.
²⁹ Should I not punish them for this?"
      declares the LORD.
   "Should I not avenge myself
      on such a nation as this?
³⁰"A horrible and shocking thing
      has happened in the land:
³¹ The prophets prophesy lies,
      the priests rule by their own authority,
   and my people love it this way.
      But what will you do in the end?

^{6:1}"Flee for safety, people of Benjamin!
      Flee from Jerusalem!

Sound the trumpet in Tekoa!
    Raise the signal over Beth Hakkerem!
For disaster looms out of the north,
    even terrible destruction.
²I will destroy the Daughter of Zion,
    so beautiful and delicate.
³Shepherds with their flocks will come against her;
    they will pitch their tents around her,
    each tending his own portion."

⁴"Prepare for battle against her!
    Arise, let us attack at noon!
But, alas, the daylight is fading,
    and the shadows of evening grow long.
⁵So arise, let us attack at night
    and destroy her fortresses!"

⁶This is what the LORD Almighty says:

"Cut down the trees
    and build siege ramps against Jerusalem.
This city must be punished;
    it is filled with oppression.
⁷As a well pours out its water,
    so she pours out her wickedness.
Violence and destruction resound in her;
    her sickness and wounds are ever before me.
⁸Take warning, O Jerusalem,
    or I will turn away from you
and make your land desolate
    so no one can live in it."

⁹This is what the LORD Almighty says:

"Let them glean the remnant of Israel
    as thoroughly as a vine;
pass your hand over the branches again,
    like one gathering grapes."

¹⁰To whom can I speak and give warning?
    Who will listen to me?
Their ears are closed
    so they cannot hear.

The word of the LORD is offensive to them;
    they find no pleasure in it.
¹¹But I am full of the wrath of the LORD,
    and I cannot hold it in.

"Pour it out on the children in the street
    and on the young men gathered together;
both husband and wife will be caught in it,
    and the old, those weighed down with years.
¹²Their houses will be turned over to others,
    together with their fields and their wives,
when I stretch out my hand
    against those who live in the land,"

                    declares the LORD.

¹³"From the least to the greatest,
    all are greedy for gain;
prophets and priests alike,
    all practice deceit.
¹⁴They dress the wound of my people
    as though it were not serious.
'Peace, peace,' they say,
    when there is no peace.
¹⁵Are they ashamed of their loathsome conduct?
    No, they have no shame at all;
they do not even know how to blush.
So they will fall among the fallen;
    they will be brought down when I punish them,"

                    says the LORD.

¹⁶This is what the LORD says:

"Stand at the crossroads and look;
    ask for the ancient paths,
ask where the good way is, and walk in it,
    and you will find rest for your souls.
    But you said, 'We will not walk in it.'
¹⁷I appointed watchmen over you and said,
    'Listen to the sound of the trumpet!'
    But you said, 'We will not listen.'
¹⁸Therefore hear, O nations;
    observe, O witnesses,
    what will happen to them.

¹⁹ Hear, O earth:
I am bringing disaster on this people,
the fruit of their schemes,
because they have not listened to my words
and have rejected my law.
²⁰ What do I care about incense from Sheba
or sweet calamus from a distant land?
Your burnt offerings are not acceptable;
your sacrifices do not please me."

²¹ Therefore this is what the LORD says:

"I will put obstacles before this people.
Fathers and sons alike will stumble over them;
neighbors and friends will perish."

²² This is what the LORD says:

"Look, an army is coming
from the land of the north;
a great nation is being stirred up
from the ends of the earth.
²³ They are armed with bow and spear;
they are cruel and show no mercy.
They sound like the roaring sea
as they ride on their horses;
they come like men in battle formation
to attack you, O Daughter of Zion."

²⁴ We have heard reports about them,
and our hands hang limp.
Anguish has gripped us,
pain like that of a woman in labor.
²⁵ Do not go out to the fields
or walk on the roads,
for the enemy has a sword,
and there is terror on every side.
²⁶ O my people, put on sackcloth
and roll in ashes;
mourn with bitter wailing
as for an only son,
for suddenly the destroyer
will come upon us.

²⁷"I have made you a tester of metals
and my people the ore,
that you may observe
and test their ways.
²⁸ They are all hardened rebels,
going about to slander.
They are bronze and iron;
they all act corruptly.
²⁹ The bellows blow fiercely
to burn away the lead with fire,
but the refining goes on in vain;
the wicked are not purged out.
³⁰ They are called rejected silver,
because the LORD has rejected them."

THIS SECTION OF Jeremiah is essentially a collection of prophecies concerning judgments to befall Judah. It is interspersed, however, with quotations attributed to Jeremiah, God, Jerusalem, and the people, all of which give this section a dialogical character (e.g., 4:10; 5:1—6).

As with the previous section, the individual prophecies in this collection likely date from various times in Jeremiah's public ministry. The primary theme is judgment on Judah and Jerusalem through the historical process as God sends disasters and enemies against his people. A few "catchword topics" provide links between some of the oracles and assist with the thematic coherence of the collection. Among these topics are descriptions of a foe (often "from the north")¹ who will wreak havoc on Judah, the senselessness of the people, the corruption of the "heart" (*leb*), and a call for the people to lament insofar as God is judging them.

As to its dialogical character, there is little indication how this conversational material was presented to the prophet's contemporaries in Judah (or even if all of it was made public orally). For readers, however, these interchanges are intended to be instructive, setting forth a depiction of the prophetic office as the location of pain and prayer, not just the source of accusation and judgment. The prophet laments over the pain he observes and over the inability of his hearers to comprehend the true nature of their predicament.

4:3–4. It is difficult to know whether these two verses conclude the Lord's reply concerning repentance in 4:1—2 or if they originated indepen-

---

1. See the discussion of the "foe from the north" in the introduction ("Jeremiah's Place in the Last Years of the Judean State and Its Destruction").

dently of 4:1–2. The Hebrew particle *ki* ("for") with which verse 3 begins can be a linking particle—meaning "therefore" or something similar—or it can be an emphasizing particle introducing something new. In either case, the basic point of these two verses can be appreciated: Repentance toward God is symbolized by a circumcision of the heart.

Genesis 17 provides an etiology for the role of circumcision in the religious life of ancient Israel. In that account the removal of the foreskin from the male genitalia is a sign (17:11; *ʾot*) of the covenant, a mark in the flesh that represents the bond established by God with Abraham and his descendants. Males so marked bore a permanent sign in their flesh of their acceptance of and membership in God's covenant. Circumcision of the heart, the organ of understanding and will, is obviously a metaphor for preparing a "wholehearted" commitment to the Lord and proper obedience to the revelation of his will. This metaphor in Jeremiah presupposes that the fleshly mark is inadequate apart from personal commitment.

There are similar references elsewhere in Jeremiah and in Deuteronomy to the significance of both the terms *circumcision* and *heart*. In Jeremiah 17:1–10 the sin of Judah is described as engraved on the tablets of their hearts. One way in which God assesses character and commitment is through examining the heart; according to 17:9–10, the heart of the people is desperately sick. In 24:7 God promises to give a new heart to his people (this assumes the fatal fallibility of the "old" one!). Similarly, Deuteronomy 10:16 preserves the imperative to Israel to circumcise their hearts, much like the command here in Jeremiah 4:4, and Deuteronomy 30:1–10 preserves the prophecy that after the coming judgment, the Lord will circumcise the hearts of his people so that they will love him with all their heart and soul.

These various references presuppose that Israel must make a radical commitment to God but also that God's people will be unable to fulfill that commitment unless he acts decisively to renew and transform them. In the previous chapter (3:22), Jeremiah has already indicated that healing and restoration come only from the Lord. The call in 4:3–4 takes seriously the role of the people and their affections, but it does not assume that a mere act of the will on their part will make everything restored. Elsewhere Jeremiah puts this dynamic in the context of the new covenant that God will make with Israel and Judah, a transforming act that will include writing his Torah on their hearts (31:31–34).[2]

---

2. In this context one should compare also Ezekiel's prophecy that God will remove the heart of stone from his people and replace it with a heart of flesh (Ezek. 11:18–21). Stone is inanimate and incapable of yielding or responding, but flesh is alive and responsive. When put in the context of the "new spirit" that God will give them (11:19), a fleshly heart is then ready to respond to God.

4:5–13. Judah and Jerusalem are called to assemble, to put on sackcloth, and to lament the approach of a foe from the north. The approach of this enemy is in reality the approach of the Lord, who comes against the people like a lion or whose blast of anger is like a searing wind. God is a warrior (Ex. 15:3), but in this context the divine warrior comes against his own people.

Verse 10 is an autobiographical comment that accuses God of deceiving the people by giving a word of "peace" (*šalom*) when in actuality a mortal threat is at hand. Just what this means is not clear, although it is a frank indication that Jeremiah and God engage each other pointedly! Perhaps the prophet's charge assumes the words of the prophets and priests mentioned in the previous verse, who may have assured the people in the name of the Lord that deliverance will come (cf. 6:13–14; 8:11–12). Elsewhere, Jeremiah shows respect to a prophet who proclaims a word of deliverance, even if he repudiates that message after further reflection and prayer (Jer. 28). A related possibility is that Jeremiah's own words about judgment to come have been proclaimed for several years, but, as yet, no catastrophic blow has fallen. Those prophets and priests who have proclaimed peace have been right (so far), and in both frustration and alarm, Jeremiah wonders how God can allow these circumstances to exist.

4:14–22. These verses continue the sentiments of 4:5–13. The prophet beseeches Jerusalem to cleanse her heart and remove her wicked thoughts. Note the reference to the heart—one of the "catchwords" in this collection of oracles. Those who would besiege her are approaching. God reminds Jerusalem of the dire consequences of her activity. Her own "conduct and actions" (v. 18) have brought these appalling circumstances to light.

In his own *heart* (note again the catchword) Jeremiah expresses horror at the realization of Jerusalem's impending doom (4:19–22). In striking fashion his emotional reaction to this doom is translated into physical reaction, with "writhing in pain." One wonders if the prophet somehow publicly acts out this physical reaction or if a recognition of such horror is left to the inference of hearer and reader. If he does, it will add illustration and poignancy to his role. Even as "the voice" reflects the pain of judgment, the prophet lays the responsibility for failure with the people, who are described as "fools" and "senseless children."

A close reading of this section brings together the voices of Jeremiah, God, and the people in an amazing way. It begins with Jeremiah addressing Jerusalem in almost frantic fashion. The emotion fits that of the prophet, but the refrain of 4:17 ("declares the LORD") indicates that this concern for the city is also that of God. The writhing pain of 4:19–20 may be that of Jerusalem as she watches her land and inhabitants being consumed, or perhaps it is that of the prophet, who has begun to grasp the enormity of the tragedy to come. The third party to this emotion-laden conversation is God himself. The sad comment in 4:22 that the people "do not know *me*" can be no other than the voice of God himself, as represented through the prophet. The conversation and mixing of voices are such that they blend together. In the final analysis, no one—people, prophet, or God—remains aloof from the horror of it all.

4:23–26. In the visionary perspective of the prophet, the Judean landscape is transformed into something "formless and empty," as if judgment on Judah will undo the very goodness and order of creation. "Formless and empty" are the same two terms used in Genesis 1:2 to describe the chaos of creation before the creative Spirit of God began its work and God spoke order into existence. Judah's sinfulness takes on a type of cosmic context in this visionary account, as if the people's folly makes them complicit in a consuming cosmic chaos. Four times comes the refrain "I looked," followed each time by a vision of the unraveling of creation. The passage functions as a horrible visionary interlude, as the prophet pauses from his projection of the foe coming on Jerusalem and casts his Spirit-aided eye toward a looming chaos.

4:27–31. The prophet returns to the horror that will befall Jerusalem. God will speak and judgment will come, just as surely as in the creation account God spoke and order was brought out of chaos. Verse 28 states that the earth will "mourn" (*ʾabal*) or languish. This sad comment reflects a synthetic understanding of existence, whereby the personified land is affected by the folly of the people's sinfulness.[3] The folly and failure of the people affect more than their historical circumstances; it extends to their whole cultural and environmental setting.

In 4:31 the prophet depicts Jerusalem's cries like those of birth pains. It is not, however, the joy of giving birth but the fear of death that is on her lips. She is in collapse before murderers! Again, did Jeremiah publicly present this message? Such emotion is not presented well through smooth modulation but through identification with the pain that arouses it.

5:1–9. This section contains an interchange between God and the audience in Jerusalem, mediated by the prophet, who offers commentary in verses 3–6. The passage begins with a challenge for people to search Jerusalem for anyone who "deals honestly and seeks the truth." One can also translate "deals honestly" as "does justice" (*mišpaṭ*). Apparently no one fits these requirements. Although judgment has already struck Jerusalem (death of Josiah? drought? first Babylonian onslaught?), there has been no repentance.

In 5:3–6 Jeremiah himself attempts a search of people, both the poor and great, but "their rebellion is great." God's reply is that forgiveness is not presently an option (cf. 5:9 with 5:29).

---

3. This same motif is found in Hos. 4:3 and Joel 1:10 (see text note).

5:10–17. Jerusalem is now personified as the possessor of vines and branches, which symbolize people (cf. Isa. 5:1–7, where the vines of a vine-yard represent the people). Not only have both Israel and Judah refused to accept that their misfortune is the Lord's judgment on them; there is even a sense among some that the Lord is not active and will not judge in the future either. Verse 12 places a quotation in their mouth to the effect that neither sword nor famine will strike them. Apparently these sentiments are provoked by "prophets" (v. 13), since Jeremiah replies that these prophets "are but wind." Underlying a text like this is heated debate among prophets, all of whom claim to represent the will of God.

The Lord makes Jeremiah's prophetic word of judgment like a fire con-suming wood (v. 14). More specifically, the Lord declares that a foreign nation is coming to devastate the people (vv. 15–17). This depiction is one of the "catchword topics" used repeatedly in chapters 4–6. One result of their onslaught is that the people will be carried away and serve foreigners in a strange land (i.e., the Exile).

5:18–19. In this short prose section the Lord offers commentary on the previous verse and its reference to exile. Two sentiments are expressed suc-cinctly. (1) Exile from the Promised Land does not bring an end to the exis-tence of the people. In context, that is "good news." (2) The Lord also reinforces the Exile as a just reward for the polytheistic deviations of the people in forsaking him. In the Exile they will serve foreigners.

5:20–31. Jeremiah describes the people as "senseless"[4] and employs the rhetorical device of describing them as possessing eyes that do not see and ears that do not hear. According to Isaiah 6:9–10, prophetic preaching of judgment actually confirms that the people are dull of sight and sound, appearing heedless of their predicament.[5] Jeremiah's invective continues by noting that they refuse to "fear" the Lord; that is, they do not hold the Lord in awe and serve him with reverence, as is befitting a holy and righteous God, who has always blessed them with regular crops and rain. Verse 25 then underscores the correspondence between act and consequence: "Your sins have deprived you of good." The Lord indicts both priest and prophet for misleading God's people in the concluding verses of the chapter (cf. 2:8; 6:13–14; 8:11).

A general breakdown of common decency, not to mention the covenant responsibilities of an elect nation, is described in 5:26–28. Greed and vio-lence go hand in hand. Here Jeremiah joins his work with that of other prophets who call for social rectitude among the people.

---

4. Lit., "without heart" (cf. 4:22 on foolishness). Jer. 5:23 describes the heart of the peo-ple as "stubborn and rebellious."

5. Cf. Matt. 13:1–17.

6:1–9. Chapter 6 functions like a summary of chapters 4–5. It contains calls to flee from the enemy (6:1) and to mourn the fall of the city (6:26). One cannot tell from the poetry if the depiction of the siege and fall is proleptic, projecting what will come in the near future, or if these words are offered during one of the times when the city of Jerusalem is surrounded by the Babylonians. Because the text contains no reference to dates, the effect of the call to flee and mourn is to remind the readers that Jeremiah announced in advance what befell the nation.

Disaster is imminent for Judah and Jerusalem. The city is "the Daughter of Zion" (6:2), so beautiful and yet so tragic. Verse 6 depicts a siege along with a succinct statement of the reason: "This city must be punished; it is filled with oppression." In 6:9 the prophet returns to a theme articulated in 5:10: The enemy will glean the vineyard of the Lord, making sure that even a surviving remnant feels the brunt of judgment.

6:10–15. Announcements about the coming judgment have fallen on deaf ears. Jeremiah, speaking for himself and for God, wonders to whom else can he speak? He confesses that he is wearied at holding in God's wrath, and he hears the command to pour it out on the city that has known no shame. As in previous oracles, the priests and prophets come under special censure for their failures. They have led the people astray with their proclamations of "peace ... when there is no peace" (v. 14; cf. 8:11). In a memorable comment the people are judged as so corrupt and shameless that they do not know how to blush (6:15)!

6:16–26. Through his prophet, the Lord asks the people to (re-)consider the "good way," the "ancient paths," that lead to security. The prophet, as vocal mediator, represents God and the people in conversation, while the people rudely contravene or reject divine guidance. They are reminded that God raised up "watchmen" (earlier prophets? godly reformers?), who warned the people—but to no avail. The people continue to reject God's "law" (Torah, instruction, v. 19). The fate to befall them is actually the "fruit of their [own] schemes." Correspondingly, God rejects the sacrifices of the people as inadequate in light of their moral and spiritual disobedience. As part of their judgment God will put "obstacles" in their way. This may be another way to refer to the foe that is coming from the north to attack the land. Jeremiah utters a severe warning about this foe.

6:27–30. Jeremiah's prophetic role is that of a "tester of metals." The refining process of calling for repentance and announcing judgment has not separated the wicked from the righteous but simply confirmed that the people as a whole are corrupt. These verses provide something of a commentary or definition of the prophetic office. Prophets are raised up by God as refiners.

*Bridging
Contexts*

THREE CONTEXTS FOR **prophetic judgment.** The Bible offers us three broad contexts in which to set these judgmental prophecies. (1) In the context of Jeremiah 1, these prophecies in chapters 4–6 further articulate how God's words will "uproot and tear down ... destroy and overthrow" (1:10). Judah and Jerusalem face a judgment sent by God that takes shape in space and time. A foe from the north (eventually Babylon) will devastate the land, besiege the city of Jerusalem, and destroy it. Not only do these prophecies contain a startling combination of visionary depictions of judgment with detail and specificity, but one will find many additional prophecies of judgment in Jeremiah that elaborate on these same themes.

(2) We can also set these prophecies in the context of the fellowship of prophets in the Old Testament. For all the attention to detail and historical setting, Jeremiah is at one with fellow prophets such as Isaiah, Amos, Hosea, Micah, and Ezekiel. Judgment begins with the "family of God" (cf. 1 Peter 4:17). The common prophetic claim is that no generation is guaranteed security when it stands in flagrant violation of its God-given identity. The prophetic call for covenant loyalty and filial obedience to the Lord has a flip side to it of judgment on a faithless people.

With respect to a prophetic posture or profile, it is important to call attention to the dialogical way in which these prophecies are presented. They contain rhetorical questions, quotations, and indications of such physical reactions that hearers are invited to respond. On more than one occasion it is difficult to separate the reaction of the prophet from that of God, so closely are the two of them tied by textual reference. This does not stop the prophet, however, from adding his own questions to God!

(3) A final context comes in the manifold witness of the New Testament that the way is broad that leads to destruction and many find their way to it (Matt. 7:13). Jeremiah's painful prophecies are not at variance with the New Testament proclamation of the gospel; they are part of the very foundation of the gospel that begins with the conviction that the wages of sin is death (Rom. 6:23). No foundation for renewal can be built until it is recognized that corruption infects all human institutions and vitiates all human intentions for self-preservation.

Corporate thinking. These prophecies of judgment insist that hearers think corporately about human affairs. This is more difficult for modern Western people than for others. Many in the West have oriented themselves toward the autonomy of the individual in such a way that attempts to define institutions and cultures as a whole become problematic. People increasingly find themselves unable to think in these categories, and without some patient probing on the part of pastors and teachers, they will revert to a more comfortable individualism. To paraphrase Jeremiah, corporate responsibility is a theme that falls on deaf ears.

For Jeremiah, however, it is "Judah and Jerusalem," "Daughter of Zion," God's "people," the "house of Israel" who are under scrutiny and subject to judgment for their sins. Should there be a righteous person in Jerusalem, God will pardon the city (5:1), but the clear implication is that no one is righteous, no, not one (Ps. 14:1; Rom. 3:10). Perhaps there are overtones of the Sodom and Gomorrah account in Genesis 18 and the dialogue between Abraham and God. The story of the cynic philosopher Diogenes is also a parallel; he searched Athens for one honest man, only to be frustrated. Jeremiah's role as tester of metals (6:27–30) produced the same results: the corporate guilt of the people.

Modern Christians may be helped to see the relevance of these prophecies by considering them in the context of institutional life. To individuals who protest that they personally are "right with the Lord," we must stress that God also deals with the character of congregations and church bodies as a whole, just as God assesses cultures and nations. Individuals are participants in institutional life and part of its manifold character. Many individuals will tell you how they are influenced by or even victimized by institutional powers.

One of the keys to appropriating the prophetic critique of Jeremiah is to show Christians how we are all complicit in the work of larger institutions, even when we feel aloof from them. No one finally is an island (John Donne) and unconnected with institutional life. To argue the opposite—that a person was truly unconnected to institutional life—will incur the judgment that such an isolated individual ignores the demands to love one's neighbor as one's self.

"Do not be deceived: God cannot be mocked. A man reaps what he sows" (Gal. 6:7). This apostolic claim corresponds on a corporate level with these prophecies of Jeremiah. What God's people have sown they will reap (Jer. 4:18; 5:25; 6:19). It is worth a moment's reflection that the apostolic claim for a relationship between moral act and consequence comes in a letter (Galatians) most passionate about justification by grace through faith. God will not be mocked by the misunderstandings of cheap grace and divine indifference.

Jeremiah's words reflect this misunderstanding of God's character on the part of some contemporaries (Jer. 5:12). The prophet does not, however, represent a legalistic understanding of covenant faith, since God is the initiator of the covenant with his people, and God will bring healing where none can be produced by Israel. There is a hint of God's freedom in the aside comment of 4:27 that God will not destroy the land completely. What Jeremiah does represent is a prophetic claim that God will use the historical process to bring on the people the consequences of their own infidelity to his rule.

JUDGMENT TODAY. A fundamental question of theology faces any interpreter of judgmental passages like these in Jeremiah. It is not enough to affirm that Jeremiah's words fit in the larger biblical context of God's righteous judgments in history. This affirmation is what the book of Jeremiah demanded from its first readers, who looked at Judah's fall and asked "Why?" The question really is not even whether one is prepared to affirm that God will judge the failures of the current generation of his people—though this is a significant question. It is really the question of whether the interpreter can affirm that even now the decline of the moral and spiritual life in segments of the church (and the corresponding moral decline and indifference in much of the Western world) is part of God's corporate judgment, and whether one should point to further judgments to come as a consequence of this decline.

Perhaps an interpreter will hesitate to affirm the second part of this issue and want to concentrate on a theological analysis of current ecclesiastical failures. A legitimate interpretation of Jeremiah's words for the contemporary church is not required to announce judgment on the audience (as Jeremiah did to his contemporaries), but his words should drive the interpreter to note the failings of Judah and Jerusalem and then to ask if corresponding failures inhibit the life of God's people today. Even if contemporary sins differ somewhat in kind from those enunciated by Jeremiah, his words should also drive the reader to repent for failures and to seek moral and spiritual renewal.[6] What follows is a (nonexhaustive) list of interpretive proposals based on this section in Jeremiah.

In 4:23–26 Jeremiah visualizes the earth in chaos and disorder. As noted above, the imagery reflects Genesis 1:2 and the chaotic conditions of the cosmos before God spoke order into existence. "I looked, and there were no people" (Jer. 4:25), exclaims the prophet. Creation is the theater of God's glory, and people made in God's image are the crowned stewards of the land (Gen. 1:26–31; Ps. 8). Moral and spiritual failure in Judah prompt prophetic eyes to see the land and people as turned back to chaos and disorder. One wonders if this vision is something like moral entropy,[7] where the disintegration of communal life is the inevitable outworking of moral and spiritual failure.

In the modern West (the part of God's creation that I know best), there is great concern in some quarters about the decline in order and civility.

---

6. Repentance and renewal are goals of the book for readers.

7. Perhaps the modern reader will recall that the second law of thermodynamics or entropy holds that matter tends to a state of progressive disorder without the influence of mitigating factors. For example, a plant that no longer translates sunlight and water into usable energy will die; when dead, the plant will decompose.

Among many Western churches there is correspondingly concern over the diminished morality of members and declining spiritual vitality. Are these factors related, and is a visionary depiction of coming chaos an accurate assessment of trends? Jeremiah's vision of chaos emerges spiritually from his deep involvement with a people who are heedless of divine standards and skeptical that God will actually judge them. Does this not sound familiar to Western ears? Is it not the case that Western society has essentially capitulated to the demands of secular pluralism that moral and values-based judgments be restricted to the private realm, where they will not intrude on public policy decisions? And does the rising perception that society is spinning out of moral control because of its spiritual bankruptcy not point to a future chaos?

Heart. Jeremiah indicts his audience as fools who lack perception and who are stubborn and rebelliously corrupt in heart (4:22; 5:21–23; cf. 17:9–11; 18:12). By "heart" Jeremiah means the source of understanding and volition that makes a person a responsible agent to love God and one's neighbor. Fools in this sense are those who fail to grasp moral meaning and significance; it is not a question of a lack of native intelligence but of culpable failure to perceive the truth and to act accordingly. The fools whom Jeremiah depicts are those whose hearts have rebelled against the truth and who can be held morally and spiritually responsible for their failures.

Jesus speaks similarly of folly and hardness of heart when he refers to those whose thoughts and actions contradict what they know is right (Matt. 5:27–28; Mark 7:14–23). When he tells his disciples that "where your treasure is, there your heart will be also" (Matt. 6:21), Jesus affirms that the heart is the seat of the human will and that human allegiance is a moral and spiritual commitment, not a neutral lifestyle choice.

One might paraphrase Jeremiah's language about the corruption of the people's heart by saying that rebellion against the truth of God is essentially moral, not intellectual. "Although [people] claimed to be wise, they became fools" (Rom. 1:22), because they have willfully evaded God's prior claim to their allegiance. God's judgments are righteous because they take into account the moral agency of people. Jeremiah would insist that this is never more true than with God's people. An interpreter of Jeremiah's judgmental words for today would do well to emphasize that God's standards for judging are not derived from lists of forbidden activities; they result more fundamentally from his taking seriously the moral agency of people and the privileged responsibility accorded them in the high calling of their creation.

Prophetic activity. Jeremiah's words of judgment stand as a critique of immoral society and the complicity of the church as societal members. The church can hear these words of judgment as reasons why it must always insist that society's problems are at root moral failures (not technological or administrative problems), and the church can hear through Jeremiah's preaching that it must always examine its character in light of God's Word. Moreover, the church can hear his words through the gift of the gospel as it seeks to follow her Lord through the gift of regenerated hearts (Eph. 3:17). What Christians know in their hearts to be the truth, they should joyfully seek to do, not as justifying activity but as spiritual obedience grounded in gratitude.

Jeremiah's words raise the question of prophetic activity on the part of the church and by individual Christians who seek to follow the Lord. (1) Prophetic activity is in obedience to the revealed word of God. Jeremiah's "call" in chapter 1 sets the power of God's spoken message at the center of the prophet's work. In 5:14 Jeremiah's words of judgment are like fire that consumes wood. Prophetic activity brings the word of the Lord to bear on circumstances and reveals God's assessment of them. A contemporary application of Jeremiah's words means first of all that Christians have assessed a situation in light of God's standards of judgment. This is not an easy task; prophetic activity is easily misunderstood, and it may expect to get a prophet's reward (Matt. 5:11−12). So it was for Jeremiah, as other texts will make clear. The depiction of Jeremiah as a "tester of metals" (6:27−30) underscores prophetic activity as the refining of character and motives, as a means of exposing God's truth among differing options, and as a way to weigh and assess the value of human commitments.

(2) Jeremiah's dialogue with the Lord (4:10; 5:4) implies that a prophetic response to sin is active. The prophet seeks the Lord's leading so that sinfulness is not just named for what it is and judgment is not simply announced for what it is, but a prophet searches for ways to end the evil activity and its evil consequences.

(3) Prophetic activity is prayerful engagement with God about the nature and purpose of judgment. So it was with Jeremiah, and so it must be for the church. One may denounce evil and march for justice and the amelioration of societal ills; but unless one also prays that God's temporal judgments become a means to discipline and to transform evildoers, denunciation and marching are not prophetic activities according to Jeremiah's example.

Jeremiah 7:1–8:3

§

THIS IS THE word that came to Jeremiah from the LORD: ²"Stand at the gate of the LORD's house and there proclaim this message:

"'Hear the word of the LORD, all you people of Judah who come through these gates to worship the LORD. ³This is what the LORD Almighty, the God of Israel, says: Reform your ways and your actions, and I will let you live in this place. ⁴Do not trust in deceptive words and say, "This is the temple of the LORD, the temple of the LORD, the temple of the LORD!" ⁵If you really change your ways and your actions and deal with each other justly, ⁶if you do not oppress the alien, the fatherless or the widow and do not shed innocent blood in this place, and if you do not follow other gods to your own harm, ⁷then I will let you live in this place, in the land I gave your forefathers for ever and ever. ⁸But look, you are trusting in deceptive words that are worthless.

⁹"'Will you steal and murder, commit adultery and perjury, burn incense to Baal and follow other gods you have not known, ¹⁰and then come and stand before me in this house, which bears my Name, and say, "We are safe"—safe to do all these detestable things? ¹¹Has this house, which bears my Name, become a den of robbers to you? But I have been watching! declares the LORD.

¹²"'Go now to the place in Shiloh where I first made a dwelling for my Name, and see what I did to it because of the wickedness of my people Israel. ¹³While you were doing all these things, declares the LORD, I spoke to you again and again, but you did not listen; I called you, but you did not answer. ¹⁴Therefore, what I did to Shiloh I will now do to the house that bears my Name, the temple you trust in, the place I gave to you and your fathers. ¹⁵I will thrust you from my presence, just as I did all your brothers, the people of Ephraim.'

¹⁶"So do not pray for this people nor offer any plea or petition for them; do not plead with me, for I will not listen to you. ¹⁷Do you not see what they are doing in the towns of Judah and in the streets of Jerusalem? ¹⁸The children gather wood,

the fathers light the fire, and the women knead the dough and make cakes of bread for the Queen of Heaven. They pour out drink offerings to other gods to provoke me to anger. ¹⁹But am I the one they are provoking? declares the LORD. Are they not rather harming themselves, to their own shame?

²⁰"'Therefore this is what the Sovereign LORD says: My anger and my wrath will be poured out on this place, on man and beast, on the trees of the field and on the fruit of the ground, and it will burn and not be quenched.

²¹"'This is what the LORD Almighty, the God of Israel, says: Go ahead, add your burnt offerings to your other sacrifices and eat the meat yourselves! ²²For when I brought your fore-fathers out of Egypt and spoke to them, I did not just give them commands about burnt offerings and sacrifices, ²³but I gave them this command: Obey me, and I will be your God and you will be my people. Walk in all the ways I command you, that it may go well with you. ²⁴But they did not listen or pay attention; instead, they followed the stubborn inclinations of their evil hearts. They went backward and not forward. ²⁵From the time your forefathers left Egypt until now, day after day, again and again I sent you my servants the prophets. ²⁶But they did not listen to me or pay attention. They were stiff-necked and did more evil than their forefathers.'

²⁷"When you tell them all this, they will not listen to you; when you call to them, they will not answer. ²⁸Therefore say to them, 'This is the nation that has not obeyed the LORD its God or responded to correction. Truth has perished; it has vanished from their lips. ²⁹Cut off your hair and throw it away; take up a lament on the barren heights, for the LORD has rejected and abandoned this generation that is under his wrath.

³⁰"'The people of Judah have done evil in my eyes, declares the LORD. They have set up their detestable idols in the house that bears my Name and have defiled it. ³¹They have built the high places of Topheth in the Valley of Ben Hinnom to burn their sons and daughters in the fire—something I did not com-mand, nor did it enter my mind. ³²So beware, the days are coming, declares the LORD, when people will no longer call it Topheth or the Valley of Ben Hinnom, but the Valley of Slaughter, for they will bury the dead in Topheth until there is no more room. ³³Then the carcasses of this people will become food for the birds of the air and the beasts of the earth, and

there will be no one to frighten them away. ³⁴I will bring an end to the sounds of joy and gladness and to the voices of bride and bridegroom in the towns of Judah and the streets of Jerusalem, for the land will become desolate.

⁸:¹"'At that time, declares the LORD, the bones of the kings and officials of Judah, the bones of the priests and prophets, and the bones of the people of Jerusalem will be removed from their graves. ²They will be exposed to the sun and the moon and all the stars of the heavens, which they have loved and served and which they have followed and consulted and worshiped. They will not be gathered up or buried, but will be like refuse lying on the ground. ³Wherever I banish them, all the survivors of this evil nation will prefer death to life, declares the LORD Almighty.'

CHAPTER 7 CONVEYS Jeremiah's (in-)famous temple "sermon." It is prose rather than poetry; thus, chapter 7 begins a new section different from the predominantly poetic contents in chapters 2–6. Whether the sermon originally included all the material now in 7:1–8:3 or whether some additional prophecies of Jeremiah have been appended in the process of transmission and compilation, readers will recognize why Jeremiah was later restricted from preaching in the temple precincts (36:5). These words cut to the quick.

Chapter 26 preserves a similar but shorter address given at the temple. Many interpreters, therefore, have concluded that chapter 7 contains the longer form of the sermon while chapter 26 contains a summary of it, along with a description of audience reaction. This reconstruction is plausible but not certain. Jeremiah may well have delivered the gist of this somber message on more than one occasion. The temple address in chapter 26 is dated to the beginning of Jehoiakim's reign (26:1; 609/608 B.C.). If chapters 7 and 26 describe the same event, then we have one of the few indications of a specific date for material in the first half of the book of Jeremiah. The material in chapter 7 fits well with the reign of Jehoiakim.

Not only was the death of Josiah a traumatic event for the state of Judah, but the transitions that followed it were difficult as well. Jehoiakim became the third monarch on the throne in less than a year. Josiah had been followed by his son Jehoahaz, but he was removed soon afterward by the Egyptians, who favored Jehoiakim, another son of Josiah. Apparently Jehoiakim was more compliant with their wishes.[1] Jeremiah has nothing good to say about Jehoiakim and the life of the people under his regime.

The pronouncements in the sermon contain a call to repentance from evil deeds, a searing reminder of the Decalogue as the standards of communal service to God, a denial that God will defend the temple from onslaught, and a polemic attack on various polytheistic activities, including ritual practices related to human sacrifice in a valley near Jerusalem's temple mount. These prose pronouncements are similar in form to Moses' sermons of Deuteronomy; indeed, the temple sermon and Deuteronomy share an emphasis on the sanctity of the place where God's Name dwells (cf. below). One should not find this surprising. Within Jeremiah's own lifetime a book (lit., a scroll) of covenant law was discovered in the temple that became the catalyst for King Josiah's reform measures (2 Kings 22–23; 2 Chron. 34–35). Many interpreters conclude that the book discovered was Deuteronomy in either penultimate or final form.

7:1–15. Jeremiah warns worshipers not to trust in deceptive words that give them false hopes concerning the security of the temple or the efficacy of their religious activities. Three times the phrase "[this is] the temple of the LORD" is repeated in verse 4. It seems to function like a mantra, as if simply repeating it or even asserting it makes it true. Just because the temple sits in Jerusalem, worshipers should not assume that they can fail in their covenantal responsibilities to God and neighbor and then come to the temple and cry, "We are safe!"

Jeremiah has no intention of denying that the majestic temple on Mount Zion belongs to the Lord. Speaking for God, however, he asserts that the Lord is not bound to preserve the temple at all costs in the face of the people's flagrant disobedience. The prophet points to the shrine at Shiloh during the time of Samuel and Eli (1 Sam. 1–4) to say that God may send judgment even on a place of worship that bears his Name.[2]

In Deuteronomy 12:5, 11, God promised to choose a place from among the Israelite tribes "to put his Name ... for his dwelling." The site would be

---

1. See the treatment of the historical background in the introduction.

2. Although the accounts in 1 Sam. 1–4 do not record a destruction of Shiloh's worship center by the Philistines when they defeated Israel, Jeremiah's words imply such destruction. Also, interpreters often suggest that the memory of God's deliverance of Jerusalem during the time of Sennacherib's assault (2 Kings 18–19; 2 Chron. 32; Isa. 36–39) lies behind the Judean belief during Jeremiah's day that God would act similarly when Jerusalem was threatened by Egypt or Babylon. This is certainly possible, if not probable, but Jeremiah does not cite that deliverance. The biblical accounts indicate that the Lord answered the intercessions of Hezekiah and Isaiah by sending his angel to destroy the Assyrian army. God's command to Jeremiah that the prophet not intercede for the people indicates that this time (cf. Isa. 37:33–35) God will not protect the city or the temple.

designated for animal sacrifice and certain other ritual acts of worship. It would be a place for pilgrimage—the only appropriate site for these endeavors, in contrast to the Canaanite inhabitants, who had many "high places" for sacrificial worship. Deuteronomy does not give the name of the place God would choose; that Jerusalem became the location, however, is clear from the dedicatory prayer of Solomon in 1 Kings 8:23–53. His prayer acknowledges that this house is for God's Name (8:29, 44; cf. 8:20), yet that no temple encapsulates God, for not even the highest heavens can do that (8:27).

There was nothing magical about the temple in Jerusalem with respect to divine presence. The claim that God's Name dwelt there was a metaphorical way of saying that God could be personally encountered at that site. It was a place of his choosing. At the same time, God recognizes that he is not tied to the structure or somehow bound irrevocably to its fate.

The prophet refers to the basic covenant stipulations in 7:9 as they are known in the Decalogue (Deut. 4:13). Moreover in Jeremiah 7:6 the prophet charges that Judah has oppressed the alien, the widow, and the orphan. Specifically cited in verse 9 are stealing, murder, adultery, and false witness. Each of these comes from the so-called second table of the law, where communal relations are regulated. Burning incense to Baal and following other gods, however, reflects the first commandment and its charge to "have no other gods before me." Taken as a whole, the prophet charges that those attending temple service love neither God nor neighbor according to the standards of the Torah. Instead, they grasp at the magical properties of the temple in hopes that God will protect the city against the enemy.

7:16–34. Jeremiah reveals that God has commanded him not to intercede for the people (cf. 15:1–9). Why should Jeremiah intercede for the people when some of them have turned to the worship of the Queen of Heaven (cf. ch. 44)[3] and other deities? Their trust is misplaced. Jeremiah is but one in a line of prophets whom God sent to his people, each of whom was rejected. The hardhearted people have refused to heed their warnings and announcements of judgment. Sacrifices are not acceptable when flagrant breaches of covenantal ethics are rampant.[4] They are no more efficacious for a sinful, obdurate people than the temple will be in the day of assault by the enemy.

---

3. See comments on ch. 44 for discussion of the Queen of Heaven.

4. Some interpreters have concluded that Jer. 7:21–23 represents a tradition of the people's desert wandering, which did not include a sacrificial system, implying that sacrifices were not a divine mandate but a human convention. Since the pentateuchal storyline describes sacrificial worship in the desert as God's mandate, this conclusion is not likely. More probably the force of v. 22 is hyperbolic: To deny one thing is to emphasize the importance of the other. Sacrifice and offerings are the fruit of the covenant relationship, not a substitute for it.

In a nearby valley nicknamed "Slaughter," the Judeans participated in the horrifying rites of child sacrifice (cf. 19:1–15). Which valley near Jerusalem is an interesting question; probably it is the valley along the western and southern boundaries of the current "old city" known as the Wadi er Rababi. *Topheth* is a term of uncertain derivation, but it refers to a place where human sacrificial and cremation rituals took place. Some Judeans must have believed that they appeased the Lord by partaking in these rituals, since God protests through the prophet that he has not commanded such activities. Elsewhere these activities are associated with Baal and Molech (2 Kings 23:10; Jer 19:5).[5] Jerusalem itself will become a place of slaughter (like the nearby Topheth) because of her rejection of the Lord.

8:1–3. These words may have been appended to the sermon because they reflect the horror of manipulating and exposing human corpses. The Topheth rites in 7:30–34 apparently included sacrificial rites with corpses (of children). Without repentance, death will be the only future for Judah.

BEHAVIORAL MATTERS. Although there is no one-to-one correspondence between ancient Israel and the church and the duties of each under the old and new covenants respectively, their common identity as God's people means that the church should hear a word to Israel as instructive for its own life. Nevertheless, since there is no one-to-one correspondence, Christian interpreters are not forced to find exact parallels in behaviors to make Jeremiah 7 relevant. The question of corporate faithfulness in the life of faith can be (and should be!) asked from generation to generation.

To put the matter of interpretation in a broader biblical context, Jeremiah's words about the need for Judah to change its behavior or lose its place in the land of promise are part of a much broader scriptural message about relating rightly to God. The "if-then" language of 7:3–7 is like that of the introductory address of God through Moses to the people at Sinai (Ex. 19:4–6): "If you ... keep my covenant ... then ... you will be for me a kingdom of priests." It is similar to the mandates of Jesus to "repent, for the kingdom of heaven is here" (Matt. 4:17), or "seek first [God's] kingdom and his righteousness, and all these things will be given to you as well" (6:33).

Behavior matters are a powerful indicator that reveals the allegiances of the heart. The particulars of Jeremiah (lack of justice, polytheism, violation

---

5. For further details on topheths and their associations with Baal and Molech, see J. A. Dearman, "The Topheth in Jerusalem: Archaeology and Cultural Profile," *JNSL* 22 (1996): 59–71. See also comments on ch. 19.

of the Decalogue) are not new instructions for Judah but central to the covenant relationship God has granted to them. Jesus readily acknowledges that the Ten Commandments indicate the proper way to life because they bring a person into relationship with God, who alone is the Author and Giver of life (Matt. 19:16–30; Mark 10:17–31; Luke 18:18–30).

False hopes about the temple. Jeremiah's words about the false hopes associated with the temple (7:4, 10) are also part of a much broader scriptural message about ways in which God reveals himself to his people and the corresponding ways in which worshipers should honor that self-revelation of God through worship and obedience. Through the tabernacle God mediated his presence with the Israelites during their desert wandering. The Lord who redeemed them also instructed them not to take the tabernacle for granted or violate its sanctity.

Solomon's dedicatory prayer at the founding of the temple in Jerusalem (1 Kings 8; 2 Chron. 6) acknowledged the blessing that God's Name was present through the temple (1 Kings 8:16–20, 29). The Lord of creation and history was personally present among his people to instruct them and to receive their praise. This holy and gracious presence of God's Name did not mean that God was limited to the sphere of the temple or bound to its spatial limitations; on the contrary, even heaven, God's "dwelling place" (1 Kings 8:27–30), cannot truly contain him. God "lives in unapproachable light" (1 Tim. 6:16) and cannot be seen or approached except when he accommodates himself to the limitations of human capacities of perception.

Jesus' disciples spoke with wonder about the temple complex built by Herod the Great on the spot first purchased by David (Mark 13:1). Behind the continuity of centuries of worship on that sacred spot lay also the facts of temple destruction by the Babylonians and temple defilement by the forces of Antiochus Epiphanes (1 Macc. 1:11–61; cf. Dan. 11:14–35). Jesus' reply that the great complex would be destroyed does not reflect hostility to the temple or denial of its divine role, but recognizes that the physical complex itself is dispensable. History would bring an end to the temple complex but not to the significance it represented.

Jesus himself overturned the tables of the moneychangers in the temple courtyards, proclaiming that his Father's house would not be a "den of robbers" (Luke 19:45–46). That reference is to Jeremiah 7:11; it shows how Jesus had absorbed the thrust of Jeremiah's temple sermon as an indictment of the people, whose actions violated the sanctity of the temple. Judgment on the temple was judgment on those for whom the temple's purpose was perverted.

Jeremiah's address presupposes the significance of the temple as a divine dwelling. He speaks words of judgment against those who view the temple in magical terms as God's guarantee of their temporal security. John's Gospel represents Jesus as God's Word living among us (John 1:14) in language similar to the tabernacle (or temple) as God's presence among Israel of old. Indeed, the temple—like all the Old Testament—bears witness to God's approach in Jesus Christ (see John 2:14–22).

Other apostolic witnesses in the New Testament take up John's recognition of Jesus as God's temple. Both Paul and Peter proclaim the church as the body of Christ and the spiritual temple (Rom. 12:4–5; 1 Cor. 12:12, 27; Eph. 1:22–23; 2:19–22; 1 Peter 2:1–5). Individual Christians too are a temple of God's dwelling (1 Cor. 6:19–20). Thus, the imperative to Christians to "honor God with your body" (6:20) reflects a concern similar to that of Jeremiah under the old covenant: Behavior matters, for through it God is either glorified or mocked.

Worship and sacrifice. Jeremiah's temple address is also the occasion for words about worship and sacrifice. His criticism of polytheism has parallels in both Old and New Testaments. Polytheism is a religious response that fails to take seriously God's claim for exclusive worship. The Decalogue is headed by the claim that God has redeemed a people from slavery, and its first command is the prohibition of having other gods.

The particulars of Jeremiah's own critique (Queen of Heaven, other gods) show people who by their religious activities are trying to secure their fortunes in uncertain times. For them religion is the system by which they induce the gods to provide what they want. The criticism about sacrifices in 7:21–26 follows this line of critique as well. Sacrifices are not means in order to force God into a religion of compliance to the wish lists of worshipers, nor are they a substitute for a life of grateful obedience (cf. Isa. 1:10–17; Amos 5:21–26).

The child sacrifices at the Topheth are a particular case of misunderstanding the significance of sacrificial ritual. The ancient world considered the offering of a child to a deity as a supremely religious act, since it gave to the deity, the author of life, what was most precious to the worshiper (cf. Mic. 6:6–8). But God did not require such a sacrifice of Abraham (Gen. 22) or of the Exodus generation (Ex. 13:2, 11–15). In those cases God provided an effectual substitute.

THEOLOGY MATTERS. To hear Jeremiah's address today means to hear it through Jesus Christ, his gospel of forgiveness, and new life offered through him. In Jeremiah's day, the mantra of "the temple of the LORD" (7:4) meant false reliance on the temple as God's guarantee of deliverance to the people of Judah. Can such words uncover modern tendencies to equate the visible church and participation in it with true service to God?

Jeremiah's address assumes a doctrine of Israel as God's people who assemble for worship and depart for service. Similarly, worship of God is the reason for Christian assembling, and service to him in word and deed is its goal. The temple was an institution by which God made himself present and known among the people. The church is an institution by which God makes himself present in the world and known among the nations.

One hears today the phrase that "theology matters." Its proponents believe that the visible church suffers from a lack of clarity about the uniqueness of the gospel, a diminished sense of authority for the classical tenets of the faith, and an overreliance on individualism and human experience as keys to Christian identity. Jeremiah denied that the popular expressions of sacrifice were an adequate indication of how individual Judeans or the nation as a whole should relate to God. The sacrificial system was one of God's gifts to be used by the people to maintain a relationship with God, though sacrifice was not a substitute for the relationship itself.

Theology does matter, not because God insists on a rigid intellectual system, but because unless we understand who God is, we will be in basic error about everything else that is ultimately important. The church will not save anyone (nor did the temple or animal sacrifice); it is a means to a goal, not the end itself. Understood correctly it is a means to know God and be rightly related to him.

One consequence of Jeremiah's address is the acknowledgment that the temple is not defined adequately as a building. Its theological significance resides in the Lord, whom it represents and reveals. Christians may legitimately draw positive or negative conclusions from this significance, depending on the nature of the church and the particulars of the Christian life that need to be addressed. God can give (and has given) the faithless institutions of his people over to judgment. God has no need to protect a lifeless institution (as if his own security were under threat); yet the gates of hell themselves will not prevail against the church that confesses Christ as Lord.

Jeremiah's address means not only that "theology matters," but that it matters in the practical applications of the Christian life. His indictment of the immorality of the people illustrates the old adage that "I may not believe everything you say, but I believe everything you do." Behavior matters for it is a key to a person's or an institution's allegiance. Christian ethics, like the social institutions and actions of Jeremiah's day, are a means to an end: to worship and serve the living God.

Child sacrifice. The Topheth sacrifices of Jeremiah's day present the most intriguing illustration of the confession that "theology matters" as well as a graphic way of underscoring the radical uniqueness of the gospel. As noted above, child sacrifice was a supremely religious act. Specific reasons to sacrifice a child varied from extreme threat to the family to extreme devotion on the part of the parents. Jeremiah insists that God has not required this slaughter, either to get his attention or to demonstrate one's piety. Religious longing and commitment do not inherently result in good things. Such sentiments require instruction in the truth of God. This is a crucial point in an era where feelings and good intentions tend to be what really matter. Religious affections and longings need to be channeled in a proper direction. Pastors and the witness of faithful generations are vital to the cause of instruction in Christian practices.

In a Christological vein, the Topheth sacrifices remind readers that what God did not require of his people he provided in the death of his own Son. If the Topheth sacrifices gave occasion for God's insistence that he does not require the sacrifice of children either to please or appease him, then the death of Jesus Christ is the occasion where God replies back through the supremely sacrificial act of a self-offering for sin. In their misguided zeal, people who frequented the Topheth hoped to avert disaster and gain life for themselves and their families. In the death of Jesus, Christians meet God's own zeal to judge iniquity and his ardent desire to provide life for the lost.

Jeremiah 8:4–10:25

S AY TO THEM, 'This is what the LORD says:

"'When men fall down, do they not get up?
    When a man turns away, does he not return?
5 Why then have these people turned away?
    Why does Jerusalem always turn away?
They cling to deceit;
    they refuse to return.
6 I have listened attentively,
    but they do not say what is right.
No one repents of his wickedness,
    saying, "What have I done?"
Each pursues his own course
    like a horse charging into battle.
7 Even the stork in the sky
    knows her appointed seasons,
and the dove, the swift and the thrush
    observe the time of their migration.
But my people do not know
    the requirements of the LORD.

8 "'How can you say, "We are wise,
    for we have the law of the LORD,"
when actually the lying pen of the scribes
    has handled it falsely?
9 The wise will be put to shame;
    they will be dismayed and trapped.
Since they have rejected the word of the LORD,
    what kind of wisdom do they have?
10 Therefore I will give their wives to other men
    and their fields to new owners.
From the least to the greatest,
    all are greedy for gain;
prophets and priests alike,
    all practice deceit.
11 They dress the wound of my people
    as though it were not serious.
"Peace, peace," they say,
    when there is no peace.

¹² Are they ashamed of their loathsome conduct?
      No, they have no shame at all;
      they do not even know how to blush.
    So they will fall among the fallen;
      they will be brought down when they are punished,
                                    says the LORD.

¹³ "'I will take away their harvest,
                            declares the LORD.

      There will be no grapes on the vine.
    There will be no figs on the tree,
      and their leaves will wither.
    What I have given them
      will be taken from them.'"

¹⁴ "Why are we sitting here?
      Gather together!
    Let us flee to the fortified cities
      and perish there!
    For the LORD our God has doomed us to perish
      and given us poisoned water to drink,
      because we have sinned against him.
¹⁵ We hoped for peace
      but no good has come,
    for a time of healing
      but there was only terror.
¹⁶ The snorting of the enemy's horses
      is heard from Dan;
    at the neighing of their stallions
      the whole land trembles.
    They have come to devour
      the land and everything in it,
      the city and all who live there."

¹⁷ "See, I will send venomous snakes among you,
      vipers that cannot be charmed,
      and they will bite you,"
                            declares the LORD.

¹⁸ O my Comforter in sorrow,
      my heart is faint within me.
¹⁹ Listen to the cry of my people
      from a land far away:

"Is the LORD not in Zion?
Is her King no longer there?"
"Why have they provoked me to anger with their images,
with their worthless foreign idols?"

20"The harvest is past,
the summer has ended,
and we are not saved."
21 Since my people are crushed, I am crushed;
I mourn, and horror grips me.
22 Is there no balm in Gilead?
Is there no physician there?
Why then is there no healing
for the wound of my people?
9:1 Oh, that my head were a spring of water
and my eyes a fountain of tears!
I would weep day and night
for the slain of my people.
2 Oh, that I had in the desert
a lodging place for travelers,
so that I might leave my people
and go away from them;
for they are all adulterers,
a crowd of unfaithful people.

3"They make ready their tongue
like a bow, to shoot lies;
it is not by truth
that they triumph in the land.
They go from one sin to another;
they do not acknowledge me,"

declares the LORD.

4"Beware of your friends;
do not trust your brothers.
For every brother is a deceiver,
and every friend a slanderer.
5 Friend deceives friend,
and no one speaks the truth.
They have taught their tongues to lie;
they weary themselves with sinning.
6 You live in the midst of deception;
in their deceit they refuse to acknowledge me,"

declares the LORD.

7 Therefore this is what the LORD Almighty says:
"See, I will refine and test them,
    for what else can I do
    because of the sin of my people?
8 Their tongue is a deadly arrow;
    it speaks with deceit.
With his mouth each speaks cordially to his neighbor,
    but in his heart he sets a trap for him.
9 Should I not punish them for this?"
    declares the LORD.
"Should I not avenge myself
    on such a nation as this?"

10 I will weep and wail for the mountains
    and take up a lament concerning the desert pastures.
They are desolate and untraveled,
    and the lowing of cattle is not heard.
The birds of the air have fled
    and the animals are gone.

11 "I will make Jerusalem a heap of ruins,
    a haunt of jackals;
and I will lay waste the towns of Judah
    so no one can live there."

12 What man is wise enough to understand this? Who has been instructed by the LORD and can explain it? Why has the land been ruined and laid waste like a desert that no one can cross?
13 The LORD said, "It is because they have forsaken my law, which I set before them; they have not obeyed me or followed my law. 14 Instead, they have followed the stubbornness of their hearts; they have followed the Baals, as their fathers taught them." 15 Therefore, this is what the LORD Almighty, the God of Israel, says: "See, I will make this people eat bitter food and drink poisoned water. 16 I will scatter them among nations that neither they nor their fathers have known, and I will pursue them with the sword until I have destroyed them."
17 This is what the LORD Almighty says:

"Consider now! Call for the wailing women to come;
    send for the most skillful of them.
18 Let them come quickly
    and wail over us

till our eyes overflow with tears
and water streams from our eyelids.
¹⁹The sound of wailing is heard from Zion:
'How ruined we are!
How great is our shame!
We must leave our land
because our houses are in ruins.'"

²⁰Now, O women, hear the word of the LORD;
open your ears to the words of his mouth.
Teach your daughters how to wail;
teach one another a lament.
²¹Death has climbed in through our windows
and has entered our fortresses;
it has cut off the children from the streets
and the young men from the public squares.

²²Say, "This is what the LORD declares:

"'The dead bodies of men will lie
like refuse on the open field,
like cut grain behind the reaper,
with no one to gather them.'"

²³This is what the LORD says:

"Let not the wise man boast of his wisdom
or the strong man boast of his strength
or the rich man boast of his riches,
²⁴but let him who boasts boast about this:
that he understands and knows me,
that I am the LORD, who exercises kindness,
justice and righteousness on earth,
for in these I delight,"

declares the LORD.

²⁵"The days are coming," declares the LORD, "when I will punish all who are circumcised only in the flesh—²⁶Egypt, Judah, Edom, Ammon, Moab and all who live in the desert in distant places. For all these nations are really uncircumcised, and even the whole house of Israel is uncircumcised in heart."

^{10:1}Hear what the LORD says to you, O house of Israel. ²This is what the LORD says:

"Do not learn the ways of the nations
or be terrified by signs in the sky,
though the nations are terrified by them.

³For the customs of the peoples are worthless;
they cut a tree out of the forest,
and a craftsman shapes it with his chisel.
⁴They adorn it with silver and gold;
they fasten it with hammer and nails
so it will not totter.
⁵Like a scarecrow in a melon patch,
their idols cannot speak;
they must be carried
because they cannot walk.
Do not fear them;
they can do no harm
nor can they do any good."

⁶No one is like you, O LORD;
you are great,
and your name is mighty in power.
⁷Who should not revere you,
O King of the nations?
This is your due.
Among all the wise men of the nations
and in all their kingdoms,
there is no one like you.
⁸They are all senseless and foolish;
they are taught by worthless wooden idols.
⁹Hammered silver is brought from Tarshish
and gold from Uphaz.
What the craftsman and goldsmith have made
is then dressed in blue and purple—
all made by skilled workers.
¹⁰But the LORD is the true God;
he is the living God, the eternal King.
When he is angry, the earth trembles;
the nations cannot endure his wrath.

¹¹"Tell them this: 'These gods, who did not make the heavens and the earth, will perish from the earth and from under the heavens.'"

¹²But God made the earth by his power;
he founded the world by his wisdom
and stretched out the heavens by his understanding.

¹³ When he thunders, the waters in the heavens roar;
   he makes clouds rise from the ends of the earth.
He sends lightning with the rain
   and brings out the wind from his storehouses.

¹⁴ Everyone is senseless and without knowledge;
   every goldsmith is shamed by his idols.
His images are a fraud;
   they have no breath in them.
¹⁵ They are worthless, the objects of mockery;
   when their judgment comes, they will perish.
¹⁶ He who is the Portion of Jacob is not like these,
   for he is the Maker of all things,
including Israel, the tribe of his inheritance—
   the LORD Almighty is his name.

¹⁷ Gather up your belongings to leave the land,
   you who live under siege.
¹⁸ For this is what the LORD says:
   "At this time I will hurl out
   those who live in this land;
I will bring distress on them
   so that they may be captured."

¹⁹ Woe to me because of my injury!
   My wound is incurable!
Yet I said to myself,
   "This is my sickness, and I must endure it."
²⁰ My tent is destroyed;
   all its ropes are snapped.
My sons are gone from me and are no more;
   no one is left now to pitch my tent
   or to set up my shelter.
²¹ The shepherds are senseless
   and do not inquire of the LORD;
so they do not prosper
   and all their flock is scattered.
²² Listen! The report is coming—
   a great commotion from the land of the north!
It will make the towns of Judah desolate,
   a haunt of jackals.

²³ I know, O LORD, that a man's life is not his own;
   it is not for man to direct his steps.

²⁴ Correct me, LORD, but only with justice—
    not in your anger,
    lest you reduce me to nothing.
²⁵ Pour out your wrath on the nations
    that do not acknowledge you,
    on the peoples who do not call on your name.
For they have devoured Jacob;
    they have devoured him completely
    and destroyed his homeland.

THIS SECTION CONTINUES the book's proclamation of judgment on Judah and Jerusalem. It is similar to the collection of poetic oracles in chapters 4–6, which was "interrupted" by the prose sermon in 7:1–8:3; it continues with the same theme and even repeats sayings used previously. These verses are not an original unit of address but are brought together by the compilers of the book to demonstrate that Jeremiah had spoken God's word to a foolish and obdurate people. As is common throughout Jeremiah 1–25, specific dates and precise allusions to political events are seldom given. These oracles function as witnesses to the prophetic preaching that was ignored by the people of Judah and Jerusalem. In a poignant dialogical style, Jeremiah represents his sorrow and frustration as also belonging to God.

8:4–12. The prophet engages his hearers with rhetorical questions and accuses them of moral stupidity and a culpable spiritual dullness. Speaking for God, the prophet states: "I have listened attentively, but they do not say what is right" (v. 6). It is also assumed that the people of Jerusalem do not do what is right. God is almost incredulous at the stupidity of the people. Verse 7 continues a theme seen elsewhere in Jeremiah: God's people are woefully and willfully ignorant of God's "requirements"[1] of behavior, which are designed to regulate life. Even a stork knows that there are appointed seasons, yet God's own people seem clueless.

To the reply from the people in verse 8 that they are indeed "wise" and "have the law [*tora*] of the LORD," Jeremiah charges that scribal interpretation has made God's truth into a lie (*šeqer*, cf. "deception" in 7:4 [NIV "deceptive"]). The deceitful interpretation of God's instruction is explained as blunting its judgmental force against iniquity. God's Torah *is* wisdom (see Deut. 4:5–8).

---

1. The Hebrew word *mišpaṭ*, used here, is singular, so that the phrase could be translated that the people "do not know the justice [or justness] of the LORD."

Priest and prophet alike are proclaiming "peace" when all is not well. This too is a theme Jeremiah stresses elsewhere (cf. 6:14). The charge that the people are shameless and don't even know how to blush is likewise found in 6:15.

The context offers few clues for more clarity on this dispute over the interpretation of God's Torah, but possibly we have here Jeremiah's accusations about the eventual collapse of Josiah's covenant reforms. Religious leaders might have blunted the sharp edge of those reforms sparked by a (re)discovery of a book of the Torah of the Lord during temple repairs (2 Kings 22–23). It is a pity that we don't have any more clues to the sharp retort of the prophet that the lying pen of the scribes has handled the Torah falsely. Presumably the interpretive skills of the priests[2] have kept God's Word from performing its basic tasks of challenging and instructing the people, as if they have explained away the force of divine imperatives. Jeremiah himself was from a priestly family and thus familiar with the tasks of interpreting and applying divine instruction.

8:13–17. The people belatedly realize that God's judgment is upon them. Jeremiah depicts them as coming to the sudden and terrifying realization that the enemy is approaching and that God is in the process of judging them for their transgressions. The reference to the enemy horses at Dan indicates that the enemy is approaching from the north. Dan was at the northern border of the northern kingdom of Israel.

The unrealistic hope of the people for peace is now seen for what the previous passage indicated it always was: self-delusion and a rejection of God's law. "Poisoned water" in verse 14 likely refers to the problems with water stored in cisterns rather than to some form of divine action in actually poisoning wells. Sieges typically result in heavy reliance on poor resources stored in cisterns (cf. 9:15). Perhaps we should read verse 17 similarly: The "venomous snakes" that the Lord will send denote the deadly work of the invaders.

8:18–22. Scholars are divided over the compositional breakdown of these verses. Are they a single unit of poetic address, or are they joined secondarily for thematic reasons by the compilers of the book? Interpreters are also divided over the implied speakers throughout this unit, since it is difficult to tell at some points whether the voice is Jeremiah's or the Lord's. A suggested outline for 8:18–22 is as follows:

---

2. Verse 8 refers to the lying pen of the scribes. Scribes comprised a professional class of people employed for their abilities in reading and writing. Those who dealt with the interpretation of Torah were most likely priests (who could read and write) because knowledge of priestly duties was necessary in interpreting such matters as sacrificial ritual and distinguishing between clean and unclean items.

[**prophet**] O my Comforter in sorrow,
   my heart is faint within me.

Listen to the cry of my people
   from a land far away:

"Is the LORD not in Zion?
   Is her King no longer there?"

[**Lord**] "Why have they provoked me to anger with their images,
   with their worthless foreign idols?"

[**prophet**, quoting the people] "The harvest is past,
   the summer has ended,
   and we are not saved."

[**prophet**] Since my people are crushed, I am crushed;
   I mourn, and horror grips me.

Is there no balm in Gilead?
   Is there no physician there?

Why then is there no healing
   for the wound of my people?

Jeremiah's prophetic poignancy demonstrates that he is not aloof or indifferent to the suffering of the people. Indeed, three times (8:19, 21–22) the people are called "my daughter people,"[3] a phrase appropriate also in the mouth of God. This point should not be lost on the reader. The sorrow Jeremiah feels at the fate of his people is that felt by God as well. Prophetic person and prophetic message converge to reveal not only the God of righteous judgment but the God of sorrows at the plaintive cry, "We are not saved."

9:1–11. As with the previous section, readers encounter a merging of Jeremiah and God's voices. Pain over the plight of the people results in daylong weeping, yet also in the desire to be absent from their self-destructive treachery to the Lord's instructions. Verses 3 and 6 conclude with the formula "declares the LORD," marking the depiction of immorality and deceit as a communication from God. A suggestion of "voices" for 9:1–11 is as follows:

[**prophet**] 9:1–2: "Oh, that my head were a spring of water...."
[**God**] 9:3: "They make ready their tongue like a bow, to shoot lies...."

---

3. In all three instances, the NIV translates the literal phrase "daughter of my people" simply as "my people," assuming it refers to God's people. This is likely correct, although the literal translation could refer to Jerusalem. Contextually it seems more likely that the people themselves are being addressed as the vulnerable daughter of a heartsick Father. One should compare this phrase with the similar "Daughter Jerusalem" or "Daughter Zion." Both of these phrases refer to the city itself, not to one of its offspring.

[**God** to Jeremiah] 9:4–6: "Beware of your friends. . . ."

[**prophet**, speaking for God] 9:7–11: "See, I will refine and test them . . .
      I will weep and wail. . . ."

If this sequence of voices is correct, we have a conversation between God and prophet in 9:1–6, followed by an announcement of judgment on the people in 9:7–11. Note that in verse 10 God weeps and wails (like Jeremiah) for the destruction to come.

9:12–22. Picking up the theme of wisdom and judgment from chapter 8, the rhetorical question of spiritual discernment is again raised in a series of divine oracles. Note the introductory formula for divine communication (e.g., "The LORD said") in 9:13, 17, 22. Judgment has fallen on Judah for her sins. Following the Baals[4] is a blatant example of the people's folly.

Mourning cries mark the demise of shameful Judah. Exile is upon them. Death too has arrived and is personified as climbing into homes and roaming the doomed cities of Judah. Verses 17 and 20 refer to wailing women; they presuppose that women played a leading role in funeral lamentation. The poetry associated with funeral lamentation is known as *qina*.[5]

A precise context for these prophecies is not given. Perhaps they reflect the initial Babylonian constriction of Jerusalem under Nebuchadnezzar in 598/597 or the devastating drought mentioned elsewhere in Jeremiah (14:1–6).

9:23–26. These verses are further prophetic responses to the previous announcement of judgment. Verses 23–24 return again to the theme of wisdom in such a time as this. With verse 25 comes the typical introduction to a prophetic depiction of the future ("days are coming . . ."). Note that markers for divine saying are found in each of verses 23–25.

Verses 23–24 are almost proverbial in form. There is a valid form of boasting, which comes with the realization of correct priorities. True wisdom is not only the recognition that God has sent judgment on Judah; it is above all knowledge of the Lord and his character. God reveals himself as One who practices and takes delight in kindness (*ḥesed*), justice (*mišpaṭ*), and righteousness (*ṣdaqa*). As verses 25–26 make clear, those nations who spurn the moral integrity of God—whether Egypt or Israel, circumcised or not—will see his judgment. The criticism of Israel as uncircumcised of heart picks up a theme from 4:4.

10:1–16. These verses contain an extended critique of idolatry and affirmations of the Lord as Ruler over all. Idolatry is described and defined variously.[6]

---

4. Cf. 2:23 for the other reference to Baal in the plural.

5. The noun *qina* is used in 9:20 (9:19 in Heb.), where the NIV translates it as "a lament." For funeral rituals and poetry associated with them, see the introduction to the book of Lamentations.

6. Cf. Isa. 44:9–20 for another extended diatribe against idolatry.

Verse 2 refers to astrological divination ("signs in the sky"). Verses 3–5 criticize the making and veneration of a wooden image. Verse 9 notes that a wooden piece can be decorated with silver and gold and clothed in royal colors—but this does not make it divine. Verse 11 is a proverb written in Aramaic, which has been incorporated into the critique of idolatry. Perhaps it is a traditional saying that the prophet adopts here for emphasis. Divine images are succinctly judged in 10:15 with the claim that they are "worthless, the objects of mockery."

The lifeless images of other deities are contrasted with the uniqueness of the "living God," who is the Creator of heaven and earth (10:10–12). His cosmic kingship is twice affirmed (vv. 7, 10). This God, the "Maker of all things," is also the "Portion of Jacob"[7]; Israel is the tribe of his inheritance (10:16). Even the wisdom from other nations is folly compared to God's truth.

Much of this section is intended to instruct Israel and Judah in the time of the Exile. Not that it is irrelevant to the circumstances of Judah before the Babylonian onslaught, but the text is cast in a teaching mode rather than as a list of reasons why Israel is being judged. Note how the text begins. The house of Israel is called to avoid the ways of the nations. Assimilation, if not downright capitulation, to a dominant culture was a real issue for Israelites and Judeans among other nations. Idolatry is folly. When other nations talk about creation, God's people are reminded that the real Creator of heaven and earth is none other than the God of Israel.

10:17–22. The topic and setting change from the previous section. Apparently Jerusalem herself is addressed as one besieged, who recognizes that her predicament has no cure. The foe from the north will make an end to Judah. One may see the voices in 10:17–22 as follows:

> [**prophet** to Jerusalem] 10:17–18: "Gather up your belongings...."
> [**Jerusalem** to herself] 10:19–20: "Woe to me because of my injury!..."
> [**prophet** to Jerusalem] 10:21–22: "The shepherds are senseless and do not inquire of the LORD...."

As with a number of poetic oracles, the change of voices raises the question of how this material was presented in oral form. Perhaps the prophet acted out the poetry, using different voices, or he may have been assisted by someone like Baruch, his secretary and assistant.

10:23–25. The poetic collection of 8:4–10:25 concludes with the prayer of a chastened individual. The speaker is almost certainly Jeremiah; the question is whether he speaks primarily autobiographically (i.e., personally) or as a member of a wounded and judged people. The prayer contains a frank

---

7. The NIV uses uppercase letters because the translators understand the phrase to be a title for God.

admission that human resources themselves are not enough to keep a person on the pathway marked out by God. God is humbly implored to correct the errant ways of the one who prays—but in a manner that reveals God's justice and that does not continue in judgment (as is appropriate for those who do not know the Lord).

There is more wisdom than resignation in the way the prayer begins. A person does not ultimately direct his or her own pathways; rather, they are in the hands of God. Recognition of this fact is a first step toward wisdom. Much of the prayer is about justice: God is implored to judge the enemy who has devoured Jacob.

WISDOM AND FOOLISHNESS. Several of the prophetic judgments offered in this section partake of the theme of wisdom and foolishness. In doing so, the prophecies echo themes and vocabulary found elsewhere in the Bible and thus indicate broader contexts in which later readers may see the significance of Jeremiah's words.

Judah and Jerusalem are accused of a woeful ignorance in their lack of comprehension over their plight before the Lord and his coming judgment. God's people should have the moral and spiritual comprehension necessary to see the folly of their ways and the consequences to come. Birds know the times of migration, but God's people do not know his "requirements" (8:7). A wise person should understand what is happening to God's people (9:12); indeed, the truly wise person knows the Lord and the activities in which he delights (9:23–24). Even the supposed wisdom among the nations is folly compared to the Lord. The superstition (magical assumptions) of pagan religions marks them as senseless, and their idols as worthless (10:1–16).

Other prophets take up the theme of the culpable ignorance of God's people. Isaiah announces the astounding fact that God's chosen family knows less than the ox or donkey (Isa. 1:2–3). Idolatry too is a parade example of folly and lack of spiritual discernment (44:6–23). Hosea compares Ephraim to a silly dove (Hos. 7:11); true wisdom sees the righteousness of God's ways and acts accordingly (14:9). The wise should recognize that God's judgment is both punishment and tragedy; punishment is due to one who is morally responsible, yet it is a tragedy because God's people were instructed to act otherwise, and they should have known better.

The wisdom traditions of the Bible are replete with examples of the wise and foolish, the righteous and the wicked. Both Proverbs and James provide wisdom vocabulary appropriate for discerning God's ways in the world and expressing his will for the common life of his people. Jesus used the examples of wise and foolish to illustrate the importance of spiritual discernment. How is it, he asks, that people who discern weather patterns through observation cannot grasp the significance of his presence among them (Luke 12:54–56)? Those who do hear his word and act on it, however, are like the wise person who builds a house on bedrock (Matt. 7:24–27).

As with this section of Jeremiah, the wisdom traditions call for knowledge of God and discernment of the times. These two aspects go together. Knowledge of God is more than familiarity with his Word; it is the gift of discerning his will for the times at hand and committing oneself to it in joyful obedience. The wise person should be a keen observer of culture and history, using God's past dealings with people and things as examples from which to learn.

The prophet's anguish. The articulation of Jeremiah's anguish over the spiritual folly and rampant immorality of the people links these prophecies together and puts them in a larger biblical context. The prophetic office meant that those whom God called as prophets were mediators of his message to the people. This privilege did not separate them from the people but instead bound them to the people. For the brokenness of the people Jeremiah himself felt broken (8:21).

Jeremiah's weeping comes from his experience of the people's folly and his knowledge of God's resolve to judge them. It also represents God's own sorrow at their folly. "What else can I do?" God asks in sorrow (9:7). The anguish of God and prophet finds parallels in Hosea 11:1–9 and above all in the anguish of God's Son, who wept over the city that killed prophets and that would be the site of his crucifixion (Luke 13:34–35; 19:41–44).

LEARNING FROM JUDAH. To comprehend the failures of Judah and Jerusalem and to learn from them, the church should ask hard questions about its own life and witness in the contexts in which God has placed it. Jeremiah charged his contemporaries with adultery, iniquity, and immorality. Since these sins are part of the fabric of Western society, the question of the church's complicity in or tolerance of them raises serious questions about the quality of its witness and its future. Regarding the prophetic charges of idolatry and polytheism, the church may not officially promote worship of other deities,[8] but the manner of its worship and the

8. Among mainline Protestant churches in North America, the movements associated with goddess spirituality or New Age philosophy may be tantamount to polytheism. Among conservative and evangelical churches, defense of the American way, wooden pride in orthodoxy, and preoccupation with success may be tantamount to idolatry. Among some non-Western churches, overt polytheism may be a serious issue to confront.

quality of its life may indicate ways in which it gives undue allegiance to culturally relative things.

Sermons and lessons that seek to be faithful to these prophetic words of Jeremiah should not necessarily limit themselves to exposing what is wrong. Just to be "against" things may have an initial appeal, but the church has more to do than point out the failures in either its own witness or in the common life of society. Christians must also look to these texts for indications of the righteousness and worship that God expects from his people. Perhaps the biggest shock for a Western audience in hearing these words is a prediction of judgment to come; but if so, there ought to be lamentation as well, in recognition of failure before God ("harvest is past . . . and we are not saved;" 8:20), and fervent prayer that God will use judgment as correcting action (10:24).

Portraits of sin. Among these judgmental prophecies are several portraits of sin, whose profiles are instructive to believers of any age. For example, in 8:8–12 Jeremiah castigates the religious leaders whose self-conveyed wisdom blunts the force of God's Word for the present. Whatever the precise historical circumstances behind this charge (see comments above), it is likely that Jeremiah has more in mind than legitimate differences over interpreting God's Word. Jeremiah perceives a crisis in moral authority and action, an inability on the part of the people to perceive their plight before God, and a brazen refusal to consider change.

The charge to Judah that people no longer blush over shameful circumstances (8:12) should strike a resonant chord with modern Christians in the West who are confronted daily with their culture's hedonistic values. How can religious leaders proclaim that all is well when it is not? They seem to represent what a modern person might call "Band-Aid theology," a misguided understanding of God as cosmic grandparent who clucks over the foibles of grandchildren and assures them that it is only a skinned knee that will get better soon. This is a wholesale rejection of the biblical portrait of God, who indicates in his Word that people are dead in their sins apart from his intervention through acts of judgment and redemption. If one rejects the biblical message that indicates the gravity and culpability of human sinfulness, then what means are left for humankind to see its plight before the Creator, who is the Judge of heaven and earth?

Jeremiah's words indicate a lack of integrity on the part of Judah and Jerusalem. His examples include the charge that people say one thing and plan another (9:3–5, 8). Lying is a type of social treachery. James recognizes the power for good or evil that resides in the tongue and the way in which human speech can mask human pretensions for control and abuse (James 3:1–18). We do well to examine the ways in which words are used as subterfuge or code language in society to mask exploitation, the ways in which "good" words serve as poor substitutes for deeds, and ways in which words become labels to demonize and divide. If Christians are people who look to God's Word for guidance and instruction, then the integrity of their witness is measured in part by the ways in which they describe reality and treat one another.

Role of the prophet. Jeremiah's anguish over the folly of God's people indicates both the passion of the prophetic office to proclaim God's Word and the passion of God to correct and redeem that which is lost. There are two instructive parts to this side of prophet and deity. (1) The role of Christians and the church in engaging the world requires a passionate identification with the folly of the world. Those who would offer a grave spiritual diagnosis must love the patients and not stand aloof from them. This is a model of the church, which is not only the recipient of a judgmental word from Jeremiah, but also which, by God's grace, seeks a prophetic ministry among society's ills. Jeremiah may be a prophetic reminder of the deep sorrow that should meet all Christians when they reflect on the circumstances of those who do not know God. The lost are, after all, estranged siblings of the Lord, who wept and died for them.

(2) God's anguish and anger are, in reality, the only basis for hope in this world. His passions grow from love; the opposite of love is not anger but indifference. Were God indifferent to the predicament of a fallen creation, there would have been no prophetic ministry in Israel and no Son to engage evil and to die to expend its curse.

Among these prophecies of judgment readers will also find indications of what God intends for his people in their corporate life. These are the marks of the wisdom Jeremiah finds lacking among his generation, but which James calls "wisdom that comes from heaven" (James 3:17). Among such marks are the recognition of repentance as a conscious rejection of evil, an embracing of God's standards for moral integrity, a willingness to hear God's Word as judgment on human pretensions and sinfulness, a passion for those whose folly has trapped them in evil consequences, a humble boasting in the sufficiency of God whose own ways are just and right, and an aversion to idolatry whereby someone or something becomes the supreme value for people's affections rather than the one God of heaven and earth.

Jeremiah 11:1-17

THIS IS THE word that came to Jeremiah from the LORD: ²"Listen to the terms of this covenant and tell them to the people of Judah and to those who live in Jerusalem. ³Tell them that this is what the LORD, the God of Israel, says: 'Cursed is the man who does not obey the terms of this covenant—⁴the terms I commanded your forefathers when I brought them out of Egypt, out of the iron-smelting furnace.' I said, 'Obey me and do everything I command you, and you will be my people, and I will be your God. ⁵Then I will fulfill the oath I swore to your forefathers, to give them a land flowing with milk and honey'—the land you possess today."

I answered, "Amen, LORD."

⁶The LORD said to me, "Proclaim all these words in the towns of Judah and in the streets of Jerusalem: 'Listen to the terms of this covenant and follow them. ⁷From the time I brought your forefathers up from Egypt until today, I warned them again and again, saying, "Obey me." ⁸But they did not listen or pay attention; instead, they followed the stubbornness of their evil hearts. So I brought on them all the curses of the covenant I had commanded them to follow but that they did not keep.'"

⁹Then the LORD said to me, "There is a conspiracy among the people of Judah and those who live in Jerusalem. ¹⁰They have returned to the sins of their forefathers, who refused to listen to my words. They have followed other gods to serve them. Both the house of Israel and the house of Judah have broken the covenant I made with their forefathers. ¹¹Therefore this is what the LORD says: 'I will bring on them a disaster they cannot escape. Although they cry out to me, I will not listen to them. ¹²The towns of Judah and the people of Jerusalem will go and cry out to the gods to whom they burn incense, but they will not help them at all when disaster strikes. ¹³You have as many gods as you have towns, O Judah; and the altars you have set up to burn incense to that shameful god Baal are as many as the streets of Jerusalem.'

¹⁴"Do not pray for this people nor offer any plea or petition for them, because I will not listen when they call to me in the time of their distress.

¹⁵"What is my beloved doing in my temple
    as she works out her evil schemes with many?
    Can consecrated meat avert your punishment?
When you engage in your wickedness,
    then you rejoice."
¹⁶The LORD called you a thriving olive tree
    with fruit beautiful in form.
But with the roar of a mighty storm
    he will set it on fire,
    and its branches will be broken.

¹⁷The LORD Almighty, who planted you, has decreed disaster
for you, because the house of Israel and the house of Judah
have done evil and provoked me to anger by burning incense
to Baal.

THIS PASSAGE IS composed essentially in prose and
is concerned with the covenant-breaking activities of Judah and Jerusalem. Verses 15–16 are
poetry and are included with the prose material
as further commentary on the failure of the people. In these two verses a
female is addressed in judgment. Most likely it is Jerusalem in her personified role of representing the people. The text offers no specific date in Jeremiah's ministry for these words from the Lord.

A closer examination of this section indicates that there are subunits
within it. Verses 1–5 comprise the initial unit, an address from God to Jeremiah that instructs the prophet about the people's failures to maintain fidelity
to "this covenant" (vv. 2–3; cf. vv. 6, 8, 10). Jeremiah responds with the affirmation "amen" to this initial revelation from the Lord. Perhaps his response
is patterned on the list of curses for covenant disobedience in Deuteronomy
27:15–26, where an "amen" (= "indeed" or "so be it") follows each curse
listed.

Verses 6–14 offer a second communication from God given to the
prophet, the bulk of which is comprised of two paragraphs (vv. 6–8, 9–13),
each one introduced by "the LORD said to me." These verses still retain the
first-person element in the report ("me"), though their content is clearly
intended for the people. Jeremiah is the human vessel to deliver them.

The Lord recognizes that much, if not all, of Jeremiah's report to the people will fall on deaf ears and hard hearts. As a result, the prophet is commanded
not to pray for the people (11:14; cf. 7:16). We ought to remember that these
somber words are intended as instruction for the people rather than as simply

a message for the prophet. Even though one of the callings of a prophet was to intercede with the Lord in prayer, 11:14 assumes that intercession will do no good because the people will remain incorrigible (note esp. v. 17).

Scholars often point out similarities between the prose sections in this address and the words of Moses in Deuteronomy, although they differ on the degree of similarity and its significance. More specifically, scholars are divided over the historical relationship of prose material like this with the poetic oracles in the book of Jeremiah; some attribute the prose addresses to Jeremiah's editors who produced the book during the latter period of the Babylonian exile, while others see the prose style as part of Jeremiah's ministry along with the (originally) oral poetry.[1] With respect to 11:1–17, the verses appear to be a summary of reflections on the failure of Judah and Jerusalem to keep God's covenant (below) rather than a report of the prophet's actual presentation to the people. In written form they communicate to readers the essence of Jeremiah's message about the consequences of covenant infidelity.

Two conclusions may be stated from this succinct analysis. (1) God's people have broken "this covenant," and the prophet's task is to communicate that message to them. (2) There are consequences for disobedience, in that judgment will fall on the people. For readers of the material in chapters 1–10, there is little new in these two conclusions except the emphasis on the term "covenant" (*bᵉrit*).[2]

Details in 11:1–17 offer further perspective on the term *covenant*, but they also leave a number of things assumed on the part of hearers/readers. "This covenant" is something God "commanded" the ancestors of Judah and Jerusalem (11:4, 10), who were slaves in Egypt. Their redemption from such slavery is the presupposition of the covenant. Obedience to what God commanded Israel to do is expected, since he redeemed Israel and they belong to him. "This covenant" also includes as part of its content an "oath" (*šᵉbuᶜa*) God swore to the ancestors,[3] a promise that the land of Canaan would belong to their descendants. According to 11:4b God asked for obedience to his word and promised, "You will be my people, and I will be your God." This last phrase states succinctly the essence of the covenant (cf. Ex. 19:3b–6;

---

1. See the introduction to the book for further discussion on the prose materials in Jeremiah and the composition of the book.

2. For a lucid discussion of the term *covenant* and for further bibliography on the significance of the word, see J. H. Walton, *Covenant: God's Purpose, God's Plan* (Grand Rapids: Zondervan, 1994).

3. It is not clear from the context in ch. 11 whether the oath sworn to the forefathers refers to the promise of land made to Abraham and his descendants in Canaan (e.g., Gen. 12:1–7; 28:10–15) or to this same promise as it was renewed with the generation in Egyptian slavery. Stated differently, it is not clear whether the "forefathers" of 11:5 are the ancestors in Egyptian slavery or those named in Genesis 12–50.

Lev. 26:12; Jer. 24:7; 31:33; Ezek. 11:20; Zech. 8:8), from which blessings like children and land would emerge.

One may compare the basic marriage formulation ("I will be your husband, and you will be my wife") with that of the covenant between God and Israel. They are linguistically similar formulations, and both presuppose an exclusive, intimate relationship as the basis on which a broader community is built.[4] Thus, the covenant was predicated on God's gifts of deliverance and instruction, it is extended by him to the people, and it also contained curses for the people's disobedience to the covenant stipulations (11:3, 8, 11).[5] Accusations in 11:9—13 that Judah venerates other gods is a violation of the covenant God established with the people (Deut. 5:7—10) and the reason for reminding them of the curses for disobedience.

As the previous comments indicate, the particulars of 11:1—17 assume a historical and theological context for the first hearers and readers that spans the biblical storyline from the promises to Abraham and descendants, the deliverance of the ancestors from Egypt, covenant-making at Mount Sinai, and guidance to the Promised Land. But there is more to be considered with respect to Jeremiah's own lifetime. King Josiah had undertaken a movement for covenant renewal (2 Kings 22—23) by calling Judah back to the fundamental principles of the Sinai/Horeb covenant. He read to the assembled people from the newly discovered book of the covenant (probably Deuteronomy), he officiated at a ceremony of covenant-making, and the people responded affirmatively from their side (23:1—3). His reforming efforts coincided with the call of the young Jeremiah.[6]

Two elements about the role of Josiah's reforming activity may help in interpreting 11:1—17. (1) The book of Deuteronomy is essentially a covenant-renewal document, for it reports the last addresses of Moses to the Israelites prior to his death. Moses emphasized that it was time for the younger generation who came out of Egypt to respond affirmatively to the covenant claim that God had on them. He mediated with them a covenant-renewal ceremony on the plains of Moab. This set a pattern that Josiah would follow. Jeremiah, a prophet like Moses for his generation (cf. Deut. 18:18), takes up a similar role of calling the people back to their first love and reminding them of the consequences.

---

4. For additional study on the vocabulary of God's choosing Israel, with attention to the covenant and marriage formulae, see T. S. Sohn, *The Divine Election of Israel* (Grand Rapids: Eerdmans, 1991).

5. For lists of blessings and curses contained in God's covenant with Israel, see Lev. 26 and Deut. 27—30. For the covenant-ratification ceremony at Sinai see Ex. 24:3—8. The people promised obedience to the Lord's covenant, and the covenant with him was sealed in blood.

6. See the treatment of the historical setting for the book in the introduction.

(2) Moses commanded that the words of God's Torah be read every seven years at the Festival of Booths (Deut. 31:9–13). It is possible that Jeremiah's "sermon" as summarized in chapter 11 is influenced by the prophet's support for the covenant reform measures instituted earlier by Josiah (although they seem to have been short-lived) as well as by the opportunity to reflect on God's covenantal instructions as they were read periodically in Judah.[7]

COVENANT CONTEXT. This prose address has many links with other material in Jeremiah. Even where there is no reference to a covenant, much of Jeremiah's criticisms of Israel and Judah are derived from their failure to maintain the covenant responsibilities God granted them when he called them to be his people. And after judgment, when Jeremiah projects a transformed future for Israel and Judah, his prophecy depicts a "new covenant," when God will grant new privileges to his covenant-breaking but chastened people (Jer. 31:31–34). From one angle of vision, therefore, the address in chapter 11 is a summary statement of Jeremiah's criticisms of the people and indications that judgment for failure is on the horizon.

From another angle of vision, the repeated references to "this covenant" provide a broader scriptural context in which to interpret the address. For Jeremiah's audience and the Jewish generations to follow, the term *covenant* evoked strong associations with God, who had freely bound himself to them through promises. A promise extended is different from a contract mutually agreed to, although both covenant and contract in the ancient world could be sealed by sacrificial ceremony and solemn oaths. The latter are part of the covenant-making tradition in the Old Testament (Gen. 15:1–21; Ex. 24:1–8).

A covenant is somewhat different from a treaty, however, although they were similar in the ancient world. Solomon and Hiram of Tyre, for example, made an agreement between themselves that is called a covenant (*berit*, see 1 Kings 5:12[26], NIV "treaty"). The arrangement instituted between the two

---

7. In his two-volume commentary *Jeremiah*, W. Holladay proposes that several passages in Jeremiah are "counter-proclamation" to the seven-year cycle of the public reading of Deuteronomy. The years of reading would be 622, 615, 608, 601, and 594 B.C. According to Holladay, 11:1–17 is one of those counter-proclamations. See also Holladay's "A Proposal for Reflections in the Book of Jeremiah of the Seven-Year Recitation of the Law in Deuteronomy (Deut 31:10–13)," in *Deuteronomium, Entstehung, Gestalt und Botschaft*, ed. N. Lohfink (Leuven: Leuven Univ. Press, 1985), 326–28. One need not accept everything about Holladay's theory to see the possibilities of influence from Josiah and Deuteronomy on the work of Jeremiah.

individuals was likely a parity agreement. A covenant extended by God to anyone else is by definition a gift from the greater to the lesser.

The Old Testament never uses the word "covenant" in the plural to refer to the various covenants God granted to Israel[8] and sets no specific chronological limits when a covenant is instituted, although a covenant may or may not have specific conditions attached to it for the covenant partner. For example, God's covenant with creation is a promise that does not have conditions placed on creation, whereas God's covenant with Israel does have conditions associated with the promises God makes to the people. The people have obligations to meet as part of the covenant graciously granted to them.

The Old Testament frequently calls the Sinai/Horeb (or Mosaic) covenant God's covenant[9]; it is never called Israel's covenant. This contrast has important theological ramifications. The Sinai covenant was a gift from God to Israel. It was conditional in that it could be broken by Israel's disobedience. A covenant is not something that Israel might extend to God. Within the structure of the covenant granted to Israel were blessings for obedience and curses for disobedience.

In the modern Western world the term *covenant* is still used in some wedding ceremonies to depict the solemn and sacred relationship of marriage— a usage similar to that in the Old Testament prophecies of Hosea and Jeremiah—but it is not used much any more to describe social relationships. The term evokes a strong sense of commitment to a relationship. As noted above, the formula for marriage and for the covenant God established with Israel were similar. Nevertheless, a modern parity commitment differs from the biblical sense of a covenant; God grants the covenant unilaterally to someone like David or the people of Israel, and it conveys primarily a self-binding promise/oath graciously granted rather than a negotiated relationship.

The judgment Jeremiah announces for covenant disobedience has two key elements. (1) The offended party (God) has the right to judge infidelity. (2) Israel responded to God's gracious invitation to covenant fellowship with an oath of obedience and an acknowledgment of curses to fall for disobedience. Not only is God just in announcing judgment, but Israel is self-inflicted with the curses of the covenant to which it agreed were proper.

---

8. In Rom. 9:4 Paul refers to the Israelites as recipients of "covenants." Probably what the apostle has in mind is the covenant with creation (Gen. 9:8–17), the Sinai covenant (Ex. 19:3–6), the covenant with David (2 Sam. 7; cf. Isa. 55:1–3), and the eschatological promise of an everlasting covenant with Israel in Ezekiel (e.g., Ezek. 16:60–63; cf. Hos. 2:18–20), interpreted as a complementary way to refer to the eschatological "new covenant" (Jer. 31:31–34) predicted by Jeremiah. Each of these affects Israel differently.

9. In first-person speech the covenant is called by God "my covenant" (e.g., Ex. 19:5); in third-person speech it is described as "his covenant" (e.g., Deut. 4:13).

New covenant and Jesus Christ. Finally, another angle of vision sees Jeremiah's judgment speech in light of his prophecy of a new covenant (31:31–34) to come, a covenant that ultimately Christ initiated through his death and resurrection (Matt. 26:26–29; Mark 14:22–25; Luke 22:17–20; 1 Cor. 11:23–26; Heb. 8:6–13; 10:1–39). What God demanded by way of covenant fidelity (as Heb. 10:26–39 reminds Christian readers) are the very things God has given as gifts through the obedience of his Son. Here is one element of the "bridge" between Jeremiah 11:1–17 and the modern world. Christians have been given the gift of a new covenant in Christ in spite of their failures to live up to the standards God has set. This is the gospel.

Christ is God's self-binding promise, gaining for his people that which they are incapable of gaining for themselves. Through him come demands for discipleship, what one might call the gracious stipulations of the "new covenant." In reading Jeremiah 11, it is not the announcement of judgment for covenant disobedience that should cause surprise on the part of readers, old or new; rather, it is the larger biblical claim that God will continue to pursue people such as these and even to offer his own Son as a self-binding gift of new life to them. One can grasp the radical nature of grace and forgiveness only when one recognizes that judgment for failure is what we deserve and should have expected.

 EMPHASIZING THE NEGATIVE. As with all biblical texts announcing divine judgment, an interpreter of the Bible who seeks contemporary application must decide whether a similar announcement is called for or whether the text is best applied as positive instruction for the present through negative examples from the history of God's people. If the decision is the former, then Jeremiah's accusation of covenant-breaking becomes an example of prophetic preaching where the failure to heed divine instruction results in the temporal judgment of God's people.

In Christian theology, God's judgment for failure may fall on those who reject Christ's call to discipleship and spurn the truth of the gospel; God has established a covenant of peace and eternal salvation through Christ, and to reject that means of salvation is to reject the only means offered. Unrepentant Christians and faithless churches open themselves to temporal judgments (and even beyond) by their rejection of what God has offered them through Christ.

Emphasizing the positive. Jeremiah's announcement of judgment for covenant infidelity can offer positive instruction to the church through its insistence on the power of promises made. In essence, the covenant began with God's promise of commitment to his people, and it sought commitment and fidelity in return. The fragile nature of human commitment in modern society is constantly under threat as marriages end, friendships fail, churches turn their back on neighborhood needs, and fidelity to God takes a back seat to many other things clamoring for time and attention. In a mobile society where the pace of life is swift, the place of enduring commitments is easily crowded out. These things are easily illustrated from modern life; the question for reflection is the extent of the damages that such societal forces inflict on (or will eventually lead to) the life of God's people.

Two current movements in North American society illustrate the significance of human commitment to responsible life. Others could be named, and a way in which the contemporary significance of Jeremiah 11 could be explored comes in naming such movements. Both of these movements emerge from the recognition that modern society (for a variety of reasons) has devalued enduring commitments, debased the significance of personal integrity, and pushed people into the folly of the "blame game," where it is always someone else's fault.

The first illustration is the movement led by Louis Farrakhan of the Nation of Islam. This is a powerful force in the African American community, which takes seriously the potential for societal improvement based on responsible commitments of African American men and women. It is not a Christian movement, and its rhetoric against Jews is reprehensible, but it is based on solemn commitments of a theological nature. One need not embrace either Islam or the separatist nationalism of this movement to recognize that it has touched something deep in the African American community, something that guides men in the ways of responsible activity. Its deserved negative connotations should not blind Christians to its emphases on community, discipline, and piety that have made constructive differences in some of the most difficult neighborhoods in America, along with an impressive record of working with convicted felons in prisons to assist them in changing patterns of destructive behavior and in lowering the rates of recidivism.

The second illustration is the avowedly evangelical movement of the Promise Keepers, led by Bill McCartney. It calls men to commit themselves through the power of the Holy Spirit to lives of fidelity to and responsibility before God. Promise Keepers doctrine assumes that God is the primary Promise Keeper and that Christian men are called to respond in kind.

Listening carefully to Jeremiah's sermon should keep one from concentrating solely on what's wrong with society, although a critical assessment will have plenty of material with which to work. Jeremiah's critique is extended to people who should know better but who have taken the easy way out. Such a word goes first to the church, since it ought to know better on a number of fronts.

The need for transformation. It is also a mistake simply to assume that people who try harder will succeed in their commitments. There will be no lasting success apart from a lasting transformation. Such transformation as God in Christ supplies is a process that begins with a gracious acceptance of the claims of the gospel and continues unto and beyond death. The prophet addresses God's people, and his message is profoundly theological. "Trying harder" in secular terms is a Band-Aid on a mortal wound.

Human beings ultimately learn that true commitment comes from who God is and the ways in which God has revealed himself through his Word and interpreted deed. We face the true depths of human failure, self-deception, and depravity only in light of the gospel, where the light of forgiveness and acceptance most clearly illumines the failures. Jeremiah's announcement of judgment points to a redemption that only God can provide. We learn too that what God demands by way of fidelity has been fulfilled in Jesus Christ and that the nature of human commitment to God depends on the gifts of the Holy Spirit and new life in Christ. God, the Judge of all the earth, is also the ultimate Promise Keeper. The church and individual Christians, therefore, are called to keep promises made to God and to exercise godly responsibility in their respective spheres of influence.

Jeremiah 11:18–12:17

ᵂ

BECAUSE THE LORD revealed their plot to me, I knew it, for at that time he showed me what they were doing. ¹⁹I had been like a gentle lamb led to the slaughter; I did not realize that they had plotted against me, saying,

"Let us destroy the tree and its fruit;
    let us cut him off from the land of the living,
    that his name be remembered no more."
²⁰But, O LORD Almighty, you who judge righteously
    and test the heart and mind,
let me see your vengeance upon them,
    for to you I have committed my cause.

²¹"Therefore this is what the LORD says about the men of Anathoth who are seeking your life and saying, 'Do not prophesy in the name of the LORD or you will die by our hands'—²²therefore this is what the LORD Almighty says: 'I will punish them. Their young men will die by the sword, their sons and daughters by famine. ²³Not even a remnant will be left to them, because I will bring disaster on the men of Anathoth in the year of their punishment.'"

¹²:¹You are always righteous, O LORD,
    when I bring a case before you.
Yet I would speak with you about your justice:
    Why does the way of the wicked prosper?
    Why do all the faithless live at ease?
²You have planted them, and they have taken root;
    they grow and bear fruit.
You are always on their lips
    but far from their hearts.
³Yet you know me, O LORD;
    you see me and test my thoughts about you.
Drag them off like sheep to be butchered!
    Set them apart for the day of slaughter!
⁴How long will the land lie parched
    and the grass in every field be withered?
Because those who live in it are wicked,
    the animals and birds have perished.
Moreover, the people are saying,
    "He will not see what happens to us."

⁵"If you have raced with men on foot
  and they have worn you out,
  how can you compete with horses?
 If you stumble in safe country,
  how will you manage in the thickets by the Jordan?
⁶Your brothers, your own family—
  even they have betrayed you;
  they have raised a loud cry against you.
 Do not trust them,
  though they speak well of you.

⁷"I will forsake my house,
  abandon my inheritance;
 I will give the one I love
  into the hands of her enemies.
⁸My inheritance has become to me
  like a lion in the forest.
 She roars at me;
  therefore I hate her.
⁹Has not my inheritance become to me
  like a speckled bird of prey
  that other birds of prey surround and attack?
 Go and gather all the wild beasts;
  bring them to devour.
¹⁰Many shepherds will ruin my vineyard
  and trample down my field;
 they will turn my pleasant field
  into a desolate wasteland.
¹¹It will be made a wasteland,
  parched and desolate before me;
 the whole land will be laid waste
  because there is no one who cares.
¹²Over all the barren heights in the desert
  destroyers will swarm,
 for the sword of the LORD will devour
  from one end of the land to the other;
  no one will be safe.
¹³They will sow wheat but reap thorns;
  they will wear themselves out but gain nothing.
 So bear the shame of your harvest
  because of the LORD's fierce anger."

¹⁴This is what the LORD says: "As for all my wicked neighbors who seize the inheritance I gave my people Israel, I will uproot them from their lands and I will uproot the house of Judah from among them. ¹⁵But after I uproot them, I will again have compassion and will bring each of them back to his own inheritance and his own country. ¹⁶And if they learn well the ways of my people and swear by my name, saying, 'As surely as the LORD lives'—even as they once taught my people to swear by Baal—then they will be established among my people. ¹⁷But if any nation does not listen, I will completely uproot and destroy it," declares the LORD.

THIS SECTION IS COMPRISED of prayer, lamentation/complaint, sad reflection on Judah's sinful state (from both the prophet and God), and prophecies on the fate of wicked neighbors (both of Jeremiah and of Judah). It is not a unified address, but as is typical with other poetic subsections of the book, various units of speech are joined editorially because of common themes: here, lamentation and petition, persecution, and punishment. The material is undated and likely derives from various times in the prophet's ministry. The depiction of Judah's devastation in 12:7–13 probably reflects either the first (598–597) or second Babylonian assault (587–586) on Jerusalem.

In this section readers encounter the first of the prophet's prayerful reactions to persecution. Prayers related to his persecution, including his anger and despair, come at intervals in chapters 11–20. One often hears them described as Jeremiah's lamentations or complaints (11:18–23; 12:1–6; 15:10–14, 15–21; 17:14–18; 18:18–23; 20:7–13, 14–18).[1] Also, through these prophetic words the sad reflection of the Lord emerges in a lament over the loss of the

---

1. There is a large bibliography on these texts. To cite only recent studies in English, see M. S. Smith, *The Laments of Jeremiah and Their Contexts: A Literary and Redactional Study of Jer 11–20* (Atlanta: Scholars Press, 1990); K. O'Connor, *The Confessions of Jeremiah: Their Interpretation and Role in Chapters 1–25* (SBLDS 94; Atlanta: Scholars Press, 1988); A. R. Diamond, *The Confessions of Jeremiah in Context: Scenes of Prophetic Drama* (JSOTSup 45; Sheffield: JSOT Press, 1987). These titles demonstrate that the terminology varies concerning the proper term for Jeremiah's prayers. *Lament* is an English term used to describe a type of prayer in the Old Testament that comes in the context of death or tragedy as well as those that are a response to mistreatment and persecution. Some interpreters would distinguish between these two aspects and call the latter a complaint. Others call Jeremiah's prayers "confessions." Whichever term is preferred, this basic type occurs frequently in the Psalms, and Lamentations is the title to the little book of prayers that follows Jeremiah in English versions of the Bible (see introduction to Lamentations).

"one I love" (12:7–8). On occasion it is difficult to discern who is represented as lamenting, Jeremiah or the Lord. Both of them react emotionally to the folly and the failures of the people.

Jeremiah's lamentations follow the model of individual laments in the Psalter. The prophet is thereby marked as an individual who prays the prayers of Israel and as one who may confess sin, vent frustration, affirm his innocence in the face of persecution, and offer pleas for deliverance. In the account of Jeremiah's call (ch. 1), the prophet was told that persecution and opposition would come to him. His only protection was God's promise to watch over him and the word he would deliver. The fact that God called Jeremiah to a prophetic task did not mean that he was exempt from the doubts and depressions that strike those in position of high stress.

11:18–23. In a moment of consternation Jeremiah is shown the true intentions of neighbors from his hometown of Anathoth (a short distance north of Jerusalem). God reveals to him that they intend to humiliate him and to bring his prophetic work to an end. Indeed, the phrase "cut him off from the land of the living" (v. 19) indicates murder, as does the threat of verse 21.

Jeremiah describes himself, therefore, as a lamb led to slaughter. Neither the context nor the terminology necessarily implies the sacrificial imagery of the temple cult. The language may simply reflect the profane practice of slaughter for consumption. It does, however, strongly imply that Jeremiah is innocent of any wrongdoing. A lamb led to slaughter carries with it the imagery of nonaggression and nonculpability on the part of the lamb. Jeremiah's predicament is not God's judgment on him but the plot of others (including some inhabitants of Anathoth, cf. 11:21–23; 12:6) who oppose his message and seek to harm him. They want him to stop prophesying as he has been in the name of the Lord.

The short prayer of the prophet in verse 20 is based on the conviction that God is a righteous Judge. Jeremiah asks not only for deliverance[2]—which is one task a judge can perform—but also for God to judge those who persecute him unjustly. God, who is able to assess the motives of heart, mind, and will, reveals that persecution of Jeremiah comes because he has sought to deliver God's word to Judah.

Verses 21–23 reveal a judgment on those who seek Jeremiah's life. Both verses 21 and 22 contain the formula "This is what the LORD says," giving a double emphasis to the judgment to come on the persecutors of the prophet.

12:1–6. Jeremiah again addresses the Lord in prayer, stating a premise about God's righteousness similar to that expressed in 11:20. The NIV

---

2. The NIV translation "let me see your vengeance upon them" can also be rendered "let me see your vindication upon them." The Heb. word in question is *neqama*. It does indeed have the element of retribution or vengeance, but also that of vindicating the innocent or oppressed through judgment.

translation of 12:1 may be rendered differently, "(Because) you are righteous, O LORD, I would plead a case[3] with you." The case or issue that Jeremiah brings is not just that of threat to his life (although this is a primary element); it is also the question of why a righteous God allows the way of the wicked to prosper. If God is so clearly opposed to the activity of the wicked, then why not judge them and be done with it? Jeremiah prays for the destruction of the wicked because of the harm they have brought to the land and asks that they (instead of he) be taken off like sheep for the slaughter. Readers can see why this passage follows that of the description of Jeremiah's persecution in 11:18–23.

God's reply (12:5–6) does not deal with the larger question of evil's prosperity or even the more restricted question of immediate judgment on those who oppose Jeremiah and ruin the land. Instead, God speaks to Jeremiah as the one called to be a prophet to the nations. This reply is couched in terms of the conflict at hand in Judah and the heavy task of prophetic work that remains. Jeremiah may be weary already by the strain of prophetic duty, but there is yet more difficulty ahead. There is no way around either persecution or the wearying strain of prophetic work, yet there will be a way through it. Jeremiah is not to trust even his relatives; rather, he is to look to the Lord for his strength and to the vindication the Lord will reveal in the future.

Jeremiah offers a quotation of the people in 12:4 to the effect that they doubt that God sees what is happening to them since he fails to act. They too (according to Jeremiah's prayer of frustration) see a God of inactivity. God does not "take the bait" and offer a defense of his providence. He simply calls the prophet to keep on the task at hand.

12:7–13. God sets forth his own complaint and announcement of judgment over the loss of his people. Here is evidence that the Lord is pained by the folly of his house. The previously revealed reply to Jeremiah in 12:5–6 does not reflect God's indifference to the prophet's precarious circumstances but recognizes the advanced state of decay in Judah and Jerusalem, the consequences of which neither Jeremiah nor God can avoid.

Verse 7 describes Judah as God's house, as his inheritance, and as the one whom God loves. All of this is family imagery and metaphor. As the head of his household, God experiences pain at its ruination and at the perversion of his inheritance. Verse 8 describes the city as transformed into an animal against God, and God's comment is that he "hates" her. Behind the reference to "her" is the metaphor of "daughter Jerusalem," a precious member of God's household. This is the language of a betrayed father and husband grappling with the enormity of treachery in the family. In this case the hatred

---

3. The NIV correctly renders the verb *rib* as "bring a case." It is typically used for judicial affairs and matters of dispute needing judgment or arbitration.

is not the opposite of love, which is indifference, but the sad effects of betrayed and wounded love.

12:14–17. This word about the neighboring states around Judah anticipates elements in the oracles concerning foreign nations in chapters 25, 46–51. It sits somewhat surprisingly in this context, but it offers important perspective on the function of judgmental prophecies. The announcement of judgment may be in service to a larger design for blessing and reconciliation.

According to 2 Kings 24:2, bands of Arameans, Ammonites, and Moabites were marauders against Judah and Jerusalem. Psalm 137:7 quotes Edomite voices who urged the destruction of Jerusalem. The Edomites are the object of bitter feelings in Lamentations 4:21–22 and in the prophecy of Obadiah (cf. Mal. 1:2–5). The neighbors who are against Judah and who taught God's people to swear by Baal will be judged and exiled ("uprooted") along with Judah, but they may yet have a future if they should learn the ways of the Lord. This is in line with the restoration prophecy of Amos 9:11–12, that the remnants of Edom may be incorporated in the booth of David that God will rebuild.

THE LANGUAGE OF LAMENT/COMPLAINT. Jeremiah's anxiety about life and his distress over his persecution are expressed in the language of lamentation or complaint. Put differently, his prayers are similar to the individual complaints in the Psalter, from which he has drawn his vocabulary and spiritual sustenance. This is a clue to their appropriation for today.

In recent decades scholars have debated the extent to which the prayers in 11:20 and 12:1–4 (and others) reflect the personal experiences of Jeremiah. Older commentators, especially nineteenth- and twentieth-century liberals, found in these prayers the key to the inner life and religious experience of the prophet. With the advent of form-critical analysis (genre identification), it became clear that Jeremiah's prayers are "typical" in that they represent the faith posture and the language of the Psalms. In reaction to the almost romantic reading of liberal individualism, some scholars have argued that the prophet's own experience is almost completely submerged behind the standard form of typical prayers.

However one assesses this issue, Jeremiah clearly prays to God as Israelites before him had done in times of crisis and self-doubt. More particularly, not only has Jeremiah been instructed by the classical prayers of his ancestors; his own adoption of them become instruction for his readers and hearers. Perhaps this issue is more crucial for modern appropriation than a rehash of the debate over his personal experience. Jeremiah chooses a vehicle that expresses his personal experience, and that vehicle gives shape to his words. The prophet's prayers, his personal experience, his public acts, and so on are all vehicles for proclamation and instruction rather a simple reporting of his feelings.

When we affirm that Jeremiah's own particular experience is mediated through the text, we also affirm that it paradigmatic; it is the result of his being called to the prophetic office (see comments below). Jeremiah finds "his voice" among the prayers of David and other ancestors in the faith, and we are told as much about the trials of the office as of the inner life of the person.

Since these prayers do not preserve a specific public setting in the book, later readers do not know how (or even if) these words were given to Jeremiah's contemporaries in Judah. While this remains a mystery, they are obviously meant to be instructive to readers of the book since they are preserved in the book. This is their primary function, although it is certainly plausible that Jeremiah looked for ways to make his prayers a teaching device for his contemporaries.

The individual and corporate laments/complaints of the Psalter, the largest single "type" (genre) in that book, reflect the personal crises of people of faith, including even the king. They can be model prayers for the faithful, but this is not required for them to be instructive for either ancient or modern readers. They provide a vocabulary through which to articulate trial and anguish, and they point to God as sympathetic Shepherd and righteous Judge.

The majority of the psalms deal with the power of the forces arrayed against God's servant(s), the plea to the Lord for vindication and deliverance through his judging the wicked, and confidence in God's power to redeem the circumstances of those who pray. Less often they are concerned with the effects of personal transgression (e.g., Ps. 51). Jeremiah prays to God, who knows the heart and mind and who judges righteously; in boldness he reminds God of his (God's) righteousness while at the same time bringing before him observations concerning the ascendancy of evil. In all this Jeremiah prays like the saints of previous generations, including David himself, who clung to the God of righteousness in spite of outward circumstances.

The prophetic office and persecution. A second contextual reading of the prayers sees them as reflective of a dual setting: the prophetic office to which Jeremiah was called and an illustration of the persecution announced at his call as sure to come against his prophetic activity. These two elements are related. In Jeremiah 1, a variety of opponents was noted who would stand against Jeremiah and his prophetic message (1:8, 17–19). His persecution, while real and personal, came to him as a result of his prophetic work.

Jeremiah is not the only servant of God to be opposed and persecuted, for he stands in a line of suffering prophetic figures reaching back to Moses and continuing past Jeremiah to Jesus. He was granted what Jesus calls a prophet's reward (Matt. 5:11−12). Jeremiah is also one of the great cloud of scriptural witnesses, one from the line of faithful servants who endured hostility for the sake of God's call (Heb. 11). Thus, Jeremiah's persecution is linked precisely to his call as a prophet, and its intensity of degree is pronounced because of the office. One bridge from Jeremiah's world to ours runs through the exercise of prophetic ministry and its consequences.

Christological reading. A Christological reading of this section begins with this recognition that Jeremiah's opposition is linked to his role as God's prophet. On the one hand, opposition to Jeremiah was ultimately opposition to God, who sent him. Thus Jeremiah's anguish is humanly indicative of God's own anguish over rejection. This point comes out in God's own complaint over the failure of his house in 12:7−13. On the other hand, the prophetic suffering of Jeremiah was a step along the way of God's dealings with Israel that in the fullness of time would bring forth God's Son, Jesus, his suffering representative and the Messiah of Israel. Jeremiah's suffering is not redemptive as is that of Jesus, but it is representative of the prophetic office and thereby "prophetic" for the suffering of Christ.

Jesus brought the prophetic office to culmination in his call to repentance and in his suffering on behalf of righteousness.[4] In a mysterious way Jesus learned obedience from the things he suffered (Heb. 2:10; 5:8); his persecution became the way of salvation for those for whom he died. In his innocence Jesus had every right to call for judgment on those who persecuted him (as Jeremiah did), but his dependence on God's righteousness meant that he left judgment to him (1 Peter 2:20−25).

The lamb led to slaughter is Jeremiah's self-designation. John describes Jesus as "the Lamb of God, who takes away the sin of the world" (John 1:29). Scripture is rich with imagery of the lamb or sheep for slaughter (e.g., Gen. 22; Ex. 12−13), and Jeremiah's innocent prophetic suffering is one element of the biblical tapestry related to suffering and redemption. In his self-offering, Christ's redemptive work includes forgiveness of the evildoers—a miracle of grace that moves beyond Jeremiah's own words but not beyond the reach of the God who inspires the prophet.

Israel's neighbors. The word about the neighbors (12:14−17) is related both to God's concern for the nations' salvation and God's intention to judge them with righteousness. These matters are of broad interest to the biblical writers, with the New Testament emphasizing as of first importance the concern that the gospel be preached to all the nations. Jeremiah's word relates

---

4. See the remarks in the introduction about Jesus as the fulfillment of the offices of prophet, priest, and king in the Old Testament.

first of all to temporal judgment, but it holds out the possibility that the neighbors will be restored in their homeland and related to the Lord. It remains for the New Testament to spell out in more detail just what a glorious inheritance the nations may have in God's Son.

THE COST OF DISCIPLESHIP. Jeremiah's words about his persecution come from the discharge of his prophetic office. They also raise for Christians the issue of the cost of discipleship, what might be termed the relationship between Christian vocation and suffering when disciples take up their cross and follow Christ. Family and friends alike apparently opposed Jeremiah's prophetic activity. His opposition, his despair, and even the threats to his life came not from his sinfulness but from the exercise of his faith in responding to God's call. This is a perennial issue for Christians, more likely in some cultures and settings than in others, but a perennial issue nevertheless.

In the Bridging Contexts section we have already noted the fellowship of suffering that the prophet represents and in which he has a well-deserved place. To name just three current examples, Christians in Indonesia, in the Philippines, and in Sudan have been attacked simply because they believe in Christ. The treatment of some of them is horribly close to that of a lamb led to slaughter. To be fair, one should cite also the despicable treatment of Jews in the country of Iran, where many were put on trial in the summer months of 2000 and charged with being agents for the state of Israel. There is no evidence, of course, to support these charges. Their only crime seems to be that they held to their faith in the God of Israel in spite of overwhelming pressure to do otherwise.

God's righteousness. We should take note of Jeremiah's words to the Lord about God's righteousness. That righteousness is the presupposition to all that is uttered in this section, even the questioning of God's judging that comes in 12:1–2. It is the anchor to which the prophet clings in spite of his circumstances. Jeremiah will not be able to depend on his own righteousness; this is clear even though these prayers presume that Jeremiah is innocent of any wrongdoing with respect to the charges of his opponents.

Jeremiah will not be able to depend on his own patience or resourcefulness. He knows full well that his life means little except that God has made certain promises to him, and it is only because of his belief in God's righteousness (God's integrity) that he has any hope. Because of what Jeremiah believes about God's integrity, he can pray both bluntly and expectantly about the exercise of God's righteousness. In faith he can even note its seeming absence.

Jeremiah also prays for God's vindication because of what he believes about God's righteousness. Vindication for Jeremiah means deliverance from the plots of his opponents and God's judgment on them. Christians should listen carefully for what Jeremiah actually prays. He seeks the exercise of God's righteousness, not the fulfillment of his wish list for vengeance. Jeremiah has no vendetta against his opponents, and he does not seek to judge them himself; he simply holds up their activities in persecuting God's prophet before the judgment seat of God. For God to be faithful to his promise to Jeremiah as prophet to the nations, those who persecute him will fail at their task to silence him. For them to persist in persecution is to invite the very judgment of God on themselves that they have mistakenly sought to perpetrate on Jeremiah. This does not make Jeremiah invulnerable; he remains a man whose only security resides in his trust of God's righteousness.

When Christians pray for their enemies and those who persecute them, they pray that God will grant the persecutors the ability to recognize their errors and see the way to a forgiveness that is ultimately God's to give. Their deeds deserve his judgment, yet by his grace that judgment has been borne by someone else. If God's grace is spurned, then nothing else in all of creation can save them. The prayer "Your kingdom come" includes the assumption that judgment as well as mercy are part of the exercise of God's righteousness. Because Christ met suffering in a way that Jeremiah could not, there is the marvelous possibility that his enemies will meet with a transforming judgment and restoration that Jeremiah could not completely foresee.

Does this make Jeremiah's prayer for vindication and judgment wrong for Christians to use? No. But what they should pray for is the vindication of the gospel and the frustration of plans for its subversion. This is consistent with Jeremiah's own plea for the exercise of God's righteousness and the vindication of the message he has been given by God.

The ultimate answer. God's "answer" to Jeremiah in 12:5—6 is not an explanation of why evil may have its ascendant day any more than the book of Job provides an answer to evil and suffering. God's reply does not even tell Jeremiah how God will vindicate him. It is less an answer and more a somber indication that to run the race of prophetic office before him, Jeremiah will be stretched more than he can yet imagine. So he must be prepared! This is also a word about the life of discipleship, about the process of refinement and growth in grace, and about trust in God in spite of difficult circumstances. It is not a philosophical discussion about the justification of God's ways and timing to the prophet.

Christian faith is well instructed by this surprising word from Jeremiah. At most points along the journey of faith, we cannot see the twists and turns that will make up our witness. And why should we know more than that our life is hid in Christ and that our ultimate vindication rests with him? Our relationship with God is not a panacea for life's problems but the basis on which we face those problems. Our strength is not our own. Should we seek to run the race with our own resources, we will ultimately fail. Should we run the race in dependence on God, we are not guaranteed victory according to worldly standards either, only that we belong to God.

In considering this surprising word in 12:5–6, therefore, one is forcefully reminded that God has not abandoned Jeremiah. His timing and purpose are simply not revealed completely to the prophet, who is told that he must be prepared for more difficult days ahead. This is not so different from the words that the apostle Paul spoke to the Philippians about pressing on toward the goal of God's call in Christ Jesus (Phil. 3:12–14). It is an arduous journey with twists and turns throughout, but the pioneer of salvation, Jesus Christ himself (Heb. 12:2), has pointed us to the journey's end and offers his companionship along the way.

Jeremiah 13:1–27

THIS IS WHAT the LORD said to me: "Go and buy a linen belt and put it around your waist, but do not let it touch water." ²So I bought a belt, as the LORD directed, and put it around my waist.

³Then the word of the LORD came to me a second time: ⁴"Take the belt you bought and are wearing around your waist, and go now to Perath and hide it there in a crevice in the rocks." ⁵So I went and hid it at Perath, as the LORD told me.

⁶Many days later the LORD said to me, "Go now to Perath and get the belt I told you to hide there." ⁷So I went to Perath and dug up the belt and took it from the place where I had hidden it, but now it was ruined and completely useless.

⁸Then the word of the LORD came to me: ⁹"This is what the LORD says: 'In the same way I will ruin the pride of Judah and the great pride of Jerusalem. ¹⁰These wicked people, who refuse to listen to my words, who follow the stubbornness of their hearts and go after other gods to serve and worship them, will be like this belt—completely useless! ¹¹For as a belt is bound around a man's waist, so I bound the whole house of Israel and the whole house of Judah to me,' declares the LORD, 'to be my people for my renown and praise and honor. But they have not listened.'

¹²"Say to them: 'This is what the LORD, the God of Israel, says: Every wineskin should be filled with wine.' And if they say to you, 'Don't we know that every wineskin should be filled with wine?' ¹³then tell them, 'This is what the LORD says: I am going to fill with drunkenness all who live in this land, including the kings who sit on David's throne, the priests, the prophets and all those living in Jerusalem. ¹⁴I will smash them one against the other, fathers and sons alike, declares the LORD. I will allow no pity or mercy or compassion to keep me from destroying them.'"

¹⁵Hear and pay attention,
    do not be arrogant,
    for the LORD has spoken.
¹⁶Give glory to the LORD your God
    before he brings the darkness,

before your feet stumble
 on the darkening hills.
You hope for light,
 but he will turn it to thick darkness
 and change it to deep gloom.
[17] But if you do not listen,
 I will weep in secret
 because of your pride;
my eyes will weep bitterly,
 overflowing with tears,
 because the LORD's flock will be taken captive.

[18] Say to the king and to the queen mother,
 "Come down from your thrones,
for your glorious crowns
 will fall from your heads."
[19] The cities in the Negev will be shut up,
 and there will be no one to open them.
All Judah will be carried into exile,
 carried completely away.
[20] Lift up your eyes and see
 those who are coming from the north.
Where is the flock that was entrusted to you,
 the sheep of which you boasted?
[21] What will you say when the LORD sets over you
 those you cultivated as your special allies?
Will not pain grip you
 like that of a woman in labor?
[22] And if you ask yourself,
 "Why has this happened to me?"—
it is because of your many sins
 that your skirts have been torn off
 and your body mistreated.
[23] Can the Ethiopian change his skin
 or the leopard its spots?
Neither can you do good
 who are accustomed to doing evil.

[24] "I will scatter you like chaff
 driven by the desert wind.
[25] This is your lot,
 the portion I have decreed for you,"

        declares the LORD,

"because you have forgotten me
   and trusted in false gods.
²⁶ I will pull up your skirts over your face
   that your shame may be seen—
²⁷ your adulteries and lustful neighings,
   your shameless prostitution!
I have seen your detestable acts
   on the hills and in the fields.
Woe to you, O Jerusalem!
   How long will you be unclean?"

THIS CHAPTER CONTAINS a collection of judgment prophecies, each intended to expose the failure of Judah and Jerusalem before the Lord and to indicate the historical form of judgment to come as a consequence of that failure. As with most of the first half of the book, the text provides no dates in Jeremiah's ministry for either the symbolic act in 13:1–11 or the oracles that follow. Judgment appears to be looming on the historical horizon (one of the assaults by Nebuchadnezzar on Judah?). In 13:18–19 some form of destruction and depopulation is assumed.

13:1–11. This prophecy, a prose account with an autobiographical element, takes the form of a symbolic act accompanied by commentary from the Lord. The prophets often carried out symbolic acts as illustrations or reinforcements of their proclamation.[1] This is the first of several acts Jeremiah performs to portray his message.

God commands Jeremiah to take a linen waistcloth, clothe himself with it, then remove it and take it to the bank of the Perath and leave it. Scholars have debated whether the river or stream named Perath is the well-known Euphrates (ca. 300 miles from Jerusalem) or the seasonal stream near Anathoth with a similar name (cf. Josh. 18:23). In Hebrew *pᵉrat* can refer to either entity. The difficulty with concluding that Perath is the Euphrates comes when we recognize that considerable time and expense would be required for two round trips to the banks of the Euphrates River. What purpose does such a long trip have, either for the prophet who would make the trek or for the hearers/readers? If there is significance attached to the river in this symbolic act, it is implicit and not explicit in the text. The textual emphasis falls on the linen waistcloth, not on the river.

---

1. W. D. Stacey, *Prophetic Drama in the Old Testament* (London: Epworth, 1990); K. Freibel, *Jeremiah's and Ezekiel's Sign-Acts: Rhetorical Nonverbal Communication* (JSOTSup 283; Sheffield: Sheffield Academic Press, 1999).

In response to these considerations, however, note that convenience of access is not a primary consideration when considering prophetic motivation. It was not convenient for Hosea to marry a prostitute or for Ezekiel to lie on his side for weeks. If the closer-but-lesser-known stream near Anathoth is the location of the discarded waistcloth, then it is almost certainly chosen because its name reminds Jeremiah (and the audience) of the Euphrates and the mighty powers coming from the north (cf. 13:20), powers long associated with Assyria and Babylon. One can make a case in context that the allies courted by Jerusalem and mentioned in 13:21 are the Assyrians and Babylonians from across the great River Euphrates.

Just as the waistcloth was to be bound to its wearer, so Israel and Judah have been formed by God to be bound to him. The verb "be bound" (*dabaq*) in verse 11 is the same word used in Genesis 2:24 to describe the man who leaves his parents to "be united" (in Elizabethan English, "cleave") to his wife and to become "one flesh." Israel was enjoined to be united to the Lord (Deut. 10:20; 11:22; 13:4; 30:20). The soiling of the waistcloth came because Jeremiah removed it and buried it near the bank of the water. So Israel and Judah—whose separation from the Lord was caused by their faithlessness—were like the ruined waistcloth.

The conclusion in verse 11 uses the daring metaphor of bound clothing as a way of emphasizing the fall from grace of Israel and Judah. Their sad description is emphatic and corporate—the "whole house" of Israel and that of Judah have fallen away. They are ruined as surely as the waistcloth was fouled from its exposure to the elements on the riverbank. Israel and Judah were formed for God's "renown and praise and honor," but they are no better than dirty underwear.

13:12–14. The prophecy about wineskins contains a command to Jeremiah to repeat a proverbial saying: "Every wineskin should be filled with wine." Of course, this is the expectation for wineskins—they are created to hold wine. The punch line, however, is that God will fill the land's inhabitants with drunkenness so that they will crash against one another. In this scenario the intended function of the wineskins is ruined in similar fashion to the waistcloth. Neither waistcloth nor wine jars fulfill their intended functions and thus are failures.

13:15–19. Jeremiah utters judgments against the pride that leads to a fall. Verse 16 employs the unusual command to "give glory to the LORD your God" before the darkness of judgment falls on the people. Perhaps this command functions like that given to Achan in Joshua 7:19. There Achan is brought forward for execution, but before the sentence is carried out, he is asked to "give glory to the LORD." That command to Achan seems to play two roles: (1) a call to tell or admit the truth in public, and (2) an acknowledgment that God's ways and judgments are just. If these two roles lie behind the command to the people in 13:16, then it is not meant as a way to spare the people from the coming judgment; rather, it is a call for them to admit the justice of the judgment about to befall them.

It is possible, however, that the call to "give glory to the LORD" is a way to avert the disaster to come. If so, then Jeremiah's message functions as a call for repentance and change on the part of the people. Jeremiah reports that he will weep over the folly of the people whose pride is such that they are heedless of their dire circumstances.

Verses 18–19 point to a particular source of pride, the king and queen mother. Their crowns will fall from their heads as a sign of the fall of the people. These two royal figures are not specifically named. Jeremiah contains a section elsewhere (chs. 21–22) in which Judean royalty is the object of his judgmental oracles. In that section the monarchs are named. This short section is the only one in Jeremiah in which the role of the queen mother is taken up.

13:20–27. Jerusalem is called to see the foe from the north who comes in judgment. Should she wonder why destruction has come to her, Jeremiah quotes a proverbial saying (v. 23). Just as neither Ethiopians (Africans) nor leopards can change the distinctive color of their skin, so the evil propensity of God's people cannot be removed by their own hand. The evil of Jerusalem is also personified as a prostitute, whose private parts are shamefully exposed.

The concluding question, "How long will you be unclean?" (v. 27), assumes that even though Jerusalem is incapable of righting herself, she could at least recognize her plight and seek the Lord, who alone can heal her failures. The imagery of this section is similar to that of the prophecies against Jerusalem in chapters 2–3.

Bridging Contexts

AUDIENCE. THERE ARE two audiences who initially heard these judgment prophecies: (1) those who heard the oral proclamation of Jeremiah, and (2) the exilic audience to whom the *written* prophecies were directed. We have no clue as to how the symbolic act/ interpretation of 13:1–11 may have been communicated in oral form to Jeremiah's contemporaries. Did he, for example, wear the fouled waistcloth as a sign to the people, offering oral commentary when opportunity presented itself? This is possible and consistent with the enactment of other such messages. Isaiah, for example, gave his son a symbolic name, and when he sought an audience with King Ahaz, he took his son with him (Isa. 7:1–17). The account only makes sense if the name of the child (Shear-Jashub, "a remnant will return") was meant to communicate to King Ahaz. If Jeremiah wore the fouled clothing, we are not told so directly.

This silence suggests that we should begin an interpretation based on the perspective of the reading audience, who hear the account as a way to confirm God's judgment to come *and* as indications of behavior to avoid. All the prophecies in Jeremiah 13 are part of a chorus line of scriptural texts (Old and New Testament) indicating the righteous judgments of the Lord. As such these prophecies invite readers to examine themselves and their communities in light of God's call to holiness and obedience.

Enacted illustrations. For the sequential reader of the book, the enacted parable of the waistcloth is Jeremiah's first example of a symbolic act. He is one of several biblical persons whose acts illustrate concretely their message and even embody the gist of their oral communication. Jeremiah later wears a yoke (chs. 27–28) and purchases property (ch. 32) as symbolic acts; the first indicated judgment to come in the historical process, and the second foreshadowed restoration from exile.

Likewise, Isaiah and Hosea enacted parables. Both named children as embodiments of their message. Ezekiel lay on his side and burned his shorn hair to act out the siege and destruction of Jerusalem (Ezek. 4–5). In the New Testament the priest Zechariah was struck dumb to embody his impertinence before the angelic messenger (Luke 1:5–25). His son John urged the embodiment of a new relationship with God based on repentance by baptizing people in the Jordan River. Jesus' miracles were the embodiment of God's kingdom made manifest; his works of power were signs of his divine Sonship.

From a slightly different angle, Jeremiah's symbolic act illustrates the connection between word and deed. On numerous occasions Jeremiah announced God's judgment. His personal engagement with his message was such that it led him to lamentations and tears. In the symbolic act not only did his soul internalize the message, but his very actions were a physical demonstration to his audience (for those with ears to hear and eyes to see) of his prophecy. There is even a sense in which God's word is incarnate in Jeremiah's actions, so close is the connection between human activity and the portrayal of the divine message.

Clothing metaphors. The waistcloth of 13:1–11 is also part of the larger scriptural appropriation of clothing metaphors to depict the life of God's people. Since clothing was (and often remains) a recognized symbol of identity, the Bible occasionally uses it as a means of instruction. To illustrate his care for the first couple after their act of rebellion, God made them clothing of animal skin (Gen. 3:21). The rich symbolism of the priestly office is seen in the description of Aaron's vestments (Ex. 28). A believer, confident in God's grace, can exult in the "clothing" of salvation and righteousness (Isa. 61:10).

In the New Testament, Jesus declared that worry over clothing can divert attention from God's good gifts, noting that not even the finery of Solomon compares to the lilies of the field as clothed by God. Paul indicated that those baptized into Christ have clothed themselves with the risen Lord (Gal. 3:27). The righteousness of God's saints is symbolized as clean linen garments (Rev. 19:8). Indeed, John sees the risen Christ in finery like that of royalty and the priesthood, including a golden girdle or outer waistband (Rev. 1:13; 3:5; 7:9).

Modern cultures are capable of understanding the symbolism of clothing and acting as a medium of communication (plays, television, movies). The symbolic acts in Jeremiah are similar to a play, a pantomine, or street theater. Indeed, the increasing popularity of skits as part of a contemporary worship experience suggests the ability of role-playing to communicate effectively. A careful reader cannot help but notice how much Jeremiah carries his oral communication with elements of role-play and acting. How else can the change in voices be portrayed? In the modern age, this illustrative activity makes sense. The issue of God's judgment on the disobedience of his people, however, is the more difficult matter for modern Christians (below).

Giving God glory. Among the words of judgment in chapter 13 is the imperative to give God glory (13:16) rather than continue in a self-deceiving pride. As noted above, perhaps this specific word is linked to the wider scriptural injunction to acknowledge the rightness (the justice) of God's judgment. Joshua urged Achan, the soldier who had violated the ban on trophies of battle, "to give glory to the LORD" and to confess what he had done (Josh. 7:19). His confession was an integral part of giving glory to God; in acknowledging his wrong Achan also affirmed the justness of God's standards. In Acts 5 Peter accuses Ananias and Sapphira of lying before God. True, the injunction "to give God the glory" is not quoted there, but the public character of their interrogation was designed to underscore their guilt and the justness of the Lord's standards.

AS OFTEN WITH PROPHETIC JUDGMENTS, contemporary readers may seek instruction either in the announced judgment itself or in the judgment's mirror image—those hoped-for characteristics of faithfulness and obedience. God's announced judgment on the faithlessness of Judah for idolatry (13:10) is a familiar refrain in this book, and any generation of God's people must examine themselves for evidence that they have lost their first love, squandered their inheritance, or spurned the Lord. The same examination is relevant for individuals as well, even though Jeremiah's own critique is corporately based.

The unusual illustration of the waistcloth brings to consideration the claim in 13:11 that God made all of Israel and Judah to be bound to him. The qualification "whole house" is intended to describe all the people in their God-intended unity. Here one meets the mirror image of judgment. God's purpose for Israel and Judah was to be united to him as Lord, "my people for my renown and praise and honor." God's people in the Old Testament may be used as negative examples (i.e., as examples of what not to do), but their fundamental identity resides in their election by God as his people. These two things make them the spiritual ancestors of Christians today. The very oddity of comparison with a bound waistcloth helps drive one to see this glorious identity amidst the failures of that generation.

Finally, perhaps modern Christians should give more consideration to the impact of symbolic acts as part of their discipleship. The president of a North American seminary remarked recently that he had not realized the extent to which his various acts were evaluated for what they might represent with respect to his policies and commitments. After some consideration he concluded that there is justification in seeing a connection between his acts and his commitments. It made him reconsider the way in which his institution took public action, for communication is not just words but deeds.

Is not this true on both an individual and a corporate scale? A church that refuses to move from a changing neighborhood is making a statement as surely as is the church that moves. A Christian who volunteers in the nursery program "speaks" as surely as the teacher of a class. The church that refuses to play the insidious games of nationalism or racism speaks, no matter what it prints on paper.

Jeremiah 14:1–15:9

❧

THIS IS THE word of the LORD to Jeremiah concerning the drought:

2 "Judah mourns,
    her cities languish;
  they wail for the land,
    and a cry goes up from Jerusalem.
3 The nobles send their servants for water;
    they go to the cisterns
    but find no water.
  They return with their jars unfilled;
    dismayed and despairing,
    they cover their heads.
4 The ground is cracked
    because there is no rain in the land;
  the farmers are dismayed
    and cover their heads.
5 Even the doe in the field
    deserts her newborn fawn
    because there is no grass.
6 Wild donkeys stand on the barren heights
    and pant like jackals;
  their eyesight fails
    for lack of pasture."

7 Although our sins testify against us,
    O LORD, do something for the sake of your name.
  For our backsliding is great;
    we have sinned against you.
8 O Hope of Israel,
    its Savior in times of distress,
  why are you like a stranger in the land,
    like a traveler who stays only a night?
9 Why are you like a man taken by surprise,
    like a warrior powerless to save?
  You are among us, O LORD,
    and we bear your name;
    do not forsake us!

[10]This is what the LORD says about this people:

> "They greatly love to wander;
>> they do not restrain their feet.
> So the LORD does not accept them;
>> he will now remember their wickedness
>> and punish them for their sins."

[11]Then the LORD said to me, "Do not pray for the well-being of this people. [12]Although they fast, I will not listen to their cry; though they offer burnt offerings and grain offerings, I will not accept them. Instead, I will destroy them with the sword, famine and plague."

[13]But I said, "Ah, Sovereign LORD, the prophets keep telling them, 'You will not see the sword or suffer famine. Indeed, I will give you lasting peace in this place.'"

[14]Then the LORD said to me, "The prophets are prophesying lies in my name. I have not sent them or appointed them or spoken to them. They are prophesying to you false visions, divinations, idolatries and the delusions of their own minds. [15]Therefore, this is what the LORD says about the prophets who are prophesying in my name: I did not send them, yet they are saying, 'No sword or famine will touch this land.' Those same prophets will perish by sword and famine. [16]And the people they are prophesying to will be thrown out into the streets of Jerusalem because of the famine and sword. There will be no one to bury them or their wives, their sons or their daughters. I will pour out on them the calamity they deserve.

[14:17]"Speak this word to them:

> "'Let my eyes overflow with tears
>> night and day without ceasing;
> for my virgin daughter—my people—
>> has suffered a grievous wound,
>> a crushing blow.
> [18]If I go into the country,
>> I see those slain by the sword;
> if I go into the city,
>> I see the ravages of famine.
> Both prophet and priest
>> have gone to a land they know not.'"

[19]Have you rejected Judah completely?
> Do you despise Zion?

Why have you afflicted us
    so that we cannot be healed?
We hoped for peace
    but no good has come,
for a time of healing
    but there is only terror.
20 O LORD, we acknowledge our wickedness
    and the guilt of our fathers;
    we have indeed sinned against you.
21 For the sake of your name do not despise us;
    do not dishonor your glorious throne.
Remember your covenant with us
    and do not break it.
22 Do any of the worthless idols of the nations bring rain?
    Do the skies themselves send down showers?
No, it is you, O LORD our God.
    Therefore our hope is in you,
    for you are the one who does all this.

15:1 Then the LORD said to me: "Even if Moses and Samuel were to stand before me, my heart would not go out to this people. Send them away from my presence! Let them go! 2 And if they ask you, 'Where shall we go?' tell them, 'This is what the LORD says:

    "'Those destined for death, to death;
    those for the sword, to the sword;
    those for starvation, to starvation;
    those for captivity, to captivity.'

3 "I will send four kinds of destroyers against them," declares the LORD, "the sword to kill and the dogs to drag away and the birds of the air and the beasts of the earth to devour and destroy. 4 I will make them abhorrent to all the kingdoms of the earth because of what Manasseh son of Hezekiah king of Judah did in Jerusalem.

5 "Who will have pity on you, O Jerusalem?
    Who will mourn for you?
    Who will stop to ask how you are?
6 You have rejected me," declares the LORD.
    "You keep on backsliding.
So I will lay hands on you and destroy you;
    I can no longer show compassion.

> ⁷ will winnow them with a winnowing fork
>> at the city gates of the land.
> I will bring bereavement and destruction on my people,
>> for they have not changed their ways.
> ⁸ I will make their widows more numerous
>> than the sand of the sea.
> At midday I will bring a destroyer
>> against the mothers of their young men;
> suddenly I will bring down on them
>> anguish and terror.
> ⁹ The mother of seven will grow faint
>> and breathe her last.
> Her sun will set while it is still day;
>> she will be disgraced and humiliated.
> I will put the survivors to the sword
>> before their enemies,"
>
> declares the LORD.

CHAPTER 14 (and perhaps the two chapters that follow) is occasioned by the threatening circumstances of drought.[1] As is typical in the first half of Jeremiah, we have no idea when the prophet utters these prophecies since no king is mentioned, though the reference to a fast in 14:12 may hint at the historical setting. The only other reference to fasting in Jeremiah is in 36:6, 9, which is set during the reign of Jehoiakim—more specifically, the ninth month of the fifth year of his reign (Nov./Dec., 604 B.C.).[2] At this time Nebuchadnezzar's army was campaigning in the region. This threat may be in the background, though the primary concern of chapter 14 is that of drought. If the context is indeed November or December and the fall rains have not yet come, a fast would be appropriate. In the Mediterranean climate there is no rain during the summer months. But without rain at some point in the fall, drought conditions become severe.

The different speaking voices in 14:1—15:9 comprise a pattern of oracle from the prophet, followed by words from the people. The prophet, speaking for God, has the first and last word:

---

1. The Hebrew text of 14:1 actually reads "droughts," an odd term that some commentators have wanted to vocalize differently. In context, however, the basic meaning is clear: There has been no rain (14:3–4).

2. See comments on ch. 36 for additional discussion of the date and context given in 36:9. The Greek version (LXX) reads "eighth year" instead of "fifth year."

A. 14:2–6: The prophet speaks of Judah's mourning.

B. 14:7–9: The people as a whole confess sin and offer a petition.

C. 14:10–16: The Lord speaks to Jeremiah about judgment on the people and other prophets.

D. 14:17–18: At God's command, Jeremiah delivers a lament over the fate of the people.

E. 14:19–22: The people as a whole confess sin and offer a petition again.

F. 15:1–9: The Lord speaks to Jeremiah about judgment on the people.

It is difficult to know how one should read the two corporate confessions/petitions of the people (14:7–9, 19–22). Nothing appears wrong with the sentiments expressed in them, but after both comes language of divine judgment. These units include confession of sin (14:7, 20). We have at least two options in seeking to make sense of this section in the context of Jeremiah's ministry. (1) The corporate confessions/petitions of the people, which offer the appropriate words of confession and repentance, are actually insincere. This view accords with the aims of the book as a whole, since one of its primary functions is to explain the culpability of the people in facing defeat and exile. (2) These confessions/petitions are confessions that Jeremiah is offering to the people, if only they would take the confessional content to heart.

14:2–6. Judah and Jerusalem mourn over the devastating effects of a drought. Nothing in these verses links the drought with divine judgment; instead, they rehearse the pitiful circumstances of the people and animals in a common quest for water.

14:7–9. Only here do we see a link between the terrible circumstances of the people and their sinfulness before God. Jeremiah implores God to act because his name is great and because his people bear that name. The people confess that their "backsliding is great,"[3] seemingly a frank acknowledgment of sin against God. In confessional terms God is described as Israel's Hope (*miqweh*) and Savior (*mošia*^c) in troubled times (v. 8). Verse 9 reflects the tradition of God as a valiant warrior who defends and delivers his people (cf. Ex. 15:3).

Taken as a whole, this section has parallels with the Psalter and other biblical prayers. As noted above, either the people are guilty of rank insincerity in praying this way, or this prayer is Jeremiah's advice to them on how to pray appropriately in the context of a drought used in judgment against them.

14:10–16. This mostly prose section records the "give and take" between God and the prophet. Verse 10 contains a poetic oracle that God does not

---

3. The word translated as "backsliding" is *mᵉšubot*. It is a plural term. In singular form it is the same word used to describe "faithless" Israel in 3:6–13.

accept the people. He will remember their wickedness and punish them. Jeremiah 31:34 is essentially a reversal of this sentiment. When God forgives, he "forgets."

In verses 11 and 14 come autobiographical introductions: "Then the LORD said to me." As in other occasions, Jeremiah is bidden not to pray for the people (e.g., 7:16). Prophets who have led the people astray receive sustained attention. God denies having appointed them or sending them. They are obviously making Jeremiah's life more difficult by speaking in the Lord's name and contradicting his own prophecies of judgment.

14:17−18. These two verses offer an example of lament in which it is difficult to know who is speaking, Jeremiah or God. Jeremiah, of course, is commanded to speak these words to the people, but in doing so he represents God. "My virgin daughter—my people" (NIV) reflects more naturally on God as speaker than the prophet. The familiar metaphor of daughter applies to Jerusalem or the people as members of God's household.

14:19−22. The second corporate confession/petition of the people asks plaintively if God has completely rejected Judah and Zion. The sad comment, "We hoped for peace," is the prayer of all right-thinking people. With the confession of sin also comes the refrain, "for the sake of your name do not despise us" (cf. 14:7, 9), and a plea for God to remember his covenant with them and not to annul it.

15:1−9. As with the first corporate confession/petition in 14:7−9, this second one is also followed by an emphatic rejection of the people. If possible, this second rejection is even stronger than the one in 14:10−16. The text indicates the frightfulness of God's judgment in more than one way.

The reference to Moses and Samuel as mediators and intercessors (15:1) evokes memory of past events in Israel's history. When God was angry with Israel in the desert, Moses interposed himself between God and the sinful community (Ex. 32:30−35; 34:1−27); moreover, Moses was a prophet who knew God "face to face" (Ex. 33:11; Num. 12:8; Deut. 34:10), mediating God's laws to his people and guiding two generations of them toward the Promised Land.

In the period before monarchy, when the word of God was rare in the land (1 Sam. 3:1), God raised up Samuel to be prophet, priest, and judge to Israel. It was Samuel who reorganized Israel after the debacle of defeat by the Philistines at Aphek and the subsequent loss of the ark of the covenant (chs. 4−6). The people entreated Samuel to cry out to the Lord on their behalf, and eventually the Philistine threat was subdued (7:8−17). Even after the appointment of a king, the people entreated Samuel to pray for them to the Lord (12:19−25; cf. 12:7). In the work of Moses and Samuel, one finds models of intercessory prayers and accounts of the preservation of the people in spite of the divine judgment that had fallen on them.

For God to dismiss the work of Moses and Samuel as efficacious in the present moment of Judah's sin is, in effect, to say that no prophetic mediator will be accepted and that judgment cannot be averted. Judgment came on Israel during the prophetic ministries of these two leaders, but total destruction had been averted through their mediation. Now, however, it will be different. Judgment to come is announced and described graphically in verse 2. Captivity is explicitly mentioned, as are four kinds of affliction. Jeremiah cites the lingering effects of Manasseh as reasons for the inevitability of judgment. This accusation has parallels in 2 Kings 21:1–18; 23:26; 24:3–4, where the judgment to come on Judah and Jerusalem in Jeremiah's day derives from the overflowing wickedness of Manasseh's reign.[4]

JUDGMENT THROUGH DROUGHT. The common theme of Judah and Jerusalem's plight before God is given the specific coloring of the devastation of drought. Along with it will come sword, famine, and pestilence (14:12). Apart from the emphasis on the drought, the reader encounters a familiar aspect of the book of Jeremiah.

During Jeremiah's time, lack of water was a persistent experience. The weather pattern in the eastern Mediterranean is such that from late spring through mid-fall, there is no rain. Thus, the later fall and winter rains are necessary for the spring planting. Not only was drought a crippling phenomenon, it was a graphic reminder of how dependent life is on forces outside of human control. Even today, water rights and distribution are major issues in the Middle East. One of the sorest points in the peace agreement between Israel and Jordan has been the distribution of water from the Jordan River to the two countries. Israel is seeking agreements with Turkey for fresh water supplies.

In 2:13 the prophet proclaimed that Judah's sin was forsaking God (who is living water) in the vain effort to preserve water in broken cisterns (other gods). In chapter 14 the reality of drought is used to chasten and judge Judah. The failure of Judah's other prophets to interpret God's judgment is indicated in 2:8, a claim also elaborated in chapter 14.

Amos, one of Jeremiah's predecessors in the prophetic office, announced drought and famine as God's judgments on Israel (Amos 4:6–13). God's word through the prophet's refrain in 4:8–11, "yet you have not returned to me,"

---

4. The reign of the wicked Manasseh is also narrated in 2 Chron. 33:1–20. As with the account in Kings, the sins of Manasseh are described; in addition, however, his eventual repentance is also noted (33:12–16). The references in 2 Kings and Jeremiah are concerned with the continuing influence of Manasseh's apostasy on a subsequent generation.

is similar to God's word to Jeremiah that he will not respond to Judah's fast or sacrifices because they have not returned wholeheartedly to him. Amos also spoke forebodingly about the ultimate famine and thirst—the lack of a life-giving word from God (8:11–14). This was a word of judgment, so that when at last people would recognize their needs and seek to assuage them, it would be too late. Such is the intention also behind Jeremiah's words in Jeremiah 14.

In the New Testament John the seer sees God's judgments poured out on the land as the seals of the prophetic scroll are broken (Rev. 6). These judgments are depicted as different horsemen, and among them are the sword, famine, and pestilence. John's vision is very much in the mode of Old Testament prophecy, but it was also intended to instruct the church so that it could see behind the temporal judgments the hand of God moving toward an even larger deliverance. Likewise, Jeremiah's contemporaries are to see God's hand moving in judgment, but beyond judgment Jeremiah's readers should recognize that God moves toward deliverance.

God and the weather. The last line of chapter 14 ends the lament with the confession that the people will "hope . . . in" (or "wait for") God, who has done all these things. This confession is both problematic and a key link between Jeremiah's world and modernity. It is problematic because many people recoil from the belief that God causes things like droughts and famines. Weather forecasters daily explain atmospheric conditions through various media, and the connection between God and weather conditions is not clear for many people.

Perhaps it is best to distinguish between the claims of a particular passage and the continuing interplay of forces in seasonal change. Jeremiah's claim is *not* that God sends all droughts to chastise and judge people. Instead, his claim is more particular: God used the specific drought described in chapter 14 as a means to address and chastise his people. It is as perilous to universalize from the specifics of a particular text as it is to ignore the possibility that a moral and sovereign God makes use of climactic forces. Jeremiah 14 is essentially a claim that God so used the circumstances of the prophet's day to instruct Judah.

It is the same issue with the divine claim in 14:11 that Jeremiah should no longer pray for the people because God will not listen. This is not a universal affirmation about how God treats the prayers of his prophets or his people; rather, 14:11 is a specific instruction about God's intentions in bringing Judah to judgment. God's disposition toward prayer and his employment of drought are particular approaches in his approach to Judah. God had most certainly listened to the prayers of Moses and Samuel—they were renowned as intercessors. Modern readers are confronted with the claim that this is God's prerogative and that it will ultimately serve his broader purpose of (re)forming a people for himself.[5]

Admittedly, some people will recoil in horror and deny that God will ever refuse to hear the prayer of Judah or send drought on its land. Such a denial, however, is different from the error of universalizing; it is the error of assuming that they know better than God how to achieve his purposes within history. Does the thought that God is indifferent about climactic conditions provide more comfort? It is not likely that those who refuse God the avenue of drought will allow God the freedom to judge at all. It would be no different with a cross and the death of a righteous man. Why, God forbid such a thing!

THE TRUE JUDGE. The confessions/petitions of chapter 14 continue to have significance for God's people because they remind us that God alone is the true Judge of our deeds and the true Savior of our lives (14:8). Modern people act wisely when they acknowledge that they are neither masters of their destiny nor spiritually self-sufficient. This is a fundamental point for modernity: How can the chastening hand of God be recognized? How might God grasp the attention of people and seek to remove the intellectual and emotional barriers to his approach set up by the modern mindset?

Indeed, the confessions/petitions are uncomfortable reminders that people are ultimately unable to avoid an encounter with the living God. Nevertheless, the One who evoked tears in the prophet is the ultimate Hope of Israel, and it is the larger design of Jeremiah's book (as it is the larger design of God Almighty) to move the people in the direction of praise and good works.

In the first half of 1996 the author experienced a prolonged drought in central Texas. It was a humbling experience to stand on the bank of the Pedernales River that typically has flowing water and excited people engaged in recreational activities to see only a dry and cracked stream bed. It was frightening to watch things wilt, animals die, and people lose their vitality because of the scarcity of water. It was a powerful illustration of the connectedness of corporate existence. The lack of water was the impetus to a variety of

---

5. Calvin, in preaching on Jeremiah 14, said: "It is not that God does not hear the prayers of His people, for He always accepts them, but most often He does not fulfill them in the way they have requested. Their prayers are answered, but not according to their desires"; quoted from *Sermons on Jeremiah by Jean Calvin*, trans. Blair Reynolds (Lewiston, N.Y.: Edwin Mellen, 1990), 1.

changes in central Texas, both physical and emotional. It is true that people will change their lifestyle and assumptions about reality when circumstances force it! They will usually do so grudgingly, however, and more often than not they will find someone or something else responsible for the debilitating circumstances. Is this dynamic a clue to the harsh reception of the corporate confessions/petitions in 14:7−9, 19−22?

Many prayers for rain are heard frequently during months of drought. Arid conditions are an effective reminder of how easily life can get out of balance and how circumstances of drought can only be ameliorated from above. Nevertheless, when rain finally comes (as it did in August 1996), drought conditions are quickly forgotten. Jeremiah 14 is a salutary reminder of the true source of life and of the One who calls a people into existence for his glory and praise.

Jeremiah 15:10–21

¹⁰ Alas, my mother, that you gave me birth,
    a man with whom the whole land strives and contends!
I have neither lent nor borrowed,
    yet everyone curses me.

¹¹ The LORD said,

"Surely I will deliver you for a good purpose;
    surely I will make your enemies plead with you
    in times of disaster and times of distress.

¹² "Can a man break iron—
    iron from the north—or bronze?
¹³ Your wealth and your treasures
    I will give as plunder, without charge,
because of all your sins
    throughout your country.
¹⁴ I will enslave you to your enemies
    in a land you do not know,
for my anger will kindle a fire
    that will burn against you."

¹⁵ You understand, O LORD;
    remember me and care for me.
    Avenge me on my persecutors.
You are long-suffering—do not take me away;
    think of how I suffer reproach for your sake.
¹⁶ When your words came, I ate them;
    they were my joy and my heart's delight,
for I bear your name,
    O LORD God Almighty.
¹⁷ I never sat in the company of revelers,
    never made merry with them;
I sat alone because your hand was on me
    and you had filled me with indignation.
¹⁸ Why is my pain unending
    and my wound grievous and incurable?
Will you be to me like a deceptive brook,
    like a spring that fails?

¹⁹Therefore this is what the LORD says:

"If you repent, I will restore you
    that you may serve me;
if you utter worthy, not worthless, words,
    you will be my spokesman.
Let this people turn to you,
    but you must not turn to them.
²⁰I will make you a wall to this people,
    a fortified wall of bronze;
they will fight against you
    but will not overcome you,
for I am with you
    to rescue and save you,"

                                declares the LORD.

²¹"I will save you from the hands of the wicked
    and redeem you from the grasp of the cruel."

JEREMIAH 15:10–18 contain a lament/complaint on the part of the prophet with reference to divine judgment in verses 12-14, while verses 19–21 are a reply from God. In literary context this material follows upon the oracles presented in 14:1–15:9, where the people offered two corporate confessions/petitions (14:7–9, 19–22) and Jeremiah responded with a lament on behalf of God (14:17–18). One way to interpret the bitter lament/complaint in 15:10–18, therefore, is to see it as a culminating reaction to the people's failures, the impact of the drought, and the pressure on Jeremiah from prophets who were offering oracles of peace to a desperate nation—all of which are depicted in 14:1–15:9.

This section is actually structured around a give-and-take conversation between prophet and God, which unfolds as follows:

    A. 15:10: Jeremiah laments the day of his birth and the curses of people that are now directed at him.
    B. 15:11: God replies that he will deliver Jeremiah for a good purpose.
    C. 15:12–14: God pronounces judgment on the people.
    D. 15:15–18: Jeremiah expresses his frustrations to God.
    E. 15:19–21: God replies to Jeremiah.

There are difficult textual and syntactical issues involved in the translation of this section, particularly with verse 12, a verse that has a significant role in the way the lament/complaint is interpreted.[1] Parts A and B, and then parts D and E, show the pattern of prophetic lament/complaint followed by divine reply. The middle portion (15:12–14), however, both interrupts the pattern and appears addressed to Judah. Perhaps the best option is to interpret verses 12–14 as a word from the Lord pronouncing judgment on Judah.

15:10. In this verse Jeremiah laments his birth (cf. also 20:14–18, as well as the first lament of Job in Job 3:1–26).[2] This provides another, somewhat broader context in which to hear the language of personal woe. Jeremiah is similar to Job. His contemporaries curse him, and the pain of his ostracism has made even God seem deceitful and unreliable to him.

In lamenting the day of his birth, Jeremiah offers an evaluation of his life and prophetic ministry. He feels as if there is no purpose for him to continue to live. The parallel with the lament of Job suggests that we are dealing with a recognized literary motif. It is tantamount to the conclusion of the Teacher in Ecclesiastes that it would be better not to have been born (Eccl. 4:1–3). Such language should be taken seriously as an indication of despair, though not literally as the announcement of suicide. Jeremiah describes the "curses" that have come to him, even though he has neither lent nor borrowed. The troubles that come from either activity are legendary. Again, Jeremiah employs a traditional motif to make his point (cf. Job 6:22; Ps. 15:5).

15:11. God replies that he will deliver Jeremiah for a "good purpose" and will bring his enemies to a place where they will need to plead with him. This last comment perhaps leads to the further pronouncement of judgment on Judah in verses 12–14.

15:12–14. As noted above, the text of verse 12 and the interpretation of these three verses is difficult. The best overall option is to see all three verses as a judgment speech on Judah. They repeat material found in 17:3–4, where the context is clearly judgment on the people.

15:15–18. Jeremiah turns once again to the Lord. As part of his lament/complaint he notes that his enemies are also God's enemies. Jeremiah suffers his reproach because he represents God's word to the people. In verse 16 he describes his encountering of God's word with the surprising claim that he "ate" them and they became his joy. This may refer to his willing acceptance of God's previous revelation to him (cf. 1:9). Possibly verse 16 refers to a literal "finding" of a text, for the verb that the NIV translates as

---

1. One may consult Holladay, *Jeremiah*, 1:447–55, for some of the lexical and interpretational difficulties. The NIV interprets verses 12–14 as a continuation of the Lord's first reply to Jeremiah, which begins in 15:11.

2. See comments on Jeremiah's laments in 11:18–12:17. Much of the lament in Job 3:1–26 concerns the claim that it would have been better for Job not to have been born.

"came" literally means to be found.[3] Whether this means that Jeremiah was instructed by a document like the book of the covenant discovered during Josiah's reign or another preserved text (Hosea?) cannot be known. The emphasis falls on the prophet's joy at that time as opposed to the despair and rejection he now encounters.

Jeremiah confesses that it is God's hand that he feels on him, that God is the source of the indignation he experiences. As his emotions boil over, the prophet asks God why his (Jeremiah's) pain is unending and why he (God) has become like failing water.

15:19–21. God's reply is not to deal with the particulars of Jeremiah's anger but to remind him that the path of the faithful and obedient prophet is still open to him. One should not conclude that Jeremiah has failed or that God has failed the prophet, but rather that God has called him to prophesy in this historical hour of judgment. Jeremiah has received the reward typical for a prophet who announces judgment (i.e., persecution; cf. Matt. 5:10–11).

Verse 19 has two plays on the verb "turn/return" (*šub*).[4] If Jeremiah will "repent" (i.e., change his tune and direction), then God will "restore" him. These are the NIV renderings of *šub* in both cases. Moreover, using the same verb, God states that the people should "turn" to Jeremiah, but that Jeremiah should not "turn" to them. Verses 20–21 are reminiscent of Jeremiah's initial "call" in 1:18–19. He still has the same task ahead of him and the same assurance that God is with him.

Bridging Contexts

JEREMIAH'S LAMENTATION IN 15:10, 15–18 has many echoes in Scripture, including several places elsewhere in Jeremiah. Being rejected by one's contemporaries is deeply painful, and the human toll it takes is evident in the prophet's candid language. The joining of this lament with the announcement of judgment in 15:1–9 shows the link between the people's rejection of God (15:6) and their rejection of God's prophet (15:16–17). These rejections are two sides of the same coin.

Jeremiah's plea for judgment on his accusers and tormentors is a prayer for justice. If God intends to judge his people for their failures, then Jeremiah prays for a just verdict on those who slander God through attacking his prophet. Jeremiah's reproach results from his role as one called by God's

---

3. There are several other places in the Old Testament where a similar concept is expressed, using the Niphal (passive) form of the verb *maṣaʾ* (2 Kings 22:13; 23:2; 2 Chron. 34:21, 30), all of which refer to the finding of the book of the covenant during the reign of King Josiah. Ezekiel is asked to eat a scroll as part of his prophetic call (2:9–3:15).

4. See comments on this verb in ch. 3.

name and one who delights in God's Word (cf. Ezek. 3:3). Suffering comes to one who stands for God's Word in evil times.

God does not reply directly to the prayer for judgment on the oppressors; instead, he reminds Jeremiah that his restoration from humiliating circumstances is simply to return to his role as mouthpiece for the Lord.[5] There is no warrant in the prophet's lament to carry out personal retribution. The jarring language of the lament is the humanness of the prophet stretched almost to the breaking point. It is a reminder that ministry is not about success or happiness but about faithfulness. Even in his despair Jeremiah's lament is evidence that he still "fought the good fight" (1 Tim. 6:12).

ACCOUNTABILITY. Instruction for God's people today comes in various ways from these somber verses. It is necessary, first of all, to face the scriptural claim that God holds his covenant people (and ultimately all people) accountable for their actions. This is as true in the case of individuals as it is in corporate terms. Jeremiah 15:1–9 contained words of judgment in historical terms (e.g., the sword, captivity) for corporate failure. This is the context in which to read the lament of 15:10–21. They should be a lesson for any subsequent generation of God's people. A secular historian might explain Judah's demise in terms of ancient Near Eastern power politics and tragic miscalculations; the eyes of faith discern divine chastisement and discipline in the tragic events of the Babylonian assault and the Exile.

Should believers today ask about trends in the life of the church today that bode ill for the future? Are there signs even now that God has given (will soon give?) individuals or communities over to the folly of their actions? Does this include the maligning of persons who carry out their discipleship in controversial ways?

The references to Moses and Samuel in 15:1–9 served as a reminder of the great privilege of intercessory prayer, even if their prayers would not have helped the people of Jeremiah's day. Mention of these two great prophets is of no value were it not for the claim that they had, in fact, led God's people through tumultuous times and that they were valiant in prayer on behalf of the people. We should listen to Jeremiah's own prayers about himself in light of their witness. In a time of despair the prophet is inclined to think his life is a total failure, and he sees little evidence that God is with him supportively. Yet God hears all his frustration and replies.

---

5. In 15:19 Jeremiah is told literally that he will become as God's mouth.

The prophet's pain. Ministry can be painful and costly. Jeremiah's lament shows one of God's chosen vessels suffering because of his service to God. His life is an Old Testament form of Jesus' call to discipleship: Take up your cross and follow me. Even when stretched seemingly to the breaking point, God reminds Jeremiah of his call to prophetic ministry. For the prophet there is no alternative but to turn (return) once again to the Lord, who called him and promised him protection.

Jeremiah's lament is an understandably human response to mistreatment. Likely it was therapeutic for him to cry out. God does not answer directly his plea for vengeance, at least on Jeremiah's own scale of justice (15:15), any more than God will answer our own pleas for judgment according to our scale of judgment. Judgment must be left to him (Rom. 12:17–21). Jeremiah can at least understand that much; that is why he prays for God to vanquish the oppressors.

Christians can see in Jeremiah a prophetic mediator whose office points forward to a suffering Savior, the author and perfecter of our faith, who for the joy set before him endured the cross, scorning its shame (Heb. 12:2). Christ's prayers included intercession even for the oppressor, although he too experienced the mysterious absence of God as he poured out his life on the cross. Jeremiah's own prayer for vindication and judgment on the oppressor is part of his plea to God that he not violate his promise of protection to him. It takes seriously God's prerogative to deal sovereignly with evil; yet his prayer can be reframed in light of Jesus' own example of intercessory prayer.

Perhaps one of the ways to grasp the significance of Jeremiah's lament(s) for modern appropriation in North America is to take seriously the tone. His laments are not like a majestic hymn of praise from the Psalter or the enthusiastic praise music so popular in segments of the church today. They have more of a point of contact with the "blues music" spawned in the African American culture. The blues have been an important contributor to both traditional soul music and vibrant gospel singing in African American churches. With the blues comes an articulate voice for the range of human experience, particularly the down times. A classic blues composition is "The Thrill Is Gone," by the legendary B. B. King. For over thirty years that song has been a catalyst for those who have sought a voice to express their despair or grief. The tone of the song is a mournful one, and the words lament a relationship gone wrong.

Singing the blues or hearing them sung is similar to pouring out one's heart in prayer to God. That is why there is such a strong connection between blues and gospel music. King himself has stated that he wants to record a gospel album before he retires because he is convinced that the blues lead one to gospel. The same can be said for a lament like Jeremiah's. He faces his doubts and tormentors, gives voice to unease and anger, and gives all of it to God.

Adult Sunday school classes usually discuss the Lord's Prayer as a standard model for Christian prayer. One of its petitions is that God will deliver the disciple from evil. There are times in which following the claims of the gospel and practicing one's faith will lead directly into encounters with evil. One of the marvelous gifts of Jeremiah's book is the humanness of his prayers when wearied and depressed by the struggle with rejection and persecution. Zeal for the path of discipleship (in the case of Jeremiah, zeal to carry out his prophetic commission) is no guarantee of smooth sailing in life. God will hear the prayers of his disciples—unlike those prayers from the dark hour of Judah's judgment—just as God heard Jeremiah's cries.

Jeremiah 16:1–21

THEN THE WORD of the LORD came to me: ²"You must not marry and have sons or daughters in this place." ³For this is what the LORD says about the sons and daughters born in this land and about the women who are their mothers and the men who are their fathers: ⁴"They will die of deadly diseases. They will not be mourned or buried but will be like refuse lying on the ground. They will perish by sword and famine, and their dead bodies will become food for the birds of the air and the beasts of the earth."

⁵For this is what the LORD says: "Do not enter a house where there is a funeral meal; do not go to mourn or show sympathy, because I have withdrawn my blessing, my love and my pity from this people," declares the LORD . ⁶"Both high and low will die in this land. They will not be buried or mourned, and no one will cut himself or shave his head for them. ⁷No one will offer food to comfort those who mourn for the dead—not even for a father or a mother—nor will anyone give them a drink to console them.

⁸"And do not enter a house where there is feasting and sit down to eat and drink. ⁹For this is what the LORD Almighty, the God of Israel, says: Before your eyes and in your days I will bring an end to the sounds of joy and gladness and to the voices of bride and bridegroom in this place.

¹⁰"When you tell these people all this and they ask you, 'Why has the LORD decreed such a great disaster against us? What wrong have we done? What sin have we committed against the LORD our God?' ¹¹then say to them, 'It is because your fathers forsook me,' declares the LORD, 'and followed other gods and served and worshiped them. They forsook me and did not keep my law. ¹²But you have behaved more wickedly than your fathers. See how each of you is following the stubbornness of his evil heart instead of obeying me. ¹³So I will throw you out of this land into a land neither you nor your fathers have known, and there you will serve other gods day and night, for I will show you no favor.'

¹⁴"However, the days are coming," declares the LORD, "when men will no longer say, 'As surely as the LORD lives, who brought the Israelites up out of Egypt,' ¹⁵but they will

say, 'As surely as the LORD lives, who brought the Israelites up out of the land of the north and out of all the countries where he had banished them.' For I will restore them to the land I gave their forefathers.

¹⁶"But now I will send for many fishermen," declares the LORD, "and they will catch them. After that I will send for many hunters, and they will hunt them down on every mountain and hill and from the crevices of the rocks. ¹⁷My eyes are on all their ways; they are not hidden from me, nor is their sin concealed from my eyes. ¹⁸I will repay them double for their wickedness and their sin, because they have defiled my land with the lifeless forms of their vile images and have filled my inheritance with their detestable idols."

¹⁹O LORD, my strength and my fortress,
   my refuge in time of distress,
to you the nations will come
   from the ends of the earth and say,
"Our fathers possessed nothing but false gods,
   worthless idols that did them no good.
²⁰Do men make their own gods?
   Yes, but they are not gods!"
²¹"Therefore I will teach them—
   this time I will teach them
   my power and might.
Then they will know
   that my name is the LORD.

THIS CHAPTER RANGES widely over the themes of sin, judgment, and restoration. Jeremiah's own life is to be a prophetic witness to the historical judgment soon to strike the land. As is common in the first half of the book, no regnal dates are provided by which one can set these instructions in a more particular context of the prophet's life.

16:1–9. God commands Jeremiah not to marry or have children (v. 2), since judgment is coming soon and many parents and children in Judah will die. There are, perhaps, at least two reasons for including this command as part of the book. (1) In a society where marriages were arranged between families, celibacy was comparatively rare. Thus, Jeremiah's celibacy might surface as a "hot-button" issue for his detractors to seize upon. They can portray him as crazed and out of touch with reality. But Jeremiah's celibacy is not a denial of the goodness of marriage or even the voicing of his own preferences in the matter. For all we know, he may well have desired a wife and children. Yet his desires, like much about his personal circumstances, recede behind the presentation of his prophetic work.

(2) Since destruction is imminent, this is no time for marriage (vv. 3–5). His celibacy is part of his embodiment of the message he proclaims; it is a symbolic act as surely as was Hosea's marriage of a prostitute (Hos. 1–3) or Ezekiel's refusal to mourn publicly the death of his wife (Ezek. 24:15–27). Note Paul's similar statement in 1 Corinthians 7:25–35.

Jeremiah is not to enter a house for feasting or celebration either (16:8–9), for the joy of bride and groom will also be silenced in the coming devastation. Here again he bears the mark of his ministry. Perhaps the lament of 15:17–18 reflects the personal cost to the prophet of his "sitting alone."

16:10–13. This text presupposes that Jeremiah passes on the substance of the Lord's messages to him about constricting his social activities. Judgment is at hand. "Why such judgment?" the people ask. The answer is the familiar (to readers of the book) and crushing reply that both ancestors and the current generation have forsaken the Lord, been disobedient to his instruction, and served other deities. The current generation is particularly recalcitrant and motivated by an evil heart (cf. 17:1, 9). The punishment for "defiling" (v. 18) God's land is to be cast from the land and humiliated in exile by worshiping other deities.[1] Crime and punishment in this case are linked like sowing and reaping.

16:14–15. These verses announce an abrupt change through the rhetorical formula, "The days are coming." God announces that the judgment of the Exile will be matched by the saving exodus from foreign territory and back to the Promised Land. Here succinctly is the same wondrous claim as given in Isaiah 40–55. These two verses predict the formation of a new proverbial saying about God: He "who brought the Israelites up out of Egypt" will bring back the banished from their exile in the north (cf. Jer. 23:7–8).

16:16–18. These verses are difficult to interpret in context. Verse 18 makes it clear that God is speaking about bringing judgment upon the failures of Judah, so that we see a return to the language of historical judgment. The announcement of fishing and hunting for offenders in foreign lands, however, is obscure. Perhaps they are a reply to the sarcasm of people who say that in exile God will not see and judge them for their sins. Certainly Jeremiah affirms that God is not limited by geography or spatial distance in bringing to pass what he desires.

16:19–21. The chapter concludes with the voice of one who prays on behalf of himself and his sinful people. Contextually this must be Jeremiah,

---

1. One should compare Deut. 4:25–31, which also assumes that the worship of other gods in exile is a judgment that comes on Israel as a result of similar activity in the Promised Land.

for the concluding verse makes it clear that God is behind the sentiments expressed and that he intends to teach his people a lesson about his power. Along with the confession of the people's sinfulness is an affirmation that "the nations will come" to God. God is the prophet's refuge and strength—characteristics that separate him from the folly of idols. This in turn leads to the declaration that God has acted in history in order that people may know that his name is Yahweh (cf. Ex. 6:3).

PATTERN. Jeremiah 16 contains the classical pattern of this book: God announces judgment on Jeremiah's contemporaries as his righteous response to Judah's spiritual corruption; the future, however, contains the promise of redemption from the land of exile, where Judeans surviving the Babylonian onslaught will be taken. For subsequent generations these words of judgment become words of instruction on what to avoid. The prophecy about redemption provides hope for Judeans in exile (one of the first groups to read/hear parts of the written collection of Jeremiah's prophecies). For generations of God's people after the Babylonian exile, the "second exodus" of the people from Babylonian captivity was testimony to the faithfulness and forgiveness of God. It would indeed become proverbial, as 16:14–15 indicate.

In 16:18 there is a connection with the proclamation of the prophet in Isaiah 40:1–2. The vocabulary is different but the content is similar: The Exile is a complete punishment for the sinfulness of Judah and Jerusalem, a double payment for her failure to obey. The prayer of 16:19–20 draws on the spiritual resources now preserved in the book of Psalms. God the Judge is also a Fortress and Protection to his people, who have learned the folly of idolatry and who find security in the Lord, their Redeemer.

Marriage. Marriage was a mark of adulthood in ancient Israel, and families routinely arranged the marriages of their sons and daughters. The Old Testament provides no evidence of celibacy as an institution of society, although Jesus validates it as a part of discipleship (Matt. 19:10–12). Jeremiah's celibacy is wrapped up in his prophetic office and his call to embody his message. To hear that word in a modern context could mean foregoing marriage for the sake of ministry (as have priests and orders in the Catholic tradition and some missionaries in the Protestant tradition) or giving up something else as a sign of Christian faith. This can be taken on an individual level (as is required for marriage!) or on a corporate level, when a body of Christians "gives up" something for the sake of its ministry and witness.

God's will. Verse 21 emphasizes God's will to make his name known. Probably the claim is not for simple cognition, as if neither Judah nor neighboring people had previously known that God had a personal name (YHWH, usually pronounced Yahweh).[2] The personal name Yahweh was first emphasized in the saving events of the Exodus (Ex. 3:1–15; 6:1–3)—events that revealed God's commitment to his promises and his people in ways that amazed both Israelite and Egyptian. In the proclamation of Judah's demise and the bold announcement that there is redemption beyond demise, readers encounter the claim that God's name indicates his identity as God of the future and that the Lord's self-manifestation in historical events is for his honor and glory.

Typology. These verses set up a typology between ancient Israel and the church, based on their respective callings as God's people. More particularly, the expectation about the future provides a bridging mechanism for subsequent generations who find themselves in an analogous situation to the Judean remnants of Jeremiah's day. In light of Christ's first advent, Christians look in faith to a future revelation of God's glory. The companionship that God provides through the Holy Spirit and the life of the church is an interim period, like that of saints in the Old Testament who lived in eschatological hope.

TRUE KNOWLEDGE OF GOD. Interpreters can take 16:21 and find in it an angle of vision that unites the chapter. God desires to make himself known, which gives shape ultimately both to world history and the life story of an individual Christian. As noted elsewhere, knowledge of God is not mere intellectual comprehension or cognition—the devil and his minions believe that God exists (James 2:19). True knowledge of God is formed in relationship with him and in obedience to his claims of exclusive worship. God serves as a fortress and refuge to those who trust him and who humbly seek to follow his revealed will. God is also a righteous Judge, whose timing in judging iniquity should not be confused with either indifference or caprice.

John Calvin proposed in his *Institutes of the Christian Religion* that true knowledge of one's self is bound together with the relational knowledge of who God is. Many subsequent interpreters have followed his viewpoint, and it is certainly consistent with the claim of Jeremiah 16. The fall of Judah and the subsequent exile of many Judeans were not simply events of power politics in the late seventh/early sixth centuries B.C.; they were part of a judging and refining process undertaken by God the Lord, who sought to make himself known to his people.

---

2. The NIV typically renders the personal name of God as "LORD." This is a tradition reaching back into the biblical period itself.

God is both Judge and Redeemer. Knowledge of him impels one to recognize our sinfulness just as knowledge of our sinfulness can—by God's grace—lead us to know God as both Judge and Redeemer. Christians recognize a similar pattern in the events of the cross and resurrection. Through these events God made himself known as Judge of all the world and Redeemer of those who trust in him through Jesus Christ, his Son, who also bore the name Lord. "Everyone who calls on the name of the Lord will be saved" (Rom. 10:13; cf. Phil. 2:9–11).

The cost of discipleship. Jeremiah's celibacy reminds Christians of the cost of discipleship. In certain circles of the church, the family has taken on nearly idolatrous status. The good news is that Christians are rightly concerned about the dissolution of the primary social unit of society (= the family), but marriage and family are not ultimate in the life of faith. God uses those who are widowed or never married, or even those who are married and without children, in special ministries. God's kingdom is full of servants whose celibacy and/or childlessness have become more than a social mark; they have become occasions for God's kingdom to grow.

Protestants can learn something from their brothers and sisters in the Catholic tradition. The call of ministry may include celibacy. Those who answer the call are in a sense "married" to the Lord and his larger family of disciples. They are whole persons who have chosen a different "symbolic act" through which to exercise their faith.

One of the most distinguished evangelical spokesmen in the twentieth century, John R. W. Stott, never married. His personal views on the goodness of marriage and family are well known. The fruit of his rich ministry as an Anglican clergyman, including valuable publications and a long series of public travels for preaching and lectures, is testimony to the use of the time he had as a single person. He continues to embody his ministry.

Calvin's prayer at the end of his meditation on Jeremiah 16 is worth quoting and pondering.

> All-powerful God, you are not content to give only one small corner of the earth to your servants; you are pleased to extend your kingdom to the ends of the earth and make your home with us through your only Son in whatever place we are. Give us the grace that we may offer ourselves to you in sacrifice. Give us the grace to arrange our lives in obedience to your Word, that your name be glorified in us and by us, until finally we are made participants in the eternal celestial glory acquired through your Son, our Lord, Jesus Christ.[3]

---

3. Calvin, *Sermons on Jeremiah*, 140.

Jeremiah 17:1–27

¹ "Judah's sin is engraved with an iron tool,
   inscribed with a flint point,
on the tablets of their hearts
   and on the horns of their altars.
² Even their children remember
   their altars and Asherah poles
 beside the spreading trees
   and on the high hills.
³ My mountain in the land
   and your wealth and all your treasures
 I will give away as plunder,
   together with your high places,
   because of sin throughout your country.
⁴ Through your own fault you will lose
   the inheritance I gave you.
 I will enslave you to your enemies
   in a land you do not know,
 for you have kindled my anger,
   and it will burn forever."

⁵ This is what the LORD says:

 "Cursed is the one who trusts in man,
   who depends on flesh for his strength
   and whose heart turns away from the LORD.
⁶ He will be like a bush in the wastelands;
   he will not see prosperity when it comes.
 He will dwell in the parched places of the desert,
   in a salt land where no one lives.

⁷ "But blessed is the man who trusts in the LORD,
   whose confidence is in him.
⁸ He will be like a tree planted by the water
   that sends out its roots by the stream.
 It does not fear when heat comes;
   its leaves are always green.
 It has no worries in a year of drought
   and never fails to bear fruit."

⁹ The heart is deceitful above all things
   and beyond cure.
   Who can understand it?

¹⁰"I the LORD search the heart
    and examine the mind,
to reward a man according to his conduct,
    according to what his deeds deserve."

¹¹Like a partridge that hatches eggs it did not lay
    is the man who gains riches by unjust means.
When his life is half gone, they will desert him,
    and in the end he will prove to be a fool.

¹²A glorious throne, exalted from the beginning,
    is the place of our sanctuary.
¹³O LORD, the hope of Israel,
    all who forsake you will be put to shame.
Those who turn away from you will be written in the dust
    because they have forsaken the LORD,
    the spring of living water.

¹⁴Heal me, O LORD, and I will be healed;
    save me and I will be saved,
    for you are the one I praise.
¹⁵They keep saying to me,
    "Where is the word of the LORD?
    Let it now be fulfilled!"
¹⁶I have not run away from being your shepherd;
    you know I have not desired the day of despair.
What passes my lips is open before you.
¹⁷Do not be a terror to me;
    you are my refuge in the day of disaster.
¹⁸Let my persecutors be put to shame,
    but keep me from shame;
let them be terrified,
    but keep me from terror.
Bring on them the day of disaster;
    destroy them with double destruction.

¹⁹This is what the LORD said to me: "Go and stand at the gate of the people, through which the kings of Judah go in and out; stand also at all the other gates of Jerusalem. ²⁰Say to them, 'Hear the word of the LORD, O kings of Judah and all people of Judah and everyone living in Jerusalem who come through these gates. ²¹This is what the LORD says: Be careful not to carry a load on the Sabbath day or bring it through the

gates of Jerusalem. [22]Do not bring a load out of your houses or do any work on the Sabbath, but keep the Sabbath day holy, as I commanded your forefathers. [23]Yet they did not listen or pay attention; they were stiff-necked and would not listen or respond to discipline. [24]But if you are careful to obey me, declares the LORD, and bring no load through the gates of this city on the Sabbath, but keep the Sabbath day holy by not doing any work on it, [25]then kings who sit on David's throne will come through the gates of this city with their officials. They and their officials will come riding in chariots and on horses, accompanied by the men of Judah and those living in Jerusalem, and this city will be inhabited forever. [26]People will come from the towns of Judah and the villages around Jerusalem, from the territory of Benjamin and the western foothills, from the hill country and the Negev, bringing burnt offerings and sacrifices, grain offerings, incense and thank offerings to the house of the LORD. [27]But if you do not obey me to keep the Sabbath day holy by not carrying any load as you come through the gates of Jerusalem on the Sabbath day, then I will kindle an unquenchable fire in the gates of Jerusalem that will consume her fortresses.'"

Original Meaning

JEREMIAH 17 CONTINUES the pattern of collecting the prophet's disparate sayings according to topics. Readers will find more than one theme or subject matter in these verses, although they are concerned primarily to communicate the reasons for the failure of Judah and Jerusalem, primarily its sinful condition. This chapter offers no indication of a precise setting in Jeremiah's life for this report or any of the poetic material.

The prophet has adopted and adapted some well-known traditions in both poetry and prose to make his case. One theme is the corruption of the human heart (17:1, 5, 9). Another appears to be an adaptation of Psalm 1 to indicate the self-incurred failure of human pride (17:5–8). Verses 9–11 are almost proverbial in form and draw on the sapiential traditions (cf. Prov. 16:1–9). There is even praise of God in this chapter (17:12–14), which leads the prophet to lament his circumstances and to pray for judgment on his persecutors (17:15–18). Finally, in a prose report the Lord urges Jeremiah to stand in public and proclaim the significance of the Sabbath as a means of honoring God and preserving a form of spiritual order to public life (17:19–27). Failure to keep the Sabbath will result in judgment on Judah and Jerusalem; thus the chapter ends with the familiar claim of divine judgment to come.

17:1–4. This brief passage—that Judah has rejected God's instruction and will be judged accordingly—is similar to many preceding parts. For example, Jeremiah spoke metaphorically about the heart before. Judah's heart is in need of circumcision (4:4; 9:25).[1] The people are "senseless" (5:21; lit., "without heart"); they have "stubborn and rebellious hearts" (5:23; 7:24; 9:14; 11:8). Here the metaphor is also a play on the formulation of the Decalogue as the content of God's covenant with Israel: "He declared to you his covenant, the Ten Commandments, which he commanded you to follow and then wrote them on two stone tablets" (Deut. 4:13). Judah's sinfulness is described as "engraved with an iron tool ... on the tablets of their hearts." This metaphor underscores the indelible nature of sin and its corrosive effects on the people.

Verse 2 mentions the "Asherah poles" (NIV) as evidence for Judah's defection from the Lord, along with the people's embracing of false worship. The Hebrew word is *ʾašerim*, a plural word literally meaning Asherahs. The NIV assumes that the plural refers to a cultic implement, and this is likely correct, whether a pole or tree or some other totem object. Asherah is also the name of a goddess worshiped in the ancient world. In recent years several inscriptions have been discovered in and around the ancient territory of Judah that mention Asherah in the singular. On more than one occasion there is the reference to "YHWH and his Asherah." These texts demonstrate a kind of unhealthy syncretism, if not outright polytheism, from the time of Jeremiah and other prophets.[2] According to 2 Kings 23:4–7, part of King Josiah's reforming measures in the temple precincts were the destruction of vessels made for Baal and Asherah, the removal of the Asherah (an idol? NIV "Asherah pole"), and the tearing down of weaving areas for Asherah.

Once more the prophet employs the familiar metaphor of inheritance (*naḥᵃla*) to speak of judgment. Canaan is actually the Lord's inheritance, but the people were granted a life in it as part of God's covenant promises to them. Punishment means they will lose their place in his inheritance.[3] This is tantamount to saying they have lost their place in the household (i.e., family) of the Lord.

17:5–8. This passage reads like a "play" (i.e., a serious pun) on Psalm 1. Jeremiah draws a contrast between the one who is cursed (*ʾarur*) and the one who is blessed (*baruk*).[4] These two terms are used in the great listings of

---

1. See comments on 4:4.

2. J. Day, "Asherah," *ABD*, 1:483–87.

3. On the Lord's inheritance, see 2:7; 3:19; 10:16; and the Lord's plaintive lament in 12:7–9.

4. The word for "blessed" in Ps. 1:1 is *ʾašre*, not a form of the verb *barak* as in Jer. 17:7. The former is used more often in wisdom literature.

curses and blessings in Deuteronomy 27–28. The contrast is between trust in human effort and design, and reliance on God.

17:9–13. These verses elaborate on the theme of the previous unit. Human commitments, and especially the deeds that proceed from them, have consequences that an observant person should take to heart. Two verses are like a proverb in their brief "systems analysis." (1) Verse 9 represents the heart as the seat of human deceitfulness. The depths of its possible depravity are difficult to measure. Indeed, only God can accurately measure it. According to verse 10, this knowledge, which belongs to God, enables him to "reward a man according to his conduct." The connection between act and consequence is important in the wisdom traditions of the Old Testament (e.g., Proverbs). Such a connection is further elaboration of the blessing-and-curse contrast presented in the previous unit. Part of what God does in overseeing blessings and curses is to connect the disposition of the human heart and the deeds that flow from it. This is not a law of physics but the operation of a sovereign God, who cannot be bound rigidly by a formula.

(2) Verse 11 is another proverbial statement: Riches gained unjustly are like a bird hatching eggs it did not lay. Here again the connection between act and consequence is set out. Jeremiah's use of this proverb suggests a connection between Judah's "gains" from idolatry and the sad loss of its land and freedom. Only a fool (*nabal*) would want such gains.

17:12–13. These two verses join the blessing of the sanctuary (almost certainly the one in Jerusalem) with God's presence as "the spring of living water" (cf. 2:13). That God is "the hope of Israel" has been used by Jeremiah before (14:8).

17:14–18. Here is another of Jeremiah's laments. Verse 14 draws a connection between healing and saving. Healing likely means the kind of restoration of emotional spirit and physical well-being that only God can grant. Since Jeremiah has been the object of scorn and ridicule as well as physical oppression (e.g., 20:1–6; 38:1–13), his acceptance by God is crucial to his survival. In verse 15 the prophet reports to God that he has been verbally abused by those who ridicule his prophecies. Their question ("Where is the word of the LORD?") points to the as-yet unfulfilled prophecies of disaster.

In poignant fashion the prophet reminds God that he has walked the path of discipleship. He has taken no joy in announcing a day of despair. It is almost as if waiting for the prophecies of disaster to be fulfilled has made Jeremiah feel separated from God, so he prays that God will be his "refuge"[5] when disaster falls. He also prays that God will deal strictly with his perse-

---

5. Refuge (*mahseb*) is used primarily in Psalms to describe the person and work of God (cf. Ps. 62:7; 71:7; 73:28; 91:2, 9; 94:22; 142:5).

cutors, so that they will know for certain that the prophecies Jeremiah delivered have come to pass and that in opposing Jeremiah they were opposing the word and prophet sent by God.

17:19–29. This is an autobiographical report in prose. It functions like a sermon on the fourth commandment of the Decalogue (Deut. 5:12–15) to keep the Sabbath day holy. Some scholars see in this section an example of editorial work, whereby the compilers of Jeremiah's prophecies added a statement on the importance of the Sabbath for exilic or early postexilic readers. Since it is generally acknowledged that the institution of the Sabbath grew in importance in the exilic and postexilic periods, there is a certain plausibility to this conclusion.

It is just as plausible, however, that one of Jeremiah's own forms of prophetic indictment includes a reference to the people's failure to maintain the integrity of the Sabbath day and that this indictment is intended to instruct the communities in exile, who had questions about the status of their covenant relationship with the Lord. In his temple sermon, Jeremiah charged the people with several failures, including theft, murder, and perjury (7:9). These terms come from the Decalogue. The charge of violating the Sabbath is simply another example of his using normative covenant traditions in his critique of the people.

Jeremiah's minisermon on the Sabbath, furthermore, has the familiar "two-way" formulation. This is entirely in keeping with the poetic texts that precede it. For example, the blessing or curse formulation in 17:5–8 is a brief exposition of the two-way paradigm. Here, keeping the Sabbath holy will result in receiving God's blessing, while failure to do so will bring destruction on Jerusalem.

Note that Jeremiah's specific accusation concerns carrying loads on the Sabbath, (i.e., working rather than refraining from labor). Resting from work helped make the Sabbath day holy. If God's people honor him by keeping the Sabbath, then not only Jerusalem but the various regions of Judah will be inhabited, and right worship will be offered to the Lord. This is the one place in the chapter that suggests a role for repentance and renewed obedience to God's law.

Bridging Contexts

THE SINFUL HUMAN CONDITION. The repeated references to the corruption of the heart in chapter 17 indicate the seriousness of Judah's predicament; this failure is deeply rooted in the essence of Judah's identity before God. The same sense of corruption and failure is true in the broader critique in 17:5–11. Jeremiah's portrayal of human fallibility has links with other biblical writers (Old and New Testament),[6] who in varying degrees see sinfulness not just as a harmful deed or process but as a condition of human existence.

The prophetic critique, generally speaking, saw human sinfulness as a condition that mitigated against Israel or Judah's ability to reform themselves. If the human heart was corrupt and seemingly incapable of reformation, then Ezekiel, Jeremiah's younger contemporary, would proclaim nevertheless that Judah should make for itself a new heart and new spirit (Ezek. 18:31). But can reformation be done adequately from the human side? Note how this same prophet proclaimed that God would be the One to give his people a new heart and spirit so that they might walk in obedience to his commandments (Ezek. 11:19; 36:26; cf. Deut. 30:6; Jer. 24:7).

Corruption is not something to be defined in rational terms, for it can manifest itself in mysterious ways, nor is it amenable to easy explanation or removal. Indeed, sinfulness as a condition of human existence is not something to be "fixed" by human effort. Jesus noted that it is not what goes into a person that causes permanent defilement (such as a particular food), but what proceeds from the human heart (i.e., the volitional center of an individual) that demonstrates corruption (Mark 7:20—23). Paul assumed the moral and spiritual bankruptcy of the human species, and he understood the advent of Christ as God's decisive countermeasure (Rom. 1:16—3:26).

Modern Western people begin from a doctrine of individuality that makes the corporate thinking of biblical writers more difficult to grasp. One of the necessary bridges from Jeremiah's world to modernity is to work with the more individualistic mentality of the present so that people can affirm the truths of a common humanity (before God!) and the insights of someone like Reinhold Niebuhr, whose classic work on *Moral Man and Immoral Society*[7] points out how all people participate in a social identity that defines, at least in part, who they are.

A primary reason why human sinfulness is so devastating is that the condition is terminal. Corruption and sin beget more of the same, and that vicious cycle can only be broken from God's side. The rhetorical question of Paul, "Who will rescue me from this body of death?" (Rom. 7:24), has been answered from God's side. Jeremiah's own proclamation fits this orientation:

---

6. This is particularly true of Paul (see below).

7. R. Niebuhr, *Moral Man and Immoral Society: A Study in Ethics and Politics* (New York: Scribner's, 1932). Niebuhr claims that regardless of the personal commitments of people, their participation in public life and society's institutions involves them in collective failures. His modern analysis of "society" is a good way to understand how an Old Testament view of corporate personality and identity can be translated (in modified form) into concepts that modern people will recognize as influential on themselves.

Only God can heal Judah's brokenness. In Jeremiah's world (or that of the New Testament), people did not think in modern psychological terms, and such concepts as repentance or new birth were not submerged into a therapeutic model (as is often the case in modernity). It is not necessarily wrong to cast the human plight in behavioral terms such as addiction or compulsion as long as one acknowledges the terminal condition and human culpability (the scriptural claim of sinfulness).

The Sabbath. Jeremiah's words about the Sabbath partake of the larger biblical teaching about the sanctity of the seventh day and the requirement that Israel be holy as the Lord their God is holy (Lev. 19:2). The sanctification of the Sabbath is the bridge commandment in the Decalogue (Ex. 20:8—11), mediating between those commands to relate rightly to God (20:3—7) and those commands to relate rightly to one's family and neighbor (20:12—17). Sabbath-keeping is a pattern rooted in divine disclosure (Gen. 2:1—3) and an activity blessed by God. Although Jesus offered severe criticism of a legalistic interpretation of the Sabbath (e.g., Mark 2:24—3:6), he acknowledged its divine origin and purpose.

The shift on the part of most churches to worship on the first day of the week (Sunday) is an example of bridging the gap between Jeremiah's world and Christian affirmation. Christ's resurrection on the Sunday morning of the first Easter has given a new orientation to the Sabbath injunctions for rest and holiness.

THOUGHTS ON HUMAN SINFULNESS. Jeremiah's assumptions about human sinfulness contribute to a fuller biblical doctrine of sin. In contemporary Western culture, where individual culpability is seldom discussed apart from the decision of law courts, a concept of corporate human failure has also waned as a significant issue for discussion. Recovering the doctrine of the corporate nature of sin and its universal effects on individuals is a necessary condition for the proclamation that God has spoken decisively to the world in Jesus Christ.

In the modern West, among the places perhaps to start a conversation is the prevalence of addictive behavior, racism, and random violence. All three of these phenomena in Western societies are symptomatic of larger issues of human existence, and they stand under the judgment of God's Word. Nevertheless, they defy easy explanation or cure. They are irrational, and they lead to more of the same in spirals of self-destruction.

Perhaps another way to hear these words of Jeremiah for today is to see the increasing secularization of society as a judgment rooted in the hubris of the human heart. Most versions of secularization in the West (myths of progress and technological security) are ultimately foolish attempts at self-deification. Their fruits will not be technological emancipation from human problems, but like the partridge with eggs it did not hatch, humankind will find that it does not possess the key to its own salvation.

Keeping the Sabbath. Jeremiah informs his contemporaries that keeping the Sabbath is one of the keys to honoring God. In essence he says: "Don't work." There is nothing explicit about worshiping on the Sabbath in Jeremiah's minisermon. In fact, one can search the whole Bible and find little about worshiping on the Sabbath. This fact should not be misunderstood; the Bible has a lot to say about the worship of God, but the Sabbath day is not the place for that discussion. "Don't work," Jeremiah says. If you go to the Decalogue, it is the same. There is nothing direct about worship in the fourth commandment; rather, it is to set the Sabbath day apart. That is what holiness means. Even God followed that pattern in creation (Gen. 1:24–31).

For many people, it is easy to draw a negative image from the insistence on "no work," and even easier to think immediately of Jesus' reply to the Pharisees: "The Sabbath was made for man, not man for the Sabbath" (Mark 2:27). Many sermons have been preached about Jewish legalism and the Sabbath with the goal of convincing Christians that Sunday (the Christian "Sabbath") should not fall prey to Pharisaical legalism. Of course Christians don't want to be legalists, but isn't it ironic that the Sabbath commandment not to work has become identified in the minds of some Christians with works righteousness and legalism, a kind of external religion? Christians don't want to make the Sabbath rest a negative institution, but does this commendable goal also inevitably blunt the force of the Sabbath commandment for modern appropriation?

Christians don't have to identify the Sabbath day with Saturday or Sunday nor think of a Sabbath rest in a legalistic way as a twenty-four-hour period (Col. 2:16–17). But what should they do? This will vary somewhat from culture to culture, but for many middle-class Christians in North America, perhaps the Sabbath commandment can point to a way of living that says work and busy schedules do not define us. Rather than thinking about the Sabbath as a legalistic prop for works righteousness, perhaps one should think of the Sabbath rest as a supreme example of God's grace. What could be more grace oriented than a refusal to live by work and through human achievement? Perhaps a Christian Sabbath can become a sign in a busy, tension-packed world that disciples will not live by work alone but through the rest and renewal that comes from God. Perhaps the sanctifying of a day or period in the week for rest can become a provisional illustration to the world of faithful Christian existence, where one is initiated in the process of loving God and enjoying him forever.

Jeremiah 18:1–19:15

❦

THIS IS THE word that came to Jeremiah from the LORD: 2"Go down to the potter's house, and there I will give you my message." 3So I went down to the potter's house, and I saw him working at the wheel. 4But the pot he was shaping from the clay was marred in his hands; so the potter formed it into another pot, shaping it as seemed best to him.

5Then the word of the LORD came to me: 6"O house of Israel, can I not do with you as this potter does?" declares the LORD. "Like clay in the hand of the potter, so are you in my hand, O house of Israel. 7If at any time I announce that a nation or kingdom is to be uprooted, torn down and destroyed, 8and if that nation I warned repents of its evil, then I will relent and not inflict on it the disaster I had planned. 9And if at another time I announce that a nation or kingdom is to be built up and planted, 10and if it does evil in my sight and does not obey me, then I will reconsider the good I had intended to do for it.

11"Now therefore say to the people of Judah and those living in Jerusalem, 'This is what the LORD says: Look! I am preparing a disaster for you and devising a plan against you. So turn from your evil ways, each one of you, and reform your ways and your actions.' 12But they will reply, 'It's no use. We will continue with our own plans; each of us will follow the stubbornness of his evil heart.'"

13Therefore this is what the LORD says:

> "Inquire among the nations:
>   Who has ever heard anything like this?
> A most horrible thing has been done
>   by Virgin Israel.
> 14Does the snow of Lebanon
>   ever vanish from its rocky slopes?
> Do its cool waters from distant sources
>   ever cease to flow?
> 15Yet my people have forgotten me;
>   they burn incense to worthless idols,
> which made them stumble in their ways
>   and in the ancient paths.

They made them walk in bypaths
and on roads not built up.
¹⁶Their land will be laid waste,
an object of lasting scorn;
all who pass by will be appalled
and will shake their heads.
¹⁷Like a wind from the east,
I will scatter them before their enemies;
I will show them my back and not my face
in the day of their disaster."

¹⁸They said, "Come, let's make plans against Jeremiah; for
the teaching of the law by the priest will not be lost, nor will
counsel from the wise, nor the word from the prophets. So
come, let's attack him with our tongues and pay no attention
to anything he says."

¹⁹Listen to me, O LORD;
hear what my accusers are saying!
²⁰Should good be repaid with evil?
Yet they have dug a pit for me.
Remember that I stood before you
and spoke in their behalf
to turn your wrath away from them.
²¹So give their children over to famine;
hand them over to the power of the sword.
Let their wives be made childless and widows;
let their men be put to death,
their young men slain by the sword in battle.
²²Let a cry be heard from their houses
when you suddenly bring invaders against them,
for they have dug a pit to capture me
and have hidden snares for my feet.
²³But you know, O LORD,
all their plots to kill me.
Do not forgive their crimes
or blot out their sins from your sight.
Let them be overthrown before you;
deal with them in the time of your anger.

^{19:1}This is what the LORD says: "Go and buy a clay jar from
a potter. Take along some of the elders of the people and of
the priests ²and go out to the Valley of Ben Hinnom, near the

entrance of the Potsherd Gate. There proclaim the words I
tell you, ³and say, 'Hear the word of the LORD, O kings of
Judah and people of Jerusalem. This is what the LORD
Almighty, the God of Israel, says: Listen! I am going to bring a
disaster on this place that will make the ears of everyone who
hears of it tingle. ⁴For they have forsaken me and made this a
place of foreign gods; they have burned sacrifices in it to gods
that neither they nor their fathers nor the kings of Judah ever
knew, and they have filled this place with the blood of the
innocent. ⁵They have built the high places of Baal to burn
their sons in the fire as offerings to Baal—something I did not
command or mention, nor did it enter my mind. ⁶So beware,
the days are coming, declares the LORD, when people will no
longer call this place Topheth or the Valley of Ben Hinnom,
but the Valley of Slaughter.

⁷"'In this place I will ruin the plans of Judah and Jerusalem. I
will make them fall by the sword before their enemies, at the
hands of those who seek their lives, and I will give their carcasses as food to the birds of the air and the beasts of the earth.
⁸I will devastate this city and make it an object of scorn; all who
pass by will be appalled and will scoff because of all its wounds.
⁹I will make them eat the flesh of their sons and daughters, and
they will eat one another's flesh during the stress of the siege
imposed on them by the enemies who seek their lives.'

¹⁰"Then break the jar while those who go with you are
watching, ¹¹and say to them, 'This is what the LORD Almighty
says: I will smash this nation and this city just as this potter's
jar is smashed and cannot be repaired. They will bury the
dead in Topheth until there is no more room. ¹²This is what I
will do to this place and to those who live here, declares the
LORD. I will make this city like Topheth. ¹³The houses in
Jerusalem and those of the kings of Judah will be defiled like
this place, Topheth—all the houses where they burned
incense on the roofs to all the starry hosts and poured out
drink offerings to other gods.'"

¹⁴Jeremiah then returned from Topheth, where the LORD
had sent him to prophesy, and stood in the court of the
LORD's temple and said to all the people, ¹⁵"This is what the
LORD Almighty, the God of Israel, says: 'Listen! I am going to
bring on this city and the villages around it every disaster I
pronounced against them, because they were stiff-necked and
would not listen to my words.'"

THESE TWO CHAPTERS do not preserve dates in Jeremiah's career, and it is possible, but not necessary, to interpret them as recording two successive acts of the prophet. But it is also possible that the events of visiting a potter and visiting the Valley of Ben Hinnom to break a pot are separated by months or even years. Probably the two accounts are placed together as part of a catchword principle or the habit of topical collection (both deal with prophetic signs using pottery). In any case, there is much to be said for taking the two chapters together. Both function in this book as a means of illustrating the slide of Judah into irreversible failure. They are linked, furthermore, with chapter 20, where Jeremiah is publicly humiliated (cf. 20:1).

The basic literary units of the two chapters may be set out as follows:

- A. 18:1–17: The prose description of a visit to the potter's house (vv. 1–12) is followed by a poetic oracle of God's response (vv. 13–17).
- B. 18:18: Jeremiah's opponents plan an attack on him.
- C. 18:19–22: Jeremiah laments his circumstances and prays for vindication.
- D. 19:1–13: Jeremiah takes a pot to the Valley of Ben Hinnom and breaks it as a symbol of God's judgment to come.
- E. 19:14–15: Jeremiah goes to the temple to announce God's judgment on the land.

18:1–17. Readers receive an account of Jeremiah's visit to a potter's workshop and commentary on its significance. Verse 1 is clearly the work of Jeremiah's editor(s). What is reported, however, has an autobiographical element still preserved (the "I" of 18:3; the "me" of 18:5). For his contemporaries, Jeremiah's visit to the workshop and his announcement of God's word have the profile of a symbolic act, what might be termed a parable in action.[1] Jeremiah's readers and hearers can use their imagination to envisage the workshop and the efforts of a potter to shape wet clay into a vessel ready to be fired and then used as a container.

God (the potter) has the sovereign right to make and remake the clay as he sees fit. Wet clay is malleable, which means it is capable of being formed in a variety of shapes. But it is also capable of collapsing its shape or of being ill-mixed and thus unsuitable for firing. Not just any wet clay will do, and not just any individual can shape a vessel properly. It takes a correct mixture of clay and the skills of a trained artisan to form[2] a pot for successful firing.

---

1. See the discussion of symbolic acts in the comments on ch. 13.
2. The common English term for forming the clay is actually "to throw" a pot.

The meaning of this illustration is clear. Just as the potter may form and reform the same clay until he is either satisfied or decides to dump the clay completely, so God can form and reform the house of Israel. "Like clay in the hand of the potter, so are you in my hand, O house of Israel" (v. 6). This affirmation of God's sovereign right over the people he has formed is followed by the "two-way" formulation of God's dealings with any nation. If God announces judgment on a nation and that nation repents, then that judgment can be reversed or simply canceled. Correspondingly, if God has announced goodness for a kingdom and it acts faithlessly, then that good can also be reversed. The Hebrew verbs used for "uproot," "tear down," and "destroy" in verse 7 and those for "build" and "plant" in verse 9 are the same ones used in the call of Jeremiah to be a prophet to the nations (1:10).

The two-way formulation implies that a wholehearted repentance on the part of Judah can avert the judgment that looms over them. If so, it seems likely that this passage comes from an earlier period in the prophet's public ministry, when he held out the hope that Judah and Jerusalem could make the necessary changes in public life.[3] Verse 12, however, puts a quote in the mouth of the people to the effect that they will follow their own stubborn heart. This quote, of course, is Jeremiah's portrait of them, based on their actions and (non-)reception of his prophecies. Judah will not repent, and irrevocable judgment will come.

God does not take "no" for an answer easily. The poetic reply in verses 13–17 begins with an indignant question: "Who has ever heard anything like this?" (cf. also the incredulous charge in 2:10). An appalling thing has happened; God's people have forgotten him and worshiped other deities, worthless idols unable to help them. Verse 17 has a surprising metaphorical "turn" to it: In the coming day of judgment, God will show his "back" (ʿorep)[4] to the people and not his face.

18:18–23. Jeremiah's opponents are again the issue. In verse 18 they intend to attack him verbally and pay no attention to anything he says. Their persecution of the prophet shows that they have also rejected God's word to them (and to Judah) that Jeremiah represents.[5] They prefer the words of other mediators of God's will to the judgmental pronouncements of Jeremiah. Note the three forms of mediating God's will: the priest with *tora* (NIV "law"), counsel from the wise, and the word from the prophet. The point seems to be that although they reject Jeremiah, they will not lack for other sources of guidance.

---

3. See the comments about the call for repentance in ch. 3.

4. The comment is similar to 2:27, where God charges the people with turning their back (ʿorep) to him, yet in the day of trouble they turn and seek his deliverance.

5. Ch. 20 will show what kind of judgment and humiliation Jeremiah's opponents have in mind for him.

In verses 19–23, in another personal lament, Jeremiah prays for God's judgment on his enemies. His harsh words come in the context of a prayer for vindication from God and for a temporal judicial sentence by God on those who malign him. The metaphor he uses is that of a pit dug by his opponents (18:20, 22), a pit designed to catch him. It is a hunting image, a trap laid to catch prey, but also a proverbial symbol.[6] Jeremiah prays, in essence, that his enemies may fall into the pit they have dug. He asks God to oversee the consequences of their acts rather than for a personal opportunity to judge them. Since they have committed an evil in attacking an innocent person, may the evil they intend fall back on them.

19:1–13. God now instructs Jeremiah to perform another symbolic act (a parable in action), also with a pottery jar. Presumably the actions described were carried out, though only the instructions and a brief report in 19:14–15 remain. God commands Jeremiah to buy an earthenware jar and to take a group of elders and priests to the Valley of Ben Hinnom where the Topheth, a place for human sacrificial rites, is located.[7] This valley is situated immediately south of the temple mount area and continues to the western side of the old city of Jerusalem. Before he breaks the jar in the valley of slaughter and burial, Jeremiah must prophesy judgment on the kings of Judah and the inhabitants of Jerusalem. The failures of these addressees are listed as the worship of other gods, the spilling of innocent blood, and especially the worship of Baal through the burning of children in a sacrificial fire.

With the breaking of the jar, Jeremiah indicates the irrevocable judgment to come. Just as the smashed earthenware cannot be repaired, Judah cannot be reformed. For original hearers and readers there is likely added significance to the earthenware pot. The Topheth was not only the place of ceremonial slaughter; it likely also contained a section where earthenware jars with the charred remains of sacrificial victims were collected. Similar places are known in Phoenicia (Tyre and Achzib) and among Phoenician colonies in the western Mediterranean (e.g., Carthage).

Jeremiah understands the Topheth as a place of defilement and its earthenware jars as symbolic of slaughter. Indeed, he gives the valley a devastating nickname—"the Valley of Slaughter" (cf. 7:32, where the same name change is given). Judgment will come on Jerusalem in such a way that there will be no other place to bury the dead except in the Topheth, the place of ritual slaughter and cultic defilement. One of the characteristics of Topheth

---

6. The term for pit in 18:20, 22 is used in Prov. 22:14 and 23:27 to describe the seductive trap of a prostitute. Cf. Ps. 35:7, where the psalmist laments the fact that his enemies have "without cause dug a pit for me." A similar term is used in Prov. 26:27: "If a man digs a pit, he will fall into it." This is an affirmation about act and consequence.

7. See comments on ch. 7.

is the crowded nature of the burial section, where pots full of bones and charred remains are stacked together.

19:14–15. Jeremiah leaves the Topheth and goes to the courtyard of the temple to proclaim that God will "bring on this city and the villages around it every disaster I pronounced against them, because they were stiff-necked and would not listen to my words." His presence in the temple court-yard is tantamount to bringing the defilement of the Topheth into the temple, as any reader familiar with the purity laws of the Old Testament would recognize (a cemetery or a corpse rendered a person ceremonially unclean). Furthermore, the reference to "stiff-necked" people catches up the failure of the people to recognize the possibility of repentance that was announced as possible in 18:7–11.

THE EDITORIAL ARRANGEMENT of chapters 18–19 is a key to how the original acts and words of Jeremiah are to instruct later readers. From the potter's workshop, through the prophetic lament of persecution, to the shattering scene at the Topheth, the progression of the accounts confirms Judah's guilt and the irrevocable judgment on the historical horizon. Later readers are told in no uncertain terms why Judah fell to the Babylonians. It was God's just judgment. With the enumeration of Judah's sins, later readers are also asked to search their own lives to see if they too are guilty of these failings.

On interpreting prophecies. In addition to the instruction about the past, later readers are confronted with a teaching about the prophetic word that opens their present and future to God (18:7–11). How should they interpret unconditional prophecies of judgment or peace? Concerning judgment, Jeremiah announces that God will "relent" when people repent of their evil deeds. Correspondingly, God will "reconsider" the good when a people fall into sinful behavior. Some prophecies explicitly contain conditional elements within their formal structure. The issue for later readers, however, is whether unconditional prophecies should be understood as determinism (as unalterable) or as an expression of God's resolve to act in light of particular circumstances, a resolve that may change as historical circumstances themselves change and as God moves toward the fulfillment of his temporal purposes to a yet grander design.

With respect to the word "relent" (Heb. *nḥm*) in 18:8, some translations render it as "repent." The theological issue at stake is not God's repentance from evil or whether God is fickle; rather, the issue is how to account for the personal activity of God who responds as Judge and Deliverer in the historical process. Jonah, for example, did not understand God as fickle when God "relented" over Nineveh's changed circumstances. The prophet believed all along that God was slow to anger and abundant in mercy—and for that reason, he knew that God might use Jonah's own unconditional prophecy of judgment as a means by which to effect change in Nineveh (Jonah 3:1–4:11).

The question of interpreting prophecies about the future is a fundamental one for interpreters who wish to bring God's announcements about the future from the Old Testament into the present: How is God the final interpreter of his own Word? Some interpreters will see in prophecy a blueprint for things as yet unrealized; others will see primarily a teaching about God's moral resolve that preserves his freedom to act in surprising ways.

In 18:12 the indictment of the people because of their stubborn and evil heart catches up the theme of the heart's corruption in the larger context. The saying also sets the stage for the portrayal of the people as "stiff-necked" in 19:15. God will hold true to his announced judgment where an ingrained evil is in evidence; but even so, the possibility of change is open to the descendants of the evil generation as God uses even the harsh words of a previous judgment to call his people to repentance.

Potter and clay. The potter's workshop takes up the theme of God's sovereignty over the things he has made. It is the right of the potter (who knows what potential the clay has) to remake and to reform a vessel until it is suitable. At an interpretive level, this analogy of potter and clay fits the question of God and unconditional prophecy. Theological reflection begins by asking the purpose for which God sent a prophetic word in the past. God may reshape his future dealings with his people in light of what that Word accomplishes among them or among those who read it (even much later). It is not so much a single fulfillment of prophecy that Christians should look for as a constant encounter with prophecy and with the God who makes sovereign use of prophecy in different contexts.

Paul took up this analogy of potter and clay in his reflection on the state of Israel according to the flesh and God's larger design in calling the Gentiles to new life in Christ (Rom. 9–11). It is God's sovereign right as the "potter" to make a common vessel (and to judge it) as it is to select one for special service (9:19–21). The apostle saw in God's sending of Christ the outworking of a plan to bind all over "to disobedience so that he may have mercy on them all" (11:32). God's sovereign mercy is the foundation of the apostle's wrestling with the difficult subject of Israel's disobedience and her future. He was convinced that Israel's rejection of Christ as the Messiah was a hardening of the heart that God could use. It would not mean the final rejection of Israel but the opportunity for the Gentiles. God is a merciful and righteous "potter," not a puppet master pulling chains.

Persecution and vindication. In his lament over his circumstances Jeremiah once again finds himself in the setting reserved for prophets and disciples. He is persecuted and rejected by contemporaries because of his words and deeds. As a result he prays for God's judgment on the persecutors. Readers do well to remember that what Jeremiah seeks is judicial sentencing, not personal vengeance. At the same time, we see the amazing grace of the Christ who prays for his enemies when we recognize the legitimacy of Jeremiah's lament and his desire for vindication. Grace is indeed unmerited favor when someone is faced with the legitimacy of judgment.

WORDS OF JUDGMENT. As with the previous words of judgment in Jeremiah, one avenue of appropriation moves along the way of demonstrating God's righteousness in the face of ingrained evil. Since the book is filled with passages proclaiming judgment, modern readers are given many opportunities to reflect on God's ways with the world. If, for example, we see the hand of God judging the failures of communism in the fall of the Berlin Wall, are we able to see any correcting hand in the Vietnam War and its tragic aftermath or in the continuing struggles over civil rights? Some, perhaps many, North American Christians may want to equivocate in assessing these last two matters, but Christians from other cultures may want to encourage North Americans to take a second, prayerful look for a judging and correcting hand. The emphasis on judgment and on Judah's failure to repent can be instructive to modern readers, if only to remind them that it is an awesome thing to fall into the hands of the living God.

The symbolic acts of the prophet (potter's workshop, broken jar) remind us that ministry calls for the embracing of society and even the embodiment of God's message through acts of service. Jesus' own ministry, whether in judgment or deliverance, was replete with symbolic acts and signs that conveyed the essence of his message. Jeremiah's confession that he had stood before God and prayed for the people (18:20) is testimony to the cost of discipleship. A community that has not prayed for the lost and has not interceded for the wicked will not be able to have a prophetic ministry.

God's word of judgment is not unalterable for those with ears to hear and eyes to see. The wonder of Jeremiah's announcement that God can "relent" and "reconsider" is not that God can change approaches to bring about his purposes. It is the wonder that God opens up ways of transformation and change in the midst of sinful and painful circumstances. What is resistant to change is not God's messages about the future but people stuck in self-destructive activities.

God's sovereignty. Jeremiah's description of the potter opens up avenues to explore the classical doctrine of God's sovereignty. It is usually fruitless to discuss God's power and purpose in the abstract. Power for what and about whom? A philosophical description can constrict and thereby control, since it is anthropologically generated. God's power, what is often called God's omnipotence, is known in relationship. Similarly with respect to God's goodness and predestination, his power and goodness are discovered in relationship and only acknowledged adequately by those who have committed themselves to know God. The proclamation that God judged Judah is not news of interest to later readers unless it somehow instructs them about the ways of God, to whom they too are related by confession.

Confidence in the potter comes finally in knowing the potter, not in observing him spin the wheel and shape the clay from the vantage point of a supposed neutrality. The Pauline reflection on the potter (Rom. 9:18–24) develops this point profoundly and in a manner consistent with the book of Jeremiah. The clay does not have the right to question the potter; but much more significant is the claim that the potter has intentions of preparing vessels for his glory and fit for his mercy. In the process of fulfilling these purposes, vessels can be shaped and reshaped and used in ways not understood by the vessels themselves. Their "essence" is not thereby violated but taken up and used by the God of grace.

In authentic discussions about God's purpose and goodness, there is an inherent reference to a future entrusted to God; it is a future not completely understood from a finite human perspective. One is called to trust in the work of the potter, to walk by faith and not by sight, and to accept God's judgment in the present in the hope that the Potter will reshape the future.

Certainly one of the stupendous events of the twentieth century happened with the collapse of Soviet domination of Eastern Europe, beginning with the fall of the Berlin Wall in November 1989. The impact of this collapse is still being worked out. Each state has its own version of the impact as do the churches in the region. Can anyone say for sure where the collapse will lead? No Christian should doubt the role of God in this process; the contribution of the churches to the collapse is widely recognized. Here is a paradigm of the surprising providence of God being worked out. Was the collapse predicted in the Old Testament? Not precisely, but the God who reshapes history and speaks authoritatively is revealed in the Old Testament, and he is still at work.

Jeremiah 20:1–18

WHEN THE PRIEST Pashhur son of Immer, the chief officer in the temple of the LORD, heard Jeremiah prophesying these things, ²he had Jeremiah the prophet beaten and put in the stocks at the Upper Gate of Benjamin at the LORD's temple. ³The next day, when Pashhur released him from the stocks, Jeremiah said to him, "The LORD's name for you is not Pashhur, but Magor-Missabib. ⁴For this is what the LORD says: 'I will make you a terror to yourself and to all your friends; with your own eyes you will see them fall by the sword of their enemies. I will hand all Judah over to the king of Babylon, who will carry them away to Babylon or put them to the sword. ⁵I will hand over to their enemies all the wealth of this city—all its products, all its valuables and all the treasures of the kings of Judah. They will take it away as plunder and carry it off to Babylon. ⁶And you, Pashhur, and all who live in your house will go into exile to Babylon. There you will die and be buried, you and all your friends to whom you have prophesied lies.'"

⁷ O LORD, you deceived me, and I was deceived;
    you overpowered me and prevailed.
I am ridiculed all day long;
    everyone mocks me.
⁸ Whenever I speak, I cry out
    proclaiming violence and destruction.
So the word of the LORD has brought me
    insult and reproach all day long.
⁹ But if I say, "I will not mention him
    or speak any more in his name,"
his word is in my heart like a fire,
    a fire shut up in my bones.
I am weary of holding it in;
    indeed, I cannot.
¹⁰ I hear many whispering,
    "Terror on every side!
    Report him! Let's report him!"
All my friends
    are waiting for me to slip, saying,

"Perhaps he will be deceived;
  then we will prevail over him
  and take our revenge on him."

¹¹ But the LORD is with me like a mighty warrior;
  so my persecutors will stumble and not prevail.
They will fail and be thoroughly disgraced;
  their dishonor will never be forgotten.
¹² O LORD Almighty, you who examine the righteous
  and probe the heart and mind,
let me see your vengeance upon them,
  for to you I have committed my cause.

¹³ Sing to the LORD!
  Give praise to the LORD!
He rescues the life of the needy
  from the hands of the wicked.

¹⁴ Cursed be the day I was born!
  May the day my mother bore me not be blessed!
¹⁵ Cursed be the man who brought my father the news,
  who made him very glad, saying,
  "A child is born to you—a son!"
¹⁶ May that man be like the towns
  the LORD overthrew without pity.
May he hear wailing in the morning,
  a battle cry at noon.
¹⁷ For he did not kill me in the womb,
  with my mother as my grave,
  her womb enlarged forever.
¹⁸ Why did I ever come out of the womb
  to see trouble and sorrow
  and to end my days in shame?

Original
Meaning

THE CHAPTER MAY BE DIVIDED into two parts: a prose account of Jeremiah's arrest and public humiliation (20:1–6), and a lengthy and poignant personal lament/complaint (20:7–18). The poetic lament perhaps combines material from two different settings, put together with the account of his humiliating incarceration to illustrate his emotional response. There is no reason to doubt, of course, that the bitter words of the lament reflect the way a person might react to human indignities. Nevertheless, it may not have been first composed by Jeremiah while in the stocks but something he took (and adapted?) from the traditional forms of lament/complaint and applied to his circumstances. Whatever the origin(s) of these verses, they serve to illustrate the pain and frustration of the prophet as he suffers abuse at the hands of the religious establishment.

No date is provided for the chapter, but there is indirect evidence for the events in the reign of Jehoiakim (609–598 B.C.). The prediction that Pashhur will die in captivity in Babylon implies a date before 597. The majority of narrative accounts that are set in the period before Zedekiah's reign come from Jehoiakim's time as ruler. One cannot make too much of this, however, since the next chapter (which refers to a second Pashhur) dates to the reign of Zedekiah. Possibly the word against Pashhur the priest anticipates the fall of the city in 587/586. In either case, chapter 20 sums up a decisive period in Jeremiah's prophetic career as it is now laid out in the prophetic book; the painful prayer in 20:7—18 is the last in a series of personal laments/complaints, and it brings the wounded feelings of the prophet to a boiling point.

20:1–6. Pashhur,[1] the priest who orders Jeremiah beaten and placed in the stocks, is from a well-known priestly division (Immer, 1 Chron. 24:14). He represents the religious establishment, especially the priests who care for and officiate at the temple. In fact, he is described as the "chief officer" at the temple. This probably means among other things that he heads the security detail for the large complex, providing oversight for the levitical personnel who keep the gates and who restrict access to and activities within the temple courts. Perhaps his role as chief officer explains his choice of the Upper Gate of Benjamin for the place of Jeremiah's temporary incarceration in the stocks. He controls that area; moreover, that location (likely on the north side of the temple complex) bears a lot of traffic.

Pashhur is from a segment of the population who prove to be some of Jeremiah's most persistent persecutors. The humiliation of being placed in the stocks[2] and beaten by a priest may have been especially galling for Jeremiah, since he too is from a priestly family. With the temple looming in the background, Jeremiah's treatment is portrayed as God's judgment on him, carried out by the priests who care for God's house. Upon his release, Jeremiah gives

---

1. The name is known from extrabiblical inscriptions from the period of Jeremiah, including a reference in the Arad inscriptions. Since there was a sacrificial shrine at Arad (near where the ostraca were discovered), it may be that the Pashhur of Arad was also a priest. See Y. Aharoni, *Arad Inscriptions* (Jerusalem: Israel Exploration Society, 1981), inscrip. #54.

2. The word translated by the NIV as "stocks" is rather obscure. It may refer to some form of restraining device like a collar or to something like the stocks known from Europe and colonial America, where one is forced to sit, bound by fetters, in an unnatural and painful position.

Pashhur a new name, "Magor-Missabib," which in Hebrew means "terror all around." This term occurs elsewhere in Jeremiah to describe the plight of Judah when the foe from the north comes against the state and its capital city (6:25; cf. 46:5; 49:29).

Jeremiah announces in the name of the Lord that Pashhur has "prophesied lies" and that he will enter Babylon as a captive (v. 6). This is an interesting use of the verb "to prophesy." Pashhur is by profession a priest; there is no record about his speaking. Perhaps his actions against Jeremiah are a form of prophecy; they were most definitely "symbolic," in a sense not unlike Jeremiah's visit to the Valley of Hinnom and his coming to the temple complex to prophesy (19:14–15). Indeed, Jeremiah's prophetic witness in the temple may have prompted his arrest and thrashing. As a priest, however, Pashhur almost certainly took the opportunity to speak a word of judgment in public about Jeremiah and his actions. These would take the form of repudiating Jeremiah's words and actions and claiming divine judgment on him.

20:7–18. Jeremiah's lament is linked contextually to his humiliating and painful experience in the stocks. His words are by now (for sequential readers of the book) familiar, yet at the same time shocking.[3] The prophet is persecuted because of "the word of the LORD" (20:8). His persecutors lie in wait to ambush him and ridicule him with his own phrase, "terror on every side" (20:10), as if to say that Jeremiah is a deluded madman who speaks incessantly about terror to come. In his frustration and bitterness Jeremiah accuses God of "deceiving" him (20:7), a strong term that can also refer to seduction.[4] The prophet has reached his wits' end and is unable to articulate a sense that God will rescue him from this situation.

This dilemma is excruciating for Jeremiah. God's word is like a fire within him, and he is unable to resist the urge to speak, even if the "violence and destruction" of which he speaks brings ridicule and physical harassment. His frustration with God comes in the fact that Pashhur, a priest of God(!), had spoken against him and humiliated him in public. Had not God promised to be with Jeremiah and to protect him? Yet God's own official representative has carried out this attack on him.

Verse 11 affirms that God is indeed strong to save. In context this means that the prophet's persecutors will fail. The next verse affirms that God is an infallible Judge and will see to the judgment of the persecutors. Jeremiah's prayer in this respect takes on the form of setting his "cause" (*rib*) before God.

---

3. For an introduction to Jeremiah's laments/complaints, see comments on 11:18–12:17.

4. The same verb (*pth*) is used in Ex. 22:16[15] to describe the seduction of a young woman. It can also describe the actions of a suitor or someone who courts ("allures") a female with the prospects of marriage (Hos. 2:14[16]).

The prophet also rues the day he was born (20:14—18; cf. 15:10), as he, like Job, suffers unjustly. It is difficult to know whether the lament/complaint of 20:7—18 should be read sequentially, as if the movement of the prayer/complaint is significant. If so, it suggests that Jeremiah goes back and forth in his confidence and on his resolve to carry out his prophetic work. That should surprise no one who takes seriously the humiliation suffered in the Upper Gate.

PERSECUTION OF THE RIGHTEOUS. The account of Pashhur's humiliation of Jeremiah is but one in a long series of scriptural accounts of the persecution of the righteous. It is important to be clear here: Jeremiah is righteous, not perfect. There is a difference. He seeks to be faithful to the prophetic call given him by God. To this extent he is righteous. He is also innocent of criminal activity. In ancient Israel, someone who was innocent when accused of a crime was called righteous (*ṣaddiq*).

Yet when Jeremiah is ridiculed and persecuted because of his prophetic calling, he becomes moody, seeking vindication in the public's eye because of his humiliation. His laments (including 20:7—13) make clear the reason for his persecution. From Joseph to David, and in a prophetic line from Elijah straight to Jeremiah, God's servants have faced opposition and persecution. David complained to God about his circumstances with respect to Saul's irrational persecution of him. Elijah fled to Mount Horeb to inform the Lord that he was the only one left who was zealous for the Lord, and Jezebel was after him (1 Kings 19:1—18). Disciples cry to God for sustenance and deliverance because their circumstances may require it!

Indeed, one can move forward through the line of faithful witnesses to John the Baptizer and the early Christian martyrs. The English term *martyr* is based on the Greek word for those who "bear witness" in times of persecution. This Greek word was applied to early Christians who gave testimony to their faith, often at the point of the sword. Christ himself is the greatest example of the phenomenon of righteous suffering, although his suffering is redemptive in a way that the others are not (see further under Contemporary Significance).

Jeremiah's lament/complaint takes up the voice of the innocent sufferer, whose words are common in the book of Psalms. To whom else can one turn with the burdens of the heart, if not to God? Jeremiah prays like the saints of the Psalter, who pour out their hearts to God. That Jeremiah's lament/complaint turns accusatory toward God probably results from two additional factors. (1) The more certain factor is the call of Jeremiah (1:5—19), where the young prophet-to-be is assured of God's protection and ultimate vindication. "Where is God's vindication?" he must have wondered while in the stocks and the object of ridicule. (2) More subjectively perhaps, Jeremiah's human frailty makes him feel that God is finally responsible for his fate. Close to the end of his endurance, he wonders why God has led him down this path; and if God has so led him, will he be stretched beyond his limits and be abandoned after all?

Shame. Shame was a powerful mechanism in the ancient world, and Jeremiah suffers public shame for his attempt to be faithful to his prophetic call. In moving to a modern context, it may be important to explore the different ways in which shame is or (increasingly) is not influential. Is there a modern counterpart to the social force of shame in antiquity? It remains more or less in force in many non-Western settings, but it appears increasingly less influential in the modern West. In any case, Jeremiah's humanity is exposed for what it is: a condition where physical and emotional pain reach intense levels and he is in need of divine grace. Can God know how Jeremiah feels? Here is a bridge to Christology and a point of contact for all generations.

REDEMPTIVE SUFFERING. It should not take much imagination on the part of Christians to see the parallels between Jeremiah's suffering and that of Christ's humiliation and suffering. Religious leaders complained about Christ and sought to trap him. He was humiliated in public and ultimately crucified. His cry of dereliction from the cross was taken directly from a psalm of lament/complaint (Ps. 22:1; Matt. 27:46; Mark 15:34). Perhaps most important, even the fate of the Son of God was cast into the hands of the Father, who seemed withdrawn at the moment.

But we should not rob Jeremiah of his humanity and the poignancy of his life by simply jumping to the New Testament and comparing him with Christ. He and other righteous sufferers are not "just like Christ." Their suffering, however poignant and unjust, is not redemptive for other people, although it can be instructive. One may, however, describe the prophet's life as a *via dolorosa*[5] precisely because his public life and that of Christ are part of a larger pattern. Jeremiah suffers because he is a prophet of God. His suffering shares the suffering of God's people, and it is prophetic in the sense that it points to the perfect Mediator, whose suffering is representative of guilty and innocent suffering alike.

Those who oppose God's Word will oppose Jeremiah. It is the prophetic office that adorns Jeremiah's life and leads him down the path of suffering.

---

5. The phrase indicates "the sorrowful way of the cross."

In his public ministry Jesus brings the prophetic office of the Old Testament to fruition, and through his Sonship fills out the significance of a prophetic ministry in profound ways.

There is much to learn from the frank expression of Jeremiah's human limitations. One may—with Christ's help—bear innocent suffering with a certain grace. But it is no failure of Jeremiah's that he feels crushed by the burdens of the prophetic office. What he gets finally is a taste of the insidious opposition to the Word of God that cloaks itself in all manner of religiosity and patriotism. He experiences the sinking feeling that not only is all lost but that God seems involved in his pain. It will take the humiliation of Christ for the redemptive element of suffering to emerge, but in his own way Jeremiah suffers on our behalf. He demonstrates what it is like to feel the burdens of human failure and personal frustration as a part of his calling, and he does so to instruct us about the cost of discipleship and also for a testimony that God is faithful still—beyond our finite comprehension and in spite of our complaints.

Recently Carlos Lavernia, a Texan convicted of rape, had his conviction overturned after having served fifteen years in prison. Because some supporters kept pestering the relevant court system, DNA testing was finally done on the semen and blood samples taken from the scene of the rape, and the tests proved his innocence with respect to the crime. Two things stood out in his statement upon the release of the findings. (1) He expressed thankfulness to God for finally being set free from responsibility for this crime. (2) But he also felt deep anger at the cost (in terms of time, emotions, reputation) inflicted on him by a wrong conviction and punishment. He recounted briefly how many times during his incarceration he doubted whether he would ever be vindicated. He questioned God's goodness too. Time and time again he wrote letters to protest his innocence. But he never gave up on his hope or on God.

Mr. Lavernia has been convicted of other crimes, so he has not been freed from incarceration. There is a lot about him still unknown to the public; nevertheless, he has served fifteen years in jail for a crime he did not commit. For fifteen years he wrote letters and offered prayers. At times he thought no one heard them, but he was wrong. So may it be with the heartfelt laments of God's children.

Jeremiah 21:1–10

THE WORD CAME to Jeremiah from the LORD when King Zedekiah sent to him Pashhur son of Malkijah and the priest Zephaniah son of Maaseiah. They said: ²"Inquire now of the LORD for us because Nebuchadnezzar king of Babylon is attacking us. Perhaps the LORD will perform wonders for us as in times past so that he will withdraw from us."

³But Jeremiah answered them, "Tell Zedekiah, ⁴'This is what the LORD, the God of Israel, says: I am about to turn against you the weapons of war that are in your hands, which you are using to fight the king of Babylon and the Babylonians who are outside the wall besieging you. And I will gather them inside this city. ⁵I myself will fight against you with an outstretched hand and a mighty arm in anger and fury and great wrath. ⁶I will strike down those who live in this city—both men and animals—and they will die of a terrible plague. ⁷After that, declares the LORD, I will hand over Zedekiah king of Judah, his officials and the people in this city who survive the plague, sword and famine, to Nebuchadnezzar king of Babylon and to their enemies who seek their lives. He will put them to the sword; he will show them no mercy or pity or compassion.'

⁸"Furthermore, tell the people, 'This is what the LORD says: See, I am setting before you the way of life and the way of death. ⁹Whoever stays in this city will die by the sword, famine or plague. But whoever goes out and surrenders to the Babylonians who are besieging you will live; he will escape with his life. ¹⁰I have determined to do this city harm and not good, declares the LORD. It will be given into the hands of the king of Babylon, and he will destroy it with fire.'

Original Meaning

READERS ARE PROVIDED here with a date in Judah's anguished history—one of the few dates given in the first half of the book. Zedekiah is king—the first reference to the last king of Judah since the superscription to the book (1:3)—and the date is ca. 588 B.C. With the Babylonian army surrounding Jerusalem, a royal official named Pashhur the son of Malkijah and a priest named Zephaniah are sent to Jeremiah for him to inquire of the Lord. Perhaps God will work one of his "wonders," so that the Babylonians will withdraw. There is, of course, historical precedent for this hope. In a previous century God had sent a judging angel among the besieging Assyrians (2 Kings 18–19; Isa. 36–39).

The name of one of the officials (Pashhur) is the same as that of the priest in chapter 20, although they are two different people. In the proximity of the two accounts, readers will find something of the catchword principle at work in the compilation of Jeremiah's book. The two episodes are collected together through the common name of Pashhur rather than because they necessarily follow each other chronologically in Jeremiah's public acts.

Pashhur and Zephaniah ask Jeremiah to inquire of the Lord and to intercede for the nation. This is something that King Zedekiah would seek from Jeremiah on more than one occasion (37:3; 38:14). The Lord's reply is full of the judgmental language seen in virtually every previous chapter. What is new (for those reading through Jeremiah) is a specific reference to Nebuchadnezzar, king of Babylon, and the specifics of the siege of Jerusalem. Babylon itself is mentioned specifically for the first time only in the previous chapter (20:4–6). Elsewhere the agent of judgment to come was merely described as the foe or enemy from the north.

According to the divine oracle, God will not war against the Babylonian army but against Judah for its faithlessness and wickedness. Yes, God is a valiant warrior, but the enemy at the moment is Judah, not Babylon! The fall of the city, therefore, is certain. God's resolve to judge the city is described in Hebrew as "the setting of his face," an idiom for single-minded determination (21:10). The NIV paraphrases accurately with its rendering of God's "determination" to judge the city.

Jeremiah mediates part of God's reply to the state officials in language reminiscent of Deuteronomy 30:11–20. In Deuteronomy Moses set before the people "life and prosperity" or "death and destruction." Jeremiah spoke similarly in a previous context with reference to curse or blessing as part of the "two-way" formulation of wisdom theology (Jer. 17:5–13). Now Jeremiah tells the people that God is setting before them the way of life and death (21:8–9). Death is the fate of those who stay in the city; those who leave and are taken captive by the Babylonians will escape with their lives.[1] Ominously, there is no call for repentance in the text of the divine oracle. God is on the side of the Babylonians for the historical moment, and the best that can be done for the Judeans is to convince them to capitulate to the Babylonians and thereby save their lives. There is specific reference to the destruction of Jerusalem by fire.

---

1. The Heb. phrase is an idiom that describes the gift of life as a "prize of war" or "booty." Cf. the similar statement in Jer. 38:2; 39:18; 45:5.

TWO WAYS. The allusion in 21:9 to the covenant proclamation of Deuteronomy 30:19—"I have set before you life and death"—helps modern readers set the announcement of Jerusalem's doom in a broader biblical context. The inhabitants of Jerusalem have a choice of "ways" set before them. Thus, the terrible announcement of doom is placed in the context of covenantal faith with its requirement of obedience and its acknowledgment that judgment will come on the disobedient. In this hour of crisis, Judah is reminded by a prophet like Moses that it is not the only generation of God's people to face hard choices or to see the bitter fruit of wrong decisions.

The New Testament picks up on this pattern of the two ways. Jesus' admonition about the way of life and the way of destruction (Matt. 7:13–14) follows the pattern exactly. It was even delivered at a time and place that reminds us of Moses—at the end of the Sermon on the Mount, delivered by the new and greater Moses. A bridge between then and now can be built on the typological correspondence of God's people from generation to generation; for in every generation there is the call to exercise obedience to the Lord, who brought it into existence. Each generation, as with each believer, ought to embark on the right way and avoid the wrong path.

God as warrior. The language of God as warrior in 21:5–6 also evokes in hearers a broader biblical context. In defeating Pharaoh and subsequently the Canaanites in the Promised Land, God revealed himself as a warrior on behalf of his people—a God who is "mighty to save," according to the great confession of Zephaniah 3:17.[2] There is, however, no partiality with God in judging iniquity. God can enter the fight against his own people, employing the Babylonians and their mighty king in the historical process to effect temporal judgment.

THE WAY THAT LEADS TO LIFE. Christians may see in Jeremiah's hard words here an example of the "razor edge" of biblical theism. God fights against the powers of evil and corruption—and as with every fight, the results are not pretty. God will fight the powers of evil when they oppress his people, but God can also use the powers of evil in this world to judge his people. God is not indifferent to the sins of his people.

It is a remarkable word, therefore, that in the midst of hard words about Judah's doom the prophet in God's name sets forth a way of life and a way

---

2. For further elaboration on this theme, see T. Longman and D. Reid, *God Is a Warrior* (Grand Rapids: Zondervan, 1995).

of death. In spite of the harsh language, annihilation of his people is not God's goal no matter how much it appears to be a necessary option. Historical judgment can be combined with the saving of a remnant, and they can become the seeds of renewal and hope. What is spoken here to the inhabitants is repeated in 38:2. It is spoken again to Jeremiah and to Baruch (38:19; 45:5)—two people who would witness divine judgment, but also two people whose work would spawn spiritual renewal among the survivors of the Babylonian onslaught.

The book of Jeremiah and the ongoing faith of the exilic communities are the evidence that these two were successful. By God's grace they found that the way to life came as a gift. In a paradox known to the faithful, the way to life is found in the giving over of one's life to the Lord. The way to life is a gift of God whose timing cannot be forced. It is often found only after several alternate routes have proved incorrect. Such is the life of faith! There is a sense in which the whole book of Jeremiah is a long commentary on the way of life and the way of death.

Wherever there is judgment and tragedy among God's people, there will also be signs of hope for those with eyes to see and ears to hear. How hard it can be to hear what the Spirit is saying in the midst of peril. The church cannot depend on its own resources but finally must implore the Lord to open their hearts in time to the way that leads to life.

Jeremiah 21:11–22:30

M OREOVER, SAY TO the royal house of Judah, 'Hear
the word of the LORD;
[12]O house of David, this is what the LORD says:

'''Administer justice every morning;
   rescue from the hand of his oppressor
   the one who has been robbed,
or my wrath will break out and burn like fire
   because of the evil you have done—
   burn with no one to quench it.
[13]I am against you, Jerusalem,
   you who live above this valley
   on the rocky plateau,

                                    declares the LORD—

you who say, "Who can come against us?
   Who can enter our refuge?"
[14]I will punish you as your deeds deserve,

                                    declares the LORD.

   I will kindle a fire in your forests
   that will consume everything around you.'"

[22:1]This is what the LORD says: "Go down to the palace of
the king of Judah and proclaim this message there: [2]'Hear the
word of the LORD, O king of Judah, you who sit on David's
throne—you, your officials and your people who come
through these gates. [3]This is what the LORD says: Do what is
just and right. Rescue from the hand of his oppressor the one
who has been robbed. Do no wrong or violence to the alien,
the fatherless or the widow, and do not shed innocent blood
in this place. [4]For if you are careful to carry out these commands, then kings who sit on David's throne will come
through the gates of this palace, riding in chariots and on
horses, accompanied by their officials and their people. [5]But if
you do not obey these commands, declares the LORD, I swear
by myself that this palace will become a ruin.'"

[6]For this is what the LORD says about the palace of the
king of Judah:

"Though you are like Gilead to me,
    like the summit of Lebanon,
I will surely make you like a desert,
    like towns not inhabited.
⁷I will send destroyers against you,
    each man with his weapons,
and they will cut up your fine cedar beams
    and throw them into the fire.

⁸"People from many nations will pass by this city and will ask one another, 'Why has the LORD done such a thing to this great city?' ⁹And the answer will be: 'Because they have forsaken the covenant of the LORD their God and have worshiped and served other gods.'"

¹⁰Do not weep for the dead king or mourn his loss;
    rather, weep bitterly for him who is exiled,
because he will never return
    nor see his native land again.

¹¹For this is what the LORD says about Shallum son of Josiah, who succeeded his father as king of Judah but has gone from this place: "He will never return. ¹²He will die in the place where they have led him captive; he will not see this land again."

¹³"Woe to him who builds his palace by unrighteousness,
    his upper rooms by injustice,
making his countrymen work for nothing,
    not paying them for their labor.
¹⁴He says, 'I will build myself a great palace
    with spacious upper rooms.'
So he makes large windows in it,
    panels it with cedar
    and decorates it in red.

¹⁵"Does it make you a king
    to have more and more cedar?
Did not your father have food and drink?
    He did what was right and just,
    so all went well with him.
¹⁶He defended the cause of the poor and needy,
    and so all went well.

Is that not what it means to know me?"
    declares the LORD.
¹⁷"But your eyes and your heart
    are set only on dishonest gain,
  on shedding innocent blood
    and on oppression and extortion."

¹⁸Therefore this is what the LORD says about Jehoiakim son of Josiah king of Judah:

"They will not mourn for him:
    'Alas, my brother! Alas, my sister!'
  They will not mourn for him:
    'Alas, my master! Alas, his splendor!'
¹⁹He will have the burial of a donkey—
    dragged away and thrown
    outside the gates of Jerusalem."

²⁰"Go up to Lebanon and cry out,
    let your voice be heard in Bashan,
  cry out from Abarim,
    for all your allies are crushed.
²¹I warned you when you felt secure,
    but you said, 'I will not listen!'
  This has been your way from your youth;
    you have not obeyed me.
²²The wind will drive all your shepherds away,
    and your allies will go into exile.
  Then you will be ashamed and disgraced
    because of all your wickedness.
²³You who live in 'Lebanon,'
    who are nestled in cedar buildings,
  how you will groan when pangs come upon you,
    pain like that of a woman in labor!

²⁴"As surely as I live," declares the LORD, "even if you, Jehoiachin son of Jehoiakim king of Judah, were a signet ring on my right hand, I would still pull you off. ²⁵I will hand you over to those who seek your life, those you fear—to Nebuchadnezzar king of Babylon and to the Babylonians. ²⁶I will hurl you and the mother who gave you birth into another country, where neither of you was born, and there you both will die. ²⁷You will never come back to the land you long to return to."

²⁸ Is this man Jehoiachin a despised, broken pot,
    an object no one wants?
Why will he and his children be hurled out,
    cast into a land they do not know?
²⁹ O land, land, land,
    hear the word of the LORD!
³⁰ This is what the LORD says:
    "Record this man as if childless,
        a man who will not prosper in his lifetime,
    for none of his offspring will prosper,
        none will sit on the throne of David
        or rule anymore in Judah."

THIS SECTION OF JEREMIAH contains several oracles directed to (against!) the royal family and its administration of affairs in Jerusalem. These prophecies are collected together because they share a common topic, not because they come from the same period in Jeremiah's ministry. Both the dynasty of David itself (21:12; 22:1, 6) and three of its kings are addressed (22:10–30): Shallum (also known as Jehoahaz),[1] Jehoiakim,[2] and Jehoiachin ("Coniah" in the Heb. of 22:24, 28).[3] Josiah, the father of Jehoahaz and Jehoiakim as well as the grandfather of Jehoiachin, is referred to by way of contrast in 22:15–16. With the mention of Zedekiah[4] in 21:1, readers have contextual references to all the kings of Judah who reigned during Jeremiah's ministry.

In the critical evaluation of the kings in this section, readers encounter an emphasis on royal social responsibilities. The king and his administration should "administer justice" (21:12) and "do what is just and right" (22:3).[5]

---

1. See 2 Kings 23:31–34. After a brief reign of three months following Josiah's death, Jehoahaz was removed by Pharaoh Neco; he died in exile in Egypt.

2. See 2 Kings 23:34–24:6. His name was Eliakim, but it was changed to Jehoiakim by Pharaoh Neco, who placed him on the throne after removing Jehoahaz. His reign lasted from 609–598 B.C. Second Kings 24:6 simply notes that he died, while 2 Chron. 36:6 records that Nebuchadnezzar bound him in chains to take him to Babylon.

3. See 2 Kings 24:6–16; 25:27–30. He reigned only three months before being led into exile by Nebuchadnezzar. According to 2 Kings 25:27–30/Jer. 52:31–34 he survived at least thirty-seven years in Babylon.

4. See 2 Kings 24:17–25:7. He reigned approximately eleven years, from 597–587/586 B.C. The fall of Jerusalem and its destruction by the Babylonians took place at the end of his reign.

5. The list of social crimes in 22:3 is similar to that in 7:6.

The Hebrew words for "just/justice" (*mišpaṭ*) and "right" (*ṣᵉdaqa*) are recognized terms to describe social rectitude and a healthy communal life. They overlap much in their meaning and often occur together as a word pair in the Old Testament.

These two terms are derived from a social vision where institutions such as the monarchy and court system are responsible to curb oppression and to protect the more vulnerable members of society.[6] *Justice* is primarily associated with administration. In doing justice one works through social institutions (e.g., court, state agencies). *Righteousness* is more a relational term. One is considered righteous when acting faithfully toward those with whom one is related in community.[7] A monarchy and its administrative agents who do not act in accord with these standards face judgment in the historical process (21:12; 22:4–9). The failures of the royal administration are also attributed to rejection of the covenant with God and the worship of other deities (22:9).

21:11–14. These verses can be read as further commentary on Jeremiah's word to Zedekiah in 21:1–10. The NIV translation of verse 11, which begins with "moreover," implies this connection. The grammar and syntax of the verse do not require this translation, however, and the four verses in this section are more like the general assessment of the monarchy in 22:1–9, the next oracle in the section.[8] This suggests that they are meant for any and all members of the house of David who live in the palace and assist in carrying out the affairs of state. In verse 13 comes a bitter criticism of those who live above the valley floors that surround Jerusalem. These persons would be royalty and other influential inhabitants who can afford the safer location of height in times of siege.

The command in 21:12 to "administer justice every morning" and to "rescue from the hand of his oppressor the one ... robbed" has a close parallel in Micah's critique preserved in Micah 2:1–2. Micah was from the Judean countryside, and his second chapter is a devastating critique of oppression that stems from Jerusalem. Early morning was the time when people in towns and villages rose and met one another on their way to perform daily tasks.

---

6. For further comments on the cultural setting of social justice themes, see M. Weinfeld, *Social Justice in Ancient Israel and in the Ancient Near East* (Minneapolis: Fortress, 1995). Ps. 72, for example, presupposes that the king in Jerusalem is to defend the weak and to guard justice and righteousness in the land as his God-given duties.

7. "Righteous" (*ṣaddiq*) is also the term used for someone who is "innocent" of a legal charge.

8. Jer. 21:12 addresses the house of David; 22:2 speaks generally of the king of Judah who sits on David's throne, along with his "servants" and "people." Both 21:12 and 22:3 contain the injunction to "rescue from the hand of his oppressor the one who has been robbed."

When they met at the gate of the city or village, they also worked out administrative-judicial affairs and witnessed agreements. Micah complains about those who rise early and seize property because they have the "power" (*ʾel;* lit., God) in their hand. Jeremiah's charge to the royal house, therefore, is to be a court of appeal for the oppressed "every morning."

22:1–9. God commands the prophet to "go down to the palace of the king" to proclaim a message. Readers should not overlook the verb "go down." Since the palace of the king is located at one of the highest points of Jerusalem, about the only place from which Jeremiah can "go down" is from the temple mount. This incidental comment tells us much about one important place where Jeremiah receives his prompting from God. Readers learn from another incidental comment in verse 2 that the royal palace had gates. Since some matters of state and cult were carried out at the royal palace (likely located near the temple), the gates would be those entry points to a public courtyard or hall.

Monarchs and their servants should prevent the shedding of "innocent blood in this place" (22:3). The prophet offered a similar charge in his temple sermon (7:6; cf. 19:4), and it is a topic to which he comes again in the context of a critique of royalty (22:17). This is a foreboding topic since "innocent blood" required atonement and other ceremonies to deal with its expiation; otherwise, responsibility for the shedding of innocent blood fell on the whole community.[9] Part of the duty of the royal house in doing justice and righteousness was to vindicate an innocent victim and to punish the murderers, even if the latter were from the elite strata of society.

Something of the "two-way" preaching is preserved in 22:4–5. In essence, the two ways set before the royal house are the same as those set before the people.

22:10–12. Of the three kings addressed directly, the briefest prophecy concerns Shallum, that is, Jehoahaz, the son and immediate successor to Josiah. He was placed on the throne after the death of his father but was subsequently removed by the Egyptian pharaoh after a brief reign. Jeremiah calls for bitter weeping (mourning) on his behalf, although his personal evaluation of Jehoahaz is not clear (cf. 2 Kings 23:32). The fate of this king foreshadows that of the people. The call in Jeremiah 22:10 not to mourn the death of Josiah is intended only to call attention to the sad fate of Jehoahaz. According to 2 Chronicles 35:25, Jeremiah offered a lamentation for Josiah, which became a pattern for singers in Israel.

---

9. One should compare the instructions in Deut. 21:1–9, which are designed for a community to purge itself of any guilt for "innocent blood" that may derive from an unsolved murder.

22:13–23. Jeremiah pronounces a judgmental "woe" on Jehoiakim, the older brother of Jehoahaz, who succeeded his younger brother on the throne (23:13–23). Apparently the people of the land (Judean property owners?) recognized Jehoiakim's unsuitability for rule when they initially bypassed him for Jehoahaz. They were loyal to the dynasty of David but did not want the eldest son to follow Josiah. The Egyptians, however, placed Jehoiakim on the throne, perhaps for the same reason that the people of the land had passed him over. Most certainly the Egyptians wanted someone from the royal family whom they could control. The Judeans would have preferred someone of a more independent nature.

Verse 13 describes Jehoiakim's activities as "unrighteous" and as examples of "injustice." These terms, of course, are the negative counterparts to justice and righteousness (cf. 22:3). Jehoiakim's arrogant building project is described as "his palace." Almost certainly this is not a primary residence, since the royal palace in Jerusalem had been in existence as long as the temple. According to 36:22 Jehoiakim had a winter house.[10] Whether this is the house that Jeremiah describes in 22:13–14 cannot be known without further information.

By contrast with Jehoiakim, his father Josiah is described as one who lived the life of a king (he ate and drank), but who also did what was "right and just" (*ṣᵉdaqa* and *mišpaṭ*, v. 15), defending the cause of the poor and needy. Jeremiah describes this activity as an example of what it means to "know" the Lord. Josiah is the only one of the monarchs from his day whom Jeremiah praises.

The fate of the arrogant and selfish king is that he will not be mourned at his death and will not receive a proper burial. Extant sources do not give details of Jehoiakim's burial or the precise circumstances of his death. The latter came apparently during the time of the Babylonians' siege of Jerusalem in 598/597 B.C.

22:24–30. This address to Jehoiachin has several grammatical complexities. The gist of the message is that he too falls under the judgment of the historical hour. His personal failings are not listed, and it may be that the query in verse 28 recognizes the incongruence of his circumstances. More precisely he and his family will go into Babylonian exile, and the young king will be reckoned as childless—although he has descendants—since his sons[11] will not sit on the throne of David and rule as kings in Judah.

---

10. The NIV translates 36:22 as "winter apartment." This is possible, but the Heb. term at issue, *bet*, ordinarily means house. According to Mic. 3:9–10, leaders in Jerusalem had earlier built Jerusalem with bloodshed and wickedness.

11. See 1 Chron. 3:17–18, which lists Jehoiachin's sons. Five of his sons are mentioned in Babylonian administrative documents that detail the rations given to Jehoiachin while a prisoner in Babylon. See W. F. Albright, "King Jehoiachin in Exile," *BA* 5 (1942): 49–55.

JUSTICE AND RIGHTEOUSNESS. This criticism of the Davidic dynasty and the enumeration of social crimes is but a part of a larger biblical concern to advocate justice and to oppose injustice. Several of the prophets before and during Jeremiah's day announced judgment on their contemporaries because of injustice and oppression.[12] Amos, for example, castigated Israel for failing to uphold God's standards of justice and righteousness (Amos 5:7, 14–15, 21–24; 6:12). Leading citizens of Samaria oppressed weaker members of society (4:1; cf. 2:7–8), and a destructive greed was rampant (8:4–6). Amos declared God's judgment on Israel; subsequently the nation was overrun by the Assyrians, Samaria was destroyed, and many inhabitants were taken into exile.[13] As noted above, Micah's social criticism of Judah has several things in common with Jeremiah. In his attitude toward the responsibilities of the royal house and their servants, Jeremiah stands in good prophetic company.

As with the other prophets, Jeremiah was not a political reformer in the modern sense of that term. His many harsh words of denunciation are not followed by a detailed blueprint for social reforms. There are at least three reasons for this. (1) Jeremiah was not a social architect or theorist; he was a prophet who spoke under the conviction that he lived in the historical hour of judgment.

(2) There is no indication that Jeremiah believed a new political philosophy or platform should be put in place. His terminology of justice and righteousness comes directly from the normative traditions of Israel. It was not a new plan that needed implementation but the application of covenant ethics as known in the Sinai revelation or in the claim of prerogative for David's family as guardian of the social order (Ps. 72).

(3) Jeremiah came to believe that Judah would be unable on its own to reconstitute itself as a just and compassionate society simply by changing a few programs. His preaching of repentance (where it is preserved in the book) seems to have convinced him that only God could reform Judah, which in turn would require a complete transformation of the people. Nor did Jeremiah have a secular ideal on which to draw for his concerns, since the "old paths" sufficed for instruction (6:16), but he did not concentrate on the "old paths" of the covenant ethics known to him. His work was essentially a theological critique, based on God's revealed character as righteous and just and shaped by the conviction that historical judgment was irrevocable.

---

12. H. Gossai, *Justice, Righteousness and the Social Critique of the Eighth-Century Prophets* (Bern: P. Lang, 1993).

13. Compare also Isa. 1:16–17; 3:13–15; 10:1–2; Mic. 2:1–5; 3:1–12; Zeph. 3:1–5.

The New Testament also voices concerns for justice and righteousness in the church. Since the tiny church of the apostolic age had no privilege in society or institutional political influence, the emphasis of the New Testament letters is on the internal ethics of the Christian community. Nevertheless, the various writers there concur that both the church body and its leaders should reflect a gospel-oriented holiness in its administrative structures and in the witness of the church's common life.[14]

As part of his criticism of Jehoiakim, Jeremiah also recognizes that a king can be a king with all the trappings and symbolism of the office and yet reflect the required covenantal ethics. Josiah ate and drank, but he also did justice and righteousness. Jeremiah's assessment is not unlike that given in 2 Kings, where the ruler is described as one who turned to the Lord with all his heart (2 Kings 23:25). The prophet asks rhetorically if such activity is what it means to "know God" (Jer. 22:16). The answer, of course, is "yes!" Here is an intertextual echo with 9:23–24. The wise person is one who knows the Lord as the God who exercises loving-kindness, justice, and righteousness and the God who delights when others do these things. What God wants from the Davidic rulers or from any truly "wise" person is someone who knows him and who shares his delight in these attributes.

Jeremiah's prophecies concerning the royal house and its administration underscore the importance of leadership for God's people. As 1 and 2 Kings make clear, as the leadership of the people goes, so go the people. This is an important bridge between then and now. With great privilege comes great responsibility. In Judah there was no "separation of church and state," as is common in modern Western societies. Kings were responsible to use their position of influence as servants of the Lord. Christians today may hear these words and be instructed first that the church (the current generation of God's people) has responsibilities to nurture and to support those among us who are weak and mistreated. Moreover, it is incumbent particularly on the leadership to demonstrate this concern and encourage it among the people.

Christians today may also hear these words as a call to support humanitarian policies and those institutions in their society that are concerned with justice and righteousness. In this way God, the Lord of all creation, is honored, and his gifts of common grace for all peoples are acknowledged by his people.

The royal line. The sad words about Jehoiachin are a somber commentary that comes in the context of judgment on Judah as a whole. These words, however, should be heard in the larger biblical context of additional

---

14. One might compare the ethics of the letter of James or the spiritual requirements of church leaders in the Pastoral Letters (1–2 Timothy, Titus).

revelation about his family. Jehoiachin and his family represent the generation judged and sent into exile. The Babylonians cut short his brief reign as king, and he spent the rest of his life in Babylon. Since the monarchical rule of the Davidic house ceased with the destruction of Jerusalem, none of Jehoiachin's sons ever sat on the throne so briefly occupied by him. Nevertheless, the fact that Jehoiachin survived in captivity is recorded as a sign of hope (2 Kings 25:27–30; Jer. 52:31–34). Moreover, his grandson Zerubbabel was appointed governor of the early postexilic community in Jerusalem (Hag. 1:1; Ezra 3:1–13).

Jehoiachin is part of the Davidic line that continues through Zerubbabel and leads to the birth of Christ (Matt. 1:1–17). When Zerubbabel is addressed by the prophet Haggai, he is told that he is a servant and a signet ring to the Lord (Hag. 2:20–23). This oracle likely reflects the judgmental prophecy against his grandfather in Jeremiah 22:24 ("if ... Jehoiachin ... were a signet ring ...") and shows, furthermore, that the historical word of judgment can be set in a larger framework of God's transhistorical intent to preserve and transform his people through the promises made to the Davidic house. Christians should see in these details the unfolding drama of the royal office into which Christ was born ("as to his human nature ... a descendant of David," Rom. 1:3). The great promises to and failures of the royal office provide the background to Jesus' fulfillment of it as the resurrected head of the church.[15]

MORAL COMMITMENTS. A maxim among modern Christians is that "truth is first in order to goodness." The truth of who God is and the truth of what God has called the church to be entail a commitment to moral character and social ethics in the church. Moral commitments start with its leadership.

Three kings in Jeremiah's time (Jehoahaz, Jehoiakim, Jehoiachin) are addressed as failures and as examples of the corporate failure of Judah. The flip side of a commitment to moral character and social rectitude is the disintegration of communal life when these qualities are absent. As the kings failed, so failed Judah. In current North American society, one can cite any number of statistics and trends that do not bode well for communal life (e.g., crime, family disintegration, etc.). Will they lead to a larger collapse of society? If so, are the churches immune from the fallout?

One should be careful in comparing the political leadership of a modern Western nation with the fate of Judah's leadership during Jeremiah's day. The

---

15. See comments in the introduction concerning Christ as the fulfillment of the prophetic, priestly, and royal (Davidic) offices.

president of the United States, for example, does not stand in the line of Davidic kings, nor is the president elected the head of the people of God (= the church). Christians may well argue the link between moral values and the health of a nation, but the first application of God's Word to ancient Judah concerning justice and righteousness is to the current generation of God's people.

Knowing God. The harsh word to Jehoiakim also contains an affirmation of what it means to know God. In his case, the contrast with his father, Josiah, is telling. The test of knowing God is the commitment of the person to the things of God—justice and righteousness for God's people. "If you love me," said Jesus, "you will obey what I command" (John 14:15). To know God is to be committed to his revealed will in the places of responsibility (ministry) where one lives and works. Of course, to know God means also to be rightly and personally related to him.

The affirmation that Josiah "turned to the LORD with all his heart and with all his soul" (2 Kings 23:25) is testimony to this truth, but Jeremiah's particular word relates to the practice of one's faith. Such an emphasis can be easily avoided by Christians claiming a cheap grace, but its truth cannot be evaded indefinitely. An orthodox theology leads to orthopraxis. Truth is first in order to goodness, not for self-justification but as service to the Lord.

God's faithfulness. The harsh words about Jehoiachin are a lesson about judgment and providence and a profound illustration of the "ups and downs" of the royal office ultimately fulfilled in Christ. As a young man and king for only three months, Jehoiachin was swept away into exile in 597. He spent the rest of his life in exile. He embodied the fate of his people. There was no escape from responsibility for failure. God's word of judgment to him in the historical hour came in service to God's larger intent to use the judgment of exile to chasten and redeem his people. God had bound himself by covenant oath to David's family as ruler over his people (2 Sam. 7; 23:5). Jehoiachin would see the discipline that God hands out to recalcitrant children (7:12–16), and his own sons were included.

Nevertheless, God would remain true to his promise and through Jehoiachin's line would again raise up leaders for his people. His grandson Zerubbabel would play a crucial role in the early postexilic period, serving as governor in Jerusalem. From this family of many failures came the ultimate child of promise, Christ the Lord (Matt. 1:1–17). God's historical "no" to the sins of Jehoiachin and his generation was tempered by his great "yes" in Jesus Christ. In his wrath God had marked Jehoiachin down as childless—none of his sons would ever sit on the throne; nevertheless, one of his descendants has ascended the throne of rule over God's people in a far grander way than Jehoiachin would ever realize.

The word of judgment to Jehoiachin is a sobering prophecy. There are situations where historical ruin comes about or where one's hopes are never realized. His uncle Jehoahaz died in Egypt, he in Babylon. Christ, his descendant according to the flesh, died on the cross. But he was raised to new life, and Christ now demonstrates God's resolve to save that which is lost. As the Lord of the church, Christ rules now as King of kings and Lord of lords.

Jeremiah 23:1–40

WOE TO THE SHEPHERDS who are destroying and scattering the sheep of my pasture!" declares the LORD. [2]Therefore this is what the LORD, the God of Israel, says to the shepherds who tend my people: "Because you have scattered my flock and driven them away and have not bestowed care on them, I will bestow punishment on you for the evil you have done," declares the LORD. [3]"I myself will gather the remnant of my flock out of all the countries where I have driven them and will bring them back to their pasture, where they will be fruitful and increase in number. [4]I will place shepherds over them who will tend them, and they will no longer be afraid or terrified, nor will any be missing," declares the LORD.

[5]"The days are coming," declares the LORD,
    "when I will raise up to David a righteous Branch,
a King who will reign wisely
    and do what is just and right in the land.
[6]In his days Judah will be saved
    and Israel will live in safety.
This is the name by which he will be called:
    The LORD Our Righteousness.

[7]"So then, the days are coming," declares the LORD, "when people will no longer say, 'As surely as the LORD lives, who brought the Israelites up out of Egypt,' [8]but they will say, 'As surely as the LORD lives, who brought the descendants of Israel up out of the land of the north and out of all the countries where he had banished them.' Then they will live in their own land."
[9]Concerning the prophets:

My heart is broken within me;
    all my bones tremble.
I am like a drunken man,
    like a man overcome by wine,
because of the LORD
    and his holy words.
[10]The land is full of adulterers;
    because of the curse the land lies parched
    and the pastures in the desert are withered.

  The prophets follow an evil course
    and use their power unjustly.

¹¹"Both prophet and priest are godless;
    even in my temple I find their wickedness,"
        declares the LORD.
¹²"Therefore their path will become slippery;
    they will be banished to darkness
    and there they will fall.
  I will bring disaster on them
    in the year they are punished,"
        declares the LORD.

¹³"Among the prophets of Samaria
    I saw this repulsive thing:
  They prophesied by Baal
    and led my people Israel astray.
¹⁴And among the prophets of Jerusalem
    I have seen something horrible:
  They commit adultery and live a lie.
  They strengthen the hands of evildoers,
    so that no one turns from his wickedness.
  They are all like Sodom to me;
    the people of Jerusalem are like Gomorrah."

¹⁵Therefore, this is what the LORD Almighty says concerning the prophets:

  "I will make them eat bitter food
    and drink poisoned water,
  because from the prophets of Jerusalem
    ungodliness has spread throughout the land."

¹⁶This is what the LORD Almighty says:

  "Do not listen to what the prophets are prophesying to you;
    they fill you with false hopes.
  They speak visions from their own minds,
    not from the mouth of the LORD.
¹⁷They keep saying to those who despise me,
    'The LORD says: You will have peace.'
  And to all who follow the stubbornness of their hearts
    they say, 'No harm will come to you.'

¹⁸ But which of them has stood in the council of the LORD
   to see or to hear his word?
   Who has listened and heard his word?
¹⁹ See, the storm of the LORD
   will burst out in wrath,
  a whirlwind swirling down
   on the heads of the wicked.
²⁰ The anger of the LORD will not turn back
   until he fully accomplishes
   the purposes of his heart.
In days to come
   you will understand it clearly.
²¹ I did not send these prophets,
   yet they have run with their message;
I did not speak to them,
   yet they have prophesied.
²² But if they had stood in my council,
   they would have proclaimed my words to my people
and would have turned them from their evil ways
   and from their evil deeds.

²³ "Am I only a God nearby,"

                          declares the LORD,

   "and not a God far away?
²⁴ Can anyone hide in secret places
   so that I cannot see him?"

                          declares the LORD.

   "Do not I fill heaven and earth?"

                          declares the LORD.

²⁵"I have heard what the prophets say who prophesy lies in my name. They say, 'I had a dream! I had a dream!' ²⁶How long will this continue in the hearts of these lying prophets, who prophesy the delusions of their own minds? ²⁷They think the dreams they tell one another will make my people forget my name, just as their fathers forgot my name through Baal worship. ²⁸Let the prophet who has a dream tell his dream, but let the one who has my word speak it faithfully. For what has straw to do with grain?" declares the LORD. ²⁹"Is not my word like fire," declares the LORD, "and like a hammer that breaks a rock in pieces?

³⁰"Therefore," declares the LORD, "I am against the prophets who steal from one another words supposedly from me. ³¹Yes,"

declares the LORD, "I am against the prophets who wag their own tongues and yet declare, 'The LORD declares.' ³²Indeed, I am against those who prophesy false dreams," declares the LORD. "They tell them and lead my people astray with their reckless lies, yet I did not send or appoint them. They do not benefit these people in the least," declares the LORD.

³³"When these people, or a prophet or a priest, ask you, 'What is the oracle of the LORD?' say to them, 'What oracle? I will forsake you, declares the LORD.' ³⁴If a prophet or a priest or anyone else claims, 'This is the oracle of the LORD,' I will punish that man and his household. ³⁵This is what each of you keeps on saying to his friend or relative: 'What is the LORD's answer?' or 'What has the LORD spoken?' ³⁶But you must not mention 'the oracle of the LORD' again, because every man's own word becomes his oracle and so you distort the words of the living God, the LORD Almighty, our God. ³⁷This is what you keep saying to a prophet: 'What is the LORD's answer to you?' or 'What has the LORD spoken?' ³⁸Although you claim, 'This is the oracle of the LORD,' this is what the LORD says: You used the words, 'This is the oracle of the LORD,' even though I told you that you must not claim, 'This is the oracle of the LORD.' ³⁹Therefore, I will surely forget you and cast you out of my presence along with the city I gave to you and your fathers. ⁴⁰I will bring upon you everlasting disgrace— everlasting shame that will not be forgotten."

Original Meaning

JEREMIAH 23 COLLECTS a number of harsh sayings against the religious leaders who oppose Jeremiah in word and deed. As is common in the first half of the book, there are no dates associated with these prophecies. Included among the "shepherds" mentioned at the beginning of the chapter are almost certainly kings—perhaps the three kings (Jehoiakim, Jehoiachin, and Zedekiah) mentioned in the previous two chapters.[1] Priests are also mentioned (23:11, 33–34), but the brunt of the criticism falls on prophets, who have not understood the Lord correctly and who have, therefore, misled the people (cf. Deut. 13; 18). Among these words of judgment are also claims that God intends to redeem his scattered people and to raise up a shepherd in whose days Judah and Israel will find security.

---

1. Jeremiah's younger contemporary Ezekiel describes the kings as shepherds (Ezek. 34). There are several similarities between this chapter and Ezek. 34.

23:1–4. Punishment and crime are linked for the shepherds in this brief prose text. God will bring judgment on them because they have not cared for their flock. Verse 2 charges them more specifically with not caring for "my [i.e.. God's] people." The scattered flock is identified as the exiled remnant of God's people, who will be brought back to their homeland (23:3, 7–8). This passage, therefore, probably originated after the first wave of exiles was taken away to Babylon in 597 B.C. Since the fall and destruction of Jerusalem are not mentioned, it is less likely that the prophecy originated after 587/586 B.C.

23:5–6. This passage begins with a typical formula about the future: "The days are coming." God will raise up for his scattered people a shepherd who will rule justly and wisely.[2] He will be a king from David's line. His wonderful name, "The LORD Our Righteousness" (*yhwh ṣidᵉqenu*), is a pun on the name Zedekiah (= Righteous is Yahweh), the last king of Judah (who reigned from 597–587/586 B.C.). For the generation of Jeremiah, the symbolic name of this "righteous Branch" is probably a sarcastic judgment on Zedekiah; moreover, it points to God's resolve to restore his people and fulfill his promises to the Davidic line.

This prophecy, like the prose text that begins chapter 23, should be read in the context of the previous section (21:11–22:30) and its concern with the injustice and failures of the Davidic monarchs. The judgment to fall on the shepherds comes because they have failed to fulfill the duties of their office. As verse 5 proclaims, a king should "do what is just [*mišpaṭ*] and right [*sᵉdaqa*] in the land." These are the normative terms, the expected attributes of kingship (see 22:15; also Ps. 72:1–4).

The name of the king ("The LORD Our Righteousness") represents significant claims about the work of God. (1) In his days Judah and Israel "will be saved"[3] and will dwell securely. (2) The righteousness indicated in his name is for the people, even though it is not fully their own. The Lord is their righteousness. It is the integrity of the Lord, his fidelity to his promises, that is finally the people's righteousness.

23:7–8. Prophecy of a future change in the circumstances of the people continues in these two verses (see also 16:14–15). Just as something new and wonderful will emerge from David's line, so a second exodus will occur, and the exiled people will return to their land.

The criticisms of the prophets who are misleading the people are manifold. The rest of the chapter concerns their culpability in failing their office and the people. These prophecies come as part of an exchange between Jeremiah and God. The voices can be outlined as follows:

---

2. Jer. 23:5–6 is repeated in 33:14–16.

3. The verb is a passive form of *yšᶜ*. Names such as Joshua, Isaiah, Hosea, and Jesus (Matt. 1:21) are based on this word.

A. 23:9–10: Jeremiah laments the evil course of his prophetic opponents.
B. 23:11–12: God speaks of the wickedness he sees and announces judgment.
C. 23:13–14: Jeremiah refers to prophets in Samaria and Jerusalem as repulsive.
D. 23:15–24: God denies that he has sent these misleading prophets and affirms that nothing they do is secret to him.
E. 23:25–40: In this prose section Jeremiah reports God's anger at the false dreams and oracles offered in his name.

23:9–10. Perhaps the first clause of verse 9 is a heading for the materials that follow and not just for Jeremiah's anguished comments in verses 9–10. Jeremiah reacts to the dire straits of his people and the power of his prophetic opponents to mislead them. He mentions drought conditions as one element of his horror (cf. ch. 14). The magnitude of God's words of judgment have rendered the prophet like a drunken man. It is not clear whether this is metaphorical language to describe Jeremiah's strong emotional reaction or if he actually manifests physical symptoms ("all my bones tremble").

23:11–12. God's first reply notes that the wickedness of prophet and priest is in "my temple" (lit., "my house"). These verses confirm that the prophets and priests who serve there are also offering oracles of assurance that the nation will not fall.

23:13–14. Jeremiah reports a repulsive thing he has observed about the earlier prophets of Samaria (the northern kingdom): They prophesied by Baal and led God's people astray (cf. 23:27). This historical comment interprets the fall of Israel and Samaria in 722/721 B.C. Something equally heinous is then reported with respect to the prophets in Jerusalem: They are adulterers and living a lie. These observations can be attributed either to God or to Jeremiah, but the introductory formula of verse 15—"Therefore, this is what the LORD Almighty says"—implies that Jeremiah is the speaker in verses 13–14 and that the divine oracle in verses 15–24 is God's response. Verse 14 offers a familiar analogy to describe the folly of Samaria and Jerusalem; the two cities are compared to Sodom and Gomorrah, the cities on the plain that God overthrew because of their wickedness (Gen. 18:16–19:29).

23:15–24. The introductory formula of verse 15 is like that of verse 9. Concerning the prophets, it seems to introduce several oracles from the Lord. There are additional rhetorical formulae in verses 16, 23, and 24. The command "do not listen to … the prophets" is addressed to the people.[4] The prophets who prophesy "peace" is a familiar complaint in Jeremiah. There will be no peace or security for a people who "despise" God.

---

4. The "you" of verse 16 is second-person plural.

The oracle about judgment on the prophets notes that the people will better understand this matter in "days to come" (v. 20). It is the function of a book like Jeremiah, which was published in the aftermath of Judah's demise, to make clear that the people had trusted in lies.

God denies sending these prophets. The rhetorical question of verse 18—"Which of [the prophets] has stood in the council of the LORD?"—implies an emphatic negative for an answer. None of them has been privy to God's council.[5] If they had been in God's council, then they would have proclaimed the evil deeds of the people and attempted to turn them from their acts and the consequences.

The rhetorical questions of verses 23–24 are also intended for the people's hearing. Whether near or far, the people and their deeds are known to God, who fills heaven and earth (with his presence).

23:25–40. These prose comments continue the criticism of Jerusalem's prophets. One of their modes of communicating is dream reports. Verse 28 makes a distinction between the faithful reporting of God's word and the reporting of a dream. The implication is that the reception of the word is a different form of experience, but it is not further defined. In effect, it is like the hammer that shatters rock.

Verses 33–40 begin with a play on one of the words for "oracle" (*maśśaʾ*), which can also be translated as "burden" (cf. NIV note). Perhaps the link between the two meanings of the word comes from the concept of bearing or carrying something. The Greek translation of verse 33 reflects a different Hebrew text from the Masoretic Text. The question implied by the LXX reads: "What is the *maśśaʾ* [oracle] of the LORD?" and it is answered by a statement directed to the people, "You are the *maśśaʾ* [the burden]." The gist of these last verses is clear, however the wordplay is sorted out: God will judge the prophets and the people who listen to them.

It is important to note that in all the criticism of the prophets, the expression "false prophet" is not used. Some of these prophets probably deserved the description, for they looked to Baal for their inspiration or simply lied about their reception of a message from Yahweh. Some, however, might not deserve such a description. Perhaps they had been of service in the cause of the Lord in times past, and they sincerely hoped that their message of peace and security had its origin with the Lord.

These judgments against the religious leaders of the people are related to other passages in Jeremiah. Various narratives and oracles make it clear that Jehoiakim and Zedekiah failed as shepherds of the nation. That some mem-

---

5. The council is the assembly of the heavenly host (cf. 1 Kings 22:19–22), where the Lord, the cosmic King, holds court and sends appointed messengers to announce his word.

bers of the priesthood were hostile to Jeremiah is clear from 20:1–6. Jeremiah will have a memorable encounter with a prophet named Hananiah in chapter 28, and he will be involved (via letters) in debate with Judean prophets in Babylon (29:21–32). His prayers of lament are derived, in part, from his experiences of ridicule and humiliation at the hand of these leaders.

FALSE PROPHETS. The covenant-renewal document known as Deuteronomy has stipulations that parallel Jeremiah's criticisms of religious leaders and provide a broader biblical context in which to interpret the prophet's critique. One may point to the first two commandments of the Decalogue (Deut. 5:7–10), which forbid the worship of other deities. In elaboration, Deuteronomy 13 and 18 warn the people to avoid prophets who advocate the worship of other deities. They offer warnings about prophets and dreamers who will lead Israel astray. The penalty for such prophetic activity is death. Jeremiah's harsh words about the religious leaders apparently have their roots in this broader biblical context of a judicial judgment on "false prophets" for inciting a rebellion or turning people away from the Lord. Similarly, Jesus judges "false prophets" harshly because of the damage they do (Matt. 7:15–23).[6]

Deuteronomy 17:14–20 requires that the king in Israel have a copy of the covenant law and that he live by its precepts. The integrity required of the ruler is missing among the indicted shepherds, whose lack of justice and righteousness and whose failure to cling to the Lord have resulted in the scattering of the Lord's flock.

Shepherding motif. The language of shepherd and shepherding is a part of the broader biblical theme of the character of leadership in Israel, taken from the cultural role of a shepherd who tends his flocks by providing sustenance and protection from harm. Israel offers praise to God, who is the ultimate Shepherd of his people (Ps. 23:1; 80:1). Ezekiel likewise uses the specific imagery of the shepherd for a ruler in his criticism of Judean leaders (Ezek. 34). Nathan, David's prophetic advisor, received a prophetic revelation to remind David that he was anointed to shepherd God's people (2 Sam. 7:7). Here is foundational material for the Davidic covenant and the royal office ultimately filled by Christ. In the New Testament Christ identifies himself as the "good shepherd" who lays down his life for the flock (John 10; cf. 1 Peter 2:25).

---

6. Prophetic activity is known in the New Testament churches (1 Cor. 12–14; Eph. 4:11), both for good and for ill (cf. Rev. 2:20).

Jeremiah announces that God will raise up a faithful shepherd whose symbolic name indicates that the Lord is the people's righteousness. Christians recognize the truth of that prophecy in a way Jeremiah's contemporaries could not. Old Testament saints heard that prophecy as God's faithfulness to the Davidic line and his grace in saving a remnant of his people. The name, of course, is symbolic of the character of the future ruler. In Christ God has demonstrated his righteousness and also accepted Christ's righteousness on behalf of those who trust in his saving work. Christ thus fulfills the Davidic hopes and represents them in a faithful, yet also grander, way than anticipated by Jeremiah's contemporaries. Christ is, as noted in the previous chapter, the culmination of the hopes of the royal office. Even the failures of a Zedekiah (or any failures in the line of David) simply set Christ's headship over the church in bold relief.

LEADERSHIP OF GOD'S PEOPLE. Jeremiah's criticism of religious leaders touches on a sensitive and central biblical theme: that of the spiritual and moral character of leadership among God's people. The history of the church is replete with examples of good and bad leadership. Saints of the past such as Augustine, Martin Luther, and William Booth (founder of the Salvation Army) provided visionary leadership and a piety combining moral character and devotion to Christ. On the other side were Gnostics, syncretists, and libertines, who diluted the faith and argued that morals do not matter.

It is a sobering exercise for modern Christians to ask who among the church's leadership downplay the issues of moral character and soft-pedal the spiritual characteristics needed to shepherd God's people. Who among the spokespersons for the faith downplay the distinctive character of Christian faith in return for an emphasis on greater commonality with the world? What leaders say one thing and yet represent another in their personal lives? The point is not to advocate moralism at all costs but to look carefully for the consistency of the prophetic voice with the faith it defends in controversial times.

Jeremiah criticizes the prophets who proclaim that all is well when the corporate life of the people shows desperate problems. In some Christian circles it is relatively easy to paint a sordid picture of parts of human existence but more difficult to strike a balance between a negative assessment of human failure and a positive proclamation of God's ability to heal and to transform. Correspondingly, some Christian communities find it too easy to ignore problems within their midst, and they look with disfavor on those who disturb the peace and purity of the church. Those who lead the church and claim to know the direction in which it should go have a great responsibility. "By their fruit you will recognize them," said Jesus (Matt. 7:16), a practical test that is consistent with Jeremiah's criticism of his prophetic contemporaries and a test that remains crucial in the present.

A true prophet. Jeremiah was a true prophet because the word he received from the Lord was vindicated in the events of history. Clearly, the timing of the fulfillment was a point of consternation for him. He spent years proclaiming a judgment that came only after much anguish on his part. That his word about the future eventually did occur is one of the tests for true prophecy (according to Deuteronomy). With the life of the people in crisis, Jeremiah announced that Judah had to change or judgment would come. Eventually he understood that any repentance would be too little and too late. Those prophets who disagreed with him were wrong historically and theologically. In essence, their denial of judgment was a denial of the Lord at work redemptively through historical judgment. Their words diverted the people's attention from seeking the Lord to a false assurance that he would protect them.

Is this not like the turmoil over Jesus' public ministry, where he continually called people to a life of commitment and spiritual discernment in counting the cost of discipleship? Discipleship (i.e., following Christ) is also a form of leadership, and vice versa. Christ came not to be served but to serve (Mark 10:45). That is the point of Christology; it is the point for all shepherds in the church.

Jeremiah 24:1–10

AFTER JEHOIACHIN son of Jehoiakim king of Judah and the officials, the craftsmen and the artisans of Judah were carried into exile from Jerusalem to Babylon by Nebuchadnezzar king of Babylon, the LORD showed me two baskets of figs placed in front of the temple of the LORD. ²One basket had very good figs, like those that ripen early; the other basket had very poor figs, so bad they could not be eaten.

³Then the LORD asked me, "What do you see, Jeremiah?"

"Figs," I answered. "The good ones are very good, but the poor ones are so bad they cannot be eaten."

⁴Then the word of the LORD came to me: ⁵"This is what the LORD, the God of Israel, says: 'Like these good figs, I regard as good the exiles from Judah, whom I sent away from this place to the land of the Babylonians. ⁶My eyes will watch over them for their good, and I will bring them back to this land. I will build them up and not tear them down; I will plant them and not uproot them. ⁷I will give them a heart to know me, that I am the LORD. They will be my people, and I will be their God, for they will return to me with all their heart.

⁸"'But like the poor figs, which are so bad they cannot be eaten,' says the LORD, 'so will I deal with Zedekiah king of Judah, his officials and the survivors from Jerusalem, whether they remain in this land or live in Egypt. ⁹I will make them abhorrent and an offense to all the kingdoms of the earth, a reproach and a byword, an object of ridicule and cursing, wherever I banish them. ¹⁰I will send the sword, famine and plague against them until they are destroyed from the land I gave to them and their fathers.'"

JEREMIAH'S OBSERVATIONS AT the temple become a vehicle for God's address to the people. The setting is in Zedekiah's reign, sometime between 597 B.C., when Nebuchadnezzar took Jehoiachin[1] and a number of the leading citizens of Judah into exile in Babylon, and 587/586,

---

1. According to 52:31–34 Jehoiachin was kept under house arrest for thirty-seven years before being granted some additional freedom in Babylon. In 24:1 Jeconiah, an alternate form of his name, is used in the Hebrew text.

when the Babylonians besieged and destroyed Jerusalem. The date is probably close to 588, the beginning of the second Babylonian siege of Jerusalem.

Jeremiah observes two baskets of figs left as offerings at the temple, one of which contains ripe figs and the other rotten figs.[2] The Lord tells the prophet that the good figs are like the Judeans taken into exile, while the rotten figs represent Zedekiah and those who remain in Jerusalem and Judah. The Lord promises to do good to the exilic community, to bring them back from exile, and to give them a heart to know him. Concerning those remaining in Judah, however, the Lord promises judgment.

One finds in this autobiographic prophetic report a shorthand version of what the larger book of Jeremiah intends to accomplish. For those on whom the judgment of the Exile has fallen, God announces that he intends to "build them up" and to "plant" them again in the Promised Land.[3] Return to the land is not all that God intends, although the return is a sign of something more fundamental, a wholehearted return to the Lord. Thus, there is also the promise of a heart prepared by God to know him as well as the reinstitution of the covenant relationship ("they will be my people, and I will be their God," 24:7).[4] For those still mired in their failures, the announced judgments stand.

REMNANT THEOLOGY. Not only does this chapter reflect in brief the larger designs of the book of Jeremiah, but its claims of judgment and restoration are also part of a larger biblical pattern of remnant theology. Judgment upon iniquity and sociopolitical changes (e.g., statehood and monarchy; exile) brought divisions among the people of God. During the period of Elijah, for example, many in Israel fell to the seductions of the Phoenician culture and religion. God assured Elijah, however, that there were still seven thousand in Israel who had not bowed the knee to Baal (1 Kings 19:1–18).

With turmoil, intrigue, and injustice rampant, Isaiah was told not to believe what many of his contemporaries called conspiracy but to seal up his testimony among his disciples (Isa. 8:11–17). With his prophetic testimony and his disciples, Isaiah formed a remnant community in eighth-century

---

2. Amos had a vision of a basket of fruit (at a temple?), which became the occasion for a prophetic announcement of judgment on Israel (Amos 8:1–4).

3. Readers will note the correspondence in vocabulary between the call of Jeremiah (1:10) and the (re)building and (re)planting of the exilic community.

4. This formula is the shorthand version of the covenant relationship established by God with Israel at Mount Sinai/Horeb. Cf. Jer. 31:33 (and reference to heart); also Ex. 6:7; Lev. 26:12; Ezek. 11:20; 36:28; Zech. 8:8. Deut. 26:16–19 has the formula in somewhat expanded form.

Judah. In the postexilic community, Ezra and Nehemiah formed a remnant community centered in Jerusalem. Their opponents may have considered themselves part of God's people, but their actions disqualified them from membership.

In the New Testament, Jesus' choice of twelve disciples likely reflects a symbolic forming of a new Israel among the Jews of his day. The church of Jew and Gentile together is a fulfillment of the prophetic hope to raise up again the booth of David and to save remnants from among humankind (Acts 15:13–21). When Paul reflects on God's providence, he thinks of the church as a remnant saved by grace and as evidence that God's mercy will cast an even wider net (Rom. 11). A circular letter to Christians in dispersion interprets them typologically as an exiled remnant, who have been born anew to a living hope through Christ (1 Peter 1:1–9).

Christians, therefore, are part of the remnant saved by grace. This is one of the bridges linking Jeremiah's vision of the two baskets with the church. Another is typological and similar to the remnant link. In the return from exile God provides fulfillment of his concern for his people in Babylon. This does not exhaust the meaning of Jeremiah's prophecy, but it illumines the concern of God wherever and whenever his people are scattered and turn to him in faith.

 JUDGMENT AND RESTORATION. God is just in judgment and yet one who justifies (accepts as righteous) those who trust him for their salvation. This is a paraphrase of Romans 3:26; it also captures the intent of Jeremiah 24. God brings judgment on those who spurn him and reject his covenant. But he also seeks to save that which is lost and to give a new heart to those whom he calls into fellowship. The divided fate of the two communities in Jeremiah's day illustrates God's use of the historical process for judgment and restoration.

The heart. Jeremiah depicts the matter of relating to God as a matter of the heart.[5] The heart is the inner core of a person that directs the will and prompts action. This is somewhat different from the modern Western emphasis on the heart as the seat of feelings and emotions. God desires wholehearted allegiance, and by his grace he offers a new heart to his people. In its original context, the physical circumstances concern the judgment of the Exile and the future gift of return to the Promised Land. But there is more even in the original context. The reaction to God's prophetic word is a matter of the heart as it prompts the spiritual allegiances and commitments of the people. That

---

5. See comments on the heart at Jer. 4:4 and 17:9.

prophetic word concerns the possibility of spiritual change on a fundamental level, and it affirms the miraculous possibility that God will renew a covenant relationship with his people. What Jeremiah projects as God's future grace finds ultimate fulfillment in the coming of Christ and his offer of new life.

A few years ago the popular movie *Places in the Heart* concerned matters of injustice and hatred and the possibility that God would work through the lives of people for reconciliation and spiritual renewal. This film was a gripping drama because it demonstrated both the power of sin to keep people mired in tragic habits of mind and the power of the gospel to bring to life what was completely missing in personal lives and community relationships.

In its conclusion, the movie provided a powerful testimony to the work of God in human hearts and the possibilities of forgiveness and renewal. The scene depicted a worship service, where community members, both Caucasian and African American, sat in proximity to one another and partook of the one communion table. It depicted that reconciliation is more than a change of mind; it is sharing of space and common commitments to one another. It is something that requires the presence of God because God is its author.

Exile and alienation are geographic and historical entities, but they are also powerful emotional forces. Only through God's grace can either the historical realities of sin or their emotional aftermath be removed and the affections of "another" heart be set in motion.

Jeremiah 25:1–38

THE WORD CAME to Jeremiah concerning all the people of Judah in the fourth year of Jehoiakim son of Josiah king of Judah, which was the first year of Nebuchadnezzar king of Babylon. ²So Jeremiah the prophet said to all the people of Judah and to all those living in Jerusalem: ³For twenty-three years—from the thirteenth year of Josiah son of Amon king of Judah until this very day—the word of the LORD has come to me and I have spoken to you again and again, but you have not listened.

⁴And though the LORD has sent all his servants the prophets to you again and again, you have not listened or paid any attention. ⁵They said, "Turn now, each of you, from your evil ways and your evil practices, and you can stay in the land the LORD gave to you and your fathers for ever and ever. ⁶Do not follow other gods to serve and worship them; do not provoke me to anger with what your hands have made. Then I will not harm you."

⁷"But you did not listen to me," declares the LORD, "and you have provoked me with what your hands have made, and you have brought harm to yourselves."

⁸Therefore the LORD Almighty says this: "Because you have not listened to my words, ⁹I will summon all the peoples of the north and my servant Nebuchadnezzar king of Babylon," declares the LORD, "and I will bring them against this land and its inhabitants and against all the surrounding nations. I will completely destroy them and make them an object of horror and scorn, and an everlasting ruin. ¹⁰I will banish from them the sounds of joy and gladness, the voices of bride and bridegroom, the sound of millstones and the light of the lamp. ¹¹This whole country will become a desolate wasteland, and these nations will serve the king of Babylon seventy years.

¹²"But when the seventy years are fulfilled, I will punish the king of Babylon and his nation, the land of the Babylonians, for their guilt," declares the LORD, "and will make it desolate forever. ¹³I will bring upon that land all the things I have spoken against it, all that are written in this book and prophesied by Jeremiah against all the nations. ¹⁴They themselves will be

enslaved by many nations and great kings; I will repay them according to their deeds and the work of their hands."

¹⁵This is what the LORD, the God of Israel, said to me: "Take from my hand this cup filled with the wine of my wrath and make all the nations to whom I send you drink it. ¹⁶When they drink it, they will stagger and go mad because of the sword I will send among them."

¹⁷So I took the cup from the LORD's hand and made all the nations to whom he sent me drink it: ¹⁸Jerusalem and the towns of Judah, its kings and officials, to make them a ruin and an object of horror and scorn and cursing, as they are today; ¹⁹Pharaoh king of Egypt, his attendants, his officials and all his people, ²⁰and all the foreign people there; all the kings of Uz; all the kings of the Philistines (those of Ashkelon, Gaza, Ekron, and the people left at Ashdod); ²¹Edom, Moab and Ammon; ²²all the kings of Tyre and Sidon; the kings of the coastlands across the sea; ²³Dedan, Tema, Buz and all who are in distant places; ²⁴all the kings of Arabia and all the kings of the foreign people who live in the desert; ²⁵all the kings of Zimri, Elam and Media; ²⁶and all the kings of the north, near and far, one after the other—all the kingdoms on the face of the earth. And after all of them, the king of Sheshach will drink it too.

²⁷"Then tell them, 'This is what the LORD Almighty, the God of Israel, says: Drink, get drunk and vomit, and fall to rise no more because of the sword I will send among you.' ²⁸But if they refuse to take the cup from your hand and drink, tell them, 'This is what the LORD Almighty says: You must drink it! ²⁹See, I am beginning to bring disaster on the city that bears my Name, and will you indeed go unpunished? You will not go unpunished, for I am calling down a sword upon all who live on the earth, declares the LORD Almighty.'

³⁰"Now prophesy all these words against them and say to them:

"'The LORD will roar from on high;
    he will thunder from his holy dwelling
    and roar mightily against his land.
He will shout like those who tread the grapes,
    shout against all who live on the earth.
³¹The tumult will resound to the ends of the earth,
    for the LORD will bring charges against the nations;

> he will bring judgment on all mankind
>   and put the wicked to the sword,'"
>
> declares the LORD.

³²This is what the LORD Almighty says:

> "Look! Disaster is spreading
>   from nation to nation;
> a mighty storm is rising
>   from the ends of the earth."

³³At that time those slain by the LORD will be everywhere—from one end of the earth to the other. They will not be mourned or gathered up or buried, but will be like refuse lying on the ground.

> ³⁴Weep and wail, you shepherds;
>   roll in the dust, you leaders of the flock.
> For your time to be slaughtered has come;
>   you will fall and be shattered like fine pottery.
> ³⁵The shepherds will have nowhere to flee,
>   the leaders of the flock no place to escape.
> ³⁶Hear the cry of the shepherds,
>   the wailing of the leaders of the flock,
>   for the LORD is destroying their pasture.
> ³⁷The peaceful meadows will be laid waste
>   because of the fierce anger of the LORD.
> ³⁸Like a lion he will leave his lair,
>   and their land will become desolate
> because of the sword of the oppressor
>   and because of the LORD's fierce anger.

Original Meaning

AT ONE STAGE in the collection of Jeremiah's prophecies, chapter 25 likely concluded the collection or, at least, ended a section on judgment of the nations. Beginning with chapter 26, the reader of Jeremiah is provided with a series of biographical prose accounts about the prophet, which make a somewhat different impression than the preceding collections of poetic oracles. One may summarize the literary placement issue somewhat differently by observing that chapter 25 brings to a conclusion the first half of the prophetic book. The material within it assists the reader in looking back to the poetic oracles or forward to the prose accounts.

It is possible that the early form of Jeremiah's prophecies recorded in Baruch's first scroll (ch. 36) ended with the almost apocalyptic portrayal of multinational judgment in chapter 25. Note the reference to Jeremiah's "book" in 25:13. In its current form chapter 25 in Hebrew has similarities to the oracles against the nations and Babylon in chapters 46–51, which now conclude the book. The initial verse of the chapter places the prophecy in the fourth year of Jehoiakim, which was also the first year of Nebuchadnezzar's kingship.[1] This was a time of political change and uncertainty, when the political map was being redrawn by the Babylonians, and Jehoiakim, an Egyptian appointee, faced a dangerous and uncertain future. Jeremiah uses the opportunity to announce that the judgment to come on Judah is but a part of the administration of the Lord's justice in international affairs.

In the Greek version of Jeremiah's book, this chapter is much expanded to include additional oracles against the nations found elsewhere in the Hebrew version.[2] The peoples and nations named in 25:19–26 are contemporaries of Judah. They too have been assessed and founding wanting in the courts of the Lord. The language is stylized, and judgment is depicted on a universal scale. At points the depiction reflects a historical process in convulsion, as if to say that the decisive point in the judgment of the world has arrived (cf. 25:30–31). In other words, the chapter contains a combination of historical allusion and symbolic portrait, anticipating the apocalyptic language of Ezekiel, Zechariah, and Daniel and paving the way for the apocalyptic language in the New Testament.

25:1–14. This material reports oracular material that God gives to Jeremiah. That it is also a summary statement is clear from verse 3—a reference to twenty-three years of preaching on the part of the prophet. Jeremiah's work is set in the context of God's ongoing prophetic witness among the people carried out by his "servants the prophets" (26:5; cf. 2 Kings 9:7; 24:2). The refusal of the people to heed Jeremiah's warnings and earlier calls for repentance (cf. Jer. 25:5) has now led to the brink of judgment. Babylon, and more particularly Nebuchadnezzar, are identified as a foe from the north. The

---

1. That is, 605 B.C. Nebuchadnezzar had been active previously as crown prince and head of the army before assuming the throne at his father's death. With the defeat of Egypt at Carchemish in the summer of 605, the Babylonians assumed political hegemony over Syria-Palestine.

2. In the Heb. text these oracles are located in chs. 46–51. Not only does the Greek version of Jeremiah include them here after v. 13, but the order of the oracles differs in the Greek version from that of the Hebrew chs. 46–51. The transmission of this oracular material is a complicated issue. In addition to the detailed commentaries see G. Fischer, "Jer 25 und die Fremdvolkerspruche: Unterschiede zwischen hebraischem und griechischem Text," *Bib* 72 (1991): 474–99.

judgment to come on Judah and Jerusalem is only part of what Nebuchadnezzar will do. Other nations will also come under his domination.

Verse 9 describes Nebuchadnezzar as God's "servant." This is a shocking term to use but fully consistent with Jeremiah's message. The prophet portrays the historical judgment to come on Judah as God's work against his sinful people. Nebuchadnezzar is not a "loose cannon" but an agent in the employ of God. In Daniel Nebuchadnezzar will bear witness in his own frailty that God is sovereign (Dan. 4:1–37). The king's servanthood does not make him morally superior or grant him saving knowledge of God. One may compare the language of "anointed" used to describe Cyrus in his historical role of liberator from the Exile, where it is explicitly stated that the Persian king does not know the Lord (Isa. 45:1–7).

In the judgments against Judah, a servitude to Babylon of "seventy years" is projected (Jer. 25:11–12). The actual period was about sixty-six years, if one reckons from the first year of Nebuchadnezzar's kingship in 605 B.C. to the fall of Babylon in 539, or seventy years almost exactly[3] if one reckons from the destruction of the temple in 586 to its rededication in 516 (cf. Ezra 6:15). More likely, seventy is a round number representing the fulfillment of an extended period (2 Chron. 36:21; Zech. 1:12–14). It should be contrasted with the short period predicted by Hananiah for Babylonian hegemony (Jer. 28:3–4).[4]

That Nebuchadnezzar and Babylon are the Lord's servants in the historical process does not make them immune from his standards of justice, however. Babylon too will be judged for its iniquities (25:12–14). This short prophecy anticipates elements in chapters 46–49 (judgment against nations) and 50–51 (judgment against Babylon).[5] As noted above, the oracles against the nations in chapters 46–51 actually come in the Greek version after 25:13 and its reference to "things . . . prophesied by Jeremiah against all the nations."

25:15–38. This section vividly depicts the imagery of the nations drinking from the Lord's "cup" of wrath. Such a cup, which presupposes the staggering of someone inebriated and out of control, is a metaphor for the turmoil to come among the nations, when God's sword of judgment is unleashed. As a prophetic symbol of judgment, God's cup of wrath is widespread. In 51:7 Babylon herself is described as the intoxicating cup, but the cup is more usually related directly to God and his judgment.[6]

---

3. C. F. Whitely, "The Seventy Years Desolation: A Rejoinder," *VT* 7 (1957): 416–18.

4. Dan. 9:24–25 employs the seventy years as a means to project a broader scale of God's providence.

5. See further J. Hill, *Friend or Foe? The Figure of Babylon in the Book of Jeremiah MT* (Leiden: Brill, 1999).

6. See also Isa. 51:17–23; Jer. 49:12; Lam. 4:21; Ezek. 23:31–34; Hab. 2:16.

A long listing of states and rulers comprises a summary for "all the kingdoms on the face of the earth" (25:26). The exaggerated imagery continues with the naming of Babylon as Sheshach, a cryptogram or symbolic name. In turn, Babylon too will drink the cup of wrath.

All the nations are caught up in the description of the judgment to come. It is not just Jerusalem, "the city that bears [God's] Name" (v. 29), who will bear judgment. God is depicted as cosmic Judge, and the imagery employed suggests a type of sweeping judgment beyond the circumstances of the late seventh/early sixth centuries B.C. The face of the earth is strewn about with the effects of destruction. Here is prophetic proclamation like that in Daniel and Zechariah, which depict cataclysmic change in apocalyptic form.

ORACLES AGAINST NATIONS. Oracles against nations are a common part of prophetic books (e.g., Isa. 13–23; Amos 1–2). There does not seem to be one reason for the judgments announced against these peoples. Perhaps they oppressed Israel or Judah, or perhaps their inhumanity, broadly distributed in their neighbors' suffering, has provoked the Lord to anger. But common to all these oracles is the assumption that the Lord is sovereign over all the nations (including Babylon). Jeremiah 25 makes this assumption plain by the radical claim that Nebuchadnezzar is the Lord's "servant" (25:9). Nebuchadnezzar's work in subjecting Judah (or other nations) to his rule is not against God's designs but part of them. That is the extent of his servanthood; he is a tool to carry out God's larger designs.

That such oracles are part of prophetic books is also part of God's design. The reference to God's "servants the prophets" (25:4) reflects God's commitment to interpreting his acts for his people through appointed means. The broader message seems to be: Listen and learn the ways of the Lord, who shapes history, judges iniquity, and seeks to form a people for himself from among the nations. In the stylized language of judgment (e.g., the cup of wrath or judgment, 25:17, 28; cf. 51:7), one encounters a mode of prophecy that will find echoes at Gethsemane (Matt. 26:39) and in John's visions (Rev. 16–17).

Jeremiah and Nebuchadnezzar. One might see the relevance of these differing claims about servants by thinking of "a tale of two servants" (Nebuchadnezzar and Jeremiah). With apologies to Charles Dickens, one might see in Nebuchadnezzar's role the "best of times" for him and in Jeremiah's prophetic service "the worst of times" for the prophet. But there is an important caveat here. Nebuchadnezzar's historical success is no reason to think that he labors to be faithful to God, nor is Jeremiah's rejection and seeming failure any reason to think he has been faithless to God. On the contrary, readers should note carefully that the chapter is intended to explain why disaster overtook Judah and also to demonstrate that God is Lord of all nations.

There is a pattern portrayed in chapter 25 that will repeat itself in history. Injustice and infidelity on the part of God's people lead to historical judgment. Yet how things change when seen in the light of God's plan to use whatever means necessary to carry out his judgment amid his larger redemptive purposes! Nebuchadnezzar's kingdom is now in the trash bin of history, but the heirs of Jeremiah's word are still the recipient of God's grace.

HISTORICAL PROVIDENCE. The claims of chapter 25 play a significant role in assessing what is meant by God's historical providence. (1) The prophetic perspective on God's historical judgments is not so much a blueprint about the future as it is a revelation about God's purpose. Judgment in the historical process can be self-incurred, but its moral dimension is shaped by the Creator in surprising ways.

(2) While God's purpose in judging and reforming his people takes shape in the historical process, God's providence was not limited to Israel, nor is it now limited to the church. Other nations, as part of God's universal purpose are judged and shaped as well.

(3) Judgment is not all that God intends for the future of nations (cf. Gen. 12:3) as his near and far purposes are worked out.

(4) The work of God is a process and not just an occasional event. Historical events are part of his proximate designs and are used in service of his eternal designs, which no one fully grasps. God's judgments are unsearchable (Rom. 11:33); they stand, however, in the service of his undeserved mercy— the ultimate goal of his providence.

In light of these affirmations Christians cannot assume that the misfortune of every nation is God's judgment and that a period of relative peace is evidence of his favor. God's work through the historical process is more complicated than that. There is no time in world history when this confession lacks application. The larger pattern can only be glimpsed by faith, and that faith must allow for a transhistorical culmination that cannot be fully grasped at any one point in history.

The book of Revelation (like Jeremiah) portrays the suffering of God's people as something that does come on the church because of some failures. Persecution of the church, however, becomes even more insidious precisely because some Christians seek to serve the risen Christ rather than Rome (symbolized in Revelation as Babylon!). The bowls of God's wrath strike universally. Nevertheless, the community of saints in the heavenly Jerusalem is drawn universally from all nations and peoples. From what angle can one possibly see the final result of God's work? Certainly not from within the span of historical existence. The full significance of God as Lord and Judge of all history is better seen at the end of history, not at its midpoint.

Perhaps one way for modern Christians to read the judgments against the nations in Jeremiah is to hear them as announcements of God's reckoning in the midst of a process that still continues and as historical signs of what the future will hold for the impenitent and unrighteous. Pertinent illustrations abound in the surprising changes of the last twenty years. Who would have predicted the dissolution of the USSR, the changes in Eastern Europe, or those in South Africa? Only time will tell their full impact, but even now God is at work in those circumstances and in the churches of these regions.

Seventy years. The prophecy of the seventy years reminds believers that God's means of testing and refining take time. As with the issues of universal justice and the fate of nations, a process of refinement is best understood at the end. How many people have confessed a quick fix in their Christian lives only to realize that God is not through with them yet? Sometimes the education and desired changes are just beginning! So it can be in the life of a congregation as well as in that of a people. God's process of sanctification has a goal, but we may never see it fully realized in our lifetime. Such was the fate of many in Jeremiah's day who trudged into exile and died there. It was also the privilege of Jeremiah to say that the process did not end with the Exile. In the cross and resurrection, believers have seen that it does not end with death either.

A profound interpretation of the cup that sends the nations reeling comes with Jesus' wrestling prayer in the Garden of Gethsemane (Matt. 26:36–46). He knows that the manifestation of God's righteous judgment is at hand. Indeed, it is about to fall on him as a sacrificial lamb. In prayer he struggles to bring his emotions into line with what he knows to be God's will. He will trust God with the immediate events to come—though they entail much suffering on his part—because he trusts God with the future of all his creation.

EARLY IN THE REIGN of Jehoiakim son of Josiah king of Judah, this word came from the LORD: 2"This is what the LORD says: Stand in the courtyard of the LORD's house and speak to all the people of the towns of Judah who come to worship in the house of the LORD. Tell them everything I command you; do not omit a word. 3Perhaps they will listen and each will turn from his evil way. Then I will relent and not bring on them the disaster I was planning because of the evil they have done. 4Say to them, 'This is what the LORD says: If you do not listen to me and follow my law, which I have set before you, 5and if you do not listen to the words of my servants the prophets, whom I have sent to you again and again (though you have not listened), 6then I will make this house like Shiloh and this city an object of cursing among all the nations of the earth.'"

7The priests, the prophets and all the people heard Jeremiah speak these words in the house of the LORD. 8But as soon as Jeremiah finished telling all the people everything the LORD had commanded him to say, the priests, the prophets and all the people seized him and said, "You must die! 9Why do you prophesy in the LORD's name that this house will be like Shiloh and this city will be desolate and deserted?" And all the people crowded around Jeremiah in the house of the LORD.

10When the officials of Judah heard about these things, they went up from the royal palace to the house of the LORD and took their places at the entrance of the New Gate of the LORD's house. 11Then the priests and the prophets said to the officials and all the people, "This man should be sentenced to death because he has prophesied against this city. You have heard it with your own ears!"

12Then Jeremiah said to all the officials and all the people: "The LORD sent me to prophesy against this house and this city all the things you have heard. 13Now reform your ways and your actions and obey the LORD your God. Then the LORD will relent and not bring the disaster he has pronounced against you. 14As for me, I am in your hands; do with me whatever you think is good and right. 15Be assured, however,

that if you put me to death, you will bring the guilt of innocent blood on yourselves and on this city and on those who
live in it, for in truth the LORD has sent me to you to speak all
these words in your hearing."

¹⁶Then the officials and all the people said to the priests and
the prophets, "This man should not be sentenced to death! He
has spoken to us in the name of the LORD our God."

¹⁷Some of the elders of the land stepped forward and said
to the entire assembly of people, ¹⁸"Micah of Moresheth
prophesied in the days of Hezekiah king of Judah. He told all
the people of Judah, 'This is what the LORD Almighty says:

> "'Zion will be plowed like a field,
>> Jerusalem will become a heap of rubble,
>> the temple hill a mound overgrown with thickets.'

¹⁹"Did Hezekiah king of Judah or anyone else in Judah put
him to death? Did not Hezekiah fear the LORD and seek his
favor? And did not the LORD relent, so that he did not bring
the disaster he pronounced against them? We are about to
bring a terrible disaster on ourselves!"

²⁰(Now Uriah son of Shemaiah from Kiriath Jearim was
another man who prophesied in the name of the LORD; he
prophesied the same things against this city and this land as
Jeremiah did. ²¹When King Jehoiakim and all his officers and
officials heard his words, the king sought to put him to death.
But Uriah heard of it and fled in fear to Egypt. ²²King
Jehoiakim, however, sent Elnathan son of Acbor to Egypt,
along with some other men. ²³They brought Uriah out of
Egypt and took him to King Jehoiakim, who had him struck
down with a sword and his body thrown into the burial place
of the common people.)

²⁴Furthermore, Ahikam son of Shaphan supported Jeremiah,
and so he was not handed over to the people to be put to death.

CHAPTER 25 IS prose and poetry; it served as a
concluding portion to the first half of this book.
Chapter 26 begins a series of narratives in
chronological order about the prophet and his
public ministry, along with references to specific kings and their reigns.

Chapter 26 contains a portion of a message delivered at the temple in the
beginning of Jehoiakim's reign (609/608 B.C.), along with an extended account

of the audience reaction. Jehoiakim was the third king to rule in less than a year's time. Upon Josiah's death, the people of the land had appointed Jehoahaz, the son of Josiah and younger brother of Jehoiakim, as king. The Egyptians removed him and put Jehoiakim on the throne (2 Kings 23:29–35). It was a time of uncertainty for the direction of the Judean state. The previous chapter concerns a message from the fourth year of Jehoiakim.

Jeremiah's oral message is summarized in 26:1–6. This sounds like an abbreviated form of the longer message delivered at the temple and recorded in Jeremiah 7. Whether or not chapter 26 and chapter 7 are two accounts of the same "sermon" is debated among interpreters.[1] The primary difference between the chapters comes in the attention given to audience reaction. Here Jeremiah engages his audience in debate (26:7–19) over the validity of his prophetic word. A summary comment is appended in 26:20–24 that describes the martyrdom of the prophet Uriah and the crucial support given Jeremiah by Ahikam the son of Shaphan. In any case, chapter 7 preserves the longer form of the same message, whether or not it is the same incident.

26:1–6. Jeremiah warns the people that if they fail to follow the instruction (*tora*, v. 4)[2] of the Lord, they will bring calamity on themselves. This is a typical form of the act-consequence claim: Disobedience brings disaster. Not following the Lord's instruction is the same thing as not listening to the Lord and not heeding the words of his "servants the prophets."[3] As Jeremiah will argue in the debate with his audience, he stands in this line of prophets sent (*šlḥ*) by the Lord because, like them, the Lord has also "sent" (*šlḥ*) him (26:12–15). The temple will be destroyed in the coming judgment, just like the destruction of the worship center at Shiloh during the days of the judges and the prophet Samuel.[4]

Jeremiah's words about the temple strike a chord with his audience. It is God's "house," and the assumption of many in the audience is that God will protect it no matter what. Also, for some in the audience, to speak against the temple is tantamount to speaking against God himself. This is blasphemy. The form of Jeremiah's proclamation, however, is a warning and a call for repentance. The historical fate of the temple is actually influenced by the actions of the people.

---

1. Note that ch. 7 does not contain a reference to the date or reign of a king.

2. The NIV translates the Heb. word *tora* as "law." The choice for an English equivalent is difficult. It is not clear if the *tora* of 26:4 refers to a state-mandated code or the Sinai covenant code, since we do not know what was the state-mandated religious code under Jehoiakim. If 26:4 assumes the Sinai covenant code, then its authoritative nature as divine instruction should be recognized in the temple above all places. It may not have been the "law of the land."

3. See the reference to "his servants the prophets" in 25:4.

4. See the comments about Shiloh in the interpretation of ch. 7.

26:7—19. Opposition to the "temple sermon," with its prediction that the temple will be destroyed, is widespread and intense. Priests and prophets (cf. 26:16), as well as "the people," propose the death sentence for what appears to them as both blasphemy and treason. The essentials of a public trial ensue, when certain officials take their seat in the New Gate of the temple complex (26:10). Such a location lends gravity to the situation and the charges against the prophet. He will be judged in the context of the temple complex against which he himself has just announced the possibility of judgment (cf. also ch. 20).

Jeremiah defends himself as one in the line of prophets whom the Lord has sent to warn his people about the consequences of disobedience to his instruction (cf. 26:5). He recognizes that he is "in [their] hands" (26:14)— that is, he is on trial—but he warns them that if they execute him, they will incur the judgment of bringing "innocent blood on yourselves." There are two implications of this claim. (1) The shedding of innocent blood will bring guilt on the assembly and the place. The Old Testament is strongly oriented to the claim that unrequited blood brings a community or people into the sphere of guilt. (2) Jeremiah is thereby reminding the people indirectly that as "innocent" of their charges, he is one of the prophets sent by the Lord. To put it in a kind of syllogism: If Jeremiah speaks a word against the temple in the name of the Lord, yet is innocent of blasphemy, then the word he speaks must come from the Lord.

This second point, at least, gains a hearing for Jeremiah among some of the people. He has spoken to them in the name of the Lord (as opposed to the prompting of another deity or offering his own political commentary). He meets, therefore, at least one of Deuteronomy's criteria for judging prophecy (Deut. 13). Some elders of the land add that Jeremiah is no different from Micah of Moresheth, who prophesied in Hezekiah's reign that Jerusalem would be destroyed (26:18 = Mic. 3:12). Apparently they agree that Micah was one of God's servants the prophets. King Hezekiah, they remind the court, did not execute Micah; instead, he feared the Lord, and the Lord relented concerning the announced judgment. In an unintended prophecy, the elders conclude that by the present course of action (opposing Jeremiah rather than heeding his warning), the people are doing great harm to themselves. This is a tacit recognition of Jeremiah's claim that to execute him would bring guilt on the place.

In referring to the prophecy of Micah, the people engage in a type of exegesis or interpretation of their religious traditions. Just as Jeremiah drew a comparison between the Jerusalem of his day with the Shiloh of Samuel's day, so they draw a comparison of Jeremiah's message with that of Micah. The elders put the work of Micah and the response of Hezekiah together in a more explicit way than either 2 Kings or 2 Chronicles (the two narratives about Hezekiah's reign) or the book of Micah itself does. The elders do not quote Micah's prophecy about Jerusalem as part of a warning or a call to repentance. In Micah 3:12 the prophet announces judgment to come. The people understand, however, that Hezekiah's reaction to the prophecy was genuine repentance and that God used the unconditional prophecy to move the king and people toward change.

26:20–24. A prophet named Uriah, however, was not given the reprieve accorded Jeremiah. King Jehoiakim's anger against prophets who announced the Lord's judgment on Judah led to the extradition of Uriah from Egypt (where he had fled) and his execution. It should be remembered that Jehoiakim was appointed king by the Egyptians, so the Egyptian officials were likely to cooperate with him. The narrator notes incidentally that the body of Uriah was thrown in the burial place of the common people. This was intended as a further sign that Uriah was not a real prophet. In another context, Jeremiah prophesies that Jehoiakim's burial will be that of a donkey—tossed outside the gate of the city (22:19; cf. 36:30).

Jehoiakim's execution of Uriah thereby brings the judgment of "innocent blood" on himself and his administration. Jeremiah too might have been executed except that an important official, Ahikam[5] son of Shaphan, stood on his side. With Ahikam one gets a glimpse of someone who sympathized with Jeremiah and his prophetic task. His brother later lends to Baruch, Jeremiah's scribe, his office ("room") overlooking the temple complex (36:10).

Bridging Contexts

INTERPRETING SCRIPTURE WITHIN SCRIPTURE. How does one deal with a prophecy of the Lord's judgment like this one? Such is the fascinating challenge of Jeremiah 26. Readers will see in the recorded response to Jeremiah's "sermon" an example of inner-scriptural interpretation, as hearers attempt to put Jeremiah's words in historical and theological contexts. Apparently the majority of the audience believe that Jeremiah has committed blasphemy and treason because they cannot fathom why God would announce the destruction of his own house. Perhaps they also feel that Jeremiah has overreacted to some minor spiritual failings regarding the covenant responsibilities of Judah.

---

5. Shaphan was an important official under Josiah and instrumental in the finding and interpreting of the book of the *torah* discovered during Josiah's reign (2 Kings 22). Ahikam too was part of the committee sent to consult with the prophet Huldah about the book (22:12). He was the father of Gedaliah (2 Kings 25:22; Jer. 39:14). On the influence of this scribal family, see J. A. Dearman, "My Servants the Scribes: Composition and Context in Jeremiah 36," *JBL* 109 (1990): 408–17.

The primary issue according to the prophet, however, is the comparison of Jerusalem with the worship center at Shiloh (26:9). Jeremiah offers a typological comparison between the days of the judges, when the corrupt worship center at Shiloh and the priestly line of Eli were destroyed, and the circumstances of Judah under Jehoiakim. To use an anachronistic phrase, what we have here is an example of Scripture interpreting Scripture.

In his defense before the assembled court and people, Jeremiah claims membership in the line of prophets whom the Lord has sent to warn his people about the consequences of their failure. Jeremiah's opponents cannot claim ignorance of such prophets or of the use God made of them in a previous generation; the questions are whether Jeremiah's diagnosis of the times is accurate and whether he himself stands in their succession.

Another example of bridging contexts comes in the elders' citation of Micah's prophecy concerning Jerusalem during the days of Hezekiah. This is a rare example in the Old Testament of a quote now contained in another prophetic book, complete with reference to time and place. It is a second example (to be anachronistic) of Scripture interpreting Scripture. Interpreters all recognize that Jeremiah has been influenced by the prophecies of Hosea. Here, however, his prophecy is compared to that of another eighth-century prophet, Micah, who announced judgment on Jerusalem. The elders assume that Micah was a prophet sent by the Lord; furthermore, Micah induced the fear of the Lord in Hezekiah, and the king's response to the prophetic word averted that word's announced wrath from God.

Here one encounters the claim that the predictions of a "true" prophet do not always come to pass literally; if the announced judgment provokes the fear of the Lord and evidence of faithful living, then it has served a divine purpose. The response of the people to Jeremiah and, above all, the response of Jehoiakim to Uriah demonstrate that the judgment predicted by Jeremiah will ultimately come.[6] This is foreshadowed by the comment of the elders that the rejection of Jeremiah will result in great harm coming on the people (26:19).

Uriah was given a prophet's "reward" (Matt. 5:10–12) and executed. He was a martyr, whose witness would have gone unrecorded had it not been noted here. God sent a line of prophets, but the people have not listened. Uriah has an honored place in that line of witnesses.

The reform movement. Jeremiah's words have not fallen on completely deaf ears! Even if the disaster announced cannot be averted, the response of the elders is the beginnings of a reform movement and perhaps also an indication of the circles of people who "remember" his words. Ahikam too seems to be a supporter of Jeremiah's call for holy living and wholehearted obedience to the

6. Chapter 36 records the arrogant rejection of Jeremiah's words by Jehoiakim.

Lord's instructions. He is from a family of scribes with a distinguished record of service to Judah. He is another member of the (often unnamed and unmentioned) reform movement that hear Jeremiah's words and help to preserve them for posterity.

LISTENING TO A PROPHETIC WARNING. How does one listen to a prophetic warning or announcement of disaster to come? One should not simply ask about the dire circumstances of the past, as if biblical interpretation is finished when one understands what was wrong.[7] There is the responsibility also of a faithful reading where one shines the light of hard sayings on a personal or corporate present. In doing so, the issue is not to find a one-to-one correspondence between then and now but a theological link between the call to faithful living then and the call to faithful living in the present. There is also the issue of act and consequence, something the prophets specialize in uncovering. What will be the results of my life or that of a church or community if things do not change? What changes is God calling for among his people?

Jeremiah was put on trial for his warning about judgment to come. Is a clear warning about judgment to come what is required for a faithful rendering of Jeremiah 26 for today? Certainly this is possible, but it is not necessarily the case. One way to understand the contemporary significance of judgmental prophecy in Scripture is to interpret it as an example for later instruction. As such, one must decide first if it is a warning to society as a whole or to one particular community (e.g., a church), or if the application is a more personal matter.

If we conclude that the warning is to society as a whole, then one should be prepared for the question: "Why should they even listen?" Or what about the church? Should the church acknowledge its failures and weaknesses? That is easy to answer; surely, it should! And while the church has good theological reasons for being concerned about destructive trends in society, the light of God's Word should go first to the life of God's people to expose what is wrong and hurtful about its own witness.

Heeding judgment. The response of the elders of the land indicates another way in which this chapter may take on contemporary significance. Notice how carefully they listen to Jeremiah and compare his word with that of another prophet who brought a judgmental word from the Lord. They ask: What did that prophecy evoke among its hearers? Unfortunately,

---

7. See also the comments on ch. 7.

the repentance evoked in Hezekiah was not matched in Jeremiah's day by either King Jehoiakim or the people, but the question starts the search for application in the hearers' own day.

Judgmental prophecy does not reach its final goal when (or even if) a predicted disaster occurs. Micah was a true prophet in that he brought about a change in Judah, although the judgment he announced did not come to pass. Judgmental prophecy is a sharp way of defining who God is, a God who takes his people seriously as covenant partners in his work of bringing justice and redemption to the world. Does God have standards? Yes! Is he committed to the righteousness and integrity of his people? Yes! While God may vindicate his righteousness through judgment of the wicked (and thereby instruct others), such judgment (enacted in history or simply announced) may also serve the larger ends of renewing his people. Both righteousness and renewal are goals of God according to the broader scriptural witness. Attaining these goals through refinement is a consistent pattern of God's dealings with his people.

Standing with the prophets. Perhaps Christians should be wary of a too-ready identification with Jeremiah. After all, God does not call each of his people to be a prophet any more than God requires all congregations to engage consistently in prophetic witness. Ahikam, however, represents a person of some repute and influence in the larger Judean society who responds to the hostile reception of Jeremiah by standing with him. When Jeremiah's life was "on the line," in a sense the integrity of Ahikam's faith was also "on the line." This is what the prophecy evoked in his personal life. He did not take the easy way out, which in this case meant acquiescence to the majority view. In Jeremiah's hour of need Ahikam put his reputation and influence to good use. Perhaps we can say that he acted out of a shared conviction with Jeremiah that the Lord they both worshiped had rightly announced a judgment on iniquity.

The future judgment will take its course from the present realities—unless the people can be brought to their theological senses, which seems unlikely. It is more important that Ahikam stand up and be counted than that he "win the day"; although without his influence, it is likely that Jeremiah would have perished at the hands of the prophets and priests who opposed him. Ahikam is a disciple, one of the "seven thousand who have not bowed the knee to the Baal," one of those effective witnesses whose work has great influence at a crucial time but whose name is not remembered by many. He is an example of that great truth that God's Word does not return to him void, nor finally does the life of God's servants become void. By God's grace there will be someone (or some people!) who have the spiritual ears to hear what a true prophet has to say.

In April 1999 the United States was brought to a state of collective shock over the senseless murders of students and a teacher at Columbine High School in the Denver area. Much has been written about the multiple tragedies of that fateful day.[8] Two disturbed and disaffected students took senseless vengeance on their school community before turning the guns on themselves. One chilling account comes with the testimony of students who saw or heard the killers stalking their prey in the school building, then stopping and asking one young woman (according to reports, Cassie Bernall) if she believed in God. When she answered "yes," they shot her. She was one of thirteen victims to die. There are reports that the killers asked the same question of another young woman and that she answered in the affirmative before being shot.

One cannot know what went through the minds of the young women in the last seconds before their murder. One thought perhaps was that the murderers felt rage at God and the pretensions of classmates to believe and trust in him, and that now these demented boys were going to make the girls victims of that rage. Indeed, they were victims, but more than that, they were witnesses. We have only the brief reference to Uriah or to the courage of Ahikam. They did what they did and stood where they stood because they believed in God. We need not ask the modern psychological question of what they thought at the moments of decision; we should, however, give thanks that they acted on what they believed. And we should be reminded that God asks that of all disciples of his Son.

---

8. Wendy M. Zoba, "'Do You Believe in God?' Columbine and the Stirring of America's Soul," *Christianity Today* (October 4, 1999), 33–40.

Jeremiah 27:1-22

ARLY IN THE REIGN of Zedekiah son of Josiah king of Judah, this word came to Jeremiah from the LORD: ²This is what the LORD said to me: "Make a yoke out of straps and crossbars and put it on your neck. ³Then send word to the kings of Edom, Moab, Ammon, Tyre and Sidon through the envoys who have come to Jerusalem to Zedekiah king of Judah. ⁴Give them a message for their masters and say, 'This is what the LORD Almighty, the God of Israel, says: "Tell this to your masters: ⁵With my great power and outstretched arm I made the earth and its people and the animals that are on it, and I give it to anyone I please. ⁶Now I will hand all your countries over to my servant Nebuchadnezzar king of Babylon; I will make even the wild animals subject to him. ⁷All nations will serve him and his son and his grandson until the time for his land comes; then many nations and great kings will subjugate him.

⁸" ' "If, however, any nation or kingdom will not serve Nebuchadnezzar king of Babylon or bow its neck under his yoke, I will punish that nation with the sword, famine and plague, declares the LORD, until I destroy it by his hand. ⁹So do not listen to your prophets, your diviners, your interpreters of dreams, your mediums or your sorcerers who tell you, 'You will not serve the king of Babylon.' ¹⁰They prophesy lies to you that will only serve to remove you far from your lands; I will banish you and you will perish. ¹¹But if any nation will bow its neck under the yoke of the king of Babylon and serve him, I will let that nation remain in its own land to till it and to live there, declares the LORD." ' "

¹²I gave the same message to Zedekiah king of Judah. I said, "Bow your neck under the yoke of the king of Babylon; serve him and his people, and you will live. ¹³Why will you and your people die by the sword, famine and plague with which the LORD has threatened any nation that will not serve the king of Babylon? ¹⁴Do not listen to the words of the prophets who say to you, 'You will not serve the king of Babylon,' for they are prophesying lies to you. ¹⁵I have not sent them,' declares the LORD. 'They are prophesying lies in my

name. Therefore, I will banish you and you will perish, both you and the prophets who prophesy to you.'"

¹⁶Then I said to the priests and all these people, "This is what the LORD says: Do not listen to the prophets who say, 'Very soon now the articles from the LORD's house will be brought back from Babylon.' They are prophesying lies to you. ¹⁷Do not listen to them. Serve the king of Babylon, and you will live. Why should this city become a ruin? ¹⁸If they are prophets and have the word of the LORD, let them plead with the LORD Almighty that the furnishings remaining in the house of the LORD and in the palace of the king of Judah and in Jerusalem not be taken to Babylon. ¹⁹For this is what the LORD Almighty says about the pillars, the Sea, the movable stands and the other furnishings that are left in this city, ²⁰which Nebuchadnezzar king of Babylon did not take away when he carried Jehoiachin son of Jehoiakim king of Judah into exile from Jerusalem to Babylon, along with all the nobles of Judah and Jerusalem—²¹yes, this is what the LORD Almighty, the God of Israel, says about the things that are left in the house of the LORD and in the palace of the king of Judah and in Jerusalem: ²²'They will be taken to Babylon and there they will remain until the day I come for them,' declares the LORD. 'Then I will bring them back and restore them to this place.'"

THIS CHAPTER IS PART of a larger unit that includes chapters 28–29. It is influenced also by the narrative in chapter 26. It is particularly important to note the relationship between chapters 27 and 28 because text-critical problems in 27:1 and 28:1 have made interpretation more difficult. Chapters 27 and 28 are linked by the report of Jeremiah's wearing a yoke (of thongs and wooden bars) as a prophetic sign that Nebuchadnezzar's claim on Judah has been granted him by the Lord. In chapter 27 Jeremiah reports that the Lord commanded him to make a yoke and to wear it and that the Lord sent him to prophesy that Nebuchadnezzar has been granted sovereignty over nations (including Judah). Jeremiah also reports that the Lord has some sharp words for the various prophets and diviners who have prophesied differently concerning Babylonian rule (cf. ch. 13). The conflict with these prophets continues in chapters 28–29.

Readers should compare translations of 26:1; 27:1; and 28:1, along with any marginal explanations provided by the translators. Often English translations have small print or marginal notes that inform the reader that the translators have made a text-critical choice in the rendering; that is, they have chosen from different words or phrases preserved in the ancient manuscripts.

The problems for translation *and interpretation* of 27:1 lie in the variants preserved in Hebrew and Greek manuscripts.[1] The majority of Hebrew manuscripts for 27:1 preserve the rendering "in the beginning of the reign of Jehoiakim . . . the word came to Jeremiah." "Jehoiakim" is clearly wrong, perhaps mistakenly copied from 26:1, because Zedekiah is the Judean monarch addressed in the prophetic oracle (27:3, 12). The NIV translators have recognized the copy error and followed a "minority reading" in some Hebrew manuscripts, where the appropriate name Zedekiah is preserved.

Recognition that Zedekiah is the correct name in 27:1 solves only one of the problems for interpreting the chapter, however. Insofar as chapters 27 and 28 should be read together as a narrative witness to the work of Jeremiah in wearing a yoke, Jeremiah 28:1 also has a problem. In Hebrew this text begins, "and it happened in that year in the beginning of the reign of Zedekiah . . ."; then the text continues, "in the fourth month of the fifth year." The problem is that the fifth year of Zedekiah does not easily qualify as "the beginning of his reign," nor is the "fifth month" the beginning of a year.[2] Probably the phrase "beginning of the reign" (also used in 26:1) has the technical meaning of "accession year." The phrase could perhaps fit the circumstances of 27:1–3, which narrate events in the accession or initial year of Zedekiah as monarch, but it fits poorly in 28:1.[3] The more likely explanation is that the chronological headings for chapters 26–28 have become mixed during the process of transmitting the material to final written form.

A plausible solution to these difficulties is at hand if one takes the qualification of the fourth year of Zedekiah seriously in 28:1, as well as the proposal that the events of chapter 28 occur in the same year as those of chapter 27. The fourth year of Zedekiah (594/593 B.C.) coincides with a serious rebellion in the east against Babylon. If chapter 27 describes an event in the fourth year of Zedekiah, then the notation that Zedekiah and ambassadors from several neighboring states have assembled in Jerusalem (27:3) takes on

---

1. For a more complete explanation of the textual problems, see W. Holladay, *Jeremiah*, 2:112, 115.

2. The NIV translation assumes that "in the beginning" can qualify the fourth year of Zedekiah. If the phrase refers to the accession year of Zedekiah as proposed by most commentators, then the translation is incorrect.

3. This requires seeing the events of ch. 27 as occurring in the beginning of Zedekiah's reign (597/596 B.C.), while those of ch. 28 in his fourth year. The more natural reading of the narratives is to see both ch. 27 and ch. 28 as recounting events in the fourth year (594/593) of Zedekiah.

significance. This conference included discussion about the possibility of a revolt against Babylon, using a political threat to Babylonian hegemony in the east as an occasion for some states west of Babylon to meet for talk. Apparently many priests, prophets, and diviners of various kinds lent their support to this anti-Babylonian movement (27:9, 16). Jeremiah's encounter with Hananiah recorded in chapter 28, where he is still wearing the yoke mentioned in chapter 27, continues the debate among the prophets over the role Babylon will play in the Lord's economy.

In chapter 29 one finds references to prophets among the Judean exiles in Babylon who are predicting a quick end to Babylonian hegemony. This chapter too presupposes a time after the initial Babylonian siege of Jerusalem and the taking of Jehoiachin and others into exile. In other words, a date in the fourth year of Zedekiah fits the historical context nicely for chapters 27–29.

Jeremiah's message in chapter 27 is that God has given a limited historical sovereignty to Babylon and Nebuchadnezzar. This applies to the Transjordanian states of Edom, Moab, and Ammon as well as the city-states of Tyre and Sidon, all of which are mentioned in 27:3. To oppose Babylon at this time is to oppose God's will as Creator and Lord. In this style of presentation, Jeremiah shows himself to be a prophet to the nations (cf. 1:5).

In keeping with prophecies made elsewhere (25:13; 29:10), the end of Babylonian supremacy is also acknowledged. Babylon's end is noted (27:7), as is God's intent to restore the temple vessels taken by Nebuchadnezzar and those of his people now in exile (27:22).[4]

The majority of chapter 27 concerns the work of other prophets who oppose the message of Jeremiah (27:9, 14–18). One wonders at the level of interchange between these various interpreter's of God's will. The events of 598/597 B.C., when Babylon came up against Judah and Jerusalem, did not quite fulfill the prophetic words of either Jeremiah or his opponents. Jeremiah's years of proclaiming an assault on Jerusalem have proved true, but the city itself has survived. Those who prophesied "peace" have been proved wrong, but the Judean state and its capital are still intact.

Verse 9 provides an intriguing list of mediators and specialists for determining the will of the gods. Five specialists are mentioned: prophets, diviners, interpreters of dreams, mediums, and sorcerers.[5] In times of threat and calamity, such people have plenty of customers. The text does not make any

---

4. Jer. 27:22 concerns the restoration of the temple vessels taken by Nebuchadnezzar, but the restoration of the people is probably assumed (cf. 28:3–4). In any case, it is stated elsewhere that God will restore the exilic people to their land (e.g., 24:5–7).

5. Balaam was paid the diviner's fee in Num. 22:7. For a discussion of the terms listed in Jer. 27:9 in the context of divination in the ancient world, see M. S. Moore, *The Balaam Traditions: Their Character and Development* (Atlanta: Scholars Press, 1990).

distinction between those practitioners who have sought the Lord's will through their rituals and those who may have consulted another deity. All alike are rejected.

With all of the language of judgment in chapter 27, the concluding verses point to a time when God will bring back temple vessels from Babylon to Jerusalem (27:16–22). Babylon did not take them away because God was impotent—Nebuchadnezzar is God's servant, not vanquisher. The vessels will be returned when God is ready. This concluding comment makes for a transition to the account of Jeremiah's encounter with Hananiah in chapter 28. There too the concern is ostensibly about the temple vessels and related matters, but the deeper issue remains the same.

WORD AND DEED. Chapter 27 records two of the favorite devices of the Old Testament prophets: a word from the Lord and a symbolic act to embody the message. Word and deed go together in prophetic ministry, whether the deed is a sign of a particular message (as here in chs. 27–28) or whether the life of the messenger more broadly speaking is congruent with the message. This is a pattern that both the leaders of God's people and the people themselves should recognize. A consistency of word and deed do not guarantee the authenticity of a message, but it is a valuable indicator of commitment.

Jeremiah is in good company. Isaiah and Ezekiel combined word and deed on several occasions. Prophetic ministry requires a commitment of one's whole life, for even personal details such as marriage, children, and grief over personal loss become vehicles for prophetic proclamation.[6] This is true of Jeremiah's prayers. His "confessions" in chapters 11–20 are vehicles for carrying out his commission as prophet to the nations, since their place in the prophetic book means they too are part of the instructional package. The symbolic acts of prophets are part of an incarnational style of ministry, much like that of Jesus, whose words and deeds embodied his message and served as signs of his true identity.

God's sovereignty over the nations. Chapter 27 is set in the broad biblical context of God's sovereignty over creation and history. The claim is not that people and places are puppets, but that in creation and through the historical process God is working out his purposes of judgment, refinement, transformation, and redemption. Nebuchadnezzar and Babylon are God's servants, as were the Assyrians before and Cyrus and the Persians after. Rome

---

6. See comments on prophet symbolic acts in Jer. 13.

too served God in various ways, as the New Testament writers make clear. None of these historical "servants" of God can boast of moral superiority or freedom from the judgment that the historical process will ultimately bring on them. Nebuchadnezzar will have his day; even the beasts of the field are his (27:5–6)! But God also has his day, when Nebuchadnezzar eats straw like an animal and when the great Babylon eventually falls (Dan. 4:28–33).

GOD'S PRIMARY GOAL. People instinctively pull for underdogs. In political terms it is easy to be sympathetic towards those groups who have had little autonomy and whose voices are not often heard. Since the birth of the United States came about as political underdogs fought for more autonomy and religious freedom, it is easy for most North American Christians to sympathize with Zedekiah and the ambassadors from neighboring states. Indeed, most of the world's peoples understand the yearning of the Judeans and the others as they rebel against foreign domination. No more tribute! No more humiliation! Surely God wants them to be free!

A close reading of chapter 27 (and 28) reveals that God did want his people free—but free from the enslavement to sin and not just free from Babylonian hegemony. The issue first was timing (27:7), but timing pointed to a larger issue: God's relationship to a recalcitrant people. It is a process that the prophet underscores in his words. God intends to judge the people for their iniquities, to refine them through the process of political servitude, and then to use them as instructional examples to later generations of his people. This is a sobering thought, but Jeremiah's yoke does not just represent Nebuchadnezzar and Babylon; it also represents God's judgment on Judah and the neighboring states. Even more radically, the yoke represents the will of God himself to constrain his people.

A modern application of this message must be quick to deny that all peoples who languish under oppressive regimes or that all individuals who suffer emotional and physical exile are bound in these conditions by God's judgment. Scripture gives no blanket warrant for such a claim. Some people (including some Christians) find unpalatable any thought of oppression and exile as God's refining judgment. Scripture gives no warrant for that claim either. The issues with which Jeremiah 27 are concerned are those of God's timing and the larger design of his historical purposes in forming a people for himself. It is simply true that God's timing is often not "our" timing and God's ways are not our ways (Isa. 55:8). What Jeremiah calls his contemporaries to believe is that their first impulse is wrong. They have yet to see the error of their ways, and until God has dealt with that, there will be no successful liberation from political oppression or anything else.

It is ironic that the prophets and priests who oppose Jeremiah are so concerned with the temple vessels. They are so concerned with God's honor, yet they have not seen how Judah's covenantal failures have offended God's honor and spurned his love. They are convinced, furthermore, that God will act quickly to restore "his" vessels. "In good time," is Jeremiah's reply. Yes, God will restore the temple vessels, but God is more concerned with the fate of his people and the refining judgment they must undergo. Ultimately God will bring a merciful end to Babylonian supremacy and in the process will restore his people. His goal is (and remains!) to make his people fit vessels for his service, a kingdom of priests and a holy nation (1 Peter 2:9).

Over the course of centuries, any number of councils and high-level meetings have convened to influence the direction of God's people. Some have been productive; others have not. Just as Jeremiah wandered about with his yoke, so various protesters and lobbyists, preachers and prophets stand to proclaim their message. It is not always easy to tell the genuine article from the counterfeit, when considering their causes. One motive, however, remains constant: God seeks a holy people who will trust him with their lives.

Jeremiah 28:1–17

I N THE FIFTH month of that same year, the fourth year, early
in the reign of Zedekiah king of Judah, the prophet Hananiah son of Azzur, who was from Gibeon, said to me in the
house of the LORD in the presence of the priests and all the
people: ²"This is what the LORD Almighty, the God of Israel,
says: 'I will break the yoke of the king of Babylon. ³Within two
years I will bring back to this place all the articles of the
LORD's house that Nebuchadnezzar king of Babylon removed
from here and took to Babylon. ⁴I will also bring back to this
place Jehoiachin son of Jehoiakim king of Judah and all the
other exiles from Judah who went to Babylon,' declares the
LORD, 'for I will break the yoke of the king of Babylon.'"

⁵Then the prophet Jeremiah replied to the prophet Hananiah before the priests and all the people who were standing
in the house of the LORD. ⁶He said, "Amen! May the LORD do
so! May the LORD fulfill the words you have prophesied by
bringing the articles of the LORD's house and all the exiles
back to this place from Babylon. ⁷Nevertheless, listen to what
I have to say in your hearing and in the hearing of all the people: ⁸From early times the prophets who preceded you and me
have prophesied war, disaster and plague against many countries and great kingdoms. ⁹But the prophet who prophesies
peace will be recognized as one truly sent by the LORD only if
his prediction comes true."

¹⁰Then the prophet Hananiah took the yoke off the neck of
the prophet Jeremiah and broke it, ¹¹and he said before all the
people, "This is what the LORD says: 'In the same way will I
break the yoke of Nebuchadnezzar king of Babylon off the
neck of all the nations within two years.'" At this, the prophet
Jeremiah went on his way.

¹²Shortly after the prophet Hananiah had broken the yoke
off the neck of the prophet Jeremiah, the word of the LORD
came to Jeremiah: ¹³"Go and tell Hananiah, 'This is what the
LORD says: You have broken a wooden yoke, but in its place
you will get a yoke of iron. ¹⁴This is what the LORD Almighty,
the God of Israel, says: I will put an iron yoke on the necks of
all these nations to make them serve Nebuchadnezzar king of

Babylon, and they will serve him. I will even give him control over the wild animals.'"

¹⁵Then the prophet Jeremiah said to Hananiah the prophet, "Listen, Hananiah! The LORD has not sent you, yet you have persuaded this nation to trust in lies. ¹⁶Therefore, this is what the LORD says: 'I am about to remove you from the face of the earth. This very year you are going to die, because you have preached rebellion against the LORD.'"

¹⁷In the seventh month of that same year, Hananiah the prophet died.

 JEREMIAH'S ENCOUNTERS WITH HANANIAH comprise one of the best-known accounts in this prophetic book. The first verse of the chapter ties the encounter with the efforts in Zedekiah's fourth year (594/593 B.C.) to foment a rebellion against Babylonian control. Although the date in the fourth year is explicit, the reference to "early in the reign of Zedekiah" seems out of place.[1] As indicated in the commentary on chapter 27, a serious rebellion broke out against Babylon at this time in the eastern section of the empire, and other states subjected to Babylon were tempted to declare themselves independent. In chapter 27 one finds the account of a conference for state diplomats held in Jerusalem, where the discussion apparently included anti-Babylonian proposals. Jeremiah wore a yoke at that time to symbolize God's intention to place Judah in servitude to Babylon.

28:1–11. Hananiah bears all the marks of a prophet of the Lord. His name means the "The LORD is [or has been] gracious." The fact that he is from Gibeon is helpful to identify him, but that fact may have no other significance for understanding his actions. When he speaks, his words are prefaced by the announcement, "This is what the LORD Almighty, the God of Israel, says" (28:2). Hananiah prophesies that God will restore to Jerusalem the temple vessels taken by the Babylonians in 597 B.C. and the exiled Judean king. Concern about the temple vessels and the words of Jeremiah's prophetic opponents have been mentioned in 27:16–22. Hananiah, therefore, represents one of the unnamed prophets, noted in chapter 27, who are leading the people astray.

Hananiah performs a prophetic symbolic act in breaking the wooden yoke that Jeremiah is wearing; this was Hananiah's illustration of his prophecy that the Lord will break the yoke of Babylon, which is constraining and

---

1. On the translation of 28:1 and the interpretation of the phrase "early in the reign," see the introductory comments in the commentary on Jer. 27.

humiliating Judah. Hananiah believes in the power of the Lord to overcome Babylonian rule and to restore the exiled king Jehoiachin,[2] the other exiles deported in 597 B.C., and even the temple vessels taken by the Babylonian army. Throughout the chapter Hananiah is described as "the prophet" (28:1, 5, 10, 12, 15, 17).[3] In the Greek translation of Jeremiah, Hananiah is explicitly described as a "false prophet," but the Hebrew text refrains from using an equivalent term. Both the terminology and the form of his public address indicate that he is a Yahwistic prophet, perhaps even one who has served God faithfully on previous occasions. Now, however, the content of his oracle is wrong. He will be shown wrong about God's timing and about God's intentions in using Babylonian might to chastise his people.

Hananiah makes his announcement that the Lord will soon overcome the Babylonians and restore the people and temple vessels in the courtyard of the temple complex (28:2−4). This setting is important to the context of the message and also to Jeremiah's ministry. On several occasions Jeremiah publicly prophesied in the temple. At the beginning of Jehoiakim's reign he offered a scathing review of misplaced confidence in the temple and called for repentance from the evil course underway in Judah (26:1−6; cf. ch. 7; 19:14−15). After being forbidden to preach at the temple complex, Jeremiah sent his faithful secretary, Baruch, to read from a scroll of collected oracles (ch. 36). During Zedekiah's reign Jeremiah was in the temple complex and received a vision with an oracle attached to it (24:1−10).

Jeremiah's encounter with Hananiah in the temple symbolizes their differing viewpoints on what it means that God dwells in the midst of his people. Hananiah seems to think that God's presence means that God's defense of the house and the people is always near at hand.

Jeremiah's first reaction to the oracle of Hananiah ("Amen!" 28:6) seems to indicate that the prophecy impresses him. This reaction is in spite of the fact that Hananiah's proclamation goes against what he himself has prophesied. Jeremiah is open to hearing God speak through Hananiah. By way of first response, Jeremiah reminds Hananiah and their audience in the temple that prophets of the Lord have habitually announced disaster and judgment—the prophet who predicts peace will be vindicated only when that word comes to pass (28:8−9). This will indicate that it has come from God.

A prophecy of disaster or judgment, however, is evaluated differently. It is intended to evoke consternation and provoke people to action. The cita-

---

2. Some English translations give the name as Jeconiah, which approximates the Hebrew name in 28:4. The name is an alternative to the better-known name Jehoiachin. For consistency, the NIV uses Jehoiachin.

3. In 28:8 Jeremiah makes a reference to the prophets "who preceded you and me." The "you" is masculine singular and likely refers to Hananiah. Thus Jeremiah too included Hananiah in the category of a Yahwistic prophet.

tion of Micah 3:12 in Jeremiah 26:18 is a good illustration of the point. Micah of Moresheth announced the coming destruction of Jerusalem. The proclamation was unconditional in form, yet what it provoked in Hezekiah and the people was enough for the Lord to relent and to keep from bringing the announced destruction to pass (26:19; see comments on ch. 26).

28:12–17. When Hananiah breaks the yoke worn by Jeremiah, Jeremiah does not reply immediately. This is another indication of the seriousness with which he takes Hananiah's prophetic efforts. It may also indicate that Jeremiah is humiliated by his first encounter with Hananiah. Subsequently the word of the Lord comes to him, and he confronts Hananiah with the message that Babylon rules with God's explicit assent and that Hananiah has made the people believe a "lie" (Heb. *šeqer,*[4] used several times in chs. 27–29). Indeed, Hananiah's words are a rebellion against the will of the Lord. In place of the wooden yoke broken by Hananiah, Jeremiah proclaims that God will now place the people in servitude to Babylon through an iron yoke.

In a somber word, Jeremiah announces that Hananiah will die within the year (28:12–17). That death is interpreted as judgment on him and his word. This is in accord with Deuteronomy 18:20–22, where the penalty for preaching falsely in the name of the Lord is death. The narrative about Hananiah is an illustration of the charges elsewhere in Jeremiah concerning prophets who prophesy "peace, when there is no peace."

Bridging Contexts

THE HUMAN ELEMENT IN PROPHECY. The encounters between Hananiah and Jeremiah in chapter 28 are narrated as part of the immediate context (chs. 27–29) of Judean opposition to Babylon and the claims of many that the Lord is on the Judean side in that struggle. On the contrary, however, Jeremiah insists that God has temporarily granted sovereignty over Judah to Nebuchadnezzar and Babylon. Judah will serve Nebuchadnezzar because he serves the Lord as the historical agent of judgment. This entire book is an attempt to preserve the words of an unpopular prophet whose witness is recognized more clearly after the fall of Jerusalem. Even more broadly the encounters are a part of the larger scriptural witness that God does not leave his people without guidance, even if the majority are heedless of the message or oppose its tenor.

---

4. This word is used in the Decalogue (Ex. 20:16): "You shall not give false testimony against your neighbor." Jeremiah uses it on various occasions (3:10, 23; 5:2, 31; 6:13; 7:4, 8–9; 8:10; 9:3, 5; 13:25; 14:14; 16:19; 20:6; 23:14, 25–26, 32; 37:14). In the context of prophets speaking deception or falsehood, it occurs in 27:10, 14–16; 28:15; 29:9, 21, 23, 31.

This chapter also underscores the human element in prophecy and in particular the humanness of Jeremiah. One gets no indication from the text that Hananiah has consciously deceived his audience. Presumably he truly believes his message; he cannot conceive of God as using the enemy of Judah as chastisement on Judah. Nor is Hananiah heterodox in prophetic practice—as if he depends on Baal for his inspiration. Everything about him suggests he is (and was) a prophet of Yahweh. Yet in his certainty and zeal for the Lord, he is wrong about the Lord's intentions. Moreover, he falls under the judgment of Deuteronomy 18:20–22 and its strictures against false prophecy. His word will not come true in two years' time, and he will die before that.

Jeremiah, on the other hand, has prophesied for years that God will bring judgment on Judah for its sinfulness. Is it possible that the burden he has carried for years is about to be lifted without the actual fall of Jerusalem and with the speedy return of exiled people and materials? Is the Lord telling him through Hananiah that indeed the time for judgment will soon end? From Jeremiah's reaction, he takes this possibility seriously. Here is one prophet listening carefully to another, open to the possibility that God has initiated a new phase in his dealings with his people.

In his humanness and openness, Jeremiah offers a model of the prophetic office. He does not dictate infallibly; he remains open, yet is certain of two things: God will not leave himself without a witness to the people, and God can make abrupt changes in his dealings with his people. Jeremiah is open, therefore, to the idea that the tone and thrust of his past prophetic ministry (over thirty years in duration) will come to an end because God is about to initiate a new direction for his people.

Perhaps most surprising, Jeremiah is open to the possibility that Hananiah is God's prophet to announce such changes. In this openness to God and to prophetic instruction himself, Jeremiah *the prophet* (28:5, 10, 11, 12, 15) helps subsequent readers to grasp the relational nature of true prophecy. It remains open to further guidance from God, listening carefully to the voices among God's people, and it requires self-examination before speaking.

The nature of true prophecy. But Jeremiah indicates something else that is fundamental about the prophetic office: It is the nature of true prophecy to indicate where God's people have failed and need instruction (28:8–9). This is basic to the larger collection of prophetic books in the Old Testament. The majority of their contents is critical toward the Israelite or Judean audience. Here is a job description that is always "open." A criterion of true prophecy from the past is not whether what is announced comes true. True prophets focus on the failures of the people and the corresponding judgment to come (if the failures are not dealt with adequately).

Jeremiah 26 referred to the prophet Micah, whose words about the destruction of Jerusalem were efficacious in turning Hezekiah and the nation from their self-destructive ways. Micah fits the prophetic profile as defined by Jeremiah in 28:8–9. Here also is one (among several) criterion for interpreting prophecy that speaks volumes across the centuries. The voice that speaks for God takes seriously the failures of the people. It is the prophet who announces that "all will be well" whose word requires a literal fulfillment. Otherwise, God has not sent him or her, and the true prophet should be about the business of uncovering the failures of God's people, holding them up to the light of day and thus demonstrating the possibility of judgment to come. Hananiah's death confirms his "lie."

Perhaps an instructive way to bridge the gap between the ancient setting and modern appropriation is to ask readers/hearers: With which of the prophets in the account do they identify? The question will not only require that they know something about the issues at stake for Jeremiah and Hananiah; it will also force them to account for why Hananiah is so adamant and sincere and why initially Jeremiah is open to considering his message.

GOD'S WILL TO SAVE. Hananiah speaks forthrightly about God's sovereignty in a time of flux and uncertainty. According to this prophet from Gibeon, not only is the Lord of history capable of delivering his people from the hand of persecutors; it is his gracious desire to save them. Who would wish to quarrel with this? Certainly not Jeremiah! According to Jeremiah, Babylon is but a tool in the hands of the sovereign Lord, and when Babylon's appointed task is complete, its worldly hegemony will come to an end. Moreover, the Lord will redeem his people and bring them back from exile. Hananiah and Jeremiah could agree on these central tenets.

Furthermore, did not God later do what Hananiah predicted when he moved Cyrus to release the exiles and the temple vessels so that both could return to their rightful home? Who among God's people today would dispute Hananiah's basic affirmation that God would deliver Judah? In light of God's subsequent radical reach into human history, his encounter with human sinfulness in Christ, his costly dealings with human failure at the cross, and his glorious triumph over death itself in raising Christ from the dead, God demonstrates his resolve to save. Yes, Hananiah was right about God's will to save.

Who speaks the truth? One sees a strange paradox in the dispute between Hananiah and Jeremiah. Hananiah's certainty about the Lord is ill-timed, while Jeremiah's human hesitation in light of Hananiah's initial prophecy is part of his care in listening for the Lord's leading. Such leading can and does come from prophetic voices, but how can one know who speaks the truth? In Hananiah's case, his certainty is ill-timed because he has failed to recognize the gravity of Judah's failures. Yes, his sense of God as strong Deliverer is accurate, but his sense of God's timing is wrong. Hananiah has an inadequate grasp of Judah's predicament before the Lord, and because of this he has an inadequate grasp of what the Lord of history intends in adopting Babylon as his historical agent.

Is Judah's predicament in 594/593 B.C. reflective of a mild miscalculation? Have the ongoing failures of Judah and the deportations of 597 been acknowledged by the people and dealt with adequately? Are the deportations of 597 the needed "slap on the wrist," the "mid-course correction" to set Judah again on the path of righteousness in relationship to her Lord, so that all that remains is God's liberation of the exiles and the temple vessels? No, unfortunately the true prophet sees that Judah has not comprehended adequately either its failures or the consequences of its failures, and the people as a whole have not been receptive to divine instruction. Hananiah is right to believe that God wants the return of his people, but his timing is wrong. In Christian terms, he wants to proclaim a resurrection without an acknowledgment of the necessity of the cross. Are there movements today within the church that "heal lightly the wound of the people"? The issue is not one of sincerity, but of truth.

An authentic prophet cannot overlook the barriers between what God has called his people to be and what they in their human fallibility actually represent. Wherever there is an automatic reliance on God's will to save without an acceptance of his refining judgments as a process of sanctification, there is the real possibility of misrepresenting God to any generation.

One is driven to ask about the state of the church in the modern West. It is on the decline in several areas. Should one think and pray and proclaim that renewal is just around the corner—that God is waiting to pour out his Spirit and to bless the church? Or should one think and pray and proclaim that God will (continue to?) give the church over to its self-incurred failures until some disaster or another has prepared the church to hear again the good news? Perhaps it is not wise to choose strictly between the two options, since God may have both judgment and renewal working mysteriously hand in hand. Nevertheless, we should look carefully for the modern-day Hananiahs because they do exist.

Jeremiah 29:1–32

T HIS IS THE text of the letter that the prophet Jeremiah sent from Jerusalem to the surviving elders among the exiles and to the priests, the prophets and all the other people Nebuchadnezzar had carried into exile from Jerusalem to Babylon. ²(This was after King Jehoiachin and the queen mother, the court officials and the leaders of Judah and Jerusalem, the craftsmen and the artisans had gone into exile from Jerusalem.) ³He entrusted the letter to Elasah son of Shaphan and to Gemariah son of Hilkiah, whom Zedekiah king of Judah sent to King Nebuchadnezzar in Babylon. It said:

⁴This is what the LORD Almighty, the God of Israel, says to all those I carried into exile from Jerusalem to Babylon: ⁵"Build houses and settle down; plant gardens and eat what they produce. ⁶Marry and have sons and daughters; find wives for your sons and give your daughters in marriage, so that they too may have sons and daughters. Increase in number there; do not decrease. ⁷Also, seek the peace and prosperity of the city to which I have carried you into exile. Pray to the LORD for it, because if it prospers, you too will prosper." ⁸Yes, this is what the LORD Almighty, the God of Israel, says: "Do not let the prophets and diviners among you deceive you. Do not listen to the dreams you encourage them to have. ⁹They are prophesying lies to you in my name. I have not sent them," declares the LORD.

¹⁰This is what the LORD says: "When seventy years are completed for Babylon, I will come to you and fulfill my gracious promise to bring you back to this place. ¹¹For I know the plans I have for you," declares the LORD, "plans to prosper you and not to harm you, plans to give you hope and a future. ¹²Then you will call upon me and come and pray to me, and I will listen to you. ¹³You will seek me and find me when you seek me with all your heart. ¹⁴I will be found by you," declares the LORD, "and will bring you back from captivity. I will gather you from all the nations and places where I have banished you," declares the LORD, "and will bring you back to the place from which I carried you into exile."

¹⁵You may say, "The LORD has raised up prophets for us in Babylon," ¹⁶but this is what the LORD says about the king who sits on David's throne and all the people who remain in this city, your countrymen who did not go with you into exile—¹⁷yes, this is what the LORD Almighty says: "I will send the sword, famine and plague against them and I will make them like poor figs that are so bad they cannot be eaten. ¹⁸I will pursue them with the sword, famine and plague and will make them abhorrent to all the kingdoms of the earth and an object of cursing and horror, of scorn and reproach, among all the nations where I drive them. ¹⁹For they have not listened to my words," declares the LORD, "words that I sent to them again and again by my servants the prophets. And you exiles have not listened either," declares the LORD.

²⁰Therefore, hear the word of the LORD, all you exiles whom I have sent away from Jerusalem to Babylon. ²¹This is what the LORD Almighty, the God of Israel, says about Ahab son of Kolaiah and Zedekiah son of Maaseiah, who are prophesying lies to you in my name: "I will hand them over to Nebuchadnezzar king of Babylon, and he will put them to death before your very eyes. ²²Because of them, all the exiles from Judah who are in Babylon will use this curse: 'The LORD treat you like Zedekiah and Ahab, whom the king of Babylon burned in the fire.' ²³For they have done outrageous things in Israel; they have committed adultery with their neighbors' wives and in my name have spoken lies, which I did not tell them to do. I know it and am a witness to it," declares the LORD.

²⁴Tell Shemaiah the Nehelamite, ²⁵"This is what the LORD Almighty, the God of Israel, says: You sent letters in your own name to all the people in Jerusalem, to Zephaniah son of Maaseiah the priest, and to all the other priests. You said to Zephaniah, ²⁶'The LORD has appointed you priest in place of Jehoiada to be in charge of the house of the LORD; you should put any madman who acts like a prophet into the stocks and neck-irons. ²⁷So why have you not reprimanded Jeremiah from Anathoth, who poses as a prophet among you? ²⁸He has sent

this message to us in Babylon: It will be a long time. Therefore build houses and settle down; plant gardens and eat what they produce.'"

²⁹Zephaniah the priest, however, read the letter to Jeremiah the prophet. ³⁰Then the word of the LORD came to Jeremiah: ³¹"Send this message to all the exiles: 'This is what the LORD says about Shemaiah the Nehelamite: Because Shemaiah has prophesied to you, even though I did not send him, and has led you to believe a lie, ³²this is what the LORD says: I will surely punish Shemaiah the Nehelamite and his descendants. He will have no one left among this people, nor will he see the good things I will do for my people, declares the LORD, because he has preached rebellion against me.'"

29:1–3. CHAPTER 29 IS LINKED with the previous chapter by literary proximity, historical context, and common vocabulary. As these first three verses make clear, Jeremiah writes a letter to the Judean community in Babylonian exile, that is, to those Judeans taken into exile with Jehoiachin[1] in 597 B.C. Although much of the chapter is taken up with the substance of that letter, it contains references to other messages that have gone back and forth from the two communities of Judeans. Jeremiah entrusts his letter to the Judeans in Babylon to Elasah the son of Shaphan (presumably the brother of Ahikam, who had earlier kept Jeremiah from the lynch mob)[2] and to Gemariah the son of Hilkiah the priest—two official Judean messengers (ambassadors?) sent by Zedekiah to Babylon on state business.

Several prophets and diviners among the Judean exiles have provoked the community with announcements of the imminent demise of Babylon and a return of the exiles to Judah (29:8–9, 15, 21–28). They are like Hananiah (ch. 28) in their orientation. Some of the agitators are named (Ahab and Zedekiah, 29:21–22; Shemaiah, 29:24), although nothing else is preserved about them beside what is contained in this chapter. Most likely they are prominent figures among the exiles. Shemaiah, for example, has communicated directly with the priest named Zephaniah, who is in charge of the house of the Lord in Jerusalem (29:25–26). These figures show awareness that Jeremiah's prophecies are known in Babylon.

---

1. Some English translations give the name as Jeconiah, which approximates the Hebrew name in 29:2. The name is an alternative to the better known name Jehoiachin. For consistency, the NIV uses Jehoiachin.

2. Cf. comments in 26:24 about the family of Shaphan.

The prophet's letter reinforces his previous prophecies that God has granted Babylon hegemony, that the duration of Babylonian sovereignty has decades to run (cf. 25:12), and that only then will there be restoration (cf. 24:6–7). What is new in chapter 29 is the instruction to settle down in Babylon and to pray for the city. The exiles are to "seek the peace and prosperity of the city to which I have carried you into exile. Pray to the LORD for it, because if it prospers, you too will prosper" (29:7).[3]

Chapter 29 contains the same charges against the exilic prophets as was made against Hananiah in chapter 28. They cause the people to trust in a lie (28:15; 29:9, 21, 23, 31; cf. 7:4),[4] and their words are, in effect, rebellion against the Lord (29:31–32; cf. 28:15–16). Jeremiah's struggle against prophets who prophesy falsely in the Lord's name extends even to the exilic community. The book of Ezekiel carries on this struggle to present the exilic community with God's word.

29:4–9. The first line of the letter contains a shocking truth, but it points to the good news to follow. God is the subject of the phrase "all those *I* carried into exile." Of course, the previous verses noted that Nebuchadnezzar was the historical agent who took the people into exile, but in verse 4 the theological point is made that it is actually the work of God himself. The affirmation is followed by the commands to settle down in exile and to carry out such functions of sedentary existence as building, planting, and marriage. Exile is not the end of existence as God's people, but the beginning of a new phase of relating to God. The people are not to rebel against the authority of Babylon because, in effect, it is the authority of God over them for a prescribed time. More positively, the people are to seek the prosperity of Babylon because it will affect them as well. Most important, they are to pray for their captors.

29:10–14. These hopeful verses help prepare readers for the section that follows in the prophetic book, a section known to interpreters as the Book of Consolation. Jeremiah notes that the future of the people in exile rests on God's "gracious promise" (v. 10; lit., God's "good word"). In verse 11 the gracious promise is described as plans God has for the people, plans for a "prosperity" (*šalom*, peace) that provides a future and "hope" (*tiqwa*). A tangible element to the future consists in the restoration of the people to their homeland. The restoration, however, is predicated on their seeking God with their whole heart.

---

3. The NIV translators have interpreted the Hebrew term *šalom*, traditionally rendered as "peace," as expressive of more than the absence of conflict and the presence of security; it is expressive also of material well-being ("prosperity," "prosper").

4. See the references to the Heb. term *šeqer* (lie, deception) in the comments of the previous chapter.

29:15–23. Certain prophets are agitating among the exiles in Babylon. From the message about judgment on the king and people who remain in Judah, one infers that these prophetic agitators believe no more disaster will befall Judah and Jerusalem. Jeremiah describes God as making King Zedekiah and the people in Jerusalem like "poor figs that ... cannot be eaten" (29:17). This metaphor is the same one as given to Jeremiah in 24:1–10. Because the king in Jerusalem and his people refuse to acknowledge God's judgment and refuse to embrace his covenant stipulations, they will be given over to the disasters of the sword and plague. The last part of this section warns the exiles not to listen to these prophetic agitators.

29:24–32. A particular opponent of Jeremiah, Shemaiah the Nehelamite, is singled out for criticism and announced judgment. He is a prophet who has proclaimed lies to the people in exile. He will not, therefore, see the "good things" that God will do for the people because he has "preached rebellion" against God (v. 32). This last element is the same charge leveled against Hananiah in 28:16.[5]

GOD'S PEOPLE AS ALIENS. Jeremiah's prophetic ministry extends even to God's people taken into exile. While his influence was profound in the decades after the final destruction of Jerusalem (through his book!), he also communicated to the early exiles via letters during the interim between the first deportation in 597 B.C. and the demise of the city in 587/586. The book of Jeremiah exhibits concern for the exiles in a variety of ways, since a broad goal is to demonstrate that Jeremiah is a true prophet to the nations (including the exiles and Babylon itself). Thus chapter 29 finds itself in the broader context of prophetic texts from Isaiah and Ezekiel that address the city-state of Babylon and the Judean exiles there.

This chapter also finds itself a part of the scriptural witness to God's people who are addressed as pilgrims, as wandering people, even as aliens, whose true home is with the Lord. From the perspective of the New Testament, God's people are both "at home" as members of the body of the risen Christ (regardless of their geographical location) and "in transit" as they live out their witness in this age (regardless of their geographical location).[6] The exiles in Babylon have not been ejected from their place among God's people; rather, they have been called to reconsider their place in God's economy in light of

---

5. The Hebrew word in 28:16 and 29:32 is *sara*. It reflects a conscious turning away from something, an overt rejection of someone.

6. See, e.g., Phil. 3:7–21; Heb. 11:1–40.

new temporal circumstances. Here potentially is a bridge to any generation of God's people.

Prayers for Babylon. It is helpful to see the letter of Jeremiah in the context of the New Testament letters. Paul and other apostles wrote to congregations about particular matters of the faith. From their remarks later readers can discern something of the debates of the congregations, the dynamics of their ministries, and the other voices that claimed divine inspiration.

Likewise Jeremiah writes to a specific situation in Babylon and offers faithful instruction in light of what he knows to be God's will for the common life of the exiles. He urges prayer for the welfare of Babylon and efforts toward the care for families because there will be no quick return from exile. He assures the exiles that God has not forgotten them or become subservient to the power of Babylon. Temporal submission to Babylon is submission to the work of God, who brought them to Babylon in the first place. The exiles should ignore the self-proclaimed prophets who stir the community with their rhetoric but have not been sent by God.

With the injunction to pray for Babylon, readers encounter an Old Testament form of Jesus' teaching (Matt. 5:43–48) to pray for one's enemies. Jeremiah's instruction to pray does not assume a generic prayer to be transported whole cloth from one setting in the life of God's people to another. It assumes that God has spoken definitively about Babylon's role in the divine economy so that his people located there should pray accordingly and live accordingly. It also assumes that the "enemy" is not simply an opponent and that the exiles are not simply victims.

In a perverse sort of way, the exiles might become comfortable thinking of themselves only as victims and the Babylonians only as the enemy. If so, the exiles would not go through the self-examination process that was necessary. If the Babylonians were only the "enemy," then they could be blamed for all of Judah's failures. Instead, the exiles should pray for Babylon because it is their home and because in the near future, the fate of Babylon will be the fate of the people as well. God will continue to use the enemy to instruct his people. Perhaps the people will offer some witness to the "enemy" and thereby lead to another aspect of God's instruction—to be a light to the nations (Isa. 42:6; 49:6; 51:4).

God's plans. In a justly famous "reminder" the prophet writes that God knows the plans that he has for the exiles—plans for a future, for hope, and for restoration (29:11–14). The first context in which to hear these words comes in the next two chapters of Jeremiah's book, where future hope and restoration in the Promised Land are given fuller expression. The same kind of confidence in God's saving purposes is available to any generation of his people who, as Jeremiah writes, seek him "with all [their] heart" (29:13).

Contemporary
Significance

TO PRAY OR NOT TO PRAY? If that is the question for Christians, then the book of Jeremiah offers some surprising answers. On occasion Jeremiah is enjoined by the Lord not to pray for his people because they are intransigent and for the moment irredeemable (7:16; 11:14; 14:11). This somber communication is not, of course, for Jeremiah's private consumption; instead, this word of the Lord becomes part of his public proclamation, designed to shock and to evoke change. The people's time is up and the consequences of failure will be severe. But what about the enemy? Surely God's people should pray for the defeat of their enemies, shouldn't they? Otherwise, they themselves will be overtaken. "Not so this time," says Jeremiah about Babylon.

There are some surprising things to be learned from and experienced through prayer. Such is the rich testimony of Scripture and saints alike. As a general rule, communities and individuals who do not regularly pray indicate by this that they do not have an adequate theology. The command for Jeremiah not to pray is thus a special case and comes as a radical illustration of the spiritual deadness of the people. Fervent prayer means confidence in God and an openness to his surprising leading. Prayer is a form of applied theology. The issue here is not belief in God, but communion with God through prayer. The devil and his assistants do not pray to God, but they believe in his existence.

Prayer is not for the benefit of God, although both praise and petition belong in a relationship with God. Prayer changes both the perceptions of those who pray and their actions. Surely this is the case in ancient Babylon. As Judeans pray for the welfare of the city, God's people will learn that no one is only an enemy. In the case of Babylon, their doom is sure to come, but in a radical way God has bound the fortunes of his people with their enemy. There is something profound at work in such circumstances. What comes with clarity in the gospel is already adumbrated in the Old Testament. Through prayer one can look at opponents or problems as more than someone or something to be overcome. They can become also a means of education and sanctification, the agents through whom one finds growth in relationship with God.

Praying for peace. "Their peace is your peace." Certainly the tremendous changes in relations between East and West—the end of the so-called "cold war"—is an illustration of this truth. The fall of the Iron Curtain and the dissolution of the Soviet empire in the last few years has brought home to millions in the East and West that the "other" is not necessarily an enemy. Subsequently it has become clear that in the prosperity of the one lies the prosperity of the other. For Christians in both East and West this truth hits home with particular force. As former enemies now seek a better coexistence, Christians on both sides can see that God has done more than instruct them about an enemy—there is now a foundation for a new community of faith. Praying for the "other" has changed those who pray as surely as it has affected the "other."

How many tensions would be alleviated, how many problems set on the road to solution, if Christians would pray for the welfare of their opponents? Prayer for an opponent does not forbid action that may keep each other in relational tension. It does not guarantee a solution. But since prayer is applied theology, it will change one's attitude toward opponents.

Prayer is the bedrock of confidence in God. It was in Jeremiah's day, and it remains a key to seeking God with all one's heart. God's promises are freely given, but not all of them can be freely accepted—that is, they have little relevancy to an indifferent people. For those in dire straits, it should come as good news that God knows the future and is committed to the redemption of his people. "Seek and you will find" (Matt. 7:7) is the Lord's gracious command, not "resign and do nothing."

Interspersed in the scriptural word of Jeremiah 29 are indications of particular judgment on individuals. It is important for Christians to remember that judgment is God's affair. Jeremiah does not take judgment into his own hands, nor does he urge others to do so. He simply notes that the work of people like Ahab, Zedekiah, and Shemaiah is opposed to the purposes of God and that God will deal with them.

Jeremiah 30–33

\(\emoji\)

Introduction to Jeremiah 30–33

THESE FOUR CHAPTERS comprise a distinct subsection in Jeremiah. They are not, however, a simple unity. Chapters 30–31 are largely poetry, while 32–33 are prose. Chapters 30–31 are often called by interpreters the "Book of Consolation" or the "Book of Hope"[1] because they contain proclamations of Israel and Judah's restoration to the Promised Land. Restoration—or better said, the creation of a new relationship with the Lord—is also central here. The same restoration-oriented hope is part of chapters 32–33, so that their interpretation is linked with the two previous chapters. Nevertheless, no concrete setting in Jeremiah's ministry is given for the proclamation of chapters 30–31 (see below) as there is with chapters 32–33. The latter are set in the last days of the Judean state (587 B.C.), the tenth year of Zedekiah and the eighteenth of Nebuchadnezzar (32:1; 33:1).

Since there is a range of interpretive possibilities regarding Jeremiah's future hope, it is best to list the most common of them and to comment on them briefly at the outset of this subsection. Individual details are discussed more fully with the specific chapter.

(1) Some modern interpreters have concluded that major portions of the hopeful prophecies in the book originated not with Jeremiah but with his editors in the later exilic period, as deported Judeans looked for the possibility of restoration to their homeland.[2] According to some proponents of this view, the historical Jeremiah was essentially a prophet of doom, or an individual so far removed from the book that bears his name that the origin of most of these restoration prophecies comes from people in exile (and perhaps even in the postexilic period) who hoped for future change.

One may begin a response with the affirmation that there is no reason, a priori, why those who edited and produced the book of Jeremiah could not also have contributed prophecies to the finished product. After all, if God can

---

1. There is a reference to a book (scroll) in 30:2. Cf. 25:13; 36:4, 28, 32. See further B. Bozak, *Life Anew: A Literary-Theological Study of Jer. 30–31* (Roma: Editrice pontificio instituto, 1991).

2. See the relevant sections in R. P. Carroll, *Jeremiah: A Commentary* (Philadelphia: Westminster, 1986). A reasonable and theologically sensitive representative of a related view may be found in W. Brueggemann, *Jeremiah 26–52: Exile and Homecoming* (ITC; Grand Rapids: Eerdmans, 1991), 39–47. Brueggemann is reticent about the precise historical origin of much of the material in chs. 30–31. He is more concerned to interpret the voice of God within these texts, which give hope to the hopeless.

call Jeremiah as a prophet, then God can also use editors! The question is simply one of evaluating the relevant evidence for secondary material and weighing the balance of probability.

As noted in the introduction, it seems more likely to the present writer that Jeremiah's circle of supporters reworked and updated material that originated with the prophet himself, and less likely that some of the most creative and compelling material in all the book originated with these anonymous laborers. Perhaps this circle of supporters even had the assistance of the prophet himself in the earlier stages of editing before the book reached its final form. As editors, this circle would have arranged the material in line with the hope enunciated by Jeremiah himself, even if the sequencing of materials and the final form of the book came after the prophet's death.

Clearly the destruction of Jerusalem and the deportation of many of Judah's inhabitants impact the entire book of Jeremiah, including the hopeful oracles in chapters 30–33. In final form the restoration texts in this section are addressed to those Judeans who lived after Judah's demise and Jerusalem's destruction. In addressing a future hope for God's people, this Book of Consolation points beyond judgment and geographic restoration to an even grander future renewal (cf. [3], below).

(2) Some interpreters have deduced from the various references to Israel, Samaria, Jacob, Rachel, and Ephraim in chapters 30–31 that these chapters contain elements of the young Jeremiah's preaching to the northern territories taken earlier by the Assyrians.[3] As with the previous view, the application of historical analysis has led some to claim precise settings for the origins of particular oracles within the two chapters.

In this view, some of the "hopeful" prophecies originated early in Jeremiah's prophetic ministry[4] as addresses to the northern territories rather than (as in the first view) with editors in the exilic period. Apparently Josiah sought to reincorporate parts of the northern territory and population in his religious and political reforms (2 Chron. 34:29–33; 35:16–18), and it is certainly plausible to see the young Jeremiah as a supporter of these goals. After all, the prophetic hope is founded on a belief that the full complement of God's

---

3. An influential article representing this view is by N. Lohfink, "Der junge Jeremia als Propagandist und Poet: Zum Grundstock von Jer 30–31," *Le livre de Jérémie*, ed. P. M. Bogaert (Leuven: Leuven Univ. Press, 1981), 351–68. W. Holladay, *Jeremiah* 2 (Hermenia; Minneapolis: Fortress, 1989), 155–67, reconstructs earlier recensions of chs. 30–31, directed first to Israel and then to Judah. Most recent commentators who hold to a traditional dating for Jeremiah's public ministry do associate some of these prophecies with his preaching during the period of Josiah's reform. Obviously those who believe that Jeremiah began his prophetic ministry in 609 or later do not equate any of the texts in chs. 30–31 with the period of Josiah's reforms.

4. See comments on "faithless Israel" in ch. 3.

people could never be limited solely to Judah. Thus the northern territory and its inhabitants are among the people addressed in these two chapters along with Judah (who can be addressed separately).

The question here is whether the restoration of the northern territories (i.e., Israel, Ephraim) was originally addressed separately during an early period of Jeremiah's career or only in the period after 609 B.C., when the announcements of Judah's imminent demise were also delivered and both Israel and Judah were no more than remnants of their former political entities. Some of the material in chapters 30–31 would fit well in the late seventh century as Josiah instituted his reforms, but since the impact of the Judean exile is also in view, perhaps it is better to view this entire section as the result of a topical collection (i.e., prophecies of restoration) that dates from different periods in Jeremiah's ministry and that was updated and set in a broader literary context in the process of preservation.[5]

Like many of the judgment prophecies in chapters 1–20, which in written form are removed from a precise historical context and now function more broadly to explain the demise of Judah, the restoration prophecies in chapters 30–31 are now somewhat isolated from an original historical context and function as indications of the mercy of God and his power to transform both the near and the distant future.

(3) As with all true prophecy, predictions about the future are intended to effect change in the hearers as well as inform them about the future. In light of the comments above (see [2]), the collection of prophecies in chapters 30–31 is actually the prediction of a new world, that is, a new age and a new time unlike that known to the hearers. It includes restoration of exiles from Assyrian and Babylonian territories, surely a hopeful and gracious word to Jeremiah's contemporaries.

But there is more to the prophetic depictions of a new world than that, for nothing less than an ideal community (a new Jerusalem and new David) and a fully realized covenant relationship with God are announced. Such predictions, therefore, gave content to the hope for national healing in the postexilic period and also served as the beginnings of a new community in a restored Jerusalem. At the same time, the prophecies point beyond those marvelous "beginnings" to a day and time qualitatively different from either the postexilic period or that of the contemporary reader.

The new world envisioned in chapters 30–33 is indeed far grander and more sublime than the communities of faith formed after the Exile. Stated

---

5. These chapters have a complicated textual history, perhaps suggesting a lengthy process of preservation. In addition to the study of Bozak cited above, see B. Becking, "Jeremiah's Book of Consolation: A Textual Comparison: Notes on the Masoretic Text and the Old Greek Version of Jer 30–31," *VT* 44 (1994): 145–69.

somewhat differently, the Jews of the exilic and postexilic periods would not see the significance of chapters 30–31 exhausted in the return to Judea from Babylon. God has yet more to accomplish with and through his people. The future depicted in these chapters still has hopes as yet unrealized. At a fundamental level this puts modern readers in a similar context to that of the first hearers/readers: All alike wait in anticipation of the fuller realization of God's grand design.

Ultimately chapters 30–31 are eschatological in nature, depicting in the language and thought-forms of the day a prophecy that God will gain ultimate victory over alienation and sin. The postexilic restoration was the firstfruits of the promises, the prelude to and a type of the greater restoration to come. In light of Christ's first advent, the New Testament provides further guidance on the significance of these prophecies; nevertheless, modern Christians still await (in hope, just like their spiritual ancestors of Jeremiah's day) the final consummation of the new world glimpsed by Jeremiah. Here is a perspective that places the current generation of God's people in a mode of expectation similar to that of Jeremiah's own day.

Modern Christians may find an instructive analogy in the eschatological discourse of Jesus with his disciples (Matt. 24; Mark 13; Luke 21). The destruction of Jerusalem and conflict in the region after Jesus' death are graphically depicted, but so are the hardships and threats sure to afflict believers in subsequent years. Moreover, these predictions do more than simply depict the Roman devastation of the region, for they point beyond that imminent tragedy to the difficulties expected at the end of the age. Jeremiah 30–31 can be interpreted similarly—the turning of God's judgment is seen in the restoration from the Exile, but these things point beyond to a restoration yet to be fully realized.

The New Testament is reticent about a final restoration of Israel (cf. Acts 1:6–8). That "all Israel will be saved" (Rom. 11:26) is affirmed, quite apart from defining more closely who that Israel will be (ethnic/national? modern state? Jews who eventually accept Jesus as the Messiah?). Interpreters, therefore, differ on the question of interpreting Old Testament promises of Israel's restoration and transformation. Are they inherited by the church and thus reach their eschatological fulfillment through it, or do they represent a fulfillment to come for "Israel" that is distinct from the future promised for the church?

This is a much bigger question than that of interpreting Jeremiah 30–33, but the basic stance of interpreting Jeremiah is the same as that for other eschatological texts in the prophetic corpus. As indicated in the introduction to this commentary, the author opts for fulfillment in and through the church. This is based on the conviction that there is no other eternal connection of God's people to him except that which has been founded through Christ's cross and resurrection. Readers are invited to investigate the resources listed in the introduction for further study and to examine carefully the comments in the Bridging Contexts and Contemporary Significance for chapter 31.

Jeremiah 30:1–24

¹This is the word that came to Jeremiah from the LORD: ²"This is what the LORD, the God of Israel, says: 'Write in a book all the words I have spoken to you. ³The days are coming,' declares the LORD, 'when I will bring my people Israel and Judah back from captivity and restore them to the land I gave their forefathers to possess,' says the LORD."

⁴These are the words the LORD spoke concerning Israel and Judah: ⁵"This is what the LORD says:

"'Cries of fear are heard—
 terror, not peace.
⁶ Ask and see:
 Can a man bear children?
Then why do I see every strong man
 with his hands on his stomach like a woman in labor,
 every face turned deathly pale?
⁷ How awful that day will be!
 None will be like it.
It will be a time of trouble for Jacob,
 but he will be saved out of it.

⁸"' In that day,' declares the LORD Almighty,
 'I will break the yoke off their necks
and will tear off their bonds;
 no longer will foreigners enslave them.
⁹ Instead, they will serve the LORD their God
 and David their king,
 whom I will raise up for them.
¹⁰"'So do not fear, O Jacob my servant;
 do not be dismayed, O Israel,'

declares the LORD.

'I will surely save you out of a distant place,
 your descendants from the land of their exile.
Jacob will again have peace and security,
 and no one will make him afraid.
¹¹ I am with you and will save you,'
 declares the LORD.

'Though I completely destroy all the nations
    among which I scatter you,
I will not completely destroy you.
I will discipline you but only with justice;
    I will not let you go entirely unpunished.'

¹²"This is what the L ORD says:

"'Your wound is incurable,
    your injury beyond healing.
¹³ There is no one to plead your cause,
    no remedy for your sore,
    no healing for you.
¹⁴ All your allies have forgotten you;
    they care nothing for you.
I have struck you as an enemy would
    and punished you as would the cruel,
because your guilt is so great
    and your sins so many.
¹⁵ Why do you cry out over your wound,
    your pain that has no cure?
Because of your great guilt and many sins
    I have done these things to you.

¹⁶ "'But all who devour you will be devoured;
    all your enemies will go into exile.
Those who plunder you will be plundered;
    all who make spoil of you I will despoil.
¹⁷ But I will restore you to health
and heal your wounds,'

                    declares the L ORD,

'because you are called an outcast,
    Zion for whom no one cares.'

¹⁸ "This is what the L ORD says:

"'I will restore the fortunes of Jacob's tents
    and have compassion on his dwellings;
the city will be rebuilt on her ruins,
    and the palace will stand in its proper place.
¹⁹ From them will come songs of thanksgiving
    and the sound of rejoicing.
I will add to their numbers,
    and they will not be decreased;
I will bring them honor,
    and they will not be disdained.

²⁰ Their children will be as in days of old,

and their community will be established before me;

I will punish all who oppress them.

²¹ Their leader will be one of their own;

their ruler will arise from among them.

I will bring him near and he will come close to me,

for who is he who will devote himself

to be close to me?'

declares the LORD.

²² '"So you will be my people,

and I will be your God.'"

²³ See, the storm of the LORD

will burst out in wrath,

a driving wind swirling down

on the heads of the wicked.

²⁴ The fierce anger of the LORD will not turn back

until he fully accomplishes

the purposes of his heart.

In days to come

you will understand this."

30:1–3. Although the text does not provide a specific setting for these prophecies in Jeremiah's life, the command in 30:2 to write them in a scroll suggests that they are to stand as instruction and witness for the future. The summary statement in 30:3 uses a typical prophetic introduction for predictions of future change—"the days are coming" (cf. 30:8, 24). The primary claim about the future is that the affliction of "Jacob" (30:7, 10, 18) will be removed and the people will be restored to their land and to a better relationship with God. Apparently "Jacob" is a covenant term for God's people that includes both Israel and Judah (30:4). In the restoration God will raise up "David their king" (30:9).[6] Jerusalem also is addressed in 30:12–17.

These prophecies presuppose a unity to God's people that transcends their current political and geographical circumstances. Not only are there predictions that Israel and Judah will be restored to their land and that God

---

6. Cf. 30:21; 33:17; also 23:5–6. In 30:9 "David" stands symbolically for someone from David's dynasty. Jeremiah stands in line with several of the prophets who predict that God's promises to the Davidic house have not failed, regardless of the quality of the current ruler or even if no descendant currently serves as king. Cf. Isa. 9:1–7; 11:1–9; Ezek. 34:23; 37:24; Hos. 3:5; Amos 9:11–12.

will raise up for them a king from David's line, but the restoration of Zion (= Jerusalem) is also predicted (30:17–18). Moreover, Jeremiah announces a restoration of the covenant relationship between God and his people that assumes a unity for that people (30:22; 31:1; cf. 32:38).

30:4–7. This portion of chapter 30 is a bit cryptic with respect to the future turmoil it presupposes. A rhetorical question in verse 6 suggests that the dismay on the part of human beings will not be permanent. The point is that Jacob will be saved from a time of trouble.

30:8–11. The introductory phrase "in that day" is a rhetorical device used by prophets to speak of a decisive time in the future. Yokes and bonds will be removed from Jacob, and the people will no longer be enslaved by foreigners. By "David their king" is most likely meant someone from David's line. Such a hope is drawn from texts like 2 Samuel 7 and prophetic texts that rely on God's promised fidelity to the Davidic line.[7] Since no king from David's line ruled Jacob in the postexilic period, this hope finds its ultimate fulfillment in the New Testament proclamation that Jesus is David's greater Son (cf. Matt. 1:1–17; Luke 1:26–33; Rom. 1:3), not in the leadership of the restored community in the Persian period.

The injunction "do not fear," addressed to Jacob as God's "servant" (v. 10), reminds the reader of the exilic prophecies in the book of Isaiah (Isa. 41:8–10; 43:1–7; 44:1–5; 54:4). The nations among whom Jacob has been exiled are subject to judgment. Jacob too has received judgment, but his judgment has been disciplinary in form. A day of reckoning still awaits the nations.

30:12–17. In these verses humiliated Jerusalem is addressed. The description of her guilt and her helplessness remind the reader/hearer of the book of Lamentations. Judgmental language predominates in these verses, but its effects on Jerusalem are not without merciful limits. There is also announcement that Zion's enemies will be destroyed and that the city will be restored.

30:18–22. The announcement that Zion will be restored continues in the proclamation that Jacob's fortunes will be reconstituted. That Jacob and Zion are closely related can be seen from verse 18b. There is also an allusion to future leadership that will spring up from among the people (v. 21). The concluding verse reiterates the covenant formula (cf. 24:7). Restoration above all is a restoration of the relationship between God and his people.

30:23–24. This surprising section puts the future under the claim of God's righteous judgment and also in the context of divine intentions that cannot be fully grasped. The final verse (v. 24) is cryptic. Only the future (lit., "in the latter days") will reveal the extent of God's purposes in restoring Jacob

---

7. See the texts listed in the footnote above and the comments on Jer. 23:5–6.

and in punishing iniquity, for God's intentions to judge iniquity are most certainly part of the future when his people are "restored."[8]

Thus, the earliest recipients of these prophecies are informed that the full significance of these prophecies will only be realized at considerable distance from their time of origin. Perhaps this last verse should be read together with verses 1–2: The cryptic words of chapter 30 will be preserved in a book to serve not only as a witness from the past, but also as inspired prediction about a future where God will judge human iniquity, a future not yet fully understood or realized by Jeremiah's contemporaries. The full impact of these predictions will best be seen at the conclusion of God's intended future.

As noted in the introduction to the hopeful prophecies in chapters 30–33, some scholars have denied that the same Jeremiah who so consistently announced judgment could simply switch directions and announce, like Hananiah in chapter 28, that God's restoring activity was on the historical horizon. These scholars speculate that these verses and others like them in Jeremiah must come from editors in the exilic and postexilic period who wished to supplement Jeremiah's words for the next generation.

But let's note again that these are not the only words of hope in Jeremiah's book. Why could not Jeremiah himself have understood God to be both a righteous Judge and the One who intends to restore a chastened and punished people? We must acknowledge, however, that neither in this chapter nor elsewhere in the book are we provided with enough detail to reconstruct when Jeremiah first announced that God would restore his people after a time of judgment. His reaction in his encounter with Hananiah demonstrates that he was open to the fresh and surprising word of the Lord that would move beyond the necessary corrective judgment to the healing balm of restoration. Since the contents of Jeremiah are not arranged chronologically, it apparently was not important for later readers to have a chronology of his theological development; it was sufficient merely to indicate topically and thematically that the prophet announced both judgment and restoration as the work of the same Lord.

Bridging Contexts

GOD AND THE FUTURE. The chapter contains prophecies that range into the near future and into the far future from the perspective of Jeremiah's contemporaries. This realization helps us with interpreting the texts. Regarding the near future, God worked through

---

8. One might compare the concluding words to the book of Ecclesiastes: "Fear God and keep his commandments, for this is the whole duty of man. For God will bring every deed into judgment, including every hidden thing, whether it is good or evil" (Eccl. 12:13b–14). The point of intersection with this passage in Jeremiah comes in the claim that the future will cast a different light on matters now hidden or misunderstood.

the historical process to overcome the power of Babylon and to provide a way for his exiled people to return to their ancestral land. With the rise of Cyrus the Persian, later known as Cyrus the Great, a different political order was established in the latter half of the sixth century B.C. Under the leadership of Sheshbazzar and Zerubbabel, several groups of Jews made their way back to the land of promise. They began the process of rebuilding the temple complex and their lives (Ezra 1–3).

These people were not free from Persian control, but they laid more than a physical foundation; along with the preaching of prophets like Haggai and Zechariah, they also laid a spiritual foundation for greater renewal to come. The unfortunate breach between the returnees and many of the other inhabitants of the area (particularly those led by Sanballat, the governor of the province of Samaria) meant that reconciliation between the descendants of Israel and Judah was not accomplished. Nevertheless, elements of chapter 30 find fulfillment in the miraculous ways in which life in Jerusalem and Judah were restored after the Babylonian exile.

The chapter as a whole indicates avenues through which God's announced intent in chapter 1 "to uproot and tear down" and "to build and to plant" is actualized. Restoration took place in the postexilic period, but this example of God's faithfulness does not exhaust the claims of chapter 30. There is also the indication that God's people should not forget the necessity of a righteous judgment and that they should recognize their own inadequacies in healing their own failures. Such claims give subsequent generations of God's people cause for reflection as they ask: Are there still ways in which we exhibit failure and incur judgment?

A claim like that addressed to Zion in 30:12 ("your wound is incurable") pushes past a mere historical reading to interrogate any generation. It is a theology at one with a later biblical claim of death apart from divine grace (Eph. 2:1; Col. 2:13). The conclusion to chapter 30 points further forward to a time (times?) of broad reckoning, where God will judge iniquity on a wider scale. Such language calls any generation of God's people to anticipate more from the Lord of history.

Chapter 30 also predicts the restoration of the covenant relationship between God and his people (30:22). This claim should cause current readers to reflect on the centuries that have passed since these words were first proclaimed. Subsequent biblical history and that of the church are evidence that God still pursues this goal among his people. In Christ God has bound himself to his people and provided all the means necessary to overcome their failures. The future remains open to a greater fulfillment of these words, just as it was for Jeremiah's contemporaries.

Contemporary
Significance

ESCHATOLOGY. WHAT DOES the future hold for the church and the world in which it carries out its ministry? Theologians use the term *eschatology* to describe the expectations about the end of the age. As these words are being written, there is much in the popular culture about transition to a new millennium. The year 2000 is popularly understood as the beginning of a new millennium (even though it is actually the end of a century and also the end of a millennium). Does this transition year bring us closer to *the Millennium* on earth, or is that scriptural hope best understood through the life of the Spirit in the church of Jesus Christ? As always, the future will be the best vantage point from which to see the significance of the present! At a distance from the pressure of the "now," the puzzles of the present begin to show new meaning.

Sociologists chart the strange behaviors that often come at transition points such as a new year. Some of it is lawless or antisocial, and some of it is the nervousness that comes with the times, even if such nervousness lies below the conscious surface. This was especially true of the transition to the year 2000, which was a milestone as modern people measure time. But what about God's ways of evaluating the state of the world and of working out his ultimate purposes? One wonders if each new year has any particular significance in God's scheme.

God's faithfulness, present and future. Yes, eschatological speculation will be profitable in the near future, but will it be helpful for the church? A glance at biblical prophecy confirms that God has been faithful to his promises, but his faithfulness comes in surprising ways. It is true that God announced through prophets both the exile of his people and their return. But the return did not usher in the final age. God also announced that a new David would come to lead the people, but not everyone could accept that Jesus was the fulfillment of this hope. In this regard, oftentimes it is at some distance that people of faith can see more clearly what God has done. Perhaps what is more important for people of faith today is to concentrate on the "constants" in the eschatological prophecy of the Bible rather than on a blueprint mentality that believes it can "figure out the future in advance."

What are some of those constants? One is certainly that God is the Judge of all people. In addition, God has called a people into fellowship and has promised to be their God. These two things will not change, whether something in the year 2000 makes it a special year or not. A typical year is one in which God judges and purifies a people in various ways. If 2000 and beyond are typical years, then they will reveal many small fulfillments of the greater purpose God has given in Scripture and has not yet brought to culmination. When all is finally accomplished, it will be more clear. The church is called every year to have expectation and hope. God has indicated the shape of prophetic hope for all time in the person of Jesus Christ, who is the same yesterday, today, and tomorrow (Heb. 13:8).

During the last week of 1999 the present writer watched a few people load up their cars and trailers and head out to the rural areas of Texas. They did so because they feared the apocalyptic changes that might be ushered in with the coming of the new year. What was it about the biblical message that so frightened them? Most likely it was the expectation that if the end of history is coming, it would have disastrous proportions (cf., e.g., Matt. 24; Mark 13). All of us should be reminded that when the end is near, whether it is accompanied by the death throes of civilization or not, the consistent teaching of the biblical text is that God will save his people.

Jesus told his disciples to watch for the signs of the times; that is good advice in any situation. It is certainly so with the concern about the future: Watch for signs of the times. The ultimate shape of the future, however, can be discerned from those things that Scripture constantly espouses: God is working out his near and far purposes to judge iniquity, to redeem a people, and to create a new world where death and sin are banished. Maranatha!

Jeremiah 31:1–40

[1]"At that time," declares the LORD, "I will be the God of all the clans of Israel, and they will be my people."
[2]This is what the LORD says:

> "The people who survive the sword
> will find favor in the desert;
> I will come to give rest to Israel."

[3]The LORD appeared to us in the past, saying:

> "I have loved you with an everlasting love;
> I have drawn you with loving-kindness.
> [4]I will build you up again
> and you will be rebuilt, O Virgin Israel.
> Again you will take up your tambourines
> and go out to dance with the joyful.
> [5]Again you will plant vineyards
> on the hills of Samaria;
> the farmers will plant them
> and enjoy their fruit.

⁶There will be a day when watchmen cry out
    on the hills of Ephraim,
'Come, let us go up to Zion,
    to the LORD our God.'"

⁷This is what the LORD says:

"Sing with joy for Jacob;
    shout for the foremost of the nations.
Make your praises heard, and say,
    'O LORD, save your people,
    the remnant of Israel.'
⁸See, I will bring them from the land of the north
    and gather them from the ends of the earth.
Among them will be the blind and the lame,
    expectant mothers and women in labor;
    a great throng will return.
⁹They will come with weeping;
    they will pray as I bring them back.
I will lead them beside streams of water
    on a level path where they will not stumble,
because I am Israel's father,
    and Ephraim is my firstborn son.

¹⁰"Hear the word of the LORD, O nations;
    proclaim it in distant coastlands:
'He who scattered Israel will gather them
    and will watch over his flock like a shepherd.'
¹¹For the LORD will ransom Jacob
    and redeem them from the hand of those stronger than they.
¹²They will come and shout for joy on the heights of Zion;
    they will rejoice in the bounty of the LORD—
the grain, the new wine and the oil,
    the young of the flocks and herds.
They will be like a well-watered garden,
    and they will sorrow no more.
¹³Then maidens will dance and be glad,
    young men and old as well.
I will turn their mourning into gladness;
    I will give them comfort and joy instead of sorrow.
¹⁴I will satisfy the priests with abundance,
    and my people will be filled with my bounty,"
                        declares the LORD.

¹⁵This is what the LORD says:

"A voice is heard in Ramah,
　　mourning and great weeping,
Rachel weeping for her children
　　and refusing to be comforted,
because her children are no more."

¹⁶This is what the LORD says:

"Restrain your voice from weeping
　　and your eyes from tears,
for your work will be rewarded,"

　　　　　　　　　　　　declares the LORD.
　　"They will return from the land of the enemy.
¹⁷So there is hope for your future,"

　　　　　　　　　　　　declares the LORD.
　　"Your children will return to their own land.

¹⁸"I have surely heard Ephraim's moaning:
　　'You disciplined me like an unruly calf,
　　and I have been disciplined.
Restore me, and I will return,
　　because you are the LORD my God.
¹⁹After I strayed,
　　I repented;
after I came to understand,
　　I beat my breast.
I was ashamed and humiliated
　　because I bore the disgrace of my youth.'
²⁰Is not Ephraim my dear son,
　　the child in whom I delight?
Though I often speak against him,
　　I still remember him.
Therefore my heart yearns for him;
　　I have great compassion for him,"

　　　　　　　　　　　　declares the LORD.

²¹"Set up road signs;
　　put up guideposts.
Take note of the highway,
　　the road that you take.
Return, O Virgin Israel,
　　return to your towns.

²²How long will you wander,
>   O unfaithful daughter?
The LORD will create a new thing on earth—
>   a woman will surround a man."

²³This is what the LORD Almighty, the God of Israel, says: "When I bring them back from captivity, the people in the land of Judah and in its towns will once again use these words: 'The LORD bless you, O righteous dwelling, O sacred mountain.' ²⁴People will live together in Judah and all its towns— farmers and those who move about with their flocks. ²⁵I will refresh the weary and satisfy the faint."

²⁶At this I awoke and looked around. My sleep had been pleasant to me.

²⁷"The days are coming," declares the LORD, "when I will plant the house of Israel and the house of Judah with the offspring of men and of animals. ²⁸Just as I watched over them to uproot and tear down, and to overthrow, destroy and bring disaster, so I will watch over them to build and to plant," declares the LORD. ²⁹"In those days people will no longer say,

>   'The fathers have eaten sour grapes,
>   and the children's teeth are set on edge.'

³⁰Instead, everyone will die for his own sin; whoever eats sour grapes—his own teeth will be set on edge.

>   ³¹"The time is coming," declares the LORD,
>   "when I will make a new covenant
>   with the house of Israel
>   and with the house of Judah.
>   ³²It will not be like the covenant
>   I made with their forefathers
>   when I took them by the hand
>   to lead them out of Egypt,
>   because they broke my covenant,
>   though I was a husband to them, "
>   declares the LORD.
>   ³³"This is the covenant I will make with the house of Israel
>   after that time," declares the LORD.
>   "I will put my law in their minds
>   and write it on their hearts.
>   I will be their God,
>   and they will be my people.

³⁴No longer will a man teach his neighbor,
 or a man his brother, saying, 'Know the LORD,'
because they will all know me,
 from the least of them to the greatest,"

declares the LORD.

"For I will forgive their wickedness
 and will remember their sins no more."

³⁵This is what the LORD says,

he who appoints the sun
 to shine by day,
who decrees the moon and stars
 to shine by night,
who stirs up the sea
 so that its waves roar—
 the LORD Almighty is his name:
³⁶"Only if these decrees vanish from my sight,"
 declares the LORD,
"will the descendants of Israel ever cease
 to be a nation before me."

³⁷This is what the LORD says:

"Only if the heavens above can be measured
 and the foundations of the earth below be searched out
will I reject all the descendants of Israel
 because of all they have done,"

declares the LORD.

³⁸"The days are coming," declares the LORD, "when this city
will be rebuilt for me from the Tower of Hananel to the Corner Gate. ³⁹The measuring line will stretch from there straight
to the hill of Gareb and then turn to Goah. ⁴⁰The whole valley where dead bodies and ashes are thrown, and all the terraces out to the Kidron Valley on the east as far as the corner
of the Horse Gate, will be holy to the LORD. The city will
never again be uprooted or demolished."

31:1 POETIC DEPICTIONS of the future continue from chapter 30. Verse 1—likely a summary of the chapter's contents—repeats the promise of covenant restoration (cf. 30:22; 31:31–34) as something that will occur "at that time."[9] This chronological phrase is a typical part of the prophetic repertoire for speaking about the future, and it fits well in the context of the repeated references in chapters 30–31 to the future.

"That time" is a reference to a decisive time of divine activity and the resulting changes brought to fruition as a result. The previous verse (30:24) refers to the "days to come," and elsewhere chapter 31 contains three references to "the days are [time is] coming" (31:27, 31, 38). How far into the future is not specified by such references; the emphasis is on the *qualitative* changes between the present grim circumstances and the future God has promised. In the chapter are also predictions of a restoration of Israel[10] to its land, so that return from the Exile is part of the future that God promises to the generation of judgment in Jeremiah's "day."

Israel's restoration provides a thematic coherence to chapter 31, but it is unlikely that the chapter originated as a literary unity; rather, various predictions from the prophet about the future are collected together to convey to hearer and reader alike that God intends a transformed future for his people. As noted in the introductory comments to chapters 30–33, readers should not think of a single event or discrete period as the only fulfillment of these future hopes. It is the quality of God's intended future that stands out in the chapter. The poetic nature and variety of claims for the future are best understood as indications of the multiple ways in which the Lord will bring (even future for us today) these words to fulfillment.

Chapter 31 can be subdivided into nine different units of speech (vv. 2–6, 7–9, 10–14, 15–20, 21–26, 27–30, 31–34, 35–37, 38–40). Several of the units have introductory and/or concluding formulae that mark the units.[11]

---

9. Jer. 31:1 is likely a summary heading for the prophecies contained in ch. 31. The introductory formula that begins verse 2 ("This is what the LORD says") is for a particular oracle (cf. also 31:7, 15, 23; footnote 11 below).

10. *Israel* is but one of several terms used to signify the people of God. It is used several times (e.g., 31:1–2, 4, 10, 21, 23, 27, 31, 36–37) as are the terms *virgin* (31:4, 21), *Judah* (31:23, 27, 31), *Jacob* (31:7, 11), *Ephraim* (31:6, 18, 20), and *Rachel* (31:15). *Zion* (31:6, 12; cf. 38–40) and even *Samaria* (31:5) are also employed to refer to the people in their various political and geographical forms.

11. See "This is what the LORD says" in 2, 7, 15, 35; "declares the LORD" in 1, 27, 31, 38; "hear the word of the LORD" in 10. It must be admitted that there is still ambiguity where some units of speech end and others begin. One can, for example, read 31:15–22 as one poetic unit, and see 31:23–26 as a separate prose unit.

This is prophetic speech that places the emphasis on divine communication. Jeremiah has receded into the background, and his circumstances are hardly mentioned (except for the cryptic comment in 31:26). Perhaps this mysterious verse indicates that some or all of the preceding prophecies in the chapter are the result of dreams.

31:2–6. God's people are addressed in familiar imagery. He reminds them that they can find his favor even in the desert (*midbar*). This should probably be understood in two senses: (1) as a typological comparison with the spiritual history of their ancestors, when that generation found favor with God in the desert, and (2) as a reference to the experience of exile and the hope that God would bring his people home through the desert. The future rebuilding of "Virgin Israel" (a metaphorical reference to the people)[12] indicates that God has loved them with an "everlasting love" and drawn them back to himself with "loving-kindness" (*ḥesed*). This latter term refers to commitments that spring from affection and loyalty rather than those prescribed by law. The language and thought forms are like those of Hosea (Hos. 2:14–23), who depicted God's covenant renewal with Israel in terms of an "alluring" of Israel in the desert and the betrothal of her to him with loving-kindness (*ḥesed*).

Zion will play an important role in the future restoration. Those in Ephraim will call to one another with the request to "go up to Zion." There they will come to the Lord their God. This is pilgrimage language.

31:7–9. The Lord proposes a song of praise for a saved remnant. In the poetry of this short prophecy, there is parallelism between the expressions "your people" and "the remnant of Israel" (v. 7). Readers should take note of the term *Israel* in context. Verse 9 uses the term to refer specifically to the former northern kingdom by way of comparison with Ephraim, God's "firstborn" (cf. Ex. 4:22; Hos. 11:1). Perhaps the remnant reference here has a particular focus on those exiled by the Assyrians in the eighth century.

31:10–14. The nations are to take note that God intends to redeem his people. God, who scattered the people in judgment, is a shepherd who will gather them. The poetry of verse 11 links two terms to describe God's reacquisition of his people. The NIV translates *pdh*, the first verb, as "ransom." Indeed it does mean purchase. This word is used in Exodus 13:13 to refer to the substitutionary sacrifice for a firstborn animal; the Israelites could ransom or redeem a firstborn animal among their flocks by offering (in one sense, "paying" with) a substitute. The term is used also for the ransom of a slave (Ex. 21:8).[13]

---

12. The term is female and can refer to the capital city as indicative of the people. Since "Virgin Israel" will plant vineyards on the hills of Samaria (v. 5), it is unlikely that this reference is a metaphor for Samaria.

13. Note, e.g., Deut. 7:8, which uses the verb to describe God's redeeming Israel from slavery in Egypt.

The second verb, a synonym of *pdh*, is *g'l*, translated by the NIV as "redeem." The word has its roots in family custom, where a relative could use his possessions and influence to extricate other family members from such difficulties as debts or other social obligations.[14]

As with a previous prophecy, Zion is one of the goals of a rejoicing people. In its primary sense the passage refers to the new exodus, which God is about to accomplish by bringing his scattered people back to their homes. The language of joy and delight in verses 12–14 is every bit as extravagant as the thorough language of judgment used elsewhere in Jeremiah. "Mourning" will be turned into "gladness."

31:15–20. The mourning of the Promised Land for the loss of "her" children is described through the metaphor of Rachel weeping. Rachel was the favorite wife of Jacob and mother of Joseph and Benjamin (Gen. 29–30). She died in childbirth with Benjamin and was buried between Bethel and Bethlehem (35:16–26). A monument was built to mark her tomb. Jeremiah's reference to weeping in Ramah (meaning "hill" in Heb.) apparently refers to the place of this monument. Ramah may refer to the hilltop mentioned in the Samuel narratives as the home of Hannah, Elkanah, and the prophet Samuel, or perhaps to another hilltop shrine known to the audience in Jeremiah's day.

Rachel's children are coming home. This means that there is a hope for Rachel's future. Here again the first element in the renewal of Israel comes in the restoration of exiles to their ancestral home.[15]

Verses 18–20 can be taken as a separate oracle from verses 15–17. The speaker changes from Rachel to Ephraim. The sentiment, however, in these verses is similar. The Israelites who have sinned and been cast from their land are personified in Ephraim, who confesses his failures. God tenderly accepts his repentance, describing Ephraim as his "dear son" (cf. 31:9), a child for whom his heart yearns. God's parental mercy is paramount in these verses.

---

14. The acts of Boaz in redeeming family property, marrying Ruth, and providing an heir to the family line of Elimelech are the acts of a family or kinsman-redeemer. In Heb. such a one is called a *go'el*, lit., "one who redeems." The verb *ga'al* is also used to describe God's liberation of his people from slavery in Egypt (Ex. 6:6; 15:13).

15. Verse 15 is quoted in Matt. 2:17–18. Herod the Great's slaughter of the young boys in Bethlehem provoked lamentation among the bereaved. Matthew reminds readers of his Gospel that this is not the first time that children among God's people have been killed. The dastardly work of Herod and the sorrows it produced are part of a larger scriptural pattern already adumbrated in Rachel's weeping. See the study by M. J. J. Menken, "The Quotation from Jeremiah 31(38).15 in Matthew 2.18: A Study of Matthew's Scriptural Text," in *The Old Testament in the New Testament: Essays in Honour of J. L. North*, ed. S. Moyise (Sheffield: Sheffield Academic Press, 2000), 106–25. Menken notes a quote from a rabbi preserved in *Genesis Rabbah* 82:10: "We find Israel called after Rachel, as it says, 'Rachel weeping for her children.'" The location of Rachel's tomb is thought to be near Bethlehem (cf. Gen. 35:19–20; 48:7), and this may also have given Matthew reason to see significance in the Jeremiah quote for the sad event in Bethlehem during Herod's reign.

31:21–26. This section is combined of both poetry and prose. The poetry (vv. 21–22) calls for highway markers to be erected so that "Virgin Israel" can find her way home. In this metaphorical expression she is also personified as God's "unfaithful daughter." In context it is difficult to know whether the referent behind Virgin Israel is the city of Samaria or the people. In either case, the female gender is important to the poetry. The text describes her return to her homeland as a new thing that God will create— "a woman will surround a man."

This imagery has caused difficulties and significant divergence for interpreters, as a perusal of commentaries will show.[16] Contextually the emphasis seems to fall on the newness that only the Lord can create. (1) This is indicated by the verb *bara'* (to create), used in verse 22 to describe what the Lord will do. This verb is used in Genesis 1:1 to describe God's creation of the heavens and the earth. Of all the occurrences of this verb in the Old Testament where the meaning is "to create," God is the only subject.[17]

(2) The phrase "a woman will encompass [or surround] a man" is a reversal of what was expected in male-female relations in ancient Near Eastern society. The phrase may have a sexual connotation (i.e., the woman initiates intimate relations); it certainly is surprising and indicates initiative and the exercise of authority or power. Already in context the reader has encountered Rachel, the personified land, who weeps for her children. Perhaps it is she or the renewed Virgin Israel who encompasses the man Ephraim. In any case, the phrase points to a surprising and compassionate act of God in making new life possible for those who were estranged in exile.

Restoration of the people is the theme of verses 23–25. While this theme is familiar in the immediate context, it is still important to note that God is the subject of the verbs "bring back," "refresh," and "satisfy." He is the chief actor in the drama of the return.

31:27–30. The introductory formula indicates that a change is coming in the future. The language is that of Jeremiah's commission to prophesy in 1:10. Not only will God pluck up and destroy Judah, but he will also build and plant Israel and Judah. The use of both names conveys totality (cf. 31:31). The form of their life together is not stated. Furthermore, the future will bring an end to the complaints that corporate judgment is unjust (31:29–30). Each person will indeed bear his or her own sins in God's judgment of the people.[18]

---

16. See the survey in W. Holladay, "Jer. xxxi 22b Reconsidered: The Woman Encompasses the Man,'" *VT* 16 (1966): 236–39, and his further elaborations in his *Jeremiah*, 2:192–95.

17. God is the subject of the verb when used in the simple (Qal) and Niphal stems. This is not the case in Piel and Hiphil.

18. The same proverb is quoted in Ezek. 18:2 as part of an extended discussion on the nature of corporate judgment and individual responsibility. J. S. Kaminsky, *Corporate Responsibility in the Hebrew Bible* (JSOTSup 196; Sheffield: Sheffield Academic Press, 1995), 139–78.

31:31–34. This well-known passage, with its proclamation of a new covenant (*bᵉrit ḥᵃdaša*), is a summary of Jeremiah's message. It moves from the righteous judgment that has come on Israel and Judah because of their disobedience to the restoration of God's people in a new relationship with him. God's *torah* ("law," the verbal expression of his will) will become a constituent part of a person/people when God writes it on their hearts. This striking claim is a play on God's writing of the Ten Commandments on tablets of stone (Ex. 32:9–16). Furthermore, the effects of sin to spoil relationships are completely done away with in the incredible claim that God will no longer remember them (and their destructive influence).

The objects of God's restoration are "the house of Israel and . . . the house of Judah." As in the previous section (31:27), these terms denote inclusivity as referring to all of God's people. They do not disqualify any other peoples among the nations from being included, but such possibilities are not mentioned either. What is "new" about the new covenant is not the covenant partner but the quality of the community created by God's amazing acts.

The passage contains frank recognition of previous failure, even though God initiated a first covenant with the people. That covenant was at Mount Sinai—a covenant that the people collectively broke. The NIV translates the conclusion of verse 32 as "though I was a husband to them." This is an acceptable rendering of the verb *baʿal* in the Hebrew text, a verb that means to marry, to own, or to be master over. The imagery is similar to that used in 2:2, where the prophet reminds the people of the bridal period of their youth, when God brought his people to himself in the desert and entered into a covenant with them (cf. Ezek. 16:8).[19]

It is the quality of the covenant bond between God and his people that gives the essential "newness" to the coming new covenant. As noted above, the imagery is the writing of God's instruction on the human heart rather than on the tablets of stone. Knowledge of God, therefore, is internalized. Furthermore, the ability of sin to disrupt the relationship is made obsolete by the astounding announcement that God will not remember sins and their effects on the relationship.

The phrase "new covenant" occurs only this once in the Old Testament, although Jeremiah twice announces an "everlasting covenant" (*bᵉrit ʿolam*) that God will establish with his people (32:40; 50:5). Several prophetic books refer to a renewal of the Mosaic (Sinai) covenant with Israel and Judah in similar terms. Hosea 2:14–23 speaks metaphorically of God's bringing Israel again into the desert and reclaiming the people in a covenantal bond likened to marriage. Ezekiel (Ezek. 16:60; 37:26) and Isaiah (Isa. 55:3) have references to an "everlasting covenant" that point to the same future for God's people as Jeremiah.

---

19. One should compare also the use of the term *baʿal* in Jer. 3:14.

This famous "new covenant" passage proclaims that an ultimate restoration of the covenant relationship between God and his people includes the transformation of corporate existence. In essence, it is a summary of all that God will accomplish in the renewing of his covenant relationship with his people (see comments on "the new covenant" in the Bridging Contexts section).

31:35–40. The fidelity of God to his people is cast by analogy with the fixed order of the cosmos. Just as the order of the cosmos is sure, so is God's commitment to his people. The final claim is for the rebuilding of Jerusalem, but the text needs careful consideration in its context. It is not a simple rebuilding of the city that is envisioned; the city, like the people of the new covenant, is to be transformed and will never again be overthrown (cf. Ezek. 40–48).

Bridging Contexts

THE ULTIMATE STATE. As noted above, this chapter concentrates in various ways on the quality of the renewed relationship with the Lord that Israel will experience. Also, as part of its original setting, the chapter presupposes the particularities of Israel and Judah in the humiliation of their failure and the resulting physical collapse of their respective states. As part of the Book of Consolation, chapter 31 projects a future in which God's righteous judgment is superseded by his sovereign work of redemption. Israel is called on to accept in faith that this future is sure and to live in anticipation of the coming redemption.

Here is a key for hearing these ancient words as instructive for the church. The current circumstances of God's people do not reflect their ultimate estate. They are called to confess their sins, to respond obediently as disciples of the risen Christ, and to anticipate the culmination of the reign of God to come with the second advent of Christ. Thus, Christians should interpret the future proclaimed to Israel in Jeremiah 31 in the context of the covenant established in Christ for all believers, Jew and Gentile alike.

The new covenant. Jeremiah's inspired expression "new covenant" has been used for centuries as the heading or title to the twenty-seven documents that form the second half of the Christian Bible, that is, the New Testament. The Latin word *testamentum*, which underlies the English term *testament*, translates the Hebrew word *bᵉrit* ("covenant"). Early Christians, therefore, made an interpretive bridge between the proclamation of the prophet and the content of the gospel of God set forth in Jesus Christ.[20]

---

20. One cannot determine who was the first early Christian to equate the gospel message of new life in Christ with the phrase "the new covenant." Melito, bishop of Sardis in western Turkey from ca. A.D. 170–90, made a list of books that he placed under the category of "the old covenant," implying that the Christian faith could be placed in the cate-

One sees this understanding as well within the pages of the New Testament. At the Last Supper Jesus describes the cup as a representation of the "new covenant in my blood" (Luke 22:20; 1 Cor. 11:25). Two other Gospel writers record the phrase "blood of the covenant" (Matt. 26:28; Mark 14:24), which reflects the initial covenant ceremony at Sinai (Ex. 24).

The apostle Paul understands the gospel of new life in Christ to be a fulfillment of the hope expressed in Jeremiah's prediction of the new covenant (2 Cor. 3:1–18). As an apostle, Paul describes himself as a servant of a new covenant, not of the letter but of the Spirit (3:6). His emphasis on the work of God's Spirit shows that he understands Jeremiah's prediction of a transformed heart to be the work of God's Spirit in the life of a Christian. Nevertheless, the coming of Christ and the gift of the Spirit do not exhaust the promises made in the new covenant; the complete transformation of God's people is still in the future.

Finally, the anonymous letter to the Hebrews likewise boldly proclaims that Christ's great salvific work as a high priest on behalf of his people is based on the "new" and "better" covenant announced by Jeremiah (Heb. 8–9).

What all the New Testament references have in common is a belief that the future redemption promised by God through Jeremiah (or any of the prophets) has dawned in the ministry of Jesus Christ and will be brought to an ultimate fulfillment in his second coming at the end of the age. Jeremiah's promise to the house of Israel and the house of Judah (31:31) is applied to Jewish and Gentile Christians alike, who comprise the church. Because of Christ's advent and through the continuing ministry of the Spirit, the church has tasted an "already" of the future Jeremiah foresaw.

Nevertheless, there is a "not yet" as the current age runs its course. This interplay of "already" and "not yet" places the church in an anticipatory posture similar to that of Jeremiah's own contemporaries. The prophet's announcement that God intended a transformed future for his people was an "already" that believers could trust. It was a goal for their future that they could use to chart their course in the present. One may interpret similarly Jeremiah's announcement of the restoration of the people in their land. It was a tangible expression, an "already" that pointed beyond itself to a complete transformation of God's people as he worked out his eschatological purposes among them.

---

gory of "new covenant." The reference to his list comes from Eusebius's *Ecclesiastical History* (4.26.14). Clement of Alexandria used "new covenant" to refer to Christian faith, and the term became more widespread in the third and fourth centuries. See further, H. von Campenhausen, *The Formation of the Christian Bible* (Philadelphia: Fortress, 1972), 262–68.

GOD'S REDEMPTIVE ACTION. Evidence for God's redemptive action will have a shape and form to it. This is true wherever a scriptural word is taken to heart. Those persons are right who emphasize that salvation in Christ is by grace alone through faith; salvation is God's work, whether we talk of individuals or of the final advent of Christ and the full manifestation of his kingdom (which will include the transformation of the heavens and the earth as we now know them). God calls people to respond to what he has already accomplished through Christ, to grow in their faith and their identity as one of Christ's own (sanctification), and to live in anticipation of the final advent of Christ and the glorious unveiling of his reign in full triumph over evil and death itself.

Jeremiah 31 is the voice of an inspired spiritual ancestor who spoke to his contemporaries about the shape that God's action would take in their lives and that of their descendants (e.g., return from exile, a purified worship, knowledge of forgiveness). Perhaps in the present we can think of things in our lives that are "signs" of God at work, things whose shape and function portray the work of God. These things may be personal; they may concern the family; they may be part of the life of fellowship one enjoys among friends and in the activities of a congregation. Signs of redemption should point not only to what has already been accomplished in Christ but also to what still lies ahead. There is always a future tense to the life of believers.

Mother Teresa died in Calcutta in September 1997. A commentator on her life noted that in a speech she delivered a few years previously to the American Congress, Mother Teresa had offended nearly everyone in the assembly by talking about the neglect of the poor in society. She went on to remark that abortion was the most egregious example of evil against the defenseless, thereby offending yet another segment of the audience. She chided those of Protestant persuasion that faith without works made for a lifeless religion, doing yet more "damage." Her point? There should be a form to and tangible evidence of God at work in his people. She was popularly described as a social activist, but she preferred to be called "religious." In the classical Catholic sense, that meant she lived out her vocation as a response to the call and claim of God. When the gospel of forgiveness and new life in Christ take root in a person or community, there will be change—and any changes will be but steps along the way toward the future that God will usher in. "For in this hope we were saved" (Rom. 8:24).

The Christian life comes with the gift of familiarity and even spiritual intimacy among believers. Jeremiah's prediction that God will write his *torah*, that is, his instruction, on human hearts takes shape in the church through the work of the Holy Spirit. "To know God" in an intimate and corporate way is not just a future promise. There is an "already" to this experience in the Christian life through the agency of God's Spirit just as there is the exciting anticipation of things "not yet" realized and only intimated. Forgiveness is something that can be experienced in the present; it is a promise of God that can and should give shape and substance to the present reality of Christian existence. Forgiveness helps one anticipate a future where even the remembrance of sin and failure have no role.

God's promises regarding Israel. God's redemptive work gives shape and substance to the life of his people. In various ways the New Testament claims the promises to Israel as promises to the church. One sees this in the use of the "new covenant" passage in the Gospels and letters. Modern Christians have differed considerably over how to read the Old Testament in light of Christ and in the way they interpret the promises to Israel as a future yet unrealized. No one can "solve" all the issues of this topic in a sermon or brief reflection. Nevertheless, Jeremiah's promise of Israel's restoration and its security before the Lord should compel modern Christians to ask about the contemporary significance of believing Judaism (as opposed to an ethnic definition) and the place of the modern state of Israel in God's economy.

"All Israel will be saved" (Rom. 11:26). Paul could write this because the Old Testament proclaimed a future for God's people, a future not realized in Paul's day any more than in Jeremiah's day. Indeed, there was no state called Israel in Paul's day. Jews lived scattered throughout the Roman Empire, and those Jews who lived within the former boundaries (which changed over the centuries) of Israel were subject to the power of Roman administration. The reason to hear this quote from Paul is a theological one, whether or not the interpreters who stand before this claim know what Paul means by Israel. It takes seriously the shape of God's promises. God has made promises to a people, albeit a people whose political shape and religious profile have changed over the centuries. They are the spiritual ancestors of Christians today.

If the church has inherited the promises made to Israel (as I believe), does this mean that God has simply turned his back in righteous judgment on Jews because they have failed to recognize Jesus as God's Son and Redeemer? The answer is "no." Certainly modern Christians have the responsibility to proclaim the gospel to Jews just as to any who do not know Christ as Savior and Lord. Christians should do so, however, with confidence that God has made promises to his people Israel (historically his "first love"), and that these promises will have an ultimate fulfillment. Those promises will have shape and substance in this age, and their influence will extend even beyond that.

Does this mean that modern Christians should have special concern for the modern state of Israel (a political entity, not to be identified with believing Judaism)? Again the answer is "no"; but God's promises to Israel do mean that Christians should have a special affinity for believing Judaism, and they should recognize that God is still at work among believing Jews in a mysterious way. God's promises hold out a future in which his people will be redeemed and constituted as a transformed community with Christ as its head. This is the future of all of God's people (the Israel of God), including Jews who confess Jesus as the Christ.

Jeremiah 32:1–44

¹THIS IS THE word that came to Jeremiah from the LORD in the tenth year of Zedekiah king of Judah, which was the eighteenth year of Nebuchadnezzar. ²The army of the king of Babylon was then besieging Jerusalem, and Jeremiah the prophet was confined in the courtyard of the guard in the royal palace of Judah.

³Now Zedekiah king of Judah had imprisoned him there, saying, "Why do you prophesy as you do? You say, 'This is what the LORD says: I am about to hand this city over to the king of Babylon, and he will capture it. ⁴Zedekiah king of Judah will not escape out of the hands of the Babylonians but will certainly be handed over to the king of Babylon, and will speak with him face to face and see him with his own eyes. ⁵He will take Zedekiah to Babylon, where he will remain until I deal with him, declares the LORD. If you fight against the Babylonians, you will not succeed.'"

⁶Jeremiah said, "The word of the LORD came to me: ⁷Hanamel son of Shallum your uncle is going to come to you and say, 'Buy my field at Anathoth, because as nearest relative it is your right and duty to buy it.'

⁸"Then, just as the LORD had said, my cousin Hanamel came to me in the courtyard of the guard and said, 'Buy my field at Anathoth in the territory of Benjamin. Since it is your right to redeem it and possess it, buy it for yourself.'

"I knew that this was the word of the LORD; ⁹so I bought the field at Anathoth from my cousin Hanamel and weighed out for him seventeen shekels of silver. ¹⁰I signed and sealed the deed, had it witnessed, and weighed out the silver on the scales. ¹¹I took the deed of purchase—the sealed copy containing the terms and conditions, as well as the unsealed copy— ¹²and I gave this deed to Baruch son of Neriah, the son of

Mahseiah, in the presence of my cousin Hanamel and of the witnesses who had signed the deed and of all the Jews sitting in the courtyard of the guard.

¹³"In their presence I gave Baruch these instructions: ¹⁴'This is what the LORD Almighty, the God of Israel, says: Take these documents, both the sealed and unsealed copies of the deed of purchase, and put them in a clay jar so they will last a long time. ¹⁵For this is what the LORD Almighty, the God of Israel, says: Houses, fields and vineyards will again be bought in this land.'

¹⁶"After I had given the deed of purchase to Baruch son of Neriah, I prayed to the LORD:

¹⁷"Ah, Sovereign LORD, you have made the heavens and the earth by your great power and outstretched arm. Nothing is too hard for you. ¹⁸You show love to thousands but bring the punishment for the fathers' sins into the laps of their children after them. O great and powerful God, whose name is the LORD Almighty, ¹⁹great are your purposes and mighty are your deeds. Your eyes are open to all the ways of men; you reward everyone according to his conduct and as his deeds deserve. ²⁰You performed miraculous signs and wonders in Egypt and have continued them to this day, both in Israel and among all mankind, and have gained the renown that is still yours. ²¹You brought your people Israel out of Egypt with signs and wonders, by a mighty hand and an outstretched arm and with great terror. ²²You gave them this land you had sworn to give their forefathers, a land flowing with milk and honey. ²³They came in and took possession of it, but they did not obey you or follow your law; they did not do what you commanded them to do. So you brought all this disaster upon them.

²⁴"See how the siege ramps are built up to take the city. Because of the sword, famine and plague, the city will be handed over to the Babylonians who are attacking it. What you said has happened, as you now see. ²⁵And though the city will be handed over to the Babylonians, you, O Sovereign LORD, say to me, 'Buy the field with silver and have the transaction witnessed.'"

²⁶Then the word of the LORD came to Jeremiah: ²⁷"I am the LORD, the God of all mankind. Is anything too hard for me?

²⁸Therefore, this is what the LORD says: I am about to hand this city over to the Babylonians and to Nebuchadnezzar king of Babylon, who will capture it. ²⁹The Babylonians who are attacking this city will come in and set it on fire; they will burn it down, along with the houses where the people provoked me to anger by burning incense on the roofs to Baal and by pouring out drink offerings to other gods.

³⁰"The people of Israel and Judah have done nothing but evil in my sight from their youth; indeed, the people of Israel have done nothing but provoke me with what their hands have made, declares the LORD. ³¹From the day it was built until now, this city has so aroused my anger and wrath that I must remove it from my sight. ³²The people of Israel and Judah have provoked me by all the evil they have done—they, their kings and officials, their priests and prophets, the men of Judah and the people of Jerusalem. ³³They turned their backs to me and not their faces; though I taught them again and again, they would not listen or respond to discipline. ³⁴They set up their abominable idols in the house that bears my Name and defiled it. ³⁵They built high places for Baal in the Valley of Ben Hinnom to sacrifice their sons and daughters to Molech, though I never commanded, nor did it enter my mind, that they should do such a detestable thing and so make Judah sin.

³⁶"You are saying about this city, 'By the sword, famine and plague it will be handed over to the king of Babylon'; but this is what the LORD, the God of Israel, says:

³⁷I will surely gather them from all the lands where I banish them in my furious anger and great wrath; I will bring them back to this place and let them live in safety. ³⁸They will be my people, and I will be their God. ³⁹I will give them singleness of heart and action, so that they will always fear me for their own good and the good of their children after them. ⁴⁰I will make an everlasting covenant with them: I will never stop doing good to them, and I will inspire them to fear me, so that they will never turn away from me. ⁴¹I will rejoice in doing them good and will assuredly plant them in this land with all my heart and soul.

⁴²"This is what the LORD says: As I have brought all this great calamity on this people, so I will give them all the prosperity I have promised them. ⁴³Once more fields will be bought

in this land of which you say, 'It is a desolate waste, without men or animals, for it has been handed over to the Babylonians.' ⁴⁴Fields will be bought for silver, and deeds will be signed, sealed and witnessed in the territory of Benjamin, in the villages around Jerusalem, in the towns of Judah and in the towns of the hill country, of the western foothills and of the Negev, because I will restore their fortunes, declares the LORD."

THIS CHAPTER CONTINUES the hopeful section of Jeremiah. The hope is in the power of God to overcome the self-destructive consequences of Judah's folly. Chapter 32 has three major sections: Jeremiah's purchase of property as a prophetic sign (32:1–15), his prayer to the Lord (32:16–25), and a commentary from the Lord on Judah's fate and future (32:26–44).

32:1–15. The chronological reference in verse 1 has caused some difficulties for interpreters. Nebuchadnezzar's eighteenth year on the reckoning of the Babylonian system would be 587/586, while the tenth year of Zedekiah, which has its own problems for interpreters, is 588/587. As noted in the introduction to the commentary, the problems associated with regnal years beginning in the spring or fall and with whether an accession year is assumed make for some problematic chronological reconstructions for the two kings in question.

The historical setting of chapter 32, however, is clear. Babylon has besieged Jerusalem for a second time, and Jeremiah is confined in the city by a royal guard. Apparently the Babylonians began the siege late in the year 588. Subsequently an Egyptian force began a march toward Palestine and caused a temporary easing of the siege (cf. Jer. 37:5). It is plausible that at this time (spring 587?) Jeremiah is visited by his cousin Hanamel, and they carry out the transaction narrated at the chapter's beginning.

Jeremiah's continual prophecies about the sovereignty of Babylon over Judah and Jerusalem have been perceived as seditious, and as a result he is imprisoned or confined on several occasions. His announcement to Zedekiah here (32:3–4) that Jerusalem and the king will be handed over to Babylon is essentially repeated in 34:2–3. Once he is arrested for attempting to leave Jerusalem (37:11–14). Perhaps Hanamel's visit to him in Jerusalem is in response to Jeremiah's failed attempt to reach his ancestral home and to carry out his personal affairs. In any case, family business at a time of crisis becomes the occasion for a prophetic symbolic act.

Jeremiah purchases (*gʾl*; lit., redeems) some family property.[21] It should be remembered that much of an Israelite family's identity was tied to its possessions. A "household" (an extended family) was defined not merely by a list of its members but also by its property and the related functions of its members. Indeed, "household" (*bayit*)[22] is the closest term in Hebrew to what modern people call a family. A particularly significant element of what defined most families was its patrimony or its inheritance. This property, unlike perhaps other things the family possessed, was not to be sold to those outside of the clan (the kin of the family).[23] Thus, when there were economic difficulties or other types of hardship, the property could be used as collateral and sold to members within the clan (or even tribe), but it was not to be alienated permanently from the family of possession.

According to Jeremiah 32:7 the prophet has the "right of redemption"[24] to the property "owned" by Hanamel. His right comes by virtue of family ties. For Jeremiah to redeem the property means either that the property already has a *lien* (to use a modern term) against it and the family of Hanamel still needs money desperately, or similarly, that the needs of Hanamel's family are such that they will "sell" the property to Jeremiah in order to satisfy some of their other obligations. Needless to say, a time of siege is not the time to be buying property. Whatever the specific reason behind the request of Hanamel, such a request reflects a time of desperation as families seek whatever means they can to keep life and limb together.

Jeremiah's purchase of Hanamel's property becomes a vehicle, a symbolic act, intended to illustrate his message. At one of the darkest moments in Judah's history, when the Babylonian reduction of the country is in an advanced state and the successful siege of Jerusalem seems merely a matter of time, Jeremiah purchases the property because "houses, fields and vineyards will again be bought in this land" (32:15). There will be a future for God's people, including restoration to their land after the pain of defeat and the trauma of exile.

Baruch assists Jeremiah in carrying out the purchase and the preparation of the necessary records. He is a scribe (36:32); that is, the preparation, reading, and preservation of documents are skills of his profession. Baruch will

---

21. On matters related to writing and transfer of property, see P. King, *Jeremiah: An Archaeological Companion* (Louisville: Westminster-JohnKnox, 1993), 85–91. King specifically treats Jeremiah's purchase as part of this section of the book.

22. Most English readers will recognize the construct form (= "house of") of the word *bayit* in the more familiar term *bet*. Bethlehem, e.g., means "house of bread."

23. Cf. Lev. 25:25–28 on the significance of a family's inheritance.

24. The word for redemption is *geʾulla*, derived from the verb *gaʾal*, to redeem. A kinsman-redeemer was called a *goʾel*, someone who could buy back or acquire family property or even family members who had been acquired by someone else (cf. comments on 31:11).

assist Jeremiah in the preparing of a scroll of prophecies in chapter 36. His patronymic is supplied in 32:12: He is "son of Neriah, the son of Mahseiah."[25] The preservation of the purchase documents is described in some detail. In time to come they will serve as verification of Jeremiah's prophecy that land and fields will again be bought.[26]

32:16–25. In a prayer Jeremiah praises God as Creator, as merciful and righteous Judge in the historical process, and as the true God who chose Israel as his own. Also he acknowledges that the Babylonian siege is God's work. As a prose prayer it is not unlike that of Nehemiah 9:5–37. Both prayers intersperse hymnic elements that praise God with frank confession of sins.

This prayer ends abruptly with the statement that God has commanded Jeremiah to go and buy the field. It is a sign of the times. When others have lost hope, the "pessimistic" Jeremiah is called to signify a future, and his prayer testifies to readers that God, the Lord of history, is still at work.

32:26–44. God speaks to Jeremiah after the prophet's prayer concludes. His communication is a summary of what Jeremiah has proclaimed for years, that a righteous judgment will befall Judah and Jerusalem and that it will proceed not from God's weakness over against the powerful Babylonian deities, but from his intention to discipline and purge his people. Considerable space is devoted to the articulation of God's anger at the failures of the people. Verse 37 describes God's response as "furious anger and great wrath."

In addition to the articulation of wrath, God reiterates the significance of Jeremiah's land purchase as a sign of the Lord's resolve to restore and bless his people. Both current calamity and future blessing are the work of God. In his prayer, Jeremiah confessed in awe that "nothing is too hard" for God (32:17). In his answer, God's rhetorical question asks: "Is anything too hard for me?" (32:27). Through this God reassures the people that what he has promised he can deliver.

God's announced future holds forth the miraculous promises of an "everlasting covenant" (32:40), a changed heart for the people (32:39), and life again in the Promised Land (32:41). These prose promises are related to the poetic announcements in chapters 30–31, which also concern the people's

---

25. Two clay bullae (lumps of clay impressed with a seal) have been discovered in the vicinity of Jerusalem that preserve a reference to Baruch the scribe (see comments on ch. 36). Apparently Baruch had a brother who was a government official (51:59): Seraiah, the son of Neriah, the son of Mahseiah had duties that most likely required literacy. Scribal activity may have been a family trait. Seraiah too worked in conjunction with Jeremiah.

26. Isaiah sealed up his testimony (Isa. 8:16), apparently so that it might be consulted in the future. Daniel's vision also is sealed for the future (Dan. 12:4), perhaps for the same reason: At the end of days it will verify his prophetic word.

future. The "everlasting covenant" is essentially a synonym for the "new covenant" in 31:31–34. The qualitative changes depicted for the new covenant, once brought to fruition, will be everlasting.[27]

The chapter ends as it began. As Jeremiah has bought a field, so shall others buy property in the future. In Jeremiah's "purchase" God's promised future has already begun to take symbolic shape.

IN TIMES OF THREAT. Judah and Jerusalem find themselves under threat. Such can be the common lot of humankind in its corporate life. Circumstances of threat and danger come periodically. Theological questions are inevitable in times of trouble; they are not as frequent in times of blessing and security. Where is God in these horrible circumstances, and what must be done in response to the predicament?

Judah's circumstances are the result of its own moral and spiritual failures. This is a scenario that has been and will be repeated in the history of God's people, for they are not immune to the threatening circumstances that come periodically. Although moral and spiritual failures are by no means the only cause of suffering (personal or corporate), they are the reasons in this case. God is not absent in the process whereby Judah reaps what it has sown but is present to move the process beyond self-incurred judgment. God has given the people over to their folly and has used the historical process as judgment on them. Is this God's final word to the "fallen"? No; judgment is a penultimate word, a stage in God's dealings with his people that leads to a future that only God can bring about.

Word and deed. Jeremiah's prophetic sign comes about in the context of family duty and solidarity. He exercises the "right of redemption" that belongs to him as a member of an extended family. His payment to Hanamel is a tangible expression of his faith and an act that is commensurate with his message. Indeed the two are inseparable. Word and deed go together as a hallmark of Old Testament prophecy. During a time of national calamity and spiritual depression, Jeremiah expends his resources, making a statement about God's intention to redeem and to restore. He does so through the circumstances of his membership in a family. It is a family where some of its members have opposed his message and sought to persecute him (12:5–6). Similar dynamics occur periodically among God's people in any age. Ministry often arises from the debris of cherished plans gone awry.

In the larger scriptural narrative Jeremiah's prophetic act is like that of Elijah on Mount Carmel, straining to see the first signs of rain clouds in a

27. Cf. Jer. 33:20–26; Ezek. 16:60–62; 37.

drought-stricken region (1 Kings 18:1–46). He looked for the cloud because water had been used as a sign that God was the Lord of the drought. Drought was on everyone's mind, and God would deal with his people through these circumstances. When finally a small cloud appeared, the prophet ran to signify that rain was on the way. Similarly, with defeat on everyone's mind, Jeremiah buys property to signify that through God's grace, property will again be bought and sold in the land by God's people. One might call this activity a tangible sign of God's grace. Here is a bridge to cross for any generation of God's people: What are the tangible signs of God's grace that you have chosen to illustrate your Christian hope?

One thing leads to another in chapter 32. The making of commitments leads by way of provisional signs to something even greater. God's reply to Jeremiah's prayer becomes a reminder not only of small steps in a time of judgment but of redemption on a grand scale. This is a dynamic of the text that runs all the way from an imprisoned prophet to the announcement of an everlasting covenant. The same dynamic exists in the exercise of Christian faith. Small steps in the right direction point ahead to even greater things God has in store.

VEHICLES FOR COMMUNICATION. As a college student I heard that one definition of an apologist for the Christian faith is a person who takes the thinking of the day and turns it into a defense of Christianity. There is a sense in which Jeremiah takes the circumstances of his day, particularly the crushing reminder of imminent failure that the siege of Jerusalem signifies for Judeans, and turns them and the mindset of the day into a vehicle for proclaiming God's truth. Viewed from this angle, the signs of the times become vehicles for communicating the signs of the kingdom. It is a perennial question: "How do I (we) exercise our faith in relevant fashion in my (our) particular context?" Perhaps one needs to look no further than the circumstances of family and community that so frequently occupy our minds.

One can be quite specific. In the case of my own community, a rapidly growing area with escalating housing costs, so-called affordable housing has become a common problem. There is more than one organization dedicated to the search for affordable housing, and even to the building of such housing, for those in need. Some of these organizations are Christian, and they intend their efforts to be signs of the kingdom, examples of Christian commitment to a vision of wholeness in the community and opportunities to demonstrate provisionally the ethics of the kingdom. Those involved, from the builders to the occupants, are invited to trust the Lord and to dedicate themselves to his service in the community in which they live. These Christians build in hope in places where many others have despaired over their circumstances, present and future.

Prayer. Prayer is a key ingredient to the exercise of one's faith. Not only did Jeremiah buy, he prayed. To praise God as Creator, Judge, and Redeemer is to focus not on one's resources but on God, who calls one to obedience. Prayer (as in the case of Jeremiah and the purchase of property) is an acknowledgment that God is at work in the world and not aloof from the circumstances of his people. It is a reminder that the dominant concerns of a people or community may be the key to the most effective ways of ministry. Finally, prayer is the opportunity for petition. To trust God in difficult circumstances and to ask for guidance and deliverance becomes both a privilege and a responsibility.

Redemption. Redemption always costs something. This is a truth that should never be ignored. Whether it is the purchase of property or a theory to explain the atonement, the whole concept of redemption rests in the dynamics of a gift on behalf of those unable to gain something for themselves. For redemption to work, it requires those who have to give on behalf of those who don't. It is usually easier to argue about the faults of those who don't have rather than to celebrate that God has provided the opportunity to give so that others might live. Evangelism and social ethics both work best when they follow the scriptural pattern of joyful giving without concern for an accounting of merits. It is amazing what can be "redeemed" by the simple giving of talents bestowed by the Lord.

Western print media have recently noted the efforts on the part of some school-age children in the United States to collect money in order to purchase Christian boys and girls in Sudan who are held by Muslims there as slaves. Some members of the public have complained that the children are manipulated and that the situation in Sudan is too complex for making clear moral judgments. For example, it is argued that to purchase the children from slavery merely encourages the practice of kidnapping Christian children so that more money (ransoms) can be collected by the slave-traders. Perhaps there is some truth to this point about not encouraging slave-traders. But ask the question: How would you feel if you were a Christian Sudanese slave? Would you prefer continued debate on the ambiguities of the situation or that someone, somewhere, would take a stand?

In most debates, not all options are open for careful deliberation, as if someone is perusing a giant shopping list with virtually all options available and leisurely looking for the best bargain. I suggest the American children are to be commended for taking a real step, for making tangible efforts at securing the freedom of Christian slaves. While the debate continues on whether or not their purchase is a wise move, let it be said that some persons are willing to pay a price in an uncertain atmosphere simply because they believe that God wants the freedom of his people. While others continue to talk and wring their hands, they pray that God's kingdom and will may be done, on earth as it is in heaven.

Jeremiah acted on the opportunity that came his way. It was definitely not a good business deal. His purchase symbolized, however, that God would redeem his people.

Jeremiah 33:1–26

¹WHILE JEREMIAH WAS still confined in the courtyard of the guard, the word of the LORD came to him a second time: ²"This is what the LORD says, he who made the earth, the LORD who formed it and established it—the LORD is his name: ³'Call to me and I will answer you and tell you great and unsearchable things you do not know.' ⁴For this is what the LORD, the God of Israel, says about the houses in this city and the royal palaces of Judah that have been torn down to be used against the siege ramps and the sword ⁵in the fight with the Babylonians: 'They will be filled with the dead bodies of the men I will slay in my anger and wrath. I will hide my face from this city because of all its wickedness.

⁶"'Nevertheless, I will bring health and healing to it; I will heal my people and will let them enjoy abundant peace and security. ⁷I will bring Judah and Israel back from captivity and will rebuild them as they were before. ⁸I will cleanse them from all the sin they have committed against me and will forgive all their sins of rebellion against me. ⁹Then this city will bring me renown, joy, praise and honor before all nations on earth that hear of all the good things I do for it; and they will be in awe and will tremble at the abundant prosperity and peace I provide for it.'

¹⁰"This is what the LORD says: 'You say about this place, "It is a desolate waste, without men or animals." Yet in the towns of Judah and the streets of Jerusalem that are deserted, inhabited by neither men nor animals, there will be heard once more ¹¹the sounds of joy and gladness, the voices of bride and bridegroom, and the voices of those who bring thank offerings to the house of the LORD, saying,

"Give thanks to the LORD Almighty,
    for the LORD is good;
    his love endures forever."

For I will restore the fortunes of the land as they were before,'
says the LORD.

¹²"This is what the LORD Almighty says: 'In this place, desolate and without men or animals—in all its towns there will
again be pastures for shepherds to rest their flocks. ¹³In the
towns of the hill country, of the western foothills and of the
Negev, in the territory of Benjamin, in the villages around
Jerusalem and in the towns of Judah, flocks will again pass
under the hand of the one who counts them,' says the LORD.

¹⁴"'The days are coming,' declares the LORD, 'when I will
fulfill the gracious promise I made to the house of Israel and
to the house of Judah.

¹⁵"'In those days and at that time
    I will make a righteous Branch sprout from David's line;
    he will do what is just and right in the land.
¹⁶In those days Judah will be saved
    and Jerusalem will live in safety.
This is the name by which it will be called:
    The LORD Our Righteousness.'

¹⁷For this is what the LORD says: 'David will never fail to have
a man to sit on the throne of the house of Israel, ¹⁸nor will the
priests, who are Levites, ever fail to have a man to stand
before me continually to offer burnt offerings, to burn grain
offerings and to present sacrifices.'"

¹⁹The word of the LORD came to Jeremiah: ²⁰"This is what
the LORD says: 'If you can break my covenant with the day
and my covenant with the night, so that day and night no
longer come at their appointed time, ²¹then my covenant with
David my servant—and my covenant with the Levites who are
priests ministering before me—can be broken and David will
no longer have a descendant to reign on his throne. ²²I will
make the descendants of David my servant and the Levites
who minister before me as countless as the stars of the sky and
as measureless as the sand on the seashore.'"

²³The word of the LORD came to Jeremiah: ²⁴"Have you not
noticed that these people are saying, 'The LORD has rejected
the two kingdoms he chose'? So they despise my people and

no longer regard them as a nation. ²⁵This is what the LORD says: 'If I have not established my covenant with day and night and the fixed laws of heaven and earth, ²⁶then I will reject the descendants of Jacob and David my servant and will not choose one of his sons to rule over the descendants of Abraham, Isaac and Jacob. For I will restore their fortunes and have compassion on them.'"

33:1–3. THIS CHAPTER concludes the "Book of Consolation" (chs. 30–33). Verse 1 links this chapter with chapter 32. God speaks a "second time" to Jeremiah while he is confined under guard and the Babylonians are besieging the city of Jerusalem. Thus one should probably read the prose narratives in chapters 32 and 33 as scene 1 and scene 2 in the narration of Jeremiah's prison experiences.

There are also links between chapter 33 and the largely poetic oracles in chapters 30–31. For example, they have in common the phrase *šub šᵉbut*²⁸ (NIV "bring back from captivity, restore the fortunes"), which succinctly captures much of the emphasis on corporate renewal. The phrase occurs three times in chapter 33 (vv. 7, 11, 26) alone, serving as a thread of continuity in the prose speeches of the Lord.

The emphasis in this chapter is on God speaking (33:2, 10, 12, 17, 19, 23), almost as if the divine commentary that concluded chapter 32 is picked up again, with continued emphasis on the future turning of Judah's fortune. Readers and hearers should note that God's communication to the prisoner is meant for them. The narrator intends for readers to be instructed by what is said to the prophet. Even as a "listener," therefore, Jeremiah is in the prophetic mode of conveying the Lord's message to his contemporaries by repeating what he hears.

33:4–9. God reiterates his promise to redeem Judah and Jerusalem. The turning fortunes of the people are here described as God's "healing" them.²⁹ Healing also includes forgiveness, along with such tangible signs of restoration as resettlement in the land of promise, rebuilding Jerusalem ("this city"

---

28. This Hebrew phrase uses the verb *šub* (turn, return) with a cognate accusative—more literally translated, "to turn the turning." It is a common phrase for corporate restoration and renewal (e.g., Deut. 30:3; Ps. 14:7; 53:6; 85:1; Amos 9:14; Zeph. 2:7), although it can be used for an individual (cf. Job 42:10). In addition to Jer. 33, the phrase also occurs in 29:14; 30:3, 18; 31:23; 32:44; 48:47; 49:6; 49:39. Ezekiel likewise uses the phrase (Ezek. 16:53; 29:14; 39:25).

29. In 33:6 the lexeme *rpʾ* ("heal") occurs in both noun and verb form.

in v. 9), and security while dwelling there. These promises reiterate those made in previous chapters. Other peoples will learn to fear (hold in awe) God because of Judah's restoration. Here again the theme of Jeremiah as "prophet to the nations" comes to the fore.

33:10–13. These verses continue to emphasize a joyful future for the people as a reversal of the judgment on and the misery suffered by Judah. Cities in Judah will again be inhabited. The temple will again have worship. Verse 11 contains a familiar refrain from the temple liturgy: "Give thanks to the LORD Almighty, for the LORD is good; his love [*hesed*] endures forever." This is the characteristic phrase of the temple singers appointed by David (1 Chron. 16:41) and is known from the praises of the Psalter (Ps. 106:1; 118:1, 29; 136; cf. 100:4). For someone who had been as critical about the temple as Jeremiah, such a text reminds us that his criticisms presuppose no enduring hostility to the temple, only toward its misuse and corruption.

33:14–18. There is more than one chronological moment to the "good word" that God provides. These verses are introduced by the prophetic formula for the future: "The days are coming." Both Israel and Judah are included in the future transformation. In addition to the corporate restoration of the people, Jeremiah announces that "a righteous Branch ... from David's line" will arise and execute justice and righteousness (see also 23:5–6). This promise is messianic in that it depends on the promises made by God to David's family (see below). Jerusalem will even receive a new symbolic name: "The LORD [is] Our Righteousness."[30]

33:19–22. The work of Davidic rule and that of priestly ministry will not cease. These announcements indicate that God's promises (when finally realized in their completeness) will never end. God will undergird two fundamental institutions of the people in perpetuity. Someone from David's line will be head of the people, and descendants of Levi, the priestly tribe, will always be available to officiate in public worship.[31]

---

30. In 23:6 the future Ruler from David's line bears the (symbolic) name "The LORD our Righteousness." The NIV translates 33:16 as "the name by which it will be called," with a note that indicates "it" can also be "he" (i.e., the future ruler). Although there are variant readings among early manuscripts, the MT preserves the rendering "the name by which *she* [i.e., the city] will be called." Jeremiah's contemporaries will hear the name for either ruler or city as a play on the name of Zedekiah, the last Judean king, which means "The Lord is righteous." The prophecy does not indicate a saving role for Zedekiah (whom Jeremiah and Ezekiel criticize severely); instead, his name is used to declare that its unrealized promise will be fulfilled by different means and by someone else from his family.

31. One should compare the promise to the Levitical priesthood with the judgment speech against Eli and his priestly house at Shiloh (1 Sam. 2:27–35). Note esp. the statement in v. 35 that the faithful priest whom God will raise up is to serve with God's "anointed."

There is an allusion to the promises made to Abraham. He was promised descendants like the stars of heaven and the sand on the seashore (Gen. 15:5; 22:17); here God promises innumerable descendants to the Davidic line and the Levitical priests.

33:23–26. God has heard the despair and cynicism of his people. Those who conclude that God has simply rejected them are wrong. God has not broken his covenant with day and night (cf. 33:20), nor has he rejected his people. The use of covenant language in this context is appropriate. A covenant (*bᵉrit*) is a solemn promise often undergirded by an oath. God's covenant with day and night is not an agreement with those inanimate parties but the expression of his sovereign resolve to maintain a beneficent order.[32] Because of his mercy, the people still have a future.

THE WORD FOR THE FUTURE. God's word about the future is usually built on the prevailing circumstances of the first recipients. His word in Jeremiah 33 presupposes the circumstances of his people in the despair of defeat and in the (soon-to-come) trauma of exile. There is a sense in which Jerusalem is like Jeremiah; as the prophet is detained by guards and his movement restricted, so the city is under siege and its movement constricted—and defeat is imminent.

What is corporate life to be like for Judah when its cities are deserted, its temple in ruins, and its king in exile? Judah and Jerusalem are called on to trust that all these circumstances can be reversed in God's good time. God will deal with the present predicament and reverse the judgment it contains. God takes seriously the particulars of their plight and promises to deal with them. Modern readers should take heart at this pattern and trust that God knows the particulars of their situation (and that of the communities in which his people live).

As noted above, the promises of chapter 33 about the future can be found elsewhere in Jeremiah (esp. chs. 30–32). Thus, chapter 33 should not be read in isolation from other sections of Jeremiah and indeed from other sections of those prophets that speak about the restoration of the people.[33] Although these elaborations have variation in vocabulary and detail, they are consistent with claims elsewhere in the Old Testament that speak about transformations to come.

Although these promises are not new to modern readers, we should not be lulled into complacency because "we know how it all comes out." God has made promises to the house of David[34] and vows that there will always be

---

32. Cf. Gen. 8:22 in the context of the Noachic covenant in Gen. 9:1–17.
33. See comments about interpreting prophecy in the introductory section to chs. 30–33.
34. See comments on 23:5–6.

priestly worship. Thus, on the one hand, God deals with the particulars of his people in the trauma of defeat and exile. The future he has promised contains the institutions of monarchy and temple and the renewed gift of the land. On the other hand, there is surprise in store for God's people as the shape of those promises is reconfigured in Christ (David's Son and heir of the promises) and through the people who are "in Christ."

A veil on the panorama of God's promised future is partially lifted in the New Testament, but in doing so, the full realization of God's promises is still future-oriented. Christ is the promised Ruler from David's line, and his ministry on behalf of his people as a great high priest[35] discloses the depth of God's commitment to the future of his people. Then as now, they are called to trust in God's promise and to live according to the hope revealed to them.

Christian hope is structured essentially like that of Old Testament prophetic hope: It has a "future tense" while it maintains itself through responsible engagement in the present. The future restoration predicted by Jeremiah is even now still "in process," long after initial realizations in the return from exile and the rebuilding of Jerusalem and the temple. Contemporary Christians should be prepared for surprise and wonder when God brings in his kingdom in its fullness.

WORKING FOR THE LORD IN ADVERSE SITUATIONS. One wonders what it is about prison life that gives rise to such deep reflections as those given in the Bible to prisoners. Joseph, Jeremiah, Paul, and John (the seer of the Apocalypse) come immediately to mind. Recent years have contributed powerful testimony to the ways of God from prison cells (e.g., Aleksandr Solzhenitsyn, Charles Colson, Nelson Mandela, Karla Faye Tucker).[36] Perhaps the obvious answer is "time." Prisoners typically have "time on their hands," since their movements and activities are forcibly restricted. Perhaps also it is the quality of the experience of God during incarceration. Though some prisoners become bored and irrational in their confinement, others are motivated to develop certain skills and mental fac-

---

35. See esp. the New Testament letter to the Hebrews. In Rom. 8:34 the risen Christ is depicted as standing at God's right hand and interceding for his people.

36. Karla Faye Tucker is not as well known as the others listed here. In 1999 she was executed by the state of Texas for a murder she committed as a young woman under the influence of drugs and alcohol. She underwent a conversion experience in prison and served Christ faithfully for years while there. She was a model of Christian fortitude in the weeks before her execution. Her case was much discussed in the national media, raising questions about the necessity of carrying out her sentence when it was obvious to all that God had changed her life.

ulties as they are able. God has found this setting to be a propitious time to approach his chosen ones and to teach his people through them.

Contemporary Christians, particularly in the West, may find this dynamic an odd one: Lose your freedom and find out more about God; be in despair and find yourself instructed about the power and mercy of God. God often finds an opportunity to reconstitute people's horizons about themselves when they are suddenly limited in their freedom. So it was for Judah, so it was for John on the isle of Patmos and the suffering churches of Asia Minor.

Charles Colson is a modern example of someone whose freedom was taken from him by the state because he had broken the law. While there, Colson dealt with more than the humiliation of imprisonment; he wrestled with his sinfulness before God and emerged from prison with Christian zeal. The lives of many prisoners and congregations have been dramatically changed because of his witness. God's promised future has the power to change the present circumstances of people as they yield themselves to the leading of the Holy Spirit.

In the last few years, the country of South Africa has undergone tremendous change. Nelson Mandela, a black South African and former political prisoner, was elected president of the country in 1994. With its former policies of apartheid and a past full of violence, the country had much to atone for and to overcome. Both partial blame for the past and the call to ministry in the present rest on the churches in the country. One wonders if the national Truth and Reconciliation Commission (established by the government to deal with past faults)[37] will be able to lead the country forward and help it prepare for the future.

Note well the title of that commission: truth and reconciliation. In God's economy the two go together. Since three-quarters of South Africans (of all races) confess Christ, there is the exciting and challenging prospect of Christian faith as the unifying center of the population. What opportunities lie before the churches at this crossroads in the history of that country! How does a Christian (or the church) see the future from a broken past? Will past sinfulness continue to work its destructive way, or, with God's grace, will the vision of reconciliation and the possibility of a transformed future find root in the present?

God's promise that someone from David's line will reign over his people is made eternal in the resurrection of his Son (born of the house of David). He is the ultimate head of God's people. Truth and reconciliation, whether in South Africa or elsewhere, can take lasting shape only if they are understood by people to be joined in Christ, the head of the church.

---

37. The Commission is chaired by Desmond Tutu, retired archbishop and winner of the Nobel Peace Prize.

Jeremiah 34:1–22

WHILE NEBUCHADNEZZAR KING of Babylon and all his army and all the kingdoms and peoples in the empire he ruled were fighting against Jerusalem and all its surrounding towns, this word came to Jeremiah from the LORD: ²"This is what the LORD, the God of Israel, says: Go to Zedekiah king of Judah and tell him, 'This is what the LORD says: I am about to hand this city over to the king of Babylon, and he will burn it down. ³You will not escape from his grasp but will surely be captured and handed over to him. You will see the king of Babylon with your own eyes, and he will speak with you face to face. And you will go to Babylon.

⁴"'Yet hear the promise of the LORD, O Zedekiah king of Judah. This is what the LORD says concerning you: You will not die by the sword; ⁵you will die peacefully. As people made a funeral fire in honor of your fathers, the former kings who preceded you, so they will make a fire in your honor and lament, "Alas, O master!" I myself make this promise, declares the LORD.'"

⁶Then Jeremiah the prophet told all this to Zedekiah king of Judah, in Jerusalem, ⁷while the army of the king of Babylon was fighting against Jerusalem and the other cities of Judah that were still holding out—Lachish and Azekah. These were the only fortified cities left in Judah.

⁸The word came to Jeremiah from the LORD after King Zedekiah had made a covenant with all the people in Jerusalem to proclaim freedom for the slaves. ⁹Everyone was to free his Hebrew slaves, both male and female; no one was to hold a fellow Jew in bondage. ¹⁰So all the officials and people who entered into this covenant agreed that they would free their male and female slaves and no longer hold them in bondage. They agreed, and set them free. ¹¹But afterward they changed their minds and took back the slaves they had freed and enslaved them again.

¹²Then the word of the LORD came to Jeremiah: ¹³"This is what the LORD, the God of Israel, says: I made a covenant with your forefathers when I brought them out of Egypt, out of the land of slavery. I said, ¹⁴'Every seventh year each of you

must free any fellow Hebrew who has sold himself to you. After he has served you six years, you must let him go free.' Your fathers, however, did not listen to me or pay attention to me. ¹⁵Recently you repented and did what is right in my sight: Each of you proclaimed freedom to his countrymen. You even made a covenant before me in the house that bears my Name. ¹⁶But now you have turned around and profaned my name; each of you has taken back the male and female slaves you had set free to go where they wished. You have forced them to become your slaves again.

¹⁷"Therefore, this is what the LORD says: You have not obeyed me; you have not proclaimed freedom for your fellow countrymen. So I now proclaim 'freedom' for you, declares the LORD—'freedom' to fall by the sword, plague and famine. I will make you abhorrent to all the kingdoms of the earth. ¹⁸The men who have violated my covenant and have not fulfilled the terms of the covenant they made before me, I will treat like the calf they cut in two and then walked between its pieces. ¹⁹The leaders of Judah and Jerusalem, the court officials, the priests and all the people of the land who walked between the pieces of the calf, ²⁰I will hand over to their enemies who seek their lives. Their dead bodies will become food for the birds of the air and the beasts of the earth.

²¹"I will hand Zedekiah king of Judah and his officials over to their enemies who seek their lives, to the army of the king of Babylon, which has withdrawn from you. ²²I am going to give the order, declares the LORD, and I will bring them back to this city. They will fight against it, take it and burn it down. And I will lay waste the towns of Judah so no one can live there."

Original Meaning

CHAPTER 34 IS PART of a series of narratives about the siege and fall of Jerusalem. It is linked with chapters 32–33 by the common setting of the Babylonian siege during Zedekiah's reign, although chapters 32–33 are also typically grouped with chapters 30–31 as part of the theme of restoration. A date sometime in 588 B.C. or early 587 fits the historical context of the events narrated in chapter 34. Chapter 35 is set in the time of King Jehoiakim, several years earlier, so its contents are related to chapter 34 by the theme of Judah's failures, not that of chronology.

The narrative in chapter 34 has two primary parts. Verses 1–5 are a word from the Lord to Jerusalem and Zedekiah, and verses 8–22 report an emancipation ceremony (lit., a covenant) for Judean slaves and a subsequent reneging on the proclamation by slave owners. The failure of the people to honor their covenant oath becomes the occasion for the Lord again to announce his judgment on Judah, Jerusalem, and Zedekiah.

34:1–5. This passage should be read in the context of 38:17–18; 39:7; 52:8–11; and 2 Kings 25:1–7. The fate of Zedekiah and of the city and nation are bound together. The statements about the future should be understood as announcements contingent on the reactions of king and people to the Babylonian siege. Verses 2–3 voice a familiar word of judgment on the city and its king. Their present course of disaster will lead (as it were) inevitably to a tragic conclusion. Verses 4–5, likewise, should be understood as contingent on some response of Zedekiah, even at this late date. Although not formulated in the classical form of a call to repentance, these prophecies indicate the possible mitigation of the king's threatening circumstances.

Later on, Zedekiah was captured while fleeing the besieged city. His last days were spent in darkness because the Babylonians blinded him—a cruel act that came after the execution of members of his family (39:5–7). One should note the information provided in 34:21. It is a commentary (an update) on the word to Zedekiah in 34:4–5, perhaps anticipating the king's continuing recalcitrance and his sorry fate. Zedekiah's actions condemned him to the same fate as the rebellious city.

34:6–7. These verses seem to be an incidental comment regarding the timing of Jeremiah's communication to Zedekiah. As a result of archaeological work, however, they have become an interesting commentary on the formation of the book. According to verses 6–7, the two cities of Azekah and Lachish were still holding out against the Babylonian forces when Jeremiah made his prophecies to Zedekiah. The site of ancient Lachish is at modern *Tell ed Duweir* in the Shephelah hills southwest of Jerusalem. During the 1930s an expedition sponsored by the British School of Archaeology excavated at the site. Near the gate and near the interior fortress the excavation team found several ostraca (letters written on pottery shards) from stratum II, dating from the time of Jeremiah. One of the letters states that the signals from Azekah, located a few kilometers to the north of Lachish, could no longer be seen.[1]

---

1. For bibliography and details, see King, *Jeremiah: An Archaeological Companion*, 78–84. Letter 4 contains the information that the writer has been watching for the fire signals of Azekah and Lachish, and that the signal from Azekah is no longer visible. This last comment may indicate that the letter to the garrison at Lachish was written toward the end of the Babylonian campaign, when Azekah had finally fallen to the siege and only Lachish remained untaken.

34:8–22. King Zedekiah had initiated a covenant with his subjects regarding their Judean slaves, that they were to be set free. The reason is not stated, but most likely the dire circumstances of the Babylonian siege lay behind the ceremony. Some scholars have speculated that with the scarcity of food, the manumission of the slaves meant that the owners were no longer obligated to feed them. It is also possible that freed slaves were more likely to defend their freedom in the struggle with Babylon. In any case, after the release of the slaves circumstances apparently improved enough so that the solemn oath of the covenant was broken and the slaves were taken back by their owners. Apparently there was a temporary lifting of the siege (cf. 37:7–8). This is the best interpretation of the comment in 34:21–22 that the Lord will "bring . . . back" the Babylonian army that "has withdrawn."

No context or background is given for the first acquisitions of the slaves, but their enslavement is primarily debt related. Debts and warfare were the two most common reasons for someone to become a slave in antiquity. In a caustic response to the events, God (through Jeremiah) alludes to the debt-slavery laws of Deuteronomy 15[2] and perhaps also to the custom of a royal proclamation of "freedom" (*deror*) from indebtedness.[3] In the indictment for breaking their word and reenslaving the slaves, the people are also accused of breaking the covenant God made with them when he brought them out of Egypt. Verse 14 includes the just treatment of slaves (and thus the allusion to Deut. 15) as part of the covenant obligations assumed by Israel. The verse also states categorically that Israel has not met that obligation adequately.

Scholars debate whether the covenant release of Jeremiah 34:8–22 was part of the sabbatical (i.e., seven-year) cycle of debt forgiveness mandated by Deuteronomy 15 or part of a special freedom proclamation initiated by King Zedekiah (on analogy with Assyrian and Babylonian rulers) as a response to the crisis of the siege.[4] One cannot be dogmatic in these matters, but perhaps the role of Zedekiah in making the covenant with the people tips the balance toward a special royal proclamation rather than the

---

2. Cf. Jer. 34:14 with Deut. 15:12–18 and Ex. 21:1–6. Deut. 15:12 begins with the circumstance ("If a fellow Hebrew, a man or a woman, sells himself to you . . .") and concludes with the sabbatical stipulation that he or she shall go forth "free" in the seventh year. Moreover, the slave shall not be sent forth without provisions (15:13–14).

3. The Hebrew word *deror* (release, liberty, freedom) is used in 34:8, 15, 17. Elsewhere it is used in Lev. 25:10 as a designation of the Jubilee release of land sold for debts, in Isa. 61:1 as a description of the freedom announced by God's messenger, and as a reference in Ezek. 46:17 to a "year of release" when parts of a royal inheritance are to return to the owner. The Heb. word is cognate to an Akkadian term used in periodic royal proclamations of debt annulments and slave manumission. See J. Lewy, "The Biblical Institution of *deror* in the Light of Akkadian Documents," *Eretz-Israel* 5 (1958): 21–31.

4. Cf. discussion and bibliography in Holladay, *Jeremiah*, 2:236–43.

regular sabbatical release. In either case, the covenant ceremony is carried out at the temple (v. 15). This is a solemn context in which to make an oath or ratify a promise, since it brings the presence of the Lord to the process.

The allusion to Deuteronomy 15 in Jeremiah 34:14–15 is also important to understanding God's anger over the injustice done to the slaves, since the pentateuchal legislation links the obligation of justice toward slaves with the content of the covenant stipulations given to their ancestors. Jeremiah underscores this same dynamic. The ancestors of the Judeans were slaves in Egypt, and God brought them out of the house of slavery. God has not gone back on his good word and work, so neither should the slave owners in Judah.

The indictment of the people contains a play on the word *deror* (34:8, 15, 17). If the people can "proclaim freedom" for the slaves, only to take them back when it is convenient, then God will "proclaim freedom" for Judah and Jerusalem. Readers will detect the sarcasm in this proclamation easily enough. God's freedom proclamation to Judah and Jerusalem is "freedom" to fall to Babylon. In this announcement of judgment, the punishment to come fits the crime. There is a link between crime and punishment.

Verses 18–19 refer to the owners and officials who pass between the parts of the calf; this probably indicates a self-imprecation and promissory oath as part of the solemn covenant ceremony. The best parallel to the report comes in Genesis 15:7–21, where Abram prepares for a sacrificial ceremony by slaying the proper animals and dividing their carcasses.[5] In such ceremonies, those who walked between the parts of the slain animals enacted symbolically their passing through death and dismemberment as a pledge to keep their word. "Passing through the pieces" thus became a symbolic act to bind the word of promise as an imprecatory oath. Since the Judeans passed between the parts of the calf when making an oath to free the slaves but subsequently did not keep their word, they themselves will be like the sacrificial animals.

CRISIS MORALITY. Jeremiah 34, with all its specificity regarding time and circumstances, raises the issue of crisis conversions or what some people call "deathbed confessions." Desperate circumstances can lead to desperate measures. As noted, the emancipation of the slaves during Zedekiah's reign was apparently prompted by the harsh

---

5. Readers should note that in the Gen. 15 ceremony God is represented by the smoking torch that passes between the divided carcasses. This symbolizes God's self-binding oath to fulfill his word to Abram. The latter is in a deep sleep and unable to participate in the ceremony other than to witness the passing of the torch and to receive the freely given promise made by God.

circumstances of the Babylonian siege. Apparently the obligations the owners had to their slaves were not carried out fairly in the past (34:13–15), so why enact a covenant ceremony now? It is hard to escape the conclusion that the ceremony was one of desperation, carried out because of the grim circumstances of the city. Was this inherently wrong? Nothing in the text indicates that the ceremony itself was wrong; if anything, the text implies that the emancipation was long overdue (cf. 34:15). The point seems to be that there really was no conversion, only desperation.

The covenant God granted Israel at Mount Sinai obligated the people to certain norms of behavior toward God and one another. Obedience, however, was not only an act but also a matter of the heart (and soul). Neither an individual nor a group honors God solely with outward obedience, although obedience is a key indicator of a person or group's true allegiance. For Judah in Zedekiah's day, it was not a case of learning something new about God's covenant stipulations but of carrying them out as a means to honor God. The people made a solemn promise before God to treat their slaves fairly and to grant them freedom. This is a dynamic that crosses time and culture regardless of the particular issue under consideration. God is served and honored when his claim on his people is demonstrated through their obedience to his revealed will.

Slavery. Slavery was an accepted institution in ancient Israel. Most slaves in the ancient Near East became such through indebtedness or capture in war (not kidnapping, as was the case for Africans brought to the United States).[6] The stipulations about slavery in the Old Testament are mostly about ways to ameliorate the conditions of servitude and/or ways to treat slaves (servants)[7] humanely. It should be noted that God is on the side of the slaves, not on the side of the crass owners. Of course, the indebtedness incurred by slaves had to be dealt with fairly, but the indebted persons themselves were expected to receive just treatment.

PROMISE KEEPERS, THEN **and now.** On October 4, 1997, close to a million men gathered in Washington, D.C., to proclaim themselves Promise Keepers for the Lord. Bill McCartney, formerly a college football coach at the University of Colorado, began a ministry seven years previously for men, which grew in a few years to become a large and

---

6. Kidnapping and then selling a person was a capital crime (Ex. 21:16).

7. The distinction between slave (a person owned by another) and servant (a person socially or institutionally obligated to another—e.g., an indentured servant) cannot be gained from the Heb. term ʿebed, which is used for both categories.

influential ministry. The premise of the evangelical organization known as The Promise Keepers is that men should ground their Christian faith in their responsibilities to love their wives and children. McCartney has also made a strong push to overcome the effects of racism in Christian organizations by reaching out to men of different color and ethnic origins. Moreover, in this movement there is a strong emphasis on repentance from past failures to live up to God's standards and to trust in Jesus Christ to change a man's life.

It is an amazing commentary on modern life when public interest groups question both the motives and the values of the Promise Keepers. Particularly strident have been the comments from the National Organization of Women. Its president stated on national television that the goals of Promise Keepers were detrimental to the freedom and health of women and that the movement was a servant to "right-wing causes." How odd! The stated purpose of Promise Keepers is to call men to be obedient to the claims of the gospel and to take godly responsibility for their lives and those of their families. These principles are not new; they are basic evangelical tenets and classical Christian teaching.

In a perceptive comment published in national newspapers, Martin Marty (professor of church history at the University of Chicago) said that perhaps the Promise Keepers were simply who they said they were: men seeking to be faithful to the gospel by keeping promises made before God to be responsible in their spheres of influence (family, work, society). Such men are not antiwomen, right-wing zealots, or puppets for sinister causes; after all, the core tenets of the movement are conservative in nature. Marty's point is an important one in a time when all commitments and allegiances seem only temporary or to have strings attached. One need not agree with all the theological underpinnings of the Promise Keepers movement to see the value of keeping commitments made before God.

Such debate illustrates the cost of discipleship for Christians as well as the nature of social commitments in a highly individualistic culture. Obedience to God will look strange in a world dedicated to individual freedom and moral relativism. In such a world people will look for their advantage and see a plot wherever people are living in a community of faith and acting out of moral conviction.

But a community of faithful obedience is what God has called his people to be. It is always easier to undergo a public ritual of moral and spiritual obligation (like a covenant before God to release slaves in Jeremiah's day or the signing of a statement of Christian outrage over the abuse of children) than it is to keep a promise made before God and to carry through one's obligation. But God has called his people to be people of their (and his) word. Repentance and embracing the gospel are not negative acts but positive, joyful responses to a higher calling. God is the ultimate Promise Keeper. God's people are called to honor him by keeping their commitments made in his name.

One wonders what later historians will say of the tumultuous social changes that have swept through much of the Western world (and affected other parts of the globe as well) in the last half of the twentieth century. Surely the accelerated pace of change itself will be seen as one of the remarkable characteristics of the period. Perhaps future generations will be making the necessary adaptations to cope with the pace of societal changes. Change seems to dictate for many people that they keep their options open, that they try to remain flexible, and that they make no commitments unless an easy point of extrication is identified. Perhaps the Christians of the future will have the courage of conviction to point out that promises, divine and human, are the rock on which all relationships stand.

Jeremiah 35:1–19

THIS IS THE word that came to Jeremiah from the LORD during the reign of Jehoiakim son of Josiah king of Judah: ²"Go to the Recabite family and invite them to come to one of the side rooms of the house of the LORD and give them wine to drink."

³So I went to get Jaazaniah son of Jeremiah, the son of Habazziniah, and his brothers and all his sons—the whole family of the Recabites. ⁴I brought them into the house of the LORD, into the room of the sons of Hanan son of Igdaliah the man of God. It was next to the room of the officials, which was over that of Maaseiah son of Shallum the doorkeeper. ⁵Then I set bowls full of wine and some cups before the men of the Recabite family and said to them, "Drink some wine."

⁶But they replied, "We do not drink wine, because our forefather Jonadab son of Recab gave us this command: 'Neither you nor your descendants must ever drink wine. ⁷Also you must never build houses, sow seed or plant vineyards; you must never have any of these things, but must always live in tents. Then you will live a long time in the land where you are nomads.' ⁸We have obeyed everything our forefather Jonadab son of Recab commanded us. Neither we nor our wives nor our sons and daughters have ever drunk wine ⁹or built houses to live in or had vineyards, fields or crops. ¹⁰We have lived in tents and have fully obeyed everything our forefather Jonadab commanded us. ¹¹But when Nebuchadnezzar king of Babylon invaded this land, we said, 'Come, we must go to Jerusalem to escape the Babylonian and Aramean armies.' So we have remained in Jerusalem."

¹²Then the word of the LORD came to Jeremiah, saying: ¹³"This is what the LORD Almighty, the God of Israel, says: Go and tell the men of Judah and the people of Jerusalem, 'Will you not learn a lesson and obey my words?' declares the LORD. ¹⁴Jonadab son of Recab ordered his sons not to drink wine and this command has been kept. To this day they do not drink wine, because they obey their forefather's command. But I have spoken to you again and again, yet you have not obeyed me. ¹⁵Again and again I sent all my servants the

prophets to you. They said, "Each of you must turn from your wicked ways and reform your actions; do not follow other gods to serve them. Then you will live in the land I have given to you and your fathers." But you have not paid attention or listened to me. ¹⁶The descendants of Jonadab son of Recab have carried out the command their forefather gave them, but these people have not obeyed me.'

¹⁷"Therefore, this is what the LORD God Almighty, the God of Israel, says: 'Listen! I am going to bring on Judah and on everyone living in Jerusalem every disaster I pronounced against them. I spoke to them, but they did not listen; I called to them, but they did not answer.'"

¹⁸Then Jeremiah said to the family of the Recabites, "This is what the LORD Almighty, the God of Israel, says: 'You have obeyed the command of your forefather Jonadab and have followed all his instructions and have done everything he ordered.' ¹⁹Therefore, this is what the LORD Almighty, the God of Israel, says: 'Jonadab son of Recab will never fail to have a man to serve me.'"

CHAPTER 35 IS set in the reign of King Jehoiakim (609–598 B.C), a period earlier than the events described in the previous chapter. Nevertheless, the two chapters have a common theme (the significance of obedience to one's word) and a common setting (Jerusalem and pressure from outside forces).

This chapter has two major parts. In verses 1–11 God commands Jeremiah to go to the Recabites and to bring them to the temple complex. He commands them to drink wine, and they protest. In verses 12–19 God commands Jeremiah to speak hard words to Judah and Jerusalem, based on the prophet's interaction with the Recabites. The prophet contrasts Recabite obedience to communal standards with the faithlessness of Judah and Jerusalem.

35:1–11. Uncertainty remains over how best to describe the Recabites.[1] Some scholars have seen them as an anti-Canaanite faction and also as conservative representatives of a "nomadic ideal" from Israel's past. This is due mainly to their rejection of wine, agriculture, and houses (cf. 35:6–10), plus

---

1. F. Frick, "The Rechabites Reconsidered," *JBL* 90 (1971): 279–87; W. McKane, "Jeremiah and the Rechabites," *ZAW* 100 (1988): 106–23. Jonadab, the founder of the Recabites, assisted Jehu in his overthrow of the Omrides (2 Kings 10:15–28). The Recabites are named as descendants of the Kenites in 1 Chron. 2:55.

the account in 2 Kings 10 that links Jonadab, the founder of the Recabites, with Jehu's revolt against the Omrides. Others have seen them more as an alternative community or commercial guild associated with the design and building of chariots. The Hebrew term *rkb* means "(to) ride," and the noun *merkaba* refers to a chariot. Since the Kenites (to whom the Recabites are related; 1 Chron. 2:55) may have been smiths, the combination of name and possible vocation suggests the possibility that the Recabites were itinerant metalworkers.

Verse 3 raises an interesting question with respect to the formation of the Recabite community. Jeremiah reports that he went to Jaazaniah, the head of the community, to offer them the opportunity to drink wine. That community is comprised of Jaazaniah's brothers and sons, "the whole family[2] of the Recabites." One cannot tell from this description whether the community is literally comprised of Jaazaniah's biological extended family or whether the kinship terminology of brothers and sons serves to identify a close-knit community. Jonadab, the founder of the Recabites, is described as the group's "forefather" in verse 8. Literally, the term can be translated as "father" (*'ab* in Heb.).[3]

Whatever the origin of the Recabites, their constancy regarding their community's values becomes a prophetically appropriated sign against the lack of integrity in Judah and Jerusalem. According to their self-designation, Recabites do not live in houses, plant crops, or drink wine. Instead, they live in tents (and apparently trade goods for grain and other agricultural products). Their presence in Jerusalem is the result of pressure put on the Judean countryside by the Babylonian army and their Aramean companions (v. 11). Jerusalem is a place of refuge for them because of its stout walls. This indicates that otherwise the Recabites would normally have lived in tents outside the city in obedience to the command of their founder, Jonadab.

The prophetic symbolism of the account is accentuated by the scene of wine cups set before the Recabites in the chambers of Hanan's sons (v. 4; their family was founded by Igdaliah, "a man of God" = prophet). Their reply— that they do not drink wine—is narrated for the effect such a scene will have on the larger community of Judah and Jerusalem.

35:12–19. God instructs Jeremiah to report the encounter with the Recabites to the people of Judah and Jerusalem. The fact that Jeremiah has invited the Recabites to meet him at a room near the temple (v. 4) ensures that they are observed by other members of the community. The incident

---

2. So NIV. The Heb. term is the familiar one for a family—*bayit*, lit., "house, household."

3. The word *'ab* can refer to someone in authority over a group and not simply the biological head of a family (cf. 2 Kings 2:12; 5:13; 6:21).

contrasts Recabite obedience to their community standards with the faithlessness of Judeans to theirs. It is part of a history of disobedience, for Judah has consistently disobeyed the word of God's servants, the prophets (v. 15). The prophetic communication, therefore, concludes that a call to repentance is neither timely nor warranted. God spoke (in the past), but Judah did not listen; he called, but they did not answer.

The final word of the chapter is addressed to the Recabites. They are promised that they will always have someone to "stand before" the Lord; that is, they will never be forgotten by God, and their place with him is secure.[4]

THE LESSON OF THE RECABITES. Surprisingly, nothing directly is said about the piety of the Recabites, although one can safely assume that they believe in the Lord, the God of Israel. The main issue, rather, is obedience to a lifestyle to which the Recabite community has committed itself. That the Recabites pursue their lifestyle as part of their piety is clear by the chapter's conclusion, but the emphasis is on their constancy and commitment to the integrity of their community. The particulars of their vows are not universally applicable in Jeremiah's day any more than they would be in modern times. Houses, for example, are neither good nor bad in themselves; but the manner in which houses are used is a moral and spiritual matter. The same can be said of wine, vineyards, and fields. Jeremiah was not a Recabite. Moreover, he owned property, probably lived in a house, and probably drank wine. He affirms the Recabite lifestyle without himself being bound by its requirements.

The Recabites, therefore, pursue their communal ideals within a society that has not adopted all of their ways. Some of their activities may have been related to the particulars of their vocation. If, for example, they itinerated as smiths, their avoidance of houses (or house ownership) is understandable. They may also have carried out certain responsibilities as part of a vow of dedication to the Lord, and their service may have related them to prophets or priests in ways not preserved for later readers. They may have functioned like Nazirites, who took certain vows of abstinence as part of a community ideal.

Nevertheless, their value as an example for Judah may be like that of the "unjust steward" in Jesus' parable (Luke 16:1–13), who is praised for his industry and shrewdness (16:8), even if the particulars of his actions are not to be

---

4. The promise is similar to those given to the Levites in 33:18. It is not a promise that the Recabite community will continue on indefinitely; it is a promise that some representative of that community will always "stand" (lit.) before the Lord.

emulated. Obedience to the community's standards, even if the broader populace is indifferent or hostile, is the key characteristic of the Recabites. This kind of commitment can be understood by an individual or a church in a variety of settings.

CHRIST AND CULTURE. Just after World War II, H. Richard Niebuhr published a series of essays on the subject of Christian faith as it is defined and exercised in a cultural context.[5] It has become something of a classic in Western Christianity because it takes up an issue central to Christian faith: How does the church offer its witness within its cultural context? In the volume Niebuhr takes up five different models of the relationship between Christian faith and its cultural context: Christ against culture, Christ of culture, Christ above culture, Christ and culture in paradox, and Christ the transformer of culture. Since the shape of corporate human existence varies so dramatically, the response of Christian faith to and within any particular culture may also vary. The relationship, however, between faith and culture is symbiotic. There is no cultureless Christianity any more than there is cultureless human existence. In any given context, the issue turns on the exercise of faithful living on the part of the believing community.

In recent years, especially in the evangelical communities of North America, one hears the expression "culture wars" being used to describe the polarizing debates in Western society about morality and education. Since Christians have convictions about morality and education that can run counter to the relativistic pluralism endemic to Western culture, the issue of Christian witness in society is a "hot topic."

Several things can be said about the nature of faithful witness on the basis of Jeremiah 35 (and the book of Jeremiah as a whole). (1) Faith in God is expressed by living in community with other believers. The community of faith (i.e., the church) helps give shape not only to what one believes but how one lives responsibly as a result of faith. (2) God has called people to lead public lives of obedience to his revealed will. Obedience is not just pleasing to God; it can be an effective witness to the larger culture in which believers find themselves. (3) The exercise of the Christian faith may entail giving up certain practices common to a culture for the sake of the gospel.

To separate or not to separate. Separation from society is not by definition a good thing or a bad thing for Christians; like so many other things, the value of separation depends on the motives and circumstances of the

---

5. H. Richard Niebuhr, *Christ and Culture* (New York: Harper & Row, 1951).

community that separates itself. In Roman Catholicism and the Eastern Orthodox churches, orders and monasteries give expression to the devotion of prayer, holiness, seclusion, and service to God. Protestants of various persuasions have not often followed this model, preferring instead to engage society more directly with the claims of the gospel. Perhaps a Protestant or free-church analogy to the Recabites would be the Amish—Mennonite pacifists who live in communities that forego certain characteristics of modern life in order to serve God more faithfully.

A visit to a monastery, however, often reminds Christians (whether Catholic or not) how influenced they are by the society and culture in which they live. The Amish (Pennsylvania Dutch as some have called them) are heirs of the radical Reformation movements in Europe of the sixteenth and seventeenth centuries. In the radically pluralistic North American culture, these Christian pacifists have refused to participate in segments of the larger institutional life of the United States because those elements divert them from pursuing their path of discipleship and communal life. Instead, they practice a form of corporate discipline and separateness that reflects well on their commitments.

The shape of the monastic life, the discipline of an order dedicated to the service of God, or the influence of alternative Christian communities can serve as effective witnesses to the power of God in directing his people to fulfill their calling as disciples. In any case, it is a great question to ask: Just what are the marks of the church that announce its commitments within the broader culture in which it takes root?

In 1993 the horror of the Branch Davidian separatists was revealed to the world. A self-appointed leader, David Koresh, named a farmstead near Waco, Texas, as *Ranch Apocalypse*. His followers separated themselves from the evils of society to follow him. The community had discipline, strict rules about behavior, and time set aside for worship and teaching from the Bible. Many of the community's members simply wanted to live in a Christian community untainted by the world and uncompromising in its commitments to uphold the word of God.

So what went so tragically wrong? The people were misled by Koresh, who saw himself as a messiah[6] and whose authority was used to twist biblical teaching and to engage in sexual relations with many of the women in the community. Instead of a holy love, he used fear to motivate his flock. Instead of pointing to Christ as the cornerstone of faith, he pointed to himself as the

---

6. *Koresh* is the Hebrew pronunciation of Cyrus. The leader of the Branch Davidians took his name from a twisted reading of Isa. 45:1, where Cyrus (i.e., *Koresh*) is called God's anointed one and is taken by the right hand.

interpreter of God's will. In April 1993, the community was largely consumed by fire that broke out when the FBI bungled a raid on the Ranch headquarters.

The Branch Davidians (and other groups could be named) are testimony that a strong, religiously based community is not infallible. Neither the Recabites of old nor more modern counterparts reflect perfection. One can cite examples of both healthy and sick communities that seek to bind themselves to a religious ideal. Obedience to fundamental values is in and of itself instructive. But how much more pleasing to God is joyful obedience to the kingdom values revealed in his Son!

The Recabites lived according to the standards of their founder. They did so as faithfully as they could, depending on the circumstances of the society in which they lived. It seems too simple to say, but the church is called to the same task. Jesus Christ, the risen Lord, is the foundation of the community of faith we call the church. The life of the church provides a witness to the larger society, whether it withdraws in protest or actively engages its cultural context. The promise of the risen Lord is even grander than that of God to the Recabites, for the gates of hell will not prevail against the community that confesses Christ.

Jeremiah 36:1-32

IN THE FOURTH year of Jehoiakim son of Josiah king of Judah, this word came to Jeremiah from the LORD: ²"Take a scroll and write on it all the words I have spoken to you concerning Israel, Judah and all the other nations from the time I began speaking to you in the reign of Josiah till now. ³Perhaps when the people of Judah hear about every disaster I plan to inflict on them, each of them will turn from his wicked way; then I will forgive their wickedness and their sin."

⁴So Jeremiah called Baruch son of Neriah, and while Jeremiah dictated all the words the LORD had spoken to him, Baruch wrote them on the scroll. ⁵Then Jeremiah told Baruch, "I am restricted; I cannot go to the LORD's temple. ⁶So you go to the house of the LORD on a day of fasting and read to the people from the scroll the words of the LORD that you wrote as I dictated. Read them to all the people of Judah who come in from their towns. ⁷Perhaps they will bring their petition before the LORD, and each will turn from his wicked ways, for the anger and wrath pronounced against this people by the LORD are great."

⁸Baruch son of Neriah did everything Jeremiah the prophet told him to do; at the LORD's temple he read the words of the LORD from the scroll. ⁹In the ninth month of the fifth year of Jehoiakim son of Josiah king of Judah, a time of fasting before the LORD was proclaimed for all the people in Jerusalem and those who had come from the towns of Judah. ¹⁰From the room of Gemariah son of Shaphan the secretary, which was in the upper courtyard at the entrance of the New Gate of the temple, Baruch read to all the people at the LORD's temple the words of Jeremiah from the scroll.

¹¹When Micaiah son of Gemariah, the son of Shaphan, heard all the words of the LORD from the scroll, ¹²he went down to the secretary's room in the royal palace, where all the officials were sitting: Elishama the secretary, Delaiah son of Shemaiah, Elnathan son of Acbor, Gemariah son of Shaphan, Zedekiah son of Hananiah, and all the other officials. ¹³After Micaiah told them everything he had heard Baruch read to the people from the scroll, ¹⁴all the officials sent Jehudi son of

Nethaniah, the son of Shelemiah, the son of Cushi, to say to Baruch, "Bring the scroll from which you have read to the people and come." So Baruch son of Neriah went to them with the scroll in his hand. ¹⁵They said to him, "Sit down, please, and read it to us."

So Baruch read it to them. ¹⁶When they heard all these words, they looked at each other in fear and said to Baruch, "We must report all these words to the king." ¹⁷Then they asked Baruch, "Tell us, how did you come to write all this? Did Jeremiah dictate it?"

¹⁸"Yes," Baruch replied, "he dictated all these words to me, and I wrote them in ink on the scroll."

¹⁹Then the officials said to Baruch, "You and Jeremiah, go and hide. Don't let anyone know where you are."

²⁰After they put the scroll in the room of Elishama the secretary, they went to the king in the courtyard and reported everything to him. ²¹The king sent Jehudi to get the scroll, and Jehudi brought it from the room of Elishama the secretary and read it to the king and all the officials standing beside him. ²²It was the ninth month and the king was sitting in the winter apartment, with a fire burning in the firepot in front of him. ²³Whenever Jehudi had read three or four columns of the scroll, the king cut them off with a scribe's knife and threw them into the firepot, until the entire scroll was burned in the fire. ²⁴The king and all his attendants who heard all these words showed no fear, nor did they tear their clothes. ²⁵Even though Elnathan, Delaiah and Gemariah urged the king not to burn the scroll, he would not listen to them. ²⁶Instead, the king commanded Jerahmeel, a son of the king, Seraiah son of Azriel and Shelemiah son of Abdeel to arrest Baruch the scribe and Jeremiah the prophet. But the LORD had hidden them.

²⁷After the king burned the scroll containing the words that Baruch had written at Jeremiah's dictation, the word of the LORD came to Jeremiah: ²⁸"Take another scroll and write on it all the words that were on the first scroll, which Jehoiakim king of Judah burned up. ²⁹Also tell Jehoiakim king of Judah, 'This is what the LORD says: You burned that scroll and said, "Why did you write on it that the king of Babylon would certainly come and destroy this land and cut off both men and animals from it?" ³⁰Therefore, this is what the LORD says about Jehoiakim king of Judah: He will have no one to sit on the

throne of David; his body will be thrown out and exposed to the heat by day and the frost by night. ³¹I will punish him and his children and his attendants for their wickedness; I will bring on them and those living in Jerusalem and the people of Judah every disaster I pronounced against them, because they have not listened.'"

³²So Jeremiah took another scroll and gave it to the scribe Baruch son of Neriah, and as Jeremiah dictated, Baruch wrote on it all the words of the scroll that Jehoiakim king of Judah had burned in the fire. And many similar words were added to them.

THIS CHAPTER CONTAINS yet another account of Jehoiakim's failure. Two precise dates are given (36:1, 9), which span about a year in Jeremiah's personal history and which also place the events in the context of a broader history of the Babylonian threat to Judah. Several officials in Jerusalem are named (36:10–12, 26), thereby giving a context to the account for later Judean readers.[1] The conclusion to the account, however, points beyond the circumstances of Jeremiah and Baruch, his scribal companion; the callous response of King Jehoiakim to the words of Jeremiah indicate Judah's disobedience (rejection) of God's message to the nation.

36:1–7. Jehoiakim's fourth year (36:1) is 605 B.C.[2] In that year Nabopolassar, the ruler of Babylon, died; his young son, Nebuchadnezzar, ascended the Babylonian throne, and his forces defeated the Egyptians in battle at Carchemish. Since Jehoiakim had been placed on the throne in Judah by the Egyptians (2 Kings 23:34–37), this defeat was potentially an ominous sign for him and the Judean leadership. Jeremiah 25:1 bears the same date as the heading to a chapter of judgmental sayings against Jerusalem and Judah.

Just why Jeremiah had been banned from preaching in the temple is a mystery (36:5). Since his words were often judgmental and divisive, a restriction on his preaching in the temple precincts could have come at almost any time in the reign of Jehoiakim. Possibly the temple sermon Jeremiah delivered at the beginning of Jehoiakim's reign (26:1; cf. ch. 7) led to his restriction from delivering oracles at that site. It should be recalled that Jeremiah narrowly escaped a lynch mob at that time. Ahikam, the son of Shaphan, stood on the prophet's side in that setting (26:24). In the narrative of

---

1. On the officials named, their context in Judean history, and their portrayal of scribal activity in interpreting documents, see J. Andrew Dearman, "My Servants the Scribes: Composition and Context in Jeremiah 36," *JBL* 109 (1990): 403–21.

2. For additional details, see comments on Jer. 1:1–3.

chapter 36, other descendants of Shaphan are instrumental in Baruch's delivery of Jeremiah's words (36:10–12; cf. 29:3). The influential family of Shaphan appears sympathetic to Jeremiah, and its members may be part of the largely anonymous group who have preserved the words of the prophet.

Baruch is a scribe (36:26); that is, his profession is in recording and interpreting documents.[3] In a way he is a disciple of Jeremiah. Since Jeremiah is restricted from preaching in the temple precincts, Baruch is commissioned with delivering the prophet's message in the temple. This comes, however, after Baruch has copied Jeremiah's oracles onto a scroll. He knows the material intimately and is able to represent the prophet in his absence.

Here readers encounter another theme of the chapter. The written scroll of Jeremiah's prophecies is an adequate substitute for the living voice of the prophet. Baruch's brother Seraiah also assisted Jeremiah in delivering prophecy to Babylon (51:59–64). Probably scribal activity was a family profession; both the father and grandfather of Baruch and Seraiah are named (51:59), as if the family and its work were well known in Judah.

Jeremiah hopes that the hard words he wants delivered to the people will be a catalyst for repentance and change (36:7). Ominously, the possibility of repentance is not mentioned in the summary statements of 36:27–31. One function of the narrative in chapter 36 is to confirm the obduracy of Judean leadership and even the collective will of the people.

36:8–19. In the ninth month of Jehoiakim's fifth year (i.e., December 604 B.C.), a solemn fast is declared, and many people in Judah stream to the temple to pray (v. 9).[4] This is a year or so later than the chronological notice in 36:1. The solemn fast becomes the occasion for Baruch to deliver the prophetic message of Jeremiah. At this time Nebuchadnezzar's army was on the Palestinian coast, and the Philistine city of Ashkelon was sacked

---

3. An impression in fired clay (a "bulla") of a seal with the reading "belonging to Berekyahu son of Neriyahu, the scribe," has been published by N. Avigad, *Hebrew Bullae from the Time of Jeremiah* (Jerusalem: Israel Exploration Society, 1986), #9 (pp. 28–29). A second bulla of the seal is in the possession of an antiquities dealer; see H. Shanks, "Fingerprints of Jeremiah's Scribe," *BAR* 22.2 (1996): 36–38. Baruch is a short form of the name Berekyahu, like Will for William or Andy for Andrew. The Heb. word *brk* means "to bless," and the name Baruch (modern English spelling) means "blessed." Most probably the two seal impressions were attached in ancient times to papyrus or animal skin documents prepared by Baruch, Jeremiah's companion. For additional references to scribal figures, such as Gemariah the son of Shaphan, whose bullae have come to light in modern times, see Dearman, "My Servants the Scribes."

4. The LXX reads eighth year rather than fifth. See Holladay, *Jeremiah*, 2:255–56, for reasons why he prefers this reading to that of the Heb. text. Although one cannot be dogmatic, it seems to me that the MT should be preferred on this point. The fifth-year date illumines the historical context, and the Greek text can be explained plausibly as a copy error.

by the Babylonians. The text does not say why the fast is called, so the link with the ominous arrival of the Babylonians is speculative, but some perceived threat prompts this assembly. Another possibility is the effects of a prolonged drought.[5]

A close reading of the text shows that the words of the scroll delivered orally by Baruch are accorded the same prophetic authority as that of Jeremiah. Baruch is asked in an initial interrogation whether these are the words from the mouth of Jeremiah; he replies that they are (36:17–18). Pointedly, the narrator (Baruch?) gives no account of the people's reaction to Baruch's oral recital in verse 10. He seems to assume that the words are familiar and that the people have not responded as hoped, although the words of the scroll aimed for repentance (36:3). The only one described as hearing anything at the temple is Micaiah the son of Gemariah, the son of Shaphan, who "heard all the words of the LORD from the scroll" (36:11, italics added). This detail is not coincidental. The chain of authority runs backward from Baruch to Jeremiah to the Lord. The prophetic word rejected by the people is ultimately that of the Lord.

It is unlikely that the officials named in 36:10–14 are simply listed for verisimilitude. On the one hand, they represent Judean leadership. On the other, some of them represent people sympathetic to Jeremiah. Gemariah has taken a big risk in allowing Baruch to use his office as the location for preaching to the crowds in the temple courtyard (v. 10). This suggests that he, like his sibling Ahikam (26:24), has heard something authentic in Jeremiah's preaching. His risk is consistent with what is known elsewhere about his family. His father and brother were cabinet-level officials under Josiah, and they were involved in the discovery of the book of the law and its promulgation (2 Kings 22).

After hearing for themselves the contents of the prophetic scroll, the officials request that Baruch and Jeremiah go into hiding. In taking that advice, Baruch and Jeremiah may have preserved their lives until the turmoil around the oracles dies down a bit (see below).

36:20–26. The callous rejection of Jeremiah's words by Jehoiakim is described in a manner intended to remind readers of his father Josiah and to contrast father and son. When Josiah heard the words of the book of the Torah, a book discovered during temple repairs, he tore (Heb. qr^c) his garments as a sign that he recognized the authority of the prophetic scroll to judge him and his nation (2 Kings 22). In contemptuous fashion, Jehoiakim

---

5. Jeremiah 14 is a series of oracles related to the effects of drought. Verses 7–9 are a repentance liturgy and the kind of confessional prayer that would be enjoined in a "time of fasting."

cuts (Heb. *qr^c*) the scroll in pieces and does not rend his garments (Jer. 36:23–24).

The use of a knife to cut the scroll probably indicates a scroll that contained more than one piece of tanned animal skin. Typically sections of tanned animal skins (probably that of a lamb) were sewn together to make a continuous roll for written contents. The easiest way for Jehoiakim (or anyone else) to cut a scroll would be to slice along the join of two sections where thread held them together. If this is correct, this also indicates that Baruch has copied a number of different oracles for presentation to the temple crowds.

36:27–32. Jehoiakim and Judah's fate is sealed by their indifference and even hostility to the prophetic word. According to 26:20–23, Jehoiakim became upset with the preaching activity of Uriah and sent a delegation to Egypt to arrest him. Subsequently, Uriah was executed for his prophetic activity. Baruch's reading of Jeremiah's scroll is the second recorded time that the prophet's words have been given at the temple and incite consternation; the delegation to arrest Baruch and Jeremiah may not itself have been empowered to execute the two men, but had they been found, execution may have been the conclusion to their arrest. The narrator notes, almost in passing, that the Lord had hidden them.[6]

One supposes that the Lord's command to compile another scroll comes while Jeremiah and Baruch are hiding from the royal officials searching for them. Along with the command comes a revelation to Jeremiah that judgment will come particularly on Jehoiakim and that it will be extended broadly to Judah and Jerusalem. No mention is made of any hope that they will repent.

The second scroll is longer than the first. Its contents are not otherwise revealed except to say that the additions are similar to what was included in the first scroll.

FUNCTIONS OF JUDGMENT PROPHECY. A primary claim of the chapter is that judgment is coming on Jerusalem and Judah for their failure to heed the word of the Lord. Since this is a common claim in Jeremiah, one must look more closely at the particulars of chap-

---

6. No details are given about the hiding of Jeremiah and Baruch. Almost certainly, however, it took cooperation from others to keep the two hid successfully. The comment of the narrator is a theological one. God willed their survival. In this context it is interesting to note the account of the Lord's prophets being hidden during the time of Ahab and Jezebel. According to 1 Kings 18:3–4, Obadiah, the official in charge of the royal palace, had hidden two groups of prophets in caves and provided them with sustenance.

ter 36. Initially, the word from God to Jeremiah contains a hope that the people will repent. As the narrative progresses, it becomes evident that no repentance is forthcoming. Thus, two of the functions of judgmental prophecy are set forth: It is usually designed to evoke change among God's people, and when change is not forthcoming, the prophecy indicates the consequences of disobedience.

Authority of a prophetic word. This account also emphasizes the authority of a prophetic word even when the prophet himself or herself is absent. As with the discovered scroll in 2 Kings 22, the king and people are called to hear a timely word from the Lord whether the human "author" is present or absent. This emphasis has probably shaped this account as it was intended for early readers (who did not know Jeremiah), but who were asked to affirm that God had spoken through him. The issue, therefore, is not access to an inspired personality (whether prophet or apostle), but recognition that God stands behind his word given to a human vessel.

Hearing the word. Chapter 36 also gives a somber and ironic account of worship at the temple. People have come there to fast and pray, apparently out of fear for the future direction of the nation. A solemn fast, almost by definition, includes calls for repentance. Indeed, the very word they need to hear is provided for them, but they lack the corporate will and spiritual discernment to hear it. What an illustration of Jesus' trademark saying: "Whoever has ears to hear . . ." (cf. Matt. 11:15; 13:13; John 5:24; 12:47; Rev. 3:20). In the disappointment over the word's reception, it is a blessing to note that some did hear. Micaiah "heard"; Baruch "heard."

One way of hearing chapter 36 is to see its function like that of Acts 6:7– 7:60. Stephen offers a witness to the people that is rebuffed. He suffers the ultimate rejection in that he is martyred for his prophetic stance. His word confirms the spiritual blindness of those who reject him. Eventually, however, his witness is confirmed in the life of one of those who persecuted him, namely, Saul of Tarsus (the apostle Paul). This is an important lesson for readers in any age: One cannot know the impact that his or her work will have, even if the initial reaction to it is negative. God may use that work in ways a disciple will never know.

Leadership. Leadership of the people is crucial for its life. Jehoiakim represents the kind of callous, amoral, arrogant, and spiritually dull leadership that is a disaster for God's people. The failure of its leadership is often a significant contribution to a systemic failure of the people. The narrator contrasts Jehoiakim with his father Josiah. Thanks be to God that there were other people of the time who had the courage to protect Jeremiah and Baruch and to follow the words that the Lord had given them.

WORSHIP. In an oral interview some years ago Mother Teresa was asked about her "success." One wonders if "success" is the right word to use, though it is a term common to the news profession. Mother Teresa replied that she spent an hour a day in prayer and didn't "do anything that she knew was wrong." Her answer was deceptively simple. Worship is intended as an encounter with God and to bring a person/group into closer relationship with God. One result of worship should be greater knowledge of God's will and motivation to do that will. Human nature being what it is (sinful), however, a person cannot simply will to do what is right or know infallibly what is right. It takes God at work in the lives of individuals and churches in order to bring them into more conformity with his will and purpose. Prayer that seeks God's will must also earnestly seek the strength of the Spirit to discern that will and empower seekers to carry it out.

In Christian terms the worship of God should lead to sanctification and holiness; to put it succinctly, the purpose of the Christian life is to become conformed to the image of God's Son, Jesus Christ (Rom. 8:28–30; Eph. 4:13–16). There is (or should be) a symbiosis between God, the one to whom worship and service are directed, and his people, who offer to him their worship and service. God gives more than guidance and comfort; through Jesus Christ and his Holy Spirit, God has given us a share in his divine life. Repentance is a biblical word that entails turning from a sinful orientation or activity and embracing God and doing his will.

The paradox of Jeremiah 36 is a people at worship who do not hear and who, therefore, do not respond to the word of instruction and change that God provides them. There is no repentance because there is no recognition that God has addressed them through the words of the prophetic scroll. The issue for Judah of old apparently was not their presence in worship—one gains the impression that many were there in the time of crisis. Rather, it was Judah's inability to see their failure before God and to seek fervently his assistance in changing their actions. A similar dilemma may take various shapes in individual lives and in portions of Christ's church. Attendance at worship is hardly even an acknowledgment that God exists or that his Word is reliable unless those who worship seek to glorify God through word and deed.

Obedience. A learned discussion about modern theology once concluded with a respondent's statement that "much about God is a mystery." Undoubtedly that is true. But the response of yet another partner in the discussion caught the predominant tone of the biblical witness in saying: "It is not what I don't know about God that troubles me; it is what I do know that impels me to action." There is no excuse for individuals or churches being unresponsive to God's call to discipleship. God has declared his will and purpose sufficiently through his Word. His instruction can only be grasped through faith. Success is not the goal of the devout life; obedience is.

The account of the prophetic scroll in Jeremiah 36 illustrates the old English word "heedless." Neither people nor king were prepared to heed (i.e., hear and obey) the word of the Lord. Thus, at one level the account becomes a testimony to the consequences of heedlessness. But at another level, there were those who did heed the word of the Lord. They preserved the account for posterity, so that God's judging word from the past might be God's correcting and instructive word to future generations. It is the nature of God's Word that it always accomplishes its purpose. This question is valid for all of us today: Who recognizes the judging, correcting, and restorative nature of God's Word?

Jeremiah 37–45

❦

Introduction to Jeremiah 37–45

CHAPTERS 37–45 FORM a subsection in the book of Jeremiah dealing primarily with the reign of Zedekiah and the fall of Jerusalem. Most of this material concerns the details of the Babylonian siege during the last two years of Zedekiah's reign (588–586 B.C.), his capture and ignominious transport to Babylon (39:4–7), and the tragic aftermath of the city's capture when Gedaliah, the Babylonian-appointed governor, is assassinated and Jeremiah is dragged to Egypt with a pitiful Judean contingent (chs. 40–44). A word of hope granted to Baruch concludes the section (ch. 45), dated to the fourth year of Jehoiakim (i.e., 605/604 B.C.). These narratives, therefore, did not form an original literary unity. They are a collection of accounts that have a thematic coherence to them.[1]

Some scholars have called this narrative section a "passion narrative" because the suffering and oppression of the prophet are central to the accounts.[2] More important, however, is the fact that there are literary and thematic parallels in these chapters with the accounts of Jesus' suffering. This is the real reason to consider using the expression. "Passion narrative" is accurate enough as a description of Jeremiah's tragic setting, even if some may think that parallels to the passion accounts in the Gospels are overdrawn. The prophet is passionate enough about the fate of the people and tragically drawn into its consequences; nevertheless, it is unlikely that the expression would be used much without the New Testament connections.

It is important to stress that the suffering and oppression that Jeremiah experiences are not atoning or salvific for others. *Atonement* and *salvation* are wonderful terms to describe what Christ has accomplished for his people through his suffering. Those terms, however, do not describe what Jeremiah accomplishes (if that is even the right term to use) on behalf of God's people. Jeremiah's "passion narrative" describes the work of a prophet whose sensitivity toward a lost people results in a deep identification with them and their suffering, and also the work of a prophet whose innocent suffering is caught up in the fate of those same people. The Gospels describe a

---

1. Chapter 45 fits thematically with the accounts of the fall of Jerusalem and its aftermath, but it is out of place chronologically with the previous chapters (see comments on ch. 45). Chapter 39 has verbal parallels with ch. 52 and 2 Kings 25. It seems that accounts of the fall of the city have been refracted in several literary settings.

2. See G. von Rad, *Old Testament Theology* (2 vols.; New York: Harper & Row, 1965), 2:206–10, and references there.

public ministry, and particularly narratives of a last tragic week in Jerusalem, that richly reflects the passion of our Lord, whose suffering *is* on behalf of his people. Jeremiah's story is simply (and profoundly) a pointer in that direction.

We should also stress that these chapters are not the only accounts of Jeremiah's persecution, either in prose (e.g., 20:1–6) or poetry (e.g., 20:7–12), nor is the prophet the only figure of suffering in the accounts. Baruch, Gedaliah, and Ebed-Melech are caught up in the drama as well.

Fundamentally, Jeremiah's "passion narrative" continues the somber unfolding of self-incurred judgment on Judah and Jerusalem, a story deeply embedded in the minds of those who compiled Jeremiah's poetry. Tragic dissolution is the central theme to the accounts, although they are not without words of hope (e.g., the word to Baruch in ch. 45). A city is largely destroyed, a royal family is decimated by execution, a governor is treacherously murdered, and the prophet and his scribal companion are taken against their will to Egypt. As a story of suffering, there is plenty of illustrative material, and perhaps this is the point on which to start building a satisfactory interpretation.

The fate of the nation is a massive tragedy. The consequences of the Babylonian siege and destruction continue on in vicious cycles after the city has quit smoldering and the Babylonian army has departed. At several levels no one is exempt from the dark influence of the nation's fall. At another level, there are words of promise and protection to Ebed-Melech (39:15–18) and Baruch (45:1–5) that cast God's care in personal terms in spite of the upheaval. Others among the remnant are pointed to a better way (42:7–12), but they choose the wrong path.

These are chapters to ponder and to read together, even if their prehistory suggests diverse origins. If we seek "good news" from them, there will surely be some disappointment with their overwhelmingly negative tone. They take on a different hue, however, when placed in the larger context of Israel's history and the broader biblical witness, but we must be prepared to grapple theologically with the enormity of failure and with massive suffering. Only then will we sense the miracle of Jeremiah's preservation until his forced exile to Egypt; only then will we grasp some sense of the cost of discipleship carried by God's servants (Jeremiah, Gedaliah, Baruch, Ebed-Melech); only then will the gift of grace that comes undeserved be appreciated for what it is.

Jeremiah 37:1–21

¹ZEDEKIAH SON OF JOSIAH was made king of Judah by Nebuchadnezzar king of Babylon; he reigned in place of Jehoiachin son of Jehoiakim. ²Neither he nor his attendants

nor the people of the land paid any attention to the words the LORD had spoken through Jeremiah the prophet.

³King Zedekiah, however, sent Jehucal son of Shelemiah with the priest Zephaniah son of Maaseiah to Jeremiah the prophet with this message: "Please pray to the LORD our God for us."

⁴Now Jeremiah was free to come and go among the people, for he had not yet been put in prison. ⁵Pharaoh's army had marched out of Egypt, and when the Babylonians who were besieging Jerusalem heard the report about them, they withdrew from Jerusalem.

⁶Then the word of the LORD came to Jeremiah the prophet: ⁷"This is what the LORD, the God of Israel, says: Tell the king of Judah, who sent you to inquire of me, 'Pharaoh's army, which has marched out to support you, will go back to its own land, to Egypt. ⁸Then the Babylonians will return and attack this city; they will capture it and burn it down.'

⁹"This is what the LORD says: Do not deceive yourselves, thinking, 'The Babylonians will surely leave us.' They will not! ¹⁰Even if you were to defeat the entire Babylonian army that is attacking you and only wounded men were left in their tents, they would come out and burn this city down."

¹¹After the Babylonian army had withdrawn from Jerusalem because of Pharaoh's army, ¹²Jeremiah started to leave the city to go to the territory of Benjamin to get his share of the property among the people there. ¹³But when he reached the Benjamin Gate, the captain of the guard, whose name was Irijah son of Shelemiah, the son of Hananiah, arrested him and said, "You are deserting to the Babylonians!"

¹⁴"That's not true!" Jeremiah said. "I am not deserting to the Babylonians." But Irijah would not listen to him; instead, he arrested Jeremiah and brought him to the officials. ¹⁵They were angry with Jeremiah and had him beaten and imprisoned in the house of Jonathan the secretary, which they had made into a prison.

¹⁶Jeremiah was put into a vaulted cell in a dungeon, where he remained a long time. ¹⁷Then King Zedekiah sent for him and had him brought to the palace, where he asked him privately, "Is there any word from the LORD?"

"Yes," Jeremiah replied, "you will be handed over to the king of Babylon."

¹⁸Then Jeremiah said to King Zedekiah, "What crime have I committed against you or your officials or this people, that you have put me in prison? ¹⁹Where are your prophets who prophesied to you, 'The king of Babylon will not attack you or this land'? ²⁰But now, my lord the king, please listen. Let me bring my petition before you: Do not send me back to the house of Jonathan the secretary, or I will die there."

²¹King Zedekiah then gave orders for Jeremiah to be placed in the courtyard of the guard and given bread from the street of the bakers each day until all the bread in the city was gone. So Jeremiah remained in the courtyard of the guard.

CHAPTER 37 PROVIDES yet another account (like ch. 36) of royal failure and the continued rejection of the prophetic word. The royal culprit this time is Zedekiah, the last king of Judah, who is the pathetic leader of the doomed city.

37:1–2. According to verse 1, Zedekiah was placed on the throne in Judah by the Babylonians. They had surrounded Jerusalem in the winter months of 598/597 B.C. In March 597 the city surrendered to the Babylonians, and Jehoiachin, who had been king only a few months, was deported to Babylon and Nebuchadnezzar placed Jehoiachin's uncle Zedekiah on the throne. The deporting of Jehoiachin (sometimes called Coniah) and the appointing of Zedekiah as king were parts of a "divide and conquer" strategy on the part of the Babylonians. With two different men in two different communities claiming title to the Judean kingship, there was much occasion for internal tensions among the Judeans of Babylon and Palestine. The Babylonians hoped this would lessen the possibility of rebellion against their policies.

These two verses are actually a summary statement of Zedekiah's eleven years of reign. Details of his kingship and of his relationship with Jeremiah are picked up in verse 3 and continue through the end of chapter 38. The section 37:3–38:28 concern only the period of the Babylonian siege of Jerusalem during the years 588–587/586.

37:3–10. An Egyptian army is moving toward Judah in a manner intended to threaten the Babylonian army. This is probably part of the Pharaoh Hophra's scheme to regain control of affairs in Judah in the spring or summer of 588.³ According to verse 4, Jeremiah was not confined or

---

3. See the discussion of this period from the perspective of international history in A. Malamat, "Twilight of Judah," *VT* 25 (1974): 123–45.

imprisoned during all of Zedekiah's reign, but the rest of chapter 37 confirms that he was confined in a variety of circumstances.

Verses 6–10 report on a revelation given Jeremiah by the Lord, a message that he is to transmit to Zedekiah: Babylon will succeed in taking the city. Even the language of verse 8 is paralleled almost exactly in 34:22. What is new in the revelation is the prediction that the Egyptian army will not turn the tide of the Babylonian intent to take Judah and Jerusalem.

37:11–15. The appearance of the Egyptian army causes a temporary lifting of the Babylonian siege. Possibly Jeremiah's futile attempt to leave Jerusalem at this time is the prelude to the visit of his cousin during his imprisonment (32:1–14). According to the summary statement in 37:12, Jeremiah wants to go to the Benjamite tribal area in order to get his share of the property there. With the (temporary) lifting of the siege must have come a lot of frenetic activity among the inhabitants of the region. In Jeremiah's case, the guards of the city are suspicious that the prophet wants to leave the city in order to desert to the Babylonians. He is beaten and placed in confinement.

37:16–21. Zedekiah appears to be a classic case of a divided mind under pressure. On the one hand, he desperately seeks guidance for the difficulties of Judah, including his requests that Jeremiah pray to God (37:3) and that Jeremiah mediate God's will to him (37:17; see also ch. 21). On the other hand, the word of the Lord causes him consternation and demands of him what his self-serving and vacillating nature will not allow. Indeed, in his irrational behavior Zedekiah mistreats the very prophet he approaches for help.

Jeremiah is confined to a house belonging to a scribe (37:15) and later to a place associated with a guardhouse (37:21). Neither place appears to be a prison in the modern sense of the word, although Jeremiah's personal circumstances are painful. He is beaten at the scribe's house, and his rations in the guardhouse quarters are minimal. Later still, he will be thrown into a cistern (38:6). In 37:18 Jeremiah inquires of the king in what way he has sinned against the king or the people that he should be treated in this manner. He has consistently preached what God has given him to deliver, and he has responded whenever the king has inquired of him. The implied point is that he has told the truth and that Zedekiah is persecuting him for it.

Bridging Contexts

ZEDEKIAH AND A WORD FROM THE LORD. Zedekiah turns to the appropriate source in seeking answers to his dilemma: He seeks a word from the Lord. He fails, however, to listen to the word God communicates. Appropriately for the national crisis, he advocates prayer (37:3) and seeks a message from the Lord through Jeremiah (37:17). The problem is that God has previously informed Zedekiah that his actions and those of the people are unacceptable, and nothing seems to have changed—nothing from the side of God or that of Zedekiah. God has not changed his mind regarding the assessment of king and people, and Zedekiah seems oblivious to the prophet's message. For his part, Zedekiah seems to have followed a form of the proverbial advice to "shoot the bearer of bad news."

Hindsight is usually better than foresight. The tragedy of this account is that God makes known the near future, and Zedekiah is simply incapable of hearing and responding.

Persecution and the prophets. Persecution comes to prophets. In a variety of ways the book of Jeremiah is one long testimony to the cost of prophetic activity. His imprisonment is one of several in the Bible for prophets; Joseph, Micaiah ben Imlah, John the Baptist, Peter, Paul, and John the seer of the Apocalypse are all companions in faith incarcerated for their role in delivering God's word. Some who represent the message of the Lord suffer the ultimate human judgment of death (e.g., Uriah the son of Shemaiah, 26:20–23). Indeed, as is made clear in Jesus Christ, were God himself to advocate his Word, the reaction does not necessarily differ.

THE PRAYERS OF GOD'S PEOPLE. When is prayer for deliverance not acceptable? The question initially seems out of place since a loving God is typically open to the cries of his people, even if the timing of his response remains mysterious. Jesus taught his disciples to pray that they not be led into temptation but that God will deliver them from evil (Matt. 6:13). But there is a difference between Zedekiah and Moses, and between Jesus' disciples and the Judeans of Jeremiah's day. Disciples of Jesus cannot blatantly disregard his Word and then assume that a prayer for deliverance is efficacious; correspondingly, Zedekiah cannot assume that his rejection of God's Word will somehow induce God to send a different word of instruction.

There are circumstances where prayer is not what God desires. Although this sounds like a radical statement, it is worth some moments of reflection. Prayer is a staple of the Christian life, but it cannot be used as a reason for shirking one's responsibility or as an excuse for not being obedient to divine instruction.

A widely told anecdote concerns a man caught in his house during a period of heavy rains and flooding. As the water began to rise around his house, a neighbor came by to take him to higher ground and safety. The man refused to go, saying that he would wait out the storm and trust the Lord. As the water began to pour into the house, the man moved to the second story of the house. A police officer in a small boat came back and called to the man in the second-story window. The man replied similarly that he would wait out the storm and trust in the Lord. As the water continued to rise, the man climbed to his roof. A helicopter came by, and the man motioned for it to go on. After several frustrating minutes, the helicopter departed.

The man waited to see what would transpire next, and when the water continued to threaten, he began to pray to the Lord. He got an answer: "I sent a neighbor, a police officer, and a helicopter. Why didn't you listen?"

This seemingly trite story illustrates an important scriptural lesson. When God sends his servants to proclaim his message, and the servants and their message are rejected, then what other recourse is open? Unfortunately in many crises, no other avenue is open except that of failure and self-incurred destruction.

Stories of the recalcitrant and the disobedient (e.g., Zedekiah) in Scripture are not told so that a different generation can gleefully note how stupid "they" were. They are recorded so that any generation of God's people who read them can be instructed. After all, somebody among the faithful got it right and preserved the accounts for posterity. The foolish finally point by way of contrast to what is healthy among the people. It is far more instructive to read the accounts sympathetically, giving due attention to the possibility that in one way or the other we have become Zedekiah or Judah in our day.

It is important to remember how easy it is to assault the messenger rather than to listen carefully and to learn humbly from him or her. It is more convenient to reject an "unfriendly" assessment than it is to look in the mirror of God's Word.

Paradoxically, there is also hope in this disquieting account. Even in judging Zedekiah and the people, God is still at work to keep his promises. Zedekiah's family (i.e., that of David) will still be privileged to play a crucial role in God's economy. Moreover, what most Judeans think is an awful tragedy—the fall of the state and the resulting exile—is also the seedbed of new beginnings.

Jeremiah 38:1–28a

¹SHEPHATIAH SON OF Mattan, Gedaliah son of Pashhur, Jehucal son of Shelemiah, and Pashhur son of Malkijah heard what Jeremiah was telling all the people when he said, ²"This is what the LORD says: 'Whoever stays in this city will die by the sword, famine or plague, but whoever goes over to the Babylonians will live. He will escape with his life; he will live.' ³And this is what the LORD says: 'This city will certainly be

handed over to the army of the king of Babylon, who will capture it.'"

⁴Then the officials said to the king, "This man should be put to death. He is discouraging the soldiers who are left in this city, as well as all the people, by the things he is saying to them. This man is not seeking the good of these people but their ruin."

⁵"He is in your hands," King Zedekiah answered. "The king can do nothing to oppose you."

⁶So they took Jeremiah and put him into the cistern of Malkijah, the king's son, which was in the courtyard of the guard. They lowered Jeremiah by ropes into the cistern; it had no water in it, only mud, and Jeremiah sank down into the mud.

⁷But Ebed-Melech, a Cushite, an official in the royal palace, heard that they had put Jeremiah into the cistern. While the king was sitting in the Benjamin Gate, ⁸Ebed-Melech went out of the palace and said to him, ⁹"My lord the king, these men have acted wickedly in all they have done to Jeremiah the prophet. They have thrown him into a cistern, where he will starve to death when there is no longer any bread in the city."

¹⁰Then the king commanded Ebed-Melech the Cushite, "Take thirty men from here with you and lift Jeremiah the prophet out of the cistern before he dies."

¹¹So Ebed-Melech took the men with him and went to a room under the treasury in the palace. He took some old rags and worn-out clothes from there and let them down with ropes to Jeremiah in the cistern. ¹²Ebed-Melech the Cushite said to Jeremiah, "Put these old rags and worn-out clothes under your arms to pad the ropes." Jeremiah did so, ¹³and they pulled him up with the ropes and lifted him out of the cistern. And Jeremiah remained in the courtyard of the guard.

¹⁴Then King Zedekiah sent for Jeremiah the prophet and had him brought to the third entrance to the temple of the LORD. "I am going to ask you something," the king said to Jeremiah. "Do not hide anything from me."

¹⁵Jeremiah said to Zedekiah, "If I give you an answer, will you not kill me? Even if I did give you counsel, you would not listen to me."

¹⁶But King Zedekiah swore this oath secretly to Jeremiah: "As surely as the LORD lives, who has given us breath, I will

neither kill you nor hand you over to those who are seeking your life."

¹⁷Then Jeremiah said to Zedekiah, "This is what the LORD God Almighty, the God of Israel, says: 'If you surrender to the officers of the king of Babylon, your life will be spared and this city will not be burned down; you and your family will live. ¹⁸But if you will not surrender to the officers of the king of Babylon, this city will be handed over to the Babylonians and they will burn it down; you yourself will not escape from their hands.'"

¹⁹King Zedekiah said to Jeremiah, "I am afraid of the Jews who have gone over to the Babylonians, for the Babylonians may hand me over to them and they will mistreat me."

²⁰"They will not hand you over," Jeremiah replied. "Obey the LORD by doing what I tell you. Then it will go well with you, and your life will be spared. ²¹But if you refuse to surrender, this is what the LORD has revealed to me: ²²All the women left in the palace of the king of Judah will be brought out to the officials of the king of Babylon. Those women will say to you:

"'They misled you and overcame you—
  those trusted friends of yours.
Your feet are sunk in the mud;
  your friends have deserted you.'

²³"All your wives and children will be brought out to the Babylonians. You yourself will not escape from their hands but will be captured by the king of Babylon; and this city will be burned down."

²⁴Then Zedekiah said to Jeremiah, "Do not let anyone know about this conversation, or you may die. ²⁵If the officials hear that I talked with you, and they come to you and say, 'Tell us what you said to the king and what the king said to you; do not hide it from us or we will kill you,' ²⁶then tell them, 'I was pleading with the king not to send me back to Jonathan's house to die there.'"

²⁷All the officials did come to Jeremiah and question him, and he told them everything the king had ordered him to say. So they said no more to him, for no one had heard his conversation with the king.

²⁸And Jeremiah remained in the courtyard of the guard until the day Jerusalem was captured.

Original Meaning

CHAPTER 38 CONTINUES the narrative account begun in chapter 37 of Jeremiah's imprisonments during the final stages of the second Babylonian siege of Jerusalem. Jeremiah says nothing new about Judah's fate to Zedekiah (who wants desperately to have an authoritative but "positive" word on which to act). The choice that God has set before Zedekiah is described clearly, including words about the king's personal circumstances (38:17–23).[4] The fear expressed by Zedekiah that he will be abused by fellow Judeans if he surrenders suggests that Zedekiah's concern about himself is stronger than that for his people.

38:1–6. The men named in verse 1 are "officials" (cf. v. 4). Two of them are named elsewhere in the book. Jehucal is the NIV rendering of Hebrew *Yukal.* The latter is a variant of the name Jehucal, a son of Shelemiah mentioned in 37:3; they are almost certainly the same person. Pashhur is one of Zedekiah's servants (21:1). These officials have much autonomy in dealing with Jeremiah, as Zedekiah concedes in verse 5.

The officials are angry with Jeremiah because his words about Babylonian supremacy are "discouraging" (v. 4; lit., "weaken the hands"). This is not a common phrase in the Old Testament, but it occurs in a secular letter from the time of Jeremiah, where it describes the effect of bad news.[5] The officials lower Jeremiah into a cistern that has mud but no water. This is vindictive treatment by his opponents. Indirectly this comment tells the reader about the desperate circumstances of the siege. An empty cistern indicates water scarcity. Jeremiah is trapped in the cistern and unable to move easily or to rest.

38:7–13. One of the palace officials, a eunuch from Ethiopia,[6] courageously approaches Zedekiah to overturn the order consigning Jeremiah to a slow and painful death. He secures an agreement from the king (who is holding court in the gate of Benjamin) and goes with thirty men to pull the weakened prophet from the muddy cistern. The need for thirty men is not for the task of pulling Jeremiah out of the cistern but for controlling any attempts to stop Ebed-Melech.

---

4. One should compare these words with chs. 21 and 27; 38:2 and 21:9 are essentially the same quotation.

5. The only other occurrence of the phrase (the verb used is *rph* in Piel) in the Old Testament is Ezra 4:4. The phrase occurs in Lachish letter 6:6.

6. The palace official is called Ebed-Melech, which means "servant of the king" in Hebrew. The "name" may be nothing more than his title. Jer. 38:7 describes him as a man from Cush and a *saris.* Cush is the biblical term for the territory associated with Egypt and descended from Ham (Gen. 10:6–7). The LXX sometimes translates Cush as "Ethiopia." The Hebrew term *saris* likely means that the African man was castrated (i.e., a eunuch). The NIV translates the term as "official," which is accurate, but provides the alternative "eunuch" in a footnote.

One gains an idea of how weak the prophet has become from the description of Ebed-Melech's manner of extricating him from the mire. The men provide some worn-out rags to place under Jeremiah's arms so that the rope harness will not injure him. Jeremiah is freed from his sentence of slow death, but he is still kept under confinement with Zedekiah's guards. The actions of Ebed-Melech later receive a commendation of God and the promise of personal deliverance when the Babylonians finally take the city (see 39:15–18).[7]

38:14–28. The chapter concludes with the notice that Jeremiah remains in the court of the guard (cf. 37:20–21; 39:11–14) until the day that Jerusalem is captured. But Zedekiah is not through with the prophet. As in earlier cases (21:1; 37:3), the king seeks spiritual advice from him. Initially, Jeremiah seeks assurance that he will not be killed, and the king swears not to hand the prophet over to those who want to kill him.

Readers learn from the narrative that Zedekiah is as worried about his personal safety and future as he is about the city and the state. Jeremiah sets before the king the alternatives of surrendering and trusting the Lord for his safety or holding out and seeing the Babylonians victorious. The latter scenario includes the burning of the city (v. 23).

Zedekiah asks Jeremiah not to reveal their conversation. This is another indication of the king's divided mind and his vacillation with respect to listening to the prophet. One gains the impression from all this that both Jeremiah and Zedekiah are the subject of rumor and conspiracy and that Zedekiah has precious few people whom he can trust. The chapter concludes with the comment that Jeremiah remains in the courtyard of the guard until the Babylonians take the city. This last comment sets the stage for the narrative in chapter 39.

FUNDAMENTAL CONVICTIONS. "Choose for yourselves this day whom you will serve" (Josh. 24:15). Much of the book of Jeremiah is about God's corporate judgment on Judah for her failures. Such a theological conviction is the presupposition of chapter 38, yet this account also shines the light of inspired testimony on individual lives. Here the personal is at center stage. One sees how people variously react to fear and courage and how they view God's work in their circumstances.

The circumstances of the siege and the awful predicament in which the inhabitants of Jerusalem find themselves lead to personal crises. The time has

---

7. The word of grace to Baruch in 45:5 uses the same image as 39:18 (cf. also 21:9). Even though Jerusalem would fall to the Babylonians (and thus suffer defeat), both Ebed-Melech and Baruch would survive. Their life would be like the gift that comes from military victory.

come for people to act on their fundamental convictions, be they "orthodox" or not. Some officials hear Jeremiah's prophetic word as a threat, undermining the resolve of the people necessary to their continued survival. The officials believe that the Lord should strengthen the people in time of need, not announce judgment to them through a prophet. As a result, they take action against the prophet.

Zedekiah hears the message repeatedly but is unable to face up to its demands. Pressure from various quarters has resulted in his doing little more than fretting over his personal safety.

Ebed-Melech too hears much of the debate, and he likewise acts on his fundamental convictions. In the midst of tragedy and suffering, hard choices, and even personal fear, Ebed-Melech stands with the prophet. As a result, God will stand with Ebed-Melech (39:15–18). Since action is a key indicator of a person's disposition, we should recognize in this man spiritual discernment as well as the courage of his convictions. Such discernment and moral courage are elements that can instruct Christians of any generation.

Readers may ask the question: Why would such an account as chapter 38 be preserved? Here are several answers. (1) It helps to explain the obdurate nature of Judah in refusing to see the hand of the Lord at work in judgment. (2) Moreover, it explains why Judah and Jerusalem fell. (3) But the account is also preserved in order to instruct readers and hearers in being open to God's corrective word and in trusting that dark days will lead to something better.

FEAR. Fear does strange things to people. Some are almost superstitious in their avoidance of "negative talk." It is almost as if they believe that to silence the words means to avoid the reality to which they may point. The phenomenon is one reason for the proverbial saying that "one may kill the messenger but not the message." That is, if you throw Jeremiah into the cistern, his message will not be heard and hopefully will not come to pass. Better for Jesus to die than for the people to get stirred up. So-called "gag orders" are intended to keep someone from stating a truth publicly when it may prove to be injurious.

Some people are frozen by fear, unable to make a decision because they cannot clearly see a resolution. Not to decide on a course of action may be prudent, just as staying a familiar course can be the better of options, but neither is satisfactory when God has called his people to accountability and to action. In the case of Zedekiah, not to act decisively and obediently to Jeremiah's prophetic word means simply keeping on with the old and tired policies of failure. In his case, not to decide is actually to make a fateful decision.

God's providence is so designed that people may inevitably face their fears and choose among difficult options. This is not necessarily "bad news." The issue is first discernment and then trusting God, who sends such matters our way. The Gospel narratives provide us with portraits of a Jesus who spoke his word in season and stood by his claims. It is true that he prayed for the cup of suffering and shame to be taken away (Luke 22:39–44). Yet what remained paramount for Jesus (and remains so for us) is the discerning of God's will. And once his will is discerned, trust in God is a conviction about life and our place in it.

Courage. Courage can be simply a noble human trait. But it can also be a gift of God in due season, and its manifestation in the lives of God's people are markers along the path of discipleship. It is for the combination of wisdom and courage that all Christians should pray, knowing that it is only a matter of time until they must make some difficult choices.

In December 1997, a disturbed fourteen-year-old boy in West Paducah, Kentucky, shot and killed four girls at the conclusion of a prayer meeting held before school hours. Hearing the shots and seeing the bodies fall, a boy at the scene stood his ground and finally convinced the attacker to drop his firearm. Why didn't he run from the killer, who still had a loaded weapon in his hand? A devout Christian, the boy stated simply that he felt that God wanted him to stand there and to reach out to the troubled attacker. Courage! It can be God's gift, and its exercise can become a testimony to the grace of the Giver.

In a story like this, one does not first ask about the lives of the four girls who were killed or the life of the disturbed teenager who shot them. All of this is relevant, of course, to understand something of the background to the tragic shootings, but none of that was useful in the quick moment when a decision had to be made. Like so many things in life, events can force decisions on us when we don't have the gift of time and leisurely reflection. If Christ's disciples have not spent time in the practice of discerning God's will and in being open to the leading of God's Spirit, then the pressure of the moment will seem all the more constricting.

Jeremiah 38:28b–39:18

28bThis is how Jerusalem was taken: 39:1In the ninth year of Zedekiah king of Judah, in the tenth month, Nebuchadnezzar king of Babylon marched against Jerusalem with his whole army and laid siege to it. 2And on the ninth day of the fourth month of Zedekiah's eleventh year, the city wall was broken through. 3Then all the officials of the king of Babylon came and took seats in the Middle Gate: Nergal-Sharezer of Sam-

gar, Nebo-Sarsekim a chief officer, Nergal-Sharezer a high
official and all the other officials of the king of Babylon.
⁴When Zedekiah king of Judah and all the soldiers saw them,
they fled; they left the city at night by way of the king's garden, through the gate between the two walls, and headed
toward the Arabah.

⁵But the Babylonian army pursued them and overtook
Zedekiah in the plains of Jericho. They captured him and took
him to Nebuchadnezzar king of Babylon at Riblah in the land
of Hamath, where he pronounced sentence on him. ⁶There at
Riblah the king of Babylon slaughtered the sons of Zedekiah
before his eyes and also killed all the nobles of Judah. ⁷Then
he put out Zedekiah's eyes and bound him with bronze shackles to take him to Babylon.

⁸The Babylonians set fire to the royal palace and the houses
of the people and broke down the walls of Jerusalem. ⁹Neb-
uzaradan commander of the imperial guard carried into exile to
Babylon the people who remained in the city, along with those
who had gone over to him, and the rest of the people. ¹⁰But
Nebuzaradan the commander of the guard left behind in the
land of Judah some of the poor people, who owned nothing;
and at that time he gave them vineyards and fields.

¹¹Now Nebuchadnezzar king of Babylon had given these
orders about Jeremiah through Nebuzaradan commander of
the imperial guard: ¹²"Take him and look after him; don't harm
him but do for him whatever he asks." ¹³So Nebuzaradan the
commander of the guard, Nebushazban a chief officer, Nergal-
Sharezer a high official and all the other officers of the king of
Babylon ¹⁴sent and had Jeremiah taken out of the courtyard of
the guard. They turned him over to Gedaliah son of Ahikam,
the son of Shaphan, to take him back to his home. So he
remained among his own people.

¹⁵While Jeremiah had been confined in the courtyard of the
guard, the word of the LORD came to him: ¹⁶"Go and tell
Ebed-Melech the Cushite, 'This is what the LORD Almighty,
the God of Israel, says: I am about to fulfill my words against
this city through disaster, not prosperity. At that time they will
be fulfilled before your eyes. ¹⁷But I will rescue you on that
day, declares the LORD; you will not be handed over to those
you fear. ¹⁸I will save you; you will not fall by the sword but
will escape with your life, because you trust in me, declares
the LORD.'"

Original
Meaning

THIS CHAPTER HAS PARALLELS with the accounts in
Jeremiah 52:1–16 and 2 Kings 25:1–12. As noted
in the introduction, the year of the fall of Jerusalem
is disputed. The eleventh year of Zedekiah (39:2)
was either 587 or 586 B.C., probably the latter. The city wall was breached in
the fourth month, which would be July/August (according to a spring new
year). The temple was not burned until a month later (52:6–14).[8]

38:28b–39:7. The first line of this section introduces the account of
Jerusalem's fall, but the narrative quickly shifts to a description of Zedekiah's
fate. To put it succinctly, his fate is essentially the same as that of the city and
people (39:4–7). He attempts to escape the consequences of Jerusalem's fall
by fleeing to the Jordan Valley. He is caught by the Babylonian army with
gruesome results. First he is taken to Riblah in Syria, where Nebuchadnezzar
is in residence. The Babylonian king personally gives Zedekiah his sentence.
His sons (and potential heirs) are slain in his presence along with other Judean
nobles. The Judean king is then blinded so that the last thing he sees is the
death of family and friends. He is then bound in fetters like other Judean
exiles and taken to Babylon. Nothing else is preserved about him.

39:8–10. These verses describe succinctly the actual burning of the city.
Named in particular are the royal palace and houses of the people. The walls
are also pulled down. Nothing is mentioned about the temple here.

Nebuzaradan, a high Babylonian official, organizes much of the surviving population into a group for exile. Some of the poorest people in Judah
(probably those who do not own land) are left to tend the land. Thus the former state of Judah is not totally depopulated, and the Babylonians will be able
to extract tribute from those who remain to tend the land.

39:11–14. Nebuchadnezzar himself orders that Jeremiah be released
from confinement. Reasons for his release are not cited, but Jeremiah's confinement serves no Babylonian purpose, and perhaps Nebuchadnezzar has
heard secondhand that a Judean prophet proclaimed his supremacy. Moreover, the Babylonians[9] turn him over to Gedaliah son of Ahikam, son of
Shaphan. In the next chapter we learn that Nebuchadnezzar will appoint
Gedaliah as governor of Judah. Here we see again the illustrious family of
Shaphan, whose members had been supportive of Jeremiah.[10] Gedaliah's fate

---

8. At some point after the destruction of the city, Jews began a public ceremony of
lamentation to recall its fall. That ceremony now takes place on the ninth of Ab (which falls
in August). See the introduction to the book of Lamentations.

9. Chapter 39 names several Babylonian officials. For a treatment of their names and
titles, see Holladay, *Jeremiah*, 2:291.

10. See comments on Jer. 26:24 and ch. 36.

also mirrors the Judean tragedy, even though his personal commitments are closer to those of Jeremiah than Zedekiah's.[11]

39:15–18. The narrator provides a retrospective account of an oracle Jeremiah received about Ebed-Melech, the eunuch who saved his life during the darker moments of the siege. God has granted Ebed-Melech his life.[12] Even though he is an official of the despised Zedekiah, he will not be handed over to the Babylonians.

WHEN READ IN THE CONTEXT of the book as a whole, chapter 39 seems not only tragic but also somewhat anticlimactic. The fall of Jerusalem predicted by Jeremiah does, in fact, come to pass, and the faithless Zedekiah is treated harshly by the Babylonians. All we read are the bare details of the account, something like the brief report of the fall of Samaria in 2 Kings 17:1–6.[13]

Bilevel reading. One function of this chapter is the somber confirmation that Jeremiah's prophetic word has reached fulfillment concerning the city and the king. Zedekiah pays the price for his moral and spiritual weakness. He had worried about reprisals from his countrymen if he surrendered to the Babylonians (38:19) only to find that he was unable to avoid the prophetic word that he would have to account for his failures. According to the prophet, Zedekiah could have avoided an awful fate and saved the city from destruction (38:17–18), but it was not to be.

One can see this account working on at least two levels. On the one hand, hindsight demonstrates that Zedekiah chose the path that ultimately failed him. He was a responsible agent who acted irresponsibly. On the other hand, his path also confirmed the prophetic word that announced judgment on such a path. Act and consequence are tragically bound together. Both of these elements can be instructive to later readers who seek to learn from the past.

This bilevel reading also works for the report of Jeremiah's word to Ebed-Melech. The eunuch chose his difficult path and discovered that God was with him. He was an agent who acted responsibly on his spiritual and moral convictions. He received his life rather than exile or execution, like many

---

11. See also comments on chs. 40–41.

12. The Heb. idiom states that his life is granted as a prize of war. It is the same phrase used in 21:9; 38:2; and 45:5.

13. It will be recalled that prophets like Amos and Hosea devoted much of their public prophetic work to announcing the fall of Israel and Samaria. Moreover, the majority of 2 Kings 17 is devoted to a polemic against Samaria and its inhabitants. Perhaps the reason that Jer. 39 and 2 Kings 17 give such a brief narration of the actual event of the fall of the cities is that they paraphrase official notices preserved in royal or state annals.

associated with the royal house (cf. Matt. 16:24–26). One cannot universalize from these two examples, but they are instructive nevertheless to God's people.

TRAGEDY AND JUDGMENT. Is there such a thing as an *expected* tragedy? So often what makes an event or circumstance "tragic" is its unexpectedness. Certainly readers of the Old Testament can point to the account of Jerusalem's fall and say that the city's fate was announced beforehand. A tragedy that is anticipated and yet comes to pass is, in some sense, doubly tragic, because if it is anticipated, there should be ways of mitigating its harshness.

In Judah's case, we may question why one would even call such an event a tragedy rather than simply a reflection of God's judgment. It is really both, and therein lies something for us to think about. Tragedy suggests that an event or process does not have to turn out that way. In theological terms it suggests that God may have preferred it otherwise (cf. Ezek. 18:32), that he took no pleasure in the fall—indeed, that he sent a string of prophets to try and turn Judah from its self-destructive folly. Whether tragedy or judgment, the circumstances of Judah's fall were both allowed and then used by God in the history of his people.

Yet there can be a personal word from God that comes in the midst of tragedy or judgment. One sees it in the gift of life to Ebed-Melech. Such a word just comes. Is it expected? Hardly so, if one calls such a thing a word of grace. Grace happens, but it cannot be presumed upon. God is the God of new beginnings as well as the God of historical destiny. How judgment and new life work out in God's economy is what gives shape to the Christian life and confirms God as Lord of all circumstances.

End and beginning. On December 7, 1941, President Franklin D. Roosevelt gave his famous "a day that will live in infamy" speech. It was his reaction to the Japanese bombing of Pearl Harbor, an event that occasioned the official entrance of the United States into World War II. What tragedies and judgments resulted from that event! The attack on Pearl Harbor took place early on a Sunday morning. But is it only a past act, or was it really the ending of an old form of existence and the beginning of something new, something that is still working out its effects decades after the fact? It is both![14]

---

14. One might compare in this context the speech of President Lincoln that a "house divided cannot stand," in which he reflects also on the fact of divine judgment in history. The ripple effects of the Civil War are still working themselves out in the history of North America.

The fall of Jerusalem is analogous. It brought several things to an end. Yet it was the beginning of something new, something that would continue on for decades. One might even argue that its effects are still being worked out in the history of Judaism and events occurring in the Middle East. Christians should see the outlines of a pattern here: God at work to use circumstances, even tragedy, for different and life-giving purposes.

Jeremiah 40:1–41:18

¹THE WORD CAME to Jeremiah from the LORD after Nebuzaradan commander of the imperial guard had released him at Ramah. He had found Jeremiah bound in chains among all the captives from Jerusalem and Judah who were being carried into exile to Babylon. ²When the commander of the guard found Jeremiah, he said to him, "The LORD your God decreed this disaster for this place. ³And now the LORD has brought it about; he has done just as he said he would. All this happened because you people sinned against the LORD and did not obey him. ⁴But today I am freeing you from the chains on your wrists. Come with me to Babylon, if you like, and I will look after you; but if you do not want to, then don't come. Look, the whole country lies before you; go wherever you please." ⁵However, before Jeremiah turned to go, Nebuzaradan added, "Go back to Gedaliah son of Ahikam, the son of Shaphan, whom the king of Babylon has appointed over the towns of Judah, and live with him among the people, or go anywhere else you please."

Then the commander gave him provisions and a present and let him go. ⁶So Jeremiah went to Gedaliah son of Ahikam at Mizpah and stayed with him among the people who were left behind in the land.

⁷When all the army officers and their men who were still in the open country heard that the king of Babylon had appointed Gedaliah son of Ahikam as governor over the land and had put him in charge of the men, women and children who were the poorest in the land and who had not been carried into exile to Babylon, ⁸they came to Gedaliah at Mizpah—Ishmael son of Nethaniah, Johanan and Jonathan the sons of Kareah, Seraiah son of Tanhumeth, the sons of Ephai the Netophathite, and Jaazaniah the son of the Maacathite, and their men. ⁹Gedaliah son of Ahikam, the son of Shaphan,

took an oath to reassure them and their men. "Do not be afraid to serve the Babylonians," he said. "Settle down in the land and serve the king of Babylon, and it will go well with you. ¹⁰I myself will stay at Mizpah to represent you before the Babylonians who come to us, but you are to harvest the wine, summer fruit and oil, and put them in your storage jars, and live in the towns you have taken over."

¹¹When all the Jews in Moab, Ammon, Edom and all the other countries heard that the king of Babylon had left a remnant in Judah and had appointed Gedaliah son of Ahikam, the son of Shaphan, as governor over them, ¹²they all came back to the land of Judah, to Gedaliah at Mizpah, from all the countries where they had been scattered. And they harvested an abundance of wine and summer fruit.

¹³Johanan son of Kareah and all the army officers still in the open country came to Gedaliah at Mizpah ¹⁴and said to him, "Don't you know that Baalis king of the Ammonites has sent Ishmael son of Nethaniah to take your life?" But Gedaliah son of Ahikam did not believe them.

¹⁵Then Johanan son of Kareah said privately to Gedaliah in Mizpah, "Let me go and kill Ishmael son of Nethaniah, and no one will know it. Why should he take your life and cause all the Jews who are gathered around you to be scattered and the remnant of Judah to perish?"

¹⁶But Gedaliah son of Ahikam said to Johanan son of Kareah, "Don't do such a thing! What you are saying about Ishmael is not true."

⁴¹:¹In the seventh month Ishmael son of Nethaniah, the son of Elishama, who was of royal blood and had been one of the king's officers, came with ten men to Gedaliah son of Ahikam at Mizpah. While they were eating together there, ²Ishmael son of Nethaniah and the ten men who were with him got up and struck down Gedaliah son of Ahikam, the son of Shaphan, with the sword, killing the one whom the king of Babylon had appointed as governor over the land. ³Ishmael also killed all the Jews who were with Gedaliah at Mizpah, as well as the Babylonian soldiers who were there.

⁴The day after Gedaliah's assassination, before anyone knew about it, ⁵eighty men who had shaved off their beards, torn their clothes and cut themselves came from Shechem, Shiloh and Samaria, bringing grain offerings and incense

with them to the house of the LORD. 6Ishmael son of Nethaniah went out from Mizpah to meet them, weeping as he
went. When he met them, he said, "Come to Gedaliah son of
Ahikam." 7When they went into the city, Ishmael son of
Nethaniah and the men who were with him slaughtered them
and threw them into a cistern. 8But ten of them said to Ishmael, "Don't kill us! We have wheat and barley, oil and
honey, hidden in a field." So he let them alone and did not
kill them with the others. 9Now the cistern where he threw
all the bodies of the men he had killed along with Gedaliah
was the one King Asa had made as part of his defense
against Baasha king of Israel. Ishmael son of Nethaniah filled
it with the dead.

10Ishmael made captives of all the rest of the people who
were in Mizpah—the king's daughters along with all the others who were left there, over whom Nebuzaradan commander
of the imperial guard had appointed Gedaliah son of Ahikam.
Ishmael son of Nethaniah took them captive and set out to
cross over to the Ammonites.

11When Johanan son of Kareah and all the army officers
who were with him heard about all the crimes Ishmael son of
Nethaniah had committed, 12they took all their men and went
to fight Ishmael son of Nethaniah. They caught up with him
near the great pool in Gibeon. 13When all the people Ishmael
had with him saw Johanan son of Kareah and the army officers who were with him, they were glad. 14All the people
Ishmael had taken captive at Mizpah turned and went over
to Johanan son of Kareah. 15But Ishmael son of Nethaniah
and eight of his men escaped from Johanan and fled to the
Ammonites.

16Then Johanan son of Kareah and all the army officers
who were with him led away all the survivors from Mizpah
whom he had recovered from Ishmael son of Nethaniah after
he had assassinated Gedaliah son of Ahikam: the soldiers,
women, children and court officials he had brought from
Gibeon. 17And they went on, stopping at Geruth Kimham
near Bethlehem on their way to Egypt 18to escape the Babylonians. They were afraid of them because Ishmael son of
Nethaniah had killed Gedaliah son of Ahikam, whom the king
of Babylon had appointed as governor over the land.

THE TRAGEDY ASSOCIATED with Judah's demise continues after the destruction of the city. Chapters 40–41 revolve around the ill-fated Gedaliah son of Ahikam, the son of Shaphan, who is appointed governor of the province by the Babylonians (40:5, 7) and who will die at the hands of a Judean zealot named Ishmael (41:1–3). Gedaliah is already mentioned in 39:14 as the one to whom Jeremiah is released from custody.[15] He was from an influential family and one friendly to Jeremiah. His grandfather, Shaphan, had been a member of Josiah's cabinet, and his father, also related to Josiah's administration, had been of crucial support to Jeremiah after a disastrous temple sermon (26:24; cf. 2 Kings 22).

Thus, the Babylonians appoint someone known to those remaining in the land and someone with administrative and political experience. It is possible, indeed likely, that Gedaliah agreed with Jeremiah's claim that God had employed Babylon as chastisement on Judah, and so he was prepared to do what seemed best for Judah in the months after Jerusalem's fall. He advises those around him to "not be afraid to serve the Babylonians," for in so doing it may go well with them (40:9; cf. the prophet's words to the exiles in Babylon, 29:4–7).

40:1–6. Nebuzaradan, a Babylonian official, addresses Jeremiah (39:9), stating that God has given Judah and Jerusalem into the hands of Babylon in order to judge them. This may sound strange to modern readers, but many people in antiquity affirmed the power of a local deity in its sphere of influence. There is no reason to suspect sarcasm or insincerity on the part of Nebuzaradan.[16]

---

15. The narrator's report in 39:14 about Jeremiah's release into the hands of Gedaliah is likely proleptic, i.e., it anticipates the conversation between Jeremiah and Nebuzaradan in 40:1–6. With respect to the identity of Gedaliah, it is probable that two Iron Age seal impressions that name a certain Gedaliah as "over the house" (from Lachish) and "servant of the king" (origin unknown) refer to this Gedaliah, who was appointed governor by the Babylonians. Both phrases from the seals are titles for officials in a state administration. Given the roles of his father and grandfather, it is understandable that Gedaliah had such titles before his appointment by the Babylonians. For references to the Iron Age inscriptions and brief discussion, see Dearman, "My Servants the Scribes," 412–14. A more cautionary note regarding the equation of Gedaliah, governor of Judah, with the Gedaliah of the two inscriptions is given by B. Becking, "Inscribed Seals As Evidence for Biblical Israel? Jeremiah 40:7–41:15 par example," in *Can a 'History of Israel' Be Written?* ed. L. L. Grabbe (Sheffield: Sheffield Academic Press, 1997), 75–78. Becking also evaluates the possibility of identifying Ishmael and Baalis from extrabiblical inscriptions, 78–83.

16. Readers should compare this communication of Nebuzaradan with that of the Assyrian Rabshakeh to Jerusalem in 2 Kings 18:19–25, 28–35.

Jeremiah is also given a choice whether to go to Babylon or remain in the land with Gedaliah. From the point of view of personal security, it would likely be better for Jeremiah to accompany Nebuzaradan to Babylon, but he chooses to remain with the remnant in the land. In this choice the prophet signals a commitment to the land and to renewal, just like his symbolic purchase of property during the Babylonian siege of Jerusalem (32:1–15). So Jeremiah becomes a member of the remnant band associated with Gedaliah. He seems to know nothing about the plot against the governor. That Jeremiah is given provisions and a "present" by the Babylonians (40:5) is recognition on their part that the prophet predicted their success.

40:7–16. Remnants of Judeans begin to gather around Gedaliah at Mizpah, about five miles north of Jerusalem.[17] Included in the group are Ishmael son of Nethaniah and Johanan son of Kareah, two people whose actions will affect decisively the fortunes of both the little province and the prophet Jeremiah. Johanan is a member of the Judean army but also seemingly well-connected to the remaining officials in Judah. Ishmael is related to the royal family of Judah (41:1). Johanan discovers (we know not how) that Baalis, king of the Ammonites (40:14), has concocted a plot with Ishmael to assassinate Gedaliah.[18] Indeed, Johanan apprises Gedaliah of his knowledge, but Gedaliah does not believe the report.

Verses 10–11 remind us of the continuing impact of the Babylonian siege. When the Babylonian army first marched into the area, a number of Judeans had fled their homes to take up residence in surrounding territories. Now that the Babylonians have completed their siege and the main elements of the army returned to Babylon, many of these Judeans now return to see what remains of their former property. Upon doing so, they also find that additional property needs tending. Gedaliah's comment to them—"Live in the towns you have taken over"—indicates that the control of land has now passed to them and to others who remain.

---

17. For the possibilities of its identification, see P. Arnold, "Mizpah," *ABD*, 4:879–81. Two sites are commonly suggested: Nebi Samwil or Tell en-Nasbeh.

18. An Ammonite seal bearing the Semitic equivalent of the name Baalis was discovered in an excavation south of Amman. See L. G. Herr, "The Servant of Baalis," *BA* 48 (1985): 169–72. The biblical text provides no reasons behind the nefarious plot of Baalis and Ishmael. Perhaps the Ammonite king saw an opportunity to expand his influence in the region now that the Judean government had been overthrown. For his part, Ishmael may have seen in Baalis the kind of support he needed to carve out his own sphere of influence once the main body of the Babylonian army left the region. He was, after all, a member of the Judean royal family. Zedekiah and his sons were gone, so perhaps Ishmael intended to play on his Davidic heritage in a bid for power.

All in all, it is a precarious time for those who remain in the land. They can be called the "remnant of Judah" (40:15), and the tasks of bringing corporate life back to a more even keel are daunting. Gedaliah may well have been able to represent the interests of the remnant to the Babylonian provincial administration. Unfortunately, this will never be known because of his tragic and untimely demise.

41:1–3. Chapter 41 narrates quickly Ishmael's treacherous murder of Gedaliah. Treachery is the correct description of murder during a mealtime, since the "eating together" of Ishmael and Gedaliah presupposes social bonding and hospitality. The massacre is both a strike against the Babylonians and an attempt by Ishmael to usurp power. In addition to Gedaliah (the appointed governor) Ishmael murders "all the Jews" with Gedaliah and the Babylonian soldiers present. By "all the Jews" is probably meant the Judean men who work with Gedaliah in administrative affairs. Verses 10 and 16 report the survival of some persons from the town of Mizpah.

41:4–18. The day after the murder at Mizpah, a group of pilgrims from Shiloh, Shechem, and Samaria come south on the hill-country road to Jerusalem. They have cut their beards and torn their clothes as signs of ritual humiliation, and they intend to worship at the site of the temple in Jerusalem (41:4–8). Here is unintended commentary on the importance of the temple for people who lived outside the territory of Judah. The pilgrims from the north want to present grain offerings and incense at the temple in Jerusalem; does this mean that part of the temple cult continues even after the destruction of the temple itself? Perhaps an altar has been erected and repositioned in the courtyard, or perhaps the ceremony envisioned by the pilgrims is for prayer and lamentation, and their gifts symbolic gesture. The text does not say, and interpreters should be wary of speculation.

In yet another treacherous act, Ishmael gains their confidence and brings them to Mizpah, only to murder most of them and then to cast their bodies into the large cistern built by a former king. A few are spared, who offer him provisions they have hidden in a field. Ishmael then gathers the townspeople and sets out to cross over the Jordan River to the Ammonites. Among his captives are daughters of the king. Most likely these are daughters of Zedekiah from marriages with women of prominent local families. Johanan and his soldiers attempt to intercept Ishmael. The two groups met near Gibeon, with the result that most of the captives taken by Ishmael are recovered by Johanan and his officers, but Ishmael and eight of his men escape.

The question faced by Johanan and his band is, "What now?" Their fear of Babylonian reprisal and the treachery of men like Ishmael lead them toward a decision to flee the region. Their choice of venue is Egypt, where already a sizable group of Judeans live.

HUMAN TENDENCY TO self-destruction. Why would an exilic audience find this sad account instructive? The material is not provided only to explain to exiles (or later generations) what happened in the past, but also to demonstrate the tragic consequences of Judah's folly as they continue to play themselves out after the fall of Jerusalem. In a related way the account confirms that the prophet of God does not have a saving word for every occasion. Although it is clear that Jeremiah did not support the assassination of Gedaliah, he says nothing about the plot beforehand (he may have known nothing about it). He will also be ineffective in seeking to convince Johanan and company to stay in the land (ch. 42). The prophet is thus caught up in the circumstances of the tragedy, and he will bear some of its consequences.

In some ways these two chapters are the saddest in the whole book of Jeremiah. Babylon has clearly demonstrated its mastery over Judah, confirming a word Jeremiah proclaimed for years; yet Gedaliah, the one figure who may have facilitated reconstruction of life in the land and become a symbol of hope, is senselessly killed. God will, of course, be able to overcome these bitter ashes of defeat, but it comes at considerable cost.

The account of life in the land after the fall of the city is a clear illustration of human community gone bad, with no mechanism to help it right itself. Part of the impact of reading these chapters is simply to sigh and be reminded of the human tendency toward self-destruction. Only the larger context of God's superabounding grace, based on his resolve to stay with such a people, provides any hope beyond the tragedy.

REBUILDING AFTER DEFEAT. "The wages of sin is death" (Rom. 6:23). For North American readers, the depressing account of Gedaliah's murder and the continuing downward spiral in Judah may strike a responsive chord in their historical memory. Abraham Lincoln announced that a "house divided against itself cannot stand." He knew he was quoting a biblical text (cf. Mark 3:24–25), and he believed that God would judge the United States for its folly in the slave trade and its continuing bitter conflict over ways to resolve the matter.

After four years of civil war (1861–1865), with the southern states in tatters and the whole nation exhausted from the senseless bloodletting, Lincoln began to look for ways to rebuild the nation and to reconcile its various factions. He went public with his conviction that God had judged the affairs of the nation, and he refused to take the moral high ground of exemption when it came to confessing the judging hand of God. Lincoln was not perfect (nor was Gedaliah!), but he represented the possibility of moving past the consequences of moral and spiritual failure. A twisted soul named John Wilkes Booth assassinated Lincoln before he could put his plans for reconciliation into effect, and the resulting turmoil in the southern states over harsh reconstruction policies was extremely costly.[19]

What does one say to such a "lesson"? One should begin by affirming that the painful historical process came about as self-incurred failure. Its effects linger on. The issues are not just "in the past." Christians, however, should go on further and, like Lincoln, confess the hand of God at work in judgment.

Are there not additional things that we as Christians can confess? One of them is that Lincoln (like Gedaliah and Jeremiah) is something of a tragic figure. In a mysterious way, he bore corporate failure in his person and suffered along with the nation—and not just in his death. The Christological analogy is not complete: Lincoln (Gedaliah or Jeremiah) did not atone for the sins of others, but they did suffer as part of their "calling."

Their tragedy raises interesting questions. If God uses their tragic circumstances to instruct his people and to evoke measures of repentance and sympathy, then they serve a larger purpose. Moreover, failure can be the prelude to and even the beginning of new directions. In the midst of a national humiliation Gedaliah advises his contemporaries not to fear. Jeremiah chooses the more difficult road rather than setting off to Babylon. Do those who have tasted new life in the crucified and risen Lord have eyes to see and ears to hear what the Spirit is saying?

Jeremiah 42:1–43:7

[1]THEN ALL THE ARMY OFFICERS, including Johanan son of Kareah and Jezaniah son of Hoshaiah, and all the people from the least to the greatest approached [2]Jeremiah the prophet and said to him, "Please hear our petition and pray to the LORD your God for this entire remnant. For as you now see, though we were once many, now only a few are left. [3]Pray that the LORD your God will tell us where we should go and what we should do."

[4]"I have heard you," replied Jeremiah the prophet. "I will certainly pray to the LORD your God as you have requested; I

---

19. The Marshall Plan instituted by the United States after World War II did not get derailed and illustrates how a positive policy after war and tragedy can have repercussions for stability that continue to have influence in current times.

will tell you everything the LORD says and will keep nothing
back from you."

⁵Then they said to Jeremiah, "May the LORD be a true and
faithful witness against us if we do not act in accordance with
everything the LORD your God sends you to tell us. ⁶Whether
it is favorable or unfavorable, we will obey the LORD our
God, to whom we are sending you, so that it will go well with
us, for we will obey the LORD our God."

⁷Ten days later the word of the LORD came to Jeremiah.
⁸So he called together Johanan son of Kareah and all the army
officers who were with him and all the people from the least
to the greatest.

⁹He said to them, "This is what the LORD, the God of
Israel, to whom you sent me to present your petition, says:

¹⁰'If you stay in this land, I will build you up and not tear
you down; I will plant you and not uproot you, for I am
grieved over the disaster I have inflicted on you. ¹¹Do not be
afraid of the king of Babylon, whom you now fear. Do not be
afraid of him, declares the LORD, for I am with you and will
save you and deliver you from his hands. ¹²I will show you
compassion so that he will have compassion on you and
restore you to your land.'

¹³"However, if you say, 'We will not stay in this land,' and
so disobey the LORD your God, ¹⁴and if you say, 'No, we will
go and live in Egypt, where we will not see war or hear the
trumpet or be hungry for bread,' ¹⁵then hear the word of the
LORD, O remnant of Judah. This is what the LORD Almighty,
the God of Israel, says: 'If you are determined to go to Egypt
and you do go to settle there, ¹⁶then the sword you fear will
overtake you there, and the famine you dread will follow you
into Egypt, and there you will die. ¹⁷Indeed, all who are determined to go to Egypt to settle there will die by the sword,
famine and plague; not one of them will survive or escape the
disaster I will bring on them.' ¹⁸This is what the LORD
Almighty, the God of Israel, says: 'As my anger and wrath have
been poured out on those who lived in Jerusalem, so will my
wrath be poured out on you when you go to Egypt. You will
be an object of cursing and horror, of condemnation and
reproach; you will never see this place again.'

¹⁹"O remnant of Judah, the LORD has told you, 'Do not go
to Egypt.' Be sure of this: I warn you today ²⁰that you made a

fatal mistake when you sent me to the LORD your God and said, 'Pray to the LORD our God for us; tell us everything he says and we will do it.' ²¹I have told you today, but you still have not obeyed the LORD your God in all he sent me to tell you. ²²So now, be sure of this: You will die by the sword, famine and plague in the place where you want to go to settle."

⁴³:¹When Jeremiah finished telling the people all the words of the LORD their God—everything the LORD had sent him to tell them—²Azariah son of Hoshaiah and Johanan son of Kareah and all the arrogant men said to Jeremiah, "You are lying! The LORD our God has not sent you to say, 'You must not go to Egypt to settle there.' ³But Baruch son of Neriah is inciting you against us to hand us over to the Babylonians, so they may kill us or carry us into exile to Babylon."

⁴So Johanan son of Kareah and all the army officers and all the people disobeyed the LORD's command to stay in the land of Judah. ⁵Instead, Johanan son of Kareah and all the army officers led away all the remnant of Judah who had come back to live in the land of Judah from all the nations where they had been scattered. ⁶They also led away all the men, women and children and the king's daughters whom Nebuzaradan commander of the imperial guard had left with Gedaliah son of Ahikam, the son of Shaphan, and Jeremiah the prophet and Baruch son of Neriah. ⁷So they entered Egypt in disobedience to the LORD and went as far as Tahpanhes.

Original Meaning

THE PREVIOUS CHAPTER ended with the note that Johanan and company were worried about Babylonian reprisals for the death of Gedaliah and thus considered an escape to Egypt (41:17–18). The current section (42:1–43:7) narrates a discussion between Jeremiah and the group, which takes place over a ten-day period and eventuates in the flight to Egypt. Jeremiah offers both a prophetic oracle and his personal word against such a flight.

One of the mysteries of the narrative is the location of Jeremiah and Baruch at the time of the massacres at Mizpah. According to the last reference to Jeremiah in the narrative, he left the presence of Nebuzaradan in Jerusalem and went to Gedaliah at Mizpah (40:1–6). Most likely, Jeremiah placed himself under the administrative authority of Gedaliah. But before the treacherous murders perpetrated by Ishmael at Mizpah, he and Baruch have probably settled elsewhere. In any case, the meeting of Johanan and Jeremiah apparently takes place after the arrival of Johanan and company at Geruth Kimham near Bethlehem.[20] Through this account, we are given some context for the surprising fact that Jeremiah and Baruch eventually go to Egypt.

42:1–6. Should the remnant associated with Johanan (and until recently with Gedaliah) flee to Egypt or not? They seek the counsel of God through Jeremiah and promise obedience to the prophetic word. There is an implied self-curse in 42:5, should the company of Judeans not heed the Lord's instruction. Jeremiah agrees to seek counsel from the Lord and to tell them everything the Lord reveals.

42:7–22. Jeremiah's reply to the request of Johanan takes two forms. After ten days he begins with the preface, "This is what the LORD ... says," where the gist of the message is that God will preserve the remnant of Judeans if they stay in the land. In language associated with Jeremiah's call, God promises to build and to plant them in the land and there to protect them from the wrath of Nebuchadnezzar (42:10–12). Should they choose to disregard his word and to flee to Egypt, judgment will come on them there.

This indication of judgment should be read in light of 42:5, where the people ask that God be a "true and faithful witness" against them if they disobey his revealed word. Jeremiah adds his personal word to the group (42:19–22), indicating that a choice for Egypt means that they are self-deceived and will not escape judgment.

43:1–7. Members of the group accuse Jeremiah of lying to them and of engaging in a conspiracy with Baruch, who wants the group to stay in the land. Why Baruch might be an agent of subterfuge is not clear from their accusation. Their reaction to Jeremiah's prophetic oracle is similar to that of Zedekiah. The latter specifically asked Jeremiah for a word from the Lord, but when he didn't like what Jeremiah provided, he simply refused to obey.

The end result is that Johanan leads the group to Tahpanhes in Egypt. Jeremiah and Baruch are taken with them, but not willingly. Tahpanhes (cf. 2:16) is located in the eastern section of the Nile Delta. It is one of the first communities that a traveler from Palestine would encounter when approaching the Nile Delta from the east. As 44:1 makes clear, it was one of several cities in Egypt with a Judean population.

---

20. This is the only reference to Geruth Kimham in the Old Testament; nothing else is known about it. Possibly Jeremiah and Baruch went to the prophet's family property (cf. 32:1–15; 37:12). Another possibility is that Jeremiah and Baruch were living on property belonging to Baruch. Baruch came from a prominent scribal family. One supposes the family had significant property holdings.

THIS EXCHANGE BETWEEN the group and the prophet is one of the clearest examples in Jeremiah of an overt disobedience to God's revealed will. The conversation makes the issues relatively clear, if not ominous. The group wants to escape reprisal from the Babylonians. Jeremiah counsels them to be more attentive to what God has to say about their circumstances. Thus a primary reason to preserve the account is to explain the failure of and the judgment on the nation that continues among disobedient survivors of the Babylonian campaigns.

It is worth noting here that a decision to flee to Egypt likely seems the safer of the two choices, at least in appearance. Nebuchadnezzar would not take kindly to the assassination of his hand-picked governor, and there is every reason to expect reprisals in some form. Furthermore, Egypt is not (yet!) under the control of the Babylonians, so if Johanan and the group make it safely there, they may have some expectation of continued security from the Babylonians.

Both the group solicitation of Jeremiah and his prophetic reply to them are couched in the language of path and obedience. There is similarity in language and theme with the great sermons of Deuteronomy as well as with elements within Jeremiah's own previous utterances. Readers are invited, therefore, not just to take note of the "why" of the continuing tragedy but to see in the language of path and obedience a calling to make their own. Jeremiah is not unconcerned about prevailing circumstances. Rather, he places concern for the safety of the group in the larger context of listening to the guidance of the Lord and having the courage to follow it.

"NOT EVERYONE WHO says to me, 'Lord, Lord' ..." (Matt. 7:21–23; cf. Luke 6:46). It is difficult to talk about obedience in modern North America, whether in secular terms or as part of the life of discipleship. Our dominant culture is one of freedom of choice and avoiding lasting commitments; it also places a premium on "happiness" (whatever that might mean). In spite of these cultural traits, modern Christians should not understand obedience to God's revealed will as an irrelevant burden or needless constriction; obedience is the proper response needed to fulfill one's calling. In biblical terms obedience is virtually a synonym for the path of discipleship.

It is certainly easy to complain that we don't always know God's will and to offer that as a reason why we don't do something. One should not make light of the intellectual difficulties associated with discerning God's will, but it is more frequently the case that the hindrance to discipleship comes from moral sloth and failure to trust than from inability to discern at least the basics of a course of action.

A former teacher once said that truth is only known through commitment. What he meant is that the intellectual approach to God or the dialogical form of inquiry can be helpful, but personal commitment to God (and being known by God) is where the truth of God's sovereignty and goodness is revealed. What a tragedy that Jeremiah's companions could commit themselves in advance to following God's will, only to reject it when it did not suit their predilections.

Jeremiah 43:8–44:30

⁸IN TAHPANHES THE word of the LORD came to Jeremiah: ⁹"While the Jews are watching, take some large stones with you and bury them in clay in the brick pavement at the entrance to Pharaoh's palace in Tahpanhes. ¹⁰Then say to them, 'This is what the LORD Almighty, the God of Israel, says: I will send for my servant Nebuchadnezzar king of Babylon, and I will set his throne over these stones I have buried here; he will spread his royal canopy above them. ¹¹He will come and attack Egypt, bringing death to those destined for death, captivity to those destined for captivity, and the sword to those destined for the sword. ¹²He will set fire to the temples of the gods of Egypt; he will burn their temples and take their gods captive. As a shepherd wraps his garment around him, so will he wrap Egypt around himself and depart from there unscathed. ¹³There in the temple of the sun in Egypt he will demolish the sacred pillars and will burn down the temples of the gods of Egypt.'"

⁴⁴:¹This word came to Jeremiah concerning all the Jews living in Lower Egypt—in Migdol, Tahpanhes and Memphis—and in Upper Egypt: ²"This is what the LORD Almighty, the God of Israel, says: You saw the great disaster I brought on Jerusalem and on all the towns of Judah. Today they lie deserted and in ruins ³because of the evil they have done. They provoked me to anger by burning incense and by worshiping other gods that neither they nor you nor your fathers ever knew. ⁴Again and again I sent my servants the prophets, who said, 'Do not do this detestable thing that I hate!' ⁵But they did not listen or pay attention; they did not turn from their wickedness or stop burning incense to other gods. ⁶Therefore, my fierce anger was poured out; it raged against

the towns of Judah and the streets of Jerusalem and made them the desolate ruins they are today.

[7]"Now this is what the LORD God Almighty, the God of Israel, says: Why bring such great disaster on yourselves by cutting off from Judah the men and women, the children and infants, and so leave yourselves without a remnant? [8]Why provoke me to anger with what your hands have made, burning incense to other gods in Egypt, where you have come to live? You will destroy yourselves and make yourselves an object of cursing and reproach among all the nations on earth. [9]Have you forgotten the wickedness committed by your fathers and by the kings and queens of Judah and the wickedness committed by you and your wives in the land of Judah and the streets of Jerusalem? [10]To this day they have not humbled themselves or shown reverence, nor have they followed my law and the decrees I set before you and your fathers.

[11]"Therefore, this is what the LORD Almighty, the God of Israel, says: I am determined to bring disaster on you and to destroy all Judah. [12]I will take away the remnant of Judah who were determined to go to Egypt to settle there. They will all perish in Egypt; they will fall by the sword or die from famine. From the least to the greatest, they will die by sword or famine. They will become an object of cursing and horror, of condemnation and reproach. [13]I will punish those who live in Egypt with the sword, famine and plague, as I punished Jerusalem. [14]None of the remnant of Judah who have gone to live in Egypt will escape or survive to return to the land of Judah, to which they long to return and live; none will return except a few fugitives."

[15]Then all the men who knew that their wives were burning incense to other gods, along with all the women who were present—a large assembly—and all the people living in Lower and Upper Egypt, said to Jeremiah, [16]"We will not listen to the message you have spoken to us in the name of the LORD! [17]We will certainly do everything we said we would: We will burn incense to the Queen of Heaven and will pour out drink offerings to her just as we and our fathers, our kings and our officials did in the towns of Judah and in the streets of Jerusalem. At that time we had plenty of food and were well off and suffered no harm. [18]But ever since we stopped burning incense to the Queen of Heaven and pouring out drink offerings to her, we have had nothing and have been perishing by sword and famine."

¹⁹The women added, "When we burned incense to the Queen of Heaven and poured out drink offerings to her, did not our husbands know that we were making cakes like her image and pouring out drink offerings to her?"

²⁰Then Jeremiah said to all the people, both men and women, who were answering him, ²¹"Did not the LORD remember and think about the incense burned in the towns of Judah and the streets of Jerusalem by you and your fathers, your kings and your officials and the people of the land? ²²When the LORD could no longer endure your wicked actions and the detestable things you did, your land became an object of cursing and a desolate waste without inhabitants, as it is today. ²³Because you have burned incense and have sinned against the LORD and have not obeyed him or followed his law or his decrees or his stipulations, this disaster has come upon you, as you now see."

²⁴Then Jeremiah said to all the people, including the women, "Hear the word of the LORD, all you people of Judah in Egypt. ²⁵This is what the LORD Almighty, the God of Israel, says: You and your wives have shown by your actions what you promised when you said, 'We will certainly carry out the vows we made to burn incense and pour out drink offerings to the Queen of Heaven.'

"Go ahead then, do what you promised! Keep your vows! ²⁶But hear the word of the LORD, all Jews living in Egypt: 'I swear by my great name,' says the LORD, 'that no one from Judah living anywhere in Egypt will ever again invoke my name or swear, "As surely as the Sovereign LORD lives." ²⁷For I am watching over them for harm, not for good; the Jews in Egypt will perish by sword and famine until they are all destroyed. ²⁸Those who escape the sword and return to the land of Judah from Egypt will be very few. Then the whole remnant of Judah who came to live in Egypt will know whose word will stand—mine or theirs.

²⁹"'This will be the sign to you that I will punish you in this place,' declares the LORD, 'so that you will know that my threats of harm against you will surely stand.' ³⁰This is what the LORD says: 'I am going to hand Pharaoh Hophra king of Egypt over to his enemies who seek his life, just as I handed Zedekiah king of Judah over to Nebuchadnezzar king of Babylon, the enemy who was seeking his life.'"

THIS SECTION NARRATES the work of Jeremiah (and Baruch) in Egypt. They are taken by their Judean compatriots to Tahpanhes in the eastern Nile Delta. Although implicit, Jeremiah and Baruch have been forced to accompany the group. In Egypt Jeremiah performs a symbolic act in preparation for judgment to come and informs the Judeans there of his activities (43:8–13). Chapter 44 records Jeremiah's second judgmental prophecy against Judeans in Egypt (44:1–14), a reply on the part of his Judean audience (44:15–19), and then a third judgment speech of the prophet (44:20–30).

43:8–13. At God's initiative, Jeremiah takes some large stones and buries them in the courtyard of a government building in Tahpanhes. He explains this act by saying that God will grant his "servant Nebuchadnezzar" a seat over these stones when the Babylonian king spreads out his royal canopy. Jeremiah's prophetic depiction of Nebuchadnezzar's presence is an indication that Babylon will conquer Egypt. Moreover, judgment will come on those Judeans who think they have escaped the reach of the Babylonians by fleeing to Egypt.[21] The prophet also predicts that the Babylonians will set fire to temples in the land of Egypt and break the obelisks (standing stones) in the city of the sun, that is, Heliopolis, located just northeast of modern Cairo.

Readers may wonder what the local Egyptians thought about a Judean prophet burying stones in a public courtyard. The narrative, however, does not tell us. As the instructions to the prophet make clear, he is to take the stones and bury them while fellow Jews are watching. The symbolic act and accompanying oracle are intended as instruction for Jews, not Egyptians.

44:1–14. The bitter exchange between prophet and people in chapter 44 underscores the deep cultural and religious fissures in the Judean community. These verses are Jeremiah's prophetic invective against Judean people in Egypt.[22] They concentrate on Judean idolatry and syncretism, if not outright apostasy against their ancestral faith. Included is the (by now) familiar charge that God had sent prophets to warn them, yet their words of warning were rejected.

Verse 7 contains a rhetorical question: "Why bring such great disaster on yourselves?" The point is another one familiar to readers of the book: Acts have consequences; the idolatry and apostasy of Judeans in Egypt will have the same self-incurred consequences as did idolatry and apostasy in Judah.

---

21. In his thirty-seventh year as king (567) Nebuchadnezzar did conduct a successful campaign against Pharaoh Ahmosis II.

22. The places named in 44:1 are in different parts of Egyptian territory, indicating a comprehensive address to the Judeans in Egypt.

The prophet concludes with a statement that Judeans in Egypt seem not to have associated the fall of Judah and Jerusalem as judgment on their faithlessness to the Lord. As the following reply to the prophet makes clear, some have not made the connection.

44:15–19. The people's testy reply to the prophet's judgment speech—that they will indeed continue to worship the Queen of Heaven[23]—reflects two significant assumptions about religious practice on the part of Judeans. (1) Religion has the primary function of securing the health and safety of a group. (2) The worship of the Queen of Heaven was stopped earlier in Judah (by Josiah?) and subsequently resumed. The fortunes of the people, so they claim, have turned out better with her than with the Lord. "At that time we had plenty of food and were well off and suffered no harm" (v. 17). As a result, the Judeans in Egypt intend to maintain the worship of the Queen of Heaven as did their ancestors and their kings in Judah.

In particular, the Judean women reply that their worship of the Queen of Heaven was done with the acquiescence of their husbands (44:19). The crowd assembled with Jeremiah contains representatives from different communities in Egypt, women as well as men. Although Jeremiah's previous comments have not singled out either Judean women or worship of the Queen of Heaven, their role in her cult takes center stage as the example of idolatry[24] and apostasy. Perhaps the occasion for the prophet's challenge to the Judeans comes at a time of public ceremony or festival, when people gather for public ritual.

44:20–30. Jeremiah's reply to the people's resolve to commit apostasy is that judgment will come on them for their act of faithlessness toward the Lord. He judges implicitly their claim that things are better with the Queen of Heaven than with the Lord.

Jeremiah recognizes that his give-and-take with the crowd has set out both their resolve to remain worshipers of the Queen of Heaven and God's resolve that his word of judgment will come to pass. He predicts, therefore, that Pharaoh Hophra, the current ruler of Egypt, will be given over to the hands of his enemies as a sign of God's mastery of affairs, even in Egypt. In 569 B.C. Hophra was killed by one of his officials in a military coup.

---

23. Queen of Heaven is a title for a goddess. She is mentioned in 7:18 as a deity worshiped in Jerusalem. Just which goddess is a disputed question. The three primary candidates are Anat, Astarte, or Asherah—to cite Canaanite deities—or possibly Ishtar, the east Semitic goddess who was popular among the Assyrians and the whole region annexed by Babylon. To make matters even more complicated, it is possible that there was some fusion between Ishtar and Astarte (the names are similar in Semitic) or some fusion between the different Canaanite goddesses. The practices of baking cakes for a goddess has been identified in the worship of Ishtar. For further discussion, see M. Smith, *The Early History of God* (New York: Harper & Row, 1990), 88–94, 145.

24. Note the reference in v. 19 to making cakes in the image of the Queen of Heaven.

The prophet does identify a future for a Jewish remnant, a future in which the remnant will recognize whose word stands the test of time. Jeremiah predicts that it will be the word of the Lord that stands the test of time, not that of the Queen of Heaven and her worshipers.

BLINDNESS CONTINUES. The Judeans in Egypt exhibit a pattern of behavior similar to that of Judah and Jerusalem before the Babylonian siege and destruction; that is, they ignore the words of the prophet, God's servant. The consequences for them will be similar to those in Judah, thereby illustrating one of the larger themes of chapters 37–45. Unfortunately, spiritual blindness and political shortsightedness have not ceased among Judeans with the hammer blows of the Babylonians, and so the consequences of this blindness will be severe.

There is little in this section of the book about judgment that has not been said elsewhere in Jeremiah. It is as if the prophet is destined to face recalcitrance and intransigence among his Judean contemporaries all the days of his prophetic work. Readers should not despair over these somber reports, however. Some indeed take Jeremiah's words to heart, preserve them, and prepare for the future on the basis of their authority.

It is illuminating to compare Jeremiah's words to the Egyptian Judeans in chapter 44 with his word to Baruch in chapter 45. The prophet declares that there is no safe haven for Judean iniquity, even in Egypt and (temporarily) away from the reach of the Babylonians. For Baruch, by contrast, the promise is that wherever he goes, God is with him for protection.

In neither case should we read these prophecies and draw blanket conclusions for any situation—Babylon will not be the end of Judean existence in Egypt, nor does chapter 45 guarantee Baruch a blissful existence—but both judgment and promise tell us something fundamental about God. The Lord was (and remains) committed to the judgment of failure among his people as well as to the vindication of his servants. How these truths work themselves out in a given scenario will vary, but God's commitments do not.

Religion that works. Judean presumptions about the efficacy of religious activities dedicated to the Queen of Heaven have their counterparts among modern people. (1) There are people for whom influencing the divine world (however defined) is the paramount reason to engage in religious activities. Religion is "whatever works," rather than the worship and service of the one true God who spoke to Jeremiah and who was fully revealed in Christ. A similar form of religion is the "health and wealth" teaching that makes faith a work to guarantee personal health and material gain.

(2) Some modern interest has developed in goddess worship and spirituality as a way to supplement the worship of a so-called "patriarchal" God of the Bible. God, of course, may have "maternal" instincts (to use anthropopathic language) along with his "paternal" role, but the God of the Bible does not have a sexual identity. The newer interest among progressive Western religions for the feminine divine or goddess spirituality may be driven, in part, by a developing feminist consciousness. Even so, modern seeking for and worship of a goddess is essentially an update of the misplaced concerns of the Judean worshipers of the Queen of Heaven.

EXERCISING DESPERATE MANEUVERS. The somber words of Jeremiah are eloquent reminders of what life can be like when one is estranged from God and has little clue to the power of inherited corruption. Especially hard to deal with are those people who insist they know something about God; for them, being sent into exile (or whatever difficulty) cannot be his work. It would be nice (so human reflection might go) if we could discover the key to saving ourselves consistent with what we think we know about God. Perhaps (so human reflection might continue) the key to self-saving comes in recognizing a new religious impulse whereby the divine world is invoked for protection; perhaps the key lies in the advance of science to meet God; or perhaps the key lies in the flight from problems in the hope that they will not reach us where we have gone. All of these things are overtly a seeking of life, but the end result will be death.

Desperate people will do desperate things. On July 24, 1998, Russell Weston attempted to enter the United States Capitol building without going through the required metal detector. When met by a uniformed officer, he pulled out a pistol and shot the officer, inflicting a mortal wound. A brief gunfight ensued within the hallways of the Capitol in which a second officer was killed trying to stop Weston from advancing any farther. Both Weston and a tourist were wounded in the exchange, with Weston felled by multiple gunshot wounds from officers who returned his fire. Perhaps time and investigation will reveal the degrees to which Weston's senseless attack was precipitated by mental sickness, paranoia,[25] and anger. Apparently he wanted to make his point and fix what he thought was wrong about the government. Everyone acknowledges that his actions were disastrously wrong, even if he himself was too ill to grasp right from wrong.

Weston's sad case illustrates how often desperate maneuvers lead only to failure. Is he not ultimately a sad and twisted illustration of the human

---

25. Weston previously had been diagnosed as a paranoid schizophrenic.

propensity to go to any length to make a "point" and to "fix it" ourselves? Sadly for him (and for all of us), the only avenue of "fixing things" comes by accepting God's diagnosis of failure and his free gift of life.

In a related fashion, the modern movements toward worship of one or more goddesses may be motivated by true spiritual hunger. There is no reason to doubt that the Judeans' worship of the Queen of Heaven resulted from pressing spiritual needs. They simply looked in the wrong direction to meet those needs. In a similar manner the modern counterparts will be judged. The hunger is real, but so is the spiritual blindness that keeps people from seeing their true home with the Lord.

"The fear of the LORD is the beginning of knowledge" (Prov. 1:7). The pathway to life begins by acknowledging that every road leads to death except the one charted by God. Jeremiah's contemporaries in Egypt simply could not face the fact that they had been (and remained) part of a failed political and religious enterprise. Tragically, they were willing to do almost anything to hear from God: kidnap Jeremiah and Baruch, worship the Queen of Heaven, and so on. What they refused to do is to acknowledge their failure and depend on the God of grace, who can make all things new.

Jeremiah 45:1–4

¹THIS IS WHAT Jeremiah the prophet told Baruch son of Neriah in the fourth year of Jehoiakim son of Josiah king of Judah, after Baruch had written on a scroll the words Jeremiah was then dictating: ²"This is what the LORD, the God of Israel, says to you, Baruch: ³You said, 'Woe to me! The LORD has added sorrow to my pain; I am worn out with groaning and find no rest.'"

⁴The LORD said, "Say this to him: 'This is what the LORD says: I will overthrow what I have built and uproot what I have planted, throughout the land. ⁵Should you then seek great things for yourself? Seek them not. For I will bring disaster on all people, declares the LORD, but wherever you go I will let you escape with your life.'"

THE PROPHECY CONCERNING Baruch is out of place chronologically with the preceding chapters (chs. 37–44). Verse 1 provides a date in the fourth year of Jehoiakim (605 B.C.), which coincides with the command from the Lord in 36:1 for Jeremiah to prepare a scroll of his prophecies. The fallout over Baruch's reading from the scroll may have been an early occasion for public persecution of this scribe, who was Jeremiah's secretary and companion. According to 36:19, 26, Baruch was forced into hiding because of his reading of the scroll at the temple complex. After the fall of Jerusalem, the Judeans accused him of playing loose with the truth (43:3). Subsequently he and Jeremiah were taken to Egypt by a band of Judeans.

Why does this account come at the end of the description of the Egyptian sojourn of Jeremiah and Baruch? Some commentators suggest that the chronological citation in 45:1 is an error (inadvertent or otherwise) and that the assurance to Baruch that God will spare his life originated as a timely assurance during the tense period in Egypt. This solution is possible, but not satisfactory. Although the prophecy does follow the narratives about life in Egypt, there are no compelling text-critical reasons to remove or to overlook the chronological citation in 45:1. Readers should take seriously the setting of the oracle during the reign of Jehoiakim.

Other commentators agree that the account is an earlier statement, but they suggest it is repeated "literarily" in this context to inform readers that God does take care of his own. This is a more satisfactory reading. These words to and about Baruch owe their literary placement to their thematic and theological value as a divine confirmation that Baruch served God and would be enabled to perform his calling. Moreover, the placement of this prophecy as a conclusion to the narratives about life in Egypt serves to reinforce the claim that Baruch's presence in Egypt is not the result of God's disfavor. Thus, although neither prophet nor companion will escape the fate of the nation, God will vindicate them nevertheless.[26]

Baruch's "woe" (45:3) is a counterpart to the laments of Jeremiah. There is a cost to serving the Lord in times such as these—as Uriah (26:20–23) and Jeremiah discovered. The divine oracle to Baruch repeats the language of uprooting and tearing down used at Jeremiah's commission to the prophetic office (1:10). In the tragic affairs of Judah and Jerusalem, God has been at work to uproot and tear down. Baruch has no more "right" (to use modern Western language) than anyone else to expect that he will escape the consequences of corporate and historical judgment that have swept through the region.

In that light, all that can be said is that God calls Baruch to be faithful and that his personal safety resides with God. God promises him that his life has been granted to him "wherever" he might go. Readers are given no additional information about where his service to Jeremiah and to God may take him. His life is a gift, and he has been called to use it well.

---

26. The promise in 45:5 that Baruch will have his life as a prize of war is an idiom used for Ebed-Melech in 39:18. God the warrior (against his sinful people) is also the gracious deliverer of his servants.

INCARNATIONAL MINISTRY. The last word from Egypt in chapter 45 is actually a reminder of an earlier word of assurance. That word remained valid for Baruch wherever he went. Christian discipleship often requires people to identify with the circumstances in which God has placed them. If they do not commit themselves to the circumstances at hand, then it is possible that their looking ahead (usually a good thing) will keep them from exercising a discriminating witness in the present.

Not only is this a characteristic of discipleship; it is a form of incarnational ministry—to be there in person. Disciples are called to be salt and light wherever they are. Baruch's call as scribe and companion to Jeremiah put him in more than one precarious situation. There is nothing wrong with his cry of "woe," for such woeful circumstances were the common lot of the day as the tumult of Judean persecution and Babylonian conquest spread their tentacles. "Woe," while understandable, cannot be the last word of discipleship. God will have the last word in the evaluation of one's work and of one's fate. The last word (literarily) from Egypt, where Baruch and Jeremiah have gone and from whom we will not hear again, is a reminder of an earlier word of assurance. Just as God was watching over his word to fulfill it (1:12), so God is watching over Baruch. Like Ebed-Melech, Baruch has received his life as a gift, so that in return he may serve the Lord in difficult circumstances.

In the Bible Egypt is a strange place for God's people. Consider Abraham, Joseph, the Hebrew slaves, and Moses. Jeremiah offers judgment on Egypt (cf. 46:2–26) and the Judeans there. But his word should also be compared with that of Isaiah, who sees Egypt as a future blessing for the world (Isa. 19:23–25). In the New Testament the family of Jesus flees to Egypt as political refugees (Matt. 2:19–23). Egypt is not home to God's people, but a lot of formation for ministry is accomplished there, and God's resolve to bless comes from there.

SERVING IN EXILE. According to Coptic Church[27] tradition, Jeremiah and Baruch chose a spot to come and pray while in Egypt. It was the same place that Moses had used centuries earlier for the same purpose. Later, the holy family would utilize that same spot when they fled to Egypt to escape the wrath of Herod (cf. Matt. 2:13–15). This

---

27. The Coptic Church traces its heritage to St. Mark (the Gospel writer), who (according to tradition) came to Egypt in A.D. 45. Currently the Coptic Church is the largest group of Christians in Egypt, and they follow the monophysite wing of the church, dating from its earliest centuries. Monophysites are those Christians who believe that the earthly Jesus had but one nature (divine). As a minority group, Coptic Christians suffer periodic persecutions in Egypt and daily pressures of various kinds from their neighbors.

legendary tradition reveals a larger truth: God is a source of strength and encouragement to those serving "in exile."

Christians who feel isolated or depressed over their circumstances, who have been forced into unfamiliar territory, or who are caught up in destructive forces that overwhelm their lives are invited to measure their lives against a scriptural pattern including saints such as Abraham, Joseph, Moses, Jeremiah, and Baruch. Abraham made mistakes in Egypt. Joseph was unjustly imprisoned there. Moses committed murder there and struggled against Pharaoh and his minions to mobilize his people to leave. Jeremiah and Baruch were kidnapped and brought to Egypt.

None of these saints, however, lacked the attention of God, who remained faithful to them in times of upheaval. This did not cause their pain to go away. Their lives were gifts in service to the Lord in and through the difficulties. And through their difficulties God formed disciples. No wonder that the idiom for Baruch is that his life is a prize of war. It is certainly given to him in the midst of struggle.

In Baruch's case, he assisted in the formation of a book that now instructs us all. That is his greatest gift.

Jeremiah 46–51

❧

Introduction to Jeremiah 46–51

LIKE OTHER PROPHETIC BOOKS, Jeremiah contains a series of prophecies (or oracles) about other nations. And as with these other books,[1] Jeremiah's oracles are largely collected into one section (Jer. 46–51; cf. 25:19–26). The location of the collected oracles, however, is one of the biggest differences between the Hebrew and Greek versions of the book. In the Greek versions, the oracles against the nations come after 25:13.[2] Moreover, the order of the oracles differs somewhat between the versions. The Hebrew manuscripts begin with oracles against Egypt, while the Greek begins with the oracle against Elam.

English versions of the Bible generally follow the chapter arrangements of the Hebrew Bible (the Masoretic Text). This is not necessarily the earliest order of the oracles or placement in a Jeremiah book. Scholars cannot say with certainty what was the original order or placement in the larger collection. Indeed, that question is not nearly as important as that of the collection's contents. Possibly the prophet's oracles against the nations circulated in more than one order from an early time in their literary history.[3] In fact, most likely some of the oracles were given individually and only later assembled into a literary collection.

Scholars are divided over which institutions in ancient Israel fostered the public utterance of such prophecies and thereby helped shape their form and concerns. The two most prominent suggestions are cultic festivals, when communities gathered for worship, or councils assembled for war.[4] Both settings were locations where presentations about God's judgment or curses against evildoers would be made. Prophets and priests are naturally associated with cultic festivals as well as with the public decisions about going to war (cf. 1 Kings 22). In the case of Jeremiah 46–51, the oracles preserve almost nothing about their institutional setting(s). They sit like an appendix at the end of the book, preserving only a few clues as to their origin in the prophet's ministry.

---

1. See, e.g., Isa. 13–23; Ezek. 25–32; Amos 1–2.

2. Readers should consult ch. 25 for additional comments on the oracles against the nations.

3. See the first part of the introduction to Jeremiah, where there is additional discussion of the textual history of this book.

4. See R. E. Clements, *Prophecy and Tradition* (Atlanta: John Knox, 1975), 58–72, for a judicious discussion of the prophets and the nations. On Jeremiah's oracles about the nations in chs. 46–51, see D. Christensen, *Transformations of the War Oracles in Old Testament Prophecy: Studies in the Oracles Against the Nations* (Missoula, Mont.: Scholars, 1975), 183–280.

A handful of chronological indicators are preserved in the oracles. For example, 46:2 provides a date that prompted a prophecy against Egypt (605 B.C.), and 49:34 refers to a prophecy early in Zedekiah's reign (597 B.C.). Thus, what has been said about the book of Jeremiah as a whole also applies to the collection of the oracles about the nations: The prophecies were gathered over a period of time and were placed together because of their common focus on other peoples. They preserve much of their oral flavor but little of the life-settings in Jeremiah's ministry. As a published collection, they bear the marks of editing, such as brief introductory formulae and (apparently) some elaboration/updating in the final text.[5]

The purpose of the collection of oracles in Jeremiah 46–51 appears to be to preserve for posterity the prophet's words about God's judgment in the historical process. Martial language is replete throughout the oracles,[6] which depict God's wrath as operating through the warfare between neighboring states. Individually and as a collection, these oracles demonstrate the designation of Jeremiah as "a prophet to the nations" (1:5). They presuppose that God is the Lord of history and the moral Judge (and potential Deliverer) of all peoples.

These prophecies are not to be read as blueprints for international events to come in the late seventh/early sixth centuries B.C. any more than they are to be read as blueprints for the twenty-first century A.D. They do indicate elements of historical relations during Jeremiah's day, but more fundamentally they indicate God's resolve to judge idolatry, hubris, and cruelty through the historical process and his intention to use that same process to reveal his glory. In this regard the oracles about the nations function like the prophecies to Israel, Judah, and Jerusalem. They mediate judgment (actualized or to come) and, in some cases, indicate the possibilities of restoration and renewal.

Jeremiah's prophecies about other nations have within them some words addressed to or about God's people (e.g., 46:27–28; 50:4–5, 17–20; 51:5–10). Also, at the end of chapter 51 comes a prose account of instructions that Jeremiah gave to Seraiah, Baruch's brother, when Seraiah went to Babylon on a diplomatic mission (51:59–64). Seraiah was to take a scroll with written

---

5. Some examples of introductory formulae for reading include 46:2, 13; 47:1; and 49:34. The combination of poetry and prose and the length of the prophecies against Egypt and Moab suggest the editing of oral presentations. The oracles against Babylon in chs. 50–51 may have circulated separately (even in written form) before being joined with the others in chs. 46–49. There are also quotations or "echoes" of earlier prophetic material (cf. 49:18 with Zeph. 2:8–9; Jer. 49:27 with Amos 1:3–5).

6. There are references to "the sword" (e.g. 46:10; 47:6), bows and arrows (50:14), the war club (51:20), God's "arsenal" (50:25), and the proverbial "cup" of wrath (49:12).

prophecies about Babylon, tie a stone to the scroll, and then throw it in the Euphrates River as a sign that Babylon would sink like the weighted scroll.

Not only should the oracles about the nations in Jeremiah be read in conjunction with oracles about Judah and Jerusalem, but also the fate of the nations themselves cannot finally be separated from what God has in store for his covenant people. Judgment and deliverance alike belong to God. Indeed, judgment on the nations is mere preparation for the announcement of good news that will be spread among them by early Christians (see below).

The prophecies about the nations[7] come in the following sequence:

About Egypt	46:2–26
A word to God's people	46:27–28
About the Philistines	47:1–7
About Moab	48:1–47
About Ammon	49:1–6
About Edom	49:7–22
About Damascus	49:23–27
About Kedar (Arabs)	49:28–33
About Elam	49:34–39
About Babylon	50:1–51:64

A recent phenomenon from the Middle East may help modern readers understand the role of the oracles against neighbor states in Jeremiah 46–51. In 1990 hostilities broke out in the region when Iraq threatened and then invaded Kuwait. Eventually several Western nations were drawn into the fray in what became known as the Gulf War. The struggle between Kuwait and Iraq was carried out in more ways than through fighting or diplomatic wrangling. Both states also carried on a propaganda war by several means, including the hiring of bedouin poets who adapted classical Arabic verse on the radio to sting the opposition. The oracles or poems announced divine judgment on the enemy, and their authors used sarcasm and parody in order to belittle the opposition. The poets' efforts became popular radio programs, and both Kuwaiti and Iraqi poets competed for acclaim as the best in concocting such oracles. "Going public" with such oracles stated a case against the opponent and set them up for the predicted fall to come.

Jeremiah's oracles against neighbor states also adapted classical forms of Hebrew poetry used for oracles against nations since at least the time of

---

7. For information on the Egyptians, Philistines, Transjordanian states (Ammon, Moab, Edom), Damascus, Arabs (Kedar was an oasis where some Arabs had settlements), Elam, and Babylon, see A. J. Hoerth et al., ed., *Peoples of the Old Testament World* (Grand Rapids: Baker, 1994). Also helpful is King, *Jeremiah: An Archaeological Companion*, 45–63.

Amos. These oracles too announce divine judgment and use sarcasm to reveal the hubris and cruelty of the opponents. They are witnesses against injustice as well as advocates of justice to be meted out by God.

One of the striking things about these oracles in Jeremiah (and in the other prophetic books) is that they are primarily concerned with God's just judgment to come. They offer a vantage point of universal judgment on Gentiles (= nations) for such matters as their oppression of God's people or of their more general inhumanity in conduct. It is instructive to put this emphasis beside that of the New Testament when the latter addresses the fate of the nations. The New Testament documents have two major foci in this regard. (1) The nations will be judged by God and by the risen Christ. One sees this most clearly in Jesus' teaching, both in apocalyptic discourses (e.g., Matt. 24; Mark 13; Luke 21) and elsewhere (e.g., Matt. 25; Luke 10:1–15). The New Testament letters also reflect this conviction (e.g., 2 Peter 3:1–13; Rev. 19:11–21).

(2) The gospel of redemption through the death and resurrection of Christ is to be preached among the nations because Jew and Gentile alike are called to repent and to receive new life in Christ (e.g., Acts 3:17–26; Rom. 15:7–22; Rev. 5:9–10). In speaking about the gospel among the nations, the New Testament sometimes refers to the Old Testament promise that through Abraham's seed "all peoples on earth will be blessed" (Gen. 12:3) or that Israel is to be "a light for the Gentiles" (Isa. 49:6).[8]

By way of summary, the oracles against the nations in the Old Testament prophets are part of a larger biblical concern. They set up standards of judgment and express concern for justice and the need for repentance. The broader biblical concern for the salvation of the nations is predicated on their need for repentance and the gift of God's transforming grace.

Jeremiah 46:1–49:39

¹THIS IS THE WORD of the LORD that came to Jeremiah the prophet concerning the nations:

²Concerning Egypt:

This is the message against the army of Pharaoh Neco king of Egypt, which was defeated at Carchemish on the Euphrates River by Nebuchadnezzar king of Babylon in the fourth year of Jehoiakim son of Josiah king of Judah:

³"Prepare your shields, both large and small,
    and march out for battle!

---

8. Cf. Acts 3:24–26; 13:47–48; Gal. 3:8.

⁴Harness the horses,
   mount the steeds!
Take your positions
   with helmets on!
Polish your spears,
   put on your armor!
⁵What do I see?
   They are terrified,
they are retreating,
   their warriors are defeated.
They flee in haste
   without looking back,
   and there is terror on every side,"

                              declares the LORD.

⁶"The swift cannot flee
   nor the strong escape.
In the north by the River Euphrates
   they stumble and fall.
⁷"Who is this that rises like the Nile,
   like rivers of surging waters?
⁸Egypt rises like the Nile,
   like rivers of surging waters.
She says, 'I will rise and cover the earth;
   I will destroy cities and their people.'
⁹Charge, O horses!
   Drive furiously, O charioteers!
March on, O warriors—
   men of Cush and Put who carry shields,
   men of Lydia who draw the bow.
¹⁰But that day belongs to the Lord, the LORD Almighty—
   a day of vengeance, for vengeance on his foes.
The sword will devour till it is satisfied,
   till it has quenched its thirst with blood.
For the Lord, the LORD Almighty, will offer sacrifice
   in the land of the north by the River Euphrates.
¹¹"Go up to Gilead and get balm,
   O Virgin Daughter of Egypt.
But you multiply remedies in vain;
   there is no healing for you.
¹²The nations will hear of your shame;
   your cries will fill the earth.

One warrior will stumble over another;
    both will fall down together."

¹³This is the message the LORD spoke to Jeremiah the prophet about the coming of Nebuchadnezzar king of Babylon to attack Egypt:

¹⁴"Announce this in Egypt, and proclaim it in Migdol;
    proclaim it also in Memphis and Tahpanhes:
'Take your positions and get ready,
    for the sword devours those around you.'
¹⁵Why will your warriors be laid low?
    They cannot stand, for the LORD will push them down.
¹⁶They will stumble repeatedly;
    they will fall over each other.
They will say, 'Get up, let us go back
    to our own people and our native lands,
    away from the sword of the oppressor.'
¹⁷There they will exclaim,
    'Pharaoh king of Egypt is only a loud noise;
    he has missed his opportunity.'

¹⁸"As surely as I live," declares the King,
    whose name is the LORD Almighty,
"one will come who is like Tabor among the mountains,
    like Carmel by the sea.
¹⁹Pack your belongings for exile,
    you who live in Egypt,
for Memphis will be laid waste
    and lie in ruins without inhabitant.

²⁰"Egypt is a beautiful heifer,
    but a gadfly is coming
    against her from the north.
²¹The mercenaries in her ranks
    are like fattened calves.
They too will turn and flee together,
    they will not stand their ground,
for the day of disaster is coming upon them,
    the time for them to be punished.
²²Egypt will hiss like a fleeing serpent
    as the enemy advances in force;
they will come against her with axes,
    like men who cut down trees.

²³ They will chop down her forest,"

declares the LORD,

"dense though it be.
They are more numerous than locusts,
they cannot be counted.
²⁴ The Daughter of Egypt will be put to shame,
handed over to the people of the north."

²⁵ The LORD Almighty, the God of Israel, says: "I am about to bring punishment on Amon god of Thebes, on Pharaoh, on Egypt and her gods and her kings, and on those who rely on Pharaoh. ²⁶ I will hand them over to those who seek their lives, to Nebuchadnezzar king of Babylon and his officers. Later, however, Egypt will be inhabited as in times past," declares the LORD.

²⁷ "Do not fear, O Jacob my servant;
do not be dismayed, O Israel.
I will surely save you out of a distant place,
your descendants from the land of their exile.
Jacob will again have peace and security,
and no one will make him afraid.
²⁸ Do not fear, O Jacob my servant,
for I am with you," declares the LORD.
"Though I completely destroy all the nations
among which I scatter you,
I will not completely destroy you.
I will discipline you but only with justice;
I will not let you go entirely unpunished."

⁴⁷:¹ This is the word of the LORD that came to Jeremiah the prophet concerning the Philistines before Pharaoh attacked Gaza:

² This is what the LORD says:

"See how the waters are rising in the north;
they will become an overflowing torrent.
They will overflow the land and everything in it,
the towns and those who live in them.
The people will cry out;
all who dwell in the land will wail
³ at the sound of the hoofs of galloping steeds,
at the noise of enemy chariots
and the rumble of their wheels.
Fathers will not turn to help their children;
their hands will hang limp.

⁴For the day has come
    to destroy all the Philistines
 and to cut off all survivors
    who could help Tyre and Sidon.
 The LORD is about to destroy the Philistines,
    the remnant from the coasts of Caphtor.
⁵Gaza will shave her head in mourning;
    Ashkelon will be silenced.
 O remnant on the plain,
    how long will you cut yourselves?
⁶"'Ah, sword of the LORD,' you cry,
    'how long till you rest?
 Return to your scabbard;
    cease and be still.'
⁷But how can it rest
    when the LORD has commanded it,
 when he has ordered it
    to attack Ashkelon and the coast?"

⁴⁸:¹Concerning Moab:

This is what the LORD Almighty, the God of Israel, says:

 "Woe to Nebo, for it will be ruined.
    Kiriathaim will be disgraced and captured;
    the stronghold will be disgraced and shattered.
²Moab will be praised no more;
    in Heshbon men will plot her downfall:
    'Come, let us put an end to that nation.'
 You too, O Madmen, will be silenced;
    the sword will pursue you.
³Listen to the cries from Horonaim,
    cries of great havoc and destruction.
⁴Moab will be broken;
    her little ones will cry out.
⁵They go up the way to Luhith,
    weeping bitterly as they go;
 on the road down to Horonaim
    anguished cries over the destruction are heard.
⁶Flee! Run for your lives;
    become like a bush in the desert.
⁷Since you trust in your deeds and riches,
    you too will be taken captive,

and Chemosh will go into exile,
    together with his priests and officials.
[8] The destroyer will come against every town,
    and not a town will escape.
The valley will be ruined
    and the plateau destroyed,
    because the LORD has spoken.
[9] Put salt on Moab,
    for she will be laid waste;
her towns will become desolate,
    with no one to live in them.
[10] "A curse on him who is lax in doing the LORD's work!
    A curse on him who keeps his sword from bloodshed!

[11] "Moab has been at rest from youth,
    like wine left on its dregs,
not poured from one jar to another—
    she has not gone into exile.
So she tastes as she did,
    and her aroma is unchanged.
[12] But days are coming,"
    declares the LORD,
"when I will send men who pour from jars,
    and they will pour her out;
they will empty her jars
    and smash her jugs.
[13] Then Moab will be ashamed of Chemosh,
    as the house of Israel was ashamed
    when they trusted in Bethel.

[14] "How can you say, 'We are warriors,
    men valiant in battle'?
[15] Moab will be destroyed and her towns invaded;
    her finest young men will go down in the slaughter,"
    declares the King, whose name is the LORD Almighty.
[16] "The fall of Moab is at hand;
    her calamity will come quickly.
[17] Mourn for her, all who live around her,
    all who know her fame;
say, 'How broken is the mighty scepter,
    how broken the glorious staff!'

[18] "Come down from your glory
    and sit on the parched ground,
    O inhabitants of the Daughter of Dibon,

for he who destroys Moab
      will come up against you
      and ruin your fortified cities.
¹⁹ Stand by the road and watch,
      you who live in Aroer.
   Ask the man fleeing and the woman escaping,
      ask them, 'What has happened?'
²⁰ Moab is disgraced, for she is shattered.
      Wail and cry out!
   Announce by the Arnon
      that Moab is destroyed.
²¹ Judgment has come to the plateau—
      to Holon, Jahzah and Mephaath,
²²   to Dibon, Nebo and Beth Diblathaim,
²³   to Kiriathaim, Beth Gamul and Beth Meon,
²⁴   to Kerioth and Bozrah—
      to all the towns of Moab, far and near.
²⁵ Moab's horn is cut off;
      her arm is broken,"

                              declares the LORD.

²⁶ "Make her drunk,
      for she has defied the LORD.
   Let Moab wallow in her vomit;
      let her be an object of ridicule.
²⁷ Was not Israel the object of your ridicule?
      Was she caught among thieves,
   that you shake your head in scorn
      whenever you speak of her?
²⁸ Abandon your towns and dwell among the rocks,
      you who live in Moab.
   Be like a dove that makes its nest
      at the mouth of a cave.

²⁹ "We have heard of Moab's pride—
      her overweening pride and conceit,
   her pride and arrogance
      and the haughtiness of her heart.
³⁰ I know her insolence but it is futile,"

                              declares the LORD,

   "and her boasts accomplish nothing.
³¹ Therefore I wail over Moab,
      for all Moab I cry out,
      I moan for the men of Kir Hareseth.

³²I weep for you, as Jazer weeps,
O vines of Sibmah.
Your branches spread as far as the sea;
they reached as far as the sea of Jazer.
The destroyer has fallen
on your ripened fruit and grapes.
³³Joy and gladness are gone
from the orchards and fields of Moab.
I have stopped the flow of wine from the presses;
no one treads them with shouts of joy.
Although there are shouts,
they are not shouts of joy.

³⁴"The sound of their cry rises
from Heshbon to Elealeh and Jahaz,
from Zoar as far as Horonaim and Eglath Shelishiyah,
for even the waters of Nimrim are dried up.
³⁵In Moab I will put an end
to those who make offerings on the high places
and burn incense to their gods,"

declares the LORD.
³⁶"So my heart laments for Moab like a flute;
it laments like a flute for the men of Kir Hareseth.
The wealth they acquired is gone.
³⁷Every head is shaved
and every beard cut off;
every hand is slashed
and every waist is covered with sackcloth.
³⁸On all the roofs in Moab
and in the public squares
there is nothing but mourning,
for I have broken Moab
like a jar that no one wants,"

declares the LORD.
³⁹"How shattered she is! How they wail!
How Moab turns her back in shame!
Moab has become an object of ridicule,
an object of horror to all those around her."

⁴⁰This is what the LORD says:

"Look! An eagle is swooping down,
spreading its wings over Moab.

⁴¹Kerioth will be captured
    and the strongholds taken.
  In that day the hearts of Moab's warriors
    will be like the heart of a woman in labor.
⁴²Moab will be destroyed as a nation
    because she defied the LORD.
⁴³Terror and pit and snare await you,
    O people of Moab,"

declares the LORD.

⁴⁴"Whoever flees from the terror
    will fall into a pit,
  whoever climbs out of the pit
    will be caught in a snare;
  for I will bring upon Moab
    the year of her punishment,"

declares the LORD.

⁴⁵"In the shadow of Heshbon
    the fugitives stand helpless,
  for a fire has gone out from Heshbon,
    a blaze from the midst of Sihon;
  it burns the foreheads of Moab,
    the skulls of the noisy boasters.
⁴⁶Woe to you, O Moab!
    The people of Chemosh are destroyed;
  your sons are taken into exile
    and your daughters into captivity.

⁴⁷"Yet I will restore the fortunes of Moab
in days to come,"

declares the LORD.

Here ends the judgment on Moab.

^{49:1}Concerning the Ammonites:

This is what the LORD says:

  "Has Israel no sons?
    Has she no heirs?
  Why then has Molech taken possession of Gad?
    Why do his people live in its towns?
  ²But the days are coming,"
    declares the LORD,

"when I will sound the battle cry
    against Rabbah of the Ammonites;
it will become a mound of ruins,
    and its surrounding villages will be set on fire.
Then Israel will drive out
    those who drove her out,"

                says the LORD.

³ "Wail, O Heshbon, for Ai is destroyed!
    Cry out, O inhabitants of Rabbah!
Put on sackcloth and mourn;
    rush here and there inside the walls,
for Molech will go into exile,
    together with his priests and officials.
⁴ Why do you boast of your valleys,
    boast of your valleys so fruitful?
O unfaithful daughter,
    you trust in your riches and say,
    'Who will attack me?'
⁵   I will bring terror on you
    from all those around you,"

            declares the Lord, the LORD Almighty.

"Every one of you will be driven away,
    and no one will gather the fugitives.

⁶ "Yet afterward, I will restore the fortunes of the Ammonites,"

               declares the LORD.

⁷ Concerning Edom:

This is what the LORD Almighty says:

"Is there no longer wisdom in Teman?
    Has counsel perished from the prudent?
    Has their wisdom decayed?
⁸ Turn and flee, hide in deep caves,
    you who live in Dedan,
for I will bring disaster on Esau
    at the time I punish him.
⁹ If grape pickers came to you,
    would they not leave a few grapes?
If thieves came during the night,
    would they not steal only as much as they wanted?
¹⁰ But I will strip Esau bare;
    I will uncover his hiding places,

    so that he cannot conceal himself.
  His children, relatives and neighbors will perish,
    and he will be no more.
¹¹Leave your orphans; I will protect their lives.
  Your widows too can trust in me."

¹²This is what the LORD says: "If those who do not deserve to drink the cup must drink it, why should you go unpunished? You will not go unpunished, but must drink it. ¹³I swear by myself," declares the LORD, "that Bozrah will become a ruin and an object of horror, of reproach and of cursing; and all its towns will be in ruins forever."

¹⁴I have heard a message from the LORD:
    An envoy was sent to the nations to say,
  "Assemble yourselves to attack it!
    Rise up for battle!"
¹⁵"Now I will make you small among the nations,
    despised among men.
¹⁶The terror you inspire
    and the pride of your heart have deceived you,
  you who live in the clefts of the rocks,
    who occupy the heights of the hill.
  Though you build your nest as high as the eagle's,
    from there I will bring you down,"
                declares the LORD.
¹⁷"Edom will become an object of horror;
    all who pass by will be appalled and will scoff
    because of all its wounds.
¹⁸As Sodom and Gomorrah were overthrown,
    along with their neighboring towns,"
             says the LORD,
  "so no one will live there;
    no man will dwell in it.
¹⁹"Like a lion coming up from Jordan's thickets
    to a rich pastureland,
  I will chase Edom from its land in an instant.
    Who is the chosen one I will appoint for this?
  Who is like me and who can challenge me?
    And what shepherd can stand against me?"
²⁰Therefore, hear what the LORD has planned against Edom,
    what he has purposed against those who live in Teman:

The young of the flock will be dragged away;
he will completely destroy their pasture because of them.
²¹ At the sound of their fall the earth will tremble;
their cry will resound to the Red Sea.
²² Look! An eagle will soar and swoop down,
spreading its wings over Bozrah.
In that day the hearts of Edom's warriors
will be like the heart of a woman in labor.

²³Concerning Damascus:

"Hamath and Arpad are dismayed,
for they have heard bad news.
They are disheartened,
troubled like the restless sea.
²⁴ Damascus has become feeble,
she has turned to flee
and panic has gripped her;
anguish and pain have seized her,
pain like that of a woman in labor.
²⁵ Why has the city of renown not been abandoned,
the town in which I delight?
²⁶ Surely, her young men will fall in the streets;
all her soldiers will be silenced in that day,"

declares the LORD Almighty.
²⁷"I will set fire to the walls of Damascus;
it will consume the fortresses of Ben-Hadad."

²⁸Concerning Kedar and the kingdoms of Hazor, which
Nebuchadnezzar king of Babylon attacked:

This is what the LORD says:

"Arise, and attack Kedar
and destroy the people of the East.
²⁹ Their tents and their flocks will be taken;
their shelters will be carried off
with all their goods and camels.
Men will shout to them,
'Terror on every side!'
³⁰"Flee quickly away!
Stay in deep caves, you who live in Hazor,"

declares the LORD.

"Nebuchadnezzar king of Babylon has plotted against you;
    he has devised a plan against you.

³¹ "Arise and attack a nation at ease,
    which lives in confidence,"

                        declares the LORD,

"a nation that has neither gates nor bars;
    its people live alone.
³² Their camels will become plunder,
    and their large herds will be booty.
I will scatter to the winds those who are in distant places
    and will bring disaster on them from every side,"

                        declares the LORD.

³³ "Hazor will become a haunt of jackals,
    a desolate place forever.
No one will live there;
    no man will dwell in it."

³⁴ This is the word of the LORD that came to Jeremiah the prophet concerning Elam, early in the reign of Zedekiah king of Judah:

³⁵ This is what the LORD Almighty says:

"See, I will break the bow of Elam,
    the mainstay of their might.
³⁶ I will bring against Elam the four winds
    from the four quarters of the heavens;
I will scatter them to the four winds,
    and there will not be a nation
    where Elam's exiles do not go.
³⁷ I will shatter Elam before their foes,
    before those who seek their lives;
I will bring disaster upon them,
    even my fierce anger,"

                        declares the LORD.

"I will pursue them with the sword
    until I have made an end of them.
³⁸ I will set my throne in Elam
    and destroy her king and officials,"

                        declares the LORD.

³⁹ "Yet I will restore the fortunes of Elam
    in days to come,"

                        declares the LORD.

46:1.[9] THERE ARE two prophecies against Egypt:[10] 46:2–12 and 46:14–26. Only the first one is dated. The fourth year of Jehoiakim was 605 B.C., the year of the fateful battle at Carchemish (in northern Syria) between the forces of Pharaoh Neco and of Nebuchadnezzar (mentioned explicitly in 46:26). The Egyptians were routed, and Babylon began the process of claiming hegemony over the states in the eastern Mediterranean. Egyptian demise is predicted as part of the judgment in the historical process but not the end of the Egyptians themselves.

46:2–12. This oracle is directed to the army of Pharaoh Neco. In 609 B.C. Pharaoh's army had marched from Egypt toward Syria in order to join forces with the remnants of the Assyrian army and to oppose the emerging power of Babylon. At that time Josiah had attempted to head off the Egyptian army at Megiddo and was mortally wounded in the unsuccessful effort to thwart the Egyptian advance (2 Kings 23:29–30; 2 Chron. 35:20–24).

As noted above, the date of this oracle against the Egyptian army is the fourth year of Jehoiakim (605 B.C.). Jehoiakim was the Egyptian choice among Josiah's sons to follow his father in rule. The martial language of the oracle depicts elements of the Egyptian army preparing to fight and then fleeing in terror. Furthermore, the boastful pride of the Egyptians is described in imperialistic terms (v. 8), only to be reversed by divine judgment on a day that "belongs to the LORD" (v. 10). It is a day of vengeance to be directed against the Lord's foes, of which Egypt is one. In fact, the language of judgment on that decisive day is described in sacrificial terms.

Egypt is also described in familial terms as "Virgin Daughter" (v. 11). She who seeks a balm in Gilead will find that there is no healing for her.

46:13–26. Verse 13 is a prose introduction to the prophecy that follows. Unlike the companion oracle in 46:2–12, this prophecy is undated. Nebuchadnezzar did not invade Egypt until 570 B.C., late in his reign, but there were periodic encounters of various kinds between Egypt and Babylon throughout Jeremiah's lifetime. Essentially the prophecy announces that Babylon will work God's judgment on Egypt. At a basic interpretive level, such a claim is little different from those Jeremiah directed at Judah. In both instances Babylon and Nebuchadnezzar serve as the rod of historical judgment used by the Lord.

The disastrous event is a day in the future (v. 21). For some in Egypt it will be defeat and exile. As in the previous oracle, Egypt is personified as a female

---

9. See the introduction to Jeremiah for discussion of historical references. A thorough treatment of the oracles in chs. 46–49 can be found in B. Huwyler, *Jeremia und die Völker: Untersuchungen zu den Völkerrsprüchen in Jeremia 46–49* (Tübingen: Mohr Siebeck, 1997).

10. Cf. Isa. 19:1–25; Ezek. 29–30, 32.

("Daughter ... Egypt," v. 24),[11] who will be put to shame by a people from the north. Part of the judgment to come is directed at Amon, one of the Egyptian deities (v. 25). Judgment, however, is not the end of Egypt as a nation; it will again be inhabited (v. 26).

46:27–28. Following the oracles against Egypt is a prediction of the restoration of God's people. Those on whom God's judgment has fallen have been disciplined justly, but in his mercy God will not make an end of them. Correspondingly, those whom God used to discipline his people (such as the Egyptians) will suffer the fate of those whose hubris, cruelty, and idolatry have kept them from acknowledging the work of God.

47:1–7. The Philistines[12] lived in some of the cities on the coast of Palestine. They had been neighbors and often enemies of Judah since the days of the judges. They were immigrants to the area, having come from some of the Aegean islands and southwestern Turkey in the twelfth century B.C.

Two Philistine cities are named here: Gaza and Ashkelon. The occasion for the oracle against the Philistines possibly comes with Nebuchadnezzar's preparations to attack Gaza (cf. v. 2, "waters ... rising in the north"). No extrabiblical records survive of a Babylonian attack on Gaza, but it is completely understandable that the Babylonians either fought against Gaza and subdued it or received the city's surrender. Gaza was a trading center and an important point of contact between Egypt, the states immediately to the north and east (e.g., Judah, Moab), and the Arab tribes from Sinai and the fringes of sedentary existence.

The assault in question could have been perpetrated by the Egyptians between 609 B.C., when Necho moved from Egypt to north Syria and 605, when the Egyptians were defeated at Carchemish. A first reading of 47:1 refers explicitly to an attack by an unnamed Pharaoh. There are two problems with this interpretation, although neither are insurmountable: (1) The Greek version of this verse omits the reference to the Pharaoh; (2) there is no record of an Egyptian attack on Gaza or Ashkelon in the period 609 and later. According to Herodotus (*Histories* 2.157) the Pharaoh before Necho did attack the Philistine city of Ashdod at some point before 610 B.C. At the present state of knowledge, therefore, it is difficult to place this oracle in a specific historical context, but there are several plausible options because of frequent military actions in the region.

In form and vocabulary, the oracle against the Philistines is similar to the preceding oracles against Egypt. The Philistines will be defeated on some

---

11. In v. 24 the NIV translates the Hebrew idiom as "Daughter *of* Egypt." Although this is grammatically permissible, it seems more likely that Egypt itself is being personified, rather than something (e.g., a city) about the nation.

12. Cf. Ezek. 25:15–17; Amos 1:6–8.

future day (v. 4). People will mourn for Gaza and Ashkelon. God's historical judgment is personified through a poetic address to his sword (v. 6).

48:1–25. The Moabites[13] receive an extensive address in 48:1–47 that preserves a significant knowledge of geography. Over twenty different cities (settlements) are named in the poetic indictment of Judah's eastern neighbor. Moab occupied much of the tableland east of the Dead Sea. According to Genesis 19:30–38, a drunken Lot slept with his two daughters, and as a result they bore Moab and Ben-Ammi.[14] The child named Moab is the ancestor of the Moabite people. Thus the Moabites and Israelites were distant relatives. Later, David's family was related to the Moabites through Ruth, his great-grandmother (Ruth 4:13–22). Solomon married a Moabite princess and built for her a temple to Chemosh, the chief Moabite deity, on the hill east of the temple mount in Jerusalem (1 Kings 11:7).

The repetition of a concluding prophetic formula ("declares the LORD") in 48:25, 30, 35, 38, 43, 44, 47 suggests that more than one prophetic announcement has been collected in Jeremiah 48. Correspondingly, Isaiah 15–16 has lengthy prophecies against Moab, from which some of this material in Jeremiah has been derived and elaborated upon.

Apart from 48:1a and the last phrase of verse 25, this long section does not have introductory or concluding formulae to break up the sequence of verses. It is possible that 48:1b–25 is a single unit of speech, offering mourning language, prediction of judgment and exile, and sarcasm in poetry, all designed to humiliate Moab.

Verse 7 mentions Chemosh. One way to refer to Moab was to call them "the people of Chemosh" (Num. 21:29). He, like his people, will suffer defeat and go into exile. In the future Moab will be ashamed of Chemosh, just as Israel was ashamed when trusting Bethel (v. 13). The name "Bethel" here likely refers to a deity rather than a place. He is known from Assyrian, Babylonian, and Jewish sources.[15]

Some of the judgment language in this section is frightful. There are references to salt (v. 9), an agent that ruins agricultural products, and to curses (v. 10) on whoever is lax in doing the Lord's work of execution. As with Egypt and Judah, Jeremiah uses familial language for Moab as a daughter

---

13. Cf. Isa. 15–16; Ezek. 25:8–11; Amos 2:1–3; Zeph. 2:8–11; and B. Jones, *Howling Over Moab: Irony and Rhetoric in Isaiah 15–16* (Atlanta: Scholars Press, 1996).

14. Lot is the nephew of Abraham. The strange episode of Gen. 19:30–38 comes in the aftermath of God's destruction of Sodom (where Lot and his family were living) and the death of Lot's wife. His daughters were motivated by concern for the continuation of the family and used the occasion of their father's drunkenness to become pregnant.

15. For convenient references to texts, see the discussion in Holladay, *Jeremiah*, 2:358; and W. Röllig, "Bethel," in *Dictionary of Deities and Demons in the Bible*, ed. K. van der Toorn (Leiden: Brill, 1999), 173–75.

(NIV has "Daughter of Dibon"). Her cities will be ruined, and she will wail a funeral lament. Even physical mutilation is mentioned. Moab's "horn," a metaphor for strength, will be cut off and her arm broken.

48:26–47. These prophecies continue the depiction of Moab's humiliation and degradation. As with the previous oracle, the language is graphic. Moab will wallow in vomit (v. 26), cries of dereliction will be heard (vv. 34, 38), fire will scorch the country (v. 45), and the children of the nation will be taken into exile (v. 46).

So moved is the prophet by the intensity of depicting Moab's downfall that he portrays himself in mourning (vv. 31–32). The historical agent of all this destruction is not named explicitly (see comments below). Moab will be judged because "she defied the LORD" (v. 42).

The last line of these intricate poetic prophecies is one of restoration: God "will restore the fortunes of Moab in days to come" (v. 47). This is the same phrase God uses elsewhere in predicting the restoration of Israel.[16]

49:1–6. The oracle against the Ammonites[17] is much briefer than the one against Moab. According to Genesis 19:30–38, Ben-Ammi, the ancestor of the Ammonites, was the incestuous son of Lot. The country of Ammon is located immediately north of Moab and east of the Jordan River. Ammon's chief deity was Milcom. Solomon married an Ammonite princess and built a temple for its worship on the hill east of the temple mount in Jerusalem (1 Kings 11:7). Baalis, king of Ammon at the time of Jerusalem's fall, plotted with Ishmael to murder Gedaliah, the Judean governor appointed by the Babylonians (Jer. 40–41).

Rabbah is the capital city of Ammon. Its remains form part of the impressive citadel at the heart of modern day Amman, Jordan. The judgment to come on Ammon is depicted as defeat and exile. No biblical or Babylonian accounts exist to document an official defeat of Ammon (or Moab), but both states fell under the control of Babylon.[18]

In verses 1 and 3 the NIV refers to "Molech" as having taken possession of Gad and then being sent into exile with his priests and officials. Elsewhere in Jeremiah, Molech is the name of the deity to whom child sacrifices are offered in Judah (32:35; cf. Lev. 20:2–5; 2 Kings 23:10). The NIV translators

---

16. Deut. 30:3; Jer. 29:14; 30:18; 31:23; 32:44; 33:7. It is also used to describe the restoration of Ammon in Jer. 49:6.

17. Cf. Ezek. 25:1–7; Amos 1:13–15; Zeph. 2:8–11.

18. The first-century Jewish historian Josephus (*Ant.* 10.9.7) preserves an account that has the Babylonians campaigning in Transjordan after the defeat of Judah in 582 B.C. Perhaps this campaign is also the occasion for a third group of exiles taken to Babylon (cf. Jer. 52:28–30). Most certainly the Ammonites should expect reprisals for their role in the murder of Gedaliah.

have rendered the Hebrew term *malkam* (lit., "their king") in 49:1, 3 as Molech, based on the reference to Molech as the Ammonite deity in 1 Kings 11:7 (but cf. NIV note). This seemingly logical move, however, concerns a complicated matter over which considerable uncertainty remains.

As a name, Molech is a polemical hybrid because it combines the consonants of the word king (*m-l-k*) with the vowels from the word "shame." Molech and Milcom have the same consonants. In comparing the biblical references to Molech, it is not clear whether Milcom is the same deity as Molech. Jeremiah also refers to the deity of child sacrifice as Baal (19:5). In brief, the Hebrew term *malkam* in 49:1, 3 can be rendered "their king," "Milcom," or (by inference from 1 Kings 11:7) "Molech."[19]

As with Moab (with whom the Ammonites are sometimes linked), the Lord promises to restore the fortunes of Ammon.[20]

49:7–22. Edom[21] lies south of Moab in a high and remote region of Transjordan. It too will fall in judgment. Like Ammon and Moab, the Edomites are related to God's people—in their case, through Esau (Gen. 36). Esau is mentioned explicitly in Jeremiah 49:8, 10 as a synonym for Edom. The bitterness reflected in the relationship between Jacob and Esau was reflected later in the relationship between Judah and Edom in the days of Jeremiah and into the postexilic period. According to the lamentation of Psalm 137:7, Edom gleefully celebrated the fall of Jerusalem. A main goal of the short prophetic book of Obadiah is the announcement of judgment on Edom (cf. Mal. 1:2–5). Unlike the prophecies to Moab and Ammon, Jeremiah makes no reference to Edom's restoration.[22]

The polemic against Edom begins with a reference to wisdom. Those who lived east of Palestine were celebrated as wise (cf. Job 1:3). Jeremiah's polemic against the Edomites depicts its day of judgment as the loss or failure of its wisdom. The region of Dedan (v. 8) is in the Arabian desert, but its inhabitants were linked with Edom through trade.

Bozrah (vv. 13, 22) is the capital city of Edom. Its ruins are located near the modern Jordanian village of Buseirah. Bozrah will drink the cup of wrath.[23]

---

19. For further discussion see E. Puech, "Milcom," in *Dictionary of Deities and Demons in the Bible*, 575–76; also G. Heider, "Molech," in *Dictionary of Deities and Demons in the Bible*, 581–85.

20. Relationships between Israel/Judah and their eastern "cousins" were rocky at times. According to 2 Kings 24:2, both Ammon and Moab raided Judean territory in the last days of the Judean state.

21. Cf. Isa. 21:11–12; Ezek. 25:12–14; 35:1–15; Amos 1:11–12.

22. Nevertheless, in Amos 9:11–12 Edom is named as a nation that bears God's name and that will be incorporated into the renewed kingdom of David's descendant. One should see also the citation of this text (via the LXX) in Acts 15:12–21.

23. See comments on the "cup of wrath" in ch. 25.

Edom's strongholds on mountains and in cliffs will not save them from destruction. Verse 19 depicts God as a lion coming upon Edom. His plan is to destroy them, which will come on a day that strikes fear into the heart of a warrior.

49:23–27. Damascus[24] (i.e., the capital of Aramean southern Syria) is another object of prophetic judgment. Perhaps Damascus is named among the oracles because of the Aramean raids reported in 2 Kings 24:2. Damascus suffered devastating attacks from the Assyrians in the ninth and eighth centuries because it was a persistent ringleader in the region for anti-Assyrian activities. History repeated itself when Babylon took Damascus.

Hamath and Arpad, two cities in northern Syria, are named in this oracle as regional cities who will be dismayed by the bad news of judgment to fall on the area. Damascus is personified as a weak woman with pain like that which comes with labor. The reference to Ben-Hadad (v. 27) comes in an "update" of Amos's prophecy (Amos 1:3–4) against Damascus. Hadad is a well-known Aramean deity, and the name Ben-Hadad designates a king as the adopted "son" (*ben* means "son") of the deity. Several kings from Damascus had this name/title (e.g., 2 Kings 6:24).

49:28–33. Kedar[25] is a region of northern Arabia; the Kedarites are mentioned in Psalm 120:5 and Isaiah 42:11. Hazor is something of a mystery since no location with that name is known in northern Arabia.[26] In any case, Kedar and Hazor most likely refer to Arab tribesmen who were attacked by the Babylonians in Nebuchadnezzar's sixth year (winter of 599 B.C.).[27] The "people of the East" are associated with Kedar. They live in tents, travel using camels, and keep sheep and goats. These peoples are known in other sources as Arabs.[28]

49:34–39. The prophecy against Elam[29] is dated early in the reign of Zedekiah. Just why Elam is singled out is a mystery. In the Greek version of the oracles, Elam comes first. Perhaps the reason Elam is cited is that it was the object of a campaign by Nebuchadnezzar. If so, only suggestive evidence survives regarding the campaign. Elam will also be restored by God. As with other matters of grace, no merit or reason is cited for this announcement.

---

24. Cf. Isa. 17:1–14; Amos 1:3–5.

25. Cf. Isa. 21:13–17.

26. See the discussion in Holladay, *Jeremiah*, 2:382–84.

27. Wiseman, *Chronicles of Chaldean Kings*, 72–73.

28. See I. Ephal, *The Ancient Arabs: Nomads on the Border of the Fertile Crescent, 9th–5th Centuries B.C.* (Jerusalem: Magnes, 1982).

29. Elam is the southern part of Iran. Its capital was at Susa.

THEOLOGY BEHIND THE ORACLES. The fact that the oracles against the nations are collected together and placed at the end of the book of Jeremiah suggests that they are preserved as witnesses to God's sovereign justice and are to be read and pondered by those who come after the prophet. They demonstrate that Jeremiah was a prophet to the nations. Some of the things they announce (e.g., Egypt's capitulation to Babylon or Moab's forced acceptance of foreign domination) give evidence for the ongoing efficacy of God's Word in shaping and interpreting history. Other elements (e.g., the hubris of Ammon) indicate what kind of attitudes and activities are displeasing to the Lord.

With proper acknowledgment of the contingent and the particular, these oracles continue to bear witness to the outworking of God's Word and against the corporate character traits that God disdains. They are valuable for more than simply compiling a checklist to see how and when, or if, judgment befell the nations addressed. Like all announcements of judgment, these oracles get the attention of audiences and warn them; they may serve other tasks than as simple predictors of what must unalterably come to pass.

Two assumptions of the oracles can be transferred to different times and places. (1) They assume without argument that God is the Creator of the broader historical process in which the nations find themselves. This is tantamount to the claim that God is Creator of the world, since creation in the Bible is not simply about a past act but about the ongoing interaction with God and the historical process. For example, God may employ the Egyptians for purposes unknown by them, and he may work through them to accomplish future plans.

(2) The oracles assume that there are recognized standards of conduct to which any group may be held accountable. God has the right to judge the nations, his standards are just, and he may restore the nations as part of a future in which his mercy is as surprising as his judgment.

Prophecy in this mode plays the role of protest against institutional injustice. It is Egypt as a nation and Ammon as a collection of tribes who are judged by God. In some ways the oracles against nations are the most public form of theological discourse in the Old Testament because they use moral standards by which to evaluate public policies and state-sponsored activities on an international scale.

Restoration possible. The oracles against the nations in Jeremiah should be read in light of other prophetic oracles against nations and also in light of the missionary concern of the New Testament that the gospel be preached among all nations.[30] Thus, one function of the Old Testament oracles is to indicate the "fallen" condition of institutional life and the need for both moral strictures and a mercy that leads to repentance and new life.

Even though the predominant note of the oracles in the Old Testament toward the nations is negative—that is, they have been weighed in the balance of divine justice and found wanting—it is crucial to note that the redeemed in John's vision come from every tribe and tongue (Rev. 5:9–10; cf. Dan 7:14). God's sovereignty over the nations does not leave them without hope and fit only for retributive justice; in the good news of the New Testament (anticipated by the mysterious restoration passages in the oracles against the nations) the nations find healing for their sicknesses and spiritual strength to overcome the horrors of their inhumanity.

PUBLIC MORALITY. Early in 1999 NATO forces made the decision to attack Yugoslavia because of charges that Serbian forces sponsored by Yugoslavia were involved in the "ethnic cleansing" of the Kosovo province where ethnic Albanians live. The Kosovo Albanians are predominantly Muslim in religion while the Serbs are predominately Orthodox Christians. The government rhetoric emanating from Washington was harsh on the Serbs and the Yugoslavian president, Slobodan Milosevic. We can debate the accuracy of the charges made by NATO or the Serbs, but the rhetoric is instructive in the ways in which standards of behavior are publicly and internationally judged.

A broad debate in the United States over the behavior of President Clinton centered around the issue of private versus public morality. The charges against the Serbs was that they had violated international standards of conduct and that their treatment of persons in their country could not be considered a private matter. To be sure, there are differences between the behavior of one public figure with citizens and that of an army against its own citizens, but the debate over moral standards and their application to public policies was similar.

Christians may differ over the degree to which they wanted President Clinton to answer for his indiscretions and over the way in which they wished to hold President Milosevic accountable in the international arena for actions taken against his own people. But Christians cannot give in to the argument that private indiscretions or internal oppressions are off-limits to broader scrutiny and evaluation. God is a moral Judge, and there are no "purely" private acts or internal policies that lack wider implications.

---

30. See introductory section to chs. 46–51.

Interestingly, in the fall of 2000 Yugoslavian citizens took to the streets to denounce the way that Milosevic had attempted to thwart a democratic election process. Eventually he was forced out of the presidency. Many churches in Yugoslavia supported the nonviolent protests against Milosevic. Justice in corporate terms is never perfect or final, but because God is committed to it, God's people should be committed to it.

Christians in North America must face up to the fact that it is increasingly difficult (some would say philosophically and practically impossible) to have public discussions about the moral nature of public acts. It is difficult enough to have the discussion in the church! In broader society the pluralism is so vast that discussion is very, very difficult. The long tradition of oracles against the nations in the Old Testament are reminders, however, that God is not mocked. The wheels of justice employed by God may grind slowly and leave much unanswered from the limited vantage point of any generation, but a glance at the long histories of Egypt or Rome are solemn reminders that political power itself is no guarantee of right or continuing might.

For all of their particularity and stridency, the oracles against the nations are a good catalyst for the kind of discussions that Christians need to have about public values and their place in institutional life. The oracles put the emphasis on God, who evaluates rather than seeks an easy consensus on what the values are. Perhaps in North American society one cannot get consensus on the values, but this should not stop Christians from claiming that normative values exist and that they play an important role in the moral evaluation that history (and ultimately God) provides of nations. History, in this sense, is a penultimate method used by God to bring down the proud and the cruel.

Restoration. Mysterious affirmations come at the end of the oracles against Egypt, Moab, Ammon, and Elam, which proclaim restoration after their judgment. The good news is that God's judgment is often in the service of a wider saving purpose. His church will be comprised of people from every nation. In heaven this joyful fact is part of a song sung by the redeemed (Rev. 5). Should this not also be a song of the church on earth?

After prayer and study, a local congregation in Texas has adopted a plan to engage in mission work in the former Soviet province of Kazakhstan. There are few churches in this large area, which is located to the south of Russia and east of the Caspian Sea. To put it bluntly, the history of the region has been bleak in recent centuries. Most of the inhabitants are nominally Muslim, but the practice of religion was not encouraged in the region when the former USSR controlled it and sought to exploit its resources. When one thinks of the grim history of this broad section of Asia, it is easy to shudder and to wonder about moral purpose and justice in history. Christians, however, are called to look past the failures and dashed hopes that inhabit the region; they are called on to acknowledge the mysteries of God's judgment and rule, but most importantly, to believe that God's glory is to be revealed among the nations.

Attempts to discern meaning and purpose in the fate of nations is a most difficult task. Read any of the oracles against the nations in Jeremiah and one is reminded instantly that injustice and cruelty are constant historical companions. But so are the words of grace and future hope. The Texas congregation that has committed itself to mission work in Kazakhstan is seeking to follow the leading of the Holy Spirit and to be part of the work to which God has called all his people.

Jeremiah 50:1–51:64

¹THIS IS THE WORD the LORD spoke through Jeremiah the prophet concerning Babylon and the land of the Babylonians:

> ²"Announce and proclaim among the nations,
>> lift up a banner and proclaim it;
>> keep nothing back, but say,
> 'Babylon will be captured;
>> Bel will be put to shame,
>> Marduk filled with terror.
> Her images will be put to shame
>> and her idols filled with terror.'
> ³A nation from the north will attack her
>> and lay waste her land.
> No one will live in it;
>> both men and animals will flee away.
>
> ⁴"In those days, at that time,"
>> declares the LORD,
> "the people of Israel and the people of Judah together
>> will go in tears to seek the LORD their God.
> ⁵They will ask the way to Zion
>> and turn their faces toward it.
> They will come and bind themselves to the LORD
>> in an everlasting covenant
>> that will not be forgotten.
>
> ⁶"My people have been lost sheep;
>> their shepherds have led them astray
>> and caused them to roam on the mountains.

They wandered over mountain and hill
    and forgot their own resting place.
⁷Whoever found them devoured them;
    their enemies said, 'We are not guilty,
for they sinned against the LORD, their true pasture,
    the LORD, the hope of their fathers.'

⁸"Flee out of Babylon;
    leave the land of the Babylonians,
    and be like the goats that lead the flock.
⁹For I will stir up and bring against Babylon
    an alliance of great nations from the land of the north.
They will take up their positions against her,
    and from the north she will be captured.
Their arrows will be like skilled warriors
    who do not return empty-handed.
¹⁰So Babylonia will be plundered;
    all who plunder her will have their fill,"

                                        declares the LORD.

¹¹"Because you rejoice and are glad,
    you who pillage my inheritance,
because you frolic like a heifer threshing grain
    and neigh like stallions,
¹²your mother will be greatly ashamed;
    she who gave you birth will be disgraced.
She will be the least of the nations—
    a wilderness, a dry land, a desert.
¹³Because of the LORD's anger she will not be inhabited
    but will be completely desolate.
All who pass Babylon will be horrified and scoff
    because of all her wounds.

¹⁴"Take up your positions around Babylon,
    all you who draw the bow.
Shoot at her! Spare no arrows,
    for she has sinned against the LORD.
¹⁵Shout against her on every side!
    She surrenders, her towers fall,
    her walls are torn down.
Since this is the vengeance of the LORD,
    take vengeance on her;
    do to her as she has done to others.

¹⁶Cut off from Babylon the sower,
   and the reaper with his sickle at harvest.
Because of the sword of the oppressor
   let everyone return to his own people,
   let everyone flee to his own land.

¹⁷"Israel is a scattered flock
   that lions have chased away.
The first to devour him
   was the king of Assyria;
the last to crush his bones
   was Nebuchadnezzar king of Babylon."

¹⁸Therefore this is what the LORD Almighty, the God of
Israel, says:

"I will punish the king of Babylon and his land
   as I punished the king of Assyria.
¹⁹But I will bring Israel back to his own pasture
   and he will graze on Carmel and Bashan;
his appetite will be satisfied
   on the hills of Ephraim and Gilead.
²⁰In those days, at that time,"
   declares the LORD,
"search will be made for Israel's guilt,
   but there will be none,
and for the sins of Judah,
   but none will be found,
   for I will forgive the remnant I spare.

²¹"Attack the land of Merathaim
   and those who live in Pekod.
Pursue, kill and completely destroy them,"
                declares the LORD.
"Do everything I have commanded you.
²²The noise of battle is in the land,
   the noise of great destruction!
²³How broken and shattered
   is the hammer of the whole earth!
How desolate is Babylon
   among the nations!
²⁴I set a trap for you, O Babylon,
   and you were caught before you knew it;

you were found and captured
    because you opposed the LORD.
²⁵ The LORD has opened his arsenal
    and brought out the weapons of his wrath,
for the Sovereign LORD Almighty has work to do
    in the land of the Babylonians.
²⁶ Come against her from afar.
    Break open her granaries;
    pile her up like heaps of grain.
Completely destroy her
    and leave her no remnant.
²⁷ Kill all her young bulls;
    let them go down to the slaughter!
Woe to them! For their day has come,
    the time for them to be punished.
²⁸ Listen to the fugitives and refugees from Babylon
    declaring in Zion
how the LORD our God has taken vengeance,
    vengeance for his temple.

²⁹ "Summon archers against Babylon,
    all those who draw the bow.
Encamp all around her;
    let no one escape.
Repay her for her deeds;
    do to her as she has done.
For she has defied the LORD,
    the Holy One of Israel.
³⁰ Therefore, her young men will fall in the streets;
    all her soldiers will be silenced in that day,"
                         declares the LORD.

³¹ "See, I am against you, O arrogant one,"
    declares the Lord, the LORD Almighty,
"for your day has come,
    the time for you to be punished.
³² The arrogant one will stumble and fall
    and no one will help her up;
I will kindle a fire in her towns
    that will consume all who are around her."

³³ This is what the LORD Almighty says:

"The people of Israel are oppressed,
    and the people of Judah as well.

All their captors hold them fast,
    refusing to let them go.
³⁴ Yet their Redeemer is strong;
    the LORD Almighty is his name.
He will vigorously defend their cause
    so that he may bring rest to their land,
    but unrest to those who live in Babylon.

³⁵ "A sword against the Babylonians!"
    declares the LORD—
"against those who live in Babylon
    and against her officials and wise men!
³⁶ A sword against her false prophets!
    They will become fools.
A sword against her warriors!
    They will be filled with terror.
³⁷ A sword against her horses and chariots
    and all the foreigners in her ranks!
    They will become women.
A sword against her treasures!
    They will be plundered.
³⁸ A drought on her waters!
    They will dry up.
For it is a land of idols,
    idols that will go mad with terror.

³⁹ "So desert creatures and hyenas will live there,
    and there the owl will dwell.
It will never again be inhabited
    or lived in from generation to generation.
⁴⁰ As God overthrew Sodom and Gomorrah
    along with their neighboring towns,"
                declares the LORD,
"so no one will live there;
    no man will dwell in it.

⁴¹ "Look! An army is coming from the north;
    a great nation and many kings
    are being stirred up from the ends of the earth.
⁴² They are armed with bows and spears;
    they are cruel and without mercy.
They sound like the roaring sea
    as they ride on their horses;

they come like men in battle formation
 to attack you, O Daughter of Babylon.
⁴³ The king of Babylon has heard reports about them,
 and his hands hang limp.
Anguish has gripped him,
 pain like that of a woman in labor.
⁴⁴ Like a lion coming up from Jordan's thickets
 to a rich pastureland,
I will chase Babylon from its land in an instant.
 Who is the chosen one I will appoint for this?
Who is like me and who can challenge me?
 And what shepherd can stand against me?"
⁴⁵ Therefore, hear what the LORD has planned against Babylon,
 what he has purposed against the land of the Babylonians:
The young of the flock will be dragged away;
 he will completely destroy their pasture because of them.
⁴⁶ At the sound of Babylon's capture the earth will tremble;
 its cry will resound among the nations.

^{51:1} This is what the LORD says:

"See, I will stir up the spirit of a destroyer
 against Babylon and the people of Leb Kamai.
² I will send foreigners to Babylon
 to winnow her and to devastate her land;
they will oppose her on every side
 in the day of her disaster.
³ Let not the archer string his bow,
 nor let him put on his armor.
Do not spare her young men;
 completely destroy her army.
⁴ They will fall down slain in Babylon,
 fatally wounded in her streets.
⁵ For Israel and Judah have not been forsaken
 by their God, the LORD Almighty,
though their land is full of guilt
 before the Holy One of Israel.

⁶ "Flee from Babylon!
 Run for your lives!
 Do not be destroyed because of her sins.
It is time for the LORD's vengeance;
 he will pay her what she deserves.

⁷Babylon was a gold cup in the LORD's hand;
   she made the whole earth drunk.
The nations drank her wine;
   therefore they have now gone mad.
⁸Babylon will suddenly fall and be broken.
   Wail over her!
Get balm for her pain;
   perhaps she can be healed.

⁹'''We would have healed Babylon,
   but she cannot be healed;
let us leave her and each go to his own land,
   for her judgment reaches to the skies,
   it rises as high as the clouds.'

¹⁰'''The LORD has vindicated us;
   come, let us tell in Zion
   what the LORD our God has done.'

¹¹"Sharpen the arrows,
   take up the shields!
The LORD has stirred up the kings of the Medes,
   because his purpose is to destroy Babylon.
The LORD will take vengeance,
   vengeance for his temple.
¹²Lift up a banner against the walls of Babylon!
   Reinforce the guard,
station the watchmen,
   prepare an ambush!
The LORD will carry out his purpose,
   his decree against the people of Babylon.
¹³You who live by many waters
   and are rich in treasures,
your end has come,
   the time for you to be cut off.
¹⁴The LORD Almighty has sworn by himself:
   I will surely fill you with men, as with a swarm
      of locusts,
   and they will shout in triumph over you.

¹⁵"He made the earth by his power;
   he founded the world by his wisdom
   and stretched out the heavens by his understanding.

¹⁶When he thunders, the waters in the heavens roar;
    he makes clouds rise from the ends of the earth.
He sends lightning with the rain
    and brings out the wind from his storehouses.

¹⁷"Every man is senseless and without knowledge;
    every goldsmith is shamed by his idols.
His images are a fraud;
    they have no breath in them.
¹⁸They are worthless, the objects of mockery;
    when their judgment comes, they will perish.
¹⁹He who is the Portion of Jacob is not like these,
    for he is the Maker of all things,
including the tribe of his inheritance—
    the LORD Almighty is his name.

²⁰"You are my war club,
    my weapon for battle—
with you I shatter nations,
    with you I destroy kingdoms,
²¹with you I shatter horse and rider,
    with you I shatter chariot and driver,
²²with you I shatter man and woman,
    with you I shatter old man and youth,
    with you I shatter young man and maiden,
²³with you I shatter shepherd and flock,
    with you I shatter farmer and oxen,
    with you I shatter governors and officials.

²⁴"Before your eyes I will repay Babylon and all who live in Babylonia for all the wrong they have done in Zion," declares the LORD.

²⁵"I am against you, O destroying mountain,
    you who destroy the whole earth,"

                      declares the LORD.

"I will stretch out my hand against you,
    roll you off the cliffs,
    and make you a burned-out mountain.
²⁶No rock will be taken from you for a cornerstone,
    nor any stone for a foundation,
    for you will be desolate forever,"

                      declares the LORD.

²⁷"Lift up a banner in the land!
    Blow the trumpet among the nations!
Prepare the nations for battle against her;
    summon against her these kingdoms:
    Ararat, Minni and Ashkenaz.
Appoint a commander against her;
    send up horses like a swarm of locusts.
²⁸Prepare the nations for battle against her—
    the kings of the Medes,
their governors and all their officials,
    and all the countries they rule.
²⁹The land trembles and writhes,
    for the LORD's purposes against Babylon stand—
to lay waste the land of Babylon
    so that no one will live there.
³⁰Babylon's warriors have stopped fighting;
    they remain in their strongholds.
Their strength is exhausted;
    they have become like women.
Her dwellings are set on fire;
    the bars of her gates are broken.
³¹One courier follows another
    and messenger follows messenger
to announce to the king of Babylon
    that his entire city is captured,
³²the river crossings seized,
    the marshes set on fire,
    and the soldiers terrified."

³³This is what the LORD Almighty, the God of Israel, says:

"The Daughter of Babylon is like a threshing floor
    at the time it is trampled;
    the time to harvest her will soon come."

³⁴"Nebuchadnezzar king of Babylon has devoured us,
    he has thrown us into confusion,
    he has made us an empty jar.
Like a serpent he has swallowed us
    and filled his stomach with our delicacies,
    and then has spewed us out.
³⁵May the violence done to our flesh be upon Babylon,"
    say the inhabitants of Zion.

"May our blood be on those who live in Babylonia,"
    says Jerusalem.

³⁶Therefore, this is what the LORD says:

"See, I will defend your cause
    and avenge you;
I will dry up her sea
    and make her springs dry.
³⁷Babylon will be a heap of ruins,
    a haunt of jackals,
an object of horror and scorn,
    a place where no one lives.
³⁸Her people all roar like young lions,
    they growl like lion cubs.
³⁹But while they are aroused,
    I will set out a feast for them
    and make them drunk,
so that they shout with laughter—
    then sleep forever and not awake,"
                    declares the LORD.
⁴⁰"I will bring them down
    like lambs to the slaughter,
    like rams and goats.

⁴¹"How Sheshach will be captured,
    the boast of the whole earth seized!
What a horror Babylon will be
    among the nations!
⁴²The sea will rise over Babylon;
    its roaring waves will cover her.
⁴³Her towns will be desolate,
    a dry and desert land,
a land where no one lives,
    through which no man travels.
⁴⁴I will punish Bel in Babylon
    and make him spew out what he has swallowed.
The nations will no longer stream to him.
    And the wall of Babylon will fall.

⁴⁵"Come out of her, my people!
    Run for your lives!
    Run from the fierce anger of the LORD.

⁴⁶ Do not lose heart or be afraid
> when rumors are heard in the land;
> one rumor comes this year, another the next,
> rumors of violence in the land
> and of ruler against ruler.
⁴⁷ For the time will surely come
> when I will punish the idols of Babylon;
> her whole land will be disgraced
> and her slain will all lie fallen within her.
⁴⁸ Then heaven and earth and all that is in them
> will shout for joy over Babylon,
> for out of the north
> destroyers will attack her,"

> declares the LORD.

⁴⁹ "Babylon must fall because of Israel's slain,
> just as the slain in all the earth
> have fallen because of Babylon.
⁵⁰ You who have escaped the sword,
> leave and do not linger!
> Remember the LORD in a distant land,
> and think on Jerusalem."

⁵¹ "We are disgraced,
> for we have been insulted
> and shame covers our faces,
> because foreigners have entered
> the holy places of the LORD's house."

⁵² "But days are coming," declares the LORD,
> "when I will punish her idols,
> and throughout her land
> the wounded will groan.
⁵³ Even if Babylon reaches the sky
> and fortifies her lofty stronghold,
> I will send destroyers against her,"

> declares the LORD.

⁵⁴ "The sound of a cry comes from Babylon,
> the sound of great destruction
> from the land of the Babylonians.
⁵⁵ The LORD will destroy Babylon;
> he will silence her noisy din.

Waves of enemies will rage like great waters;
the roar of their voices will resound.
⁵⁶ A destroyer will come against Babylon;
her warriors will be captured,
and their bows will be broken.
For the LORD is a God of retribution;
he will repay in full.
⁵⁷ I will make her officials and wise men drunk,
her governors, officers and warriors as well;
they will sleep forever and not awake,"
declares the King, whose name is the LORD Almighty.

⁵⁸ This is what the LORD Almighty says:

"Babylon's thick wall will be leveled
and her high gates set on fire;
the peoples exhaust themselves for nothing,
the nations' labor is only fuel for the flames."

⁵⁹ This is the message Jeremiah gave to the staff officer Seraiah son of Neriah, the son of Mahseiah, when he went to Babylon with Zedekiah king of Judah in the fourth year of his reign. ⁶⁰ Jeremiah had written on a scroll about all the disasters that would come upon Babylon—all that had been recorded concerning Babylon. ⁶¹ He said to Seraiah, "When you get to Babylon, see that you read all these words aloud. ⁶² Then say, 'O LORD, you have said you will destroy this place, so that neither man nor animal will live in it; it will be desolate forever.' ⁶³ When you finish reading this scroll, tie a stone to it and throw it into the Euphrates. ⁶⁴ Then say, 'So will Babylon sink to rise no more because of the disaster I will bring upon her. And her people will fall.'"

The words of Jeremiah end here.

THESE TWO CHAPTERS are a collection of poetic oracles interspersed with brief prose units of speech. They concern Babylon and God's just judgment on that nation for its arrogance and its oppression of others.³¹ They are not an original unity, but the material is

---

31. K. T. Aitken, "The Oracles Against Babylon in Jeremiah 50–51: Structures and Perspectives," *TynBul* 35 (1984): 25–63; D. J. Reimer, *The Oracles Against Babylon in Jeremiah 50–51: A Horror Among the Nations* (Lewiston, N.Y.: Edwin Mellen, 1992); J. Hill, *Friend or Foe?*

brought together as testimony to the role that Babylon had played and would play in the divine economy. These chapters complete the collection of oracles about the nations begun in chapter 46.

These are not the only texts in Jeremiah to take up the topic of Babylon. Indeed, the impact of Babylon lies behind every line of the book as it now exists. In terms of historical context, the Babylonian threat has been a primary concern of Judah's government since the defeat of Egypt at the battle of Carchemish in 605 B.C. In 597 the Babylonian army surrounded Jerusalem and received a surrender from young king Jehoiachin. There were many contacts between Judah and Babylon between 597 and the second siege and tragic destruction of Jerusalem in 588–586. Explicit references to Babylon and to Nebuchadnezzar occur in chapters 21, 24–25, 27–29, 32, 34–35, 37–44. The Babylonian defeat of Judah and the fall of Jerusalem are what shape this book.

The theme of the oracles in chapters 50–51 is the downfall of Babylon, sometimes depicted as already accomplished and sometimes represented as a future event. In this they differ from most of the other references to Babylon in Jeremiah, which assume that Babylonian supremacy has been divinely given and exercised in judgment against Judah and Jerusalem.[32] The city of Babylon fell in October 539 B.C. to invaders led by Cyrus the Great.

In a remarkable turnaround, chapters 50–51 portray Babylon's fall in language similar to that used elsewhere in Jeremiah to portray Judah's fall to Babylon. Hostile forces will be arrayed against Babylon, and there will be no deliverance from them. Thus, some scholars have wondered how the prophet, who so assiduously announced Babylonian supremacy, could have made such a complete turnaround. Indeed, a close reading of modern commentaries shows that some authors think these oracles against Babylon come from the prophet's editors rather than the prophet himself.[33]

But there is no compelling reason why Jeremiah, who announced the defeat of Judah at the hands of Babylon, could not also have announced the defeat of tyrant Babylon. The two claims are not inconsistent with each other, and there is no objection on the basis of the content of the chapters to assigning the oracles a place in Jeremiah's own lifetime. As noted above, they probably did originate over a period of time—probably they were put

---

The Figure of Babylon in the Book of Jeremiah MT (Leiden: Brill, 1999). The city of Babylon is personified as a female in several of the poetic oracles (cf. "Daughter [of] Babylon" in 51:33).

32. Jer. 25:12–14 announces that God will judge the Babylonians after the period of Babylonian hegemony is complete. Chapter 25 dates to the fourth year of Jehoiakim/first year of Nebuchadnezzar (i.e., 605 B.C.).

33. Holladay, *Jeremiah*, 2:401–15, has a lengthy discussion on the form, authenticity, and setting of these two chapters.

---

together by the prophet's editors—but the theology that undergirds the oracles is vintage Jeremiah. God used Babylon to judge Judah. But Babylon had exercised its role with extreme arrogance and cruelty and had done so in mocking defiance of Jeremiah's claim that it served the Lord, the God of Israel.

Chapter 50 intersperses the doom oracles against Babylon with briefer affirmations of Judah's deliverance (e.g., 50:4–5). The prophecy to strike Babylon is part of the Lord's plan and purpose (51:45). Even as Judah ultimately will be delivered, a foe from the north will wreak havoc on Babylon (50:3, 41). This is a classic reversal motif—previously Jeremiah had spoken of the foe from the north who would threaten Judah (1:13–14; 5:15–17; 6:22). The sword will flash against Babylon (50:35–37) and all her inhabitants.[34] Babylon, which was a tool in the hands of the Lord, exercised an arrogance that provoked him to judgment (50:14–15, 29–31).

One of the ways in which the judgment is depicted is sarcasm. Babylon is lampooned as a rebellious city (*Merathaim*, 50:21) and as punishment (*Pekod*, 50:21). Both names are puns on aspects of Babylonian geography or tribesmen.[35] Another way is the symbolism of battle forces arrayed against the city (50:14, 35). Babylon will be destroyed because of idolatry (50:2).

50:1–10. The fall of Babylon is to be proclaimed among the nations. Perhaps this is because Babylon had subjugated a number of them, and there will be rejoicing in more than one corner of the former empire. Another reason perhaps is the public declaration of the Lord's sovereignty by announcing the fact in public and in advance.

As in the prophecies in the book of the covenant (chs. 30–31), remnants from Israel and Judah will seek the Lord and a way back to Zion. They are currently like lost sheep, but they will return to their true Shepherd, "the hope of their fathers." The prophet urges them to flee out of Babylon (cf. 51:6). This is not contradictory to the advice given in 29:4–9, that the exiles should build houses in Babylon and pray for the welfare of the city. That same chapter indicated a coming time when God will restore his people. The defeat of Babylon will indicate that restoration is on the horizon.

50:11–17. Babylon's joy in pillaging Judah (God's "inheritance") will be turned to great shame. Babylon is personified here as the mother of the Babylonian people. Potraying cities as female persons is common in the Old Testament, but this imagery will be taken up in the New Testament, where Babylon is portrayed as a great prostitute (Rev. 17–18).

---

34. Another name for Babylon is Chaldea. Inhabitants of Babylonia are sometimes called Chaldeans.

35. In 51:41 the name Sheshach for Babylon is another wordplay. It is used also in 25:26.

In poetic reversal pattern, Babylon will be besieged and defeated. Verse 15 is a somber cry: "Since this is the vengeance of the LORD, take vengeance on her; do to her as she has done to others." This proclamation is also an example of the "act and consequence" theology espoused by many biblical writers. What Babylon has set in motion will come around to her.

50:18–32. Imperialistic Babylon is compared to Assyria, the earlier conqueror of Israel and much of the Near East. As with Assyria, so with Babylon—God will judge the oppressor. Twice the language of judgment against Babylon uses the verb *ḥrm* ("to devote to ritual destruction").[36] Vengeance on God's part is another motive for judgment (v. 28; cf. 51:11).

50:33–46. God is strong, not just as Judge of iniquity, but as the Redeemer of his people. Verse 34 celebrates God as the One who vindicates his people's cause.[37]

The overthrow of Babylon is compared to that of Sodom and Gomorrah. Again the prophet uses the language of military attack and siege to describe the coming fall of Babylon. Verse 44 alludes to either a people or an individual who will do God's bidding and take Babylon. Possibly this refers to the Medes and Persians or even to Cyrus himself (cf. Isa. 45:1), but one cannot be sure. As Jeremiah 50:9; 51:27–28 indicate, God has summoned several groups against Babylon. These claims elaborate on the theme that a foe from the north will attack Babylon.

51:1–23. Chapter 51 continues the contrast between the coming deliverance of Judean exiles and the judgment to befall Babylon. Much of the imagery of judgment on Babylon and redemption for Israel is repeated from or similar to that in chapter 50. One of the poetic symbols Jeremiah uses is that of the "cup," a vessel that indicates the future when its contents are consumed. In 51:7 Babylon itself is depicted as a cup from which Judah and the nations drank, but now it is ready to be smashed.[38]

Verses 15–19 celebrate the creative power and wisdom of God. The sentiments expressed here are similar to those in chapter 10, where again the character of the true God is set in the context of the foolishness and idolatry of the nations. In contrast to human idol-makers, God is "the Maker of all things."

51:24–58. These verses portray four of Babylon's neighbors as threats.[39] The Medes are mentioned twice (51:11, 28). They were a people to the

---

36. Verses 21, 26.

37. The Heb. term is *rib*, a legal term. God will act to defend a proper cause.

38. See comments on the image of the cup in 25:15–29. The "cup" becomes something of a proverbial symbol in the New Testament (cf. Mark 10:35–40). In Rev. 18:6 Babylon, the harlot, is to drink from the "cup" of judgment. The symbolism in Rev. 18 draws heavily on Jer. 51.

39. For background information, see entries on these names in the *Anchor Bible Dictionary*.

north and east of Babylon who were incorporated into the Persian state created by Cyrus the Great. Ararat, Minni, and the Ashkenaz (51:27–28) were also peoples from the north and northeast of Babylon. Along with the Medes and the Persians, they may reflect collectively the "foe from the north" who will strike Babylon.

In 51:34–40 personified Jerusalem speaks, and the Lord replies that judgment will come on Babylon. In this context she (Jerusalem) speaks of the torment she has received from Babylon. Her first-person speech is similar to that found in the book of Lamentations.

The gods of Babylon are also judged in the fall of the city. Specifically mentioned is Bel (v. 44; cf. Isa. 46:1–2). The imagery of judgment against Babylon alludes to the tower of Babylon (Babel) in Genesis 11:1–9. God will send destroyers against Babylon, even if the city reaches the sky (Jer. 51:53).

51:59–64. The chapter concludes with a prose account of Seraiah, brother of Baruch, who traveled to Babylon in Zedekiah's fourth year (594/593). Apparently he was sent to Babylon on diplomatic business; Seraiah was from a family of scribes and was capable of writing and interpreting documents.[40] While in Babylon he performed a symbolic act to depict the judgment that would ultimately befall Babylon. Just as the written scroll sank when Seraiah threw it into the river, so will Babylon sink and rise no more.

The last line of the chapter states that "the words of Jeremiah end here." Readers do well to recall the way in which Jeremiah's work began. He was called to be a prophet to the nations. The literary arrangement of his words concludes with an extended prophecy against Babylon, the great imperial power of the day. But note how Jeremiah's words in collected form have lasted much longer than the great political and military foe of his day.

Bridging Contexts

JUDGING THE OPPRESSOR. Chapters 50–51 deal with God's judgment on Babylon, a judgment that came on the city in 539 B.C., when Cyrus the Great and his forces occupied the city and put the Babylonian Empire out of business. The influence of this word of judgment continued as the prophetic texts bore witness to the contrast between the ongoing life of the Judean exiles and the continuing decline of the once-proud city. Ultimately the city itself would be abandoned, giving additional confirmation of the prophetic depiction of its demise. Thus, at one level, chapters 50–51 are not only about announcing God's judgment but also

---

40. N. Avigad, "The Seal of Seraiah (Son of) Neriah," *Eretz Israel* 14 (1978): 86–87 [in Hebrew]; and J. R. Lundbom, "Baruch, Seraiah, and Expanded Colophons in the Book of Jeremiah," *JSOT* 36 (1986): 89–114.

serve as witness to the truthfulness of the claim that God has judged the oppressor in the historical process. Modern application of these sentiments may begin by asking: Which current political entities offend the justice and moral order of God, and which afflict God's people who live among them?

Babylon as a symbol. Chapters 50–51 also serve as reminders that Jeremiah represented a dual theme with regard to Babylon. According to chapter 25, already in the time of Jehoiakim, when Babylon first loomed on the horizon as political master, the prophet announced not only that Babylon would be the agent of God's judgment but that it would also be the recipient of God's judgment. Thus, on another level, these chapters are part of that broader scriptural teaching concerning the ubiquity of sin and of fallen human nature. Babylon becomes a symbol—that is, both a historical illustration and a reminder—of the self-destructive consequences of arrogance, pride in wealth, oppression, and idolatry. They are destructive because they offend the moral order created by God and because they are ruinous to public, institutional life.

One will find additional confirmation of this in the book of Daniel, where Nebuchadnezzar and Babylon are one example of a type of oppressive government that arises periodically. Both Jeremiah and Daniel affirm that God has granted all of them historical supremacy for a time, yet they are—and their type always will be—subject to his judgment for their failures. Nahum similarly affirms God's judgment on Assyria as a great judicial act that frees Judah and others from the oppressive yoke of the tyrant.

Babylon, the evil and arrogant female, is a scriptural symbol that lives on in the inspired imagination of John, prophetic seer of the book of Revelation (Rev. 17–18). He uses the imagery of Babylon as a prostitute, oppressing the world over and drunk with the blood of the saints, as a means to describe the lethal power of imperial Rome. Here is an example of earlier biblical texts being interpreted and reapplied. The older prophetic word lives on in a new key, as again the greatest political and military power of the era persecutes God's people. Furthermore, John's apocalyptic depiction points Christians toward the future. Before the current age runs its course, there may be other arrogant powers that seek to dominate their neighbors. Readers are invited to see a pattern at work in the ebb and flow of the broad historical process.

MORAL RESPONSIBILITY. GOD'S judgment of Babylon is but a past act unless it is put in the broader contexts of God's historical purposes and the continuing validity of belief in a moral order through which he holds nations and institutions responsible for their actions. It is important to note that God's judgment is not simply a righteous reaction to arrogance and oppression; at the same time it is also zeal to defend his own. Notice how many times the deliverance of Israel and Judah is mentioned in these two chapters. Judgment comes in the historical process not only from God, the righteous Judge, but from God the zealous Defender of his people. This is a confession of faith that Christians are called to make in spite of the "messiness" and ambiguity of history.

Forms of deliverance. It is a sad fact that at the beginning of the twenty-first century Christians are being persecuted for their faith in several places around the world. When members of the church universal pray for the safety and deliverance of persecuted brothers and sisters, they do well to remember what forms deliverance takes in the historical process. Deliverance and freedom for God's people may well come through difficult and violent historical circumstances.

It is sobering to think of the military and political struggles in the last few years and their effects. The year 1989 brought the collapse of the Berlin Wall. December of that same year saw the Romanian dictator felled. The so-called "Gulf War" in 1991 may have prevented a wider conflagration from breaking out.

In 1999 there was much debate in the Western world about ways to react to the lethal and oppressive policies of Slobodan Milosevic, president of Yugoslavia and the architect of a brutal campaign by Serbians against the largely Muslim province of Kosovo. A primary debating point concerned the legitimacy of Western intervention in what seemed to be internal strife. One may debate the various reasons why Western forces ultimately began an air campaign against the Serbian forces, but one of them was the belief that universal standards of justice and decency had been violated by the Serbian aggression. Some persons argued, correctly it seems, that similar patterns of horrific ethnic persecution had happened recently in Rwanda between Hutu and Tutsi tribes, but no one had taken any action. It is this sense of a moral standard to which all can be held that partially underlies the claims of Jeremiah 50–51.

In pondering the judgments of history, perhaps no region is more strife-ridden and more difficult to understand than the Middle East. While Israelis and Arabs debate and fight—which they seem to do at the same time—there is the ongoing exodus of Arab Christians from the region. Understandably, Christians in other parts of the world lament the fact that brothers and sisters from the land of the Messiah are fleeing in such numbers that if current projections continue, in fifty years virtually all churches in Israel and Jordan will be museums.

Yes, the fleeing of Arab Christians is a tragedy. It may also be one of the ways in which God saves his people from a more terrible historical fate looming on the horizon. Hindsight often improves judgment, even for the church. Christians may find much about judgment in Jeremiah 50–51, but it is the hidden work of God to which we should also be drawn.

In all these questions about the judgment of oppressing nations, the Christian church finds itself caught up in debates about morality and the just exercise of force. These debates are good when they remind Christians that God is not mocked and that no nation or ethnic group will have the final say on Judgment Day. They can mislead if they allow people to think that it is only the "other side" that is wrong and sinful in God's assessment.

No group comes out unscathed in the book of Jeremiah. There is plenty of folly and failure to go around, whether in Judah or in Babylon. God's promise to rescue his people comes not because they are morally perfect, but because of the grace of his promise to them. His standards of judgment are a stark reminder of how much grace is needed for the rescue of the saints in any generation.

Jeremiah 52:1–34

ZEDEKIAH WAS TWENTY-ONE years old when he became king, and he reigned in Jerusalem eleven years. His mother's name was Hamutal daughter of Jeremiah; she was from Libnah. ²He did evil in the eyes of the Lord, just as Jehoiakim had done. ³It was because of the LORD's anger that all this happened to Jerusalem and Judah, and in the end he thrust them from his presence.

Now Zedekiah rebelled against the king of Babylon.

⁴So in the ninth year of Zedekiah's reign, on the tenth day of the tenth month, Nebuchadnezzar king of Babylon marched against Jerusalem with his whole army. They camped outside the city and built siege works all around it. ⁵The city was kept under siege until the eleventh year of King Zedekiah.

⁶By the ninth day of the fourth month the famine in the city had become so severe that there was no food for the people to eat. ⁷Then the city wall was broken through, and the whole army fled. They left the city at night through the gate between the two walls near the king's garden, though the Babylonians were surrounding the city. They fled toward the Arabah, ⁸but the Babylonian army pursued King Zedekiah and overtook him in the plains of Jericho. All his soldiers were separated from him and scattered, ⁹and he was captured.

He was taken to the king of Babylon at Riblah in the land of Hamath, where he pronounced sentence on him. ¹⁰There at Riblah the king of Babylon slaughtered the sons of Zedekiah before his eyes; he also killed all the officials of Judah. ¹¹Then he put out Zedekiah's eyes, bound him with bronze shackles and took him to Babylon, where he put him in prison till the day of his death.

¹²On the tenth day of the fifth month, in the nineteenth year of Nebuchadnezzar king of Babylon, Nebuzaradan commander of the imperial guard, who served the king of Babylon, came to Jerusalem. ¹³He set fire to the temple of the LORD, the royal palace and all the houses of Jerusalem. Every important building he burned down. ¹⁴The whole Babylonian army under the commander of the imperial guard broke down all the walls around Jerusalem. ¹⁵Nebuzaradan the commander

of the guard carried into exile some of the poorest people and those who remained in the city, along with the rest of the craftsmen and those who had gone over to the king of Babylon. ¹⁶But Nebuzaradan left behind the rest of the poorest people of the land to work the vineyards and fields.

¹⁷The Babylonians broke up the bronze pillars, the movable stands and the bronze Sea that were at the temple of the LORD and they carried all the bronze to Babylon. ¹⁸They also took away the pots, shovels, wick trimmers, sprinkling bowls, dishes and all the bronze articles used in the temple service. ¹⁹The commander of the imperial guard took away the basins, censers, sprinkling bowls, pots, lampstands, dishes and bowls used for drink offerings—all that were made of pure gold or silver.

²⁰The bronze from the two pillars, the Sea and the twelve bronze bulls under it, and the movable stands, which King Solomon had made for the temple of the LORD, was more than could be weighed. ²¹Each of the pillars was eighteen cubits high and twelve cubits in circumference; each was four fingers thick, and hollow. ²²The bronze capital on top of the one pillar was five cubits high and was decorated with a network and pomegranates of bronze all around. The other pillar, with its pomegranates, was similar. ²³There were ninety-six pomegranates on the sides; the total number of pomegranates above the surrounding network was a hundred.

²⁴The commander of the guard took as prisoners Seraiah the chief priest, Zephaniah the priest next in rank and the three doorkeepers. ²⁵Of those still in the city, he took the officer in charge of the fighting men, and seven royal advisers. He also took the secretary who was chief officer in charge of conscripting the people of the land and sixty of his men who were found in the city. ²⁶Nebuzaradan the commander took them all and brought them to the king of Babylon at Riblah. ²⁷There at Riblah, in the land of Hamath, the king had them executed.

So Judah went into captivity, away from her land. ²⁸This is the number of the people Nebuchadnezzar carried into exile:

in the seventh year, 3,023 Jews;
²⁹in Nebuchadnezzar's eighteenth year,
832 people from Jerusalem;
³⁰in his twenty-third year,
745 Jews taken into exile by Nebuzaradan the
commander of the imperial guard.
There were 4,600 people in all.

³¹In the thirty-seventh year of the exile of Jehoiachin king of Judah, in the year Evil-Merodach became king of Babylon, he released Jehoiachin king of Judah and freed him from prison on the twenty-fifth day of the twelfth month. ³²He spoke kindly to him and gave him a seat of honor higher than those of the other kings who were with him in Babylon. ³³So Jehoiachin put aside his prison clothes and for the rest of his life ate regularly at the king's table. ³⁴Day by day the king of Babylon gave Jehoiachin a regular allowance as long as he lived, till the day of his death.

CHAPTER 52, THE CONCLUSION to the book of Jeremiah, largely parallels the conclusion to the book of 2 Kings (2 Kings 24:20b–25:30). That the two accounts are similar is obvious; what is not at all obvious is the literary relationship between the two. Were details from one of the accounts copied for the other; and if so, which is the earlier of the two? The answer to either question is difficult to answer with any confidence—and neither question is as important as the role of the account in 2 Kings and in Jeremiah.

(1) We begin by observing that at least two scriptural writers/editors believed that a *narrative* account of Jerusalem's tragic fall, coupled with the report that the exiled king Jehoiachin was still in Babylon until the reign of Evil-Merodach, was the appropriate place to conclude their respective "books."

(2) The book of Jeremiah is not historical narrative in the sense that 1–2 Kings is, but its presentation of the prophet's work presupposes the historical context provided in Kings.

(3) Not only is this last chapter of Jeremiah tragic in its details; it is somewhat repetitive and therefore anticlimactic. This may be a small clue to the literary relationship between Kings and Jeremiah. For sequential readers of this book, Jeremiah 37–44 has already provided details of the fall of Jerusalem and its aftermath, some of which get repeated in chapter 52 (cf. 39:1–10 with 52:4–16). The account in 2 Kings 25, however, follows the chronologically arranged, unfolding scheme of the larger work entitled 1–2 Kings. Perhaps, therefore, it was the compilers of Jeremiah who made a conscious decision to end the prophet's book in similar fashion to that of 2 Kings, even if that meant repeating material already used in the book.

If the scenario above is correct, it does not solve the issue of the literary relationship between the two accounts, as if it is certain that Jeremiah's compiler(s) copied from 2 Kings; it only suggests that the way 2 Kings concludes influenced the way Jeremiah's compiler(s) concluded the prophet's book. There are, after all, significant differences between the two prose accounts. Given the fact that generally speaking the prose traditions of Jeremiah are similar linguistically to those in 1–2 Kings—suggesting to a number of scholars that the compilers of the two works were somehow related[1]—it is more likely that the particular relationship between 2 Kings 25 and Jeremiah 52 goes back to the prehistory of the texts as we now have them rather than with one essentially copying the other. Both chapters contain prose traditions that have been shaped by the respective needs of the larger work in which they are included, and both were likely compiled in the exilic period.

To summarize: The ending of Jeremiah was likely influenced by the way 2 Kings concludes. It is difficult to discern if 2 Kings 25 is earlier in literary form than Jeremiah 52, since the prose traditions in Jeremiah's book have a lot in common with those in 1–2 Kings.

There are several minor differences between the Jeremiah and Kings accounts and one major difference. The major one is the omission of Gedaliah's assassination in Jeremiah 52 (cf. 2 Kings 25:22–26). The circumstances surrounding his death are certainly known to Jeremiah's compiler(s), since they are given a much fuller account in Jeremiah 40–41.

One minor difference comes in 52:11, where we read that Nebuchadnezzar put Zedekiah in prison until his death. The parallel in 2 Kings 25:7 simply notes that Zedekiah was blinded by the Babylonians, bound in fetters, and sent to Babylon. There is also a difference between the numbers of exiles cited in Jeremiah 52:28–30 when compared to the parallel data in 2 Kings.[2] Moreover, Jeremiah 52:30 records another wave of exiles in Nebuchadnezzar's twenty-third year (582 B.C.), a detail not provided in 2 Kings. This deportation could be punishment for the assassination of Gedaliah, but the reason is not given.[3]

Jeremiah 52 provides a retrospective of approximately thirty years. It begins with the account of the Babylonian siege in 588 B.C. and concludes with the notice in 52:31–34 that Evil-Merodach had released Jehoiachin from prison and allowed him to eat at the royal table. Evil-Merodach is the Hebrew version of *Amel Marduk*, son and successor of Nebuchadnezzar, who

---

1. See comments in the introduction to Jeremiah.

2. The numbers given in 2 Kings 24:13–16 for the deportation at the time of Jehoiachin (the seventh year of Nebuchadnezzar) are higher than those cited in Jer. 52:28. The smaller number given in Jeremiah may include only males.

3. As noted in the introduction, Josephus records that the Babylonian army campaigned in Ammon as punishment for the murder of Gedaliah (*Ant.* 10.9.7). Perhaps this campaign is linked to the deportation noted in 52:30. The problem is that we do not have a firm date for the death of Gedaliah. It may have come shortly after the fall of the city in 586 B.C.

had a short reign from 562−560 B.C. Jehoiachin would have been approximately fifty-three years old at the time of his release.[4] This last reference in chapter 52 gives the reader a likely indication of the date for the final compiling of the material in the book of Jeremiah.

Two different dates are given in Jeremiah 52 for the fall of the city to the Babylonians. They contribute directly to the differences one finds among scholars for the reconstructed date—either 587 or 586 B.C. In 52:12 the date is the nineteenth year of Nebuchadnezzar (so also 2 Kings 25:8), while in 52:29 it is assigned to the eighteenth year. These look like—and perhaps are—contradictory dates. One solution to the problem is to posit a copyist error. But which date is the error? Those who posit a date for the destruction in 587 B.C. suggest that the nineteenth year is a mistake, whether one of improper calculation on the part of the writer or simply a copyist error. Another suggestion is to see the date in 52:12 (nineteenth year) as reflecting a nonaccession-year dating scheme for Nebuchadnezzar, while interpreting the eighteenth year of 52:29 as assuming an accession-year dating for his regnal years. This would make 586 B.C. the date of the city's fall.[5]

52:1−11. The date of the ninth day and fourth month (v. 6) refers to the last year of Zedekiah's reign. The details of Zedekiah's capture should be compared with 39:1−7 and 2 Kings 25:1−7. Second Chronicles contains no narrative of Zedekiah's capture.

52:12−16. This brief description of the city's fall should be compared with 39:8 and 2 Kings 25:8−12. A reader only of Jeremiah 39 would not know that Nebuzaradan was the official in charge of burning the city and the temple. Indeed, 39:8 does not even mention the burning of the temple, as do the other two accounts.

52:17−23. This is a brief report of the looting of the temple (see also 2 Kings 25:13−17). A comparison of the two is fascinating. Each begins with a report that the Babylonians broke the bronze pillars, and there are similar details preserved between them. Nevertheless, each account preserves some distinctive elements. The Jeremiah account, which is the longer of the two, has more details about the carved pomegranates and the bronze pillars.

52:24−27a. These verses closely parallel 2 Kings 25:18−21.

52:27b−30. These verses preserve references to two waves of exiles during the reign of Nebuchadnezzar. The first wave came during the reign of Jehoiachin (597 B.C.), the second in 582 (see comments above).

---

4. According to 2 Kings 24:8, he was eighteen years old when he became king in Judah. He was exiled to Babylon in 597 B.C. after a reign of only three months. As noted in the introduction, archaeologists excavating the ruins of Babylon discovered ration tablets that mention the name of Jehoiachin and his five sons. See W. F. Albright, "King Jehoiachin in Exile," *BA* 5 (1942): 49−55.

5. See the discussion of chronology in the introduction.

52:31–34. This notice about Jehoiachin, which concludes Jeremiah, is paralleled in 2 Kings 25:27–30, which also concludes 2 Kings. It is far more than a simple report about a minor monarch being long-exiled. The report undergirds a type of muted but stubborn faith. Even when the land of Judah and the city of Jerusalem lie in ruins, one from David's line still lives.

Bridging Contexts

THE SIGNIFICANCE OF JEHOIACHIN'S RELEASE. Jeremiah 52 has a peculiar combination of a narrative that records recent events of a traumatic past with a concluding report that Jehoiachin, a member of the Davidic line and formerly king in Jerusalem for three months, was released from imprisonment in Babylon. This combination points to a way of reading the account as a lesson about the price of failure combined with an indication of a future open to the continuing efficacy of God's earlier promises made to David (2 Sam. 7; Jer. 23:5–6; 33:19–22).

Unless readers can draw continuing significance from narration about the past, past acts remain simply events that lie behind the present. Since a retelling of the past is typically done to uncover ways in which to understand the present, we should ask why the account of Jerusalem's fall is rehearsed (again). One reason is reflected in the widely quoted maxim, "Those who do not remember the past are doomed to repeat it." In the retelling of the story, we are instructed to live and learn from the mistakes of others. Such a reading can be instructive on the personal or the corporate level. It may point us toward introspection regarding our personal histories ("unfinished business") as well as the history of our nation and church.

The account of Jehoiachin's release comes like the small cloud of Elijah's ministry during a time of drought (1 Kings 18:41–46). There is the possibility of change and deliverance to come. The shape of that change is indicated by the person released. He is David's "son." Even though the final paragraph likely presupposes the death of Jehoiachin in Babylon, he is the agent of continuity in the Davidic line and thus the family history of the Messiah, which reaches its culmination in the birth of Jesus. A Christological reading of the chapter's conclusion grows out of the historical concerns of the compilers themselves. They wanted readers to know that all hope was not gone. Jehoiachin and his family were still living. And while the shape of any hope was inchoate, readers are invited to do more than simply acknowledge the judgment of the past. They are invited to be open to a future predicated on God's promises to the Davidic house.

The basic point is this: The original readers of Jeremiah 52 looked back on judgment, but through the notice concerning Jehoiachin they were invited to look ahead to ways in which God would fulfill his promises to them. This posture can be similar to that of any generation of God's people. Christians, for example, look back on the founding events of their faith—the death and resurrection of David's greater Son—but they also look forward to the second coming of Christ, when he will bring God's promised redemption to its final stage. Christians, like the generations of the Judean exile, live between promise and fulfillment.

BETWEEN THE TIMES. Because of his own and his people's failure, Moses did not enter the Promised Land. He did, however, see it from a distance. One might characterize his final point of view at Mount Pisgah as one between promise and fulfillment. He had the experience of having been led from Egypt, via Mount Sinai and the desert, to the edge of the Promised Land. He had tasted both victory and defeat, and though he himself gained a glimpse of the future, he ended his days before the surviving Israelites settled in the land promised to their ancestors.

Similarly, the point of view of Jeremiah 52 is that between the promise that judgment is not the end and the fulfillment of the promises of a better future and a ruler from David's line to come. This kind of dynamic in the lives of peoples and generations fits the profile of Christians. We are those who live "between the times," in the "already" of Christ's initial coming and in the "not yet" of his second advent, where sin and death still have their influence but where it is known that the future belongs to God. "For in this hope we were saved" (Rom. 8:24), wrote Paul. In the short term we are not invulnerable to failure and weakness, but the future realization of God's promised deliverance is sure—as sure and indestructible as Christ's resurrection from the dead.

God and the future. It is possible for those who "wait on the LORD" to renew their strength. It is possible because God provides the strength we need in our times of need. It is possible because no matter how strong or resilient the enemy, the future belongs to God, who is faithful. How this happens is the mystery of grace. One cannot explain it by a formula; one can only point to the God of new beginnings as the faithful God and Lord of life and death.

Matthew's genealogy of Jesus runs through the line of Jehoiachin (Matt. 1:11–12). What a story is packed into that simple genealogical list. Here is inspired commentary on sacred history. It is a reminder of how decades and centuries play a part in God's redemptive work, even when their twists and turns seem only confusing. Who would have thought that a king exiled for thirty-seven years meant much of anything other than years of frustration?

Jeremiah 52 is the final word about an influential epoch in sacred history. It is the final witness of the prophet Jeremiah's book. What we do with the witness is the way in which the ending of the book becomes an instructional piece in the unfolding drama of our lives. Jehoiachin died in captivity, yet he provided the means by which the Davidic family and the promises to it could continue. Jehoiachin's greater Son arrived in the fullness of time only to die at the hands of another imperial power. The story of which the book of Jeremiah is a part is still unfolding because Christ is alive and because he calls the current generation of God's people to discipleship and faithful living. So comfort one another with these words.

Introduction to Lamentations

Occasion and Date

THE BOOK OF LAMENTATIONS consists of five chapters of Hebrew poetry, joined together by the common themes of sorrow over the destruction of Jerusalem in 586 B.C. and the humiliation of Judah's population.[1] Individual poems within the book may have been compiled soon after the destruction of the city or anytime between that date and the rebuilding of the temple in 520–515 B.C. None of them gives any indication that the temple has been rebuilt at the time of composition.

Whether the individual poems were all composed in Palestine or in one or more of the exilic communities of Jews in Egypt or Babylon cannot be determined conclusively. Scholars also differ over whether one author wrote all five chapters or a compiler brought together laments of different provenance for a liturgical purpose. The poetic style of the chapters is classical, with a vocalized rhythm characteristic of a lament,[2] and it fits historically in the exilic period.

Authorship

NO AUTHOR IS named in the Hebrew version, and the book appears not in the prophetic section of the Hebrew Bible but in the last section, entitled "the Writings." Both of these points are understandable; much of the book gives voice to communal experience, there are few clues within the poetry itself to its human author(s), and the function of the book is different from that of a prophetic corpus.

The issue of authorship—regardless of who is responsible for it—is further complicated in that there are different voices expressed within the book.[3]

---

1. For the events leading up to the Babylonian capture and destruction of Jerusalem, see the introduction to the book of Jeremiah.

2. That the Hebrew poetry of chs. 1–4 in Lamentations contains an uneven poetic meter, defined as couplets with uneven lengths of line, was first proposed by K. Budde, "Das Hebraische Klagelied," *ZAW* 2 (1882): 1–22. He described it as the *qinah* meter, based on the Hebrew noun for lament/lamentation, and suggested that it can be seen in some other biblical laments where the imagery of a funeral is carried by the meter. See also W. R. Garr, "The *Qinah*: A Study of Poetic Meter, Syntax and Style," *ZAW* 95 (1983): 54–75. Current scholarship, however, uses the term *meter* less frequently and talks more about rhythm.

3. See further W. F. Lanahan, "The Speaking Voice in the Book of Lamentations," *JBL* 93 (1974): 41–49. The voices are that of the poet, personified Jerusalem, an unidentified man in ch. 3 (who may or may not be the poet personified), and the communal voice of Jerusalem's inhabitants.

In chapters 1–2 Jerusalem is personified as "Daughter ... Zion" (1:6; 2:1, 4, 8, 10, 13, 18) and speaks on occasion (e.g., 1:9b, 11b–16; 2:22) to supplement the poet's voice. An anonymous individual in chapter 3, who possibly should be identified with the poet of the book, speaks through a first-person lament. Plural forms are used in chapter 4, where there are references to "our eyes" (4:17) and (lit.) "our steps" (4:18). The first-person plural voice continues in chapter 5 in what is essentially a communal lament. The creativity of the human author(s) recedes behind the primary function of these poems, which is to articulate grief over the loss of Jerusalem and to speak aloud the devastating effects of Judah's sinfulness.

The earliest claim to human authorship comes in the Greek translation, where the first verse explicitly attributes the book to the weeping prophet Jeremiah.[4] In some Greek and Latin manuscripts attribution to Jeremiah is repeated at the beginning of chapter 5, as if that chapter needed additional comment. Chapter 5 is essentially a communal lament, with much of it "voiced" in first-person plural.

Such an association with Jeremiah is an ancient and plausible one, but that the prophet actually wrote the poems is historically unlikely. On the surface it is plausible, given the fact that the prophecy of Jeremiah itself contains laments/complaints, both for himself and for Jerusalem/Judah.[5] However, some of the emphases in Lamentations are different from the prophet's book,[6] and the thrust of the poetry is prayerful and liturgical, not prophetic. In

---

4. Lam. 1:1 in the LXX begins as follows: "After the captivity of Israel and the destruction of Jerusalem, Jeremiah sat weeping and composed this lament, saying...." The Babylonian Talmud tractate *B. Batra* 15a holds that Jeremiah wrote his book, that of Kings, and *Qinot*. *Qinot* is the plural form of *qina* and refers to the book of Lamentations. See note 2 above.

5. For Jeremiah's personal laments, see Jer. 11:18–12:6; 15:10–21; 17:14–18; 18:18–23; 20:7–13; 20:14–18. During a devastating drought Jeremiah takes up the people's lament in 14:1–9. In 8:18–9:3 Jeremiah expresses deep grief and weeps over the fate of the people. The way that he expresses himself seems also to present God's tearful grief over the people's fate (note the first-person complaint by God in 9:3). God laments the loss of "his house" in 12:7–13.

6. For a judicious assessment of the book's authorship and date, see the discussion by D. Hillers, "Lamentations, Book of," *ABD*, 4:138–39, and his commentary on *Lamentations* (AB; Garden City, N.Y.: Doubleday, 1992), 9–15. The haunting recollection of Zedekiah, Judah's last king, in 4:20 is far different from Jeremiah's sad but harsh denunciation of him. Similarly, Jeremiah's criticism of the temple and prediction of its demise are different from the plaintive comment in 1:10. In ch. 3 the poet is quite aware of his complicity in the failures of Zion. One scholar has gone so far as to suggest that parts of Lamentations are written to counteract some of Jeremiah's emphatic preaching on the judgment of Jerusalem and Judah. Cf. G. Brunet, "Une interpretation nouvelle du livre biblique des Lamentations," *RHR* 175 (1969): 115–17. While the poems of Lamentations are not inappropriate for Jeremiah, their tone is somewhat different from the "confessions" he offers.

2 Chronicles 35:25 Jeremiah is credited with a lamentation for King Josiah (640–609 B.C.), and its recitation by singers became a custom in Israel, but this is not likely a reference to the book of Lamentations.[7] The early association of Lamentations with Jeremiah is the reason that it appears in most modern versions after the prophetic book. As a part of Scripture Lamentations has a complementary function with Jeremiah's prophecies, providing yet another inspired assessment of Judah's fate.

Although it is unlikely that Jeremiah is the author of Lamentations, its association with him is one of several indications that the work fits into the broader context of the prophet's later life and times. The effects of the Babylonian army in besieging Jerusalem and in finally burning the city and temple precincts are everywhere reflected in the poignancy of the poetry. Someday Judah's humiliation will end (4:22), but there is nothing in the poems to indicate that either Jerusalem or the temple have been rebuilt. In short, the perspective of the voices in Lamentations is that of the Babylonian exile.

At some point in the Exile Judeans began to lament corporately and publicly in order to remember Jerusalem, the capital city, the location of the temple, and the symbolic mother of the people. Already in Jeremiah (Jer. 41:4–8), there is the account of pious men from the former Israelite territories traveling to the ruins of the temple in Jerusalem in order to worship. Their beards were shaved, their clothes torn, and their bodies gashed in order to mourn its destruction. According to Zechariah 7:1–7, there was traditional mourning in the fifth month of the year, and the prophet was asked about its efficacy and whether it should continue. The fifth month is the month of Ab (July/August), the same month of the temple's destruction.[8] Thus within the lifetime of those who witnessed the temple's destruction, there developed ceremonial lamentation to bewail and remember the tragedy, and the book of Lamentations is one result of these rituals.

Structure and Literary Style of the Book

THE FIVE POETIC CHAPTERS do not have a narrative base or reflect a literary plot. As noted above, it is not clear whether the five chapters were always joined in a collection or if one or more of them originated independently of the others. Thus, the effect of reading them sequentially is that of artful repetition, where the themes of suffering, judgment, confession of sin, and divine abandonment reappear.

---

7. This passage does, however, undergird the view that Jeremiah held King Josiah in great esteem, something that the book of Jeremiah also indicates (Jer. 22:15–16).

8. The temple was destroyed in the fifth month (2 Kings 25:8–9). The setting for the question to the prophet Zechariah is the fourth year of the Persian king Darius (7:1), which would be 518 B.C.

The book does have, however, clear subunits based on the five chapters. Each of the chapters is arranged in a recognizable pattern—that is, they are in poetry[9]—and each follows an aspect of the Semitic alphabet. Chapters 1–4 are known as acrostics because the poetic verses are arranged in a pattern following the sequence of the twenty-two letters in the Hebrew alphabet.[10] The first word of each verse in chapters 1 and 2 begins with a different letter of the alphabet and follows the alphabetic sequence of twenty-two letters from beginning to end. That is, 1:1 and 2:1 begin with a word whose initial letter is *aleph* (א), and 1:22 and 2:22 begin with a word whose initial letter is *taw* (ת). Chapter 3 has sixty-six verses but follows the same acrostic pattern, in three-verse units.[11] Chapter 4 follows the pattern outlined for chapters 1 and 2.[12]

Chapter 5 is somewhat different; it has twenty-two verses—as do chapters 1, 2, and 4—but the initial word of each verse in chapter 5 does not follow the alphabetical sequence. For this reason, most scholars do not describe chapter 5 as an acrostic. Although technically correct, the number of verses in chapter 5 is not likely coincidence.

Readers are left to infer the significance of the alphabetic pattern. Perhaps the best explanation is that the pattern is meant to signify fullness or completeness, something like the English expression "from A to Z" or the expression in the Revelation to John that the risen Lord is "the Alpha and the Omega . . . the Beginning and the End" (Rev. 22:13; cf. 1:8). The acrostic provides a structure for the public expression of emotion and the development of a theme. Once hearers or readers know that a communication is following an acrostic pattern, they may anticipate its length and know something of the medium of the message.

Within the literature of the Old Testament, the book of Lamentations has literary parallels with funeral laments, the psalms of lament/complaint, Job's complaints against God and friends, and prophetic oracles against nations. On hearing the account of Saul and Jonathan's death, for example, David composed a poetic funeral oration (2 Sam. 1:19–27). It contains themes that

---

9. For a good introduction to the characteristics of Hebrew poetry, with many bibliographical references, see the entry by A. Berlin, "Parallelism," *ABD*, 5:155–62. For Lamentations in particular, see Hillers, *Lamentations*, 16–31.

10. Several Psalms (Ps. 9–10, 25, 34, 37, 111, 112, 119, 145) and Proverbs 31:10–31 are also acrostics.

11. The first word in each verse of 3:1–3 begins with a word whose initial letter is *aleph*, and the first word in each verse of 3:64–66 has *taw* for its initial letter.

12. Actually chs. 2, 3, and 4 alter the traditional sequence of letters, putting the *pe* (פ) before the *ayin* (ע). This would be like putting the English letter *p* before the letter *o*. There is limited but suggestive evidence that some in Syria-Palestine followed an alphabet with the *pe* before the *ayin*. For details, see Hillers, "Lamentations, Book of," 4:139.

one also finds in Lamentations. For example, 2 Samuel 1:19 begins with reference to Saul as the "glory" of Israel, who "lies slain"; Lamentations 4:20 describes King Zedekiah as the "LORD's anointed, our very life breath," as caught in the captors' trap. Twice the oration cries out that "the mighty have fallen" (2 Sam. 1:25, 27), in tragic contrast to the praise of Saul and Jonathan's royalty (1:23–24). Repeatedly the book of Lamentations refers to the fall and humiliation of Jerusalem, who is personified as a princess (Lam. 1:1, 6), one cast down from heaven (2:1), and as perfect in beauty (2:15).[13]

Approximately half of Psalms is comprised of individual and corporate laments/complaints, with those of individuals being the most frequent.[14] These psalms have some or all of the following formal characteristics: complaints and/or cries of dereliction, petitions for deliverance and/or judgment on the enemies, confessions of sin, expressions of trust, and vows. Lamentations 3 and 5 have enough of these formal characteristics to be described as an individual and a corporate lament respectively, quite apart from their place in the book.

A poignant parallel to the voices of Lamentations comes in the defiant voice of the exiles in Psalm 137, where the pain over the fall of Jerusalem is raw and the anger toward the Edomites is palpable (v. 7). Edom too is remembered in Lamentations (Lam. 4:21–22). The individual voice of chapter 3 finds parallels in the psalms of individual lament/complaint,[15] the complaints of Jeremiah, and those of Job to God.

There are city laments in ancient Near Eastern literature, which are also related to the book of Lamentations. These are compositions that reflect on the fall of a city and its temple(s). The best-known examples are much earlier than the sixth century B.C. and come from Mesopotamia.[16] In some of them a prominent place is given to the patron goddess of the city, who

---

13. Amos offers a *Qinah* (a funeral lament) against Israel in 5:1–2, saying that the "Virgin Israel" is fallen, no more to rise. The term *virgin* is female and honorific and likely refers to the capital city of Samaria. F. W. Dobbs-Allsopp, *Weep, O Daughter of Zion: A Study of the City-Lament Genre in the Hebrew Bible* (Rome: Pontifical Biblical Institute, 1993), 97–154, demonstrates the broad connections between prophetic judgment speeches and the description of humiliated Jerusalem.

14. A classic treatment of the lament in the Old Testament is given in C. Westermann, *Praise and Lament in the Psalms* (Atlanta: John Knox, 1981), 165–213.

15. Hillers, *Lamentations*, 124, cites a number of the thematic and verbal parallels.

16. For further discussion see W. C. Gwaltney, "The Biblical Book of Lamentations in the Context of Near Eastern Lament Literature," in *Scripture in Context II: More Essays on the Comparative Method*, ed. W. W. Hallo et al. (Winona Lake, Ind.: Eisenbrauns, 1983), 191–211; Dobbs-Allsopp, *Weep, O Daughter of Zion*. A convenient translation of some Sumerian city-laments can be found in *ANET*, 611–19. Dobbs-Allsopp proposes that the book of Lamentations as a whole is an example of a city-lament genre. Hillers, *Lamentations*, 32–39, speaks more broadly of the "city-lament tradition."

mourns the fall of her city. Since there is no counterpart to the patron goddess in Judah (at least not among the circles responsible for the Old Testament), it is possible that the prominence given to personified Jerusalem as "Daughter ... Zion"[17] and the symbolic mother of the faithful is the Israelite counterpart to the broader, ancient Near Eastern tradition of patron goddesses. Recognition of Jerusalem's voice and personification is crucial to an adequate grasp of the book's style and its message.

A common category among prophetic books is that of oracles against foreign nations. The language is typically poetic, often mixed with sarcasm and invective, and holds out the claim of God's judgment to fall on the arrogance and cruelty of the states. Isaiah 47:1–15 is a splendid example of judgment depicted to fall on Babylon, the same power that besieged Jerusalem and brought Judah to a sorrowful end. The city of Babylon ("Virgin Daughter ... Babylon", 47:1) is depicted as a humiliated queen, bereft of her symbols of royalty and exposed shamefully. Widowhood will be her fate as judgment for her oppression and cruelty falls on her. The personification of Babylon as an exposed female, as a widow bereft of children, and as helpless before the onslaught are all portrayals repeated for Jerusalem in Lamentations.

The characteristics noted above are sufficient to indicate that Lamentations' contents are *traditional* in the typical cultural sense of the term. In the Israelite funeral, in individual and corporate laments, and in the broad tradition of lamenting the demise of a city, there are recognized formal characteristics and terminology that bear the emotions fit for the particular occasion. Lamentations brings these traditional elements together as a result of Judah's demise at the hands of the Babylonians.

Theology and Significance

ONE INDICATION OF LAMENTATIONS' significance comes in its use. As suggested above, the poetry provided a vehicle for a communal voice to lament the horror of Judah's fall. At some point in the exilic or postexilic period,

---

17. Some English translations (e.g., NIV) render the Hebrew phrase *bat ṣiyyon* (בַּת צִיּוֹן) as "daughter of Zion" while others render "Daughter Zion." There are complex grammatical matters in the discussion, but the better rendering in my judgment is the latter. "Daughter Zion" is the personified symbol of Jerusalem herself (cities are feminine in Hebrew); "Daughter *of* Zion" leaves open the possibility that it is someone who belongs to the city that is being described or addressed as the daughter. See the following helpful studies on this matter: M. E. Biddle, "The Figure of Lady Jerusalem: Identification, Deification and Personification of Cities in the Ancient Near East," in *The Biblical Canon in Comparative Perspective*, ed. K. Lawson Younger et al. (Lewiston, N.Y.: Edwin Mellen, 1991), 173–94; E. Follis, "Zion, Daughter of," *ABD*, 6:1103; and T. Frymer-Kensky, *In the Wake of the Goddesses: Women, Culture and the Biblical Transformation of Pagan Myth* (New York: Fawcett, 1992), 168–78.

God's people used the poetry that now comprises the book in public ceremonies of lamenting the temple's destruction. Whether initially or as a later
development, these ceremonies became regularized as an annual event (cf.
discussion in previous section). Likely the annual ceremony took place in
certain exilic communities and among Jews who returned to rebuild the
city and temple during the Persian period.

With the tragedy of the Roman capture and destruction of Jerusalem in
A.D. 70, the mourning ritual over the Babylonian destruction was supple-
mented with mourning for the later Roman destruction. That destruction of
Jerusalem and the temple complex was every bit as traumatic as the earlier
devastation wrought by the Babylonians. The joining of the two events
through the memory of ritual lamentation is the result of "telescoping"; that
is, a ceremony occasioned by an earlier event becomes the focal point for also
remembering a later and similar event. Thus, in classical Judaism the ninth
of Ab is a one-day ceremony (in August) in which Jews read the book of
Lamentations, and through its mournful language, worshipers recall the two
destructions of the temple.[18]

Articulation of Grief

ALL HUMAN BEINGS have a deep-seated need to process grief, death, and loss,
or to put it colloquially, "to come to grips with grief." The prevalent mode
of doing so in modern Western culture has been through psychological
understanding and therapeutic practices.[19] Many in modern society, therefore, are inclined to a psychological interpretation of the ritual mourning
for the loss of the temple as described above. There is something to that
analysis; anthropologists and cultural historians will point to the formative
power of public ceremony to provide symbolic meaning for participants. It
bears repeating, however, that premodern cultures did not process these

---

18. On this issue, see the discussion in M. Ydit, "Av, The Ninth of," in *Encyclopedia
Judaica* (16 vols.; Jerusalem: MacMillan, 1971), 3:936–40. According to the Talmud (*b.
Ta'an.* 30b), this commemoration of the temples' destructions is as important as Yom Kip-
pur (= the Day of Atonement).

19. One thinks of the impact in modern culture of the studies on death and dying by
E. Kubler-Ross, and more particularly the ways in which she has assisted people in pro-
cessing their grief. This is not to endorse all that has been claimed for her studies; rather,
it is to note how influential she has been in her psychological analysis of the process.
Indeed, there is a whole industry related to grief, death, and dying in Western culture.
Among her works are: *On Death and Dying* (New York: MacMillan, 1969); *Questions and
Answers on Death and Dying* (New York: Collins, 1974); *Death: The Final Stage of Growth* (Engle-
wood, N.J.: Prentice-Hall, 1975); *To Live Until We Say Goodbye* (Englewood, N.J.: Prentice-
Hall); *Living With Death and Dying* (New York: MacMillan, 1981); and *On Children and Death*
(New York: MacMillan, 1983).

matters psychologically—at least, not in the modern, Western sense of that term—but through various forms of ritual and symbolic performance.

Most likely, Lamentations gave form and procedure to mourning on the part of Judeans, but it did so without the self-consciousness and introspection that comes so "naturally" to modern readers and their analysts. Apparently the poetry (in ceremony) worked so effectively that its performance became an annual ritual. One should not read a negative evaluation into either the term "performance" or "ritual." While moderns think rightly of Lamentations as a form of literature, Judeans in exile understood the poetry as something to be performed. They recited it, sang it, and prayed it. This process brought to mind the continuing influence of a formative event. Furthermore, it helped define Judean corporate identity.

Grief, Complaint, and Hope in God

CLAUS WESTERMANN HAS PROPOSED that the enduring value of the book of Lamentations comes at just the point of its voice in the mourning over and protesting against the tragic events of 586 B.C.:

> It is highly significant that there is no attempt anywhere in Lamentations to request restoration. All that is asked for is God's return. God continues to be remembered, and the memory is kept alive in the complaints. They are placed before God in the hope that God's compassion will be aroused.[20]

Westermann helpfully calls attention to the roles of prayer and memory in forming an expectant people before God. In a public and prayerful way, Judeans were gifted with the opportunity to bring their pain and grief before the same God who had used the Babylonians to judge them and their ancestors. Like the insistent visitor at midnight (Luke 11:5–8) or the widow appealing to the judge (Luke 18:1–8), those who prayed the Lamentations brought the circumstances of their corporate identity before God.

Suffering and Confession of Sin

LAMENTATIONS HOLDS TOGETHER the grief that comes from tragedy and the pain that comes in acknowledging sin and its consequences. When one thinks corporately, the question is not, "How is this event a response to *me*?" but "How is this event a response to *us*?" Both tragedy and judgment are

---

20. C. Westermann, "The Complaint Against God," in *God in the Fray: A Tribute to Walter Brueggemann*, ed. T. Linafelt and T. Beal (Minneapolis: Fortress, 1998), 233–41 (quote on p. 236). See also his *Lamentations: Issues and Interpretation* (Minneapolis: Fortress, 1994).

voiced in Lamentations. Those voices speak first about a historical catastrophe and a judgment that fell on a particular people. Language about "feelings" is in service to this broader perspective. Weeping comes from both catastrophic loss[21] and the consequences of failure. Even those people who may not have lived in Judah during the tragic events of 586 B.C. are invited to find their place in the community affected by them. Indeed, by taking up the voices offered them in Lamentations, they are asked to learn from them. In this respect Lamentations has a function similar to certain "spirituals" in the African American community, since these songs continue to instruct a community long after the demise of slavery.

Clearing Ground for New Growth

THERE IS A sense in which the liturgical poetry of Lamentations plays a role similar to that of Ecclesiastes in the wisdom tradition. Ecclesiastes reminds readers of the limits of wisdom, of what the wise among humankind still cannot know or explain, of the inequities of life and its disappointments. To be sure, Ecclesiastes notes the joy that is associated with the Lord; moreover, the conclusion to the book reminds readers that it is best to fear God and keep his commandments, for in the future God will bring every secret matter to judgment. But having said these things, Ecclesiastes is primarily a book about limits and about what does not work. In the service of a greater revelation to come, it clears the ground of obstacles to new growth.

Lamentations similarly takes up the traditions of funeral poetry and prayers of anguish to clear away every vestige of self-righteousness, to close avenues of escape from responsibility for failure, and to drive home the uncomfortable truth that no one is finally exempt from God's searching judgments. To be sure, Lamentations confesses that God's mercies are new every morning (3:22–24), but the weight of the poems is to plumb the depths of human anguish and despair and to speak about such experiences to the Lord.[22] In the service of a greater revelation to come from God, Lamentations speaks both for and to human suffering.

---

21. F. W. Dobbs-Allsopp, "Tragedy, Tradition, and Theology in the Book of Lamentations," *JSOT* 74 (1997): 29–60, proposes that Lamentations is a work about tragedy. He points out that the book contains more complaints addressed to God than confessions of sin on the part of the community. Judgment on sin, he maintains, *is* a claim of the book, but the perspectives associated with tragedy and suffering are dominant. He understands that one contribution of the book is the heroic response to tragedy, i.e., the community should not react passively to suffering. Another is the compassion that the articulation of suffering brings. A third is the possibility that healing comes with the recitation of the laments.

22. K. Heim, "The Personification of Jerusalem and the Drama of Her Bereavement in Lamentations," in *Zion, City of Our God*, ed. R. S. Hess and G. J. Wenham (Grand Rapids: Eerdmans, 1999), 129–69.

Lamentations and the New Testament

IT IS NONE OTHER than Jesus who provides the primary place for lament in the New Testament. Apart from his practice, lamentation is not common in the New Testament. Jesus wept over Jerusalem as a sign of his grief regarding its unbelief and the consequences to come from it (Luke 19:41–44). In his Gethsemane prayer he sweated and prayed for the cup of suffering to be removed from him, but he finally placed himself in God's hands (22:39–46). This is a posture similar to the prayers in Lamentations—similar in the sense that one resolutely casts his or her fate into the hands of a God who seems absent at a moment of great need or perhaps remote and inscrutable.

Jesus' painful death on the cross is punctuated by the cry of dereliction (Mark 15:34): "My God, my God, why have you forsaken me?" This is, moreover, a quotation from a psalm of lament/complaint (Ps. 22:1). Here, it seems, the cry is not only a reflection of Jesus' own suffering but also a testimony to the power of Scripture to define human experience in light of God's self-revelation. A psalm of lament/complaint was a voice offered to those who suffer.

Psalm 22 had been instructive in this regard for centuries. Even David, the king after God's own heart and the psalmist for Israel, experienced judgment and forsakenness, and yet vindication in God's own timing (cf. Ps. 22:25–31). Jesus' passion is a salutary reminder that suffering and grief are endemic to the human race and that he is no exception. Indeed, one element of the atonement accomplished in Jesus' passion is his identification with human suffering. Jesus represents his own in all things, including tragedy and suffering. This is neither to deny or minimize the sacrificial mode of his death, only to note that his representative death is both sacrificial and tragic.[23]

Lamentation as a form of prayer is not common in the letters of the New Testament. Paul, for example, enjoins giving thanks in all circumstances with the advice to make petitions known to God (1 Thess. 5:16–18; cf. Rom. 12:12; Phil. 4:4–7). How strongly he may also have petitioned the Lord is hinted at in his thrice-made appeal to God to remove a physical affliction, his "thorn in the flesh" (2 Cor. 12:7b–10). He also urged believers to have solidarity with one another, and when appropriate, to "mourn with those who mourn" (Rom 12:15).

A form of lamentation, although somewhat different from the book of Lamentations, comes in the Revelation of John. After a stunning vision of the

---

23. In some Christian liturgies portions of Lamentations are read during Holy Week, including the Tenebrae service. Making Lamentations a part of the scriptural lesson for Holy Week entails an interpretation of the book as a witness to human suffering that Jesus has taken up and made his own.

heavenly throne room and the scroll with seven seals (Rev. 4:1–5:3), John weeps bitterly because no one is worthy to take the scroll (i.e., the book of life) and break its seals. This is a powerful depiction of human fallibility and its consequences apart from the intervening and redeeming acts of God. However, the Lamb, standing as though slain, is able to take the scroll and to receive the praise of those in heaven. Chapter 5 ends with songs of praise to God and to the Lamb who was slain to purchase the lives of the saints. Yet even in their redeemed state, those who were martyred can still ask, "How long?" concerning a fuller cosmic redemption that God has promised (6:10).

Perhaps the reason that the voice of lamentation is muted in the New Testament letters comes with the conviction that in Christ God has demonstrated decisively that he is for his people and that in spite of continuing judgment and refinement through the historical process God will not be thwarted in saving them. A book like Lamentations is a powerful indicator of the travail of human existence and of the way a particular historical experience can shape the perspective of many generations of people. In depicting God as strong in anger and judgment, the book takes its place in an unfolding revelation that points to a God who is more strongly resolute to save. Calvin's comment at the end of his own lectures on Lamentations is still worth pondering:

> The faithful, even when they bear their evils and submit to God's scourges, do yet familiarly deposit their complaints in his bosom, and thus unburden themselves.... Let us, then, know, that though the faithful sometimes take this liberty of expostulating with God, they yet do not put off reverence, modesty, submission, or humility.[24]

---

24. J. Calvin, *Commentaries on the Prophet Jeremiah and Lamentations* (Grand Rapids: Eerdmans, 1950), 513.

Outline of Lamentations

I. **The Royal City of Jerusalem Mourns Like a Widow** (1:1–22)
    A. The Poet Speaks about Her Destruction (1:1–9a)
    B. She Speaks in Anguish to the Lord (1:9b)
    C. The Poet Speaks Again of Her Suffering (1:10–11a, 17)
    D. Jerusalem Speaks in Mourning (1:11b–16, 18–22)

II. **Jerusalem Mourns the Day of the Lord's Anger That Fell on Her** (2:1–22)
    A. Destruction Is Described (2:1–10)
    B. The Poet Laments the Destruction of the People (2:11–13)
    C. The Poet Describes the Tragedy of Her Demise (2:14–19)
    D. God Is Addressed About His Work of Judgment (2:20–22)

III. **The Poet Speaks of Judgment and Mercy** (3:1–66)
    A. God's Judgment Has Fallen on the Poet (3:1–20)
    B. God Is Yet Merciful and Just (3:21–39)
    C. God's People Are Called to Examine Their Way, and God Examines the Poet's Way (3:40–66)

IV. **Jerusalem Is Examined Before and After Destruction** (4:1–22)
    A. Her Judgment Is Greater Than That of Sodom (4:1–11)
    B. Kings and Others Are Astounded At Jerusalem's Fall (4:12–16)
    C. The Poet Speaks of the People's Suffering and Loss (4:17–20)
    D. God Will Judge the Cruelty of Edom but Grant Jerusalem a Future (4:21–22)

V. **The Community Remembers and Asks God to Remember What Happened to Them** (5:1–22)

Bibliography

Biddle, M. E. "The Figure of Lady Jerusalem: Identification, Deification and Personification of Cities in the Ancient Near East." Pp. 173–94 in *The Biblical Canon in Comparative Perspective*. Ed. K. Lawson Younger et al. Lewiston, N.Y.: Edwin Mellen, 1991.

Brunet, G. "Une interpretation nouvelle du livre biblique des Lamentations." *RHR* 175 (1969): 115–17.

Budde, K. "Das hebraische Klagelied." *ZAW* 2 (1882): 1–22.

Cohen, C. "The Widowed City." *Journal of the Ancient Near Eastern Society of Columbia University* 5 (1973): 75–81.

Dobbs-Allsopp, F. W. "Tragedy, Tradition, and Theology in the Book of Lamentations." *JSOT* 74 (1997): 29–60.

_____. *Weep, O Daughter of Zion: A Study of the City-Lament Genre in the Hebrew Bible*. Rome: Pontifical Biblical Institute, 1993.

Garr, W. R. "The *Qinah*: A Study of Poetic Meter, Syntax and Style." *ZAW* 95 (1983): 54–75.

Gwaltney, W. C. "The Biblical Book of Lamentations in the Context of Near Eastern Lament Literature." Pp. 191–211 in *Scripture in Context II. More Essays on the Comparative Method*. Ed. W. W. Hallo et al. Winona Lake, Ind.: Eisenbrauns, 1983.

Heim, K. "The Personification of Jerusalem and the Drama of Her Bereavement in Lamentations." Pp. 129–69 in *Zion, City of Our God*. Ed. R. S. Hess and G. J. Wenham. Grand Rapids: Eerdmans, 1999.

Hillers, D. *Lamentations*. AB. Garden City, N.Y.: Doubleday, 1992.

Lanahan, W. F. "The Speaking Voice in the Book of Lamentations." *JBL* 93 (1974): 41–49.

Mintz, A. "The Rhetoric of Lamentations and the Representation of Catastrophe." *Prooftexts* 2 (1982): 1–17.

Moore, M. S. "Human Suffering in Lamentations." *RB* 90 (1983): 534–55.

Provan, I. *Lamentations*. NCB. Grand Rapids: Eerdmans, 1991.

Renkema, J. *Lamentations*. Leuven: Peeters, 1998.

Westermann, Claus. "The Complaint Against God." Pp. 233–41 in *God in the Fray: A Tribute to Walter Brueggemann*. Ed. T. Linafelt and T. Beal. Minneapolis: Fortress, 1998.

_____. *Lamentations: Issues and Interpretation*. Minneapolis: Fortress, 1994.

_____. *Praise and Lament in the Psalms*. Atlanta: John Knox, 1981.

Lamentations 1:1–22

¹ How deserted lies the city,
    once so full of people!
How like a widow is she,
    who once was great among the nations!
She who was queen among the provinces
    has now become a slave.
² Bitterly she weeps at night,
    tears are upon her cheeks.
Among all her lovers
    there is none to comfort her.
All her friends have betrayed her;
    they have become her enemies.
³ After affliction and harsh labor,
    Judah has gone into exile.
She dwells among the nations;
    she finds no resting place.
All who pursue her have overtaken her
    in the midst of her distress.
⁴ The roads to Zion mourn,
    for no one comes to her appointed feasts.
All her gateways are desolate,
    her priests groan,
her maidens grieve,
    and she is in bitter anguish.
⁵ Her foes have become her masters;
    her enemies are at ease.
The LORD has brought her grief
    because of her many sins.
Her children have gone into exile,
    captive before the foe.
⁶ All the splendor has departed
    from the Daughter of Zion.
Her princes are like deer
    that find no pasture;
in weakness they have fled
    before the pursuer.
⁷ In the days of her affliction and wandering
    Jerusalem remembers all the treasures
    that were hers in days of old.

When her people fell into enemy hands,
 there was no one to help her.
Her enemies looked at her
 and laughed at her destruction.
⁸Jerusalem has sinned greatly
 and so has become unclean.
All who honored her despise her,
 for they have seen her nakedness;
she herself groans
 and turns away.
⁹Her filthiness clung to her skirts;
 she did not consider her future.
Her fall was astounding;
 there was none to comfort her.
"Look, O LORD, on my affliction,
 for the enemy has triumphed."
¹⁰The enemy laid hands
 on all her treasures;
she saw pagan nations
 enter her sanctuary—
those you had forbidden
 to enter your assembly.
¹¹All her people groan
 as they search for bread;
they barter their treasures for food
 to keep themselves alive.
"Look, O LORD, and consider,
 for I am despised."
¹²"Is it nothing to you, all you who pass by?
 Look around and see.
Is any suffering like my suffering
 that was inflicted on me,
that the LORD brought on me
 in the day of his fierce anger?
¹³"From on high he sent fire,
 sent it down into my bones.
He spread a net for my feet
 and turned me back.
He made me desolate,
 faint all the day long.

14"My sins have been bound into a yoke;
     by his hands they were woven together.
They have come upon my neck
     and the Lord has sapped my strength.
He has handed me over
     to those I cannot withstand.
15"The Lord has rejected
     all the warriors in my midst;
he has summoned an army against me
     to crush my young men.
In his winepress the Lord has trampled
     the Virgin Daughter of Judah.
16"This is why I weep
     and my eyes overflow with tears.
No one is near to comfort me,
     no one to restore my spirit.
My children are destitute
     because the enemy has prevailed."
17Zion stretches out her hands,
     but there is no one to comfort her.
The LORD has decreed for Jacob
     that his neighbors become his foes;
Jerusalem has become
     an unclean thing among them.
18"The LORD is righteous,
     yet I rebelled against his command.
Listen, all you peoples;
     look upon my suffering.
My young men and maidens
     have gone into exile.
19"I called to my allies
     but they betrayed me.
My priests and my elders
     perished in the city
while they searched for food
     to keep themselves alive.
20"See, O LORD, how distressed I am!
     I am in torment within,
and in my heart I am disturbed,
     for I have been most rebellious.

Outside, the sword bereaves;
  inside, there is only death.
²¹"People have heard my groaning,
  but there is no one to comfort me.
All my enemies have heard of my distress;
  they rejoice at what you have done.
May you bring the day you have announced
  so they may become like me.
²²"Let all their wickedness come before you;
  deal with them
as you have dealt with me
  because of all my sins.
My groans are many
  and my heart is faint."

AS NOTED IN the introduction, this chapter is an acrostic. Each verse begins with a word whose initial letter follows the twenty-two-letter sequence of the Hebrew alphabet. The first word in verse 1, *ʾeka* ("How"), begins with *aleph*. As the initial word in the book, *ʾeka* is also the traditional name of the book for Hebrew-speaking people.

More than one voice speaks in chapter 1. The poet (the author's voice) begins, and it is complemented by that of personified Jerusalem. When the chapter is read as a unit, the "back and forth" of the two voices mutually reinforces the tragic dilemma of Jerusalem. Possibly the two voices offer a clue to the performance of the poetry among the survivors of Jerusalem's downfall. A poetic recital would give the opportunity not only to descriptive language— that is, that of the poet—but also that of the aggrieved herself, ravaged Jerusalem. The two voices are arranged as follows:

A. Verses 1–9a are the voice of the poet.
B. A quotation is attributed to personified Jerusalem in verse 9b.
C. Verses 10–11a are the voice of the poet.
D. An extended quotation is attributed to personified Jerusalem in verses 11b–16.
E. Verse 17 is the voice of the poet.
F. An extended quotation is attributed to personified Jerusalem in verses 18–22.

Verse 1 indicates the theme of the chapter; it depicts the noble city of Jerusalem in the mourning position of a widow. Not only is she described, but she will speak. The imagery for the city is drawn from three cultural traditions: (1) cities described as female, (2) the funeral tradition of public mourning, and (3) a tradition of using uncleanness and nakedness as metaphors for sinful behavior.[1]

The imagery for Jerusalem, personified and otherwise, runs throughout the chapter. She is a widow, once a noble woman and now a slave (1:1). The NIV rendering in verse 1, "she who was queen," translates the Hebrew noun *śara*, which indicates nobility or royalty but does not necessarily refer to a queen. It is the word used for the name of Abraham's wife, Sarah.

In verse 2 *śara* is forsaken by her "lovers." The term has a sexual overtone when used in a similar context by the prophets (e.g., Jer. 2:25b; Ezek. 16:36; Hos. 2:1–13), where it refers either to other gods pursued illicitly or to stronger neighbors with whom Israel or Judah sought to ingratiate themselves. The city's name is actually used for the first time in verse 4, where she is called "Zion" (also in 1:17). Elsewhere the city is named as "Daughter [of] Zion" (1:6), "Jerusalem" (1:7, 8, 17), and "Virgin Daughter of Judah" (1:15). Because of her sinfulness, the Lord has judged her, and her children have gone into exile (1:5; cf. 1:16, 18). Among her children are named "priests" (1:4, 19), "maidens" (1:4, 18), "people" (1:7, 11), and "young men" (1:15, 18).

The feminine personification runs throughout the chapter, with one exception. In 1:17 the lament is that the "LORD has decreed for Jacob that *his* neighbors become his foes." Here the name of the ancestor, which in previous years had sometimes been used for the northern kingdom,[2] serves to personify the nation of Judah and its capital as a covenant partner gone bad. Otherwise, the female imagery extends remarkably even to Judah in verse 3.[3] Jerusalem is the metaphorical daughter/princess in the Lord's realm and/or the daughter of Judah (i.e., the name of the state).

The language of chapter 1 refers to the sinfulness of Judah and to a resulting sorrow and suffering. These things are related to one another; sinfulness has led to judgment and suffering. Their link is expressed succinctly in 1:5, "the LORD has brought her [i.e., Zion] grief because of her many

---

1. On the cultural habit of depicting cities as female and on the language of funeral, see the introduction. "Unclean" and "nakedness" are used by the prophets (e.g., Ezek. 7:19–20; ch. 16) to depict sinful behavior. Whether such usage developed as part of the prophetic speech repertoire or whether they borrowed it from another rhetorical tradition is unknown. Judgments about clean and unclean are the work of priests and Levites. In 2 Chron. 29:5 Levites are asked to remove the "defilement" (so NIV) from the sanctuary. It is the same term translated "unclean" in Lam. 1:17.

2. In Amos 7:2, 5, Jacob is a synonym for Israel and refers to the northern kingdom and its capital city of Samaria. Cf. Lam. 2:2–3.

3. In the Heb. text of v. 3, the verbs associated with Judah are inflected as feminine.

sins" (cf. 1:8, 14, 18, 20, 22). The emphasis falls, however, on the grief, the suffering, and the pitiful nature of the city. She "weeps" (1:1–2, 16) and "groans" (1:8, 21–22), and is "in bitter anguish" (1:4) and "distress" (1:20–21). Nothing here points to the relief of the city's woes.

The ongoing nature of the city's suffering is underscored by the fivefold repetition of the phrase, "there is [was] none [no one] to comfort her" (1:2, 9, 16, 17, 21), and the concluding comment of the chapter that her "heart is faint."[4] In the comment that "her friends have betrayed her" (1:2), the city takes up a familiar theme from the psalms of lament/complaint (Ps. 38:11; 88:8). The chapter falls short of claiming that God has betrayed the city, but it seems clear that the experience of divine judgment has shattered the emotions of the poem's speakers.

The voice of the poet depicts Jerusalem in the posture of "remembering" her days of affliction (1:7). This posture of remembering or bringing to mind again captures much of the reason for the book of Lamentations as a whole. What is depicted for Jerusalem is actually what the readers (or performers) do when reciting the poem.

In verse 16 Jerusalem weeps, for there is no one to comfort her. This is certainly true with respect to the poems of the book. Apart from the marvelous affirmation in 3:22–24, the tenor of the poems is almost unrelieved in its anguish. One gets only a hint of the other side of judgment in 4:21–22, which envisions judgment on the ravagers of Jerusalem and an end to the exile of Judah and Jerusalem. The same term "comfort" (*nḥm*), however, is used in Isaiah 40:1 in the imperative form as a command to "comfort" Jerusalem, since her anguish will come to an end and because she has paid double for her sins. Possibly there is a scriptural "echo" at work in Isaiah 40:1–2, whereby the cry of Jerusalem in Lamentations is taken up in the prophetic call to comfort the bereaved city.

In verse 22 Jerusalem asks that the evil done to her by her enemies be brought before God so that he can deal with them. An answer to this sentiment also lies largely outside the book. In texts like Obadiah and Isaiah 47 readers again may get an intertextual echo of Lamentations and the desire for vindication.

AN INTERPRETER MAY EXTRACT certain "themes" from chapter 1 and then seek to apply them to a setting in ministry today. That exercise would be unhelpful without more consideration of how chapter 1 says what it says. Put another way, there is more to the text than the simple extrapolation of anguish as a result of an ancient tragedy. How "it

---

4. This last phrase can refer to physical illness or emotional distress (cf. Isa. 1:5; Jer. 8:18).

says what it says" is a primary clue to its meaning for earlier readers, and with proper attention to detail and context, the "how" element can instruct modern readers as well.

(1) The female language points to a familial and corporate depiction of the capital city. By familial is meant the metaphor of membership in God's family. As the royal "daughter," she is a member of Yahweh's family and an intimate covenant partner with him. Jerusalem is also the political and cultural center of Judah. Reference to her is tantamount to a corporate reference to Judah. In that sense, to mention Jerusalem is *pars pro toto* (a part representing the whole). Her failures, therefore, are failures against a family identity and responsibility. Her shame reflects negatively on her failure to maintain a proper family identity and obedience to its standards of behavior.

(2) Zion laments with respect to her fall from grace and to her anguish. Her mourning reflects in almost ritual fashion a pattern of funeral lament. Rather than first reading this in psychological terms, it is important to read the text as an indication of social status. Daughter Zion has lost her status as virgin princess and as family member. At certain levels of relationship, she has died. Deadly judgment and public shame are mixed together. Her humiliation reflects also the shame of rejection by God and that of violation by her (and finally God's) enemies. In this case, the shame and anguish are heightened because her enemies have laughed at or celebrated her downfall. As is common with the laments/complaints of the Psalter, the celebrations and taunts of the enemy are particularly bitter to take.[5]

(3) Zion brings her lament and anguish directly to God. It is a dynamic worthy of careful attention. God has brought the shame and humiliation on her, but he is also the One to whom she turns in lamentation. It is almost as if she reminds God that her humiliation also means his loss as well. Her ridicule could become his as well. She can deny neither her failure nor her neediness. Her neediness is something that only God can fully grasp and only God can fully heal. One function of her lamentation is to give voice to her failures, so that God will recognize in her voice an indication of confession and an appeal for mercy.

It is important to remember that the "she" in this chapter is a corporate reference. Personified Zion is the people. Here we have finally an ecclesiology. God judges his people through their sin and suffering, and they offer their pain to the Lord.

---

5. Cf. 4:21—22 and the caustic language about Edom.

IN THE SUMMER OF 1999 John F. Kennedy Jr. died in a tragic airplane crash. Subsequent investigation concluded that he had likely miscalculated his navigational skills for night-time flight. He, his wife, and her sister were killed in the single plane crash. For American readers, JFK Jr. was close to royalty. With regard to his tragic death, one headline read: "The End of Camelot." Adding to the grief was the fate of his father, President John Kennedy, himself a victim of tragedy when he was shot and killed in November 1963.

It all seemed so senseless. John Jr. was young, handsome, and rich. The public outpouring of grief, however, was out of proportion to what JFK Jr. had accomplished in life. This comment is not meant to denigrate his life but to illustrate the public persona that JFK Jr. had become. Tragically, an American prince had died. His name and family represented much in the realms of American public life and national identity, and with his demise came an end for some people in their way of perceiving American identity.

The demise of Jerusalem brought with it the end of certain ways of perceiving a relationship with the Lord. How difficult it was (and is!) to grasp meaning in the context of tragedy. Just as some could now ask, "What will life be like without the ideals represented by JFK Jr.?" so God's ancient people asked, "What will life be like without Zion and Judah?" How difficult it is for God's people to see themselves in light of their failures. They first must know that to be God's people is a precious privilege, and then that it is possible for something to threaten that privilege so that they cannot take it for granted. Separation and exclusion from the family of God are painful. Shock is added to the pain with the subsequent recognition that failure has separated people from God in such a way that the rift cannot be healed from Daughter Zion's side any more than it can be healed from the church's side. It can only be healed from God's side.

The subsequent history of Jerusalem demonstrates that God can restore what Judah's failures had corrupted. In Jesus Christ the God who judged Jerusalem and worked through her destruction was himself judged. Christ bore the failures of the world as well as judged them. The poetry of Lamentations is one of the most articulate voices for confession of sin and lament over failure. The poems themselves point first to the consequences of failure; as tragedy they loom larger than life and seemingly out of proportion to the failure. But most important, they are directed to the only One who can hear them fully and adequately respond.

Lamentations 2:1–22

¹ How the Lord has covered the Daughter of Zion
     with the cloud of his anger!
He has hurled down the splendor of Israel
     from heaven to earth;
he has not remembered his footstool
     in the day of his anger.
² Without pity the Lord has swallowed up
     all the dwellings of Jacob;
in his wrath he has torn down
     the strongholds of the Daughter of Judah.
He has brought her kingdom and its princes
     down to the ground in dishonor.
³ In fierce anger he has cut off
     every horn of Israel.
He has withdrawn his right hand
     at the approach of the enemy.
He has burned in Jacob like a flaming fire
     that consumes everything around it.
⁴ Like an enemy he has strung his bow;
     his right hand is ready.
Like a foe he has slain
     all who were pleasing to the eye;
he has poured out his wrath like fire
     on the tent of the Daughter of Zion.
⁵ The Lord is like an enemy;
     he has swallowed up Israel.
He has swallowed up all her palaces
     and destroyed her strongholds.
He has multiplied mourning and lamentation
     for the Daughter of Judah.
⁶ He has laid waste his dwelling like a garden;
     he has destroyed his place of meeting.
The LORD has made Zion forget
     her appointed feasts and her Sabbaths;
in his fierce anger he has spurned
     both king and priest.
⁷ The Lord has rejected his altar
     and abandoned his sanctuary.

He has handed over to the enemy
 the walls of her palaces;
they have raised a shout in the house of the LORD
 as on the day of an appointed feast.
⁸ The LORD determined to tear down
 the wall around the Daughter of Zion.
He stretched out a measuring line
 and did not withhold his hand from destroying.
He made ramparts and walls lament;
 together they wasted away.
⁹ Her gates have sunk into the ground;
 their bars he has broken and destroyed.
Her king and her princes are exiled among the nations,
 the law is no more,
and her prophets no longer find
 visions from the LORD.
¹⁰ The elders of the Daughter of Zion
 sit on the ground in silence;
they have sprinkled dust on their heads
 and put on sackcloth.
The young women of Jerusalem
 have bowed their heads to the ground.
¹¹ My eyes fail from weeping,
 I am in torment within,
my heart is poured out on the ground
 because my people are destroyed,
because children and infants faint
 in the streets of the city.
¹² They say to their mothers,
 "Where is bread and wine?"
as they faint like wounded men
 in the streets of the city,
as their lives ebb away
 in their mothers' arms.
¹³ What can I say for you?
 With what can I compare you,
 O Daughter of Jerusalem?
To what can I liken you,
 that I may comfort you,
 O Virgin Daughter of Zion?
Your wound is as deep as the sea.
 Who can heal you?

¹⁴ The visions of your prophets
    were false and worthless;
they did not expose your sin
    to ward off your captivity.
The oracles they gave you
    were false and misleading.
¹⁵ All who pass your way
    clap their hands at you;
they scoff and shake their heads
    at the Daughter of Jerusalem:
"Is this the city that was called
    the perfection of beauty,
    the joy of the whole earth?"
¹⁶ All your enemies open their mouths
    wide against you;
they scoff and gnash their teeth
    and say, "We have swallowed her up.
This is the day we have waited for;
    we have lived to see it."
¹⁷ The LORD has done what he planned;
    he has fulfilled his word,
which he decreed long ago.
    He has overthrown you without pity,
he has let the enemy gloat over you,
    he has exalted the horn of your foes.
¹⁸ The hearts of the people
    cry out to the Lord.
O wall of the Daughter of Zion,
    let your tears flow like a river
    day and night;
give yourself no relief,
    your eyes no rest.
¹⁹ Arise, cry out in the night,
    as the watches of the night begin;
pour out your heart like water
    in the presence of the Lord.
Lift up your hands to him
    for the lives of your children,
who faint from hunger
    at the head of every street.
²⁰ "Look, O LORD, and consider:
    Whom have you ever treated like this?

Should women eat their offspring,
the children they have cared for?
Should priest and prophet be killed
in the sanctuary of the Lord?
²¹"Young and old lie together
in the dust of the streets;
my young men and maidens
have fallen by the sword.
You have slain them in the day of your anger;
you have slaughtered them without pity.
²²"As you summon to a feast day,
so you summoned against me terrors on every side.
In the day of the LORD's anger
no one escaped or survived;
those I cared for and reared,
my enemy has destroyed."

CHAPTER 2 CONTINUES the mournful tone of the previous chapter. The poet again frequently refers to Jerusalem as "Daughter,"[1] and the pronoun "her" is used throughout to designate things that belong to or are associated with the city. Covenant terms such as *Jacob* and *Israel* also occur (2:1–3) to refer to those whom God has judged. Each of these terms emphasizes that the city, the state, and their inhabitants were and are members of God's people.

Careful examination of chapter 2 reveals several changes in the speaker's form of address. Verses 1–10 describe, in the third person, the suffering and anguish of the city through what God has done to them. God has covered the city with "the cloud of his anger" (2:1); he has "burned in Jacob like a flaming fire" (2:3; cf. 2:5); God has "handed over to the enemy the walls of her palaces" (2:7); and so on. Verses 9–10 describe Jerusalem in her pathetic state.

In verse 11 the poet uses the first-person "I" to describe his weeping and torment with respect to the awful condition of "my people." This is a most interesting verse, since the pattern from chapter 1 suggests that the first-person speech belongs to that of personified Jerusalem. Indeed, some commentators take it that way. However, the first person of 2:13 is that of the poet addressing Jerusalem, and it seems best overall to take 2:11 as also the

---

1. Lam. 2:1, 4, 8, 10, 18 = Daughter Zion; 2:13 = Virgin Daughter Zion; 2:2, 5 = Daughter Judah; 2:13, 15 = Daughter Jerusalem.

voice of the poet. The alternation between description and first-person lament gives poignancy to the circumstances of Jerusalem's humiliation.

First-person references come also in verses 13 and 22. The former is the voice of the poet addressing Jerusalem, but verses 20–22 are perhaps better taken as the voice of Jerusalem. Verse 22 refers to those whom the speaker has cared for and raised—verbs associated with child-rearing. Since Jerusalem is frequently personified as a mother, it seems best to see her as the final speaker of chapter 2. In fact, verses 18–19 seem to address the wall(s) of Jerusalem with the urge to cry out. If correct—and verse 18 is textually difficult—this call to the wall(s) of Jerusalem is an example of metonymy, a literary device whereby something is represented or personified by a constituent part.

We may therefore set out the chapter's voices as follows:

A. Verses 1–10 are the poet's description of Jerusalem's anguish and humiliation.
B. Verses 11–13 are the poet's first-person response to Jerusalem's wretchedness.
C. Verses 14–17 are again the poet's description of Jerusalem.
D. Verses 18–19 are a call to Jerusalem's walls to cry out to God.
E. Verses 20–22 are addressed to God by Jerusalem (perhaps more specifically her "walls"; cf. v. 18).

Both the city (2:13–19) and God (2:20–21) are addressed directly. These are second-person references ("you ... your"). The effect overall of this chapter is to move beyond a surface description to give a more nuanced and personal portrait of those judged and bereaved and to ask God about the rightness of the devastation.

The great distinction of Zion's calling is reflected in 2:1. She is the "splendor" (*tip'eret*) of Israel. This word can be used of an ornament or jewel. In Isaiah 60:7 God describes the temple as "my glorious house" (*bet tip'arti*). In Psalm 99:5 the ark of the covenant is described as God's "footstool," a term also used in in 2:1 in parallel with Israel's splendor. The city was "the perfection of beauty, the joy of the whole earth" (2:15; cf. Ps. 48:2), until it came crashing down.

In 2:3 the poet laments the fact that God has "cut off every horn of Israel." The term *horn* can be used as a metaphor for strength or honor, though it can also refer to the upraised corner or protrusions at the ends of a sacrificial altar (Ex. 29:12; Lev. 4:7; Ps. 118:27). It was customary in Israel that those who "grasped the horns of the altar" had asylum and would not be slain (cf. 1 Kings 1:49–53). Thus the comment that God has cut off every horn in Israel can mean that God has destroyed the pride and nobility of the people and/or that God has removed any means of seeking asylum from the judgment fallen on Jerusalem and Judah.

God is so angry with Jerusalem that he is destroying "his" things that are within her. God has "laid waste his dwelling" and "destroyed his place of meeting" (2:6). Verse 7 elaborates on this matter: God has "rejected his altar and abandoned his sanctuary." The presence of the sacred temple in the midst of Jerusalem was no guarantee of God's benevolence or protection. The so-called "temple sermon" of Jeremiah made this view quite clear (Jer. 7 and 26). Even parts of the city are personified to underscore the horror of what has befallen God's jewel. The walls of the city lament and weep over their destruction (2:8, 18).

Judgment is unsparing on those leaders who should have led the people in a different direction. The king is rejected and exiled (2:6, 9); the visionary task of the prophets failed them and their people (2:9, 14, 20). Priests are spurned, and now Torah is gone (2:6, 9, 20).

God used the enemy to judge his people and his city. In remarkably pointed and anguished language, the poet asks God whether he has ever treated anyone else like this (2:20). It is as if God has become the enemy by using the enemy.

THE LANGUAGE OF JUDGMENT and destruction in Lamentations is almost a mirror image, a tragic reversal, of the language of the Zion psalms. Those psalms celebrate the greatness of Jerusalem as an agent of God's election and as the secure home of the faithful. A refrain from Psalm 46 says, "The LORD Almighty is with us; the God of Jacob is our fortress" (46:7, 11; cf. 46:1). God is in the midst of the holy city; she shall not be moved (46:5). In the midst of the temple precincts, a worshiper ponders God's steadfast love (48:9). Visitors are encouraged to walk around the ramparts of Jerusalem in order to tell the next generation that "this is God" (48:12–14). But now the security of the city of God has been rolled away by God himself, who has aided Jerusalem's enemies in destroying the city.

The function of this mirror image is to critique a theology of election as privilege and to underscore the necessity of responsibility. Here is a hermeneutical clue for one way to read the book of Lamentations, broadly speaking, and more particularly, to appropriate chapter 2. As with the harsh words of Jeremiah 7, Lamentations confesses that one cannot assume God will protect his own at all cost. No one can stand on holy ground and assert that nothing will overcome it/them. The fall of the city in 586 B.C. is proof of that. Chapter 2 portrays the royal city of God as destitute because of her failures.

Within the language of pain and despair are references to familiar failures. The leadership of God's people has failed miserably to educate and to serve the people responsibly. Here is a theme with wide scriptural endorsement—one that is of paramount concern in any age. It is important to note, however, that with all the language of failure and even accusatory language toward God, there is no suggestion that God has brought into being a turn of events incompatible with his will.

Certainly it is also important to note that modern readers should not universalize from the historical experience of 586 B.C. and the poetry of despair it produced. Not every situation of despair, whether of a group of people or an individual, is God's judging hand. Moreover, the almost defiant tone one picks up among the laments can be a spur to resist attempts to be defined solely as victims seeking pity. Defining oneself or one's group as victims with trampled rights can be both accurate and proper, but such defining can also lead to self-righteousness.

 LAMENTATIONS 2 TEACHES both an important historical lesson and one way to pray. The historical lesson, stated succinctly, is that nothing made by human hands can save—not even something as significant as the house of the Lord. Yes, God can give up on an institution founded at his instruction and capable of mediating his grace to generations of worshipers. God can even make war against it. That somber news is tempered by the truth that God can raise the dead and that God's ultimate will to save cannot be thwarted by the historical demise of a central "saving" institution. Congregations, denominations, and nations (including the modern state of Israel) need to hear this. They should hear both tones of the lesson. They are not indispensable to God, but God is gracious nevertheless.

The frankness of the language in Lamentations should persuade people that God is open to their real feelings and their honest reactions to tragedy. There is no "answer" in the immediacy of overwhelming tragedy, and one's prayers ought to reflect that. The great miracle of the gospel is that the One to whom despair and bitterness are directed is the One whose only Son suffered the travail of the cross. God, who strove against Jerusalem and Judah, also engaged the principalities and powers to gain an eternal victory for his people.

Yes! All things work together for good to those who love God and who are called according to his purpose (Rom. 8:28). His purpose is to conform us to the image of his Son. That means quite a bit of chiseling and disciplining for us. Not everything is good, but things that happen work toward the good purpose of our incorporation into Christ.

Lamentations 3:1–66

¹I am the man who has seen affliction
   by the rod of his wrath.
²He has driven me away and made me walk
   in darkness rather than light;
³indeed, he has turned his hand against me
   again and again, all day long.
⁴He has made my skin and my flesh grow old
   and has broken my bones.
⁵He has besieged me and surrounded me
   with bitterness and hardship.
⁶He has made me dwell in darkness
   like those long dead.
⁷He has walled me in so I cannot escape;
   he has weighed me down with chains.
⁸Even when I call out or cry for help,
   he shuts out my prayer.
⁹He has barred my way with blocks of stone;
   he has made my paths crooked.
¹⁰Like a bear lying in wait,
   like a lion in hiding,
¹¹he dragged me from the path and mangled me
   and left me without help.
¹²He drew his bow
   and made me the target for his arrows.
¹³He pierced my heart
   with arrows from his quiver.
¹⁴I became the laughingstock of all my people;
   they mock me in song all day long.
¹⁵He has filled me with bitter herbs
   and sated me with gall.
¹⁶He has broken my teeth with gravel;
   he has trampled me in the dust.
¹⁷I have been deprived of peace;
   I have forgotten what prosperity is.
¹⁸So I say, "My splendor is gone
   and all that I had hoped from the LORD."
¹⁹I remember my affliction and my wandering,
   the bitterness and the gall.

²⁰ I well remember them,
 and my soul is downcast within me.
²¹ Yet this I call to mind
 and therefore I have hope:
²² Because of the LORD's great love we are not consumed,
 for his compassions never fail.
²³ They are new every morning;
 great is your faithfulness.
²⁴ I say to myself, "The LORD is my portion;
 therefore I will wait for him."
²⁵ The LORD is good to those whose hope is in him,
 to the one who seeks him;
²⁶ it is good to wait quietly
 for the salvation of the LORD.
²⁷ It is good for a man to bear the yoke
 while he is young.
²⁸ Let him sit alone in silence,
 for the LORD has laid it on him.
²⁹ Let him bury his face in the dust—
 there may yet be hope.
³⁰ Let him offer his cheek to one who would strike him,
 and let him be filled with disgrace.
³¹ For men are not cast off
 by the Lord forever.
³² Though he brings grief, he will show compassion,
 so great is his unfailing love.
³³ For he does not willingly bring affliction
 or grief to the children of men.
³⁴ To crush underfoot
 all prisoners in the land,
³⁵ to deny a man his rights
 before the Most High,
³⁶ to deprive a man of justice—
 would not the Lord see such things?
³⁷ Who can speak and have it happen
 if the Lord has not decreed it?
³⁸ Is it not from the mouth of the Most High
 that both calamities and good things come?
³⁹ Why should any living man complain
 when punished for his sins?
⁴⁰ Let us examine our ways and test them,
 and let us return to the LORD.

⁴¹ Let us lift up our hearts and our hands
    to God in heaven, and say:
⁴² "We have sinned and rebelled
    and you have not forgiven.
⁴³ "You have covered yourself with anger and pursued us;
    you have slain without pity.
⁴⁴ You have covered yourself with a cloud
    so that no prayer can get through.
⁴⁵ You have made us scum and refuse
    among the nations.
⁴⁶ "All our enemies have opened their mouths
    wide against us.
⁴⁷ We have suffered terror and pitfalls,
    ruin and destruction."
⁴⁸ Streams of tears flow from my eyes
    because my people are destroyed.
⁴⁹ My eyes will flow unceasingly,
    without relief,
⁵⁰ until the LORD looks down
    from heaven and sees.
⁵¹ What I see brings grief to my soul
    because of all the women of my city.
⁵² Those who were my enemies without cause
    hunted me like a bird.
⁵³ They tried to end my life in a pit
    and threw stones at me;
⁵⁴ the waters closed over my head,
    and I thought I was about to be cut off.
⁵⁵ I called on your name, O LORD,
    from the depths of the pit.
⁵⁶ You heard my plea: "Do not close your ears
    to my cry for relief."
⁵⁷ You came near when I called you,
    and you said, "Do not fear."
⁵⁸ O Lord, you took up my case;
    you redeemed my life.
⁵⁹ You have seen, O LORD, the wrong done to me.
    Uphold my cause!
⁶⁰ You have seen the depth of their vengeance,
    all their plots against me.
⁶¹ O LORD, you have heard their insults,
    all their plots against me—

⁶²what my enemies whisper and mutter
　　against me all day long.
⁶³Look at them! Sitting or standing,
　　they mock me in their songs.
⁶⁴Pay them back what they deserve, O LORD,
　　for what their hands have done.
⁶⁵Put a veil over their hearts,
　　and may your curse be on them!
⁶⁶Pursue them in anger and destroy them
　　from under the heavens of the LORD.

CHAPTER 3 EXPANDS on the acrostic pattern of the first two chapters. Instead of a chapter of twenty-two verses, where the initial word in each verse follows the sequence of letters in the Hebrew alphabet, this chapter has sixty-six verses, compiled of twenty-two stanzas, where the stanzas follow the sequence of the Hebrew alphabet. Thus each stanza has three verses, and the initial word of each verse in a stanza begins with the same letter of the alphabet.

Chapter 3 is dominated by first-person references, the language of "I" and "we." This raises the question of authorship in a way the previous two chapters do not. The emphasis of the previous two chapters on the tragic fate of Jerusalem is in the background of chapter 3; front and center is the travail of an individual. Some scholars have taken a cue from this chapter and seen a reference to Jeremiah in the first-person voice. Although possible, most scholars have not found that view convincing.[1] With respect to this individual, there is much language about judgment and the need for repentance that sets his voice apart from that of Jeremiah. In any case, chapter 3 has several of the constituent elements of a lament/complaint so well known from the book of Psalms.[2]

It is worth asking whether in chapter 3 we as readers are dealing with an individual voice in the fully modern sense of that term (i.e., an individual whose suffering and experience is provided in autobiographical form), or whether the "I" is the poet's voice in service to the larger community of

---

1. See the discussion in the introduction regarding authorship.

2. Among these elements are: description of dire circumstances, references to the persecution of the enemy, plea for God to judge the enemies, plea to God for protection or deliverance, invitation to repentance. Two examples can be cited for comparison. Psalm 56 speaks of the persecutions of the enemies and implores God to be gracious and to deliver the psalmist. Psalm 88 speaks of travail as the threats of the "pit" (cf. Lam. 3:53, 55).

readers and those who pray the Lamentations. The balance of probability favors the latter. This view does not deny that the suffering voiced in chapter 3 is real; it assumes that the suffering is real and not imagined or choreographed, but it understands that the presentation of the suffering is paradigmatic and that the voice of suffering invites those who hear and read to make it their voice. Put another way, the individual voice of chapter 3, which includes "we" and "our," speaks in order to provide a voice for the suffering members of his community. The first generations of readers would understand the formulaic language of chapter 3 (by way of the laments in the Psalter) to be paradigmatic of the poet's time and generation.

The "I" of chapter 3 is likely the poet of the book. He has seen the destruction of the city and its people, and the language of pain and suffering is filtered through both self-reference and shared experience ("we" and "our"). The language of individual travail is also reminiscent of Job,[3] whose "speeches" are much like psalms of individual lament/complaint, especially in the description of his sufferings, in the recounting of the machinations of his "friends," and in his appeal to God for deliverance. Likewise, the affirmation of God's benevolent faithfulness is derived from the central confessions of the Old Testament (see below).

The poet first sees God as the source of trouble, who has turned his rod and hand against the poet (3:1–3). God has besieged and walled him in (3:4–9), as if the fate of the city and the poet are the same. God is a lion or bear, or more menacingly, an archer taking aim at the poet (3:10–12).

In slightly different language the enemies of Zion have condemned and hunted the poet (3:46–54). They plot, insult, and mock him (3:58–63). He recapitulates in his person the suffering endured by the city and its inhabitants. Because his experience is shared by his contemporaries, it is relatively easy to follow the shift in the language from "I" to "we."

As noted above, the terminology of what is essentially an individual lament abounds in scriptural echoes. Darkness is a place of judgment and anguish (3:2, 6).[4] Barring of a way is evidence of judgment (3:9).[5] Divine judgment is compared to the assaults of lions and bears (3:10)[6] and arrows (3:12).[7] The persecution of the enemies is like being hunted or immersed in water (3:52–54).[8]

---

3. See, e.g., Job 9:34 and 21:9 (3:1); Job 19:8 (3:2); Job 7:18 (3:3); Job 3:23 (3:7); Job 30:20 (3:8); Job 7:20 (3:12); Job 6:4 (3:13). Other examples could be cited.

4. See Mic. 7:8–10, where sitting in darkness is a sign of judgment (see also Job 23:16–17).

5. See Hos. 2:6, where God builds a wall so that the wayward mother (Israel) cannot find her way.

6. Ps. 10:9; 22:13; Hos. 13:7–8.

7. Ps. 7:12–13; 38:2–3.

8. Ps. 11:1; 69:1–2; 124:2–7; 140:5.

Memory plays an important role in a lament. Sometimes the poet asks God to remember and sometimes he himself remembers or recalls the previous deeds of the Lord. Such is the case in 3:19–24. Both suffering and redemption are part of the poet's experience, and he sets their memories side by side. God is the source not only of judgment but also of deliverance. Since he knows that God is strong to save, he says he has "hope" (3:21, 24). The word in Hebrew is a verb (*yḥl*), which has the sense of waiting with expectancy.[9] This means that the resignation seen elsewhere in Lamentations is tempered by the realization that God, who has struck both Jerusalem and the poet, is the same One who can overturn the shame of public judgment and humiliation.

In 3:22 the "great love" of the Lord renders the Hebrew term *ḥesed*. While love is not a wrong translation, the term also carries the meaning of kindness and loyalty.[10] *Ḥesed* is the kind of act that is not required by civil law but springs from the concerned character of the one who acts. A good place to see its focus is in the saying of Hosea 6:6, that God prefers *ḥesed* to sacrifice and the *knowledge of God* rather than burnt offerings. *Ḥesed* and knowledge of God are paired together in the poetic couplet, and both are contrasted with ritual acts that, while good and proper, must proceed from something deeper and more fundamental than a sense of obligation. Stated differently, sacrifice is a requirement of the Torah and therefore good and proper in context, but *ḥesed* is something that can be freely given but not defined by requirements.

Closely related to the term *ḥesed* is that of compassion(s)—*raḥᵃmim* in the Hebrew of 3:22. The best analogy is that of parental concern, for in the singular *reḥem* can mean womb.[11] Finally, the poet confesses that God is great in faithfulness (*ᵉmuna*; 3:23). One finds these three terms in the great self-definition that God offers of himself to Moses in Exodus 34:6–7:

> The LORD, The LORD, the compassionate [*raḥum*][12] and gracious God, slow to anger, abounding in love [*ḥesed*] and faithfulness [*ᵉmet*],[13] maintaining love [*ḥesed*] to thousands, and forgiving wickedness, rebellion and sin. Yet he does not leave the guilty unpunished; he punishes the children and their children for the sin of the fathers to the third and fourth generation.

One can read the claims of Lamentations about judgment and mercy and see them as the outworking of this great self-definition of God. The

---

9. Cf. Job 6:11; also 1 Sam. 10:8; 13:8.
10. D. A. Baer and R. P. Gordon, "חֶסֶד," *NIDOTTE*, 2:211–18.
11. M. Butterworth, "רחם," *NIDOTTE*, 3:1093–97. Lam. 3:32 pairs the words *ḥesed* and *rḥm* (vb. in Piel, to have compassion).
12. *Raḥum* is an adjective formed from the basic root *rḥm*.
13. Heb. *ᵉmet* is a variant form of the basic term *ᵉmuna*.

corporate judgment that fell on Judah and Jerusalem is like the judgment that falls to the third and fourth generation, since what is likely meant by them is the claim of completeness. To judge the third and fourth generation is to deal with all involved. By contrast, to show mercy and forgiveness to thousands is to claim that mercy and forgiveness abound further than the third and fourth generation of complete retribution.

As with psalms of lament/complaint, the poet speaks of the "pit," which seeks to claim his life (3:53, 55). In the stanzas of 3:52–57, the poet prays like the beginning of Psalm 130: "Out of the depths I cry to you, O LORD." The poet then reminds God that he has seen and heard what the enemies have done. His own life is like a judicial case (3:58), where God the Judge should rule in his favor. The chapter, again like some of the psalms of lament/complaint, concludes with the plea of the poet for God to judge the enemies. In this the poet is also reminiscent of Jeremiah, who sought judgment on his tormenters (Jer. 11:20; 15:15; 17:18; 18:19–23; 20:12).

As is sometimes also the case with psalms of lament/complaint, the poet is moved to speak about repentance (Lam. 3:40–45). Significantly, the language is first-person plural: "Let us examine . . . let us return . . . let us lift." This indicates that the poet's experience is linked with that of his community. They become one before God. It also signifies the function or impact of Lamentations as a whole. The poems move readers to consider their lives in light of God's holiness and his cleansing judgment.

HUMAN SUFFERING AND RESPONSE. If one looks for an overall impression of chapter 3, it is its similarity to the psalms of individual lament/complaint and to the complaints of Job. These parallels also provide the first indications of how they may be interpreted in modern contexts. Job and Lamentations are fundamentally oriented toward two issues: God's character in the face of human suffering, and the human response to God in the context of its suffering. Chapter 3 offers several windows on these two issues.

(1) God was not absent from the travail and tragedy that accompanied the fall of Jerusalem. God was present as Judge, using historical circumstances in the process of judging and refining his people. The enemies, who in stylized language afflicts the poet, are also agents of God's approach to the poet and the poet's lamenting community. "Why should any living man complain when punished for his sins" (3:39)? Correspondingly, repentance is one response that the poet advocates to his contemporaries. It is characterized by self-examination in light of God's holiness and by a return to the Lord and

his covenant stipulations. Judgment on the poet's enemies is still an option for God, even if he has used the "enemy" as a means to reach the poet.

(2) God is also present as someone who loves his wayward people in spite of their sinfulness. There is more than affirmation of divine judgment in this chapter. If this was not also the experience of the poet before God, he could not have written 3:22–24, and he could not have affirmed that "though [God] brings grief, he will show compassion, so great is his unfailing love" (3:32). Note that the poet's affirmation comes at the center of the book, in the midst of the middle chapter. Perhaps this placement is a clue, although a small one, that God's loyalty is ultimately the center of existence for a believer.

(3) The way into the future and the way back to God remain open. In addition to repentance the poet gives voice to a plea that God will hear his voice and act (3:56). Job-like in his despair and in his persistent seeking of an audience with God, the poet reminds God that he (God) had defended the poet's case and is his Redeemer. Without a full explanation for his pitiful circumstances, the poet clings to God and asks him to remove the injustice done to him. Only someone with a robust confidence in God's ability to hear and act can speak and pray in this fashion.

In a larger canonical context, one can see the circumstances of the poet similarly portrayed in the life of Christ. The paradigmatic Psalm 22, a classical lament/complaint, helped the early church see meaning in Christ's death and resurrection. Much of the poet's experience in chapter 3—especially persecution, suffering, and alienation—are also part of Christ's experience. More importantly, he endured them on behalf of those he loved. Whether receiving the judgment due to sinners or suffering the fate of the unjustly accused, Christ represented it all in his atoning work, just as he had made it part of his own lived experience. The God to whom the poet prayed and to whom the poet wished to return is the God revealed in and through Jesus Christ.

QUEST FOR SPIRITUALITY. It is illuminating to set the language of Lamentations 3 in the context of the modern quest for (in some cases almost an obsession with) spirituality. We must distinguish carefully between interest in a subject and the particular content or truthfulness of the subject material. There can be no doubt about the rising interest in spirituality in North America, just as there can be no doubt that for many people the topic has been loosened from any connection with a church (i.e., group or corporate identity) or historic form of theology. A recent headline in a secular magazine read "God Dethroned." The point of the piece was that the quest for a personal spirituality and religious experience in the Western world is increasingly being pursued apart from the traditional means of Christian grace.

In a recent phone conversation a pastor friend told me of a conference she was organizing for her congregation around the theme *The People of God*. A steering committee at the church was eager to explore several issues related to the practice of spirituality in daily life. One committee member reported that his neighbor would be a good person to make a presentation about modern spirituality. When the pastor inquired a bit about the neighbor, she discovered that it was the neighbor's intense interest in spirituality that had impressed the congregation member, even though he didn't know whether the neighbor was a Christian or not.

Chapter 3 of Lamentations comes in the context of historical experience and inherited revelation. It has several marks of authentic spirituality. The language of the text is thoroughly imbued with terms and concepts found elsewhere in the Old Testament. There is no doubt in the poet's mind that he is dealing with the living God, who revealed himself to his ancestors and acted in judgment in the destruction of Jerusalem. The questions for the poet are how to make sense of his tragic circumstances and how to approach his future in relationship to this God.

The poet looks at his circumstances squarely and sees them as God's approach to him and to his community. In response, the poet sees the circumstances as indications of a way forward in his spirituality. (1) He sees the tragedy of Jerusalem's fall as a revelation of the Lord, not as the entry of a new and foreign deity into his life or the stubborn arrival of an irrational mystery. Judgment is consistent with the character of God revealed in Torah, prophecy, and the psalms.

(2) He learns that prayer and confession directed toward God bring him into fellowship with God.

(3) He finds that repentance is more than a concept, that it is a tangible way of relating to God. Repentance is not a magical elixir but a series of steps taken toward God in obedience to his will. For many people, failure to acknowledge the truth about God is less an intellectual matter and more a moral matter; and more particularly a matter of the will. That is why confession and repentance are integral to authentic spirituality.

(4) He seeks God for deliverance and healing. He is able to see that his circumstances are the occasion for fresh prayers and newfound vows.

(5) It probably never occurs to him that his spirituality can be a private matter. His confession that God is faithful also includes affirmation that "we" are not consumed. His call to repentance offers steps for "us" to return to the Lord.

(6) For the poet "waiting" on the Lord includes the practices of prayer and repentance and does not assume that waiting is merely marking time.

Obedience. One of the mysterious sayings in the New Testament is the affirmation in Hebrews 5:8 that Jesus learned obedience through things suffered. Clearly the obedience that Jesus embraced did not emerge from his earlier sinfulness. Instead, his incarnation and the life he lived gave shape to a kind of spirituality he shared with his followers. The poet of Lamentations 3 learns a kind of obedience from the things he has suffered. He gives voice to them because his experience is meant to be shared. Christian spirituality has a goal: to be conformed to the image of Christ. By the incarnation of his Son, God has given us a Savior, who was fashioned to draw us to himself. Suffering and travail can be means to that end, not in a masochistic or pain-denying way, but in ways that the poet of Lamentations is just beginning to grasp.

Lamentations 4:1–22

¹ How the gold has lost its luster,
   the fine gold become dull!
The sacred gems are scattered
   at the head of every street.
² How the precious sons of Zion,
   once worth their weight in gold,
are now considered as pots of clay,
   the work of a potter's hands!
³ Even jackals offer their breasts
   to nurse their young,
but my people have become heartless
   like ostriches in the desert.
⁴ Because of thirst the infant's tongue
   sticks to the roof of its mouth;
the children beg for bread,
   but no one gives it to them.
⁵ Those who once ate delicacies
   are destitute in the streets.
Those nurtured in purple
   now lie on ash heaps.
⁶ The punishment of my people
   is greater than that of Sodom,
which was overthrown in a moment
   without a hand turned to help her.
⁷ Their princes were brighter than snow
   and whiter than milk,
their bodies more ruddy than rubies,
   their appearance like sapphires.
⁸ But now they are blacker than soot;
   they are not recognized in the streets.
Their skin has shriveled on their bones;
   it has become as dry as a stick.
⁹ Those killed by the sword are better off
   than those who die of famine;
racked with hunger, they waste away
   for lack of food from the field.
¹⁰ With their own hands compassionate women
   have cooked their own children,

who became their food
    when my people were destroyed.
¹¹ The LORD has given full vent to his wrath;
    he has poured out his fierce anger.
He kindled a fire in Zion
    that consumed her foundations.
¹² The kings of the earth did not believe,
    nor did any of the world's people,
that enemies and foes could enter
    the gates of Jerusalem.
¹³ But it happened because of the sins of her prophets
    and the iniquities of her priests,
who shed within her
    the blood of the righteous.
¹⁴ Now they grope through the streets
    like men who are blind.
They are so defiled with blood
    that no one dares to touch their garments.
¹⁵ "Go away! You are unclean!" men cry to them.
    "Away! Away! Don't touch us!"
When they flee and wander about,
    people among the nations say,
    "They can stay here no longer."
¹⁶ The LORD himself has scattered them;
    he no longer watches over them.
The priests are shown no honor,
    the elders no favor.
¹⁷ Moreover, our eyes failed,
    looking in vain for help;
from our towers we watched
    for a nation that could not save us.
¹⁸ Men stalked us at every step,
    so we could not walk in our streets.
Our end was near, our days were numbered,
    for our end had come.
¹⁹ Our pursuers were swifter
    than eagles in the sky;
they chased us over the mountains
    and lay in wait for us in the desert.
²⁰ The LORD's anointed, our very life breath,
    was caught in their traps.

> We thought that under his shadow
>> we would live among the nations.
> ²¹Rejoice and be glad, O Daughter of Edom,
>> you who live in the land of Uz.
> But to you also the cup will be passed;
>> you will be drunk and stripped naked.
> ²²O Daughter of Zion, your punishment will end;
>> he will not prolong your exile.
> But, O Daughter of Edom, he will punish your sin
>> and expose your wickedness.

CHAPTER 4 VARIES the presentation of the city's fall from that given in chapters 1–2 or 3. A dominant motif here is a chronological contrast or what may be called a "then and now" contrast. The poet contrasts the former splendor of the city and its inhabitants with the pitiful conditions of his own day.

Verses 1–2 set a tone for the poem, where he compares the presiege city and its inhabitants to gold, the most precious metal in the ancient world. The postsiege and destroyed city is dull metal and scattered jewels, and its sons are pots of clay, subject to breaking at any moment.

With verse 3 comes a depressing comparison. The carrion-eating jackal cares enough to suckle its young, but the poet's people are like the ostrich. This is not a self-evident comparison to modern readers. Perhaps the ostrich's habit of burying eggs and leaving them gave it the reputation of being heartless (cf. Job 39:13–16). In any case, the dehumanizing effects of oppression continue their deadly work among a spent people.

One shocking effect of the Babylonian siege was the enormity of the changes that happened to families with children. There was no food for the children to eat (4:4), so they had to beg for sustenance.[1] Indeed, since there is nothing for anyone to eat, some mothers even cooked their own children (4:10). Although the comment about cannibalism is made without elaboration, the emotional impact can hardly be overestimated.[2]

---

1. Note the brief (but ominous) comment about famine in 2 Kings 25:3. Lam. 2:11–12 also reminds the reader of the insidious affliction of famine.

2. Deut. 28:53–57 lists cannibalism as a curse to come on God's people should they break the covenant God granted them. Lev. 26:29 similarly speaks of the eating of children as a curse to come on Israel for disobedience to the Lord. Since in Lam. 4:11 the poet speaks of God's venting his anger on Zion, it may be that he links the cannibalism of 4:10 with God's judgment and not only with a tragedy brought on by Zion's enemies. In any case, it is almost certain that he understands the fall of Zion and its horrific aftermath as the outworking of Zion's failures (i.e., breach of covenant faithfulness).

Such dire circumstances give rise to a speculative thought concerning death. The poet suggests that those who died from the sword are better off than those who died from famine (4:9). It is not clear whether the poet really believes this is so or whether he states the comparison for its effectiveness in depicting the horror of Zion's fall. One may compare the author of Ecclesiastes, a master of rhetoric in making a point, in his claims that the dead have it better than the living, and that better than either is the one never born (Eccl. 4:1–6). The logic of such a statement is, of course, suicide. But since Ecclesiastes does not advocate suicide elsewhere or opt for it in his own case, presumably he is exaggerating to make a point about life's inequities.

Similarly, the poet of Lamentations underscores the pain and despair of his generation rhetorically by noting how much longer and more painful it is to starve than to die by the sword. Perhaps we should interpret similarly the comment about the punishment on Zion as greater than that for Sodom (4:6). Sodom—it should be recalled—was wholly consumed in fire in a way that Zion was not. God's judgment on Sodom was proverbial as an example of swift and total punishment, and this is the reason for its employment in the poetry of Lamentations 4.[3]

The poet picks up a strand of teaching about Jerusalem's failure that is given elsewhere in the Old Testament, namely, that the leadership of the people shed "the blood of the righteous" (4:13, i.e., innocent blood). Whether this means by active persecution or by allowing injustice is not stated. One finds this charge against Manasseh in 2 Kings 21:16, against Jehoahaz in Jeremiah 22:17, and against princes and officials in Ezekiel 22:6, 27.[4]

There is a reflection of the popular "theology of Zion" in 4:12, a belief that Jerusalem was sacrosanct and that God would not allow the city to fall. By "popular" is meant that it was well-received by the populace and thus a well-known sentiment. We should add immediately that this view was *not* held in such a simplistic formulation by inspired prophets such as Isaiah, Jeremiah, and Ezekiel, who spoke a word of the Lord against a number of popular (mis)conceptions of their contemporaries. Jeremiah, in particular, railed against a blind belief in the inviolability of the temple area (see Jer. 7; 26). The poet of Lamentations notes (perhaps rhetorically) that foreign kings were surprised at Zion's fall, as if everyone knew of Zion's special status.

Lamentations 4:17 picks up on another theme given in prophetic accounts, namely, that help from another state would not save Zion. Jeremiah

---

3. See Deut. 29:23; Isa. 1:9–10; Jer. 49:18; 50:40; cf. Matt. 11:20–24.

4. Ps. 106:38–39 states that the shedding of innocent blood defiles a land and the perpetrating state.

notes that the Babylonian siege was temporarily lifted because of an approaching Egyptian army (Jer. 34:21–22; 37:5–11). Hopes for relief, however, quickly died when the siege was reinstated.

The poet speaks movingly of Zedekiah, Zion's reigning monarch at the time of the city's fall (4:20). He uses a striking phrase to describe his royal role—that Zedekiah was the very "life breath" of the people. Comparison of this statement with the strong polemic of Jeremiah against Zedekiah is one reason why some scholars conclude that Jeremiah cannot be the author of Lamentations. However one decides that issue, verse 20 reflects poignant appreciation for the royal office ("the LORD's anointed"). The royal messiah (i.e., "anointed one") represented and gave life to the people. Metaphorically his "shadow" provided security for the people like the shadow or wings of the Lord for the righteous (cf. Ruth 2:12; Ps. 17:8; 91:1, 4).

Finally, verses 21–22 refer to an end to Zion's punishment and the beginning of Edom's judgment from the Lord. Apparently, the assistance Edom gave the Babylonians in taking Zion was a particularly bitter pill for Judeans. After all, Judah and Edom were joined by blood.[5] Nothing is said directly about an Edomite role in the fall of Jerusalem, but the vitriolic language of Psalm 137:7; Joel 3:19–21; and Obadiah 10–14 make it clear that Edom had committed treachery.

This oracle-like conclusion to chapter 4 has a strong ironic bite to it. Edom is actually called on to rejoice and be glad [in the present] because the cup is about to be passed, and they will be harshly judged in the future. Partaking of a celebratory cup—which turns on its drinker and leads to drunkenness and judgment—is a proverbial motif of judgment throughout the Old Testament. The content of the cup initially tastes good, but it contains the wrath of judgment soon to be dispensed.[6]

The judgment that fell on Zion was severe, but it will have an end (4:22a). In succinct fashion the two parts of this affirmation show the major function of Lamentations. On the one hand, judgment has fallen, and the resulting tragedies are everywhere in evidence. On the other hand, a confession on the part of the people helps prepare the way for the new thing God will do in bringing an end to Jerusalem's bereavement and humiliation.

---

5. Judah traced her lineage back to Jacob and Edom to Esau (cf. Gen. 36:1, where Esau is explicitly equated with Edom).

6. Jeremiah uses the image several times (Jer. 13:13; 25:15–29; 48:26; 49:12; 51:7, 39). The majority of these references come in oracles against the wickedness of other nations. Cf. Hab. 2:15–16 and esp. Obad. 15–16: "The day of the LORD is near for all nations. As you [Edom] have done, it will be done to you. . . . Just as you drank on my holy hill, so all the nations will drink continually; they will drink . . . and be as if they had never been."

THEN AND NOW. The "then and now" mode of presentation of chapter 4 is a basis on which to proceed toward a modern appropriation of the text. Jerusalem's demise at the hands of the Babylonians (and Edomites!) came as the result of sweeping historical forces used by the Lord to judge and discipline his people. Assumed in this presentation of great privilege and great fall is Jerusalem's place in the divine economy. It was a marvelous place because God had chosen it for the seat of Davidic rule and the location of the temple, where his name and glory dwelt. Any destruction of human life and limb is tragic, but the fall of Jerusalem is particularly poignant because she is "Daughter ... Zion," God's chosen vehicle.

There is a pattern to be discerned and prayerfully contemplated in the "then and now" motif: The church is an object of God's gracious choice, formed through the hammer and anvil of the historical process and intended as the spiritual home and sustenance of believers. Comprised of God's people, the church has taken a variety of forms in the unfolding revelation we call history. It has suffered grievously at times, and in the power of the Holy Spirit it has given birth to redemptive miracles. God has granted the church, or parts thereof, more than one angle of vision to see its past and present set before the seat of assessment.

Correspondingly, individual believers will recognize the pattern of tragedy and triumph, a kind of "then and now" too, as part of the Christian life. Christian lives are grounded in God's gracious call and subject to the various fits and turns known as providence.

It is important to note the way this chapter ends. The poet notes that God will not prolong the exile of Daughter Zion. At a time he has determined, Jerusalem and Judah will be reconstituted. It was and remains an ongoing process. For both individuals and the church, the future lies open to God's redeeming grace and his judgment on wickedness.

ACCEPTING RESPONSIBILITY. *The New York Times* carried an editorial for July 5, 2000, written by Thomas Lynch entitled "A Man's Right to Choose." His first point has to do with the essence of adulthood in modern America, which is to exercise choice among options. He notes that his three sons and daughter can choose their sexual partners and how much to invest in the broader relationship that comes with sexual activity. Mr. Lynch knows that such choices/commitments are not easy, and he hopes (as do all parents) that his children will choose wisely, including the taking of precautions to avoid unwanted pregnancies. Lynch wonders, however—and this is his next point—that since his daughter can legally avail herself of the option to terminate a pregnancy, why cannot also his three sons legally avail themselves of the option to disallow responsibility for an unwanted child. As he puts it:

> If the choice as to when one is ready, willing and able to parent is a good thing, wouldn't it be good for my sons as well? And if that choice may be exercised by women after conception, then shouldn't men have the same option: to proclaim, legally and unilaterally, the end of their interest in the tissue or fetus or baby or whatever it is that sex between a man and a woman sometimes produces?

Lynch reminds the reader that Roe versus Wade gave a woman the right to choose, but that once a child is born, the father is forced minimally into eighteen years of fiscal responsibility. He thinks it better if men as well as women can choose whether to be a parent or not, and that the state should not compel men any more than women to be parents.

The point of this quick summary is not to say that Lamentations 4 is an antiabortion, profamily piece, nor is it to vilify Mr. Lynch (with whom this author emphatically disagrees). It is to show how presuppositions about individual freedom and options of withdrawal of responsibility sit so differently beside a text like Lamentations 4, with its heartfelt concern for the inhabitants of Zion who have died or who are suffering, and above all its presupposition that God has placed them in places of moral and spiritual responsibility in which they will be held accountable.

Zion's (then) recent tragedy is set in the context of a history in which God called the city and its inhabitants to exercise their covenant responsibilities, to be a city set on a hill as a light to the nations, and to show forth God's praise. The poet laments the loss of people, great and small, while acknowledging communal responsibility for her demise. Everywhere it is assumed that God's people are called to exercise a moral and spiritual life in the public realm and that there have been and will be consequences to moral choices. This is not just an Old Testament conviction; it is broadly biblical and as relevant today as in the past.

In the twenty-first century it is still the case that there is no evading of responsibility in God's economy, so that it is false and misleading to view life as comprised primarily of morally neutral choices to be made by autonomous people. We have no right to move in and out of social commitments like stock options in building a portfolio.

The past, present, and future alike come under the judging, refining, and transforming work of God. We are called to moral and spiritual accountability.

We, as creatures made in the image of God, are much more than "the tissue or fetus or baby or whatever it is that sex between a man and a woman sometimes produces" (the terminology of Mr. Lynch). All of us have a past as well as a future in which we are held morally and spiritually accountable. There will be harsh and tragic words in the future for those who think that freedom and pleasure are the goals of human existence. By God's grace they can be gifts in due season, but that is a far different matter than the goal of radical autonomy. The latter is a false god and leads ultimately to catastrophe.

God grants joy and peace in the Holy Spirit, but the freedom of his children comes through embracing a gospel of redemption and renewal—redemption from the effects of sin and selfishness, and renewal in the image and likeness of Christ. God will not prolong "your exile," but "wickedness" will be exposed. That was true then, and it will remain so.

Lamentations 5:1–22

¹ Remember, O LORD, what has happened to us;
   look, and see our disgrace.
² Our inheritance has been turned over to aliens,
   our homes to foreigners.
³ We have become orphans and fatherless,
   our mothers like widows.
⁴ We must buy the water we drink;
   our wood can be had only at a price.
⁵ Those who pursue us are at our heels;
   we are weary and find no rest.
⁶ We submitted to Egypt and Assyria
   to get enough bread.
⁷ Our fathers sinned and are no more,
   and we bear their punishment.
⁸ Slaves rule over us,
   and there is none to free us from their hands.
⁹ We get our bread at the risk of our lives
   because of the sword in the desert.
¹⁰ Our skin is hot as an oven,
   feverish from hunger.
¹¹ Women have been ravished in Zion,
   and virgins in the towns of Judah.
¹² Princes have been hung up by their hands;
   elders are shown no respect.
¹³ Young men toil at the millstones;
   boys stagger under loads of wood.
¹⁴ The elders are gone from the city gate;
   the young men have stopped their music.
¹⁵ Joy is gone from our hearts;
   our dancing has turned to mourning.
¹⁶ The crown has fallen from our head.
   Woe to us, for we have sinned!
¹⁷ Because of this our hearts are faint,
   because of these things our eyes grow dim
¹⁸ for Mount Zion, which lies desolate,
   with jackals prowling over it.
¹⁹ You, O LORD, reign forever;
   your throne endures from generation to generation.

²⁰ Why do you always forget us?

Why do you forsake us so long?

²¹ Restore us to yourself, O LORD, that we may return;

renew our days as of old

²² unless you have utterly rejected us

and are angry with us beyond measure.

 THE FINAL CHAPTER of Lamentations is a corporate lament, a mournful address to God, seeking his recognition of his people's sufferings and reminding him of the continuing effects of these sufferings on them. The text is not arranged as an acrostic in the ways that the first four chapters are, but the number of verses is twenty-two, the same as chapters 1–2 and 4. Perhaps the use of twenty-two verses is a final reminder that this communal response to the suffering of Judah and Jerusalem moves once more, like the previous chapters, from beginning to end.

The dominant voice in this chapter is first-person plural. There are pleas to God (5:1, 20–21), descriptions of dire circumstances and their ongoing oppressiveness (5:2–18), confession of sin (5:16), and affirmation of God's majesty (5:19). Verse 1 calls on God to remember what has happened to the people, and verse 20 comes back to the matter of what God knows or remembers by asking: "Why do you always forget us?" Between 5:1 and 5:20, only verse 19 does not describe the people's circumstances. In content there is little new from the previous chapters but much that remains poignant about the fall of Jerusalem and its effects on Judah.

The tone, indeed the very grammar, of the chapter with its challenge for God to remember and its plea for God to restore invites conversation between the people and God.[1] In some ways this tone is a primary function of Lamentations as a poetic collection, but it is especially characteristic of the concluding chapter. By conversation is meant much more than the exchange of pleasantries or of recent news. A corporate call to God typically comes in the context of worship, and the topic of conversation here—the very possibility of an ongoing relationship between Judah and God—is best approached through prayer and confession.

---

1. Verse 1 contains three imperatives: "Remember . . . look, and see." Verse 20 has the interrogative "why," which occurs once in the Hebrew text, but it is probably assumed to do double duty with the next poetic line as well: "[Why] do you forsake us so long?" The imperative of 5:21 deserves some scrutiny. It is the Hiphil imperative of *šub*, a primary term meaning "turn" or "repent." What God can demand, i.e., repentance, is something that God can also effect by working in and through the people's circumstances. Cf. 3:40, where the poet proposes that the community "return" (*šub*) to the Lord.

There are formal parallels (the constituent parts) and common concerns with Psalm 44, a corporate lament/complaint. In 44:24 God is asked: "Why do you ... forget our misery and oppression?"[2] In 44:1–8 God is extolled.[3] One function of the psalm's initial praise of God is to remind both God and people that he has been their Protector and Redeemer in the past. In 44:20–22 the people note that they have not "forgotten" God, implying that perhaps God has forgotten them. A few verses later (44:23–24), they utter the plea for God to rouse himself from sleep.[4] We are dealing here with metaphor and rhetoric. Psalm 44 does not, however, understand the devastation on God's people (whatever it was) as the consequence of sinfulness and faithlessness. On the contrary, that devastation comes from the evildoers as a result of the people's attempt to be faithful to God (44:17–18, 22).[5]

The poet of Lamentations 5 offers a catalogue of characters whose lives have been shattered by the loss of Jerusalem. Women were assaulted, princes and elders abused, and men of various ages in calamity (5:11–14). Corporately the joy is gone from the people's hearts (5:15). The voices of the text sound weary, resigned, and accusatory.

One acknowledgment is that it was futile to seek aid from Egypt and Assyria (5:6). This was a familiar prophetic charge that God's people looked too quickly for deliverance from a neighbor,[6] and the poet confirms its truthfulness.

The last verse both raises a question and provides an implied answer. There is no doubt in the mind of the poet that God has rejected and judged his people. But has God irrevocably and utterly rejected them, and is his anger beyond measure and without appeasement? No final answer can come solely from the side of the people, for they are not capable of restoring themselves to God. An answer, nevertheless, is intimated, even though only God can bring it to pass. It is intimated in the confession of God's daily mercy (3:22–24), in the claim that Judah's exile will not be forever (4:22), and in the request for God to restore the people to himself (5:21).

Bridging Contexts

WEARY AND OUTCAST. "With what shall I come before the LORD?" asks the prophet Micah in Micah 6:6. There are occasions when confession of sin and articulations of grief and concern are the order of the day. Lamentations 5 gives a historical voice for one such occasion. It serves as a summary of much of the previous book, yet it can also stand alone as a communal lament to God.

---

2. Cf. Lam. 5:20; also Ps. 13:1.
3. Cf. Lam. 5:19.
4. Cf. Lam. 5:1.
5. Lam. 5:16, by contrast, has: "Woe to us, for we have sinned!" (cf. 5:7).
6. Cf. Hos. 7:11; also Jer. 2:18.

The abiding value of chapter 5 (which is essentially a concluding prayer) is not likely to be found by a modern group trying to match up exactly its problems with those enunciated in the chapter. It is more likely to be discovered through contemplation on the weariness (5:5b) that human failure and fallibility typically produce. It is even more likely to be found when a believing community finds itself not only weary but also feeling outcast, and where there is no longer any joy in the Lord. If there is presence of mind among God's people on such occasions, some will articulate their feelings and find that God seems absent or judgmental. It may take a long time to discover any or all of the reasons why. But those reasons do exist. Furthermore, the language of biblical lamentation may provide just the kind of resources needed for the articulation of pain and the spiritual discernment to push beyond the spiritual malaise.

Another clue to the application of the chapter's teaching is the fact that a number of medieval Hebrew manuscripts repeat 5:21 after 5:22, so that the reading or chanting of the book does not end on a down note. A consequence of this reading is to end the book with a recognition that God is able to restore a wayward people (or person) and that there is a history to the issue of divine judgment and restoration.

MEMORY. The congregational voices in Lamentations 5 work on several levels, two of which may be held up for special consideration. One common element is memory. With regard to God's memory, when the ancient congregation asks God to remember its decrepit state, it does not literally believe that God has forgotten their circumstances. To remember in this instance means to bring to mind again a matter whose import should induce one to act. That is why the call for God to remember in the prayer is immediately connected with a plea for God to see and take notice. The assumption is that once the circumstances are noted, they will induce action on God's part.

With regard to the people's memory, the shameful and oppressive nature of what happened at the hands of the Babylonians was kept in memory and thus (it was hoped) became instructional for later generations. The circumstances functioned as a teaching device, explaining why Jerusalem had fallen and warning of the consequences. Lamentations functions to keep a sad and oppressive period alive in memory and influence so that it may not get repeated.

Visitors to the concentration-camp complexes at Auschwitz-Birkenau in Poland report that plaques have been erected on the rubble of one of the crematoriums. Of all the concentration camps established by the Nazis, Auschwitz seems to evoke the most horror. Each plaque says essentially the same thing, although each is inscribed in a different language. The English plaque reads: "Forever let this place be a cry of despair, a warning to humanity." The complexes at Auschwitz-Birkenau serve a crucial educational role. No visitor can avoid the feeling of evil that pervades the place, even though the camp has not been used in over half a century.

Despair and hope. One cannot visit that site without experiencing despair and warning. In recent years Polish Catholics have placed crosses near a part of the complex as a witness of their Christian faith and as a sign that Christ too shared the pain of the thousands of Jews and other "undesirables" executed in the gas chambers and burned in the crematoriums. Some Jewish groups have been offended at their witness and have insisted that nothing divert attention from the task of remembering and warning.

Reading the book of Lamentations evokes similar emotions to those expressed on the plaques at Auschwitz. The main reasons are that much of the language of this book is that of despair and that the destruction of Jerusalem had an impact on ancient Jews similar to that of the Holocaust on modern Jews. To be sure, there are clear differences between occasions for the Judean war with Babylon and those for the Second World War, chief among them being Judean responsibility for the disaster in 586 B.C. Judeans of that time brought the tragedy on themselves in ways that European Jews did not bring the Holocaust on themselves. But despair was and remains a common product of both events.

Whatever one makes of the propriety of Polish Catholics erecting crosses at Auschwitz, a Christian interpreter cannot help but read Lamentations in light of the cross and resurrection, since these two teachings are foundational to the gospel. In some ways the destruction of Jerusalem and the downfall of Judah were tantamount to the death of Judah and the people of God. Only a God who raises the dead can speak adequately to that generation.

The book of Lamentations preaches the cross in a historically based typological sense. In doing so, it unmasks the pretense and hypocrisy of humankind in any generation, pushing all who read its despairing poetry to reflect on the meaning and purpose of their own lives. Within the dominant despair of the book are indications that God has spoken a renewing and redeeming Word. In the fullness of time that Word was enfleshed, crucified, and resurrected. Through his Word God is not aloof toward despair, even despair of its own making, but has taken despair into and upon himself through the cross and resurrection of his Son, expending its death-dealing curse and bringing healing and immortality to light.

Calvin's words to introduce the reading of Lamentations are appropriate also as a conclusion to our own reading: "Though nothing in the land appeared but desolation, and the temple being destroyed, the covenant of God appeared as made void, and thus all hope of salvation had been cut off, yet hope still remained, provided the people sought God in true repentance and faith."[7]

---

7. Calvin, *Commentaries on the Prophet Jeremiah and Lamentations*, 300.

Scripture Index

Subject Index

Bring ancient truth to modern life with the
NIV Application Commentary *series*

Covering both the Old and New Testaments, the **NIV Application Commentary** series is a staple reference for pastors seeking to bring the Bible's timeless message into a modern context. It explains not only what the Bible means but also how that meaning impacts the lives of believers today.

Genesis
This commentary demonstrates how the text charts a course of theological affirmation that results in a simple but majestic account of an ordered, purposeful cosmos with God at the helm, masterfully guiding it, and what this means to us today.

John H. Walton
ISBN: 0-310-20617-0

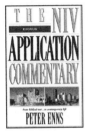

Exodus
The truth of Christ's resurrection and its resulting impact on our lives mean that to Christians, the application of Exodus is less about how to act than it is about what God has done and what it means to be his children.

Peter Enns
ISBN: 0-310-20607-3

Judges, Ruth
This commentary helps readers learn how the messages of Judges and Ruth can have the same powerful impact today that they did when they were first written. Judges reveals a God who employs very human deliverers but refuses to gloss over their sins and the consequences of those sins. Ruth demonstrates the far-reaching impact of a righteous character.

K. Lawson Younger Jr.
ISBN: 0-310-20636-7

Available at your local Christian bookstore

ZONDERVAN™

GRAND RAPIDS, MICHIGAN 49530
WWW.ZONDERVAN.COM

Esther

Karen H. Jobes shows what a biblical narrative that never mentions God tells Christians about him today.

Karen H. Jobes
ISBN: 0-310-20672-3

Ecclesiastes, Song of Songs

Ecclesiastes and Songs of Songs have always presented particular challenges to their readers, especially if those readers are seeking to understand them as part of Christian Scripture. Revealing the links between the Scriptures and our own times, Iain Provan shows how these wisdom books speak to us today with relevance and conviction.

Iain Provan
ISBN: 0-310-21372-X

Ezekiel

Discover how, properly understood, this mysterious book with its obscure images offers profound comfort to us today.

Ian M. Duguid
ISBN: 0-310-20147-X

Daniel

Tremper Longman III reveals how the practical stories and spellbinding apocalyptic imagery of Daniel contain principles that are as relevant now as they were in the days of the Babylonian Captivity.

Tremper Longman III
ISBN: 0-310-20608-1

Available at your local Christian bookstore

GRAND RAPIDS, MICHIGAN 49530
WWW.ZONDERVAN.COM

Hosea, Amos, Micah

Scratch beneath the surface of today's culture and you'll find we're not so different from ancient Israel. Revealing the links between Israel eight centuries B.C. and our own times, Gary V. Smith shows how the prophetic writings of Hosea, Amos, and Micah speak to us today with relevance and conviction.

Gary Smith
ISBN: 0-310-20614-6

Mark

Learn how the challenging Gospel of Mark can leave recipients with the same powerful questions and answers it did when it was written.

David E. Garland
ISBN: 0-310-49350-1

Luke

Focus on the most important application of all: "the person of Jesus and the nature of God's work through him to deliver humanity."

Darrell L. Bock
ISBN: 0-310-49330-7

John

Learn both halves of the interpretive task. Gary M. Burge shows readers how to bring the ancient message of John into a modern context. He also explains not only what the book of John meant to its original readers but also how it can speak powerfully today.

Gary M. Burge
ISBN: 0-310-49750-7

Available at your local Christian bookstore

ZONDERVAN™

GRAND RAPIDS, MICHIGAN 49530

WWW.ZONDERVAN.COM

Acts

Study the first portraits of the church in action around the world with someone whose ministry mirrors many of the events in Acts. Biblical scholar and worldwide evangelist Ajith Fernando applies the story of the church's early development to the global mission of believers today.

Ajith Fernando
ISBN: 0-310-49410-9

Romans

Paul's letter to the Romans remains one of the most important expressions of Christian truth ever written. Douglas Moo comments on the text and then explores issues in Paul's culture and in ours that help us understand the ultimate meaning of each paragraph.

Douglas J. Moo
ISBN: 0-310-49400-1

1 Corinthians

Is your church struggling with the problem of divisiveness and fragmentation? See the solution Paul gave the Corinthian Christians over 2,000 years ago. It still works today!

Craig Blomberg
ISBN: 0-310-48490-1

2 Corinthians

Often recognized as the most difficult of Paul's letters to understand, 2 Corinthians can have the same powerful impact today that it did when it was first written.

Scott J. Hafemann
ISBN: 0-310-49420-6

Available at your local Christian bookstore

ZONDERVAN™

GRAND RAPIDS, MICHIGAN 49530

WWW.ZONDERVAN.COM

Galatians

A pastor's message is true not because of his preaching or people-management skills, but because of Christ. Learn how to apply Paul's example of visionary church leadership to your own congregation.

Scot McKnight
ISBN: 0-310-48470-1

Ephesians

Explore what the author calls "a surprisingly comprehensive statement about God and his work, about Christ and the gospel, about life with God's Spirit, and about the right way to live."

Klyne Snodgrass
ISBN: 0-310-49340-4

Philippians

The best lesson Philippians provides is how to encourage people who actually are doing quite well. Learn why not all the New Testament letters are reactions to theological crises.

Frank Thielman
ISBN: 0-310-49340-4

Colossians/Philemon

The temptation to trust in the wrong things has always been strong. Use this commentary to learn the importance of trusting only in Jesus, God's Son, in whom all the fullness of God lives. No message is more important for our postmodern culture.

David E. Garland
ISBN: 0-310-48480-4

Available at your local Christian bookstore

ZONDERVAN™

GRAND RAPIDS, MICHIGAN 49530

WWW.ZONDERVAN.COM

1&2 Thessalonians

Paul's letters to the Thessalonians say as much to us today about Christ's return and our resurrection as they did in the early church. This volume skillfully reveals Paul's answers to these questions and how they address the needs of contemporary Christians.

Michael W. Holmes
ISBN: 0-310-49380-3

1&2 Timothy, Titus

Reveals the context and meanings of Paul's letters to two leaders in the early Christian Church and explores their present-day implications to help you to accurately apply the principles they contain to contemporary issues.

Walter L. Liefeld
ISBN: 0-310-50110-5

Hebrews

The message of Hebrews can be summed up in a single phrase: "God speaks effectively to us through Jesus." Unpack the theological meaning of those seven words and learn why the gospel still demands a hearing today.

George H. Guthrie
ISBN: 0-310-49390-0

James

Give your church the best antidote for a culture of people who say they believe one thing but act in ways that either ignore or contradict their belief. More than just saying, "Practice what you preach," James gives solid reasons why faith and action must coexist.

David P. Nystrom
ISBN: 0-310-49360-9

Available at your local Christian bookstore

ZONDERVAN™

GRAND RAPIDS, MICHIGAN 49530

WWW.ZONDERVAN.COM

1 Peter

The issue of the church's relationship to the state hits the news media in some form nearly every day. Learn how Peter answered the question for Christians surviving under Roman rule and how it applies similarly to believers living amid the secular institutions of the modern world.

Scot McKnight
ISBN: 0-310-49290-4

2 Peter, Jude

Introduce your modern audience to letters they may not be familiar with and show why they'll want to get to know them.

Douglas J. Moo
ISBN: 0-310-20104-7

Letters of John

Like the community in John's time, which faced disputes over erroneous "secret knowledge," today's church needs discernment in affirming new ideas supported by Scripture and weeding out harmful notions. This volume will help you show today's Christians how to use John's example.

Gary M. Burge
ISBN: 0-310-486420-3

Revelation

Craig Keener offers a "new" approach to the book of Revelation by focusing on the "old." He stresses the need for believers to prepare for the possibility of suffering for the sake of Jesus.

Craig S. Keener
ISBN: 0-310-23192-2

Available at your local Christian bookstore

GRAND RAPIDS, MICHIGAN 49530

WWW.ZONDERVAN.COM

We want to hear from you. Please send your comments about this book to us in care of the address below. Thank you.

GRAND RAPIDS, MICHIGAN 49530

WWW.ZONDERVAN.COM